Volume

o. 4

N.A.D.A.

OFFICIAL USED CAR GUIDE®

Published Quarterly by the
National Automobile Dealers Association
Used Car Guide Company
8400 Westpark Drive, McLean, Virginia 22102
Telephone: (703) 821-7080 www.NADAguides.com

Customer Service Department 800-544-6232
Subscription Information .... guideinfo@nada.org

CONTENTS

PASSENGER CAR SECTION

LIGHT-DUTY TRUCK SECTION

HIGH RETAIL

A High Retail vehicle should be in flawless condition. All power equipment should be functional. The paint should match and have a high gloss finish. The carpet and seat upholstery should be clean and have minimal wear. The engine should start quickly and run smoothly. The tires should be like new with a spare and jack. The mileage should be significantly below the mileage range for the model year (refer to Mileage Range Chart). A High Retail vehicle on a dealer lot should be fully reconditioned and is likely to include a warranty, guarantee or manufacturer certification and current safety and/or emission inspection (where applicable).

RETAIL

A Retail vehicle should be clean and without glaring defects. Tires and glass should be in good condition. The paint should match and have a good finish. The interior should have wear in relation to the age of the vehicle. Carpet and seat upholstery should be clean and all power options should work. The mileage should be within the range noted for the model year (refer to Mileage Range Chart). A Retail vehicle on a dealer lot may include a limited warranty or guarantee, and possibly a current safety and/or emission inspection (where applicable).

TRADE-IN

A Trade-In vehicle should be clean and without glaring defects. Tires and glass should be in good condition. The paint should match and have a good finish. The interior should have wear in relation to the age of the vehicle. Carpet and seat upholstery should be clean and all power options should work. The mileage should be within the noted range for the model year (refer to Mileage Range Chart).

Certified Pre-Owned Information

Certification and Extended Warranties

Used vehicles that carry an extended warranty or have been certified by a manufacturer or dealer may command a premium value. Due to the wide variety of certification programs and extended warranties available in the marketplace today, this Guide makes no attempt to provide a value adjustment. Manufacturer program details can be found in the chart on the following page.

Certification Chart Column Explanations

Inspection Points: Number of items inspected on the vehicle before achieving certification. Most manufactures will provide a list of inspection points.

Eligible Age: Maximum number of model years a vehicle may have and still achieve certification.

Eligible Mileage: Maximum mileage a vehicle may have and still achieve certification.

Warranty Months: Length of warranty.

Warranty Mileage: Number of miles covered under warranty.

Comp/PT: Designates whether the warranty is comprehensive or limited to powertrain components only.

Extra Warranty: In these cases, manufacturers offer an extended powertrain warranty in addition to a comprehensive warranty.

Transfer: Designates whether the manufacturer allows the warranty to be transferable among owners.

Roadside: Designates whether the manufacturer offers roadside assistance. Manufacturer programs may vary widely.

Make	Insp Points	Eligible Age	Eligible Mileage	Warranty Months	Warranty Mileage	Comp/ PT	Extra Warranty	Transfer	Road Side
Acura	150	6	80,000	12	12,000	Comp	7Y/100 PT	Y	Y
Audi	300+	5	70,000	72*	100,000 total	Comp		Y	Y
BMW	N/A	5	60,000	24	100,000 total	Comp		Y	Y
Buick	110+	5	60,000	3	3,000	Comp		Y	Y
Cadillac	110+	4	50,000	72*	100,000 total	Comp		Y	Y
Chevrolet	110+	5	60,000	3	3,000	Comp		Y	Y
Chrysler	125	5	65,000	96*	80,000 total	PT	3M/3 COMP**	Y	Y
Dodge	125	5	65,000	96*	80,000 total	PT	3M/3 COMP**	Y	Y
Ford	115	5	50,000	72*	75,000 total	PT		Y	Y
GMC	110+	5	60,000	3	3,000	Comp		Y	Y
Honda	150	6	80,000	12	12,000	Comp	7Y/100 PT	Y	N
Hyundai	120	4	48,000	12	15,000	Comp		Y	Y
Infiniti	142	6	70,000	36*	100,000 total	Comp	5/110 Comp 2/10,000	Y	Y
Jaguar	140	5	60,000	72*	100,000 total	Comp	8Y/100	Y	Y
Jeep	125	5	65,000	96*	80,000 total	PT	3M/3 COMP**	Y	Y
Land Rover	140	7	75,000	12	12,000	Comp	3Y/36,000 3Y/50,000	Y	Y
Lexus	161	5	60,000	36	100,000 total	Comp		N	Y
Lincoln	141	5	50,000	72*	75,000 total	Comp		Y	Y
Mazda	100	5	62,000	12	12,000	Comp	7/8/100 PT***	Y	Y
Mercedes	130+	6	75,000	12	100,000 total	Comp	1Y & 2Y	Y	Y
Mercury	115	5	50,000	72*	75,000 total	PT		Y	Y
Nissan	142	6	72,000	36*	100,000 total	PT	36, 48, 60/100 Comp	Y	Y
Oldsmobile	110+	5	60,000	3	3,000	Comp		Y	Y
Pontiac	110+	5	60,000	3	3,000	Comp		Y	Y
Porsche	100+	8	100,000	72* or 24	100,000 total	Comp		Y	Y
Saab	110+	5	60,000	72*	100,000 total	Comp		Y	Y
Saturn	150+	4	60,000	12	12,000	Comp		Y	Y
Suzuki	144	5	70,000	12	12,000	Basic	7Y/100 PT	Y	Y
Toyota	160	6	65,000	72*	100,000 total	PT	72/100 COMP	Y	Y
Volkswagen	112	5	75,000	24	24,000	Comp		Y	Y
Volvo	130	6	80,000	72*	100,000 total	Comp	7Y & 8Y	Y	Y

***From in-service date of vehicle. Certified warranty encompasses remainder of new vehicle warranty.**
****Includes 2003 model year vehicles and newer.**
*****7/100k on 2000, 2001 and 2002 models and 8/100k on 2003 from first in service date.**

Warranty information may differ depending upon the model, model year, mileage or other factors, and is subject to change. Contact the manufacturer for the most recent and detailed warranty information. Roadside assistance programs often vary on the length and scope of coverage. Program duration can range from the length of certified coverage to the lifetime of the vehicle. Program scope can range from towing on warranted components to unlimited roadside assistance. Contact the manufacturer for the most recent and detailed roadside assistance information. Special financing may be available through the manufacturer. Contact the manufacturer for financing details.

ACURA	www.acura.com	800-862-2872
AUDI	www.audiusa.com	800-822-2834
BMW	www.bmwusa.com	800-831-1117
BUICK	www.buick.com	800-521-7300
CADILLAC	www.cadillac.com	800-458-8006
CHEVROLET	www.chevrolet.com	800-222-1020
CHRYSLER	www.chrysler.com	800-992-1997
DODGE	www.dodge.com	800-992-1997
FORD	www.fordvehicles.com	800-392-3673
GMC	www.gmc.com	800-462-8782
HONDA	www.hondacars.com	800-999-1009
HUMMER	www.hummer.com	800-732-5493
HYUNDAI	www.hyundaiusa.com	800-633-5151
INFINITI	www.infiniti.com	800-662-6200
ISUZU	www.isuzu.com	800-255-6727
JAGUAR	www.jaguarusa.com	800-452-4827
JEEP	www.jeep.com	800-992-1997
KIA	www.kia.com	800-333-4542
LAND ROVER	www.landroverusa.com	800-637-6837
LEXUS	www.lexus.com	800-255-3987
LINCOLN	www.lincolnvehicles.com	800-392-3673
MAZDA	www.mazdausa.com	800-222-5500
MERCEDES-BENZ	www.mbusa.com	800-222-0100
MERCURY	www.mercuryvehicles.com	800-392-3673
MINI	www.miniusa.com	866-467-6464
MITSUBISHI	www.mitsucars.com	800-222-0037
NISSAN	www.nissanusa.com	800-647-7261
OLDSMOBILE	www.oldsmobile.com	800-442-6537
PONTIAC	www.pontiac.com	800-762-2737
PORSCHE	www.porsche.com	800-545-8039
SAAB	www.saabusa.com	800-955-9007
SATURN	www.saturn.com	800-553-6000
SCION	www.scion.com	866-707-2466
SUBARU	www.subaru.com	800-782-2783
SUZUKI	www.suzuki.com	800-934-0934
TOYOTA	www.toyota.com	800-331-4331
VOLKSWAGEN	www.vw.com	800-822-8987
VOLVO	www.volvocars.us	800-458-1552

Mileage may be a very important factor in determining the value of a used vehicle. The effect of mileage will vary according to the class, age and condition of the vehicle. Mileage adjustments should be made with vehicle condition taken into consideration. Any mileage adjustment made without considering vehicle condition may result in an inappropriate valuation.

Mileage can be misleading in certain situations. It is possible for a lower mileage vehicle to be in poor condition or a higher mileage vehicle to be in very good condition. In these cases, the overall condition of the vehicle should be considered when adjusting vehicle value for mileage.

Mileage Range Chart

Model Year	Fall 2005
2004	29,500 - 32,500
2003	41,500 - 44,500
2002	53,500 - 56,500
2001	65,500 - 68,500
2000	77,500 - 80,500
1999	89,500 - 92,500
1998	101,500 - 104,500
1997	111,500 - 114,500
1996	121,500 - 124,500
1995	131,500 - 134,500

Please read your Guide carefully when determining the value of optional equipment. N.A.D.A.'s editors believe that most optional equipment has little or no value on older vehicles. This is especially true of options that cost relatively little when new and which deteriorate with age or use.

Only the more popular vehicle options are listed in the Guide. As such, this guide makes little attempt at addressing non-OEM optional equipment. However, exclusion does not necessarily mean that only OEM-sourced optional equipment should be considered when arriving at a valuation.

Optional Equipment Applicability

In certain cases, a group of vehicles share a set of optional equipment listings. Cadillac, BMW and Ford F-Series pickups are a few examples. Where this occurs, a note line will appear above the optional equipment listings highlighting all applicable vehicles. The optional equipment listed beneath these note lines applies to ALL vehicles within the specified group.

2002 S80-I6					
Veh. Ident.: YV1T(Model)D()2()000001 Up.					
Sedan 4D	S92	3589	**18675**	**21900**	**23450**
Sedan 4D T-6	S91	3655	**21050**	**24425**	**26050**
2002 C70-5 Cyl. Turbo					
Veh. Ident.: YV1N(Model)D()2()000001 Up.					
Coupe 2D HT	K53	3395	**22325**	**25950**	**27625**
Convertible 2D LT	C56	3691	**25125**	**28925**	**30700**
Convertible 2D HT	C53	3668	**26575**	**30475**	**32300**
S80/C70 OPTIONS					
Add Navigation System			**550**	**625**	**625**
Add Theft Recovery System			**75**	**100**	**100**
Deduct W/out Automatic Trans.			**575**	**575**	**575**

In this case, the option value of the Theft Recovery System may be added to BOTH the S80 and the C70. In addition, the deduction without Automatic Transmission would also apply to any of the same vehicles where a manual transmission is available.

Option Adjustment Notes

Options are included in the base N.A.D.A. value if listed:

- On a Year/Series line:

1999 3000GT-V6-5/6 Spd./AT

- On a Bodystyle line:

2001 EXPLORER SPORT TRAC-1/2 Ton-V6

Utility 4D	U67	4148	**12325**	**14825**	**15800**
Utility 4D (4WD)	U77	4365	**13525**	**16125**	**17150**

*Options are considered standard on a vehicle if that vehicle is listed in parentheses following "**Std.**":*

Add Power Seat (Std. Accord V6)

In this case, the option value may be added to any vehicle EXCEPT those vehicles following "**Std**."

Option values may be added to the base N.A.D.A. value if that vehicle is listed in parentheses:

Add Left Sliding Door (Base Caravan)

In this case, the option value may be added ONLY to vehicles listed in parentheses.

*Option values should NOT be deducted from the base N.A.D.A. value if that vehicle is listed in parentheses following "**Ex.**":*

Deduct W/out AT (Ex. M, Sed 540i)

In this case, the option value may be deducted from any vehicle EXCEPT those vehicles following "**Ex**."

Vehicle Identification Numbers are printed on a small metal plate usually located on the left side of the dashboard visible through the windshield. Some models and makes place the VIN plate on the inside of the left windshield pillar.

The Vehicle Identification Number's tenth digit represents the vehicle model year. This will be true on all vehicles since 1981. Please refer to the following chart for model year indicator codes.

Code	Model Year	Code	Model Year
A	1980	S	1995
B	1981	T	1996
C	1982	V	1997
D	1983	W	1998
E	1984	X	1999
F	1985	Y	2000
G	1986	1	2001
H	1987	2	2002
J	1988	3	2003
K	1989	4	2004
L	1990	5	2005
M	1991	6	2006
N	1992	7	2007
P	1993	8	2008
R	1994	9	2009

BODY TYPE	Model No.	Weight	Trade-In	Retail	High Retail

ACURA

* Model can be identified by VIN. Please refer to the VIN Explanation Section.

ACURA

BODY TYPE	Model No.	Weight	Trade-In	Retail	High Retail
2004 RSX-4 Cyl.					
Veh. Ident.: JH4(Model)()4C000001 Up.					
Coupe 3D	DC5()8	2721	**17075**	**19775**	**20875**
Coupe 3D Type S (6 Spd.)	DC530	2778	**18700**	**21500**	**22650**
Add Leather Seats (Std. Type S)			**450**	**500**	**500**
Add Theft Recovery System			**100**	**125**	**125**
Deduct W/out Automatic Trans. (Ex. S)			**575**	**575**	**575**
2004 TSX-4 Cyl.					
Veh. Ident.: JH4(Model)()4()000001 Up.					
Sedan 4D	CL9()8	3230	**21900**	**24875**	**26275**
Sedan 4D Nav	CL9()9	3241	**22700**	**25800**	**27225**
2004 TL-V6					
Veh. Ident.: 19UUA6()()()4A000001 Up.					
Sedan 4D 3.2	UA6()()	3482	**28000**	**31200**	**32775**
Sedan 4D 3.2 Nav	UA6()()	3489	**28800**	**32050**	**33675**
TSX/TL OPTIONS					
Add Theft Recovery System			**100**	**125**	**125**
Deduct W/out Automatic Trans.			**625**	**625**	**625**
2004 RL-V6					
Veh. Ident.: JH4(Model)()4()000001 Up.					
Sedan 4D 3.5	KA965	3880	**28525**	**32650**	**34550**
Sedan 4D 3.5 Nav	KA966	3893	**29325**	**33500**	**35425**
2004 NSX-V6-6 Spd./AT					
Veh. Ident.: JH4NA()()6()4T000001 Up.					
Coupe 2D Targa	6	3153	**66550**	**73375**	**76500**
RL/NSX OPTIONS					
Add Theft Recovery System			**100**	**125**	**125**

ACURA

BODY TYPE	Model No.	Weight	Trade-In	Retail	High Retail
2003 RSX-4 Cyl.					
Veh. Ident.: JH4(Model)()3()000001 Up.					
Coupe 3D	DC5()8	2721	**15475**	**18000**	**19050**
Coupe 3D Type S (6 Spd.)	DC530	2778	**16900**	**19500**	**20600**
Add Leather Seats (Std. Type S)			**400**	**450**	**450**
Add Theft Recovery System			**75**	**100**	**100**
Deduct W/out Automatic Trans. (Ex. S)			**525**	**525**	**525**
2003 CL-V6					
Veh. Ident.: 19U(Model)()3()000001 Up.					
Coupe 2D 3.2	YA424	3470	**17025**	**19750**	**21050**
Coupe 2D 3.2 Nav	YA425	3485	**17625**	**20500**	**21825**
Coupe 2D 3.2 Type S	YA4()6	3446	**18500**	**21425**	**22775**
Coupe 2D 3.2 Type S Nav	YA4()7	3461	**19100**	**22050**	**23375**
2003 TL-V6					
Veh. Ident.: 19U(Model)()3()000001 Up.					
Sedan 4D 3.2	UA566	3494	**17900**	**20775**	**22125**
Sedan 4D 3.2 Nav	UA567	3510	**18650**	**21575**	**22950**
Sedan 4D 3.2 Type S	UA568	3538	**19225**	**22200**	**23525**
Sedan 4D 3.2 Type S Nav	UA569	3554	**19975**	**22975**	**24325**

PASSENGER CARS

BODY TYPE	Model No.	Weight	Trade-In	Retail	High Retail
CL/TL OPTIONS					
Add Theft Recovery System			75	100	100
Deduct W/out Automatic Trans.			575	575	575
2003 RL-V6					
Veh. Ident.: JH4(Model)()3()000001 Up.					
Sedan 4D 3.5	KA965	3920	23775	27475	29200
Sedan 4D 3.5 Nav	KA966	3869	24475	28225	29975
2003 NSX-V6-6 Spd./AT					
Veh. Ident.: JH4NA()()6()3()000001 Up.					
Coupe 2D Targa	6	3153	60200	66700	69625
RL/NSX OPTIONS					
Add Compact Disc Player (Std. RL)			150	175	175
Add Theft Recovery System			75	100	100
ACURA					
2002 RSX-4 Cyl.					
Veh. Ident.: JH4(Model)()2()000001 Up.					
Coupe 3D	DC5()8	2694	13800	16225	17250
Coupe 3D Type S (6 Spd.)	DC530	2767	15025	17525	18575
Add Leather Seats (Std. Type S)			350	400	400
Add Theft Recovery System			75	100	100
Deduct W/out Automatic Trans. (Ex. S)			475	475	475
2002 CL-V6					
Veh. Ident.: 19U(Model)()2()000001 Up.					
Coupe 2D 3.2	YA424	3470	14675	17200	18425
Coupe 2D 3.2 Nav	YA425	3485	15225	17800	19025
Coupe 2D 3.2 Type S	YA426	3510	15925	18525	19775
Coupe 2D 3.2 Type S Nav	YA427	3525	16475	19125	20400
2002 TL-V6					
Veh. Ident.: 19U(Model)()2A000001 Up.					
Sedan 4D 3.2	UA566	3494	15925	18525	19775
Sedan 4D 3.2 Nav	UA567	3510	16625	19275	20550
Sedan 4D 3.2 Type S	UA568	3538	16950	19650	20950
Sedan 4D 3.2 Type S Nav	UA569	3554	17650	20525	21850
CL/TL OPTIONS					
Add Theft Recovery System			75	100	100
2002 RL-V6					
Veh. Ident.: JH4(Model)()2C000001 Up.					
Sedan 4D 3.5	KA965	3920	19425	22700	24250
Sedan 4D 3.5 Nav	KA966	3869	20075	23375	24950
2002 NSX-V6-6 Spd./AT					
Veh. Ident.: JH4NA()()6()2()000001 Up.					
Coupe 2D Targa	6	3153	54425	60600	63325
RL/NSX OPTIONS					
Add Compact Disc Player (Std. RL)			125	150	150
Add Theft Recovery System			75	100	100
ACURA					
2001 INTEGRA-4 Cyl.					
Veh. Ident.: JH4(Model)()1()000001 Up.					
Coupe 3D LS	DC4()5	2643	10175	12300	13200
Coupe 3D GS	DC4()6	2639	11000	13175	14100
Coupe 3D GS-R (5 Spd.)	DC239	2672	11800	14050	15000
Coupe 3D R (5 Spd.)	DC231	2639	15150	17650	18700

BODY TYPE	Model No.	Weight	Trade-In	Retail	High Retail
Sedan 4D LS	DB7()5	2703	10275	12400	13300
Sedan 4D GS	DB7()6	2725	11100	13300	14225
Sedan 4D GS-R (5 Spd.)	DB859	2764	11900	14150	15100
Add Theft Recovery System			50	75	75
Deduct W/out Automatic Trans. (Ex. R/GS-R)			425	425	425
2001 CL-V6					
Veh. Ident.: 19U(Model)()1()000001 Up.					
Coupe 2D 3.2	YA424	3470	12650	15050	16225
Coupe 2D 3.2 Nav	YA425	3485	13100	15550	16725
Coupe 2D 3.2 Type S	YA426	3510	13775	16250	17450
Coupe 2D 3.2 Type S Nav	YA427	3525	14225	16725	17950
2001 TL-V6					
Veh. Ident.: 19U(Model)()1()000001 Up.					
Sedan 4D 3.2	UA566	3483	14075	16575	17800
Sedan 4D 3.2 Nav	UA567	3494	14725	17275	18500
CL/TL OPTIONS					
Add Theft Recovery System			50	75	75
2001 RL-V6					
Veh. Ident.: JH4(Model)()1()000001 Up.					
Sedan 4D 3.5	KA965	3858	16550	19475	20925
Sedan 4D 3.5 Nav	KA966	3869	17150	20250	21725
2001 NSX-V6-6 Spd./AT					
Veh. Ident.: JH4NA()()(Model)()1()000001 Up.					
Coupe 2D	3	3069	46225	51950	54425
Coupe 2D Targa	6	3160	49225	55100	57675
RL/NSX OPTIONS					
Add Compact Disc Player (Std. RL)			125	150	150
Add Theft Recovery System			50	75	75
ACURA					
2000 INTEGRA-4 Cyl.					
Veh. Ident.: JH4(Model)()Y()000001 Up.					
Coupe 3D LS	DC4()5	2639	8400	10300	11225
Coupe 3D GS	DC4()6	2639	9175	11200	12075
Coupe 3D GS-R (5 Spd.)	DC239	2672	9925	12000	12925
Coupe 3D R (5 Spd.)	DC231	2639	13150	15550	16550
Sedan 4D LS	DB7()5	2725	8500	10400	11325
Sedan 4D GS	DB7()6	2725	9275	11300	12200
Sedan 4D GS-R (5 Spd.)	DB859	2767	10025	12100	12975
Deduct W/out Automatic Trans. (Ex. R/GS-R)			375	375	375
2000 TL-V6					
Veh. Ident.: 19U(Model)()Y()000001 Up.					
Sedan 4D 3.2	UA566	3483	12225	14625	15775
Sedan 4D 3.2 Nav	UA567	3494	12825	15250	16425
2000 RL-V6					
Veh. Ident.: JH4(Model)()Y()000001 Up.					
Sedan 4D 3.5	KA965	3858	14475	17250	18600
Sedan 4D 3.5 Nav	KA966	3869	14975	17800	19175
2000 NSX-V6-6 Spd./AT					
Veh. Ident.: JH4NA()()(Model)()Y()000001 Up.					
Coupe 2D	3	3069	41825	47300	49625
Coupe 2D Targa	6	3113	44525	50150	52575

BODY TYPE	Model No.	Weight	Trade-In	Retail	High Retail
RL/NSX OPTIONS					
Add Compact Disc Player (Std. RL)			**100**	**125**	**125**
ACURA					
1999 INTEGRA-4 Cyl.					
Veh. Ident.: JH4(Model)()X()000001 Up.					
Coupe 3D LS	DC4()5	2643	**6950**	**8725**	**9600**
Coupe 3D GS	DC4()6	2639	**7675**	**9500**	**10375**
Coupe 3D GS-R (5 Spd.)	DC239	2667	**8375**	**10275**	**11200**
Sedan 4D LS	DB7()5	2703	**7050**	**8850**	**9750**
Sedan 4D GS	DB7()6	2725	**7775**	**9625**	**10525**
Sedan 4D GS-R (5 Spd.)	DB859	2764	**8475**	**10400**	**11325**
Deduct W/out Automatic Trans. (Ex. GS-R)			**325**	**325**	**325**
1999 CL-4 Cyl.					
Veh. Ident.: 19UYA3()5()X()000001 Up.					
Coupe 2D 2.3	YA3()5	3120	**7275**	**9250**	**10275**
1999 CL-V6					
Veh. Ident.: 19UYA225()X()000001 Up.					
Coupe 2D 3.0	YA225	3285	**8275**	**10325**	**11350**
1999 TL-V6					
Veh. Ident.: 19UUA56()()X()000001 Up.					
Sedan 4D 3.2	UA56()	3461	**10250**	**12450**	**13175**
CL/TL OPTIONS					
Deduct W/out Automatic Trans.			**375**	**375**	**375**
1999 RL-V6					
Veh. Ident.: JH4KA96()()X()000001 Up.					
Sedan 4D 3.5	KA96()	3840	**12650**	**15325**	**16625**
1999 NSX-V6-6 Spd./AT					
Veh. Ident.: JH4NA()()(Model)()X()000001 Up.					
Coupe 2D	3	3066	**37825**	**43075**	**45275**
Coupe 2D Targa	6	3160	**40275**	**45675**	**47950**
ACURA					
1998 INTEGRA-4 Cyl.					
Veh. Ident.: JH4(Model)()WS000001 Up.					
Coupe 3D RS	DC4()4	2526	**4925**	**6475**	**7375**
Coupe 3D LS	DC4()5	2640	**5700**	**7350**	**8250**
Coupe 3D GS	DC4()6	2636	**6375**	**8100**	**8950**
Coupe 3D GS-R (5 Spd.)	DC23()	2665	**6850**	**8600**	**9475**
Coupe 3D R (5 Spd.)	DC231	2595	**8475**	**10375**	**11300**
Sedan 4D LS	DB7()5	2703	**5800**	**7475**	**8375**
Sedan 4D GS	DB7()6	2722	**6475**	**8200**	**9050**
Sedan 4D GS-R (5 Spd.)	DB85()	2762	**6950**	**8725**	**9600**
Add Aluminum/Alloy Wheels (Std. GS, GS-R, R)			**50**	**75**	**75**
Add Leather Seats (Std. GS)			**175**	**200**	**200**
Deduct W/out Air Conditioning			**400**	**400**	**400**
Deduct W/out Automatic Trans. (Ex. R/GS-R)			**275**	**275**	**275**
1998 CL-4 Cyl.					
Veh. Ident.: 19U(Model)()W()000001 Up.					
Coupe 2D 2.3	YA3()4	3004	**5325**	**7100**	**8100**
Coupe 2D 2.3 Premium	YA3()5	3004	**5625**	**7425**	**8450**
1998 CL-V6					
Veh. Ident.: 19U(Model)()W()000001 Up.					
Coupe 2D 3.0	YA224	3215	**6200**	**8075**	**9075**

BODY TYPE	Model No.	Weight	Trade-In	Retail	High Retail
Coupe 2D 3.0 Premium	YA225	3215	**6500**	**8400**	**9425**
1998 TL-5 Cyl.					
Veh. Ident.: JH4UA265()W()000001 Up.					
Sedan 4D 2.5	UA265	3282	**7825**	**9825**	**10875**
1998 TL-V6					
Veh. Ident.: JH4UA364()W()000001 Up.					
Sedan 4D 3.2	UA364	3513	**8625**	**10700**	**11750**
CL/TL OPTIONS					
Deduct W/out Automatic Trans.			**325**	**325**	**325**
1998 RL-V6					
Veh. Ident.: JH4(Model)()WC000001 Up.					
Sedan 4D 3.5	KA96()*	3660	**9600**	**11900**	**13050**
Sedan 4D 3.5 Premium	KA96()*	3693	**10050**	**12375**	**13550**
1998 NSX-V6-6 Spd./AT					
Veh. Ident.: JH4NA()()(Model)()W()000001 Up.					
Coupe 2D	3	3066	**34375**	**39450**	**41550**
Coupe 2D Targa	6	3160	**36425**	**41600**	**43750**
ACURA					
1997 INTEGRA-4 Cyl.					
Veh. Ident.: JH4(Model)()VS000001 Up.					
Coupe 3D RS	DC4()4	2529	**4300**	**5800**	**6675**
Coupe 3D LS	DC4()5	2572	**4850**	**6400**	**7300**
Coupe 3D GS	DC4()6	2568	**5275**	**6900**	**7825**
Coupe 3D GS-R (5 Spd.)	DC23()	2672	**5750**	**7425**	**8325**
Coupe 3D R (5 Spd.)	DC231	2600	**7200**	**9000**	**9900**
Sedan 4D LS	DB7()5	2727	**4900**	**6450**	**7350**
Sedan 4D GS	DB7()6	2712	**5325**	**6950**	**7900**
Sedan 4D GS-R (5 Spd.)	DB85()	2751	**5800**	**7475**	**8375**
Add Leather Seats (Std. GS)			**150**	**175**	**175**
Deduct W/out Air Conditioning			**250**	**250**	**250**
Deduct W/out Automatic Trans. (Ex. R/GS-R)			**175**	**175**	**175**
1997 CL-4 Cyl.					
Veh. Ident.: 19U(Model)()VL000001 Up.					
Coupe 2D 2.2	YA1()4	3108	**4550**	**6225**	**7200**
Coupe 2D 2.2 Premium	YA1()5	3119	**4750**	**6450**	**7450**
1997 CL-V6					
Veh. Ident.: 19U(Model)()VL000001 Up.					
Coupe 2D 3.0	YA224	3278	**5100**	**6850**	**7900**
Coupe 2D 3.0 Premium	YA225	3287	**5300**	**7075**	**8075**
1997 TL-5 Cyl.					
Veh. Ident.: JH4(Model)()VC000001 Up.					
Sedan 4D 2.5	UA264	3252	**5475**	**7275**	**8300**
Sedan 4D 2.5 Premium	UA265	3285	**6125**	**8000**	**9075**
1997 TL-V6					
Veh. Ident.: JH4(Model)()VC000001 Up.					
Sedan 4D 3.2	UA364	3450	**6325**	**8225**	**9225**
Sedan 4D 3.2 Premium	UA365	3505	**6625**	**8550**	**9575**
CL/TL OPTIONS					
Deduct W/out Automatic Trans.			**250**	**250**	**250**
1997 RL-V6					
Veh. Ident.: JH4(Model)()VC000001 Up.					
Sedan 4D 3.5	KA964	3649	**7175**	**9200**	**10350**

BODY TYPE	Model No.	Weight	Trade-In	Retail	High Retail
Sedan 4D 3.5 Premium	KA96()	3693	**7525**	**9600**	**10775**
1997 NSX-V6-6 Spd./AT					
Veh. Ident.: JH4NA()()(Model)()VT000001 Up.					
Coupe 2D	3	3069	**31525**	**36225**	**38225**
Coupe 2D Targa	6	3164	**33075**	**38075**	**40125**
ACURA					
1996 INTEGRA-4 Cyl.					
Veh. Ident.: JH4(Model)()TS000001 Up.					
Coupe 3D RS	DC4()4	2529	**3725**	**5150**	**5950**
Coupe 3D LS	DC4()5	2643	**4125**	**5600**	**6450**
Coupe 3D SE	DC4()6	2638	**4325**	**5825**	**6700**
Coupe 3D GS-R (5 Spd.)	DC23()	2671	**4875**	**6425**	**7325**
Sedan 4D RS	DB7()4	2628	**3725**	**5150**	**5950**
Sedan 4D LS	DB7()5	2738	**4125**	**5600**	**6450**
Sedan 4D SE	DB7()6	2725	**4325**	**5825**	**6700**
Sedan 4D GS-R (5 Spd.)	DB85()	2769	**4875**	**6425**	**7325**
Deduct W/out Air Conditioning			**150**	**150**	**150**
Deduct W/out Automatic Trans. (Ex. GS-R)			**125**	**125**	**125**
1996 TL-5 Cyl.					
Veh. Ident.: JH4(Model)()TC000001 Up.					
Sedan 4D 2.5	UA264	3252	**4825**	**6525**	**7550**
Sedan 4D 2.5 Premium	UA265	3285	**5200**	**6975**	**8025**
1996 TL-V6					
Veh. Ident.: JH4(Model)()TC000001 Up.					
Sedan 4D 3.2	UA364	3450	**5350**	**7125**	**8125**
Sedan 4D 3.2 Premium	UA365	3505	**5650**	**7450**	**8475**
1996 RL-V6					
Veh. Ident.: JH4(Model)()TC000001 Up.					
Sedan 4D 3.5	KA964	3660	**6150**	**8100**	**9300**
Sedan 4D 3.5 Premium	KA96()	3693	**6400**	**8375**	**9600**
1996 NSX-V6-5 Spd./AT					
Veh. Ident.: JH4NA1()(Model)()TT000001 Up.					
Coupe 2D	6	3047	**30275**	**34900**	**36850**
Coupe 2D Targa	8	3142	**31425**	**36125**	**38125**
ACURA					
1995 INTEGRA-4 Cyl.					
Veh. Ident.: JH4(Model)()SS000001 Up.					
Coupe 3D RS	DC4()4	2570	**3300**	**4675**	**5550**
Coupe 3D LS	DC4()5	2685	**3500**	**4900**	**5800**
Coupe 3D SE	DC4()6	2672	**3650**	**5075**	**5875**
Coupe 3D GS-R	DC23()	2671	**4200**	**5675**	**6525**
Sedan 4D RS	DB7()4	2670	**3300**	**4675**	**5550**
Sedan 4D LS	DB7()5	2780	**3500**	**4900**	**5800**
Sedan 4D SE	DB7()6	2767	**3650**	**5075**	**5875**
Sedan 4D GS-R	DB85()	2769	**4200**	**5675**	**6525**
1995 TL-5 Cyl.					
Veh. Ident.: JH4(Model)()SC000001 Up.					
Sedan 4D 2.5	UA264	3252	**4250**	**5900**	**6875**
Sedan 4D 2.5 Premium	UA265	3285	**4425**	**6100**	**7075**
1995 LEGEND-V6					
Veh. Ident.: JH4(Model)()SC000001 Up.					
Coupe 2D L	KA8()6	3560	**5325**	**7175**	**8325**

BODY TYPE	Model No.	Weight	Trade-In	Retail	High Retail
Coupe 2D LS	KA8()7	3583	**5575**	**7450**	**8625**
Sedan 4D L	KA7()()	3560	**4825**	**6600**	**7750**
Sedan 4D SE	KA769	3576	**5075**	**6900**	**8075**
Sedan 4D LS	KA767	3583	**5075**	**6900**	**8075**
Sedan 4D GS	KA7()8	3616	**5175**	**7000**	**8175**
1995 NSX-V6					
Veh. Ident.: JH4NA1()8()ST000001 Up.					
Coupe 2D Targa	NA	3208	**29850**	**34075**	**36000**

ALFA ROMEO

ALFA ROMEO

BODY TYPE	Model No.	Weight	Trade-In	Retail	High Retail
1995 164-V6					
Veh. Ident.: ZAR(Model)()S6000001 Up.					
Sedan 4D LS	ED43E	3517	**4675**	**6375**	**7375**
Sed 4D Quadrifoglio	ED33R	3406	**4975**	**6700**	**7725**

AUDI

AUDI

BODY TYPE	Model No.	Weight	Trade-In	Retail	High Retail
2004 A4-4 Cyl. Turbo					
Veh. Ident.: WAU(Model)()8()()4()000001 Up.					
Sedan 4D 1.8T	JC	3252	**20700**	**23750**	**25125**
Sedan 4D 1.8T Quattro	LC	3406	**23200**	**26550**	**28000**
Wagon 4D 1.8T Avant Quattro	VC	3516	**24100**	**27525**	**29000**
Cabriolet 2D 1.8T	AC	3638			
2004 A4-V6					
Veh. Ident.: WAU(Model)()8()()4()000001 Up.					
Sedan 4D 3.0	JT	3462	**24600**	**28050**	**29525**
Sedan 4D 3.0 Quattro	LT	3583	**27100**	**30775**	**32325**
Wagon 4D 3.0 Avant Quattro	VT	3693	**28000**	**31725**	**33300**
Cabriolet 2D 3.0	AT	3814			
Cabriolet 2D 3.0 Quattro	DT	4013			
2004 S4-V8-6 Spd./AT					
Veh. Ident.: WAU(Model)()8()()4()000001 Up.					
Sedan 4D S4 Quattro	PL	3825			
Wagon 4D S4 Avant Quattro	XL	3936			
Cabriolet 2D S4 Quattro	RL	4090			
A4/S4 OPTIONS					
Add Sport Pkg. (Std. S4)			**950**	**1075**	**1075**
Add Bose Stereo System			**350**	**400**	**400**
Add Leather Seats (Std. A4 3.0, S4)			**525**	**600**	**600**
Add Navigation System			**650**	**725**	**725**
Add Power Seat (Std. A4 3.0, S4)			**225**	**250**	**250**
Add Power Sunroof			**625**	**700**	**700**
Add Theft Recovery System			**100**	**125**	**125**
Deduct W/out Automatic Trans. (Ex. S4)			**625**	**625**	**625**
2004 TT-4 Cyl. Turbo					
Veh. Ident.: TRU(Model)28N()41000001 Up.					
Coupe 2D 180	SC	2921	**22700**	**26350**	**28025**
Coupe 2D 225 Quattro (6 Spd.)	WT	3274	**26200**	**30075**	**31900**
Roadster 2D 180	TC	3131	**25000**	**28800**	**30575**

BODY TYPE	Model No.	Weight	Trade-In	Retail	High Retail
Roadster 2D 225 Quattro (6 Spd.)	UT	3472	**28500**	**32650**	**34550**
2004 TT-V6 Turbo					
Veh. Ident.: TRU(Model)28N()41000001 Up.					
Coupe 2D 250 Quattro	WF	3351	**29725**	**33950**	**35875**
Roadster 2D 250 Quattro	UF	3472	**32025**	**36450**	**38450**
2004 A6-V6					
Veh. Ident.: WA()(Model)()4B()4N000001 Up.					
Sedan 4D 3.0	JT	3561	**26000**	**29875**	**31675**
Sedan 4D 3.0 Quattro	LT	3880	**29200**	**33375**	**35300**
Sedan 4D 2.7T Quattro	LD	3836	**31725**	**36050**	**38050**
Sedan 4D 2.7T Quattro S-Line	CD	3958	**32725**	**37225**	**39250**
Wagon 4D 3.0 Avant Quattro	VT	4035			
Wagon 4D Allroad Quattro	YD	4178			
2004 A6-V8					
Veh. Ident.: WA()(Model)()4B()4N000001 Up.					
Sedan 4D 4.2 Quattro	ML	4024			
Wagon 4D 4.2 Allroad Quattro	YL	4277			
2004 A8-V8					
Veh. Ident.: WAUML44E()4N000001 Up.					
Sedan 4D 4.2 Quattro L	ML	4399	**52850**	**58925**	**61600**
TT/A6/A8 OPTIONS					
Add Sport Pkg. (A6 Sedan 4.2)					
Add Bose Stereo System (Std. A8)			**425**	**475**	**475**
Add Navigation System (Std. A8)			**750**	**850**	**850**
Add Power Sunroof (Model JT, YD, YL)			**725**	**825**	**825**
Add Theft Recovery System			**100**	**125**	**125**
Deduct W/o Automatic Trans. (Ex. TT)			**675**	**675**	**675**
Deduct W/out Leather Seats					
AUDI					
2003 A4-4 Cyl. Turbo					
Veh. Ident.: WAU(Model)()8()()3()000001 Up.					
Sedan 4D 1.8T	JC	3252	**17325**	**20175**	**21500**
Sedan 4D 1.8T Quattro	LC	3406	**19625**	**22600**	**23950**
Wagon 4D 1.8T Avant Quattro	VC	3516	**20475**	**23525**	**24900**
Cabriolet 2D 1.8T	AC	3660	**26225**	**29775**	**31300**
2003 A4-V6					
Veh. Ident.: WAU(Model)()8()()3()000001 Up.					
Sedan 4D 3.0	JT	3462	**20325**	**23350**	**24725**
Sedan 4D 3.0 Quattro	LT	3583	**22625**	**25950**	**27400**
Wagon 4D 3.0 Avant Quattro	VT	3693	**23475**	**26850**	**28325**
Cabriolet 2D 3.0	AT	3814	**29225**	**33025**	**34675**
A4 OPTIONS					
Add Sport Pkg.			**825**	**925**	**925**
Add Bose Stereo System			**300**	**350**	**350**
Add Leather Seats (Std. A4 3.0)			**475**	**550**	**550**
Add Navigation System			**550**	**625**	**625**
Add Power Seat (Std. A4 3.0)			**200**	**225**	**225**
Add Power Sunroof			**575**	**650**	**650**
Add Theft Recovery System			**75**	**100**	**100**
Deduct W/out Automatic Trans.			**575**	**575**	**575**
2003 TT-4 Cyl. Turbo					
Veh. Ident.: TRU(Model)28N()31000001 Up.					
Coupe 2D 180	SC	2921	**19725**	**23000**	**24575**

BODY TYPE	Model No.	Weight	Trade-In	Retail	High Retail
Coupe 2D 225 Quattro (6 Spd.)	WT	3274	**23025**	**26675**	**28375**
Roadster 2D 180	TC	3131	**22025**	**25525**	**27175**
Roadster 2D 225 Quattro (6 Spd.)	UT	3472	**25325**	**29125**	**30900**
2003 A6-V6					
Veh. Ident.: WA()(Model)()4B()3N000001 Up.					
Sedan 4D 3.0	JT	3516	**20800**	**24150**	**25750**
Sedan 4D 3.0 Quattro	LT	3770	**23100**	**26775**	**28475**
Sedan 4D 2.7T Quattro	LD	3759	**25325**	**29125**	**30900**
Wagon 4D 3.0 Avant Quattro	VT	3924	**23950**	**27675**	**29400**
Wagon 4D Allroad Quattro	YD	4167	**27500**	**31575**	**33450**
2003 A6-V8					
Veh. Ident.: WA()(Model)()4B()3N000001 Up.					
Sedan 4D 4.2 Quattro	ML	4024	**29375**	**33550**	**35475**
Sedan 4D RS6 Quattro	PV		**65025**	**71300**	**74350**
Wagon 4D S6 Avant Quattro	XU	4024	**37525**	**42275**	**44450**
2003 A8-V8					
Veh. Ident.: WAU(Model)()4D()3N000001 Up.					
Sedan 4D 4.2 Quattro	FL	4068	**33375**	**38375**	**40450**
Sedan 4D 4.2 Quattro L	ML	4156	**35850**	**41000**	**43150**
Sedan 4D S8 Quattro	GU	4068	**43350**	**48900**	**51275**
TT/A6/A8 OPTIONS					
Add Sport Pkg. (A6 Sedan 4.2)			**1125**	**1250**	**1250**
Add Bose Stereo System (Std. RS6/S6, A8)			**375**	**425**	**425**
Add Navigation System			**650**	**725**	**725**
Add Power Sunroof (Std. A6-V8, A8)			**675**	**775**	**775**
Add Theft Recovery System			**75**	**100**	**100**
Deduct W/o Automatic Trans. (Ex. TT)			**625**	**625**	**625**
Deduct W/out Leather Seats			**525**	**525**	**525**
AUDI					
2002 A4-4 Cyl. Turbo					
Veh. Ident.: WAU(Model)()8E()2()000001 Up.					
Sedan 4D 1.8T	JC	3252	**14400**	**16925**	**18175**
Sedan 4D 1.8T Quattro	LC	3406	**16500**	**19150**	**20425**
Wagon 4D 1.8T Avant Quattro	VC	3516	**17300**	**20150**	**21475**
2002 A4-V6					
Veh. Ident.: WAU(Model)()8()()2()000001 Up.					
Sedan 4D 3.0	JT	3462	**16100**	**18725**	**20000**
Sedan 4D 3.0 Quattro	LT	3583	**18200**	**21100**	**22450**
Sedan 4D S4-T Quattro (AT/6Sp)	RD	3593	**21300**	**24375**	**25775**
Wagon 4D 3.0 Avant Quattro	VT	3693	**19000**	**21950**	**23325**
Wagon 4D S4-T Quattro (AT/6Sp)	XD	3704	**22100**	**25400**	**26825**
A4 OPTIONS					
Add Bose Stereo System			**250**	**300**	**300**
Add Leather Seats (Std. S4)			**425**	**475**	**475**
Add Navigation System			**450**	**500**	**500**
Add Power Sunroof			**525**	**600**	**600**
Add Theft Recovery System			**75**	**100**	**100**
Deduct W/out Automatic Trans. (Ex. S4)			**525**	**525**	**525**
2002 TT-4 Cyl. Turbo-5 Spd.					
Veh. Ident.: TRU(Model)28N()2()000001 Up.					
Coupe 2D 180	S()	2921	**16625**	**19575**	**21025**
Coupe 2D 180 Quattro	W()	3208	**18725**	**21950**	**23500**
Coupe 2D 225 Quattro (6 Spd.)	WT	3274	**19725**	**23025**	**24600**
Roadster 2D 180	T()	3131	**18925**	**22150**	**23675**

PASSENGER CARS

PASSENGER CARS

BODY TYPE	Model No.	Weight	Trade-In	Retail	High Retail
Roadster 2D 225 Quattro (6 Spd.)	UT	3472	**22025**	**25525**	**27175**
2002 A6-V6					
Veh. Ident.: WA()(Model)()4B()2()000001 Up.					
Sedan 4D 3.0	JT	3516	**16525**	**19450**	**20900**
Sedan 4D 3.0 Quattro	LT	3748	**18625**	**21850**	**23375**
Sedan 4D 2.7T Quattro	LD	3759	**20650**	**24000**	**25600**
Wagon 4D 3.0 Avant Quattro	VT	3924	**19425**	**22700**	**24250**
Wagon 4D Allroad Quattro	YD	4167	**23450**	**27150**	**28875**
2002 A6-V8					
Veh. Ident.: WAU(Model)()4B()2()000001 Up.					
Sedan 4D 4.2 Quattro	ML	4024	**24225**	**27975**	**29725**
Wagon 4D S6 Avant Quattro	XU	4024	**31050**	**35350**	**37325**
2002 A8-V8					
Veh. Ident.: WAU(Model)()4D()2()000001 Up.					
Sedan 4D 4.2 Quattro	FL	4068	**26100**	**30350**	**32175**
Sedan 4D 4.2 Quattro L	ML	4156	**27600**	**32075**	**33950**
Sedan 4D S8 Quattro	GU	4068	**34975**	**40075**	**42200**
TT/A6/A8 OPTIONS					
Add Sport Pkg. (Std. S6, S8)			**1000**	**1125**	**1125**
Add Bose Stereo System (Std. A6-V8, A8)			**325**	**375**	**375**
Add Navigation System			**550**	**625**	**625**
Add Power Sunroof (Std. A6-V8, A8)			**625**	**700**	**700**
Add Theft Recovery System			**75**	**100**	**100**
Deduct W/o Automatic Trans. (Ex. TT)			**575**	**575**	**575**
Deduct W/out Leather Seats			**475**	**475**	**475**
AUDI					
2001 A4-4 Cyl. Turbo					
Veh. Ident.: WAU(Model)()8D()1()000001 Up.					
Sedan 4D 1.8T	AC	2998	**10500**	**12725**	**13800**
Sedan 4D 1.8T Quattro	DC	3241	**12400**	**14800**	**15950**
Wagon 4D 1.8T Avant Quattro	KC	3351	**13150**	**15600**	**16775**
2001 A4-V6					
Veh. Ident.: WAU(Model)()8D()1()000001 Up.					
Sedan 4D 2.8	AH	3263	**11825**	**14150**	**15275**
Sedan 4D 2.8 Quattro	DH	3384	**13725**	**16200**	**17400**
Sedan 4D S4-T Quattro (AT/6Sp)	RD	3593	**19025**	**21975**	**23350**
Wagon 4D 2.8 Avant Quattro	KH	3494	**14475**	**17000**	**18250**
Wagon 4D S4-T Quattro (AT/6Sp)	XD	3704	**19775**	**22775**	**24125**
A4 OPTIONS					
Add Bose Stereo System			**200**	**225**	**225**
Add Leather Seats (Std. S4)			**375**	**425**	**425**
Add Navigation System			**400**	**450**	**450**
Add Power Sunroof			**475**	**550**	**550**
Add Theft Recovery System			**50**	**75**	**75**
Deduct W/out Automatic Trans. (Ex. S4)			**475**	**475**	**475**
2001 TT-4 Cyl. Turbo-5 Spd.					
Veh. Ident.: TRU(Model)()8N()1()000001 Up.					
Coupe 2D 180	S()	2921	**14175**	**16950**	**18325**
Coupe 2D 180 Quattro	W()	3208	**16075**	**18975**	**20400**
Coupe 2D 225 Quattro (6 Spd.)	WT	3274	**16875**	**19825**	**21275**
Roadster 2D 180	T()	3131	**16475**	**19400**	**20850**
Roadster 2D 225 Quattro (6 Spd.)	UT	3472	**19175**	**22425**	**23975**

BODY TYPE	Model No.	Weight	Trade-In	Retail	High Retail
2001 A6-V6					
Veh. Ident.: WAU(Model)()4B()1()000001 Up.					
Sedan 4D 2.8	BH	3560	**13100**	**15800**	**17125**
Sedan 4D 2.8 Quattro	EH	3770	**15000**	**17825**	**19200**
Sedan 4D 2.7T Quattro	ED	3759	**16825**	**19775**	**21225**
Wagon 4D 2.8 Avant Quattro	LH	3947	**15750**	**18625**	**20025**
Wagon 4D Allroad Quattro	YP	4167	**20400**	**23725**	**25325**
2001 A6-V8					
Veh. Ident.: WAUZL()4B()1()000001 Up.					
Sedan 4D 4.2 Quattro	ZL	4024	**19925**	**23225**	**24800**
2001 A8-V8					
Veh. Ident.: WAU(Model)()4D()1()000001 Up.					
Sedan 4D 4.2 Quattro	FL	4068	**20375**	**24200**	**25800**
Sedan 4D 4.2 Quattro L	ML	4156	**21575**	**25500**	**27150**
Sedan 4D S8 Quattro	GU	4068	**28825**	**33400**	**35325**
TT/A6/A8 OPTIONS					
Add Bose Stereo System (Std. A6-V8, A8)			**275**	**325**	**325**
Add Compact Disc Player (Std. A6, A8)			**125**	**150**	**150**
Add Navigation System (Std. A8 4.2 L)			**500**	**575**	**575**
Add Power Sunroof (Std. A6 4.2, A8)			**575**	**650**	**650**
Add Theft Recovery System			**50**	**75**	**75**
Deduct W/o Automatic Trans. (Ex. TT)			**525**	**525**	**525**
Deduct W/out Leather Seats			**425**	**425**	**425**
AUDI					
2000 A4-4 Cyl. Turbo					
Veh. Ident.: WAU(Model)()8D()Y()000001 Up.					
Sedan 4D 1.8T	AC	2998	**8375**	**10450**	**11475**
Sedan 4D 1.8T Quattro	DC	3241	**10075**	**12275**	**13325**
Wagon 4D 1.8T Avant Quattro	KC	3351	**10775**	**13025**	**14100**
2000 A4-V6					
Veh. Ident.: WAU(Model)()8D()Y()000001 Up.					
Sedan 4D 2.8	AH	3164	**9550**	**11700**	**12750**
Sedan 4D 2.8 Quattro	DH	3384	**11250**	**13550**	**14650**
Sedan 4D S4-T Quattro (AT/6Sp)	DD	3593	**16175**	**18800**	**20075**
Wagon 4D 2.8 Avant Quattro	KH	3494	**11950**	**14300**	**15425**
A4 OPTIONS					
Add Bose Stereo System			**150**	**175**	**175**
Add Leather Seats (Std. S4)			**325**	**375**	**375**
Add Navigation System			**300**	**350**	**350**
Add Power Sunroof			**425**	**475**	**475**
Deduct W/out Automatic Trans. (Ex. S4)			**425**	**425**	**425**
2000 TT-4 Cyl. Turbo-5 Spd.					
Veh. Ident.: TRU(Model)()()8N()Y()000001 Up.					
Coupe 2D	T	2910	**11600**	**14125**	**15375**
Coupe 2D Quattro	U	3131	**13300**	**16000**	**17325**
2000 A6-V6					
Veh. Ident.: WAU(Model)()4B()Y()000001 Up.					
Sedan 4D 2.8	BH	3560	**9825**	**12125**	**13275**
Sedan 4D 2.8 Quattro	EH	3638	**11525**	**14050**	**15300**
Sedan 4D 2.7T Quattro	ED	3759	**13150**	**15850**	**17175**
Wagon 4D 2.8 Avant Quattro	LH	3947	**12225**	**14850**	**16125**

PASSENGER CARS

PASSENGER CARS

BODY TYPE	Model No.	Weight	Trade-In	Retail	High Retail
2000 A6-V8					
Veh. Ident.: WAUZL()4B()Y()000001 Up.					
Sedan 4D 4.2 Quattro	ZL	4024	**15575**	**18450**	**19850**
2000 A8-V8					
Veh. Ident.: WAUFL()4D()Y()000001 Up.					
Sedan 4D 4.2 Quattro	FL	4068	**15950**	**19325**	**20750**
Sedan 4D 4.2 Quattro L	FL	4156	**16850**	**20350**	**21825**
TT/A6/A8 OPTIONS					
Add Bose Stereo System (Std. A6-V8, A8)			**225**	**250**	**250**
Add Compact Disc Player (Std. A6, A8)			**100**	**125**	**125**
Add Navigation System (Std. A8 4.2 L)			**450**	**500**	**500**
Add Power Sunroof (Std. A6 4.2, A8)			**525**	**600**	**600**
Deduct W/o Automatic Trans. (Ex. TT)			**475**	**475**	**475**
Deduct W/out Leather Seats			**375**	**375**	**375**
AUDI					
1999 A4-4 Cyl. Turbo					
Veh. Ident.: WAU(Model)B()8D()X()000001 Up.					
Sedan 4D 1.8T	B	2998	**6400**	**8275**	**9025**
Sedan 4D 1.8T Quattro	C	3241	**7900**	**9900**	**10625**
Wagon 4D 1.8T Avant Quattro	G	3351	**8550**	**10625**	**11350**
1999 A4-V6					
Veh. Ident.: WAU(Model)D()8D()X()000001 Up.					
Sedan 4D 2.8	D	3164	**7275**	**9225**	**9925**
Sedan 4D 2.8 Quattro	E	3384	**8775**	**10850**	**11600**
Wagon 4D 2.8 Avant Quattro	G	3494	**9425**	**11550**	**12275**
A4 OPTIONS					
Add Bose Stereo System			**100**	**125**	**125**
Add Leather Seats			**275**	**325**	**325**
Add Power Sunroof			**375**	**425**	**425**
Deduct W/out Automatic Trans.			**375**	**375**	**375**
1999 A6-V6					
Veh. Ident.: WAU(Model)()()4()()X()000001 Up.					
Sedan 4D	A	3560	**7875**	**10000**	**10725**
Sedan 4D Quattro	B	3770	**9375**	**11650**	**12375**
Wagon 4D Avant Quattro	D	3858	**10025**	**12375**	**13100**
1999 A8-V8					
Veh. Ident.: WAU(Model)()()4D()X()000001 Up.					
Sedan 4D 3.7	A	3682	**10800**	**13550**	**14775**
Sedan 4D 4.2 Quattro	B	3902	**12875**	**16025**	**17350**
A6/A8 OPTIONS					
Add Bose Stereo System (Std. A8 4.2)			**175**	**200**	**200**
Add Power Sunroof (Std. A8)			**475**	**550**	**550**
Deduct W/out Leather Seats			**325**	**325**	**325**
AUDI					
1998 A4-4 Cyl. Turbo					
Veh. Ident.: WAU(Model)B88D()W()000001 Up.					
Sedan 4D 1.8T	B	2877	**5125**	**6875**	**7925**
Sedan 4D 1.8T Quattro	C	3130	**6425**	**8325**	**9325**
1998 A4-V6					
Veh. Ident.: WAU(Model)D88D()W()000001 Up.					
Sedan 4D 2.8	D	3087	**5850**	**7675**	**8725**
Sedan 4D 2.8 Quattro	E	3318	**7150**	**9100**	**10100**
Wagon 4D 2.8 Avant	F	3289	**6450**	**8350**	**9375**

BODY TYPE	Model No.	Weight	Trade-In	Retail	High Retail
Wagon 4D 2.8 Avant Quattro	G	3428	7750	9750	10800
1998 CABRIOLET-V6					
Veh. Ident.: WAUAA88G()W()000001 Up.					
Convertible 2D	A	3364	9125	11250	12275
A4/CABRIOLET OPTIONS					
Add Leather Seats			225	250	250
Add Power Sunroof			325	375	375
Deduct W/out Automatic Trans.			325	325	325
1998 A6-V6					
Veh. Ident.: WAU(Model)()84()()W()000001 Up.					
Sedan 4D	A	3473	6225	8175	9375
Sedan 4D Quattro	B	3704	7525	9600	10775
Wagon 4D	H		5975	7875	9100
Wagon 4D Quattro	J		7275	9325	10475
1998 A8-V8					
Veh. Ident.: WAU(Model)()84D()W()000001 Up.					
Sedan 4D 3.7	A	3682	8550	11000	12225
Sedan 4D 4.2 Quattro	B	3902	10150	12850	14050
A6/A8 OPTIONS					
Add Power Sunroof (Std. A8)			425	475	475
Deduct W/out Leather Seats			275	275	275
AUDI					
1997 A4-4 Cyl. Turbo					
Veh. Ident.: WAU(Model)BB8D()V()000001 Up.					
Sedan 4D 1.8T	B	2877	4600	6275	7275
Sedan 4D 1.8T Quattro	C	3130	5500	7300	8325
1997 A4-V6					
Veh. Ident.: WAU(Model)A88D()V()000001 Up.					
Sedan 4D 2.8	D	2976	5225	7000	8050
Sedan 4D 2.8 Quattro	E	3228	6125	8000	9075
1997 CABRIOLET-V6					
Veh. Ident.: WAUAA88G()V()000001 Up.					
Convertible 2D	A	3364	7825	9825	10875
A4/CABRIOLET OPTIONS					
Add Leather Seats			200	225	225
Add Power Sunroof			250	300	300
Deduct W/out Automatic Trans.			250	250	250
1997 A6-V6					
Veh. Ident.: WAU(Model)()84A()V()000001 Up.					
Sedan 4D	F	3428	5100	6925	8100
Sedan 4D Quattro	G	3693	6000	7900	9125
Wagon 4D	H	3582	5550	7425	8600
Wagon 4D Quattro	J	3847	6450	8425	9650
1997 A8-V8					
Veh. Ident.: WAU(Model)()84D()V()000001 Up.					
Sedan 4D 3.7	A	3682	7950	10300	11475
Sedan 4D 4.2 Quattro	B	3902	9075	11625	12775
A6/A8 OPTIONS					
Add Power Sunroof (Std. A8)			350	400	400
Deduct W/out Leather Seats			250	250	250

PASSENGER CARS

BODY TYPE	Model No.	Weight	Trade-In	Retail	High Retail
AUDI					
1996 A4-V6					
Veh. Ident.: WAU(Model)A88D()T()000001 Up.					
Sedan 4D 2.8	D	2976	**4500**	**6175**	**7150**
Sedan 4D 2.8 Quattro	E	3228	**5300**	**7075**	**8075**
1996 CABRIOLET-V6					
Veh. Ident.: WAUAA88G()T()000001 Up.					
Convertible 2D	A	3364	**6650**	**8575**	**9600**
A4/CABRIOLET OPTIONS					
Add Power Sunroof			**200**	**225**	**225**
Deduct W/out Automatic Trans.			**150**	**150**	**150**
1996 A6-V6					
Veh. Ident.: WAU(Model)()84A()T()000001 Up.					
Sedan 4D	F	3428	**4275**	**5975**	**7075**
Sedan 4D Quattro	G	3693	**5075**	**6900**	**8075**
Wagon 4D	H	3582	**4700**	**6450**	**7575**
Wagon 4D Quattro	J	3847	**5500**	**7350**	**8525**
AUDI					
1995 90-V6					
Veh. Ident.: WAU(Model)()88C()S()000001 Up.					
Sedan 4D	B	3252	**2975**	**4400**	**5275**
Sedan 4D Sport	D	3252	**3075**	**4550**	**5450**
Sedan 4D Quattro	C	3296	**3675**	**5225**	**6125**
Sedan 4D Quattro Sport	E	3296	**3775**	**5325**	**6250**
1995 CABRIOLET-V6					
Veh. Ident.: WAUB()88G()S()000001 Up.					
Convertible 2D	B	3494	**5650**	**7450**	**8475**
1995 A6-V6					
Veh. Ident.: WAU(Model)()84A()S()000001 Up.					
Sedan 4D	F	3452	**3550**	**5175**	**6175**
Sedan 4D Quattro	G	3726	**4250**	**5950**	**7050**
Wagon 4D	H	3628	**3950**	**5625**	**6700**
Wagon 4D Quattro	J	3870	**4650**	**6400**	**7525**
1995 S6-5 Cyl. Turbo					
Veh. Ident.: WAU(Model)()84A()S()000001 Up.					
Sedan 4D (AWD)	K	3825	**8950**	**11150**	**12275**
Wagon 4D (AWD)	L	3924	**9350**	**11625**	**12775**

BMW

* Model can be identified by VIN. Please refer to the VIN Explanation Section.

BODY TYPE	Model No.	Weight	Trade-In	Retail	High Retail
BMW					
2004 3 SERIES					
Veh. Ident.: WB()(Model)4()4()000001 Up.					
Coupe 2D 325Ci	B()()3*	3197	**26950**	**30900**	**32750**
Coupe 2D 330Ci	BD53	3285	**30125**	**34350**	**36300**
Coupe 2D M3 (AT/6 Spd.)	BL93	3415	**44225**	**49350**	**51750**
Sedan 4D 325i	()()3()*	3219	**25325**	**29150**	**30925**
Sedan 4D 325xi (AWD)	EU33	3461	**26825**	**30750**	**32600**
Sedan 4D 330i	EV53	3285	**29625**	**33825**	**35750**
Sedan 4D 330xi (AWD)	EW53	3483	**31125**	**35425**	**37400**
Wagon 4D 325i	()()()3*	3362	**25925**	**29775**	**31575**

BODY TYPE	Model No.	Weight	Trade-In	Retail	High Retail
Wagon 4D 325xi (AWD)	EP33	3594	**27425**	**31500**	**33375**
Convertible 2D 325Ci	BW33	3560	**34650**	**39250**	**41350**
Convertible 2D 330Ci	BW53	3616	**38100**	**42900**	**45100**
Convertible 2D M3 (AT/6 Spd.)	BR93	3781			
2004 Z SERIES					
Veh. Ident.: 4US(Model)()()4L000001 Up.					
Roadster 2D Z4 2.5i	BT33	2932	**27725**	**31800**	**33675**
Roadster 2D Z4 3.0i	BT53	2998	**31500**	**35800**	**37775**
2004 5 SERIES					
Veh. Ident.: WBA(Model)5()4B000001 Up.					
Sedan 4D 525i	NA53	3428	**36775**	**41500**	
Sedan 4D 530i	NA73	3472	**38975**	**43825**	**46050**
Sedan 4D 545i (AT/6 Spd.)	NB33	3803	**46250**	**51500**	**53950**
2004 6 SERIES					
Veh. Ident.: WBA(Model)4()4B000001 Up.					
Coupe 2D 645Ci	EH73	3781			
Convertible 2D 645Ci	EK73	4178			
2004 7 SERIES					
Veh. Ident.: WBA(Model)()()4D000001 Up.					
Sedan 4D 745i	GL63	4376	**54975**	**61175**	**63925**
Sedan 4D 745Li	GN63	4464	**57925**	**64275**	**67125**
Sedan 4D 760i	GL83	4762			
Sedan 4D 760Li	GN83	4872			
BMW OPTIONS					
Add Sport Suspension Pkg. (Std. 3 Series Coupe, 330i, M Cars, 6 Series)			**1325**	**1475**	**1475**
Add Performance Pkg. (330)			**3150**	**3375**	**3375**
Add BMW Prem/Harman Kardon Stereo (Std. 330, Z4 3.0i, 760)			**425**	**475**	**475**
Add Detachable Hardtop			**1050**	**1175**	**1175**
Add Navigation System (Std. 6 Series, 7 Series)			**750**	**850**	**850**
Add Power Sunroof (Std. 3 Series Wagon, 545i, 645 Coupe, 7 Series)			**725**	**825**	**825**
Add Rear Entertainment System			**600**	**675**	**675**
Add Theft Recovery System			**100**	**125**	**125**
Deduct 5/6 Spd. Manual Trans. (Ex. M, 545i, Performance Pkg.)			**675**	**675**	**675**
Deduct W/out Cruise Control			**250**	**250**	**250**
Deduct W/out Leather Seats			**575**	**575**	**575**
Deduct W/out Power Seat			**275**	**275**	**275**
BMW					
2003 3 SERIES					
Veh. Ident.: WB()(Model)4()3()000001 Up.					
Coupe 2D 325Ci	BN()3	3197	**24250**	**28000**	**29750**
Coupe 2D 330Ci	BN53	3285	**27175**	**31200**	**33050**
Coupe 2D M3 (AT/6 Spd.)	BL93	3415	**39975**	**44875**	**47125**
Sedan 4D 325i	()()3()*	3219	**22825**	**26475**	**28175**
Sedan 4D 325xi (AWD)	EU33	3461	**24225**	**27975**	**29725**
Sedan 4D 330i	EV53	3285	**26675**	**30575**	**32400**
Sedan 4D 330xi (AWD)	EW53	3483	**28075**	**32175**	**34050**
Wagon 4D 325i	()()()3*	3362	**23375**	**27050**	**28750**
Wagon 4D 325xi (AWD)	EP33	3594	**24775**	**28550**	**30300**
Convertible 2D 325Ci	BS33	3560	**31450**	**35750**	**37725**
Convertible 2D 330Ci	BS53	3616	**34625**	**39225**	**41325**

PASSENGER CARS

BODY TYPE	Model No.	Weight	Trade-In	Retail	High Retail
Convertible 2D M3 (AT/6 Spd.)	BR93	3781	**45200**	**50375**	**52800**
2003 Z SERIES					
Veh. Ident.: 4US(Model)4()3L000001 Up.					
Roadster 2D Z4 2.5i	BT33	2932	**24300**	**28025**	**29775**
Roadster 2D Z4 3.0i	BT53	2998	**27425**	**31475**	**33350**
2003 5 SERIES					
Veh. Ident.: WB()(Model)4()3()000001 Up.					
Sedan 4D 525i	DT()3*	3450	**28675**	**32825**	**34725**
Sedan 4D 530i	DT()3*	3494	**31000**	**35275**	**37250**
Sedan 4D 540i (AT/6 Spd.)	DN()3	3748	**38075**	**42875**	**45075**
Wagon 4D 525i	DS()3	3682	**28575**	**32700**	**34600**
Wagon 4D 540i	DR63	4056	**37975**	**42775**	**44975**
2003 M5					
Veh. Ident.: WBSDE934()3C000001 Up.					
Sedan 4D (6 Spd.)	DE93	4024	**52550**	**58625**	**61300**
2003 7 SERIES					
Veh. Ident.: WBA(Model)4()3D000001 Up.					
Sedan 4D 745i	GL63	4376	**47075**	**52850**	**55350**
Sedan 4D 745Li	GN63	4464	**49825**	**55750**	**58325**
Sedan 4D 760Li	GN83	4872	**70625**	**77675**	**80925**
BMW OPTIONS					
Add Sport Suspension Pkg. (Std. 3 Series Coupe, 330i, M Cars)			**1125**	**1250**	**1250**
Add Performance Pkg. (330i)			**2950**	**3175**	**3175**
Add BMW Prem/Harman Kardon Stereo (Std. 330, Z4 3.0i, M5, 760Li)			**375**	**425**	**425**
Add Detachable Hardtop			**975**	**1100**	**1100**
Add Navigation System (Std. M5, 7 Series)			**650**	**725**	**725**
Add Power Sunroof (Std. 3 Series Wagon, 5 Series, 7 Series)			**675**	**775**	**775**
Add Theft Recovery System			**75**	**100**	**100**
Deduct 5/6 Spd. Manual Trans. (Ex. M, Sedan 540i, Performance Pkg.)			**625**	**625**	**625**
Deduct W/out Cruise Control			**225**	**225**	**225**
Deduct W/out Leather Seats			**525**	**525**	**525**
Deduct W/out Power Seat			**250**	**250**	**250**
BMW					
2002 3 SERIES					
Veh. Ident.: WB()(Model)4()2()000001 Up.					
Coupe 2D 325Ci	BN33	3197	**20600**	**23950**	**25550**
Coupe 2D 330Ci	BN53	3285	**23325**	**27000**	**28700**
Coupe 2D M3 (AT/6 Spd.)	BL93	3415	**34775**	**39375**	**41475**
Sedan 4D 325i	E()3()	3219	**19300**	**22550**	**24100**
Sedan 4D 325xi (AWD)	EU33	3461	**20600**	**23950**	**25550**
Sedan 4D 330i	EV53	3285	**22725**	**26375**	**28075**
Sedan 4D 330xi (AWD)	EW53	3483	**24025**	**27750**	**29475**
Wagon 4D 325i	EN33	3362	**19200**	**22450**	**24000**
Wagon 4D 325xi (AWD)	EP33	3594	**20500**	**23825**	**25425**
Convertible 2D 325Ci	BS33	3560	**26600**	**30500**	**32325**
Convertible 2D 330Ci	BS53	3616	**29450**	**33625**	**35550**
Convertible 2D M3 (AT/6 Spd.)	BR93	3781	**39025**	**43875**	**46100**
2002 Z SERIES					
Veh. Ident.: ()()()(Model)4()2()000001 Up.					
Coupe 2D Z3 3.0	CK73	2943	**20900**	**24275**	**25875**

BODY TYPE	Model No.	Weight	Trade-In	Retail	High Retail
Coupe 2D M (5 Spd.)	CN93	3131	26425	30300	32125
Roadster 2D Z3 2.5	CN33	2899	20100	23425	25000
Roadster 2D Z3 3.0	CN53	2910	22350	25975	27650
Roadster 2D M (5 Spd.)	CL93	3131	28200	32325	34200
2002 5 SERIES					
Veh. Ident.: WB()(Model)4()2()000001 Up.					
Sedan 4D 525i	DT()3*	3450	23650	27350	29075
Sedan 4D 530i	DT()3*	3494	25550	29375	31175
Sedan 4D 540i (AT/6 Spd.)	DN()3	3748	31825	36150	38150
Wagon 4D 525i	DS()3	3682	23550	27250	28975
Wagon 4D 540i	DR63	4056	31725	36050	38050
2002 M5					
Veh. Ident.: WBSDE934()2B000001 Up.					
Sedan 4D (6 Spd.)	DE93	4024	45525	51200	53650
2002 7 SERIES					
Veh. Ident.: WBA(Model)4()2D000001 Up.					
Sedan 4D 745i	GL63	4376	40300	45700	47975
Sedan 4D 745Li	GN63	4464	42775	48300	50650
BMW OPTIONS					
Add Sport Suspension Pkg. (Std. 3 Series Coupe, 330i, Z Series, M Cars)			1000	1125	1125
Add BMW Prem/Harman Kardon Stereo (Std. 330, Z3 3.0, Cpe/Rdster M, M5)			325	375	375
Add Detachable Hardtop			900	1000	1000
Add Navigation System (Std. M5, 7 Series)			550	625	625
Add Power Sunroof (Std. 540i, M5, 7 Series)			625	700	700
Add Theft Recovery System			75	100	100
Ded 5/6 Spd. Manual Trans. (Ex. M, Sed 540i)			575	575	575
Deduct W/out Leather Seats			475	475	475
Deduct W/out Power Seat			225	225	225
BMW					
2001 3 SERIES					
Veh. Ident.: WB()(Model)()()1()000001 Up.					
Coupe 2D 325Ci	BN33	3252	18000	21175	22675
Coupe 2D 330Ci	BN53	3351	20275	23600	25175
Coupe 2D M3 (6 Spd.)	BL93	3415	29750	33950	35875
Sedan 4D 325i	AV33	3241	16850	19825	21275
Sedan 4D 325xi (AWD)	AV33	3494	18050	21225	22725
Sedan 4D 330i	AV53	3318	18925	22150	23675
Sedan 4D 330xi (AWD)	AV53	3527	20125	23450	25025
Wagon 4D 325i	AW33	3384	16750	19725	21175
Wagon 4D 325xi (AWD)	AW33	3627	17950	21125	22625
Convertible 2D 325Ci	BS33	3560	23050	26725	28425
Convertible 2D 330Ci	BS53	3627	25525	29350	31150
Convertible 2D M3 (6 Spd.)	BR93	3781	34050	38625	40700
2001 Z SERIES					
Veh. Ident.: WB()(Model)()()1()000001 Up.					
Coupe 2D Z3 3.0	CK73	2943	18200	21375	22900
Coupe 2D M (5 Spd.)	CN93	3131	23325	27000	28700
Roadster 2D Z3 2.5	CN33	2899	17500	20625	22100
Roadster 2D Z3 3.0	CN53	2910	19550	22825	24375
Roadster 2D M (5 Spd.)	CL93	3086	24975	28750	30525

PASSENGER CARS

BODY TYPE	Model No.	Weight	Trade-In	Retail	High Retail
2001 5 SERIES					
Veh. Ident.: WB()(Model)4()1()000001 Up.					
Sedan 4D 525i	DT()3*	3450	**19625**	**22900**	**24450**
Sedan 4D 530i	DT()3*	3494	**21250**	**24650**	**26275**
Sedan 4D 540i (AT/6 Spd.)	DN()3	3803	**26000**	**29850**	**31650**
Wagon 4D 525i	DS()3	3682	**19525**	**22800**	**24350**
Wagon 4D 540i	DR63	4056	**25900**	**29750**	**31550**
2001 M5					
Veh. Ident.: WBSDE934()1B000001 Up.					
Sedan 4D (6 Spd.)	DE93	4024	**38700**	**44000**	**46225**
2001 7 SERIES					
Veh. Ident.: WBA(Model)4()1D000001 Up.					
Sedan 4D 740i	GG83	4255	**26425**	**30700**	**32525**
Sedan 4D 740iL	GH83	4288	**26975**	**31325**	**33175**
Sedan 4D 750iL	GJ03	4597	**31350**	**36050**	**38050**
BMW OPTIONS					
Add Sport Suspension Pkg. (Std. 3 Series Coupe, xi, Z Series, M Cars)			**850**	**950**	**950**
Add BMW Prem/Harman Kardon Stereo (Std. Z3 3.0, Cpe/Rdster M, M5, 7 Series)			**275**	**325**	**325**
Add Compact Disc Player (Std. M5, 7 Series)			**125**	**150**	**150**
Add Detachable Hardtop			**825**	**925**	**925**
Add Navigation System (Std. M5, 7 Series)			**500**	**575**	**575**
Add Power Sunroof (Std. 540i, M5, 7 Series)			**575**	**650**	**650**
Add Theft Recovery System			**50**	**75**	**75**
Deduct W/out AT (Ex. M, Sed 540i)			**525**	**525**	**525**
Deduct W/out Cruise Control			**175**	**175**	**175**
Deduct W/out Leather Seats			**425**	**425**	**425**
Deduct W/out Power Seat			**200**	**200**	**200**
BMW					
2000 3 SERIES					
Veh. Ident.: WBA(Model)()()Y()000001 Up.					
Coupe 2D 323Ci	BM33	3153	**14400**	**17175**	**18525**
Coupe 2D 328Ci	BM53	3197	**16175**	**19075**	**20500**
Sedan 4D 323i	AM33	3153	**13375**	**16075**	**17400**
Sedan 4D 328i	AM53	3197	**15150**	**17975**	**19350**
Wagon 4D 323i	AR33	3351	**13275**	**15975**	**17300**
Convertible 2D 323i	BR33	3501	**18950**	**22175**	**23700**
2000 Z SERIES					
Veh. Ident.: ()()()(Model)()()Y()000001 Up.					
Coupe 2D Z3 2.8	CK53	2943	**15250**	**18100**	**19475**
Coupe 2D M (5 Spd.)	CM93	3131	**19975**	**23275**	**24850**
Roadster 2D Z3 2.3	CH93	2899	**14650**	**17475**	**18825**
Roadster 2D Z3 2.8	CH33	2910	**16500**	**19450**	**20900**
Roadster 2D M (5 Spd.)	CK93	3086	**21500**	**24925**	**26550**
2000 5 SERIES					
Veh. Ident.: WB()(Model)4()Y()000001 Up.					
Sedan 4D 528i	DM()3	3495	**15825**	**18725**	**20125**
Sedan 4D 540i (AT/6 Spd.)	DN()3	3748	**20000**	**23300**	**24875**
Wagon 4D 528i	DP()3	3726	**15725**	**18600**	**20000**
Wagon 4D 540i	DR63	4056	**19900**	**23200**	**24775**
2000 M5					
Veh. Ident.: WBSDE934()YB000001 Up.					
Sedan 4D (6 Spd.)	DE93	4024	**33150**	**38150**	**40200**

BODY TYPE	Model No.	Weight	Trade-In	Retail	High Retail
2000 7 SERIES					
Veh. Ident.: WBA(Model)4()YD000001 Up.					
Sedan 4D 740i	GG83	4255	**20000**	**23800**	**25400**
Sedan 4D 740iL	GH83	4288	**20550**	**24375**	**26000**
Sedan 4D 750iL	GJ03	4597	**24025**	**28150**	**29900**
BMW OPTIONS					
Add Sport Suspension Pkg. (Std. 3 Series Coupe, M Cars)			**725**	**825**	**825**
Add BMW Prem/Harman Kardon Stereo. (Std. Z3 2.8, Cpe/Rdster M, M5, 7 Series)			**225**	**250**	**250**
Add Compact Disc Player (Std. M5, 7 Series)			**100**	**125**	**125**
Add Detachable Hardtop			**750**	**850**	**850**
Add Navigation System (Std. M5, 7 Series)			**450**	**500**	**500**
Add Power Sunroof (Std. 540i, M5, 7 Series)			**525**	**600**	**600**
Deduct W/out AT (Ex. M, Sed 540i)			**475**	**475**	**475**
Deduct W/out Cruise Control			**150**	**150**	**150**
Deduct W/out Leather Seats			**375**	**375**	**375**
Deduct W/out Power Seat			**175**	**175**	**175**
BMW					
1999 3 SERIES					
Veh. Ident.: WBA(Model)()()X()000001 Up.					
Coupe 2D 318ti	CG()3	2778	**7550**	**9625**	**10350**
Coupe 2D 323is	BF()3	3075	**10050**	**12375**	**13100**
Coupe 2D 328is	BG()3	3142	**11875**	**14425**	**15200**
Coupe 2D M3 (5 Spd.)	BG93	3175	**17325**	**20450**	**21325**
Sedan 4D 323i	AM33	3153	**11000**	**13425**	**14175**
Sedan 4D 328i	AM53	3197	**12675**	**15325**	**16125**
Convertible 2D 323i	BJ()3	3395	**14550**	**17350**	**18150**
Convertible 2D 328i	BK()3*	3395	**16575**	**19500**	**20350**
Convertible 2D M3	BK()3*	3494	**21275**	**24650**	**25600**
1999 Z SERIES					
Veh. Ident.: ()()C(Model)()()XL000001 Up.					
Coupe 2D Z3 2.8	CK53	2943	**13725**	**16450**	**17275**
Coupe 2D M (5 Spd.)	CM93	3131	**18025**	**21200**	**22075**
Roadster 2D Z3 2.3	CH93	2899	**13025**	**15700**	**16500**
Roadster 2D Z3 2.8	CH33	2910	**14675**	**17475**	**18275**
Roadster 2D M (5 Spd.)	CK93	3086	**19225**	**22475**	**23375**
1999 5 SERIES					
Veh. Ident.: WBA(Model)()()()()X()000001 Up.					
Sedan 4D 528i	DM	3495	**13450**	**16175**	**17000**
Sedan 4D 540i (AT/6 Spd.)	DN	3748	**16825**	**19800**	**20650**
Wagon 4D 528i	DP	3726	**13350**	**16050**	**16875**
Wagon 4D 540i	DR	4056	**16725**	**19675**	**20525**
1999 7 SERIES					
Veh. Ident.: WBA(Model)()()X()000001 Up.					
Sedan 4D 740i	GG83	4255	**15075**	**18400**	**19800**
Sedan 4D 740iL	GH83	4288	**15625**	**19000**	**20425**
Sedan 4D 750iL	GJ03	4597	**18350**	**22025**	**23550**
BMW OPTIONS					
Add Sport Pkg. (Std. M Cars)			**625**	**700**	**700**
Add Aluminum/Alloy Wheels (318ti)			**175**	**200**	**200**
Add BMW Prem/Harman Kardon Stereo. (Std. Z3 2.8, Cpe/Rdster M, 750iL)			**175**	**200**	**200**
Add Detachable Hardtop			**675**	**750**	**750**

PASSENGER CARS

BODY TYPE	Model No.	Weight	Trade-In	Retail	High Retail
Add Power Sunroof (Std. 540i, 7 Series)			**475**	**550**	**550**
Ded W/out AT (Ex. Cpe M/M3, M Roadster, 540i)			**425**	**425**	**425**
Deduct W/out Cruise Control			**125**	**125**	**125**
Deduct W/out Leather Seats (Ex. 318ti)			**325**	**325**	**325**
Deduct W/out Power Seat (Ex. 318ti/323is)			**150**	**150**	**150**
BMW					
1998 3 SERIES					
Veh. Ident.: WB()(Model)()()W()000001 Up.					
Coupe 2D 318ti	CG()3	2778	**6350**	**8300**	**9500**
Coupe 2D 323is	BF()3	3075	**7875**	**9975**	**11175**
Coupe 2D 328is	BG()3	3142	**9450**	**11725**	**12875**
Coupe 2D M3 (5 Spd.)	BG93	3175	**14450**	**17225**	**18575**
Sedan 4D 318i	CC()3	2954	**7000**	**9025**	**10175**
Sedan 4D 328i	CD()3*	3131	**9150**	**11400**	**12525**
Sedan 4D M3	CD()3*	3175	**13600**	**16325**	**17675**
Convertible 2D 323i	BJ()3	3296	**12450**	**15075**	**16375**
Convertible 2D 328i	BK()3*	3395	**14150**	**16900**	**18275**
Convertible 2D M3	BK()3*	3395	**18700**	**21925**	**23475**
1998 Z SERIES					
Veh. Ident.: ()()S(Model)()()WL000001 Up.					
Roadster 2D Z3 1.9	CH73	2793	**10775**	**13175**	**14375**
Roadster 2D Z3 2.8	CJ33	2844	**12525**	**15200**	**16500**
Roadster 2D M (5 Spd.)	CK93	3086	**16875**	**19900**	**21350**
1998 5 SERIES					
Veh. Ident.: WBA(Model)()32()WB000001 Up.					
Sedan 4D 528i	DD	3450	**11275**	**13775**	**15000**
Sedan 4D 540i (AT/6 Spd.)	DE	3748	**13850**	**16600**	**17950**
1998 7 SERIES					
Veh. Ident.: WBA(Model)2()WD000001 Up.					
Sedan 4D 740i	GF83	4255	**11575**	**14425**	**15675**
Sedan 4D 740iL	GJ83	4288	**12125**	**15225**	**16525**
Sedan 4D 750iL	GK23	4553	**14275**	**17525**	**18900**
BMW OPTIONS					
Add Sport Pkg. (Std. M Cars)			**525**	**600**	**600**
Add Aluminum/Alloy Wheels (318)			**150**	**175**	**175**
Add Detachable Hardtop			**600**	**675**	**675**
Add Power Sunroof (Std. 540i, 7 Series)			**425**	**475**	**475**
Deduct W/out Automatic Trans. (Ex. Coupe M3, Roadster M, 540i)			**375**	**375**	**375**
Deduct W/out Cruise Control			**100**	**100**	**100**
Deduct W/out Leather Seats			**275**	**275**	**275**
BMW					
1997 3 SERIES					
Veh. Ident.: WB()(Model)2()V()000001 Up.					
Coupe 2D 318ti	CG()3	2745	**5325**	**7175**	**8325**
Coupe 2D 318is	BE()3	2976	**6575**	**8575**	**9800**
Coupe 2D 328is	BG()3	3120	**8275**	**10400**	**11600**
Coupe 2D M3 (5 Spd.)	BG93	3175	**12725**	**15400**	**16700**
Sedan 4D 318i	CC()3	2976	**6375**	**8350**	**9575**
Sedan 4D 328i	CD()3*	3120	**8075**	**10200**	**11375**
Sedan 4D M3	CD()3*	3175	**12525**	**15175**	**16475**
Convertible 2D 318i	BH()3	3131	**9975**	**12300**	**13475**
Convertible 2D 328i	BK()3	3362	**11875**	**14425**	**15675**

BODY TYPE	Model No.	Weight	Trade-In	Retail	High Retail
1997 Z SERIES					
Veh. Ident.: 4US(Model)2()VL000001 Up.					
Roadster 2D Z3 1.9	CH73	2701	**9750**	**12050**	**13200**
Roadster 2D Z3 2.8	CJ33	2844	**11175**	**13675**	**14900**
1997 5 SERIES					
Veh. Ident.: WBA(Model)()32()VB000001 Up.					
Sedan 4D 528i	DD	3505	**9450**	**11725**	**12875**
Sedan 4D 540i (AT/6 Spd.)	DE	3803	**11600**	**14125**	**15375**
1997 7 SERIES					
Veh. Ident.: WBA(Model)2()VD000001 Up.					
Sedan 4D 740i	GF83	4255	**9750**	**12350**	**13525**
Sedan 4D 740iL	GJ83	4288	**10300**	**13000**	**14200**
Sedan 4D 750iL	GK23	4553	**12200**	**15300**	**16600**
1997 8 SERIES					
Veh. Ident.: WBA(Model)2()VC000001 Up.					
Coupe 2D 840Ci	EF83	4167	**20850**	**24225**	**25825**
Coupe 2D 850Ci	EG43	4288	**23975**	**27700**	**29425**
BMW OPTIONS					
Add Sport Pkg. (Std. M3)			**425**	**475**	**475**
Add Aluminum/Alloy Wheels (318)			**100**	**125**	**125**
Add Detachable Hardtop			**550**	**625**	**625**
Add Power Sunroof (Std. 540i, 7/8 Series)			**350**	**400**	**400**
Ded W/out Automatic Trans. (Ex. Coupe M3, 540i)			**300**	**300**	**300**
Deduct W/out Cruise Control			**100**	**100**	**100**
Deduct W/out Leather Seats			**250**	**250**	**250**
BMW					
1996 3 SERIES					
Veh. Ident.: ()()()(Model)2()T()000001 Up.					
Coupe 2D 318ti	CG()3	2745	**4600**	**6350**	**7450**
Coupe 2D 318is	BE()3	2976	**5650**	**7525**	**8725**
Coupe 2D 328is	BG()3	3120	**7050**	**9075**	**10225**
Coupe 2D M3 (5 Spd.)	BG93	3175	**11400**	**13900**	**15150**
Sedan 4D 318i	CD()3	2976	**5450**	**7300**	**8475**
Sedan 4D 328i	CD()3	3120	**6850**	**8875**	**10125**
Convertible 2D 318i	BH()3	3362	**8375**	**10525**	**11725**
Convertible 2D 328i	BK()3	3362	**9950**	**12275**	**13450**
1996 Z SERIES					
Veh. Ident.: 4USCH732()TL000001 Up.					
Roadster 2D Z3 1.9	CH73	2690	**8675**	**10850**	**12075**
1996 7 SERIES					
Veh. Ident.: WBA(Model)2()TD000001 Up.					
Sedan 4D 740iL	GJ83	4288	**8750**	**11200**	**12325**
Sedan 4D 750iL	GK23	4533	**10400**	**13125**	**14325**
1996 8 SERIES					
Veh. Ident.: WBA(Model)2()TC000001 Up.					
Coupe 2D 840Ci	EF83	4167	**19400**	**22675**	**24225**
Coupe 2D 850Ci	EG43	4288	**22125**	**25725**	**27400**
BMW OPTIONS					
Add Sport Pkg. (Std. M3)			**350**	**400**	**400**
Add Detachable Hardtop			**500**	**575**	**575**
Add Power Sunroof (318ti, M3)			**275**	**325**	**325**
Deduct W/out Automatic Trans. (Ex. M3)			**200**	**200**	**200**

P A S S E N G E R   C A R S

BODY TYPE	Model No.	Weight	Trade-In	Retail	High Retail
BMW					
1995 3 SERIES					
Veh. Ident.: ()()()(Model)2()S()000001 Up.					
Coupe 2D 318ti	CG()3	2734	**4025**	**5700**	**6775**
Coupe 2D 318is	BE()3	3021	**4825**	**6600**	**7750**
Coupe 2D 325is	BF()3	3164	**6025**	**7950**	**9175**
Coupe 2D M3	BF()3	3175	**10175**	**12525**	**13700**
Sedan 4D 318i	CC()3	3021	**4625**	**6375**	**7500**
Sedan 4D 325i	CB()3	3164	**5825**	**7725**	**8925**
Convertible 2D 318i	BK()3	3208	**6925**	**8950**	**10225**
Convertible 2D 325i	BJ()3	3429	**8275**	**10400**	**11600**
1995 5 SERIES					
Veh. Ident.: WBA(Model)2()SG000001 Up.					
Sedan 4D 525i	HD()3	3560	**6075**	**8025**	**9200**
Sedan 4D 530i	HE()3	3693	**6800**	**8800**	**10050**
Sedan 4D 540i	HE()3	3803	**7675**	**9750**	**10950**
Touring Wagon 5D 525i	HJ63	3759	**6450**	**8425**	**9650**
Touring Wagon 5D 530i	HK23	3880	**7175**	**9200**	**10350**
1995 7 SERIES					
Veh. Ident.: WBA(Model)2()SD000001 Up.					
Sedan 4D 740i	GF63	4145	**7100**	**9125**	**10275**
Sedan 4D 740iL	GJ63	4288	**7550**	**9625**	**10800**
Sedan 4D 750iL	GK23	4234	**8950**	**11150**	**12275**
1995 8 SERIES					
Veh. Ident.: WBA(Model)2()SC000001 Up.					
Coupe 2D 840Ci	EF()3	4167	**18275**	**21475**	**23000**
Coupe 2D 850Ci	EG43	4201	**20950**	**24325**	**25950**
Coupe 2D 850CSi	EG93	4496	**26450**	**30325**	**32150**

BUICK

BODY TYPE	Model No.	Weight	Trade-In	Retail	High Retail
BUICK					
2004 CENTURY-V6					
Veh. Ident.: 2G4WS5()J()41000001 Up.					
Sedan 4D	WS5	3353	**10325**	**12475**	**13375**
Sedan 4D Custom	WS5		**10675**	**12825**	**13725**
Sedan 4D Limited	WS5		**12050**	**14350**	**15325**
Sedan 4D Special Edition	WS5		**12500**	**14850**	**15825**
Add Aluminum/Alloy Wheels (Std. Special Ed.)			**325**	**375**	**375**
Add Power Seat (Base)			**200**	**225**	**225**
Add Theft Recovery System			**100**	**125**	**125**
Deduct W/out Cruise Control			**200**	**200**	**200**
2004 REGAL-V6					
Veh. Ident.: 2G4(Model)()()()41000001 Up.					
Sedan 4D LS	WB5	3461	**12825**	**15200**	**16200**
Sedan 4D GS	WF5	3536	**16100**	**18650**	**19725**
Add Aluminum/Alloy Wheels (Std. GS)			**325**	**375**	**375**
Add Leather Seats (Std. GS)			**450**	**500**	**500**
Add Monsoon Stereo System			**300**	**350**	**350**
Add Power Sunroof			**575**	**650**	**650**
Add Theft Recovery System			**100**	**125**	**125**

BODY TYPE	Model No.	Weight	Trade-In	Retail	High Retail
2004 LESABRE-V6					
Veh. Ident.: 1G4(Model)()K()4()000001 Up.					
Sedan 4D Custom	HP5	3567	**13725**	**16200**	**17400**
Sedan 4D Limited	HR5	3591	**18175**	**21075**	**22425**
Add Aluminum/Alloy Wheels (Std. Limited)			**375**	**425**	**425**
Add Leather Seats (Std. Limited)			**525**	**600**	**600**
Add Power Sunroof			**625**	**700**	**700**
Add Theft Recovery System			**100**	**125**	**125**
2004 PARK AVENUE-V6					
Veh. Ident.: 1G4(Model)()()()44000001 Up.					
Sedan 4D	CW5	3778	**18425**	**21625**	**23150**
Sedan 4D Ultra	CU5	3909	**22525**	**26150**	**27825**
Add Compact Disc Player (Std. Ultra)			**175**	**200**	**200**
Add Power Sunroof			**725**	**825**	**825**
Add Theft Recovery System			**100**	**125**	**125**
BUICK					
2003 CENTURY-V6					
Veh. Ident.: 2G4WS5()J()31000001 Up.					
Sedan 4D Custom	WS5	3353	**8675**	**10600**	**11550**
Sedan 4D Limited	WS5		**10150**	**12275**	**13175**
Add Aluminum/Alloy Wheels			**275**	**325**	**325**
Add Compact Disc Player			**75**	**100**	**100**
Add Power Seat (Std. Limited)			**175**	**200**	**200**
Add Theft Recovery System			**75**	**100**	**100**
Deduct W/out Cruise Control			**175**	**175**	**175**
2003 REGAL-V6					
Veh. Ident.: 2G4(Model)()()()31000001 Up.					
Sedan 4D LS	WB5	3461	**10725**	**12875**	**13800**
Sedan 4D GS	WF5	3536	**13725**	**16150**	**17175**
Add Aluminum/Alloy Wheels (Std. GS)			**275**	**325**	**325**
Add Compact Disc Player (Std. GS)			**75**	**100**	**100**
Add Leather Seats (Std. GS)			**400**	**450**	**450**
Add Monsoon Stereo System			**250**	**300**	**300**
Add Power Sunroof			**525**	**600**	**600**
Add Theft Recovery System			**75**	**100**	**100**
2003 LESABRE-V6					
Veh. Ident.: 1G4(Model)()K()3()000001 Up.					
Sedan 4D Custom	HP5	3567	**11750**	**14075**	**15200**
Sedan 4D Limited	HR5	3591	**15550**	**18150**	**19400**
Add Aluminum/Alloy Wheels (Std. Limited)			**325**	**375**	**375**
Add Leather Seats (Std. Limited)			**475**	**550**	**550**
Add Power Sunroof			**575**	**650**	**650**
Add Theft Recovery System			**75**	**100**	**100**
2003 PARK AVENUE-V6					
Veh. Ident.: 1G4(Model)()()()34000001 Up.					
Sedan 4D	CW5	3778	**16000**	**18900**	**20325**
Sedan 4D Ultra	CU5	3909	**19050**	**22300**	**23850**
Add Compact Disc Player (Std. Ultra)			**150**	**175**	**175**
Add Power Sunroof			**675**	**775**	**775**
Add Theft Recovery System			**75**	**100**	**100**

PASSENGER CARS

BODY TYPE	Model No.	Weight	Trade-In	Retail	High Retail
BUICK					
2002 CENTURY-V6					
Veh. Ident.: 2G4(Model)()()()2()000001 Up.					
Sedan 4D Custom	WS5	3368	7600	9425	10300
Sedan 4D Limited	WY5	3391	9000	10975	11925
Add Aluminum/Alloy Wheels			225	250	250
Add Compact Disc Player			75	100	100
Add Power Seat (Std. Limited)			150	175	175
Add Power Sunroof			475	550	550
Add Theft Recovery System			75	100	100
Deduct W/out Cruise Control			150	150	150
2002 REGAL-V6					
Veh. Ident.: 2G4(Model)()()()2()000001 Up.					
Sedan 4D LS	WB5	3438	9150	11175	12050
Sedan 4D GS	WF5	3543	11575	13800	14750
Add Aluminum/Alloy Wheels (Std. GS)			225	250	250
Add Compact Disc Player (Std. GS)			75	100	100
Add Leather Seats (Std. GS)			350	400	400
Add Power Sunroof			475	550	550
Add Theft Recovery System			75	100	100
2002 LESABRE-V6					
Veh. Ident.: 1G4(Model)()()()2()000001 Up.					
Sedan 4D Custom	HP5	3567	9900	12075	13125
Sedan 4D Limited	HR5	3591	12700	15125	16300
Add Aluminum/Alloy Wheels (Std. Limited)			275	325	325
Add Compact Disc Player (Std. Limited)			100	125	125
Add Leather Seats (Std. Limited)			425	475	475
Add Power Sunroof			525	600	600
Add Theft Recovery System			75	100	100
2002 PARK AVENUE-V6					
Veh. Ident.: 1G4(Model)()()()24000001 Up.					
Sedan 4D	CW5	3788	13200	15900	17225
Sedan 4D Ultra	CU5	3884	15050	17875	19250
Add Compact Disc Player (Std. Ultra)			125	150	150
Add Power Sunroof			625	700	700
Add Theft Recovery System			75	100	100
BUICK					
2001 CENTURY-V6					
Veh. Ident.: 2G4(Model)()()()11400001 Up.					
Sedan 4D Custom	WS5	3368	6150	7850	8775
Sedan 4D Limited	WY5	3371	7275	9075	9925
Add Aluminum/Alloy Wheels			175	200	200
Add Compact Disc Player			50	75	75
Add Power Seat (Std. Limited)			125	150	150
Add Power Sunroof			425	475	475
Add Theft Recovery System			50	75	75
Deduct W/out Cruise Control			125	125	125
2001 REGAL-V6					
Veh. Ident.: 2G4(Model)()()()11400001 Up.					
Sedan 4D LS	WB5	3440	7525	9350	10225
Sedan 4D GS	WF5	3543	9275	11300	12200

BODY TYPE	Model No.	Weight	Trade-In	Retail	High Retail
Add Aluminum/Alloy Wheels (Std. GS)			175	200	200
Add Compact Disc Player (Std. GS)			50	75	75
Add Leather Seats (Std. GS)			300	350	350
Add Power Sunroof			425	475	475
Add Theft Recovery System			50	75	75
2001 LESABRE-V6					
Veh. Ident.: 1G4(Model)()()()1()400001 Up.					
Sedan 4D Custom	HP5	3567	8250	10300	11325
Sedan 4D Limited	HR5	3591	9925	12100	13150
Add Aluminum/Alloy Wheels (Std. Limited)			225	250	250
Add Compact Disc Player (Std. Limited)			100	125	125
Add Leather Seats			375	425	425
Add Power Sunroof			475	550	550
Add Theft Recovery System			50	75	75
2001 PARK AVENUE-V6					
Veh. Ident.: 1G4(Model)()()()14600001 Up.					
Sedan 4D	CW5	3778	10375	12725	13900
Sedan 4D Ultra	CU5	3884	11700	14225	15475
Add Compact Disc Player (Std. Ultra)			125	150	150
Add Power Sunroof			575	650	650
Add Theft Recovery System			50	75	75
BUICK					
2000 CENTURY-V6					
Veh. Ident.: 2G4(Model)()()()Y1400001 Up.					
Sedan 4D Custom	WS5	3340	4950	6500	7400
Sedan 4D Limited	WY5		5800	7475	8375
Add Aluminum/Alloy Wheels			125	150	150
Add Compact Disc Player			50	75	75
Add Power Seat (Std. Limited)			100	125	125
Add Power Sunroof			375	425	425
Deduct W/out Cruise Control			100	100	100
2000 REGAL-V6					
Veh. Ident.: 2G4(Model)()()()Y1400001 Up.					
Sedan 4D LS	WB5	3440	5850	7525	8425
Sedan 4D GS	WF5	3543	7200	9000	9900
Add Aluminum/Alloy Wheels (Std. GS)			125	150	150
Add Compact Disc Player			50	75	75
Add Leather Seats (Std. GS)			250	300	300
Add Power Seat (Std. GS)			100	125	125
Add Power Sunroof			375	425	425
2000 LESABRE-V6					
Veh. Ident.: 1G4(Model)()()()Y()400001 Up.					
Sedan 4D Custom	HP5	3566	6625	8550	9575
Sedan 4D Limited	HR5	3590	7525	9500	10525
Add Aluminum/Alloy Wheels (Std. Limited)			175	200	200
Add Compact Disc Player			75	100	100
Add Leather Seats			325	375	375
Add Power Sunroof			425	475	475
Deduct W/out Power Seat			125	125	125

ADJUST FOR MILEAGE

PASSENGER CARS

BODY TYPE	Model No.	Weight	Trade-In	Retail	High Retail
2000 PARK AVENUE-V6					
Veh. Ident.: 1G4(Model)()()()Y4600001 Up.					
Sedan 4D	CW5	3740	7850	9950	11150
Sedan 4D Ultra	CU5	3837	8675	10850	12075
Add Compact Disc Player (Std. Ultra)			100	125	125
Add Power Sunroof			525	600	600
Deduct W/out Leather Seats			375	375	375
BUICK					
1999 CENTURY-V6					
Veh. Ident.: 2G4(Model)()()()X1400001 Up.					
Sedan 4D Custom	WS5	3340	4050	5525	6375
Sedan 4D Limited	WY5	3371	4500	6000	6875
Add Aluminum/Alloy Wheels			75	100	100
Add Leather Seats			225	250	250
Add Power Seat			75	100	100
Add Power Sunroof			325	375	375
Deduct W/out Cruise Control			75	75	75
1999 REGAL-V6					
Veh. Ident.: 2G4(Model)()()()X1400001 Up.					
Sedan 4D LS	WB5	3440	4850	6400	7300
Sedan 4D GS	WF5	3543	5825	7500	8400
Add Aluminum/Alloy Wheels (Std. GS)			75	100	100
Add Leather Seats (Std. GS)			225	250	250
Add Power Seat (Std. GS)			75	100	100
Add Power Sunroof			325	375	375
1999 LESABRE-V6					
Veh. Ident.: 1G4(Model)()()()XH400001 Up.					
Sedan 4D Custom	HP5	3443	4750	6450	7450
Sedan 4D Limited	HR5	3468	5375	7150	8150
Add Aluminum/Alloy Wheels (Std. Limited)			125	150	150
Add Leather Seats			275	325	325
Deduct W/out Power Seat			100	100	100
1999 PARK AVENUE-V6					
Veh. Ident.: 1G4(Model)()()()X4600001 Up.					
Sedan 4D	CW5	3740	6175	8125	9325
Sedan 4D Ultra	CU5	3837	6725	8725	9975
Add Power Sunroof			475	550	550
Deduct W/out Leather Seats			325	325	325
1999 RIVIERA-V6					
Veh. Ident.: 1G4(Model)()()()X4700001 Up.					
Coupe 2D	GD2	3699	6275	8225	9425
Add Power Sunroof			475	550	550
BUICK					
1998 SKYLARK-V6					
Veh. Ident.: ()G4NJ5()()()W()400001 Up.					
Sedan 4D Custom	NJ5	2985	2300	3525	4275
Add Aluminum/Alloy Wheels			50	75	75
Deduct W/out Cruise Control			50	50	50
Deduct W/out Power Windows			50	50	50

BODY TYPE	Model No.	Weight	Trade-In	Retail	High Retail
1998 CENTURY-V6					
Veh. Ident.: ()G4(Model)()()()W()400001 Up.					
Sedan 4D Custom	WS5	3335	3450	4850	5750
Sedan 4D Limited	WY5	3354	3800	5225	6025
Add Aluminum/Alloy Wheels			50	75	75
Add Leather Seats			175	200	200
Add Power Seat			50	75	75
Add Power Sunroof			275	325	325
Deduct W/out Cruise Control			50	50	50
1998 REGAL-V6					
Veh. Ident.: ()G4(Model)()()()W()400001 Up.					
Sedan 4D LS	WB5	3447	4075	5525	6375
Sedan 4D GS	WF5	3562	4800	6325	7200
Add Aluminum/Alloy Wheels (Std. GS)			50	75	75
Add Leather Seats (Std. GS)			175	200	200
Add Power Seat (Std. GS)			50	75	75
Add Power Sunroof			275	325	325
1998 LESABRE-V6					
Veh. Ident.: ()G4(Model)()()()W()400001 Up.					
Sedan 4D Custom	HP5	3443	3850	5400	6325
Sedan 4D Limited	HR5	3465	4375	6025	7000
Add Aluminum/Alloy Wheels (Std. Limited)			100	125	125
Add Leather Seats			225	250	250
Deduct W/out Power Seat			75	75	75
1998 PARK AVENUE-V6					
Veh. Ident.: ()G4(Model)()()()W()400001 Up.					
Sedan 4D	CW5	3740	4775	6525	7650
Sedan 4D Ultra	CU5	3837	5275	7100	8250
Add Power Sunroof			425	475	475
Deduct W/out Leather Seats			275	275	275
1998 RIVIERA-V6					
Veh. Ident.: ()G4GD2()()()W()700001 Up.					
Coupe 2D	GD2	3699	5050	6850	8025
Add Power Sunroof			425	475	475
BUICK					
1997 SKYLARK-L4					
Veh. Ident.: 1G4(Model)()()()VC400001 Up.					
Coupe 2D Custom	NJ1	2945	1825	3000	3675
Coupe 2D Limited	NJ1		1950	3150	3850
Sedan 4D Custom	NJ5	2985	1825	3000	3675
Sedan 4D Limited	NJ5		1950	3150	3850
1997 SKYLARK-V6					
Veh. Ident.: 1G4(Model)()()()VC400001 Up.					
Coupe 2D Custom	NJ1		1975	3175	3875
Coupe 2D Limited	NJ1		2100	3325	4025
Coupe 2D Gran Sport	NJ1		2125	3350	4075
Sedan 4D Custom	NJ5		1975	3175	3875
Sedan 4D Limited	NJ5		2100	3325	4025
Sedan 4D Gran Sport	NJ5		2125	3350	4075
SKYLARK OPTIONS					
Add Leather Seats			150	175	175

BODY TYPE	Model No.	Weight	Trade-In	Retail	High Retail
Add Power Seat			50	75	75
Add Power Sunroof			200	225	225
Deduct W/out Cruise Control			25	25	25
Deduct W/out Power Windows			25	25	25
1997 CENTURY-V6					
Veh. Ident.: 2G4(Model)()()()V1400001 Up.					
Sedan 4D Custom	WS5	3364	2925	4250	5075
Sedan 4D Limited	WY5	3378	3100	4450	5300
Add Leather Seats			150	175	175
Add Power Seat			50	75	75
Add Power Sunroof			200	225	225
Deduct W/out Cruise Control			25	25	25
1997 REGAL-V6					
Veh. Ident.: 2G4(Model)()()()V1400001 Up.					
Sedan 4D LS	WB5	3473	3425	4825	5725
Sedan 4D GS	WF5	3520	3875	5325	6150
Add Leather Seats (Std. GS)			150	175	175
Add Power Seat			50	75	75
Add Power Sunroof			200	225	225
1997 LESABRE-V6					
Veh. Ident.: 1G4(Model)()()()VH400001 Up.					
Sedan 4D Custom	HP5	3441	3200	4700	5625
Sedan 4D Limited	HR5	3462	3625	5175	6075
Add Aluminum/Alloy Wheels (Std. Limited)			50	75	75
Add Leather Seats			200	225	225
Deduct W/out Cruise Control			50	50	50
Deduct W/out Power Seat			50	50	50
1997 PARK AVENUE-V6					
Veh. Ident.: 1G4(Model)()()()V4600001 Up.					
Sedan 4D	CW5	3788	4000	5675	6750
Sedan 4D Ultra	CU5	3879	4375	6100	7175
Add Power Sunroof			350	400	400
Deduct W/out Leather Seats			250	250	250
1997 RIVIERA-V6					
Veh. Ident.: 1G4GD2()()()V4700001 Up.					
Coupe 2D	GD2	3720	4025	5700	6775
Add Power Sunroof			350	400	400
Add Supercharged V6 Engine			200	225	225
Deduct W/out Leather Seats			250	250	250
BUICK					
1996 SKYLARK-L4					
Veh. Ident.: ()G4(Model)()()()T()000001 Up.					
Coupe 2D Custom	NJ1	2917	1600	2750	3400
Coupe 2D Limited	NJ1	2917	1725	2900	3575
Sedan 4D Custom	NJ5	2948	1600	2750	3400
Sedan 4D Limited	NJ5	2948	1725	2900	3575
1996 SKYLARK-V6					
Veh. Ident.: ()G4(Model)()()()T()000001 Up.					
Coupe 2D Custom	NJ1		1700	2850	3525
Coupe 2D Limited	NJ1		1825	3000	3675
Coupe 2D Gran Sport	NJ1		1850	3025	3700

BODY TYPE	Model No.	Weight	Trade-In	Retail	High Retail
Sedan 4D Custom	NJ5		1700	2850	3525
Sedan 4D Limited	NJ5		1825	3000	3675
Sedan 4D Gran Sport	NJ5		1850	3025	3700
SKYLARK OPTIONS					
Add Power Sunroof			150	175	175
1996 CENTURY-V6					
Veh. Ident.: ()G4(Model)()()()T()000001 Up.					
Sedan 4D Special (L4)	AG5	2951	1850	3025	3700
Sedan 4D Special	AG5		1950	3150	3850
Sedan 4D Custom	AG5		2050	3250	3950
Sedan 4D Limited	AG5		2125	3350	4075
Wagon 4D Special	AG8	3118	2000	3200	3900
1996 REGAL-V6					
Veh. Ident.: ()G4(Model)()()()T()000001 Up.					
Coupe 2D Custom	WB1	3232	2425	3675	4425
Coupe 2D Gran Sport	WB1		2675	3950	4750
Sedan 4D Custom	WB5	3331	2425	3675	4425
Sedan 4D Limited	WD5		2600	3875	4650
Sedan 4D Gran Sport	WF5		2675	3950	4750
Add Power Sunroof			150	175	175
1996 LESABRE-V6					
Veh. Ident.: ()G4(Model)()()()T()000001 Up.					
Sedan 4D Custom	HP5	3430	2600	3975	4875
Sedan 4D Limited	HR5	3430	2950	4375	5250
1996 ROADMASTER-V8					
Veh. Ident.: ()G4(Model)()()()T()000001 Up.					
Sedan 4D	BN5	4211	3550	5075	5975
Sedan 4D Limited	BT5		3850	5425	6350
1996 ROADMASTER ESTATE WAGON-V8					
Veh. Ident.: ()G4BR8()()()T()000001 Up.					
Wagon 4D	BR8	4563	3950	5525	6475
Wagon 4D Limited	BR8		4250	5900	6875
1996 PARK AVENUE-V6					
Veh. Ident.: ()G4(Model)()()()T()000001 Up.					
Sedan 4D	CW5	3536	3200	4775	5800
Sedan 4D Ultra	CU5	3629	3575	5200	6200
Add Power Sunroof			275	325	325
1996 RIVIERA-V6					
Veh. Ident.: ()G4GD2()()()T()000001 Up.					
Coupe 2D	GD2	3690	3450	5050	6050
Add Power Sunroof			275	325	325
Add Supercharged V6 Engine			150	175	175
BUICK					
1995 SKYLARK-Quad 4					
Veh. Ident.: ()G4(Model)()()()S()000001 Up.					
Coupe 2D Custom	NV1	2888	1300	2400	3000
Coupe 2D Limited	NV1	2888	1425	2550	3175
Sedan 4D Custom	NV5	2941	1300	2400	3000
Sedan 4D Limited	NV5	2941	1425	2550	3175

PASSENGER CARS

BODY TYPE	Model No.	Weight	Trade-In	Retail	High Retail
1995 SKYLARK-V6					
Veh. Ident.: ()G4(Model)()()()S()000001 Up.					
Coupe 2D Custom	NV1	2907	**1400**	**2525**	**3150**
Coupe 2D Limited	NV1	2907	**1525**	**2650**	**3275**
Coupe 2D Gran Sport	NV1	3005	**1550**	**2700**	**3350**
Sedan 4D Custom	NV5	2960	**1400**	**2525**	**3150**
Sedan 4D Limited	NV5	2960	**1525**	**2650**	**3275**
Sedan 4D Gran Sport	NV5	3058	**1550**	**2700**	**3350**
1995 CENTURY-L4					
Veh. Ident.: ()G4(Model)()()()S()000001 Up.					
Sedan 4D Special	AG5	2986	**1550**	**2700**	**3350**
Wagon 4D Special	AG8	3130	**1600**	**2750**	**3400**
1995 CENTURY-V6					
Veh. Ident.: ()G4(Model)()()()S()000001 Up.					
Sedan 4D Special	AG5	3004	**1650**	**2800**	**3450**
Sedan 4D Custom	AH5	2993	**1750**	**2925**	**3600**
Sedan 4D Limited	AG5		**1825**	**3000**	**3675**
Wagon 4D Special	AG8	3168	**1700**	**2850**	**3525**
1995 REGAL-V6					
Veh. Ident.: ()G4(Model)()()()S()000001 Up.					
Coupe 2D Custom	WB1	3261	**2000**	**3200**	**3900**
Coupe 2D Gran Sport	WB1	3328	**2250**	**3475**	**4200**
Sedan 4D Custom	WB5	3335	**2000**	**3200**	**3900**
Sedan 4D Limited	WD5	3463	**2175**	**3400**	**4125**
Sedan 4D Gran Sport	WF5	3406	**2250**	**3475**	**4200**
1995 LESABRE-V6					
Veh. Ident.: ()G4(Model)()()()S()000001 Up.					
Sedan 4D Custom	HP5	3442	**2300**	**3625**	**4475**
Sedan 4D Limited	HR5	3442	**2625**	**4000**	**4900**
1995 ROADMASTER-V8					
Veh. Ident.: ()G4(Model)()()()S()000001 Up.					
Sedan 4D	BN5	4211	**2925**	**4350**	**5225**
Sedan 4D Limited	BT5	4244	**3200**	**4700**	**5625**
1995 ROADMASTER ESTATE WAGON-V8					
Veh. Ident.: ()G4BR8()()()S()000001 Up.					
Wagon 4D	BR8	4563	**3550**	**5075**	**5975**
Wagon 4D Limited	BR8		**3825**	**5400**	**6325**
1995 PARK AVENUE-V6					
Veh. Ident.: ()G4(Model)()()()S()000001 Up.					
Sedan 4D	CW5	3532	**2600**	**4050**	**4975**
Sedan 4D Ultra	CU5	3642	**2950**	**4475**	**5450**
1995 RIVIERA-V6					
Veh. Ident.: ()G4GD2()()()S()000001 Up.					
Coupe 2D	GD2	3748	**2900**	**4400**	**5375**
Add Supercharged V6 Engine			**150**	**175**	**175**

BODY TYPE	Model No.	Weight	Trade-In	Retail	High Retail

CADILLAC

CADILLAC
2004 CTS-V6
Veh. Ident: 1G6(Model)()40000001 Up.

Sedan 4D 3.2L (5 Spd. MT)	DM57N	3568	**22275**	**25875**	**27550**
Sedan 4D 3.6L	DM577	3694	**23500**	**27175**	**28900**
Sedan V-Series (V8, 6 Spd.)	DN57S	3847	**34025**	**38575**	**40650**

2004 SEVILLE-V8
Veh. Ident.: 1G6KS54Y()4U000001 Up.

Sedan 4D SLS	KS5	3992	**22700**	**26325**	**28000**

2004 DEVILLE-V8
Veh. Ident.: 1G6(Model)()()()4U000001 Up.

Sedan 4D	KD5	3984	**22450**	**26075**	**27750**
Sedan 4D DHS	KE5	4048	**28150**	**32250**	**34125**
Sedan 4D DTS	KF5	4044	**29550**	**33750**	**35675**

2004 XLR-V8
Veh. Ident.: 1G6YV3()A()45000001 Up.

Roadster 2D	YV3	3647	**55175**	**61375**	**64125**

CADILLAC OPTIONS

Add Sport Package (CTS V6)	**750**	**850**	**850**
Add Bose Stereo (Std. V-Series, DHS, DTS, XLR)	**425**	**475**	**475**
Add Navigation System (Std. V-Series, XLR)	**750**	**850**	**850**
Add Power Sunroof	**725**	**825**	**825**
Add Theft Recovery System	**100**	**125**	**125**

CADILLAC
2003 CTS-V6
Veh. Ident.: 1G6DM57N()30000001 Up.

Sedan 4D (5 Spd. MT)	DM5	3509	**19975**	**23275**	**24850**
Sedan 4D	DM5	3568	**20600**	**23950**	**25550**

2003 SEVILLE-V8
Veh. Ident.: 1G6(Model)4()()3U000001 Up.

Sedan 4D SLS	KS5	3992	**18700**	**21900**	**23450**
Sedan 4D STS	KY5	4027	**22475**	**26100**	**27775**

2003 DEVILLE-V8
Veh. Ident.: 1G6(Model)()()()3U000001 Up.

Sedan 4D	KD5	3984	**19125**	**22375**	**23925**
Sedan 4D DHS	KE5	4048	**23750**	**27475**	**29200**
Sedan 4D DTS	KF5	4044	**24850**	**28650**	**30425**

CADILLAC OPTIONS

Add Sport Package (CTS)	**650**	**725**	**725**
Add Bose Stereo System (Std. DHS, DTS, STS)	**375**	**425**	**425**
Add Navigation System	**650**	**725**	**725**
Add Power Sunroof	**675**	**775**	**775**
Add Theft Recovery System	**75**	**100**	**100**

CADILLAC
2002 SEVILLE-V8
Veh. Ident.: 1G6(Model)()()()2U000001 Up.

Sedan 4D SLS	KS5	3986	**15525**	**18375**	**19775**
Sedan 4D STS	KY5	4027	**18375**	**21575**	**23100**

PASSENGER CARS

P A S S E N G E R C A R S

BODY TYPE	Model No.	Weight	Trade-In	Retail	High Retail
2002 DEVILLE-V8					
Veh. Ident.: 1G6(Model)()()()2U000001 Up.					
Sedan 4D	KD5	3978	**16850**	**19800**	**21250**
Sedan 4D DHS	KE5	4049	**19900**	**23200**	**24775**
Sedan 4D DTS	KF5	4047	**20900**	**24250**	**25850**
2002 ELDORADO-V8					
Veh. Ident.: 1G6(Model)()()()2M000001 Up.					
Coupe 2D ESC	EL1	3814	**18575**	**21775**	**23300**
Coupe 2D ETC	ET1	3865	**20725**	**24075**	**25675**
CADILLAC OPTIONS					
Add Bose Stereo System (SLS, ESC)			**325**	**375**	**375**
Add Compact Disc Player (ESC)			**125**	**150**	**150**
Add Navigation System			**550**	**625**	**625**
Add Power Sunroof			**625**	**700**	**700**
Add Theft Recovery System			**75**	**100**	**100**
CADILLAC					
2001 CATERA-V6					
Veh. Ident.: W06VR5()()()1()000001 Up.					
Sedan 4D	VR5	3770	**8400**	**10550**	**11750**
2001 SEVILLE-V8					
Veh. Ident.: ()G6(Model)()()()1()000001 Up.					
Sedan 4D SLS	KS5	3986	**12500**	**15150**	**16450**
Sedan 4D STS	KY5	4027	**14775**	**17575**	**18950**
2001 DEVILLE-V8					
Veh. Ident.: ()G6(Model)()()()1()000001 Up.					
Sedan 4D	KD5	3978	**13350**	**16050**	**17375**
Sedan 4D DHS	KE5	4049	**15775**	**18650**	**20050**
Sedan 4D DTS	KF5	4047	**16475**	**19400**	**20850**
2001 ELDORADO-V8					
Veh. Ident.: ()G6(Model)()()()1()000001 Up.					
Coupe 2D ESC	EL1	3843	**14825**	**17625**	**19000**
Coupe 2D ETC	ET1	3876	**16475**	**19400**	**20850**
CADILLAC OPTIONS					
Add Bose Stereo System (Std. DHS,DTS,ETC,STS)			**275**	**325**	**325**
Add Compact Disc Player (VR5, EL1)			**125**	**150**	**150**
Add Navigation System			**500**	**575**	**575**
Add Power Sunroof			**575**	**650**	**650**
Add Theft Recovery System			**50**	**75**	**75**
Deduct W/out Leather Seats			**425**	**425**	**425**
CADILLAC					
2000 CATERA-V6					
Veh. Ident.: W06VR5()()()Y()000001 Up.					
Sedan 4D	VR5	3770	**6625**	**8600**	**9825**
2000 SEVILLE-V8					
Veh. Ident.: ()G6(Model)()()()Y()000001 Up.					
Sedan 4D SLS	KS5	3970	**9750**	**12050**	**13200**
Sedan 4D STS	KY5	4001	**11450**	**13950**	**15200**
2000 DEVILLE-V8					
Veh. Ident.: ()G6(Model)()()()Y()000001 Up.					
Sedan 4D	KD5	3869	**10800**	**13175**	**14375**
Sedan 4D DHS	KE5	3940	**12625**	**15275**	**16575**
Sedan 4D DTS	KF5	3941	**13325**	**16025**	**17350**

BODY TYPE	Model No.	Weight	Trade-In	Retail	High Retail
2000 ELDORADO-V8					
Veh. Ident.: ()G6(Model)()()()Y()000001 Up.					
Coupe 2D ESC	EL1	3843	**11400**	**13925**	**15175**
Coupe 2D ETC	ET1	3876	**12575**	**15250**	**16550**
CADILLAC OPTIONS					
Add Bose Stereo System (Std. DHS,DTS,ETC,STS)			**225**	**250**	**250**
Add Compact Disc Player (VR5, KD5, EL1)			**100**	**125**	**125**
Add Navigation System			**450**	**500**	**500**
Add Power Sunroof			**525**	**600**	**600**
Deduct W/out Leather Seats			**375**	**375**	**375**
CADILLAC					
1999 CATERA-V6					
Veh. Ident.: W06VR5()()()X()000001 Up.					
Sedan 4D	VR5	3770	**5250**	**7075**	**8225**
1999 SEVILLE-V8					
Veh. Ident.: ()G6(Model)()()()X()000001 Up.					
Sedan 4D SLS	KS5	3970	**7875**	**9975**	**11175**
Sedan 4D STS	KY5	4001	**9150**	**11400**	**12525**
1999 DEVILLE-V8					
Veh. Ident.: ()G6(Model)()()()X()000001 Up.					
Sedan 4D	KD5	4012	**7100**	**9125**	**10275**
Sedan 4D d'Elegance	KE5	4052	**7700**	**9775**	**10975**
Sedan 4D Concours	KF5	4063	**8000**	**10125**	**11300**
1999 ELDORADO-V8					
Veh. Ident.: ()G6(Model)()()()X()000001 Up.					
Coupe 2D	EL1	3843	**8775**	**10950**	**12175**
Coupe 2D Touring	ET1	3876	**9650**	**11950**	**13100**
CADILLAC OPTIONS					
Add Bose Stereo System (Std. Touring, STS)			**175**	**200**	**200**
Add Power Sunroof			**475**	**550**	**550**
Deduct W/out Leather Seats			**325**	**325**	**325**
CADILLAC					
1998 CATERA-V6					
Veh. Ident.: W06VR5()()()W()000001 Up.					
Sedan 4D	VR5	3770	**4200**	**5900**	**7000**
1998 SEVILLE-V8					
Veh. Ident.: 1G6(Model)()()()W()900001 Up.					
Sedan 4D SLS	KS5	3972	**6625**	**8625**	**9875**
Sedan 4D STS	KY5	4001	**7525**	**9600**	**10775**
1998 DEVILLE-V8					
Veh. Ident.: 1G6(Model)()()()W()000001 Up.					
Sedan 4D	KD5	4063	**5650**	**7525**	**8725**
Sedan 4D d'Elegance	KE5	4052	**6075**	**8000**	**9225**
Sedan 4D Concours	KF5	4012	**6325**	**8275**	**9475**
1998 ELDORADO-V8					
Veh. Ident.: 1G6(Model)()()()W()600001 Up.					
Coupe 2D	EL1	3843	**6900**	**8925**	**10200**
Coupe 2D Touring	ET1	3876	**7575**	**9650**	**10825**
CADILLAC OPTIONS					
Add Bose Stereo System (Std. Touring, STS)			**150**	**175**	**175**
Add Power Sunroof			**425**	**475**	**475**
Deduct W/out Leather Seats			**275**	**275**	**275**

PASSENGER CARS

BODY TYPE	Model No.	Weight	Trade-In	Retail	High Retail
CADILLAC					
1997 CATERA-V6					
Veh. Ident.: W06VR5()()()V()000001 Up.					
Sedan 4D	VR5	3770	**3500**	**5125**	**6125**
1997 SEVILLE-V8					
Veh. Ident.: 1G6(Model)()()()V()800001 Up.					
Sedan 4D SLS	KS5	3901	**5150**	**6975**	**8150**
Sedan 4D STS	KY5	3960	**5650**	**7525**	**8725**
1997 DEVILLE-V8					
Veh. Ident.: 1G6(Model)()()()V()200001 Up.					
Sedan 4D	KD5	4015	**4925**	**6700**	**7850**
Sedan 4D d'Elegance	KE5	4050	**5225**	**7050**	**8200**
Sedan 4D Concours	KF5	4055	**5375**	**7225**	**8375**
1997 ELDORADO-V8					
Veh. Ident.: 1G6(Model)()()()V()600001 Up.					
Coupe 2D	EL1	3843	**5500**	**7350**	**8525**
Coupe 2D Touring	ET1	3876	**5950**	**7850**	**9075**
CADILLAC OPTIONS					
Add Bose Stereo System			**100**	**125**	**125**
Add Power Sunroof			**350**	**400**	**400**
Deduct W/out Leather Seats			**250**	**250**	**250**
CADILLAC					
1996 SEVILLE-V8					
Veh. Ident.: 1G6(Model)()()()T()800001 Up.					
Sedan 4D SLS	KS5	3832	**4550**	**6275**	**7375**
Sedan 4D STS	KY5	3869	**4975**	**6750**	**7900**
1996 DEVILLE-V8					
Veh. Ident.: 1G6(Model)()()()T()200001 Up.					
Sedan 4D	KD5	3959	**4050**	**5725**	**6800**
Sedan 4D Concours	KF5	3981	**4400**	**6125**	**7200**
1996 FLEETWOOD-V8					
Veh. Ident.: 1G6DW5()()()T()700001 Up.					
Sedan 4D	DW5	4461	**5400**	**7250**	**8400**
1996 ELDORADO-V8					
Veh. Ident.: 1G6(Model)()()()T()600001 Up.					
Coupe 2D	EL1	3765	**4700**	**6450**	**7575**
Coupe 2D Touring	ET1	3801	**5075**	**6900**	**8075**
CADILLAC OPTIONS					
Add Brougham (Fleetwood)			**250**	**300**	**300**
Add Power Sunroof			**275**	**325**	**325**
CADILLAC					
1995 SEVILLE-V8					
Veh. Ident.: 1G6(Model)()()()S()800001 Up.					
Sedan 4D SLS	KS5	3892	**3800**	**5450**	**6500**
Sedan 4D STS	KY5	3950	**4200**	**5900**	**7000**
1995 DEVILLE-V8					
Veh. Ident.: 1G6(Model)()()()S()200001 Up.					
Sedan 4D	KD5	3758	**3600**	**5225**	**6250**
Sedan 4D Concours	KF5	3985	**3900**	**5575**	**6625**
1995 FLEETWOOD-V8					
Veh. Ident.: 1G6DW5()()()S()700001 Up.					
Sedan 4D	DW5	4477	**4300**	**6000**	**7100**

PASSENGER CARS

BODY TYPE	Model No.	Weight	Trade-In	Retail	High Retail
1995 ELDORADO-V8					
Veh. Ident.: 1G6(Model)()()()S()600001 Up.					
Coupe 2D	EL1	3774	**4175**	**5875**	**6975**
Coupe 2D Touring	ET1	3818	**4475**	**6200**	**7300**
CHEVROLET					
CHEVROLET					
2004 AVEO-L4					
Veh. Ident.: KL1(Model)()6()4B000001 Up.					
Hatchback 5D	TD6	2348	**6925**	**8550**	**9325**
Hatchback 5D LS	TJ6		**7550**	**9250**	**9950**
Sedan 4D	TD5	2370	**6925**	**8550**	**9325**
Sedan 4D LS	TJ5		**7550**	**9250**	**9950**
Add Aluminum/Alloy Wheels			**300**	**350**	**350**
Add Compact Disc Player (Std. LS)			**100**	**125**	**125**
Add Power Door Locks (Std. LS)			**150**	**175**	**175**
Add Power Sunroof			**525**	**600**	**600**
Add Power Windows (Std. LS)			**175**	**200**	**200**
Add Theft Recovery System			**100**	**125**	**125**
Deduct W/out Air Conditioning			**575**	**575**	**575**
Deduct W/out Automatic Trans.			**475**	**475**	**475**
2004 CAVALIER-L4					
Veh. Ident.: 1G1(Model)()F()47000001 Up.					
Coupe 2D	JC1	2617	**7600**	**9300**	**10000**
Coupe 2D LS	JF1		**8625**	**10475**	**11200**
Coupe 2D LS Sport	JH1		**9725**	**11700**	**12450**
Sedan 4D	JC5	2676	**7600**	**9300**	**10000**
Sedan 4D LS	JF5		**8625**	**10475**	**11200**
Sedan 4D LS Sport	JH5		**9725**	**11700**	**12450**
Add Aluminum/Alloy Wheels (Std. LS Sport)			**300**	**350**	**350**
Add Compact Disc Player (Base)			**100**	**125**	**125**
Add Cruise Control (Base)			**175**	**200**	**200**
Add Power Door Locks (Base)			**150**	**175**	**175**
Add Power Sunroof			**525**	**600**	**600**
Add Theft Recovery System			**100**	**125**	**125**
Add Tilt Steering Wheel (Base)			**125**	**150**	**150**
Deduct W/out Automatic Trans.			**475**	**475**	**475**
2004 CLASSIC-L4					
Veh. Ident.: 1G1ND5()F()4()000001 Up.					
Sedan 4D	ND5	3033	**8575**	**10475**	**11400**
Add Aluminum/Alloy Wheels			**325**	**375**	**375**
Add Power Seat			**200**	**225**	**225**
Add Theft Recovery System			**100**	**125**	**125**
2004 MALIBU-V6					
Veh. Ident.: 1G1(Model)()()()4F000001 Up.					
Sedan 4D (4 Cyl.)	ZS5	3174	**10625**	**12775**	**13675**
Sedan 4D	ZS5		**11175**	**13375**	**14300**
Sedan 4D LS	ZT5	3297	**11825**	**14075**	**15025**
Sedan 4D LT	ZU5	3315	**13475**	**15875**	**16900**
Sedan 5D Maxx	ZS6		**12475**	**14825**	**15800**
Sedan 5D Maxx LS	ZT6	3458	**13125**	**15525**	**16525**

ADJUST FOR MILEAGE

PASSENGER CARS

BODY TYPE	Model No.	Weight	Trade-In	Retail	High Retail
Sedan 5D Maxx LT	ZU6	3476	14775	17250	18275
Add Aluminum/Alloy Wheels (Std. LS, LT)			325	375	375
Add Power Seat (Std. LT)			200	225	225
Add Power Sunroof			575	650	650
Add Rear Entertainment System			600	675	675
Add Theft Recovery System			100	125	125
Deduct W/out Cruise Control			200	200	200
2004 MONTE CARLO-V6					
Veh. Ident.: 2G1(Model)()()()49000001 Up.					
Coupe 2D LS	WW1	3340	11275	13500	14425
Coupe 2D SS	WX1	3434	14875	17375	18400
Coupe 2D Supercharged SS	WZ1	3522	16950	19575	20675
Add Aluminum/Alloy Wheels (Std. SS)			325	375	375
Add Compact Disc Player			100	125	125
Add Leather Seats			450	500	500
Add Power Seat			200	225	225
Add Power Sunroof			575	650	650
Add Theft Recovery System			100	125	125
Deduct W/out Cruise Control			200	200	200
2004 IMPALA-V6					
Veh. Ident.: 2G1(Model)()()()49000001 Up.					
Sedan 4D	WF5	3465	11325	13625	14725
Sedan 4D LS	WH5	3476	14500	17025	18225
Sedan 4D SS	WP5	3606	16975	19675	20975
Add LS Sport Appearance Pkg.			450	500	500
Add 3.8L V6 Engine (Base)			400	450	450
Add Aluminum/Alloy Wheels (Std. LS, SS)			375	425	425
Add Compact Disc Player			150	175	175
Add Leather Seats (Std. SS)			525	600	600
Add Power Sunroof			625	700	700
Add Theft Recovery System			100	125	125
Deduct W/out Cruise Control			225	225	225
Deduct W/out Power Seat			225	225	225
2004 CORVETTE-V8-6 Spd./AT					
Veh. Ident.: 1G1(Model)2()()45000001 Up.					
Coupe 2D	YY2	3246	32850	37375	39400
Hardtop 2D Z06	YY1	3118	36750	41475	43625
Convertible 2D	YY3	3248	38025	42825	45025
Add Commemorative Edition Pkg			2300	2525	2525
Add Magnetic Selective Ride Control			900	1000	1000
Add Removable Glass Roof			675	775	775
Add Theft Recovery System			100	125	125
CHEVROLET					
2003 CAVALIER-L4					
Veh. Ident.: 1G1(Model)()F()37000001 Up.					
Coupe 2D	JC1	2617	6350	7925	8750
Coupe 2D LS	JF1		7225	8900	9675
Coupe 2D LS Sport	JH1		8300	10125	10850
Sedan 4D	JC5	2676	6350	7925	8750
Sedan 4D LS	JF5		7225	8900	9675
Sedan 4D LS Sport	JH5		8300	10125	10850
Add Aluminum/Alloy Wheels (Std. LS Sport)			250	300	300

BODY TYPE	Model No.	Weight	Trade-In	Retail	High Retail
Add Compact Disc Player (Base)			75	100	100
Add Cruise Control (Base)			150	175	175
Add Power Door Locks (Base)			125	150	150
Add Power Sunroof			475	550	550
Add Theft Recovery System			75	100	100
Add Tilt Steering Wheel (Base)			100	125	125
Deduct W/out Automatic Trans.			425	425	425
2003 MALIBU-V6					
Veh. Ident.: 1G1(Model)2J()3()000001 Up.					
Sedan 4D	ND5	3106	7450	9250	10125
Sedan 4D LS	NE5	3101	8650	10575	11525
Add Aluminum/Alloy Wheels (Std. LS)			275	325	325
Add Leather Seats			400	450	450
Add Power Seat (Std. LS)			175	200	200
Add Power Sunroof			525	600	600
Add Theft Recovery System			75	100	100
Deduct W/out Cruise Control			175	175	175
Deduct W/out Power Windows			175	175	175
2003 MONTE CARLO-V6					
Veh. Ident.: 2G1(Model)()()()39000001 Up.					
Coupe 2D LS	WW1	3340	9825	11900	12825
Coupe 2D SS	WX1	3391	13400	15800	16825
Add SS High Sport Appearance Pkg.			500	575	575
Add Aluminum/Alloy Wheels (Std. SS)			275	325	325
Add Compact Disc Player			75	100	100
Add Leather Seats			400	450	450
Add Power Seat			175	200	200
Add Power Sunroof			525	600	600
Add Theft Recovery System			75	100	100
Deduct W/out Cruise Control			175	175	175
2003 IMPALA-V6					
Veh. Ident.: 2G1(Model)()()()39000001 Up.					
Sedan 4D	WF5	3308	9450	11600	12625
Sedan 4D LS	WH5	3450	12375	14775	15925
Add LS Sport Appearance Pkg.			400	450	450
Add 3.8L V6 Engine (Std. LS)			350	400	400
Add Aluminum/Alloy Wheels (Std. LS)			325	375	375
Add Compact Disc Player			125	150	150
Add Leather Seats			475	550	550
Add Power Sunroof			575	650	650
Add Theft Recovery System			75	100	100
Deduct W/out Cruise Control			200	200	200
Deduct W/out Power Seat			200	200	200
2003 CORVETTE-V8-6 Spd./AT					
Veh. Ident.: 1G1(Model)2()()35000001 Up.					
Coupe 2D	YY2	3246	29850	34075	36000
Coupe 2D 50th Anniversary	YY2		33175	37700	39750
Hardtop 2D Z06	YY1	3118	33400	37950	40000
Convertible 2D	YY3	3248	34775	39375	41475
Convertible 2D 50th Anniversary	YY3		38100	42900	45100
Add Magnetic Selective Ride Control (Std. 50th)			800	900	900
Add Removable Glass Roof			625	700	700
Add Theft Recovery System			75	100	100

BODY TYPE	Model No.	Weight	Trade-In	Retail	High Retail
CHEVROLET					
2002 PRIZM-4 Cyl.					
Veh. Ident.: 1Y1SK5()()()2Z000001 Up.					
Sedan 4D	SK5	2403	**5925**	**7475**	**8275**
Sedan 4D LSi	SK5		**6625**	**8225**	**8975**
Add Aluminum/Alloy Wheels			**200**	**225**	**225**
Add Compact Disc Player			**75**	**100**	**100**
Add Cruise Control (Std. LSi)			**125**	**150**	**150**
Add Power Door Locks (Std. LSi)			**100**	**125**	**125**
Add Power Sunroof			**425**	**475**	**475**
Add Power Windows (Std. LSi)			**125**	**150**	**150**
Add Theft Recovery System			**75**	**100**	**100**
Add Tilt Steering Wheel (Std. LSi)			**75**	**100**	**100**
Deduct W/out Automatic Trans.			**375**	**375**	**375**
2002 CAVALIER-L4					
Veh. Ident.: ()G1(Model)()()()2()000001 Up.					
Coupe 2D	JC1	2617	**5350**	**6850**	**7675**
Coupe 2D LS	JS1	2617	**5950**	**7500**	**8300**
Coupe 2D LS Sport	JH1		**7000**	**8650**	**9425**
Coupe 2D Z24	JH1	2749	**7000**	**8650**	**9425**
Sedan 4D	JC5	2676	**5350**	**6850**	**7675**
Sedan 4D LS	JF5	2676	**5950**	**7500**	**8300**
Sedan 4D LS Sport	JH5		**7000**	**8650**	**9425**
Sedan 4D Z24	JH5	2809	**7000**	**8650**	**9425**
Add Aluminum/Alloy Wheels (Std. LS Sport, Z24)			**200**	**225**	**225**
Add Cruise Control (Base)			**125**	**150**	**150**
Add Power Door Locks (Base)			**100**	**125**	**125**
Add Power Sunroof			**425**	**475**	**475**
Add Theft Recovery System			**75**	**100**	**100**
Deduct W/out Automatic Trans.			**375**	**375**	**375**
2002 MALIBU-V6					
Veh. Ident.: 1G1(Model)()()()2()000001 Up.					
Sedan 4D	ND5	3051	**6525**	**8275**	**9125**
Sedan 4D LS	NE5	3080	**7575**	**9400**	**10275**
Add Aluminum/Alloy Wheels (Std. LS)			**225**	**250**	**250**
Add Leather Seats			**350**	**400**	**400**
Add Power Sunroof			**475**	**550**	**550**
Add Theft Recovery System			**75**	**100**	**100**
Deduct W/out Cruise Control			**150**	**150**	**150**
Deduct W/out Power Windows			**150**	**150**	**150**
2002 MONTE CARLO-V6					
Veh. Ident.: 2G1(Model)()()()2()000001 Up.					
Coupe 2D LS	WW1	3340	**8675**	**10575**	**11525**
Coupe 2D SS	WX1	3395	**11850**	**14100**	**15050**
Add Aluminum/Alloy Wheels (Std. SS)			**225**	**250**	**250**
Add Compact Disc Player			**75**	**100**	**100**
Add Leather Seats			**350**	**400**	**400**
Add Power Seat			**150**	**175**	**175**
Add Power Sunroof			**475**	**550**	**550**
Add Theft Recovery System			**75**	**100**	**100**
Deduct W/out Cruise Control			**150**	**150**	**150**

BODY TYPE	Model No.	Weight	Trade-In	Retail	High Retail
2002 CAMARO-V6					
Veh. Ident.: 2G1(Model)()()()22000001 Up.					
Coupe 2D	FP2	3323	**9775**	**11850**	**12750**
Convertible 2D	FP3	3524	**11900**	**14175**	**15125**
2002 CAMARO-V8-6 Spd./AT					
Veh. Ident.: 2G1(Model)()()()22000001 Up.					
Coupe 2D Z28	FP2	3433	**13725**	**16150**	**17175**
Coupe 2D SS	FP2		**15725**	**18275**	**19325**
Convertible 2D Z28	FP3	3577	**16000**	**18550**	**19625**
Convertible 2D SS	FP3		**17850**	**20600**	**21725**
CAMARO OPTIONS					
Add Leather Seats			**350**	**400**	**400**
Add Power Seat (Std. SS, Z28 Conv.)			**150**	**175**	**175**
Add T-Top			**625**	**700**	**700**
Add Theft Recovery System			**75**	**100**	**100**
Deduct W/out Automatic Trans. (V6)			**475**	**475**	**475**
Deduct W/out Cruise Control			**150**	**150**	**150**
Deduct W/out Power Door Locks			**125**	**125**	**125**
Deduct W/out Power Windows			**150**	**150**	**150**
2002 IMPALA-V6					
Veh. Ident.: 2G1(Model)()()()2()000001 Up.					
Sedan 4D	WF5	3389	**7850**	**9850**	**10900**
Sedan 4D LS	WH5	3466	**10275**	**12475**	**13525**
Add Aluminum/Alloy Wheels (Std. LS)			**275**	**325**	**325**
Add Compact Disc Player			**100**	**125**	**125**
Add Leather Seats			**425**	**475**	**475**
Add Power Sunroof			**525**	**600**	**600**
Add Theft Recovery System			**75**	**100**	**100**
Deduct W/out Cruise Control			**175**	**175**	**175**
Deduct W/out Power Seat			**175**	**175**	**175**
2002 CORVETTE-V8-6 Spd./AT					
Veh. Ident.: 1G1(Model)()()()25000001 Up.					
Coupe 2D	YY2	3214	**26225**	**30100**	**31925**
Hardtop 2D Z06	YY1	3116	**29425**	**33600**	**35525**
Convertible 2D	YY3	3210	**30750**	**35000**	**36950**
Add Removable Glass Roof			**575**	**650**	**650**
Add Theft Recovery System			**75**	**100**	**100**
CHEVROLET					
2001 METRO-4 Cyl.					
Veh. Ident.: ()C1MR5()()()1()000001 Up.					
Sedan 4D LSi	MR5	1984	**3250**	**4500**	**5250**
Add Aluminum/Alloy Wheels			**150**	**175**	**175**
Add Compact Disc Player			**50**	**75**	**75**
Add Power Door Locks			**75**	**100**	**100**
Add Theft Recovery System			**50**	**75**	**75**
Deduct W/out Power Steering			**75**	**75**	**75**
2001 PRIZM-4 Cyl.					
Veh. Ident.: ()Y1SK5()()()1()000001 Up.					
Sedan 4D	SK5	2403	**4975**	**6425**	**7225**
Sedan 4D LSi	SK5	2403	**5575**	**7100**	**7875**
Add Aluminum/Alloy Wheels			**150**	**175**	**175**
Add Compact Disc Player			**50**	**75**	**75**

PASSENGER CARS

P A S S E N G E R C A R S

BODY TYPE	Model No.	Weight	Trade-In	Retail	High Retail
Add Cruise Control (Std. LSi)			100	125	125
Add Power Door Locks (Std. LSi)			75	100	100
Add Power Sunroof			375	425	425
Add Power Windows (Std. LSi)			100	125	125
Add Theft Recovery System			50	75	75
Add Tilt Steering Wheel (Std. LSi)			75	100	100
Deduct W/out Automatic Trans.			325	325	325
2001 CAVALIER-L4					
Veh. Ident.: ()G1(Model)()()()1()000001 Up.					
Coupe 2D	JC1	2617	4250	5625	6400
Coupe 2D Z24	JF1	2749	5900	7450	8250
Sedan 4D	JC5	2676	4250	5625	6400
Sedan 4D LS	JF5	2676	4700	6100	6875
Add Aluminum/Alloy Wheels (Std. Z24)			150	175	175
Add Compact Disc Player (Std. LS, Z24)			50	75	75
Add Cruise Control (Std. LS, Z24)			100	125	125
Add Power Door Locks (Std. Z24)			75	100	100
Add Power Sunroof			375	425	425
Add Power Windows (Std. Z24)			100	125	125
Add Theft Recovery System			50	75	75
Add Tilt Steering Wheel (Std. LS, Z24)			75	100	100
Deduct W/out Automatic Trans.			325	325	325
2001 MALIBU-V6					
Veh. Ident.: ()G1(Model)()()()1()000001 Up.					
Sedan 4D	ND5	3051	5300	6925	7850
Sedan 4D LS	NE5	3077	6225	7950	8875
Add Aluminum/Alloy Wheels (Std. LS)			175	200	200
Add Compact Disc Player (Std. LS)			50	75	75
Add Leather Seats			300	350	350
Add Power Sunroof			425	475	475
Add Theft Recovery System			50	75	75
Deduct W/out Cruise Control			125	125	125
Deduct W/out Power Windows			125	125	125
2001 LUMINA-V6					
Veh. Ident.: ()G1WL5()()()1()000001 Up.					
Sedan 4D	WL5	3330	4475	5975	6850
Add Aluminum/Alloy Wheels			175	200	200
Add Compact Disc Player			50	75	75
Add Power Seat			125	150	150
Add Theft Recovery System			50	75	75
2001 MONTE CARLO-V6					
Veh. Ident.: ()G1(Model)()()()1()000001 Up.					
Coupe 2D LS	WW1	3340	7675	9500	10375
Coupe 2D SS	WX1	3395	10125	12250	13150
Add Aluminum/Alloy Wheels (Std. SS)			175	200	200
Add Compact Disc Player			50	75	75
Add Leather Seats			300	350	350
Add Power Seat			125	150	150
Add Power Sunroof			425	475	475
Add Theft Recovery System			50	75	75
Deduct W/out Cruise Control			125	125	125

BODY TYPE	Model No.	Weight	Trade-In	Retail	High Retail
2001 CAMARO-V6					
Veh. Ident.: ()G1(Model)()()()1()000001 Up.					
Coupe 2D	FP2	3306	7925	9775	10675
Convertible 2D	FP3	3500	9775	11850	12750
2001 CAMARO-V8-6 Spd./AT					
Veh. Ident.: ()G1(Model)()()()1()000001 Up.					
Coupe 2D Z28	FP2	3439	11850	14100	15050
Coupe 2D SS	FP2		13500	15925	16950
Convertible 2D Z28	FP3	3574	13825	16275	17300
Convertible 2D SS	FP3		15475	18025	19075
CAMARO OPTIONS					
Add Aluminum/Alloy Wheels (V6)			175	200	200
Add Compact Disc Player			50	75	75
Add Leather Seats			300	350	350
Add Power Seat (Std. V8 Conv.)			125	150	150
Add T-Top			575	650	650
Add Theft Recovery System			50	75	75
Deduct W/out Automatic Trans. (V6)			425	425	425
Deduct W/out Cruise Control			125	125	125
Deduct W/out Power Door Locks			100	100	100
Deduct W/out Power Windows			125	125	125
2001 IMPALA-V6					
Veh. Ident.: ()G1(Model)()()()1()000001 Up.					
Sedan 4D	WF5	3389	6575	8475	9500
Sedan 4D LS	WH5	3466	8475	10525	11575
Add Aluminum/Alloy Wheels (Std. LS)			225	250	250
Add Compact Disc Player			100	125	125
Add Leather Seats			375	425	425
Add Power Sunroof			475	550	550
Add Theft Recovery System			50	75	75
Deduct W/out Cruise Control			150	150	150
Deduct W/out Power Seat			150	150	150
2001 CORVETTE-V8-6 Spd./AT					
Veh. Ident.: ()G1(Model)()()()1()000001 Up.					
Coupe 2D	YY2	3221	23600	27300	29025
Hardtop 2D Z06	YY1		26425	30300	32125
Convertible 2D	YY3	3248	27725	31800	33675
Add Compact Disc Player (Std. Z06)			125	150	150
Add Removable Glass Roof			525	600	600
Add Theft Recovery System			50	75	75
CHEVROLET					
2000 METRO-4 Cyl.-5 Spd.					
Veh. Ident.: ()C1(Model)()()()Y()000001 Up.					
Hatchback 2D (3 Cyl.)	MR2	1895	1900	3000	3650
Hatchback 2D LSi	MR2	1895	2200	3350	4000
Sedan 4D LSi	MR5	1984	2350	3500	4150
Add Aluminum/Alloy Wheels			100	125	125
Add Automatic Trans.			300	350	350
Add Compact Disc Player			50	75	75
Add Power Door Locks			50	75	75
Deduct W/out Air Conditioning			375	375	375
Deduct W/out Power Steering (Sedan LSi)			50	50	50

PASSENGER CARS

PASSENGER CARS

BODY TYPE	Model No.	Weight	Trade-In	Retail	High Retail
2000 PRIZM-4 Cyl.					
Veh. Ident.: ()Y1SK5()()()Y()000001 Up.					
Sedan 4D	SK5	2403	**4150**	**5525**	**6275**
Sedan 4D LSi	SK5	2403	**4625**	**6025**	**6800**
Add Aluminum/Alloy Wheels			**100**	**125**	**125**
Add Compact Disc Player			**50**	**75**	**75**
Add Cruise Control (Std. LSi)			**75**	**100**	**100**
Add Power Door Locks (Std. LSi)			**50**	**75**	**75**
Add Power Sunroof			**325**	**375**	**375**
Add Power Windows (Std. LSi)			**75**	**100**	**100**
Add Tilt Steering Wheel (Std. LSi)			**50**	**75**	**75**
Deduct W/out Automatic Trans.			**300**	**300**	**300**
2000 CAVALIER-L4					
Veh. Ident.: ()G1(Model)()()()Y()000001 Up.					
Coupe 2D	JC1	2617	**3500**	**4775**	**5575**
Coupe 2D Z24	JF1	2617	**4925**	**6350**	**7150**
Sedan 4D	JC5	2676	**3500**	**4775**	**5575**
Sedan 4D LS	JF5	2676	**3825**	**5125**	**5850**
Convertible 2D Z24	JF3	2838	**5950**	**7500**	**8300**
Add Aluminum/Alloy Wheels (Std. Z24)			**100**	**125**	**125**
Add Compact Disc Player (Std. Z24)			**50**	**75**	**75**
Add Cruise Control (Std. LS, Z24)			**75**	**100**	**100**
Add Power Door Locks (Std. Z24)			**50**	**75**	**75**
Add Power Sunroof			**325**	**375**	**375**
Add Power Windows (Std. Z24)			**75**	**100**	**100**
Add Tilt Steering Wheel (Std. LS, Z24)			**50**	**75**	**75**
Deduct W/out Automatic Trans.			**300**	**300**	**300**
2000 MALIBU-V6					
Veh. Ident.: ()G1(Model)()()()Y()000001 Up.					
Sedan 4D	ND5	3051	**4350**	**5850**	**6725**
Sedan 4D LS	NE5	3077	**5075**	**6675**	**7600**
Add Aluminum/Alloy Wheels (Std. LS)			**125**	**150**	**150**
Add Compact Disc Player (Std. LS)			**50**	**75**	**75**
Add Leather Seats			**250**	**300**	**300**
Add Power Seat (Std. LS)			**100**	**125**	**125**
Add Power Sunroof			**375**	**425**	**425**
Deduct W/out Cruise Control			**100**	**100**	**100**
Deduct W/out Power Door Locks			**75**	**75**	**75**
Deduct W/out Power Windows			**100**	**100**	**100**
2000 LUMINA-V6					
Veh. Ident.: ()G1WL5()()()Y()000001 Up.					
Sedan 4D	WL5	3330	**3900**	**5350**	**6175**
Add Aluminum/Alloy Wheels			**125**	**150**	**150**
Add Compact Disc Player			**50**	**75**	**75**
Add Power Seat			**100**	**125**	**125**
2000 MONTE CARLO-V6					
Veh. Ident.: ()G1(Model)()()()Y()000001 Up.					
Coupe 2D LS	WW1	3340	**6525**	**8275**	**9125**
Coupe 2D SS	WX1	3391	**8475**	**10375**	**11300**
Add Aluminum/Alloy Wheels (Std. SS)			**125**	**150**	**150**
Add Compact Disc Player			**50**	**75**	**75**
Add Leather Seats			**250**	**300**	**300**

BODY TYPE	Model No.	Weight	Trade-In	Retail	High Retail
Add Power Seat			100	125	125
Add Power Sunroof			375	425	425
Deduct W/out Cruise Control			100	100	100
2000 CAMARO-V6					
Veh. Ident.: ()G1(Model)()()()Y()000001 Up.					
Coupe 2D	FP2	3306	6600	8350	9225
Convertible 2D	FP3	3500	8325	10200	11125
2000 CAMARO-V8-6 Spd./AT					
Veh. Ident.: ()G1(Model)()()()Y()000001 Up.					
Coupe 2D Z28	FP2	3439	10225	12375	13275
Coupe 2D SS	FP2		11675	13925	14875
Convertible 2D Z28	FP3	3574	12050	14325	15300
Convertible 2D SS	FP3		13500	15900	16925
CAMARO OPTIONS					
Add Aluminum/Alloy Wheels (V6)			125	150	150
Add Compact Disc Player			50	75	75
Add Leather Seats			250	300	300
Add Power Seat (Std. V8 Conv.)			100	125	125
Add T-Top			525	600	600
Deduct W/out Automatic Trans. (V6)			375	375	375
Deduct W/out Cruise Control			100	100	100
Deduct W/out Power Door Locks			75	75	75
Deduct W/out Power Windows			100	100	100
2000 IMPALA-V6					
Veh. Ident.: ()G1(Model)()()()Y()000001 Up.					
Sedan 4D	WF5	3389	5725	7550	8600
Sedan 4D LS	WH5	3466	7050	9000	10050
Add Aluminum/Alloy Wheels (Std. LS)			175	200	200
Add Compact Disc Player			75	100	100
Add Leather Seats			325	375	375
Add Power Sunroof			425	475	475
Deduct W/out Cruise Control			125	125	125
Deduct W/out Power Seat			125	125	125
2000 CORVETTE-V8-6 Spd./AT					
Veh. Ident.: ()G1(Model)()()()Y()000001 Up.					
Coupe 2D	YY2	3173	20875	24250	25850
Hardtop 2D	YY1	3246	19650	22950	24500
Convertible 2D	YY3	3248	24650	28425	30175
Add Bose Stereo System (Hardtop)			225	250	250
Add Compact Disc Player			100	125	125
Add Removable Glass Roof			475	550	550
Deduct W/out Power Seat			175	175	175
CHEVROLET					
1999 METRO-4 Cyl.-5 Spd.					
Veh. Ident.: ()C1(Model)()()()X()000001 Up.					
Hatchback 2D (3 Cyl.)	MR2	1895	1500	2525	3100
Hatchback 2D LSi	MR2	1895	1775	2850	3475
Sedan 4D LSi	MR5	1984	1925	3025	3625
Add Aluminum/Alloy Wheels			50	75	75
Add Automatic Trans.			250	300	300
Deduct W/out Air Conditioning			325	325	325

PASSENGER CARS

BODY TYPE	Model No.	Weight	Trade-In	Retail	High Retail
1999 PRIZM-4 Cyl.					
Veh. Ident.: ()Y1SK5()()()X()000001 Up.					
Sedan 4D	SK5	2403	**3400**	**4650**	**5425**
Sedan 4D LSi	SK5	2403	**3650**	**4925**	**5725**
Add Aluminum/Alloy Wheels			**50**	**75**	**75**
Add Cruise Control (Std. LSi)			**50**	**75**	**75**
Add Power Sunroof			**275**	**325**	**325**
Add Power Windows			**50**	**75**	**75**
Deduct W/out Air Conditioning			**325**	**325**	**325**
Deduct W/out Automatic Trans.			**250**	**250**	**250**
1999 CAVALIER-L4					
Veh. Ident.: ()G1(Model)()()()X()000001 Up.					
Coupe 2D	JC1	2617	**2750**	**3950**	**4650**
Coupe 2D RS	JC1	2617	**2975**	**4200**	**4925**
Coupe 2D Z24	JF1	2749	**3875**	**5200**	**5925**
Sedan 4D	JC5	2676	**2750**	**3950**	**4650**
Sedan 4D LS	JF5	2676	**2975**	**4200**	**4925**
Convertible 2D Z24	JF3	2838	**4825**	**6250**	**7025**
Add Aluminum/Alloy Wheels (Std. Z24)			**50**	**75**	**75**
Add Cruise Control (Base Coupe)			**50**	**75**	**75**
Add Power Sunroof			**275**	**325**	**325**
Add Power Windows (Std. Z24)			**50**	**75**	**75**
Deduct W/out Air Conditioning			**325**	**325**	**325**
Deduct W/out Automatic Trans.			**250**	**250**	**250**
1999 MALIBU-V6					
Veh. Ident.: ()G1(Model)()()()X()000001 Up.					
Sedan 4D (4 Cyl.)	ND5	3051	**3350**	**4725**	**5600**
Sedan 4D	ND5	3051	**3625**	**5025**	**5825**
Sedan 4D LS	NE5	3077	**4150**	**5625**	**6475**
Add Aluminum/Alloy Wheels (Std. LS)			**75**	**100**	**100**
Add Leather Seats			**225**	**250**	**250**
Add Power Seat (Std. LS)			**75**	**100**	**100**
Add Power Sunroof			**325**	**375**	**375**
Deduct W/out Cruise Control			**75**	**75**	**75**
Deduct W/out Power Door Locks			**50**	**50**	**50**
Deduct W/out Power Windows			**75**	**75**	**75**
1999 LUMINA-V6					
Veh. Ident.: ()G1(Model)()()()X()000001 Up.					
Sedan 4D	WL5	3330	**3300**	**4675**	**5550**
Sedan 4D LS	WL5	3372	**3600**	**5000**	**5900**
Sedan 4D LTZ	WN5	3372	**4025**	**5475**	**6300**
Add Aluminum/Alloy Wheels (Std. LS, LTZ)			**75**	**100**	**100**
Add Leather Seats			**225**	**250**	**250**
Add Power Seat			**75**	**100**	**100**
Add Power Sunroof			**325**	**375**	**375**
1999 MONTE CARLO-V6					
Veh. Ident.: ()G1(Model)()()()X()000001 Up.					
Coupe 2D LS	WW1	3306	**4150**	**5625**	**6475**
Coupe 2D Z34	WX1	3436	**4900**	**6450**	**7350**
Add Aluminum/Alloy Wheels (Std. Z34)			**75**	**100**	**100**
Add Leather Seats			**225**	**250**	**250**
Add Power Seat			**75**	**100**	**100**

BODY TYPE	Model No.	Weight	Trade-In	Retail	High Retail
Add Power Sunroof			325	375	375
1999 CAMARO-V6					
Veh. Ident.: ()G1(Model)()()()X()000001 Up.					
Coupe 2D	FP2	3306	5425	7050	7925
Convertible 2D	FP3	3340	7000	8775	9675
1999 CAMARO-V8-6 Spd./AT					
Veh. Ident.: ()G1(Model)()()()X()000001 Up.					
Coupe 2D Z28	FP2	3446	8550	10450	11375
Coupe 2D SS	FP2		9850	11900	12825
Convertible 2D Z28	FP3	3565	10200	12350	13250
Convertible 2D SS	FP3		11500	13750	14700
CAMARO OPTIONS					
Add Aluminum/Alloy Wheels (V6)			75	100	100
Add Leather Seats			225	250	250
Add Power Seat (Std. V8 Conv.)			75	100	100
Add T-Top			475	550	550
Deduct W/out Automatic Trans. (V6)			325	325	325
Deduct W/out Cruise Control			75	75	75
Deduct W/out Power Door Locks			50	50	50
Deduct W/out Power Windows			75	75	75
1999 CORVETTE-V8-6 Spd./AT					
Veh. Ident.: ()G1(Model)()()()X()000001 Up.					
Coupe 2D	YY2	3221	18450	21650	23175
Hardtop 2D	YY1	3153	17425	20550	22025
Convertible 2D	YY3	3246	21775	25225	26875
Add Bose Stereo System (Hardtop)			175	200	200
Add Removable Glass Roof			425	475	475
Deduct W/out Power Seat			150	150	150
CHEVROLET					
1998 METRO-4 Cyl.-5 Spd.					
Veh. Ident.: ()()1(Model)()()()W()000001 Up.					
Hatchback 2D (3 Cyl.)	MR2	1895	1225	2225	2750
Hatchback 2D LSi	MR2	1895	1500	2550	3125
Sedan 4D LSi	MR5	1984	1650	2700	3300
Add Automatic Trans.			200	225	225
Deduct W/out Air Conditioning			275	275	275
1998 PRIZM-4 Cyl.					
Veh. Ident.: ()()1(Model)()()()W()000001 Up.					
Sedan 4D	SK5		2825	4025	4725
Sedan 4D LSi	SK5		3050	4275	5000
Add Cruise Control (Std. LSi)			50	75	75
Add Power Sunroof			225	275	275
Add Power Windows			50	75	75
Deduct W/out Air Conditioning			275	275	275
Deduct W/out Automatic Trans.			200	200	200
1998 CAVALIER-L4					
Veh. Ident.: ()()1(Model)()()()W()000001 Up.					
Coupe 2D	JC1	2584	2300	3450	4100
Coupe 2D RS	JC1	2584	2500	3675	4350
Coupe 2D Z24	JF1	2749	3275	4525	5275
Sedan 4D	JC5	2630	2300	3450	4100
Sedan 4D LS	JF5	2729	2500	3675	4350

PASSENGER CARS

P A S S E N G E R C A R S

BODY TYPE	Model No.	Weight	Trade-In	Retail	High Retail
Convertible 2D Z24	JF3	2899	4150	5500	6250
Add Cruise Control (Base Coupe)			50	75	75
Add Power Sunroof			225	275	275
Add Power Windows (Std. Z24)			50	75	75
Deduct W/out Air Conditioning			275	275	275
Deduct W/out Automatic Trans.			200	200	200
1998 MALIBU-V6					
Veh. Ident.: ()()1(Model)()()()W()000001 Up.					
Sedan 4D (4 Cyl.)	ND5	3100	2850	4150	4950
Sedan 4D	ND5		3075	4425	5275
Sedan 4D LS	NE5	3100	3475	4875	5775
Add Aluminum/Alloy Wheels (Std. LS)			50	75	75
Add Leather Seats			175	200	200
Add Power Seat (Std. LS)			50	75	75
Add Power Sunroof			275	325	325
Deduct W/out Cruise Control			50	50	50
Deduct W/out Power Windows			50	50	50
1998 LUMINA-V6					
Veh. Ident.: ()()1(Model)()()()W()000001 Up.					
Sedan 4D	WL5	3330	2800	4100	4900
Sedan 4D LS	WL5	3372	3000	4350	5175
Sedan 4D LTZ	WN5	3420	3325	4700	5575
Add 3.8L V6 Engine			175	200	200
Add Aluminum/Alloy Wheels (Std. LS, LTZ)			50	75	75
Add Leather Seats			175	200	200
Add Power Seat			50	75	75
Add Power Sunroof			275	325	325
Deduct W/out Cruise Control			50	50	50
Deduct W/out Power Windows			50	50	50
1998 MONTE CARLO-V6					
Veh. Ident.: ()()1(Model)()()()W()000001 Up.					
Coupe 2D LS	WW1	3239	3450	4850	5750
Coupe 2D Z34	WX1	3452	4025	5500	6325
Add Aluminum/Alloy Wheels (Std. Z34)			50	75	75
Add Leather Seats			175	200	200
Add Power Seat			50	75	75
Add Power Sunroof			275	325	325
Deduct W/out Cruise Control			50	50	50
1998 CAMARO-V6					
Veh. Ident.: ()()1(Model)()()()W()000001 Up.					
Coupe 2D	FP2	3331	4350	5850	6725
Convertible 2D	FP3	3468	5800	7475	8375
1998 CAMARO-V8-6 Spd./AT					
Veh. Ident.: ()()1(Model)()()()W()000001 Up.					
Coupe 2D Z28	FP2	3439	7050	8825	9725
Coupe 2D SS	FP2		8275	10175	11100
Convertible 2D Z28	FP3	3574	8550	10450	11375
Convertible 2D SS	FP3		9775	11825	12725
CAMARO OPTIONS					
Add Aluminum/Alloy Wheels (V6)			50	75	75
Add Leather Seats			175	200	200
Add Power Seat (Std. V8 Conv.)			50	75	75

BODY TYPE	Model No.	Weight	Trade-In	Retail	High Retail
Add T-Top			425	475	475
Deduct W/out Automatic Trans. (V6)			275	275	275
Deduct W/out Cruise Control			50	50	50
Deduct W/out Power Windows			50	50	50
1998 CORVETTE-V8-6 Spd./AT					
Veh. Ident.: ()()1(Model)()()()W()000001 Up.					
Coupe 2D	YY2	3245	16825	19775	21225
Convertible 2D	YY3	3246	19825	23100	24675
Add Removable Glass Roof			375	425	425
CHEVROLET					
1997 CAVALIER-L4					
Veh. Ident.: ()G1(Model)()()()V()000001 Up.					
Coupe 2D	JC1	2584	1950	3050	3650
Coupe 2D RS	JG1	2617	2050	3175	3800
Coupe 2D Z24	JF1	2749	2600	3775	4475
Sedan 4D	JC5	2630	1950	3050	3650
Sedan 4D LS	JF5	2729	2050	3175	3800
Convertible 2D LS	JF3	2899	2750	3950	4650
Add Power Sunroof			150	175	175
Deduct W/out Air Conditioning			150	150	150
Deduct W/out Automatic Trans.			125	125	125
1997 MALIBU-V6					
Veh. Ident.: ()G1(Model)()()()V()000001 Up.					
Sedan 4D (4 Cyl.)	ND5	3051	2425	3675	4425
Sedan 4D	ND5		2625	3900	4700
Sedan 4D LS	NE5	3077	2825	4125	4925
Add Power Seat (Std. LS)			50	75	75
Deduct W/out Cruise Control			25	25	25
Deduct W/out Power Windows			25	25	25
1997 LUMINA-V6					
Veh. Ident.: ()G1(Model)()()()V()000001 Up.					
Sedan 4D	WL5	3360	2200	3425	4150
Sedan 4D LS	WL5	3388	2300	3550	4300
Sedan 4D LTZ	WN5		2575	3850	4625
Add 3.4L V6 Engine			75	100	100
Add Leather Seats			150	175	175
Add Power Seat			50	75	75
Add Power Sunroof			200	225	225
Deduct W/out Cruise Control			25	25	25
Deduct W/out Power Windows			25	25	25
1997 MONTE CARLO-V6					
Veh. Ident.: ()G1(Model)()()()V()000001 Up.					
Coupe 2D LS	WW1	3320	2975	4300	5125
Coupe 2D Z34	WX1	3455	3300	4675	5550
Add Leather Seats			150	175	175
Add Power Seat			50	75	75
Add Power Sunroof			200	225	225
Deduct W/out Cruise Control			25	25	25
1997 CAMARO-V6					
Veh. Ident.: ()G1(Model)()()()V()000001 Up.					
Coupe 2D	FP2	3294	3875	5325	6150

BODY TYPE	Model No.	Weight	Trade-In	Retail	High Retail
Coupe 2D RS	FP2	3307	**4025**	**5475**	**6300**
Convertible 2D	FP3	3446	**5100**	**6700**	**7625**
Convertible 2D RS	FP3	3455	**5250**	**6875**	**7800**
1997 CAMARO-V8-6 Spd./AT					
Veh. Ident.: ()G1(Model)()()()V()000001 Up.					
Coupe 2D Z28	FP2	3433	**6050**	**7750**	**8675**
Convertible 2D Z28	FP3	3589	**7275**	**9075**	**9925**
CAMARO OPTIONS					
Add Leather Seats			**150**	**175**	**175**
Add Power Seat			**50**	**75**	**75**
Add T-Top			**250**	**300**	**300**
Deduct W/out Automatic Trans. (V6)			**175**	**175**	**175**
Deduct W/out Cruise Control			**25**	**25**	**25**
Deduct W/out Power Windows			**25**	**25**	**25**
1997 CORVETTE-V8-6 Spd./AT					
Veh. Ident.: 1G1YY2()()()V5100001 Up.					
Coupe 2D	YY2	3229	**15175**	**18025**	**19400**
Add Removable Glass Roof			**325**	**375**	**375**
CHEVROLET					
1996 CAVALIER-L4					
Veh. Ident.: ()G1(Model)()()()T()000001 Up.					
Coupe 2D	JC1	2617	**1650**	**2700**	**3300**
Coupe 2D Z24	JF1	2788	**2150**	**3275**	**3900**
Sedan 4D	JC5	2676	**1650**	**2700**	**3300**
Sedan 4D LS	JF5	2736	**1750**	**2825**	**3450**
Convertible 2D LS	JF3	2838	**2350**	**3500**	**4150**
Add Power Sunroof			**100**	**125**	**125**
Deduct W/out Air Conditioning			**75**	**75**	**75**
Deduct W/out Automatic Trans.			**75**	**75**	**75**
1996 BERETTA/CORSICA-L4					
Veh. Ident.: ()G1(Model)()()()T()000001 Up.					
Beretta Coupe 2D	LV1	2756	**1475**	**2500**	**3075**
Corsica Sedan 4D	LD5	2745	**1225**	**2225**	**2750**
1996 BERETTA/CORSICA-V6					
Veh. Ident.: ()G1(Model)()()()T()000001 Up.					
Beretta Coupe 2D	LV1	2896	**1575**	**2625**	**3225**
Beretta Coupe 2D Z26	LW1	2990	**1875**	**2950**	**3600**
Corsica Sedan 4D	LD5	2885	**1325**	**2350**	**2900**
BERETTA/CORSICA OPTIONS					
Deduct W/out Automatic Trans.			**75**	**75**	**75**
1996 LUMINA-V6					
Veh. Ident.: ()G1(Model)()()()T()000001 Up.					
Sedan 4D	WL5	3330	**1850**	**3025**	**3700**
Sedan 4D LS	WN5	3372	**1950**	**3150**	**3850**
Add 3.4L V6 Engine			**75**	**100**	**100**
Add Power Sunroof			**150**	**175**	**175**
1996 MONTE CARLO-V6					
Veh. Ident.: ()G1(Model)()()()T()000001 Up.					
Coupe 2D LS	WW1	3306	**2450**	**3700**	**4450**
Coupe 2D Z34	WX1	3436	**2775**	**4075**	**4875**
Add Power Sunroof			**150**	**175**	**175**

BODY TYPE	Model No.	Weight	Trade-In	Retail	High Retail
1996 CAMARO-V6					
Veh. Ident.: ()G1(Model)()()()T()000001 Up.					
Coupe 2D	FP2	3306	**3425**	**4825**	**5725**
Coupe 2D RS	FP2	3306	**3575**	**4975**	**5875**
Convertible 2D	FP3	3440	**4575**	**6100**	**6950**
Convertible 2D RS	FP3	3440	**4725**	**6250**	**7125**
1996 CAMARO-V8-6 Spd./AT					
Veh. Ident.: ()G1(Model)()()()T()000001 Up.					
Coupe 2D Z28	FP2	3466	**5325**	**6950**	**7900**
Convertible 2D Z28	FP3	3593	**6475**	**8200**	**9050**
CAMARO OPTIONS					
Add T-Top			**200**	**225**	**225**
Deduct W/out Air Conditioning			**150**	**150**	**150**
Deduct W/out Automatic Trans. (V6)			**125**	**125**	**125**
1996 CAPRICE CLASSIC-V8					
Veh. Ident.: ()G1(Model)()()()T()000001 Up.					
Sedan 4D	BL5	4061	**3700**	**5250**	**6175**
Wagon 4D	BL8	4473	**3925**	**5500**	**6450**
1996 IMPALA SS-V8					
Veh. Ident.: ()G1BL5()()()T()000001 Up.					
Sedan 4D	BL5	4036	**9800**	**11975**	**13025**
1996 CORVETTE-V8-6 Spd./AT					
Veh. Ident.: ()G1(Model)()()()T()000001 Up.					
Coupe 2D	YY2	3298	**12325**	**14975**	**16250**
Convertible 2D	YY3	3360	**14500**	**17300**	**18650**
Add LT4 Engine			**575**	**650**	**650**
Add Removable Glass Roof			**275**	**325**	**325**
Add Removable Hardtop			**325**	**375**	**375**
CHEVROLET					
1995 CAVALIER-L4					
Veh. Ident.: ()G1(Model)()()()S()000001 Up.					
Coupe 2D	JC1	2617	**1425**	**2450**	**3025**
Coupe 2D Z24	JF1	2788	**1775**	**2850**	**3475**
Sedan 4D	JC5	2676	**1425**	**2450**	**3025**
Sedan 4D LS	JF5	2736	**1500**	**2550**	**3125**
Convertible 2D LS	JF3	2838	**2075**	**3200**	**3825**
1995 BERETTA/CORSICA-L4					
Veh. Ident.: ()G1(Model)()()()S()000001 Up.					
Beretta Coupe 2D	LV1	2756	**1300**	**2325**	**2875**
Corsica Sedan 4D	LD5	2745	**1075**	**2075**	**2600**
1995 BERETTA/CORSICA-V6					
Veh. Ident.: ()G1(Model)()()()S()000001 Up.					
Beretta Coupe 2D	LV1	2896	**1375**	**2400**	**2950**
Beretta Coupe 2D Z26	LW1	2990	**1600**	**2650**	**3250**
Corsica Sedan 4D	LD5	2885	**1150**	**2150**	**2675**
1995 LUMINA-V6					
Veh. Ident.: ()G1(Model)()()()S()000001 Up.					
Sedan 4D	WL5	3330	**1575**	**2725**	**3375**
Sedan 4D LS	WN5	3372	**1675**	**2825**	**3475**
Add 3.4L V6 Engine			**75**	**100**	**100**

PASSENGER CARS

PASSENGER CARS

BODY TYPE	Model No.	Weight	Trade-In	Retail	High Retail
1995 MONTE CARLO-V6					
Veh. Ident.: ()G1(Model)()()()S()000001 Up.					
Coupe 2D LS	WW1	3276	**2100**	**3325**	**4025**
Coupe 2D Z34	WX1	3451	**2400**	**3650**	**4400**
1995 CAMARO-V6					
Veh. Ident.: ()G1(Model)()()()S()000001 Up.					
Coupe 2D	FP2	3251	**2950**	**4275**	**5100**
Convertible 2D	FP3	3342	**4025**	**5475**	**6300**
1995 CAMARO-V8					
Veh. Ident.: ()G1(Model)()()()S()000001 Up.					
Coupe 2D Z28	FP2	3390	**4575**	**6100**	**6950**
Convertible 2D Z28	FP3	3480	**5650**	**7300**	**8175**
CAMARO OPTIONS					
Add T-Top			**150**	**175**	**175**
1995 CAPRICE CLASSIC-V8					
Veh. Ident.: ()G1(Model)()()()S()000001 Up.					
Sedan 4D	BL5	4061	**3150**	**4625**	**5550**
Wagon 4D	BL8	4473	**3350**	**4850**	**5800**
1995 IMPALA SS-V8					
Veh. Ident.: ()G1BL5()()()S()000001 Up.					
Sedan 4D	BL5	4036	**7950**	**9975**	**11025**
1995 CORVETTE-V8					
Veh. Ident.: ()G1(Model)()()()S()000001 Up.					
Coupe 2D	YY2	3203	**11300**	**13800**	**15025**
Convertible 2D	YY3	3360	**13375**	**16100**	**17425**
1995 CORVETTE ZR1-V8					
Veh. Ident.: ()G1(Model)()()()S()000001 Up.					
Coupe 2D	YZ2	3512	**24800**	**28575**	**30350**
CORVETTE OPTIONS					
Add Removable Glass Roof			**200**	**225**	**225**
Add Removable Hardtop			**250**	**300**	**300**

CHRYSLER

BODY TYPE	Model No.	Weight	Trade-In	Retail	High Retail
CHRYSLER					
2004 PT CRUISER-4 Cyl.					
Veh. Ident.: 3C()F(Model)()4T000001 Up.					
Wagon 4D	Y48B	3101	**10575**	**12750**	**13650**
Wagon 4D Touring	Y58B		**11350**	**13575**	**14525**
Wagon 4D Touring Turbo	Y588		**12175**	**14525**	**15500**
Wagon 4D Limited	Y68B		**12900**	**15300**	**16300**
Wagon 4D Limited Turbo	Y688		**13725**	**16150**	**17175**
Wagon 4D Ltd. Platinum Turbo	Y688		**14150**	**16600**	**17650**
Wagon 4D GT Turbo	Y78G		**14625**	**17100**	**18125**
Add Aluminum/Alloy Wheels (Base)			**325**	**375**	**375**
Add Navigation System			**600**	**675**	**675**
Add Power Sunroof (Std. Ltd, Platinum, GT)			**575**	**650**	**650**
Add Theft Recovery System			**100**	**125**	**125**
Deduct W/out Automatic Trans.			**575**	**575**	**575**
Deduct W/out Cruise Control			**200**	**200**	**200**
Deduct W/out Power Door Locks			**175**	**175**	**175**

BODY TYPE	Model No.	Weight	Trade-In	Retail	High Retail
2004 SEBRING-4 Cyl.					
Veh. Ident.: ()C3()(Model)()()4()000001 Up.					
Coupe 2D	G42	3064	**10225**	**12350**	**13250**
Sedan 4D	L46	3094	**9425**	**11450**	**12350**
Sedan 4D LX	L46	3094	**9325**	**11350**	**12250**
Convertible 2D	L45	3357	**12250**	**14600**	**15575**
Convertible 2D LX	L45	3276	**12150**	**14500**	**15475**
2004 SEBRING-V6					
Veh. Ident.: ()C3()(Model)()()4()000001 Up.					
Coupe 2D Limited	G52	3206	**11975**	**14225**	**15175**
Coupe 2D Limited Platinum	G52	3206	**12775**	**15150**	**16150**
Sedan 4D LX	L46	3143	**9950**	**12025**	**12900**
Sedan 4D Touring	L56	3222	**10875**	**13050**	**13975**
Sedan 4D Touring Platinum	L56	3273	**11675**	**13900**	**14850**
Sedan 4D LXi	L56	3149	**11075**	**13275**	**14200**
Sedan 4D Limited	L66	3228	**12525**	**14875**	**15850**
Convertible 2D LX	L45	3327	**12675**	**15050**	**16050**
Convertible 2D GTC	L75	3325	**13975**	**16425**	**17450**
Convertible 2D LXi	L55	3338	**14400**	**16875**	**17925**
Convertible 2D Touring	L55	3419	**14850**	**17350**	**18375**
Convertible 2D Touring Platinum	L55	3474	**15000**	**17500**	**18525**
Convertible 2D Limited	L65	3369	**17250**	**19975**	**21075**
SEBRING OPTIONS					
Add Aluminum/Alloy Wheels (Base, LX)			**325**	**375**	**375**
Add CD Player (Sedan LX 4 Cyl., Conv LX)			**100**	**125**	**125**
Add Infinity Stereo System (Std. G52, L65)			**300**	**350**	**350**
Add Leather Seats (Std. Sedan/Conv Limited, Conv Touring, Platinum)			**450**	**500**	**500**
Add Power Seat (Std. L55, L65, L66, LXi, Platinum)			**200**	**225**	**225**
Add Power Sunroof			**575**	**650**	**650**
Add Theft Recovery System			**100**	**125**	**125**
Deduct W/out Automatic Trans.			**575**	**575**	**575**
Deduct W/out Cruise Control			**200**	**200**	**200**
2004 300M-V6					
Veh. Ident.: 2C3()(Model)()()4H000001 Up.					
Sedan 4D	E66	3581	**17700**	**20575**	**21900**
Sedan 4D Platinum	E66	3581	**18150**	**21050**	**22400**
Sedan 4D Special	E76	3650	**19100**	**22050**	**23375**
Add Navigation System			**650**	**725**	**725**
Add Power Sunroof			**625**	**700**	**700**
Add Theft Recovery System			**100**	**125**	**125**
2004 CONCORDE-V6					
Veh. Ident.: 2C3()(Model)()()4H000001 Up.					
Sedan 4D LX	D46	3479	**11050**	**13325**	**14425**
Sedan 4D LXi	D36	3548	**13100**	**15550**	**16725**
Sedan 4D Limited	D56	3567	**15600**	**18200**	**19450**
Add Aluminum/Alloy Wheels (LX)			**375**	**425**	**425**
Add Compact Disc Player (LX)			**150**	**175**	**175**
Add Infinity Stereo System			**350**	**400**	**400**
Add Power Sunroof			**625**	**700**	**700**
Add Theft Recovery System			**100**	**125**	**125**

PASSENGER CARS

BODY TYPE	Model No.	Weight	Trade-In	Retail	High Retail
2004 CROSSFIRE-V6					
Veh. Ident.: 1C3()N69L()4X000001 Up.					
Coupe 2D	N69	3060	**20550**	**23600**	**24975**
Add Theft Recovery System			**100**	**125**	**125**
Deduct W/out Automatic Trans.			**625**	**625**	**625**
CHRYSLER					
2003 PT CRUISER-4 Cyl.					
Veh. Ident.: 3C()F(Model)()()3T000001 Up.					
Wagon 4D	Y48	3108	**9250**	**11275**	**12175**
Wagon 4D Touring	Y58		**9975**	**12050**	**12925**
Wagon 4D Limited	Y68	3182	**11425**	**13650**	**14600**
Wagon 4D GT Turbo	Y78		**12175**	**14500**	**15475**
Add Aluminum/Alloy Wheels (Base)			**275**	**325**	**325**
Add Leather Seats (Std. Ltd)			**400**	**450**	**450**
Add Power Sunroof (Std. Ltd)			**525**	**600**	**600**
Add Theft Recovery System			**75**	**100**	**100**
Deduct W/out Automatic Trans.			**525**	**525**	**525**
Deduct W/out Cruise Control			**175**	**175**	**175**
Deduct W/out Power Door Locks			**150**	**150**	**150**
2003 SEBRING-4 Cyl.					
Veh. Ident.: ()C3()(Model)()()3()000001 Up.					
Coupe 2D LX	G42	3064	**8525**	**10425**	**11350**
Sedan 4D LX	L46	3201	**7650**	**9475**	**10350**
Convertible 2D LX	L45	3394	**10450**	**12600**	**13500**
2003 SEBRING-V6					
Veh. Ident.: ()C3()(Model)()()3()000001 Up.					
Coupe 2D LX	G42	3254	**9025**	**11025**	**11900**
Coupe 2D LXi	G52	3206	**10150**	**12275**	**13175**
Sedan 4D LX	L46		**8150**	**10025**	**10950**
Sedan 4D LXi	L56	3273	**9275**	**11300**	**12200**
Convertible 2D LX	L45		**10950**	**13150**	**14075**
Convertible 2D GTC	L75	3452	**12150**	**14475**	**15450**
Convertible 2D LXi	L55	3474	**12875**	**15275**	**16275**
Convertible 2D Limited	L65	3491	**15225**	**17750**	**18800**
SEBRING OPTIONS					
Add Aluminum/Alloy Wheels (LX)			**275**	**325**	**325**
Add Compact Disc Player (L45, L46)			**75**	**100**	**100**
Add Infinity Stereo System (Std. G52, L65)			**250**	**300**	**300**
Add Leather Seats (Std. L55, L65)			**400**	**450**	**450**
Add Power Seat (Std. L55, L56, L65)			**175**	**200**	**200**
Add Power Sunroof			**525**	**600**	**600**
Add Theft Recovery System			**75**	**100**	**100**
Deduct W/out Automatic Trans.			**525**	**525**	**525**
Deduct W/out Cruise Control			**175**	**175**	**175**
2003 300M-V6					
Veh. Ident.: 2C3()(Model)()()3H000001 Up.					
Sedan 4D	E66	3581	**15350**	**17925**	**19175**
Sedan 4D Special	E76	3650	**16600**	**19250**	**20525**
Add Power Sunroof			**575**	**650**	**650**
Add Theft Recovery System			**75**	**100**	**100**

BODY TYPE	Model No.	Weight	Trade-In	Retail	High Retail
2003 CONCORDE-V6					
Veh. Ident.: 2C3()(Model)()()3H000001 Up.					
Sedan 4D LX	D46	3479	**9275**	**11400**	**12425**
Sedan 4D LXi	D36	3548	**11200**	**13475**	**14575**
Sedan 4D Limited	D56	3567	**13100**	**15525**	**16700**
Add Aluminum/Alloy Wheels (LX)			**325**	**375**	**375**
Add Compact Disc Player (LX)			**125**	**150**	**150**
Add Infinity Stereo System			**300**	**350**	**350**
Add Power Sunroof			**575**	**650**	**650**
Add Theft Recovery System			**75**	**100**	**100**
CHRYSLER					
2002 PT CRUISER-4 Cyl.					
Veh. Ident.: 3C()F(Model)B()2T000001 Up.					
Wagon 4D	Y48	3108	**8075**	**9925**	**10825**
Wagon 4D Touring	Y58		**8750**	**10675**	**11625**
Wagon 4D Limited	Y68		**10100**	**12200**	**13100**
Add Aluminum/Alloy Wheels (Base)			**225**	**250**	**250**
Add Power Sunroof (Std. Ltd)			**475**	**550**	**550**
Add Theft Recovery System			**75**	**100**	**100**
Deduct W/out Automatic Trans.			**475**	**475**	**475**
Deduct W/out Cruise Control			**150**	**150**	**150**
Deduct W/out Power Door Locks			**125**	**125**	**125**
2002 SEBRING-4 Cyl.					
Veh. Ident.: ()C3()(Model)()()2()100001 Up.					
Coupe 2D LX	G42	3099	**7525**	**9350**	**10225**
Sedan 4D LX	L46	3201	**6725**	**8475**	**9350**
Convertible 2D LX	L45	3394	**9325**	**11375**	**12275**
2002 SEBRING-V6					
Veh. Ident.: ()C3()(Model)()()2()100001 Up.					
Coupe 2D LX	G42	3229	**7925**	**9775**	**10675**
Coupe 2D LXi	G52	3251	**9025**	**11000**	**11950**
Sedan 4D LX	L46		**7125**	**8900**	**9800**
Sedan 4D LXi	L56	3273	**8175**	**10050**	**10975**
Convertible 2D LX	L45		**9725**	**11800**	**12700**
Convertible 2D GTC	L75	3452	**10850**	**13050**	**13975**
Convertible 2D LXi	L55	3474	**11500**	**13725**	**14675**
Convertible 2D Limited	L65	3491	**13450**	**15875**	**16900**
SEBRING OPTIONS					
Add Aluminum/Alloy Wheels (LX)			**225**	**250**	**250**
Add Compact Disc Player (LX)			**75**	**100**	**100**
Add Infinity Stereo System (L45, L55, L75)			**200**	**225**	**225**
Add Leather Seats (Std. L55, L65)			**350**	**400**	**400**
Add Power Seat (Std. L55, L56, L65)			**150**	**175**	**175**
Add Power Sunroof			**475**	**550**	**550**
Add Theft Recovery System			**75**	**100**	**100**
Deduct W/out Automatic Trans.			**475**	**475**	**475**
Deduct W/out Cruise Control			**150**	**150**	**150**
2002 300M-V6					
Veh. Ident.: ()C3()(Model)()()2()100001 Up.					
Sedan 4D	E66	3581	**13225**	**15675**	**16875**
Sedan 4D Special	E76	3650	**14325**	**16850**	**18075**
Add Power Sunroof			**525**	**600**	**600**
Add Theft Recovery System			**75**	**100**	**100**

ADJUST FOR MILEAGE

BODY TYPE	Model No.	Weight	Trade-In	Retail	High Retail
2002 CONCORDE-V6					
Veh. Ident.: ()C3()(Model)()()2()100001 Up.					
Sedan 4D LX	D46	3479	**8125**	**10150**	**11175**
Sedan 4D LXi	D36	3548	**9850**	**12025**	**13075**
Sedan 4D Limited	D56	3567	**11750**	**14075**	**15200**
Add Aluminum/Alloy Wheels (LX)			**275**	**325**	**325**
Add Compact Disc Player (LX)			**100**	**125**	**125**
Add Infinity Stereo System (Std. Limited)			**250**	**300**	**300**
Add Power Sunroof			**525**	**600**	**600**
Add Theft Recovery System			**75**	**100**	**100**
CHRYSLER					
2001 PT CRUISER-4 Cyl.					
Veh. Ident.: 3C()()(Model)B()1T000001 Up.					
Wagon 4D	Y4B	3123	**6700**	**8450**	**9325**
Wagon 4D Touring	Y4B		**7175**	**8950**	**9850**
Wagon 4D Limited	Y4B		**8475**	**10375**	**11300**
Add Aluminum/Alloy Wheels (Base)			**175**	**200**	**200**
Add Compact Disc Player			**50**	**75**	**75**
Add Power Sunroof (Std. Ltd.)			**425**	**475**	**475**
Add Theft Recovery System			**50**	**75**	**75**
Deduct W/out Automatic Trans.			**425**	**425**	**425**
Deduct W/out Cruise Control			**125**	**125**	**125**
Deduct W/out Power Door Locks			**100**	**100**	**100**
2001 SEBRING-4 Cyl.					
Veh. Ident.: ()C3()(Model)()()1()100001 Up.					
Coupe 2D LX	G42	3100	**6400**	**8125**	**8975**
Sedan 4D LX	L46	3100	**5600**	**7250**	**8125**
2001 SEBRING-V6					
Veh. Ident.: ()C3()(Model)()()1()100001 Up.					
Coupe 2D LX	G42	3231	**6775**	**8525**	**9400**
Coupe 2D LXi	G52	3317	**7750**	**9575**	**10475**
Sedan 4D LX	L46	3252	**5975**	**7675**	**8600**
Sedan 4D LXi	L56	3317	**7225**	**9025**	**9875**
Convertible 2D LX	L45	3489	**8525**	**10425**	**11350**
Convertible 2D LXi	L55	3513	**10100**	**12200**	**13100**
Convertible 2D Limited	L65	3533	**11600**	**13825**	**14775**
SEBRING OPTIONS					
Add Aluminum/Alloy Wheels (Std. LXi, Ltd.)			**175**	**200**	**200**
Add Compact Disc Player (Std. LXi, Ltd.)			**50**	**75**	**75**
Add Infinity Stereo System (Conv. LX)			**150**	**175**	**175**
Add Leather Seats (Cpe LXi)			**300**	**350**	**350**
Add Power Seat (Std. 4D LXi, Conv.)			**125**	**150**	**150**
Add Power Sunroof			**425**	**475**	**475**
Add Theft Recovery System			**50**	**75**	**75**
Deduct W/out Automatic Trans.			**425**	**425**	**425**
2001 300M-V6					
Veh. Ident.: ()C3()E66()()1()100001 Up.					
Sedan 4D	E66	3598	**11175**	**13450**	**14550**
Add Power Sunroof			**475**	**550**	**550**
Add Theft Recovery System			**50**	**75**	**75**

P A S S E N G E R C A R S

BODY TYPE	Model No.	Weight	Trade-In	Retail	High Retail
2001 CONCORDE-V6					
Veh. Ident.: ()C3()(Model)()()1()100001 Up.					
Sedan 4D LX	D46	3495	6475	8375	9400
Sedan 4D LXi	D36	3566	8000	10025	11050
Add Aluminum/Alloy Wheels (Std. LXi)			225	250	250
Add Compact Disc Player (Std. LXi)			100	125	125
Add Infinity Stereo System			200	225	225
Add Leather Seats (Std. LXi)			375	425	425
Add Power Sunroof			475	550	550
Add Theft Recovery System			50	75	75
2001 LHS-V6					
Veh. Ident.: ()C3()C56()()1()100001 Up.					
Sedan 4D	C56	3581	9100	11350	12475
Add Infinity Stereo System			275	325	325
Add Power Sunroof			575	650	650
Add Theft Recovery System			50	75	75
CHRYSLER					
2000 CIRRUS-V6					
Veh. Ident.: ()C3()(Model)()()Y()100001 Up.					
Sedan 4D LX (4 Cyl.)	J46		3925	5375	6200
Sedan 4D LXi	J56	2942	4750	6275	7150
Add Aluminum/Alloy Wheels (Std. LXi)			125	150	150
Add Compact Disc Player			50	75	75
Add Leather Seats			250	300	300
Add Power Seat (Std. LXi)			100	125	125
Add Power Sunroof			375	425	425
Deduct W/out Automatic Trans.			375	375	375
Deduct W/out Power Door Locks			75	75	75
Deduct W/out Power Windows			100	100	100
2000 SEBRING-V6					
Veh. Ident.: ()C3()(Model)()()Y()100001 Up.					
Coupe 2D LX	U42	3155	4675	6200	7075
Coupe 2D LXi	U52	3155	5850	7525	8425
Convertible 2D JX	L45	3332	6500	8250	9100
Convertible 2D JXi	L55	3428	7525	9350	10225
Convertible 2D Limited	L55		8225	10125	11050
Add Aluminum/Alloy Wheels (LX, JX)			125	150	150
Add Compact Disc Player (Std. LXi, Ltd.)			50	75	75
Add Power Seat (LX)			100	125	125
Add Power Sunroof			375	425	425
2000 300M-V6					
Veh. Ident.: ()C3()E66()()Y()100001 Up.					
Sedan 4D	E66	3567	8750	10825	11875
Add Power Sunroof			425	475	475
2000 CONCORDE-V6					
Veh. Ident.: ()C3()(Model)()()Y()100001 Up.					
Sedan 4D LX	D46	3452	4975	6700	7725
Sedan 4D LXi	D36	3532	6225	8100	9100
Add Aluminum/Alloy Wheels (Std. LXi)			175	200	200
Add Compact Disc Player (Std. LXi)			75	100	100
Add Infinity Stereo System			150	175	175

PASSENGER CARS

BODY TYPE	Model No.	Weight	Trade-In	Retail	High Retail
Add Leather Seats (Std. LXi)			325	375	375
Add Power Sunroof			425	475	475
2000 LHS-V6					
Veh. Ident.: ()C3()C56()()Y()100001 Up.					
Sedan 4D	C56	3589	7125	9175	10325
Add Infinity Stereo System			225	250	250
Add Power Sunroof			525	600	600
CHRYSLER					
1999 CIRRUS-V6					
Veh. Ident.: ()C3()J56()()X()100001 Up.					
Sedan 4D LXi	J56	3168	4025	5475	6300
Add Aluminum/Alloy Wheels			75	100	100
Add Leather Seats			225	250	250
Add Power Sunroof			325	375	375
1999 SEBRING-V6					
Veh. Ident.: ()C3()(Model)()()X()100001 Up.					
Coupe 2D LX (4 Cyl.)	U42		3850	5300	6125
Coupe 2D LX	U42		4175	5650	6500
Coupe 2D LXi	U52		4825	6375	7250
Convertible 2D JX	L45	3332	5175	6800	7725
Convertible 2D JXi	L55	3428	6025	7725	8650
Convertible 2D Limited	L55		6475	8225	9075
Add Aluminum/Alloy Wheels (LX, JX)			75	100	100
Add Leather Seats (Std. JXi, Limited)			225	250	250
Add Power Seat (Std. Convertible)			75	100	100
Add Power Sunroof			325	375	375
Deduct W/out Automatic Trans.			325	325	325
Deduct W/out Cruise Control			75	75	75
Deduct W/out Power Door Locks			50	50	50
Deduct W/out Power Windows			75	75	75
1999 300M-V6					
Veh. Ident.: ()C3()E66()()X()100001 Up.					
Sedan 4D	E66	3567	6775	8700	9750
Add Power Sunroof			375	425	425
1999 CONCORDE-V6					
Veh. Ident.: ()C3()D46()()X()100001 Up.					
Sedan 4D LX	D46	3452	3925	5500	6450
Sedan 4D LXi	D46		4775	6475	7475
Add Aluminum/Alloy Wheels (Std. LXi)			125	150	150
Add Infinity Stereo System			100	125	125
Add Power Sunroof			375	425	425
1999 LHS-V6					
Veh. Ident.: ()C3()C56()()X()100001 Up.					
Sedan 4D	C56	3589	5950	7850	9075
Add Power Sunroof			475	550	550
CHRYSLER					
1998 CIRRUS-V6					
Veh. Ident.: ()C3()J56()()W()000001 Up.					
Sedan 4D LXi	J56		3175	4550	5400
Add Leather Seats			175	200	200

BODY TYPE	Model No.	Weight	Trade-In	Retail	High Retail
Add Power Seat			50	75	75
Add Power Sunroof			275	325	325
1998 SEBRING-4 Cyl.					
Veh. Ident.: ()C3()(Model)()()W()000001 Up.					
Coupe 2D LX	U42	2959	3200	4575	5425
Convertible 2D JX	L45	3344	3800	5225	6025
Convertible 2D JXi	L55	3406	4500	6000	6875
1998 SEBRING-V6					
Veh. Ident.: ()C3()(Model)()()W()000001 Up.					
Coupe 2D LX	U42		3425	4825	5725
Coupe 2D LXi	U52	3197	3950	5400	6225
Convertible 2D JX	L45		4025	5475	6300
Convertible 2D JXi	L55		4725	6250	7125
Convertible 2D Limited	L55		4975	6550	7450
SEBRING OPTIONS					
Add Aluminum/Alloy Wheels (LX, JX)			50	75	75
Add Leather Seats (Std. JXi, Limited)			175	200	200
Add Power Seat (Std. JXi, Limited)			50	75	75
Add Power Sunroof			275	325	325
Deduct W/out Automatic Trans.			275	275	275
Deduct W/out Cruise Control			50	50	50
Deduct W/out Power Windows			50	50	50
1998 CONCORDE-V6					
Veh. Ident.: ()C3()D46()()W()000001 Up.					
Sedan 4D LX	D46	3451	3275	4775	5700
Sedan 4D LXi	D46	3531	3975	5550	6500
Add Aluminum/Alloy Wheels (Std. LXi)			100	125	125
Add Infinity Stereo System (Std. LXi)			75	100	100
Add Leather Seats (Std. LXi)			225	250	250
Add Power Sunroof			325	375	375
CHRYSLER					
1997 CIRRUS-4 Cyl.					
Veh. Ident.: ()C3()J56()()V()000001 Up.					
Sedan 4D LX	J56	3099	2275	3500	4225
Sedan 4D LXi	J56		2625	3900	4700
1997 CIRRUS-V6					
Veh. Ident.: ()C3()J56()()V()000001 Up.					
Sedan 4D LX	J56		2450	3700	4450
Sedan 4D LXi	J56		2800	4100	4900
CIRRUS OPTIONS					
Add Power Seat (Std. LXi)			50	75	75
1997 SEBRING-4 Cyl.					
Veh. Ident.: ()C3()(Model)()()V()000001 Up.					
Coupe 2D LX	U42	2888	2650	3925	4725
Convertible 2D JX	L45	3350	3300	4675	5550
Convertible 2D JXi	L55	3365	3775	5200	6000
1997 SEBRING-V6					
Veh. Ident.: ()C3()(Model)()()V()000001 Up.					
Coupe 2D LX	U42	3117	2825	4125	4925
Coupe 2D LXi	U52	3197	3125	4475	5325
Convertible 2D JX	L45		3475	4875	5775
Convertible 2D JXi	L55		3950	5400	6225

PASSENGER CARS

BODY TYPE	Model No.	Weight	Trade-In	Retail	High Retail
SEBRING OPTIONS					
Add Leather Seats (Std. JXi)			150	175	175
Add Power Seat (Std. JXi)			50	75	75
Add Power Sunroof			200	225	225
Deduct W/out Automatic Trans.			175	175	175
Deduct W/out Cruise Control			25	25	25
Deduct W/out Power Windows			25	25	25
1997 CONCORDE-V6					
Veh. Ident.: ()C3()D56()()V()000001 Up.					
Sedan 4D LX	D56	3468	2325	3650	4500
Sedan 4D LXi	D56		2775	4175	5025
Add Aluminum/Alloy Wheels (Std. LXi)			50	75	75
Add Infinity Stereo System (Std. LXi)			50	75	75
Add Leather Seats (Std. LXi)			200	225	225
Add Power Sunroof			250	300	300
Deduct W/out Power Seat			50	50	50
1997 LHS-V6					
Veh. Ident.:()C3()C56()()V()000001 Up.					
Sedan 4D	C56	3625	2900	4400	5375
Add Power Sunroof			350	400	400
CHRYSLER					
1996 CIRRUS-V6					
Veh. Ident.: 1C3()J56()()T()000001 Up.					
Sedan 4D LX (4 Cyl.)	J56	3148	1875	3050	3725
Sedan 4D LX	J56		2025	3225	3925
Sedan 4D LXi	J56	3153	2150	3375	4100
Add Power Sunroof			150	175	175
1996 SEBRING-4 Cyl.					
Veh. Ident.: ()C3()(Model)()()T()000001 Up.					
Coupe 2D LX	U42	2908	1950	3150	3850
Convertible 2D JX	L45	3244	2925	4250	5075
1996 SEBRING-V6					
Veh. Ident.: ()C3()(Model)()()T()000001 Up.					
Coupe 2D LX	U42		2100	3325	4025
Coupe 2D LXi	U52	3157	2300	3550	4300
Convertible 2D JX	L45		3075	4425	5275
Convertible 2D JXi	L55		3300	4675	5550
SEBRING OPTIONS					
Add Power Sunroof			150	175	175
Deduct W/out Automatic Trans.			125	125	125
1996 CONCORDE-V6					
Veh. Ident.: ()C3()D56()()T()000001 Up.					
Sedan 4D LX	D56	3492	1900	3175	3950
Sedan 4D LXi	D56		2050	3350	4150
Add Power Sunroof			200	225	225
1996 NEW YORKER-V6					
Veh. Ident.: ()C3()C46()()T()000001 Up.					
Sedan 4D	C46	3587	2100	3475	4375
Add Power Sunroof			275	325	325

BODY TYPE	Model No.	Weight	Trade-In	Retail	High Retail
1996 LHS-V6					
Veh. Ident.: ()C3()C56()()T()000001 Up.					
Sedan 4D	C56	3596	**2400**	**3825**	**4775**
Add Power Sunroof			**275**	**325**	**325**
CHRYSLER					
1995 LEBARON-V6					
Veh. Ident.: 1C3()U453()S()000001 Up.					
Convertible 2D GTC	U45	3010	**1900**	**3100**	**3775**
1995 CIRRUS-V6					
Veh. Ident.: 1C3()J56()()S()000001 Up.					
Sedan 4D LX	J56	2911	**1775**	**2950**	**3625**
Sedan 4D LXi	J56		**1900**	**3100**	**3775**
1995 SEBRING-V6					
Veh. Ident.: ()C3()(Model)()()S()000001 Up.					
Coupe 2D LX (4 Cyl.)	U42	2816	**1600**	**2750**	**3400**
Coupe 2D LX	U42		**1750**	**2925**	**3600**
Coupe 2D LXi	U52	2980	**1900**	**3100**	**3775**
1995 CONCORDE-V6					
Veh. Ident.: ()C3()D56()()S()000001 Up.					
Sedan 4D	D56	3369	**1675**	**2900**	**3625**
Add 3.5L V6 Engine			**100**	**125**	**125**
1995 NEW YORKER-V6					
Veh. Ident.: ()C3()C46()()S()000001 Up.					
Sedan 4D	C46	3457	**1800**	**3125**	**3950**
1995 LHS-V6					
Veh. Ident.: ()C3()C56()()S()000001 Up.					
Sedan 4D	C56	3483	**2000**	**3375**	**4250**

P A S S E N G E R C A R S

DAEWOO

* Model can be identified by VIN. Please refer to the VIN Explanation Section.

BODY TYPE	Model No.	Weight	Trade-In	Retail	High Retail
DAEWOO					
2002 LANOS-4 Cyl.					
Veh. Ident.: KLAT(Model)26()2()000001 Up.					
Hatchback 3D S	A2	2447	**2125**	**3275**	**3900**
Hatchback 3D Sport	B2	2447	**2875**	**4100**	**4825**
Sedan 4D S	A5	2522	**2350**	**3525**	**4175**
2002 NUBIRA-4 Cyl.					
Veh. Ident.: KLAJ(Model)2Z()2()000001 Up.					
Sedan 4D SE	C5	2800	**3025**	**4250**	**4975**
Wagon 4D CDX	B8	2888	**3500**	**4775**	**5575**
2002 LEGANZA-4 Cyl.					
Veh. Ident.: KLAV(Model)92()2()000001 Up.					
Sedan 4D SE	()6*	3086	**4175**	**5550**	**6300**
Sedan 4D CDX	()6*	3086	**4700**	**6125**	**6900**
DAEWOO OPTIONS					
Add Aluminum/Alloy Wheels (Std. Sport, Leganza CDX)			**200**	**225**	**225**
Add CD Player (Std. Sport, Leganza CDX)			**75**	**100**	**100**
Add Cruise Control (Std. Leganza CDX)			**125**	**150**	**150**
Add Leather Seats (Std. Sport)			**250**	**300**	**300**

ADJUST FOR MILEAGE

BODY TYPE	Model No.	Weight	Trade-In	Retail	High Retail
Add Power Locks (Lanos S, Nubira SE) . .			**100**	**125**	**125**
Add Power Sunroof			**425**	**475**	**475**
Add Power Windows (Lanos S)			**125**	**150**	**150**
Add Theft Recovery System			**75**	**100**	**100**
Deduct W/out Air Conditioning			**375**	**375**	**375**
Deduct W/out Automatic Trans.			**325**	**325**	**325**
DAEWOO					
2001 LANOS-4 Cyl.					
Veh. Ident.: KLAT(Model)26()1()000001 Up.					
Hatchback 3D S.	A2	2447	**1775**	**2850**	**3475**
Hatchback 3D Sport.	B2	2447	**2350**	**3500**	**4150**
Sedan 4D S	A5	2522	**1975**	**3100**	**3700**
2001 NUBIRA-4 Cyl.					
Veh. Ident.: KLAJ(Model)2Z()1()000001 Up.					
Sedan 4D SE.	C5	2800	**2425**	**3575**	**4250**
Sedan 4D CDX	B5	2800	**2975**	**4200**	**4925**
Wagon 4D CDX.	B8	2888	**3275**	**4525**	**5275**
2001 LEGANZA-4 Cyl.					
Veh. Ident.: KLAV(Model)92()1()000001 Up.					
Sedan 4D SE.	()6*	3102	**3150**	**4375**	**5125**
Sedan 4D SX.	()6*	3102	**3600**	**4875**	**5675**
Sedan 4D CDX	()6*	3102	**4200**	**5575**	**6350**
DAEWOO OPTIONS					
Add Aluminum/Alloy Wheels (Std. Sport, CDX)			**150**	**175**	**175**
Add CD Player (Std. Sport, CDX, SX) . . .			**50**	**75**	**75**
Add Cruise Control (Leganza SE)			**100**	**125**	**125**
Add Leather Seats (Std. Sport, Leganza SX/CDX)			**200**	**225**	**225**
Add Power Locks (Lanos S, Nubira SE) . .			**75**	**100**	**100**
Add Power Sunroof (Std. Leganza CDX) .			**375**	**425**	**425**
Add Power Windows (Lanos S, Nubira SE)			**100**	**125**	**125**
Add Theft Recovery System			**50**	**75**	**75**
Deduct W/out Air Conditioning			**325**	**325**	**325**
Deduct W/out Automatic Trans.			**275**	**275**	**275**
DAEWOO					
2000 LANOS-4 Cyl.					
Veh. Ident.: KLAT(Model)26()Y()000001 Up.					
Hatchback 3D S.	A2	2447	**1425**	**2450**	**3025**
Hatchback 3D SE	B2	2447	**1575**	**2625**	**3225**
Sedan 4D S	A5	2522	**1600**	**2650**	**3250**
Sedan 4D SX.	C5	2522	**1925**	**3025**	**3625**
2000 NUBIRA-4 Cyl.					
Veh. Ident.: KLAJ(Model)2Z()Y()000001 Up.					
Sedan 4D SE.	C5	2621	**2050**	**3175**	**3800**
Sedan 4D CDX	B5	2621	**2450**	**3625**	**4300**
Wagon 4D CDX	B8	2749	**2750**	**3950**	**4650**
2000 LEGANZA-4 Cyl.					
Veh. Ident.: KLAV(Model)92()Y()000001 Up.					
Sedan 4D SE.	()6	3086	**2325**	**3475**	**4125**
Sedan 4D SX.	A6	3086	**2675**	**3850**	**4550**
Sedan 4D CDX	A6	3086	**3150**	**4375**	**5125**
DAEWOO OPTIONS					
Add Aluminum/Alloy Wheels (Std. Lanos SX, CDX)			**100**	**125**	**125**
Add CD Player (Std. SX, CDX).			**50**	**75**	**75**
Add Leather Seats (Std. Leganza SX/CDX)			**150**	**175**	**175**

BODY TYPE	Model No.	Weight	Trade-In	Retail	High Retail
Add Power Locks (Nubira SE)			50	75	75
Add Power Sunroof (Std. Leganza CDX)			325	375	375
Add Power Windows (Nubira SE)			75	100	100
Deduct W/out Air Conditioning			275	275	275
Deduct W/out Automatic Trans.			225	225	225
DAEWOO					
1999 LANOS-4 Cyl.					
Veh. Ident.: KLAT(Model)26()X()000001 Up.					
Hatchback 3D S	A2	2447	925	1875	2350
Hatchback 3D SE	B2	2447	1025	1975	2450
Hatchback 3D SX	C2	2447	1100	2100	2625
Sedan 4D S	A5	2522	1075	2050	2550
Sedan 4D SE	B5	2522	1175	2175	2700
Sedan 4D SX	C5	2522	1250	2250	2800
1999 NUBIRA-4 Cyl.					
Veh. Ident.: KLAJ(Model)2Z()X()000001 Up.					
Hatchback 5D SX	A6	2546	1300	2325	2875
Hatchback 5D CDX	B6	2546	1400	2425	3000
Sedan 4D SX	A5	2566	1500	2550	3125
Sedan 4D CDX	B5	2566	1600	2650	3250
Wagon 4D SX	A8	2694	1800	2875	3500
Wagon 4D CDX	B8	2694	1900	3000	3650
1999 LEGANZA-4 Cyl.					
Veh. Ident.: KLAV(Model)92()X()000001 Up.					
Sedan 4D SE	()6	3102	1825	2900	3525
Sedan 4D SX	A6	3157	2050	3150	3775
Sedan 4D CDX	A6	3157	2400	3550	4225
DAEWOO OPTIONS					
Add Aluminum/Alloy Wheels (Std. Lanos SX, CDX)			50	75	75
Add Leather Seats (Std. Leganza SX/CDX)			125	150	150
Add Power Sunroof (Std. Leganza CDX)			275	325	325
Deduct W/out Air Conditioning			225	225	225
Deduct W/out Automatic Trans.			175	175	175

DODGE

BODY TYPE	Model No.	Weight	Trade-In	Retail	High Retail
DODGE					
2004 NEON-4 Cyl.					
Veh. Ident.: 1B3()(Model)()()4D000001 Up.					
Sedan 4D SE	S26	2581	7425	9125	9825
Sedan 4D SXT	S56	2626	8550	10375	11100
Sedan 4D R/T (5 Spd.)	S76	2712	9825	11800	12550
Sedan 4D SRT-4 (5 Spd.)	S66	2900	15050	17550	18375
Add Aluminum/Alloy Wheels (SE)			300	350	350
Add Compact Disc Player (SE)			100	125	125
Add Cruise Control (SE, SXT)			175	200	200
Add Leather Seats			350	400	400
Add Power Sunroof			525	600	600
Add Theft Recovery System			100	125	125
Deduct W/out Air Conditioning			575	575	575
Deduct W/out Auto Trans. (Ex. R/T, SRT-4)			475	475	475

PASSENGER CARS

BODY TYPE	Model No.	Weight	Trade-In	Retail	High Retail
2004 STRATUS-4 Cyl.					
Veh. Ident.: ()B3()(Model)()()4()000001 Up.					
Coupe 2D SXT	G42	3051	**10475**	**12625**	**13525**
Sedan 4D SE	L36		**9100**	**11125**	**12000**
Sedan 4D SXT	L46	3182	**9675**	**11725**	**12625**
2004 STRATUS-V6					
Veh. Ident.: ()B3()(Model)()()4()000001 Up.					
Coupe 2D R/T	G52	3206	**13000**	**15400**	**16400**
Sedan 4D SE	L36	3175	**9625**	**11675**	**12575**
Sedan 4D SXT	L46		**10200**	**12325**	**13225**
Sedan 4D ES	L56	3225	**10950**	**13125**	**14050**
Sedan 4D R/T	L76	3230	**12200**	**14550**	**15525**
STRATUS OPTIONS					
Add Aluminum/Alloy Wheels (SE)			**325**	**375**	**375**
Add Compact Disc Player (SE)			**100**	**125**	**125**
Add Leather Seats			**450**	**500**	**500**
Add Power Seat (Std. ES)			**200**	**225**	**225**
Add Power Sunroof			**575**	**650**	**650**
Add Theft Recovery System			**100**	**125**	**125**
Deduct W/out Automatic Trans.			**575**	**575**	**575**
Deduct W/out Cruise Control			**200**	**200**	**200**
2004 INTREPID-V6					
Veh. Ident.: 2B3()(Model)()()4H000001 Up.					
Sedan 4D SE	D46	3469	**10325**	**12550**	**13625**
Sedan 4D ES	D56	3487	**12675**	**15100**	**16275**
Sedan 4D SXT	D56	3548	**12150**	**14525**	**15675**
Add Aluminum/Alloy Wheels (SE)			**375**	**425**	**425**
Add Compact Disc Player (SE)			**150**	**175**	**175**
Add Infinity Stereo System			**350**	**400**	**400**
Add Leather Seats (Std. ES)			**525**	**600**	**600**
Add Power Sunroof			**625**	**700**	**700**
Add Theft Recovery System			**100**	**125**	**125**
Deduct W/out Cruise Control			**225**	**225**	**225**
Deduct W/out Power Seat			**225**	**225**	**225**
DODGE					
2003 NEON-4 Cyl.					
Veh. Ident.: 1B3()(Model)()()3D000001 Up.					
Sedan 4D SE	S26	2581	**6225**	**7775**	**8600**
Sedan 4D SXT	S56	2626	**7100**	**8750**	**9525**
Sedan 4D R/T (5 Spd.)	S76	2712	**8450**	**10275**	**11000**
Sedan 4D SRT-4 (5 Spd.)	S66	2970	**13125**	**15525**	**16325**
Add Aluminum/Alloy Wheels (SE)			**250**	**300**	**300**
Add Compact Disc Player (SE)			**75**	**100**	**100**
Add Cruise Control (SE, SXT)			**150**	**175**	**175**
Add Leather Seats			**300**	**350**	**350**
Add Power Sunroof			**475**	**550**	**550**
Add Theft Recovery System			**75**	**100**	**100**
Deduct W/out Air Conditioning			**525**	**525**	**525**
Deduct W/out Auto Trans. (Ex. R/T, SRT-4)			**425**	**425**	**425**
2003 STRATUS-4 Cyl.					
Veh. Ident.: ()B3()(Model)()()3()000001 Up.					
Coupe 2D SE	G42	3064	**8250**	**10150**	**11075**
Coupe 2D SXT	G42		**8675**	**10600**	**11550**

BODY TYPE	Model No.	Weight	Trade-In	Retail	High Retail
Sedan 4D SE	L3/46	3200	**7375**	**9175**	**10050**
Sedan 4D SXT	L46		**7875**	**9725**	**10625**
2003 STRATUS-V6					
Veh. Ident.: ()B3()(Model)()(3()000001 Up.					
Coupe 2D SE	G42	3254	**8750**	**10675**	**11625**
Coupe 2D R/T	G52	3206	**11175**	**13375**	**14300**
Sedan 4D SE	L3/46		**7950**	**9800**	**10700**
Sedan 4D ES	L56	3269	**9100**	**11125**	**12000**
Sedan 4D R/T	L76	3294	**10375**	**12525**	**13425**
STRATUS OPTIONS					
Add Aluminum/Alloy Wheels (SE)			**275**	**325**	**325**
Add CD Player (Sedan SE 4 Cyl.)			**75**	**100**	**100**
Add Leather Seats			**400**	**450**	**450**
Add Power Seat (Std. ES)			**175**	**200**	**200**
Add Power Sunroof			**525**	**600**	**600**
Add Theft Recovery System			**75**	**100**	**100**
Deduct W/out Automatic Trans.			**525**	**525**	**525**
Deduct W/out Cruise Control			**175**	**175**	**175**
2003 INTREPID-V6					
Veh. Ident.: 2B3()(Model)()()3H000001 Up.					
Sedan 4D SE	D46	3469	**8475**	**10550**	**11600**
Sedan 4D ES	D56	3487	**10225**	**12425**	**13475**
Sedan 4D SXT	D56	3548	**10225**	**12425**	**13475**
Add Aluminum/Alloy Wheels (SE)			**325**	**375**	**375**
Add Compact Disc Player (SE)			**125**	**150**	**150**
Add Infinity Stereo System			**300**	**350**	**350**
Add Leather Seats			**475**	**550**	**550**
Add Power Sunroof			**575**	**650**	**650**
Add Theft Recovery System			**75**	**100**	**100**
Deduct W/out Cruise Control			**200**	**200**	**200**
Deduct W/out Power Seat			**200**	**200**	**200**
DODGE					
2002 NEON-4 Cyl.					
Veh. Ident.: ()B3()(Model)()(2()100001 Up.					
Sedan 4D	S1/26	2590	**4775**	**6200**	**6975**
Sedan 4D SE	S46	2630	**5200**	**6700**	**7525**
Sedan 4D ES	S56	2648	**5650**	**7175**	**7950**
Sedan 4D SXT	S56		**5850**	**7400**	**8200**
Sedan 4D R/T (5 Spd.)	S76	2709	**6625**	**8225**	**8975**
Add Aluminum/Alloy Wheels (Base, SE)			**200**	**225**	**225**
Add Compact Disc Player (Base)			**75**	**100**	**100**
Add Cruise Control (Std. R/T)			**125**	**150**	**150**
Add Leather Seats			**250**	**300**	**300**
Add Power Door Locks (Base)			**100**	**125**	**125**
Add Power Sunroof			**425**	**475**	**475**
Add Theft Recovery System			**75**	**100**	**100**
Deduct W/out Air Conditioning			**475**	**475**	**475**
Deduct W/out Automatic Trans. (Ex. R/T)			**375**	**375**	**375**
2002 STRATUS-4 Cyl.					
Veh. Ident.: ()B3()(Model)()(2()100001 Up.					
Coupe 2D SE	G42	3051	**7200**	**9000**	**9900**
Coupe 2D SXT	G42		**7800**	**9625**	**10525**
Sedan 4D SE	L36	3200	**6400**	**8125**	**8975**

PASSENGER CARS

PASSENGER CARS

BODY TYPE	Model No.	Weight	Trade-In	Retail	High Retail
Sedan 4D SE Plus	L46		6850	8600	9475
Sedan 4D SXT	L46		7000	8775	9675
2002 STRATUS-V6					
Veh. Ident.: ()B3()(Model)()()2()100001 Up.					
Coupe 2D SE	G42	3173	7600	9425	10300
Coupe 2D R/T	G52	3201	9775	11825	12725
Sedan 4D SE	L36		6800	8550	9425
Sedan 4D SE Plus	L46		7250	9050	9900
Sedan 4D ES	L56	3269	7950	9800	10700
Sedan 4D R/T	L76	3294	8975	10925	11875
STRATUS OPTIONS					
Add Aluminum/Alloy Wheels (SE)			225	250	250
Add Compact Disc Player (SE)			75	100	100
Add Leather Seats			350	400	400
Add Power Seat (Std. ES, SXT 2D)			150	175	175
Add Power Sunroof			475	550	550
Add Theft Recovery System			75	100	100
Deduct W/out Automatic Trans.			475	475	475
Deduct W/out Cruise Control			150	150	150
2002 INTREPID-V6					
Veh. Ident.: ()B3()(Model)()()2()100001 Up.					
Sedan 4D SE	D46	3469	7075	9025	10025
Sedan 4D ES	D56	3487	8700	10775	11825
Sedan 4D SXT	D56		8800	10875	11925
Sedan 4D R/T	D76	3549	10050	12225	13275
Add Aluminum/Alloy Wheels (SE)			275	325	325
Add Compact Disc Player (SE)			100	125	125
Add Infinity Stereo System			250	300	300
Add Leather Seats			425	475	475
Add Power Sunroof			525	600	600
Add Theft Recovery System			75	100	100
Deduct W/out Cruise Control			175	175	175
Deduct W/out Power Seat			175	175	175
DODGE					
2001 NEON-4 Cyl.					
Veh. Ident.: ()B3()S46()()1()100001 Up.					
Sedan 4D SE	S46	2567	4100	5450	6200
Sedan 4D ES	S46	2567	4475	5875	6675
Sedan 4D R/T (5 Spd.)	S46		5175	6650	7475
Add Aluminum/Alloy Wheels (Std. R/T)			150	175	175
Add Compact Disc Player			50	75	75
Add Cruise Control			100	125	125
Add Leather Seats			200	225	225
Add Power Door Locks (SE)			75	100	100
Add Power Sunroof			375	425	425
Add Power Windows (SE)			100	125	125
Add Theft Recovery System			50	75	75
Deduct W/out Air Conditioning			425	425	425
Deduct W/out Automatic Trans. (Ex. R/T)			325	325	325
2001 STRATUS-4 Cyl.					
Veh. Ident.: ()B3()(Model)()()1()100001 Up.					
Coupe 2D SE	G42	3012	6350	8075	8925
Sedan 4D SE	J46	3228	5550	7200	8075

BODY TYPE	Model No.	Weight	Trade-In	Retail	High Retail
2001 STRATUS-V6					
Veh. Ident.: ()B3()(Model)()()1()100001 Up.					
Coupe 2D SE	G42		6725	8475	9350
Coupe 2D R/T	G52	3188	8300	10200	11125
Sedan 4D SE	J46		5925	7600	8500
Sedan 4D ES	J56	3297	6925	8700	9575
STRATUS OPTIONS					
Add Aluminum/Alloy Wheels (Std. ES, R/T)			175	200	200
Add Compact Disc Player (Std. ES, R/T)			50	75	75
Add Leather Seats			300	350	350
Add Power Seat (Std. ES)			125	150	150
Add Power Sunroof			425	475	475
Add Theft Recovery System			50	75	75
Deduct W/out Automatic Trans.			425	425	425
2001 INTREPID-V6					
Veh. Ident.: ()B3()(Model)()()1()100001 Up.					
Sedan 4D SE	D46	3478	5575	7375	8400
Sedan 4D ES	D56	3493	6925	8850	9900
Sedan 4D R/T	D76	3563	8100	10125	11150
Add 3.2L V6 Engine (ES)			250	300	300
Add Aluminum/Alloy Wheels (Std. ES, R/T)			225	250	250
Add Compact Disc Player (Std. R/T)			100	125	125
Add Infinity Stereo System			200	225	225
Add Leather Seats			375	425	425
Add Power Sunroof			475	550	550
Add Theft Recovery System			50	75	75
Deduct W/out Power Seat			150	150	150
DODGE					
2000 NEON-4 Cyl.					
Veh. Ident.: ()B3()S46()()Y()100001 Up.					
Sedan 4D Highline	S46	2564	3400	4675	5450
Sedan 4D ES	S46	2564	3725	5025	5750
Add Aluminum/Alloy Wheels			100	125	125
Add Compact Disc Player			50	75	75
Add Cruise Control			75	100	100
Add Power Door Locks (Std. ES)			50	75	75
Add Power Sunroof			325	375	375
Add Power Windows (Std. ES)			75	100	100
Deduct W/out Air Conditioning			375	375	375
Deduct W/out Automatic Trans.			300	300	300
2000 AVENGER-V6					
Veh. Ident.: ()B3()(Model)()()Y()100001 Up.					
Coupe 2D	U42	3137	4425	5925	6800
Coupe 2D ES	U52	3137	5250	6875	7800
Add Aluminum/Alloy Wheels (Std. ES)			125	150	150
Add Compact Disc Player (Std. ES)			50	75	75
Add Power Sunroof			375	425	425
2000 STRATUS-V6					
Veh. Ident.: ()B3()(Model)()()Y()100001 Up.					
Sedan 4D SE (4 Cyl.)	J46	2942	4100	5575	6425
Sedan 4D ES	J56	3169	5175	6800	7725
Add Aluminum/Alloy Wheels (Std. ES)			125	150	150

P A S S E N G E R   C A R S

BODY TYPE	Model No.	Weight	Trade-In	Retail	High Retail
Add Compact Disc Player			50	75	75
Add Power Sunroof			375	425	425
Deduct W/out Automatic Trans.			375	375	375
Deduct W/out Cruise Control			100	100	100
Deduct W/out Leather Seats (ES)			250	250	250
Deduct W/out Power Door Locks			75	75	75
Deduct W/out Power Seat			100	100	100
Deduct W/out Power Windows			100	100	100
2000 INTREPID-V6					
Veh. Ident.: ()B3()(Model)()()Y()100001 Up.					
Sedan 4D	D46	3423	4325	5975	6975
Sedan 4D ES	D56	3518	5400	7200	8200
Sedan 4D R/T	D76		6575	8500	9525
Add 3.2L V6 Engine (ES)			225	250	250
Add Aluminum/Alloy Wheels (Std. ES, R/T)			175	200	200
Add Compact Disc Player (Std. R/T)			75	100	100
Add Infinity Stereo System			150	175	175
Add Leather Seats			325	375	375
Add Power Sunroof			425	475	475
Deduct W/out Power Seat			125	125	125
DODGE					
1999 NEON-4 Cyl.					
Veh. Ident.: ()B3()(Model)()()X()100001 Up.					
Coupe 2D Highline	S42	2389	2500	3675	4350
Coupe 2D R/T (5 Spd.)	S42		3150	4400	5150
Sedan 4D Highline	S47	2399	2500	3675	4350
Sedan 4D R/T (5 Spd.)	S47		3150	4400	5150
Add Sport Package (Std. R/T)			175	200	200
Add Aluminum/Alloy Wheels (Std. R/T)			50	75	75
Add Cruise Control			50	75	75
Add Power Sunroof			275	325	325
Add Power Windows			50	75	75
Deduct W/out Air Conditioning			325	325	325
Deduct W/out Automatic Trans. (Ex. R/T)			250	250	250
1999 AVENGER-4 Cyl.					
Veh. Ident.: ()B3()(Model)()()X()100001 Up.					
Coupe 2D	U42		3525	4925	5825
Coupe 2D ES	U42		3875	5300	6125
1999 AVENGER-V6					
Veh. Ident.: ()B3()(Model)()()X()100001 Up.					
Coupe 2D	U42		3850	5275	6100
Coupe 2D ES	U52		4200	5675	6525
AVENGER OPTIONS					
Add Aluminum/Alloy Wheels (Std. ES)			75	100	100
Add Leather Seats			225	250	250
Add Power Seat			75	100	100
Add Power Sunroof			325	375	375
Deduct W/out Air Conditioning			450	450	450
Deduct W/out Automatic Trans.			325	325	325
Deduct W/out Cruise Control			75	75	75
Deduct W/out Power Door Locks			50	50	50
Deduct W/out Power Windows			75	75	75

BODY TYPE	Model No.	Weight	Trade-In	Retail	High Retail
1999 STRATUS-V6					
Veh. Ident.: ()B3()(Model)()()X()100001 Up.					
Sedan 4D (4 Cyl.)	J46	2911	**3175**	**4525**	**5375**
Sedan 4D ES	J56		**3800**	**5225**	**6025**
Add Aluminum/Alloy Wheels (Std. ES)			**75**	**100**	**100**
Add Leather Seats			**225**	**250**	**250**
Add Power Seat			**75**	**100**	**100**
Add Power Sunroof			**325**	**375**	**375**
Deduct W/out Automatic Trans.			**325**	**325**	**325**
Deduct W/out Cruise Control			**75**	**75**	**75**
Deduct W/out Power Door Locks			**50**	**50**	**50**
Deduct W/out Power Windows			**75**	**75**	**75**
1999 INTREPID-V6					
Veh. Ident.: ()B3()(Model)()()X()100001 Up.					
Sedan 4D	D46	3423	**3525**	**5050**	**5950**
Sedan 4D ES	D56	3518	**4350**	**6000**	**7000**
Add Aluminum/Alloy Wheels (Std. ES)			**125**	**150**	**150**
Add Infinity Stereo System			**100**	**125**	**125**
Add Leather Seats			**275**	**325**	**325**
Add Power Sunroof			**375**	**425**	**425**
Deduct W/out Power Seat			**100**	**100**	**100**
DODGE					
1998 NEON-4 Cyl.					
Veh. Ident.: ()B3()(Model)()()W()000001 Up.					
Coupe 2D Highline	S42		**2025**	**3125**	**3725**
Sedan 4D Highline	S47		**2025**	**3125**	**3725**
Add Sport Package			**125**	**150**	**150**
Add Cruise Control			**50**	**75**	**75**
Add Power Sunroof			**225**	**275**	**275**
Add Power Windows			**50**	**75**	**75**
Deduct W/out Air Conditioning			**275**	**275**	**275**
Deduct W/out Automatic Trans.			**200**	**200**	**200**
1998 AVENGER-4 Cyl.					
Veh. Ident.: ()B3()(Model)()()W()000001 Up.					
Coupe 2D	U42	2888	**3050**	**4400**	**5225**
Coupe 2D ES	U42	2989	**3350**	**4750**	**5625**
1998 AVENGER-V6					
Veh. Ident.: ()B3()(Model)()()W()000001 Up.					
Coupe 2D	U42		**3275**	**4650**	**5525**
Coupe 2D ES	U52		**3575**	**4975**	**5875**
AVENGER OPTIONS					
Add Aluminum/Alloy Wheels (Std. ES)			**50**	**75**	**75**
Add Leather Seats			**175**	**200**	**200**
Add Power Seat			**50**	**75**	**75**
Add Power Sunroof			**275**	**325**	**325**
Deduct W/out Air Conditioning			**400**	**400**	**400**
Deduct W/out Automatic Trans.			**275**	**275**	**275**
Deduct W/out Cruise Control			**50**	**50**	**50**
Deduct W/out Power Windows			**50**	**50**	**50**
1998 STRATUS-4 Cyl.					
Veh. Ident.: ()B3()(Model)()()W()000001 Up.					
Sedan 4D	J46	2919	**2350**	**3600**	**4350**

PASSENGER CARS

PASSENGER CARS

BODY TYPE	Model No.	Weight	Trade-In	Retail	High Retail
Sedan 4D ES	J56	2958	2600	3875	4650
Sedan 4D ES (V6)	J56		2825	4125	4925
Add Aluminum/Alloy Wheels (Std. ES)			50	75	75
Add Leather Seats			175	200	200
Add Power Seat			50	75	75
Add Power Sunroof			275	325	325
Deduct W/out Automatic Trans.			275	275	275
Deduct W/out Cruise Control			50	50	50
Deduct W/out Power Windows			50	50	50
1998 INTREPID-V6					
Veh. Ident.: ()B3()(Model)()()W()000001 Up.					
Sedan 4D	D46	3422	2950	4375	5250
Sedan 4D ES	D56	3517	3600	5150	6050
Add Aluminum/Alloy Wheels (Std. ES)			100	125	125
Add Infinity Stereo System			75	100	100
Add Leather Seats			225	250	250
Add Power Sunroof			325	375	375
Deduct W/out Power Seat			75	75	75
DODGE					
1997 NEON-4 Cyl.					
Veh. Ident.: ()B3()(Model)()()V()000001 Up.					
Coupe 2D	S22	2389	1475	2500	3075
Coupe 2D Highline	S42	2416	1500	2550	3125
Sedan 4D	S27	2399	1475	2500	3075
Sedan 4D Highline	S47	2459	1500	2550	3125
Add Sport Package			75	100	100
Add Power Sunroof			150	175	175
Deduct W/out Air Conditioning			150	150	150
Deduct W/out Automatic Trans.			125	125	125
1997 AVENGER-4 Cyl.					
Veh. Ident.: ()B3()(Model)()()V()000001 Up.					
Coupe 2D	U42	2822	2375	3625	4375
Coupe 2D ES	U42	3084	2575	3850	4625
1997 AVENGER-V6					
Veh. Ident.: ()B3()(Model)()()V()000001 Up.					
Coupe 2D	U42		2550	3825	4600
Coupe 2D ES	U52		2750	4050	4850
AVENGER OPTIONS					
Add Leather Seats			150	175	175
Add Power Seat			50	75	75
Add Power Sunroof			200	225	225
Deduct W/out Air Conditioning			250	250	250
Deduct W/out Automatic Trans.			175	175	175
Deduct W/out Cruise Control			25	25	25
Deduct W/out Power Windows			25	25	25
1997 STRATUS-4 Cyl.					
Veh. Ident.: ()B3()(Model)()()V()000001 Up.					
Sedan 4D	J46	2911	1850	3025	3700
Sedan 4D ES	J56	2968	2050	3250	3950
Sedan 4D ES (V6)	J56		2225	3450	4175
Add Leather Seats			150	175	175
Add Power Seat			50	75	75

BODY TYPE	Model No.	Weight	Trade-In	Retail	High Retail
Deduct W/out Automatic Trans.			175	175	175
Deduct W/out Power Windows			25	25	25
1997 INTREPID-V6					
Veh. Ident.: ()B3()(Model)()()V()000001 Up.					
Sedan 4D	D46	3349	2150	3450	4275
Sedan 4D ES	D56	3440	2500	3850	4725
Add 3.5L V6 Engine (Std. ES)			100	125	125
Add Aluminum/Alloy Wheels (Std. ES)			50	75	75
Add Infinity Stereo System			50	75	75
Add Leather Seats			200	225	225
Add Power Sunroof			250	300	300
Deduct W/out Power Seat			50	50	50
DODGE					
1996 NEON-4 Cyl.					
Veh. Ident.: ()B3()(Model)()()T()000001 Up.					
Coupe 2D	S22		1175	2175	2700
Coupe 2D Highline	S42	2385	1200	2200	2725
Coupe 2D Sport	S62	2469	1275	2300	2850
Sedan 4D	S27	2343	1175	2175	2700
Sedan 4D Highline	S47	2416	1200	2200	2725
Sedan 4D Sport	S67	2456	1275	2300	2850
Add Power Sunroof			100	125	125
Deduct W/out Air Conditioning			75	75	75
Deduct W/out Automatic Trans.			75	75	75
1996 AVENGER-4 Cyl.					
Veh. Ident.: ()B3()(Model)()()T()000001 Up.					
Coupe 2D	U42	2879	1850	3025	3700
Coupe 2D ES (5 Spd.)	U42		1925	3125	3800
Coupe 2D ES (V6)	U52	3124	2200	3425	4150
Add Power Sunroof			150	175	175
Deduct W/out Air Conditioning			150	150	150
Ded W/out Automatic Trans. (Ex. ES 4 Cyl.)			125	125	125
1996 STRATUS-4 Cyl.					
Veh. Ident.: ()B3()(Model)()()T()000001 Up.					
Sedan 4D	J46	2899	1525	2650	3275
Sedan 4D ES	J56		1700	2850	3525
Sedan 4D ES (V6)	J56	3117	1850	3025	3700
Add Power Sunroof			150	175	175
Deduct W/out Automatic Trans.			125	125	125
1996 INTREPID-V6					
Veh. Ident.: ()B3()(Model)()()T()000001 Up.					
Sedan 4D	D46	3318	1725	2950	3675
Sedan 4D ES	D56	3415	2000	3275	4050
Add 3.5L V6 Engine (Std. ES)			100	125	125
Add Power Sunroof			200	225	225
1996 STEALTH-V6-5/6 Spd./AT					
Veh. Ident.: ()B3()(Model)()()T()000001 Up.					
Liftback 2D	M44	3053	4700	6400	7400
Liftback 2D R/T	M84	3153	5400	7175	8175
Liftback 2D R/T Turbo (AWD)	N74	3671	8300	10350	11375

BODY TYPE	Model No.	Weight	Trade-In	Retail	High Retail
DODGE					
1995 NEON-4 Cyl.					
Veh. Ident.: ()B3()(Model)()()S()000001 Up.					
Coupe 2D Highline	S42	2377	**1000**	**1950**	**2425**
Coupe 2D Sport	S62	2439	**1075**	**2075**	**2600**
Sedan 4D	S27	2320	**975**	**1925**	**2400**
Sedan 4D Highline	S47	2388	**1000**	**1950**	**2425**
Sedan 4D Sport	S67	2449	**1075**	**2075**	**2600**
1995 SPIRIT-4 Cyl.					
Veh. Ident.: ()B3()A46()()S()000001 Up.					
Sedan 4D	A46	2771	**1050**	**2125**	**2675**
Sedan 4D (V6)	A46	2795	**1125**	**2200**	**2775**
1995 AVENGER-4 Cyl.					
Veh. Ident.: ()B3()(Model)()()S()000001 Up.					
Coupe 2D	U42	2822	**1475**	**2600**	**3225**
Coupe 2D ES (V6)	U52	3084	**1825**	**3000**	**3675**
1995 STRATUS-4 Cyl.					
Veh. Ident.: ()B3()(Model)()()S()000001 Up.					
Sedan 4D	J46	2911	**1300**	**2400**	**3000**
Sedan 4D ES	J56		**1450**	**2575**	**3200**
Sedan 4D ES (V6)	J56	3145	**1600**	**2750**	**3400**
1995 INTREPID-V6					
Veh. Ident.: ()B3()(Model)()()S()000001 Up.					
Sedan 4D	D46	3308	**1500**	**2700**	**3400**
Sedan 4D ES	D56	3370	**1675**	**2900**	**3625**
Add 3.5L V6 Engine			**100**	**125**	**125**
1995 STEALTH-V6					
Veh. Ident.: ()B3()(Model)()()S()000001 Up.					
Liftback 2D	M44	3064	**4175**	**5825**	**6800**
Liftback 2D R/T	M84	3164	**4775**	**6475**	**7475**
Liftback 2D R/T Turbo (AWD)	N74	3792	**7275**	**9225**	**10225**

EAGLE

BODY TYPE	Model No.	Weight	Trade-In	Retail	High Retail
EAGLE					
1998 TALON-4 Cyl.					
Veh. Ident.: ()E3()(Model)()()W()000001 Up.					
Hatchback 2D	K24	2729	**3250**	**4625**	**5500**
Hatchback 2D ESi	K44	2749	**3550**	**4950**	**5850**
Hatchback 2D TSi Turbo	K54	2899	**4750**	**6275**	**7150**
Hatchback 2D TSi Turbo (AWD)	L54	3142	**5250**	**6875**	**7800**
Add Aluminum/Alloy Wheels (Std. TSi)			**50**	**75**	**75**
Add Leather Seats			**175**	**200**	**200**
Add Power Seat			**50**	**75**	**75**
Add Power Sunroof			**275**	**325**	**325**
Deduct W/out Air Conditioning			**400**	**400**	**400**
Deduct W/out Automatic Trans.			**275**	**275**	**275**
Deduct W/out Cruise Control (Ex. Base)			**50**	**50**	**50**
Deduct W/out Power Windows (Ex. Base)			**50**	**50**	**50**

PASSENGER CARS

BODY TYPE	Model No.	Weight	Trade-In	Retail	High Retail
EAGLE					
1997 TALON-4 Cyl.					
Veh. Ident.: ()E3()(Model)()()V()000001 Up.					
Hatchback 2D	K24	2729	**2650**	**3925**	**4725**
Hatchback 2D ESi	K44	2745	**2875**	**4175**	**4975**
Hatchback 2D TSi Turbo	K54	2899	**3925**	**5375**	**6200**
Hatchback 2D TSi Turbo (AWD)	L54	3142	**4350**	**5850**	**6725**
Add Leather Seats			**150**	**175**	**175**
Add Power Seat			**50**	**75**	**75**
Add Power Sunroof			**200**	**225**	**225**
Deduct W/out Air Conditioning			**250**	**250**	**250**
Deduct W/out Automatic Trans.			**175**	**175**	**175**
Deduct W/out Cruise Control (Ex. Base)			**25**	**25**	**25**
Deduct W/out Power Windows (Ex. Base)			**25**	**25**	**25**
1997 VISION-V6					
Veh. Ident.: ()E3()(Model)()()V()000001 Up.					
Sedan 4D ESi	D56	3439	**2050**	**3350**	**4150**
Sedan 4D TSi	D66	3535	**2275**	**3600**	**4425**
Add Infinity Stereo System			**50**	**75**	**75**
Add Leather Seats			**200**	**225**	**225**
Add Power Sunroof			**250**	**300**	**300**
Deduct W/out Power Seat			**50**	**50**	**50**
EAGLE					
1996 SUMMIT-4 Cyl.					
Veh. Ident.: ()E3()(Model)()()T()000001 Up.					
Coupe 2D DL	A11	2085	**1000**	**1950**	**2425**
Coupe 2D ESi	A31	2105	**1075**	**2075**	**2600**
Sedan 4D LX	A36	2195	**1025**	**2000**	**2475**
Sedan 4D ESi	A46	2250	**1100**	**2100**	**2625**
Wagon 3D DL	B30	2734	**1350**	**2375**	**2925**
Wagon 3D LX	B40	2855	**1425**	**2450**	**3025**
Wagon 3D (4WD)	C30	3064	**1500**	**2550**	**3125**
Deduct W/out Air Conditioning			**75**	**75**	**75**
Deduct W/out Automatic Trans.			**75**	**75**	**75**
1996 TALON-4 Cyl.					
Veh. Ident.: ()E3()(Model)()()T()000001 Up.					
Hatchback 2D	K24	2789	**2100**	**3325**	**4025**
Hatchback 2D ESi	K44	2789	**2250**	**3475**	**4200**
Hatchback 2D TSi Turbo	K54	2866	**3200**	**4575**	**5425**
Hatchback 2D TSi Turbo (AWD)	L54	3120	**3575**	**4975**	**5875**
Add Power Sunroof			**150**	**175**	**175**
Deduct W/out Air Conditioning			**150**	**150**	**150**
Deduct W/out Automatic Trans.			**125**	**125**	**125**
1996 VISION-V6					
Veh. Ident.: ()E3()(Model)()()T()000001 Up.					
Sedan 4D ESi	D56	3371	**1700**	**2925**	**3650**
Sedan 4D TSi	D66	3494	**1975**	**3250**	**4025**
Add Power Sunroof			**200**	**225**	**225**

P A S S E N G E R C A R S

BODY TYPE	Model No.	Weight	Trade-In	Retail	High Retail
EAGLE					
1995 SUMMIT-4 Cyl.					
Veh. Ident.: ()E3()(Model)()()S()000001 Up.					
Coupe 2D DL	A11	2085	**850**	**1775**	**2225**
Coupe 2D ESi	A31	2105	**925**	**1875**	**2350**
Sedan 4D LX	A36	2195	**875**	**1800**	**2250**
Sedan 4D ESi	A46	2250	**950**	**1900**	**2375**
Wagon 3D DL	B30	2734	**1175**	**2175**	**2700**
Wagon 3D LX	B40	2855	**1250**	**2250**	**2800**
Wagon 3D (4WD)	C40	3064	**1325**	**2350**	**2900**
1995 TALON-4 Cyl.					
Veh. Ident.: ()E3()(Model)()()S()000001 Up.					
Hatchback 2D ESi	K44	2756	**1850**	**3025**	**3700**
Hatchback 2D TSi Turbo	K54	2866	**2750**	**4050**	**4850**
Hatchback 2D TSi Turbo (AWD)	L54	3119	**3050**	**4400**	**5225**
1995 VISION-V6					
Veh. Ident.: 1E3()(Model)()()S()000001 Up.					
Sedan 4D ESi	D56	3374	**1400**	**2575**	**3250**
Sedan 4D TSi	D66	3493	**1675**	**2900**	**3625**

FORD

BODY TYPE	Model No.	Weight	Trade-In	Retail	High Retail
FORD					
2004 FOCUS-4 Cyl.					
Veh. Ident.: ()FA()P(Model)()()4()100001 Up.					
Hatchback 3D ZX3	31	2612	**8975**	**10875**	**11625**
Hatchback 3D SVT (6 Spd.)	39	2750	**12850**	**15225**	**16025**
Hatchback 5D ZX5	37	2691	**10025**	**12025**	**12750**
Hatchback 5D SVT (6 Spd.)	30		**12975**	**15375**	**16175**
Sedan 4D LX	33	2606	**8175**	**10000**	**10725**
Sedan 4D SE	34		**9275**	**11225**	**11950**
Sedan 4D ZTS	38		**10400**	**12425**	**13150**
Wagon 4D SE	36	2702	**10000**	**12000**	**12750**
Wagon 4D ZTW	35		**11325**	**13425**	**14175**
Add European Appearance Pkg. (SVT)			**800**	**900**	**900**
Add Alum/Alloy Wheels (Std. SVT, ZTS, ZTW)			**300**	**350**	**350**
Add Audiophile Stereo System			**250**	**300**	**300**
Add CD Player (LX, SE Wagon)			**100**	**125**	**125**
Add Cruise Control (ZX3, ZX5, LX, SE)			**175**	**200**	**200**
Add Leather Seats (Std. SVT)			**350**	**400**	**400**
Add Power Door Locks (ZX3, ZX5, LX)			**150**	**175**	**175**
Add Power Sunroof			**525**	**600**	**600**
Add Pwr Windows (ZX3, ZX5, LX, SE Wagon)			**175**	**200**	**200**
Add Theft Recovery System			**100**	**125**	**125**
Add Tilt Steering Wheel (ZX3, ZX5, LX, SE)			**125**	**150**	**150**
Deduct W/out Air Conditioning			**575**	**575**	**575**
Deduct W/out Automatic Trans. (Ex. SVT)			**475**	**475**	**475**
2004 MUSTANG-V6					
Veh. Ident.: 1FAFP(Model)()()4F100001 Up.					
Coupe 2D	40	3290	**11950**	**14225**	**15175**
Convertible 2D	44		**15050**	**17550**	**18600**

BODY TYPE	Model No.	Weight	Trade-In	Retail	High Retail
2004 MUSTANG-V8-5/6 Spd./AT					
Veh. Ident.: 1FAFP(Model)()()4F100001 Up.					
Coupe 2D GT	42	3347	**16750**	**19350**	**20450**
Coupe 2D MACH 1	42	3469	**20200**	**23075**	**24275**
Coupe 2D Cobra	48	3665	**25550**	**29050**	**30400**
Convertible 2D GT	45		**19650**	**22500**	**23675**
Convertible 2D Cobra	49	3780	**28450**	**32200**	**33550**
MUSTANG OPTIONS					
Add Pony Package (V6)			**275**	**325**	**325**
Add Leather Seats (Std. MACH 1, Cobra)			**450**	**500**	**500**
Add MACH Stereo (Std. MACH 1, Cobra)			**300**	**350**	**350**
Add Power Seat (Coupe V6)			**200**	**225**	**225**
Add Theft Recovery System			**100**	**125**	**125**
Deduct W/out Automatic Trans. (V6)			**575**	**575**	**575**
Deduct W/out Cruise Control			**200**	**200**	**200**
2004 TAURUS-V6					
Veh. Ident.: 1FA()P(Model)()()4()100001 Up.					
Sedan 4D LX	52	3306	**9275**	**11300**	**12200**
Sedan 4D SE	53		**9600**	**11650**	**12550**
Sedan 4D SES	55		**10650**	**12800**	**13700**
Sedan 4D SEL	56	3313	**11850**	**14100**	**15050**
Wagon 4D SE	58	3497	**10950**	**13125**	**14050**
Wagon 4D SEL	59		**12800**	**15175**	**16175**
Add 3.0L Duratec V6 Engine (Std. Sedan SEL)			**400**	**450**	**450**
Add Aluminum/Alloy Wheels (LX, SE)			**325**	**375**	**375**
Add Compact Disc Player (Std. SES, SEL)			**100**	**125**	**125**
Add Leather Seats			**450**	**500**	**500**
Add MACH Stereo System			**300**	**350**	**350**
Add Power Seat (Std. SES, SEL)			**200**	**225**	**225**
Add Power Sunroof			**575**	**650**	**650**
Add Theft Recovery System			**100**	**125**	**125**
Deduct W/out Cruise Control			**200**	**200**	**200**
Deduct W/out Third Seat (Wagon)			**275**	**275**	**275**
2004 CROWN VICTORIA-V8					
Veh. Ident.: 2FA()P(Model)W()4X100001 Up.					
Sedan 4D Police Interceptor	71		**10975**	**13225**	**14325**
Sedan 4D S	72		**10825**	**13075**	**14150**
Sedan 4D	73	4057	**11075**	**13350**	**14450**
Sedan 4D LX	74		**13300**	**15750**	**16950**
Sedan 4D LX Sport	74		**14800**	**17325**	**18550**
Sedan 4D S Extended	70		**11925**	**14250**	**15375**
Add Handling Package (Std. LX Sport)			**425**	**475**	**475**
Add Aluminum/Alloy Wheels (Std. 74)			**375**	**425**	**425**
Add Compact Disc Player (Std. 74)			**150**	**175**	**175**
Add Leather Seats (Std. LX Sport)			**525**	**600**	**600**
Add Power Sunroof			**625**	**700**	**700**
Add Theft Recovery System			**100**	**125**	**125**
Deduct W/out Cruise Control			**225**	**225**	**225**
Deduct W/out Power Seat			**225**	**225**	**225**
2004 THUNDERBIRD-V8					
Veh. Ident.: 1FAHP60A()4Y100001 Up.					
Convertible 2D	60	3780	**24925**	**28700**	**30475**
Add Removable Hardtop			**800**	**900**	**900**

BODY TYPE	Model No.	Weight	Trade-In	Retail	High Retail
Add Theft Recovery System			100	125	125
FORD					
2003 FOCUS-4 Cyl.					
Veh. Ident.: ()FA()P(Model)()()3()100001 Up.					
Hatchback 3D ZX3	31	2593	7600	9300	10000
Hatchback 3D SVT (6 Spd.)	39	2750	10975	13150	13900
Hatchback 5D ZX5	37	2675	8825	10675	11400
Hatchback 5D SVT (6 Spd.)	37	2750	11100	13300	14050
Sedan 4D LX	33	2586	6825	8425	9175
Sedan 4D SE	34		7850	9575	10300
Sedan 4D ZTS	38		8625	10475	11200
Wagon 4D SE	36	2683	8500	10325	11050
Wagon 4D ZTW	36		9550	11500	12225
Add European Appearance Pkg. (SVT)			700	800	800
Add Aluminum/Alloy Wheels (LX)			250	300	300
Add Audiophile Stereo System			200	225	225
Add CD Player (LX, SE Wagon)			75	100	100
Add Cruise Control (ZX3, ZX5, LX, SE)			150	175	175
Add Leather Seats (Std. SVT)			300	350	350
Add Power Locks (ZX3, LX, SE Wagon)			125	150	150
Add Power Sunroof			475	550	550
Add Power Windows (ZX3, LX, SE Wagon)			150	175	175
Add Theft Recovery System			75	100	100
Add Tilt Steering Wheel (ZX3, ZX5, LX, SE)			100	125	125
Deduct W/out Air Conditioning			525	525	525
Deduct W/out Automatic Trans. (Ex. SVT)			425	425	425
2003 ZX2-4 Cyl.					
Veh. Ident.: 3FAFP113()3R100001 Up.					
Coupe 2D	11	2478	6775	8375	9125
Add Compact Disc Player			75	100	100
Add Cruise Control			150	175	175
Add Leather Seats			300	350	350
Add Power Door Locks			125	150	150
Add Power Sunroof			475	550	550
Add Power Windows			150	175	175
Add Theft Recovery System			75	100	100
Add Tilt Steering Wheel			100	125	125
Deduct W/out Air Conditioning			525	525	525
Deduct W/out Automatic Trans.			425	425	425
2003 MUSTANG-V6					
Veh. Ident.: 1FAFP(Model)4()3F100001 Up.					
Coupe 2D	40	3066	10175	12300	13200
Convertible 2D	44	3208	13000	15400	16400
2003 MUSTANG-V8-5/6 Spd./AT					
Veh. Ident.: 1FAFP(Model)()()3F100001 Up.					
Coupe 2D GT	42		14850	17350	18375
Coupe 2D MACH 1	42		18000	20775	21900
Coupe 2D Cobra	48	3665	22825	26175	27450
Coupe 2D Cobra 10th Anniv.	48		23575	26950	28250
Convertible 2D GT	45		17500	20250	21375
Convertible 2D Cobra	49	3780	25475	29000	30325
Convertible Cobra 10th Anniv.	49		26225	29775	31125

BODY TYPE	Model No.	Weight	Trade-In	Retail	High Retail
MUSTANG OPTIONS					
Add Pony Package (V6)			250	300	300
Add Leather Seats (Std. MACH 1, Cobra)			400	450	450
Add MACH Stereo (Std. MACH 1, Cobra)			250	300	300
Add Power Seat (Coupe V6)			175	200	200
Add Theft Recovery System			75	100	100
Deduct W/out Automatic Trans. (V6)			525	525	525
Deduct W/out Cruise Control			175	175	175
2003 TAURUS-V6					
Veh. Ident.: 1FA()P(Model)()()3()100001 Up.					
Sedan 4D LX	52	3343	7350	9150	10025
Sedan 4D SE	53		7925	9775	10675
Sedan 4D SES	55		8600	10500	11425
Sedan 4D SEL	56	3322	9725	11775	12675
Wagon 4D SE	58	3514	9125	11150	12025
Wagon 4D SEL	59		10575	12725	13625
Add 3.0L Duratec V6 Engine (Std. Sedan SEL)			350	400	400
Add Aluminum/Alloy Wheels (LX)			275	325	325
Add Compact Disc Player (Std. SES, SEL)			75	100	100
Add Leather Seats			400	450	450
Add MACH Stereo System			250	300	300
Add Power Seat (Std. SES, SEL)			175	200	200
Add Power Sunroof			525	600	600
Add Theft Recovery System			75	100	100
Deduct W/out Cruise Control			175	175	175
Deduct W/out Third Seat (Wagon)			250	250	250
2003 CROWN VICTORIA-V8					
Veh. Ident.: 2FA()P(Model)W()3X100001 Up.					
Sedan 4D Police Interceptor	71		9825	12000	13050
Sedan 4D S	72		9700	11875	12925
Sedan 4D	73	4057	9950	12125	13175
Sedan 4D LX	74		11650	13975	15100
Sedan 4D LX Sport	74		13325	15775	16975
Sedan 4D S Extended	70		10700	12950	14025
Add Handling Package (Std. LX Sport)			375	425	425
Add Aluminum/Alloy Wheels (Std. LX Sport)			325	375	375
Add Compact Disc Player (Std. 74)			125	150	150
Add Leather Seats (Std. LX Sport)			475	550	550
Add Theft Recovery System			75	100	100
Deduct W/out Cruise Control			200	200	200
Deduct W/out Power Seat			200	200	200
2003 THUNDERBIRD-V8					
Veh. Ident.: 1FAHP60A()3W100001 Up.					
Convertible 2D	60	3775	22825	26475	28175
Add Removable Hardtop			700	800	800
Add Theft Recovery System			75	100	100
FORD					
2002 FOCUS-4 Cyl.					
Veh. Ident.: ()FA()P(Model)()()2()100001 Up.					
Hatchback 3D ZX3	31	2598	6450	8025	8775
Hatchback 3D SVT (6 Spd.)	39	2770	9300	11325	12050
Hatchback 5D ZX5	37	2699	7550	9250	9950
Sedan 4D LX	33	2604	5625	7150	7925

PASSENGER CARS

BODY TYPE	Model No.	Weight	Trade-In	Retail	High Retail
Sedan 4D SE	34	2564	**6650**	**8250**	**9000**
Sedan 4D ZTS	38	2551	**7375**	**9075**	**9775**
Wagon 4D SE	36	2717	**7475**	**9175**	**9875**
Wagon 4D ZTW	36	2717	**8375**	**10200**	**10925**
Add Aluminum/Alloy Wheels (LX)			**200**	**225**	**225**
Add Audiophile Stereo System			**150**	**175**	**175**
Add Compact Disc Player (LX)			**75**	**100**	**100**
Add Cruise Control (ZX3, LX, SE)			**125**	**150**	**150**
Add Leather Seats (Std. SVT, ZTW)			**250**	**300**	**300**
Add Power Door Locks (ZX3, LX)			**100**	**125**	**125**
Add Power Sunroof			**425**	**475**	**475**
Add Power Windows (ZX3, LX)			**125**	**150**	**150**
Add Theft Recovery System			**75**	**100**	**100**
Add Tilt Steering Wheel (ZX3, LX, SE)			**75**	**100**	**100**
Deduct W/out Air Conditioning			**475**	**475**	**475**
Deduct W/out Automatic Trans. (Ex. SVT)			**375**	**375**	**375**
2002 ESCORT-4 Cyl.					
Veh. Ident.: ()FA()P(Model)()()2()100001 Up.					
Coupe 2D ZX2	11	2464	**5425**	**6925**	**7775**
Sedan 4D	13	2510	**4900**	**6350**	**7150**
Add Aluminum/Alloy Wheels (Std. ZX2)			**200**	**225**	**225**
Add Compact Disc Player			**75**	**100**	**100**
Add Cruise Control			**125**	**150**	**150**
Add Leather Seats			**250**	**300**	**300**
Add Power Door Locks			**100**	**125**	**125**
Add Power Sunroof			**425**	**475**	**475**
Add Power Windows			**125**	**150**	**150**
Add Theft Recovery System			**75**	**100**	**100**
Add Tilt Steering Wheel			**75**	**100**	**100**
Deduct W/out Air Conditioning			**475**	**475**	**475**
Deduct W/out Automatic Trans.			**375**	**375**	**375**
2002 MUSTANG-V6					
Veh. Ident.: ()FA()P(Model)()()2()100001 Up.					
Coupe 2D	40	3114	**8675**	**10600**	**11550**
Convertible 2D	44	3254	**11300**	**13500**	**14425**
2002 MUSTANG-V8-5 Spd./AT					
Veh. Ident.: ()FA()P(Model)()()2()100001 Up.					
Coupe 2D GT	42	3273	**12825**	**15200**	**16200**
Convertible 2D GT	45	3429	**15300**	**17800**	**18850**
MUSTANG OPTIONS					
Add Leather Seats			**350**	**400**	**400**
Add MACH Stereo System			**200**	**225**	**225**
Add Power Seat (Coupe V6)			**150**	**175**	**175**
Add Theft Recovery System			**75**	**100**	**100**
Deduct W/out Automatic Trans. (V6)			**475**	**475**	**475**
Deduct W/out Cruise Control			**150**	**150**	**150**
2002 TAURUS-V6					
Veh. Ident.: ()FA()P(Model)()()2()100001 Up.					
Sedan 4D LX	52	3355	**6450**	**8175**	**9025**
Sedan 4D SE	53	3355	**7000**	**8775**	**9675**
Sedan 4D SES	55	3392	**7625**	**9450**	**10325**
Sedan 4D SEL	56	3408	**8575**	**10475**	**11400**
Wagon 4D SE	58	3519	**8075**	**9925**	**10825**

BODY TYPE	Model No.	Weight	Trade-In	Retail	High Retail
Wagon 4D SEL	59	3532	9350	11375	12275
Add 3.0L Duratec V6 Engine (Std. Sedan SEL)			300	350	350
Add Aluminum/Alloy Wheels (LX)			225	250	250
Add Compact Disc Player (Std. SES, SEL)			75	100	100
Add Leather Seats			350	400	400
Add MACH Stereo System			200	225	225
Add Power Seat (Std. SES, SEL)			150	175	175
Add Power Sunroof			475	550	550
Add Theft Recovery System			75	100	100
Deduct W/out Cruise Control			150	150	150
Deduct W/out Third Seat (Wagon)			225	225	225
2002 CROWN VICTORIA-V8					
Veh. Ident.: ()FA()P(Model)()()2()100001 Up.					
Sedan 4D Police Interceptor	71		8725	10800	11850
Sedan 4D S	72		8575	10650	11700
Sedan 4D	73	3917	8825	10925	12000
Sedan 4D LX	74	3927	10275	12475	13525
Sedan 4D LX Sport	74	3927	11425	13725	14825
Sedan 4D S Extended	70		9475	11625	12650
Add Aluminum/Alloy Wheels (Std. LX Sport)			275	325	325
Add Compact Disc Player			100	125	125
Add Leather Seats (Std. LX Sport)			425	475	475
Add Theft Recovery System			75	100	100
Deduct W/out Cruise Control			175	175	175
Deduct W/out Power Seat			175	175	175
2002 THUNDERBIRD-V8					
Veh. Ident.: ()FA()P60()()2()100001 Up.					
Convertible 2D	60	3775	20825	24175	25775
Add Removable Hardtop			600	675	675
Add Theft Recovery System			75	100	100
FORD					
2001 FOCUS-4 Cyl.					
Veh. Ident.: 1FA()P(Model)()()1()100001 Up.					
Hatchback 3D ZX3	31	2551	5325	6825	7650
Sedan 4D LX	33	2564	4700	6125	6900
Sedan 4D SE	34	2564	5475	6975	7825
Sedan 4D ZTS	38	2564	6050	7600	8400
Wagon 4D SE	36	2717	6100	7650	8450
Add Aluminum/Alloy Wheels (LX)			150	175	175
Add Compact Disc Player (LX)			50	75	75
Add Cruise Control (Std. ZTS)			100	125	125
Add Leather Seats			200	225	225
Add Power Door Locks (Std. SE, ZTS)			75	100	100
Add Power Windows (Std. SE, ZTS)			100	125	125
Add Sunroof			175	200	200
Add Theft Recovery System			50	75	75
Add Tilt Steering Wheel (Std. ZTS)			75	100	100
Deduct W/out Air Conditioning			425	425	425
Deduct W/out Automatic Trans.			325	325	325
2001 ESCORT-4 Cyl.					
Veh. Ident.: 1FA()P(Model)()()1()100001 Up.					
Coupe 2D ZX2	11	2478	4450	5850	6650

PASSENGER CARS

PASSENGER CARS

BODY TYPE	Model No.	Weight	Trade-In	Retail	High Retail
Sedan 4D	13	2468	**4000**	**5350**	**6100**
Add Aluminum/Alloy Wheels (Std. ZX2)			**150**	**175**	**175**
Add Compact Disc Player			**50**	**75**	**75**
Add Cruise Control			**100**	**125**	**125**
Add Leather Seats			**200**	**225**	**225**
Add Power Door Locks			**75**	**100**	**100**
Add Power Sunroof			**375**	**425**	**425**
Add Power Windows			**100**	**125**	**125**
Add Theft Recovery System			**50**	**75**	**75**
Add Tilt Steering Wheel			**75**	**100**	**100**
Deduct W/out Air Conditioning			**425**	**425**	**425**
Deduct W/out Automatic Trans.			**325**	**325**	**325**
2001 MUSTANG-V6					
Veh. Ident.: 1FA()P(Model)()()1()100001 Up.					
Coupe 2D	40	3066	**7425**	**9225**	**10100**
Convertible 2D	44	3208	**9750**	**11825**	**12725**
2001 MUSTANG-V8-5 Spd./AT					
Veh. Ident.: 1FA()P(Model)()()1()100001 Up.					
Coupe 2D GT	42	3241	**11150**	**13350**	**14275**
Coupe 2D Bullitt GT	42	3273	**13050**	**15425**	**16425**
Coupe 2D Cobra	47		**16200**	**18825**	**19900**
Convertible 2D GT	45	3379	**13350**	**15775**	**16800**
Convertible 2D Cobra	46		**18400**	**21325**	**22475**
MUSTANG OPTIONS					
Add Leather Seats (Std. Bullitt, Cobra)			**300**	**350**	**350**
Add MACH Stereo System (Std. Cobra)			**150**	**175**	**175**
Add Power Seat (Coupe V6)			**125**	**150**	**150**
Add Theft Recovery System			**50**	**75**	**75**
Deduct W/out Automatic Trans. (V6)			**425**	**425**	**425**
Deduct W/out Cruise Control			**125**	**125**	**125**
2001 TAURUS-V6					
Veh. Ident.: 1FA()P(Model)()()1()100001 Up.					
Sedan 4D LX	52	3355	**4900**	**6450**	**7350**
Sedan 4D SE	53	3355	**5325**	**6950**	**7900**
Sedan 4D SES	55	3392	**5800**	**7475**	**8375**
Sedan 4D SEL	56	3408	**6675**	**8425**	**9300**
Wagon 4D SE	58	3519	**6275**	**8000**	**8925**
Wagon 4D SES	58		**6750**	**8500**	**9375**
Add 3.0L Duratec V6 Engine (Std. SEL)			**275**	**325**	**325**
Add Aluminum/Alloy Wheels (LX)			**175**	**200**	**200**
Add Compact Disc Player (Std. SES, SEL)			**50**	**75**	**75**
Add Leather Seats			**300**	**350**	**350**
Add MACH Stereo System			**150**	**175**	**175**
Add Power Seat (Std. SES, SEL)			**125**	**150**	**150**
Add Power Sunroof			**425**	**475**	**475**
Add Theft Recovery System			**50**	**75**	**75**
Deduct W/out Cruise Control			**125**	**125**	**125**
Deduct W/out Third Seat (Wagon)			**200**	**200**	**200**
2001 CROWN VICTORIA-V8					
Veh. Ident.: 1FA()P(Model)()()1()100001 Up.					
Sedan 4D Police Interceptor	71		**7325**	**9275**	**10300**
Sedan 4D S	72		**7150**	**9100**	**10100**
Sedan 4D	73	3946	**7400**	**9375**	**10400**

BODY TYPE	Model No.	Weight	Trade-In	Retail	High Retail
Sedan 4D LX	74	3927	8575	10650	11700
Sedan 4D LX Sport	74		9575	11725	12775
Add Aluminum/Alloy Wheels (Std. LX Sport)			225	250	250
Add Compact Disc Player			100	125	125
Add Leather Seats (Std. LX Sport)			375	425	425
Add Theft Recovery System			50	75	75
Deduct W/out Cruise Control			150	150	150
Deduct W/out Power Seat			150	150	150
FORD					
2000 FOCUS-4 Cyl.					
Veh. Ident.: 1FA()P(Model)()()Y()100001 Up.					
Hatchback 3D ZX3	31	2551	4375	5750	6525
Sedan 4D LX	33	2564	3825	5125	5850
Sedan 4D SE	34	2564	4350	5725	6500
Sedan 4D ZTS	38	2564	4850	6275	7075
Wagon 4D SE	36	2717	4875	6300	7100
Add Aluminum/Alloy Wheels (LX)			100	125	125
Add Compact Disc Player (Std. ZX3, ZTS)			50	75	75
Add Cruise Control (Std. ZTS)			75	100	100
Add Leather Seats			150	175	175
Add Power Door Locks (Std. SE, ZTS)			50	75	75
Add Power Windows (Std. ZTS)			75	100	100
Add Tilt Steering Wheel (Std. ZTS)			50	75	75
Deduct W/out Air Conditioning			375	375	375
Deduct W/out Automatic Trans.			300	300	300
2000 ESCORT-4 Cyl.					
Veh. Ident.: 1FA()P(Model)()()Y()100001 Up.					
Coupe 2D ZX2	11	2478	3575	4850	5650
Sedan 4D	13	2454	3200	4450	5200
Add Aluminum/Alloy Wheels (Std. ZX2)			100	125	125
Add Compact Disc Player			50	75	75
Add Cruise Control			75	100	100
Add Leather Seats			150	175	175
Add Power Door Locks			50	75	75
Add Power Sunroof			325	375	375
Add Power Windows			75	100	100
Add Tilt Steering Wheel			50	75	75
Deduct W/out Air Conditioning			375	375	375
Deduct W/out Automatic Trans.			300	300	300
2000 CONTOUR-V6					
Veh. Ident.: 1FA()P(Model)()()Y()100001 Up.					
Sedan 4D SE (4 Cyl.)	66	2769	3375	4650	5525
Sedan 4D SE	66		3650	4950	5850
Sedan 4D Sport	66	2769	3950	5275	6100
Sedan 4D SVT (5 Spd.)	68	3126	5650	7450	8350
Add Aluminum/Alloy Wheels (SE)			125	150	150
Add Compact Disc Player			50	75	75
Add Power Seat (Std. SVT)			100	125	125
Add Power Sunroof			375	425	425
Deduct W/out Automatic Trans. (Ex. SVT)			375	375	375

PASSENGER CARS

BODY TYPE	Model No.	Weight	Trade-In	Retail	High Retail
2000 MUSTANG-V6					
Veh. Ident.: 1FA()P(Model)()()Y()100001 Up.					
Coupe 2D	40	3064	**6200**	**7900**	**8825**
Convertible 2D	44	3203	**8150**	**10025**	**10950**
2000 MUSTANG-V8-5 Spd./AT					
Veh. Ident.: 1FA()P(Model)()()Y()100001 Up.					
Coupe 2D GT	42	3237	**9450**	**11475**	**12375**
Convertible 2D GT	45	3375	**11400**	**13625**	**14575**
MUSTANG OPTIONS					
Add Leather Seats			**250**	**300**	**300**
Add MACH Stereo System			**100**	**125**	**125**
Add Power Seat			**100**	**125**	**125**
Deduct W/out Automatic Trans. (V6)			**375**	**375**	**375**
Deduct W/out Cruise Control			**100**	**100**	**100**
2000 TAURUS-V6					
Veh. Ident.: 1FA()P(Model)()()Y()100001 Up.					
Sedan 4D LX	52	3331	**3875**	**5300**	**6125**
Sedan 4D SE	53	3333	**4275**	**5750**	**6600**
Sedan 4D SES	55	3340	**4625**	**6150**	**7025**
Sedan 4D SEL	56	3340	**5300**	**6925**	**7850**
Wagon 4D SE	58	3540	**5100**	**6700**	**7625**
Wagon 4D SES	58		**5450**	**7075**	**7950**
Add 3.0L Duratec V6 Engine (Std. SEL)			**250**	**300**	**300**
Add Aluminum/Alloy Wheels (LX)			**125**	**150**	**150**
Add Compact Disc Player			**50**	**75**	**75**
Add Leather Seats			**250**	**300**	**300**
Add MACH Stereo System			**100**	**125**	**125**
Add Power Seat (Std. SES, SEL)			**100**	**125**	**125**
Add Power Sunroof			**375**	**425**	**425**
Deduct W/out Cruise Control			**100**	**100**	**100**
Deduct W/out Power Door Locks			**75**	**75**	**75**
Deduct W/out Third Seat (Wagon)			**175**	**175**	**175**
2000 CROWN VICTORIA-V8					
Veh. Ident.: 1FA()P(Model)()()Y()100001 Up.					
Sedan 4D Police Interceptor	71		**6475**	**8375**	**9400**
Sedan 4D S	72	3908	**6350**	**8225**	**9225**
Sedan 4D	73	3908	**6600**	**8500**	**9525**
Sedan 4D LX	74	3908	**7575**	**9550**	**10575**
Add Aluminum/Alloy Wheels			**175**	**200**	**200**
Add Compact Disc Player			**75**	**100**	**100**
Add Leather Seats			**325**	**375**	**375**
Deduct W/out Cruise Control			**125**	**125**	**125**
Deduct W/out Power Seat			**125**	**125**	**125**
FORD					
1999 ESCORT-4 Cyl.					
Veh. Ident.: ()FA()P(Model)()()X()100001 Up.					
Coupe 2D ZX2	11	2478	**2800**	**4000**	**4725**
Sedan 4D LX	10		**2425**	**3600**	**4275**
Sedan 4D SE	13	2468	**2550**	**3725**	**4400**
Wagon 4D SE	15	2531	**2800**	**4000**	**4725**
Add Aluminum/Alloy Wheels (Std. SE Wagon)			**50**	**75**	**75**
Add Cruise Control			**50**	**75**	**75**
Add Power Sunroof			**275**	**325**	**325**

BODY TYPE	Model No.	Weight	Trade-In	Retail	High Retail
Add Power Windows (Std. SE Wagon)...			50	75	75
Deduct W/out Air Conditioning			325	325	325
Deduct W/out Automatic Trans.			250	250	250
1999 CONTOUR-4 Cyl.					
Veh. Ident.: ()FA()P(Model)()()X()100001 Up.					
Sedan 4D LX	65	2774	2600	3775	4550
Sedan 4D SE	66	2774	2800	4000	4800
1999 CONTOUR-V6					
Veh. Ident.: ()FA()P(Model)()()X()100001 Up.					
Sedan 4D SE	66		3075	4300	5125
Sedan 4D SVT (5 Spd.)	68		4750	6450	7350
CONTOUR OPTIONS					
Add Aluminum/Alloy Wheels (Std. SVT)..			75	100	100
Add Leather Seats (Std. SVT)			225	250	250
Add Power Seat (Std. SVT)			75	100	100
Add Power Sunroof			325	375	375
Deduct W/out Automatic Trans. (Ex. SVT)			325	325	325
Deduct W/out Cruise Control			75	75	75
1999 MUSTANG-V6					
Veh. Ident.: ()FA()P(Model)()()X()100001 Up.					
Coupe 2D	40	3069	5325	6950	7900
Convertible 2D	44	3211	7025	8800	9700
1999 MUSTANG-V8-5 Spd./AT					
Veh. Ident.: ()FA()P(Model)()()X()100001 Up.					
Coupe 2D GT	42	3273	7950	9800	10700
Coupe 2D Cobra	47		11550	13850	14800
Convertible 2D GT	45	3429	9650	11700	12600
Convertible 2D Cobra	46		13250	15700	16700
MUSTANG OPTIONS					
Add Leather Seats (Std. Cobra)			225	250	250
Add MACH Stereo System (Std. Cobra) .			75	100	100
Add Power Seat (Std. Cobra)			75	100	100
Deduct W/out Automatic Trans. (V6)			325	325	325
Deduct W/out Cruise Control			75	75	75
1999 TAURUS-V6					
Veh. Ident.: ()FA()P(Model)()()X()100001 Up.					
Sedan 4D LX	52	3329	3125	4500	5350
Sedan 4D SE	53	3353	3350	4750	5625
Sedan 4D SHO (V8)	54		5500	7300	8175
Wagon 4D SE	58	3480	3700	5125	5925
Add Aluminum/Alloy Wheels (Std. SHO) .			75	100	100
Add Leather Seats (Std. SHO)			225	250	250
Add MACH Stereo System (Std. SHO) ..			75	100	100
Add Power Seat (Std. SHO)			75	100	100
Add Power Sunroof (Std. SHO)			325	375	375
Deduct W/out Cruise Control			75	75	75
Deduct W/out Power Door Locks			50	50	50
Deduct W/out Third Seat (Wagon)			125	125	125
1999 CROWN VICTORIA-V8					
Veh. Ident.: ()FA()P(Model)()()X()100001 Up.					
Sedan 4D Police Interceptor	71		5650	7450	8475
Sedan 4D S	72		5500	7300	8325
Sedan 4D	73	3917	5750	7575	8625

PASSENGER CARS

BODY TYPE	Model No.	Weight	Trade-In	Retail	High Retail
Sedan 4D LX	74	3927	6550	8450	9475
Add Aluminum/Alloy Wheels			125	150	150
Add Leather Seats			275	325	325
Deduct W/out Cruise Control			100	100	100
Deduct W/out Power Seat			100	100	100
FORD					
1998 ESCORT-4 Cyl.					
Veh. Ident.: ()FA()P(Model)()()W()000001 Up.					
Coupe 2D ZX2	11	2478	2350	3500	4150
Sedan 4D LX	10		2000	3100	3700
Sedan 4D SE	13	2468	2125	3250	3875
Wagon 4D SE	15	2531	2225	3375	4025
Add Cruise Control			50	75	75
Add Power Sunroof			225	275	275
Add Power Windows			50	75	75
Deduct W/out Air Conditioning			275	275	275
Deduct W/out Automatic Trans.			200	200	200
1998 CONTOUR-4 Cyl.					
Veh. Ident.: ()FA()P(Model)()()W()000001 Up.					
Sedan 4D	65		2075	3200	3900
Sedan 4D GL	65		2100	3225	3925
Sedan 4D LX	65	2769	2150	3275	3975
Sedan 4D SE	66	2769	2300	3450	4175
1998 CONTOUR-V6					
Veh. Ident.: ()FA()P(Model)()()W()000001 Up.					
Sedan 4D GL	65		2300	3450	4175
Sedan 4D LX	65		2350	3500	4225
Sedan 4D SE	66		2500	3675	4425
Sedan 4D SVT (5 Spd.)	68		3850	5425	6250
CONTOUR OPTIONS					
Add Aluminum/Alloy Wheels (Std. SVT)			50	75	75
Add Leather Seats (Std. SVT)			175	200	200
Add Power Seat (Std. SVT)			50	75	75
Add Power Sunroof			275	325	325
Deduct W/out Automatic Trans. (Ex. SVT)			275	275	275
1998 MUSTANG-V6					
Veh. Ident.: ()FA()P(Model)()()W()000001 Up.					
Coupe 2D	40	3065	4150	5625	6475
Convertible 2D	44	3264	5650	7300	8175
1998 MUSTANG-V8-5 Spd./AT					
Veh. Ident.: ()FA()P(Model)()()W()000001 Up.					
Coupe 2D GT	42	3278	6400	8125	8975
Coupe 2D Cobra	47		9600	11750	12650
Convertible 2D GT	45	3471	7900	9750	10650
Convertible 2D Cobra	46		11100	13375	14300
MUSTANG OPTIONS					
Add Leather Seats			175	200	200
Add MACH Stereo System			50	75	75
Add Power Seat (V6)			50	75	75
Deduct W/out Automatic Trans. (V6)			275	275	275
Deduct W/out Cruise Control			50	50	50

BODY TYPE	Model No.	Weight	Trade-In	Retail	High Retail
1998 TAURUS-V6					
Veh. Ident.: ()FA()P(Model)()()W()000001 Up.					
Sedan 4D LX	52	3359	**2625**	**3900**	**4700**
Sedan 4D SE	52/53	3294	**2800**	**4100**	**4900**
Sedan 4D SHO (V8)	54		**4775**	**6475**	**7375**
Wagon 4D SE	57/58	3457	**3050**	**4375**	**5200**
Add Aluminum/Alloy Wheels (Std. SHO)			**50**	**75**	**75**
Add Leather Seats (Std. SHO)			**175**	**200**	**200**
Add MACH Stereo System (Std. SHO)			**50**	**75**	**75**
Add Power Seat (Std. SHO)			**50**	**75**	**75**
Add Power Sunroof (Std. SHO)			**275**	**325**	**325**
Deduct W/out Third Seat (Wagon)			**75**	**75**	**75**
1998 CROWN VICTORIA-V8					
Veh. Ident.: ()FA()P(Model)()()W()000001 Up.					
Sedan 4D Police Interceptor	71		**5000**	**6725**	**7750**
Sedan 4D S	72		**4875**	**6575**	**7600**
Sedan 4D	73	3917	**5125**	**6875**	**7925**
Sedan 4D LX	74	3927	**5800**	**7625**	**8675**
Add Aluminum/Alloy Wheels			**100**	**125**	**125**
Add Leather Seats			**225**	**250**	**250**
Deduct W/out Cruise Control			**75**	**75**	**75**
Deduct W/out Power Seat			**75**	**75**	**75**
FORD					
1997 ASPIRE-4 Cyl.-5 Spd.					
Veh. Ident.: ()FA()T(Model)()()V()000001 Up.					
Hatchback 2D	05	2056	**1100**	**2100**	**2625**
Hatchback 4D	06	2091	**1175**	**2175**	**2700**
Add Automatic Trans.			**125**	**150**	**150**
Deduct W/out Air Conditioning			**150**	**150**	**150**
1997 ESCORT-4 Cyl.					
Veh. Ident.: ()FA()P(Model)()()V()000001 Up.					
Sedan 4D	10	2457	**1525**	**2575**	**3150**
Sedan 4D LX	13	2503	**1625**	**2675**	**3275**
Wagon 4D LX	15	2571	**1675**	**2725**	**3325**
Deduct W/out Air Conditioning			**150**	**150**	**150**
Deduct W/out Automatic Trans.			**125**	**125**	**125**
1997 CONTOUR-4 Cyl.					
Veh. Ident.: ()FA()P(Model)()()V()000001 Up.					
Sedan 4D	65		**1675**	**2725**	**3375**
Sedan 4D GL	65	2769	**1725**	**2800**	**3450**
Sedan 4D LX	66		**1825**	**2900**	**3575**
1997 CONTOUR-V6					
Veh. Ident.: ()FA()P(Model)()()V()000001 Up.					
Sedan 4D GL	65		**1850**	**2925**	**3600**
Sedan 4D LX	66	2808	**1950**	**3050**	**3725**
Sedan 4D SE	67	2994	**1975**	**3075**	**3750**
CONTOUR OPTIONS					
Add Leather Seats			**150**	**175**	**175**
Add Power Seat			**50**	**75**	**75**
Add Power Sunroof			**200**	**225**	**225**
Deduct W/out Air Conditioning			**250**	**250**	**250**
Deduct W/out Automatic Trans.			**175**	**175**	**175**

BODY TYPE	Model No.	Weight	Trade-In	Retail	High Retail
Deduct W/out Cruise Control			25	25	25
Deduct W/out Power Windows			25	25	25
1997 MUSTANG-V6					
Veh. Ident.: ()FA()P(Model)()()V()000001 Up.					
Coupe 2D	40	3084	3600	5000	5900
Convertible 2D	44	3264	4850	6400	7300
1997 MUSTANG-V8-5 Spd./AT					
Veh. Ident.: ()FA()P(Model)()()V()000001 Up.					
Coupe 2D GT	42	3288	5550	7200	8075
Coupe 2D Cobra	47	3404	8300	10350	11275
Convertible 2D GT	45	3422	6800	8550	9425
Convertible 2D Cobra	46	3540	9550	11700	12600
MUSTANG OPTIONS					
Add Leather Seats			150	175	175
Add Power Seat (Std. Cobra)			50	75	75
Deduct W/out Air Conditioning			250	250	250
Deduct W/out Automatic Trans. (V6)			175	175	175
Deduct W/out Cruise Control			25	25	25
Deduct W/out Power Windows			25	25	25
1997 PROBE-4 Cyl.					
Veh. Ident.: ()FA()T(Model)()()V()000001 Up.					
Hatchback 2D	20	2690	1825	3000	3675
Hatchback 2D GT (V6)	22	2921	2425	3675	4425
Add GTS Sport Pkg.			75	100	100
Add Leather Seats			150	175	175
Add Power Seat			50	75	75
Add Power Sunroof			200	225	225
Deduct W/out Air Conditioning			250	250	250
Deduct W/out Automatic Trans.			175	175	175
Deduct W/out Cruise Control			25	25	25
Deduct W/out Power Windows			25	25	25
1997 TAURUS-V6					
Veh. Ident.: ()FA()P(Model)()()V()000001 Up.					
Sedan 4D G	51	3329	1975	3175	3875
Sedan 4D GL	52	3329	2050	3250	3950
Sedan 4D LX	53		2275	3500	4225
Sedan 4D SHO (V8)	54	3440	3500	5025	5825
Wagon 4D GL	57	3480	2200	3425	4150
Wagon 4D LX	58		2425	3675	4425
Add Leather Seats			150	175	175
Add Power Seat (Std. LX, SHO)			50	75	75
Add Power Sunroof			200	225	225
Deduct W/out Cruise Control			25	25	25
1997 CROWN VICTORIA-V8					
Veh. Ident.: ()FA()P(Model)()()V()000001 Up.					
Sedan 4D Police Interceptor	71		3600	5125	6025
Sedan 4D S	72		3425	4950	5900
Sedan 4D	73	3776	3675	5225	6125
Sedan 4D LX	74		4150	5775	6750
Add Aluminum/Alloy Wheels			50	75	75
Add Leather Seats			200	225	225
Deduct W/out Cruise Control			50	50	50

BODY TYPE	Model No.	Weight	Trade-In	Retail	High Retail
Deduct W/out Power Seat			50	50	50
1997 THUNDERBIRD-V6					
Veh. Ident.: ()FA()P62()()V()000001 Up.					
Coupe 2D LX	62	3561	2300	3550	4300
Coupe 2D LX (V8)	62	3644	2550	3825	4600
Add Leather Seats			150	175	175
Add Power Seat			50	75	75
Add Power Sunroof			200	225	225
FORD					
1996 ASPIRE-4 Cyl.-5 Spd.					
Veh. Ident.: ()FA()T(Model)()()T()100001 Up.					
Hatchback 2D	05	2004	900	1850	2325
Hatchback 4D	06	2114	975	1925	2400
Add Automatic Trans.			75	100	100
Deduct W/out Air Conditioning			75	75	75
1996 ESCORT-4 Cyl.					
Veh. Ident.: ()FA()P(Model)()()T()100001 Up.					
Hatchback 2D	10	2323	1050	2025	2525
Hatchback 2D LX	11	2356	1150	2150	2675
Hatchback 2D GT	12	2455	1325	2350	2900
Hatchback 4D LX	14	2398	1175	2175	2700
Sedan 4D LX	13	2378	1200	2200	2725
Wagon 4D LX	15	2444	1225	2225	2750
Add Power Sunroof			100	125	125
Deduct W/out Air Conditioning			75	75	75
Deduct W/out Automatic Trans.			75	75	75
1996 CONTOUR-4 Cyl.					
Veh. Ident.: ()FA()P(Model)()()T()100001 Up.					
Sedan 4D GL	65	2773	1375	2400	3000
Sedan 4D LX	66	2815	1475	2500	3100
1996 CONTOUR-V6					
Veh. Ident.: ()FA()P(Model)()()T()100001 Up.					
Sedan 4D GL	65	2875	1500	2550	3175
Sedan 4D LX	66	2939	1600	2650	3275
Sedan 4D SE	67	2934	1625	2675	3325
CONTOUR OPTIONS					
Add Power Sunroof			150	175	175
Deduct W/out Air Conditioning			150	150	150
Deduct W/out Automatic Trans.			125	125	125
1996 MUSTANG-V6					
Veh. Ident.: ()FA()P(Model)()()T()100001 Up.					
Coupe 2D	40	3057	3175	4550	5400
Convertible 2D	44	3269	4325	5825	6700
1996 MUSTANG-V8-5 Spd./AT					
Veh. Ident.: ()FA()P(Model)()()T()100001 Up.					
Coupe 2D GT	42	3279	4925	6475	7375
Coupe 2D Cobra	47	3401	7425	9400	10275
Convertible 2D GT	45	3468	6075	7775	8700
Convertible 2D Cobra	46	3566	8575	10650	11600
MUSTANG OPTIONS					
Deduct W/out Air Conditioning			150	150	150
Deduct W/out Automatic Trans. (V6)			125	125	125

PASSENGER CARS

BODY TYPE	Model No.	Weight	Trade-In	Retail	High Retail
1996 PROBE-4 Cyl.					
Veh. Ident.: ()FA()T(Model)()()T()100001 Up.					
Hatchback 2D	20	2690	1525	2650	3275
Hatchback 2D GT (V6)	22	2921	2075	3300	4000
Add Power Sunroof			150	175	175
Deduct W/out Air Conditioning			150	150	150
Deduct W/out Automatic Trans.			125	125	125
1996 TAURUS-V6					
Veh. Ident.: ()FA()P(Model)()()T()100001 Up.					
Sedan 4D G	51		1575	2725	3375
Sedan 4D GL	52	3347	1650	2800	3450
Sedan 4D LX	53	3355	1825	3000	3675
Sedan 4D SHO (V8)	54	3544	3000	4425	5275
Wagon 4D GL	57	3511	1750	2925	3600
Wagon 4D LX	58	3531	1925	3125	3800
Add Power Sunroof			150	175	175
1996 CROWN VICTORIA-V8					
Veh. Ident.: ()FA()P(Model)()()T()100001 Up.					
Sedan 4D Police Interceptor	71		2825	4225	5075
Sedan 4D S	72	3780	2650	4025	4850
Sedan 4D	73	3780	2900	4325	5200
Sedan 4D LX	74	3791	3300	4800	5725
1996 THUNDERBIRD-V6					
Veh. Ident.: ()FA()P62()()T()100001 Up.					
Coupe 2D LX	62	3561	1975	3175	3875
Coupe 2D LX (V8)	62	3689	2200	3425	4150
Add Power Sunroof			150	175	175
FORD					
1995 ASPIRE-4 Cyl.					
Veh. Ident.: ()FA()T(Model)()()S()100001 Up.					
Hatchback 2D	05	2004	750	1675	2125
Hatchback 2D SE	07	2004	825	1750	2200
Hatchback 4D	06	2053	825	1750	2200
1995 ESCORT-4 Cyl.					
Veh. Ident.: ()FA()P(Model)()()S()100001 Up.					
Hatchback 2D	10	2316	825	1750	2200
Hatchback 2D LX	11	2355	925	1875	2350
Hatchback 2D GT	12	2459	1100	2100	2625
Hatchback 4D LX	14	2385	950	1900	2375
Sedan 4D LX	13	2404	975	1925	2400
Wagon 4D LX	15	2451	1000	1950	2425
1995 CONTOUR-4 Cyl.					
Veh. Ident.: ()FA()P(Model)()()S()000001 Up.					
Sedan 4D GL	65	2769	1075	2075	2625
Sedan 4D LX	66	2808	1175	2175	2750
1995 CONTOUR-V6					
Veh. Ident.: ()FA()P(Model)()()S()000001 Up.					
Sedan 4D GL	65		1200	2200	2775
Sedan 4D LX	66		1300	2325	2900
Sedan 4D SE	67	2994	1325	2350	2950

BODY TYPE	Model No.	Weight	Trade-In	Retail	High Retail
1995 MUSTANG-V6					
Veh. Ident.: ()FA()P(Model)()()S()100001 Up.					
Coupe 2D	40	3077	**2775**	**4075**	**4875**
Convertible 2D	44	3257	**3875**	**5325**	**6150**
1995 MUSTANG-V8					
Veh. Ident.: ()FA()P(Model)()()S()100001 Up.					
Coupe 2D GTS	42	3246	**4000**	**5450**	**6275**
Coupe 2D GT	42	3280	**4425**	**5925**	**6800**
Coupe 2D Cobra	42	3354	**6675**	**8425**	**9300**
Convertible 2D GT	45	3451	**5525**	**7175**	**8050**
Convertible 2D Cobra	45	3524	**7775**	**9600**	**10500**
MUSTANG OPTIONS					
Add Removable Hardtop			**100**	**125**	**125**
1995 PROBE-4 Cyl.					
Veh. Ident.: ()ZV()P(Model)()()S()100001 Up.					
Hatchback 2D	20	2690	**1200**	**2300**	**2875**
Hatchback 2D GT (V6)	22	2921	**1675**	**2825**	**3475**
1995 TAURUS-V6					
Veh. Ident.: ()FA()P(Model)()()S()100001 Up.					
Sedan 4D GL	52	3118	**1250**	**2350**	**2950**
Sedan 4D SE	52	3118	**1300**	**2400**	**3000**
Sedan 4D LX	53	3186	**1425**	**2550**	**3175**
Sedan 4D SHO	54	3377	**2500**	**3775**	**4550**
Wagon 4D GL	57	3285	**1350**	**2475**	**3075**
Wagon 4D LX	58	3363	**1525**	**2650**	**3275**
1995 CROWN VICTORIA-V8					
Veh. Ident.: ()FA()P(Model)()()S()100001 Up.					
Sedan 4D Police Interceptor	71		**2500**	**3850**	**4725**
Sedan 4D S	72	3762	**2275**	**3600**	**4425**
Sedan 4D	73	3762	**2575**	**3950**	**4825**
Sedan 4D LX	74	3779	**2800**	**4200**	**5050**
1995 THUNDERBIRD-V6					
Veh. Ident.: ()FA()P(Model)()()S()100001 Up.					
Coupe 2D LX	62	3536	**1600**	**2750**	**3400**
Coupe 2D LX (V8)	62	3673	**1775**	**2950**	**3625**
Super Coupe 2D	64	3758	**2350**	**3600**	**4350**

PASSENGER CARS

GEO

BODY TYPE	Model No.	Weight	Trade-In	Retail	High Retail
GEO					
1997 METRO-4 Cyl.-5 Spd.					
Veh. Ident.: 2C1(Model)()V()000001 Up.					
Hatchback 2D (3 Cyl.)	MR226	1830	**850**	**1775**	**2225**
Hatchback 2D LSi	MR229	1841	**1050**	**2025**	**2525**
Sedan 4D LSi	MR529	1995	**1150**	**2150**	**2675**
1997 PRIZM-4 Cyl.					
Veh. Ident.: 1Y1SK5()()()V()000001 Up.					
Sedan 4D	SK5	2360	**2000**	**3100**	**3700**
Sedan 4D LSi	SK5	2370	**2125**	**3250**	**3875**
GEO OPTIONS					
Add Automatic Trans. (Metro)			**125**	**150**	**150**

PASSENGER CARS

BODY TYPE	Model No.	Weight	Trade-In	Retail	High Retail
Add Leather Seats			**75**	**100**	**100**
Add Power Sunroof			**150**	**175**	**175**
Deduct W/out Air Conditioning			**150**	**150**	**150**
Deduct W/out Automatic Trans. (Ex. Metro)			**125**	**125**	**125**
GEO					
1996 METRO-4 Cyl.-5 Spd.					
Veh. Ident.: 2C1(Model)()T()000001 Up.					
Hatchback 2D (3 Cyl.)	MR226	1808	**750**	**1675**	**2125**
Hatchback 2D	MR229	1808	**850**	**1775**	**2225**
Hatchback 2D LSi (3 Cyl.)	MR226	1808	**850**	**1775**	**2225**
Hatchback 2D LSi	MR229	1808	**950**	**1900**	**2375**
Sedan 4D	MR529	1940	**950**	**1900**	**2375**
Sedan 4D LSi	MR529	1940	**1050**	**2025**	**2525**
1996 PRIZM-4 Cyl.					
Veh. Ident.: 1Y1SK5()()()T()000001 Up.					
Sedan 4D	SK5	2359	**1700**	**2775**	**3400**
Sedan 4D LSi	SK5	2370	**1825**	**2900**	**3525**
GEO OPTIONS					
Add Automatic Trans. (Metro)			**100**	**125**	**125**
Add Power Sunroof			**100**	**125**	**125**
Deduct W/out Air Conditioning			**100**	**100**	**100**
Deduct W/out Automatic Trans. (Ex. Metro)			**100**	**100**	**100**
GEO					
1995 METRO-4 Cyl.					
Veh. Ident.: 2C1(Model)()S()000001 Up.					
Hatchback 2D (3 Cyl.)	MR226	1751	**600**	**1500**	**1900**
Hatchback 2D LSi (3 Cyl.)	MR226	1784	**700**	**1600**	**2025**
Hatchback 2D LSi	MR229	1808	**800**	**1725**	**2175**
Sedan 4D	MR529	1962	**775**	**1700**	**2150**
Sedan 4D LSi	MR529	1995	**875**	**1800**	**2250**
1995 PRIZM-4 Cyl.					
Veh. Ident.: 1Y1SK5()()()S()000001 Up.					
Sedan 4D	SK5	2348	**1450**	**2475**	**3050**
Sedan 4D LSi	SK5	2395	**1550**	**2600**	**3200**

HONDA

* Model can be identified by VIN. Please refer to the VIN Explanation Section.

BODY TYPE	Model No.	Weight	Trade-In	Retail	High Retail
HONDA					
2004 CIVIC-4 Cyl.					
Veh. Ident.: ()H()(Model)()4()000001 Up.					
Hatchback 3D Si (5 Spd.)	EP33()	2782	**14675**	**16975**	**17800**
Coupe 2D DX Value	EM2()()*	2456	**11525**	**13650**	**14400**
Coupe 2D HX	EM2()()*	2441	**11975**	**14125**	**14900**
Coupe 2D LX	EM2()()*	2538	**12625**	**14800**	**15575**
Coupe 2D EX	EM2()()*	2597	**14125**	**16400**	**17225**
Sedan 4D DX (5 Spd.)	ES15()*	2449	**11075**	**13175**	**13925**
Sedan 4D DX Value	ES16()*	2544	**11925**	**14075**	**14850**
Sedan 4D LX	ES1()()*	2560	**13025**	**15225**	**16025**
Sedan 4D EX	ES2()()	2612	**14525**	**16825**	**17650**
Sedan 4D Hybrid	ES9()6	2675	**17125**	**19550**	**20400**

BODY TYPE	Model No.	Weight	Trade-In	Retail	High Retail
2004 INSIGHT-3 Cyl.-5 Spd./AT					
Veh. Ident.: JHMZE1()()()4T000001 Up.					
Hatchback 3D	ZE1()()	1850	**16300**	**18700**	
CIVIC/INSIGHT OPTIONS					
Add Aluminum/Alloy Wheels (Civic DX/LX/Value)			**300**	**350**	**350**
Add Compact Disc Player (Civic DX/HX)			**100**	**125**	**125**
Add Theft Recovery System			**100**	**125**	**125**
Deduct W/out Air Conditioning			**575**	**575**	**575**
Deduct W/out AT (Ex. Insight, Si, Sedan DX)			**475**	**475**	**475**
2004 ACCORD-4 Cyl.					
Veh. Ident.: ()H()(Model)()4()000001 Up.					
Coupe 2D LX	CM7()()*	3038	**15750**	**18275**	**19325**
Coupe 2D LX (V6)	CM822	3274	**17600**	**20325**	**21450**
Coupe 2D EX	CM7()()*	3073	**17825**	**20575**	**21700**
Coupe 2D EX Nav	CM7()7		**19075**	**21900**	**23075**
Coupe 2D EX (V6)	CM8()()*	3285	**20125**	**23000**	**24200**
Coupe 2D EX Nav (V6)	CM8()7		**20725**	**23625**	**24825**
Sedan 4D DX	CM5()1	3053	**14075**	**16500**	**17550**
Sedan 4D LX	CM5()()*	3109	**15800**	**18325**	**19375**
Sedan 4D LX (V6)	CM663	3349	**17650**	**20375**	**21500**
Sedan 4D EX	CM5()()*	3144	**17875**	**20625**	**21750**
Sedan 4D EX Nav	CM5()8		**19125**	**21950**	**23125**
Sedan 4D EX (V6)	CM665	3384	**20175**	**23050**	**24250**
Sedan 4D EX Nav (V6)	CM668		**20775**	**23675**	**24900**
Add Aluminum/Alloy Wheels (Std. Accord EX)			**325**	**375**	**375**
Add Leather Seats (Std. Accord EX V6, Nav)			**450**	**500**	**500**
Add Power Seat (Std. Accord V6, Nav)			**200**	**225**	**225**
Add Theft Recovery System			**100**	**125**	**125**
Deduct W/out Air Conditioning			**700**	**700**	**700**
Deduct W/out Automatic Trans.			**575**	**575**	**575**
2004 S2000-4 Cyl.-6 Spd.					
Veh. Ident.: JHMAP214()4T000001 Up.					
Roadster 2D	AP214	2835	**24125**	**27550**	**29025**
Add Detachable Hardtop			**875**	**975**	**975**
Add Theft Recovery System			**100**	**125**	**125**
HONDA					
2003 CIVIC-4 Cyl.					
Veh. Ident.: ()H()(Model)()3()000001 Up.					
Hatchback 3D Si (5 Spd.)	EP33()	2744	**12875**	**15050**	**15850**
Coupe 2D DX	EM2()()*	2403	**9725**	**11700**	**12450**
Coupe 2D HX	EM2()()*	2436	**10525**	**12550**	**13275**
Coupe 2D LX	EM2()()*	2474	**11025**	**13100**	**13850**
Coupe 2D EX	EM2()()*	2555	**12075**	**14225**	**15000**
Sedan 4D DX	ES1()()*	2449	**10125**	**12125**	**12850**
Sedan 4D LX	ES1()()*	2513	**11425**	**13525**	**14275**
Sedan 4D EX	ES2()()	2601	**12475**	**14625**	**15400**
Sedan 4D Hybrid	ES9()6	2661	**14450**	**16725**	**17550**
2003 INSIGHT-3 Cyl.-5 Spd./AT					
Veh. Ident.: JHMZE1()()()3()000001 Up.					
Hatchback 3D	ZE1()()	1847	**14150**	**16425**	**17250**
CIVIC/INSIGHT OPTIONS					
Add Aluminum/Alloy Wheels (Civic DX/LX/EX)			**250**	**300**	**300**
Add Compact Disc Player (Civic DX, Insight)			**75**	**100**	**100**

BODY TYPE	Model No.	Weight	Trade-In	Retail	High Retail
Add Theft Recovery System			**75**	**100**	**100**
Deduct W/out Air Conditioning			**525**	**525**	**525**
Ded W/out Automatic Trans. (Ex. Insight, Si)			**425**	**425**	**425**
2003 ACCORD-4 Cyl.					
Veh. Ident.: ()H()(Model)()3()000001 Up.					
Coupe 2D LX	CM7()()*	2994	**14200**	**16650**	**17700**
Coupe 2D LX (V6)	CM822	3250	**15825**	**18350**	**19425**
Coupe 2D EX	CM7()6	3047	**16175**	**18725**	**19800**
Coupe 2D EX Nav	CM7()7		**17250**	**19975**	**21075**
Coupe 2D EX (V6)	CM8()()*	3265	**18200**	**20975**	**22125**
Coupe 2D EX Nav (V6)	CM8()7		**18700**	**21500**	**22650**
Sedan 4D DX	CM5()1	2989	**12700**	**15050**	**16050**
Sedan 4D LX	CM5()()*	3053	**14250**	**16700**	**17750**
Sedan 4D LX (V6)	CM663	3309	**15875**	**18400**	**19475**
Sedan 4D EX	CM5()6	3109	**16225**	**18775**	**19850**
Sedan 4D EX Nav	CM5()7		**17300**	**20025**	**21150**
Sedan 4D EX (V6)	CM665	3360	**18250**	**21025**	**22175**
Sedan 4D EX Nav (V6)	CM668		**18750**	**21550**	**22700**
Add Aluminum/Alloy Wheels (Std. Accord EX)			**275**	**325**	**325**
Add Leather Seats (Std. Accord EX V6, Nav)			**400**	**450**	**450**
Add Power Seat (Std. Accord V6, Nav)			**175**	**200**	**200**
Add Theft Recovery System			**75**	**100**	**100**
Deduct W/out Air Conditioning			**650**	**650**	**650**
Deduct W/out Automatic Trans.			**525**	**525**	**525**
2003 S2000-4 Cyl.-6 Spd.					
Veh. Ident.: JHMAP114()3()000001 Up.					
Roadster 2D	AP114	2809	**21950**	**25150**	**26575**
Add Detachable Hardtop			**775**	**875**	**875**
Add Theft Recovery System			**75**	**100**	**100**
HONDA					
2002 CIVIC-4 Cyl.					
Veh. Ident.: ()H()(Model)()2()000001 Up.					
Hatchback 3D Si (5 Spd.)	EP33()	2744	**11500**	**13625**	**14375**
Coupe 2D DX	EM2()()*	2405	**8675**	**10525**	**11250**
Coupe 2D HX	EM2()7	2434	**9300**	**11225**	**11950**
Coupe 2D LX	EM2()()*	2465	**9775**	**11750**	**12500**
Coupe 2D EX	EM2()()*	2553	**10800**	**12850**	**13575**
Sedan 4D DX	ES1()()*	2421	**9075**	**11000**	**11750**
Sedan 4D LX	ES1()()*	2465	**10175**	**12175**	**12900**
Sedan 4D EX	ES2()()	2564	**11200**	**13300**	**14050**
2002 INSIGHT-3 Cyl.-5 Spd./AT					
Veh. Ident.: JHMZE1()()()2()000001 Up.					
Hatchback 3D	ZE1()()	1847	**11475**	**13600**	**14350**
CIVIC/INSIGHT OPTIONS					
Add Aluminum/Alloy Wheels (Std. Si, HX, Insight)			**200**	**225**	**225**
Add Compact Disc Player (Std. EX, Si)			**75**	**100**	**100**
Add Theft Recovery System			**75**	**100**	**100**
Deduct W/out Air Conditioning			**475**	**475**	**475**
Ded W/out Automatic Trans. (Ex. Insight, Si)			**375**	**375**	**375**
2002 ACCORD-4 Cyl.					
Veh. Ident.: ()H()(Model)()2()000001 Up.					
Coupe 2D LX	CG3()()*	2967	**11750**	**14000**	**14950**
Coupe 2D LX (V6)	CG224	3236	**13150**	**15550**	**16550**

BODY TYPE	Model No.	Weight	Trade-In	Retail	High Retail
Coupe 2D SE	CG32()*	2967	**12825**	**15200**	**16200**
Coupe 2D EX	CG3()()*	3014	**13075**	**15475**	**16475**
Coupe 2D EX (V6)	CG225	3283	**14825**	**17325**	**18350**
Sedan 4D DX	CF8()4	2943	**9850**	**11925**	**12850**
Sedan 4D Value	CF866	2943	**10225**	**12375**	**13275**
Sedan 4D LX	CG()()()*	3031	**11800**	**14050**	**15000**
Sedan 4D LX (V6)	CG164	3274	**13200**	**15600**	**16600**
Sedan 4D SE	CG()6()*	3031	**12875**	**15275**	**16275**
Sedan 4D EX	CG()()()*	3097	**13125**	**15525**	**16525**
Sedan 4D EX (V6)	CG165	3329	**14875**	**17375**	**18400**
Add Aluminum/Alloy Wheels (Std. Accord SE/EX)			**225**	**250**	**250**
Add Compact Disc Player (Accord DX)			**75**	**100**	**100**
Add Leather Seats (Std. Accord EX V6)			**350**	**400**	**400**
Add Power Seat (Std. Accord V6)			**150**	**175**	**175**
Add Theft Recovery System			**75**	**100**	**100**
Deduct W/out Air Conditioning			**600**	**600**	**600**
Deduct W/out Automatic Trans.			**475**	**475**	**475**

2002 S2000-4 Cyl.-6 Spd.
Veh. Ident.: JHMAP114()2()000001 Up.

BODY TYPE	Model No.	Weight	Trade-In	Retail	High Retail
Roadster 2D	AP114	2809	**19850**	**22875**	**24225**
Add Detachable Hardtop			**725**	**825**	**825**
Add Theft Recovery System			**75**	**100**	**100**

HONDA

2001 CIVIC-4 Cyl.
Veh. Ident.: ()H()(Model)()1()000001 Up.

BODY TYPE	Model No.	Weight	Trade-In	Retail	High Retail
Coupe 2D DX	EM2()2	2405	**7475**	**9175**	**9875**
Coupe 2D HX	EM2()7	2434	**8000**	**9750**	**10475**
Coupe 2D LX	EM2()5	2465	**8475**	**10300**	**11025**
Coupe 2D EX	EM2()9	2553	**9375**	**11300**	**12025**
Sedan 4D DX	ES1()2	2421	**7875**	**9600**	**10325**
Sedan 4D LX	ES1()5	2465	**8875**	**10725**	**11475**
Sedan 4D EX	ES2()7	2564	**9775**	**11750**	**12500**

2001 INSIGHT-3 Cyl.-5 Spd./AT
Veh. Ident.: JHMZE13()()1()000001 Up.

BODY TYPE	Model No.	Weight	Trade-In	Retail	High Retail
Hatchback 3D	ZE13()	1856	**10050**	**12025**	**12750**
CIVIC/INSIGHT OPTIONS					
Add Aluminum/Alloy Wheels (Std. HX, Insight)			**150**	**175**	**175**
Add Compact Disc Player (Std. EX)			**50**	**75**	**75**
Add Theft Recovery System			**50**	**75**	**75**
Deduct W/out Air Conditioning			**425**	**425**	**425**
Deduct W/out Automatic Trans. (Ex. Insight)			**325**	**325**	**325**

2001 ACCORD-4 Cyl.
Veh. Ident.: ()H()(Model)()1()000001 Up.

BODY TYPE	Model No.	Weight	Trade-In	Retail	High Retail
Coupe 2D LX	CG3()()*	2967	**9950**	**11950**	**12875**
Coupe 2D LX (V6)	CG224	3236	**11125**	**13350**	**14275**
Coupe 2D EX	CG3()()*	3014	**11175**	**13275**	**14200**
Coupe 2D EX (V6)	CG225	3283	**12650**	**15025**	**16025**
Sedan 4D DX	CF8()4*	2943	**8200**	**10025**	**10950**
Sedan 4D Value	CF866	2943	**8550**	**10400**	**11325**
Sedan 4D LX	CG()()()*	3031	**10000**	**12000**	**12925**
Sedan 4D LX (V6)	CG164	3274	**11175**	**13400**	**14325**
Sedan 4D EX	CG()()()*	3075	**11225**	**13350**	**14275**
Sedan 4D EX (V6)	CG165	3329	**12700**	**15075**	**16075**

BODY TYPE	Model No.	Weight	Trade-In	Retail	High Retail
2001 PRELUDE-4 Cyl.					
Veh. Ident.: JHM(Model)()1()000001 Up.					
Coupe 2D	BB6()4	2954	**12350**	**14700**	**15675**
Coupe 2D SH (5 Spd.)	BB615	3042	**13150**	**15550**	**16550**
ACCORD/PRELUDE OPTIONS					
Add Aluminum/Alloy Wheels (Std. Accord EX, Prelude)			**175**	**200**	**200**
Add Compact Disc Player (Accord DX)			**50**	**75**	**75**
Add Leather Seats (Std. Accord EX V6)			**300**	**350**	**350**
Add Power Seat (Std. Accord V6)			**125**	**150**	**150**
Add Theft Recovery System			**50**	**75**	**75**
Deduct W/out Air Conditioning			**550**	**550**	**550**
Ded W/out Automatic Trans. (Ex. Prelude SH)			**425**	**425**	**425**
2001 S2000-4 Cyl.-6 Spd.					
Veh. Ident.: JHMAP114()1()000001 Up.					
Roadster 2D	AP114	2809	**17975**	**20450**	**21775**
Add Detachable Hardtop			**675**	**750**	**750**
Add Theft Recovery System			**50**	**75**	**75**
HONDA					
2000 CIVIC-4 Cyl.					
Veh. Ident.: ()H()(Model)()Y()000001 Up.					
Hatchback 3D CX	EJ6()2*	2359	**5475**	**6975**	**7825**
Hatchback 3D DX	EJ6()4	2388	**6175**	**7725**	**8550**
Coupe 2D DX	EJ6()2*	2359	**6225**	**7775**	**8600**
Coupe 2D HX	EJ7()2	2370	**6650**	**8250**	**9000**
Coupe 2D EX	EJ8()()*	2513	**7925**	**9650**	**10375**
Coupe 2D Si (5 Spd.)	EM115	2601	**10100**	**12100**	**12825**
Sedan 4D DX	EJ6()2*	2339	**6575**	**8150**	**8900**
Sedan 4D Value	EJ661		**6925**	**8550**	**9325**
Sedan 4D LX	EJ6()7*	2410	**7475**	**9175**	**9875**
Sedan 4D EX	EJ8()4*	2513	**8275**	**10075**	**10800**
2000 INSIGHT-3 Cyl.-5 Spd.					
Veh. Ident.: JHMZE13()()Y()000001 Up.					
Hatchback 3D	ZE13()	1856	**8300**	**10125**	**10850**
CIVIC/INSIGHT OPTIONS					
Add Aluminum/Alloy Wheels (Std. HX, Si, Insight)			**100**	**125**	**125**
Add Compact Disc Player (Std. Value/EX/Si)			**50**	**75**	**75**
Deduct W/out Air Conditioning			**375**	**375**	**375**
Ded W/out Automatic Trans. (Ex. Si, Insight)			**300**	**300**	**300**
2000 ACCORD-4 Cyl.					
Veh. Ident.: ()H()(Model)()Y()000001 Up.					
Coupe 2D LX	CG3()()*	2948	**8350**	**10150**	**11075**
Coupe 2D LX (V6)	CG224	3215	**9350**	**11375**	**12275**
Coupe 2D EX	CG3()()*	2981	**9350**	**11275**	**12175**
Coupe 2D EX (V6)	CG225	3259	**10600**	**12750**	**13650**
Sedan 4D DX	CF8()4	2932	**6825**	**8425**	**9300**
Sedan 4D LX	CG()()()*	3020	**8400**	**10225**	**11150**
Sedan 4D LX (V6)	CG164	3241	**9400**	**11425**	**12325**
Sedan 4D SE	CG()6()*	3053	**8925**	**10775**	**11725**
Sedan 4D EX	CG()()()*	3064	**9400**	**11325**	**12225**
Sedan 4D EX (V6)	CG165	3285	**10650**	**12800**	**13700**
2000 PRELUDE-4 Cyl.					
Veh. Ident.: JHM(Model)()Y()000001 Up.					
Coupe 2D	BB6()4	2954	**10575**	**12725**	**13625**

BODY TYPE	Model No.	Weight	Trade-In	Retail	High Retail
Coupe 2D SH (5 Spd.)	BB615	3042	**11275**	**13500**	**14425**
ACCORD/PRELUDE OPTIONS					
Add A/A Wheels (Std. Accord SE/EX, Prelude)			**125**	**150**	**150**
Add Compact Disc Player (Std. Accord EX, Prelude)			**50**	**75**	**75**
Add Leather Seats (Std. Accord EX V6)			**250**	**300**	**300**
Add Power Seat (Std. Accord V6)			**100**	**125**	**125**
Deduct W/out Air Conditioning			**500**	**500**	**500**
Ded W/out Automatic Trans. (Ex. Prelude SH)			**375**	**375**	**375**
2000 S2000-4 Cyl.-6 Spd.					
Veh. Ident.: JHMAP114()Y()000001 Up.					
Roadster 2D	AP114	2809	**16225**	**18625**	**19900**
Add Detachable Hardtop			**625**	**700**	**700**
HONDA					
1999 CIVIC-4 Cyl.					
Veh. Ident.: ()H()(Model)()X()000001 Up.					
Hatchback 3D CX	EJ6()2*	2359	**4325**	**5700**	**6475**
Hatchback 3D DX	EJ6()4	2388	**5000**	**6450**	**7250**
Coupe 2D DX	EJ6()2*	2359	**5050**	**6500**	**7300**
Coupe 2D HX	EJ7()2	2370	**5375**	**6875**	**7700**
Coupe 2D EX	EJ8()()*	2513	**6500**	**8075**	**8825**
Coupe 2D Si (5 Spd.)	EM115	2612	**8625**	**10450**	**11175**
Sedan 4D DX	EJ6()2*	2339	**5350**	**6850**	**7675**
Sedan 4D Value	EJ661	2361	**5625**	**7150**	**7925**
Sedan 4D LX	EJ6()7*	2412	**6125**	**7675**	**8475**
Sedan 4D EX	EJ8()4*	2511	**6800**	**8400**	**9150**
Add Aluminum/Alloy Wheels (Std. HX, Si)			**50**	**75**	**75**
Deduct W/out Air Conditioning			**325**	**325**	**325**
Deduct W/out Automatic Trans. (Ex. Si)			**250**	**250**	**250**
1999 ACCORD-4 Cyl.					
Veh. Ident.: ()H()(Model)()X()000001 Up.					
Coupe 2D LX	CG3()()*	2943	**7025**	**8650**	**9525**
Coupe 2D LX (V6)	CG224	3197	**7900**	**9725**	**10625**
Coupe 2D EX	CG3()()*	2976	**7900**	**9625**	**10525**
Coupe 2D EX (V6)	CG225	3241	**9000**	**10950**	**11900**
Sedan 4D DX	CF8()4	2888	**5650**	**7175**	**8050**
Sedan 4D LX	CG()()()*	2987	**7075**	**8725**	**9600**
Sedan 4D LX (V6)	CG164	3241	**7950**	**9800**	**10700**
Sedan 4D EX	CG()()()*	3020	**7950**	**9675**	**10575**
Sedan 4D EX (V6)	CG165	3285	**9050**	**11000**	**11950**
1999 PRELUDE-4 Cyl.					
Veh. Ident.: JHM(Model)()X()000001 Up.					
Coupe 2D	BB6()4	3042	**9075**	**11050**	**11925**
Coupe 2D SH (5 Spd.)	BB615	3042	**9675**	**11725**	**12625**
ACCORD/PRELUDE OPTIONS					
Add Aluminum/Alloy Wheels (Std. Accord EX, Prelude)			**75**	**100**	**100**
Add Leather Seats (Std. Accord EX V6)			**225**	**250**	**250**
Add Power Seat (Std. Accord V6)			**75**	**100**	**100**
Deduct W/out Air Conditioning			**450**	**450**	**450**
Ded W/out Automatic Trans. (Ex. Prelude SH)			**325**	**325**	**325**

PASSENGER CARS

PASSENGER CARS

BODY TYPE	Model No.	Weight	Trade-In	Retail	High Retail
HONDA					
1998 CIVIC-4 Cyl.					
Veh. Ident.: ()H()(Model)()W()000001 Up.					
Hatchback 3D CX	EJ6()2*	2295	**3425**	**4700**	**5475**
Hatchback 3D DX	EJ6()4*	2339	**4075**	**5425**	**6175**
Coupe 2D DX	EJ6()2*	2342	**4125**	**5475**	**6225**
Coupe 2D HX	EJ7()2	2361	**4425**	**5825**	**6600**
Coupe 2D EX	EJ8()()*	2504	**5375**	**6875**	**7700**
Sedan 4D DX	EJ6()2*	2339	**4275**	**5650**	**6425**
Sedan 4D LX	EJ6()7*	2412	**4975**	**6425**	**7225**
Sedan 4D EX	EJ8()4*	2511	**5525**	**7025**	**7800**
Deduct W/out Air Conditioning			**275**	**275**	**275**
Deduct W/out Automatic Trans.			**200**	**200**	**200**
1998 ACCORD-4 Cyl.					
Veh. Ident.: 1HG(Model)()WA000001 Up.					
Coupe 2D LX	CG3()4*	2965	**5850**	**7400**	**8300**
Coupe 2D LX (V6)	CG224	3197	**6600**	**8350**	**9225**
Coupe 2D EX	CG3()()*	3009	**6625**	**8250**	**9100**
Coupe 2D EX (V6)	CG225	3241	**7550**	**9375**	**10250**
Sedan 4D DX	CF8()4*	2888	**4725**	**6175**	**7050**
Sedan 4D LX	CG5()4*	2987	**5900**	**7450**	**8350**
Sedan 4D LX (V6)	CG164	3241	**6650**	**8425**	**9300**
Sedan 4D EX	CG5()()*	3020	**6675**	**8300**	**9150**
Sedan 4D EX (V6)	CG165	3285	**7600**	**9425**	**10300**
1998 PRELUDE-4 Cyl.					
Veh. Ident.: JHM(Model)()WC000001 Up.					
Coupe 2D	BB6()4	2954	**7625**	**9450**	**10325**
Coupe 2D SH (5 Spd.)	BB615	3042	**8125**	**10000**	**10900**
ACCORD/PRELUDE OPTIONS					
Add Aluminum/Alloy Wheels (Std. Accord EX, Prelude)			**50**	**75**	**75**
Add Leather Seats (Std. Accord EX V6)			**175**	**200**	**200**
Add Power Seat (Std. Accord V6)			**50**	**75**	**75**
Deduct W/out Air Conditioning			**400**	**400**	**400**
Ded W/out Automatic Trans. (Ex. Prelude SH)			**275**	**275**	**275**
HONDA					
1997 CIVIC-4 Cyl.					
Veh. Ident.: ()H()(Model)()V()000001 Up.					
Hatchback 3D CX	EJ6()2*	2286	**3075**	**4300**	**5025**
Hatchback 3D DX	EJ6()4*	2304	**3525**	**4800**	**5600**
Coupe 2D DX	EJ6()2*	2324	**3575**	**4850**	**5650**
Coupe 2D HX	EJ7()2	2352	**3850**	**5150**	**5875**
Coupe 2D EX	EJ8()()*	2507	**4375**	**5750**	**6525**
Sedan 4D DX	EJ6()2*	2370	**3675**	**4975**	**5775**
Sedan 4D LX	EJ6()7*	2489	**4025**	**5375**	**6125**
Sedan 4D EX	EJ8()4*	2568	**4475**	**5875**	**6675**
Deduct W/out Air Conditioning			**150**	**150**	**150**
Deduct W/out Automatic Trans.			**125**	**125**	**125**
1997 DEL SOL-4 Cyl.					
Veh. Ident.: JHM(Model)()VS000001 Up.					
Coupe 2D S	EH6()4	2469	**4125**	**5600**	**6450**
Coupe 2D Si	EH6()6	2469	**4925**	**6475**	**7375**
Coupe 2D VTEC (5 Spd.)	EG217	2517	**5600**	**7250**	**8125**

BODY TYPE	Model No.	Weight	Trade-In	Retail	High Retail
1997 ACCORD-4 Cyl.					
Veh. Ident.: 1HG(Model)()VA000001 Up.					
Coupe 2D LX	CD7()3*	2855	**4150**	**5525**	**6375**
Coupe 2D SE	CD720	2921	**4625**	**6025**	**6875**
Coupe 2D EX	CD7()()*	2965	**4775**	**6200**	**7075**
Sedan 4D DX	CD5()()*	2855	**3725**	**5025**	**5825**
Sedan 4D LX	CD5()()*	2899	**4350**	**5725**	**6575**
Sedan 4D LX (V6)	CE664	3219	**5000**	**6550**	**7450**
Sedan 4D SE	CD560	2965	**4825**	**6250**	**7125**
Sedan 4D EX	CD5()()*	3009	**4975**	**6425**	**7325**
Sedan 4D EX (V6)	CE667	3285	**5775**	**7450**	**8350**
Wagon 5D LX	CE1()2	3053	**4550**	**5950**	**6825**
Wagon 5D EX	CE189	3197	**5175**	**6650**	**7550**
1997 PRELUDE-4 Cyl.					
Veh. Ident.: JHM(Model)()VC000001 Up.					
Coupe 2D	BB6()4	2954	**6400**	**8125**	**8975**
Coupe 2D SH (5 Spd.)	BB615	3042	**6750**	**8500**	**9375**
DEL SOL/ACCORD/PRELUDE OPTIONS					
Add Leather Seats (Std. Accord EX V6)			**150**	**175**	**175**
Add Power Seat (Std. Accord V6)			**50**	**75**	**75**
Deduct W/out Air Conditioning			**250**	**250**	**250**
Deduct W/out Automatic Trans. (Ex. Prelude SH, Del Sol VTEC)			**175**	**175**	**175**
HONDA					
1996 CIVIC-4 Cyl.					
Veh. Ident.: ()H()(Model)()T()000001 Up.					
Hatchback 3D CX	EJ6()2	2222	**2825**	**4025**	**4725**
Hatchback 3D DX	EJ6()4	2242	**3125**	**4375**	**5125**
Coupe 2D DX	EJ6()2	2262	**3200**	**4450**	**5200**
Coupe 2D HX	EJ7()2	2313	**3300**	**4550**	**5325**
Coupe 2D EX	EJ8()()	2483	**3775**	**5075**	**5800**
Sedan 4D DX	EJ6()2	2319	**3225**	**4475**	**5225**
Sedan 4D LX	EJ6()()	2387	**3425**	**4700**	**5475**
Sedan 4D EX	EJ8()4	2518	**3800**	**5100**	**5825**
Deduct W/out Air Conditioning			**100**	**100**	**100**
Deduct W/out Automatic Trans.			**100**	**100**	**100**
1996 DEL SOL-4 Cyl.					
Veh. Ident.: JHM(Model)()TS000001 Up.					
Coupe 2D S	EH6()4	2297	**3500**	**4900**	**5800**
Coupe 2D Si	EH6()6	2409	**4250**	**5725**	**6575**
Coupe 2D VTEC (5 Spd.)	EG217	2517	**4800**	**6325**	**7200**
1996 ACCORD-4 Cyl.					
Veh. Ident.: ()H()(Model)()T()000001 Up.					
Coupe 2D LX	CD7()()	2921	**3500**	**4775**	**5650**
Coupe 2D EX	CD7()()	3031	**4025**	**5375**	**6200**
Sedan 4D DX	CD5()()	2921	**3325**	**4575**	**5425**
Sedan 4D Anniversary	CD568	2919	**3600**	**4875**	**5775**
Sedan 4D LX	CD5()()	2965	**3700**	**5000**	**5900**
Sedan 4D LX (V6)	CE664	3219	**4175**	**5650**	**6500**
Sedan 4D EX	CD5()()	3075	**4225**	**5600**	**6450**
Sedan 4D EX (V6)	CE667	3285	**4800**	**6325**	**7200**
Wagon 5D LX	CE1()2	3053	**3900**	**5225**	**6025**
Wagon 5D EX	CE189	3197	**4425**	**5825**	**6700**

BODY TYPE	Model No.	Weight	Trade-In	Retail	High Retail
1996 PRELUDE-4 Cyl.					
Veh. Ident.: JHM(Model)()()()TC000001 Up.					
Coupe 2D S	BA8	2809	**4725**	**6250**	**7125**
Coupe 2D Si	BB2	2866	**5075**	**6675**	**7600**
Coupe 2D VTEC (5 Spd.)	BB1	2932	**5525**	**7175**	**8050**
DEL SOL/ACCORD/PRELUDE OPTIONS					
Deduct W/out Air Conditioning			**150**	**150**	**150**
Deduct W/out Automatic Trans.. (Ex. Del Sol/Prelude VTEC)			**125**	**125**	**125**
HONDA					
1995 CIVIC-4 Cyl.					
Veh. Ident.: ()H()(Model)()S()000001 Up.					
Hatchback 3D CX	EH235	2108	**2075**	**3200**	**3825**
Hatchback 3D DX	EH2()6	2264	**2275**	**3425**	**4075**
Hatchback 3D VX	EH237	2094	**2275**	**3425**	**4075**
Hatchback 3D Si	EH338	2390	**3025**	**4250**	**4975**
Coupe 2D DX	EJ2()2	2326	**2350**	**3500**	**4150**
Coupe 2D EX	EJ1()()	2502	**2800**	**4000**	**4725**
Sedan 4D DX	EG8()4	2392	**2375**	**3525**	**4175**
Sedan 4D LX	EG8()()	2440	**2525**	**3700**	**4375**
Sedan 4D EX	EH9()9	2575	**2825**	**4025**	**4725**
1995 DEL SOL-4 Cyl.					
Veh. Ident.: ()H()(Model)()()()S()000001 Up.					
Coupe 2D S	EG1	2387	**2975**	**4300**	**5125**
Coupe 2D Si	EH6	2474	**3575**	**4975**	**5875**
Coupe 2D VTEC	EG2	2562	**4075**	**5550**	**6400**
1995 ACCORD-4 Cyl.					
Veh. Ident.: ()H()(Model)()S()000001 Up.					
Coupe 2D LX	CD7()()	2888	**2950**	**4175**	**4975**
Coupe 2D EX	CD7()()	3020	**3400**	**4675**	**5550**
Sedan 4D DX	CD5()2	2866	**2825**	**4025**	**4825**
Sedan 4D LX	CD5()()	2976	**3150**	**4400**	**5225**
Sedan 4D LX (V6)	CE664	3218	**3550**	**4950**	**5850**
Sedan 4D EX	CD5()()	3075	**3600**	**4875**	**5775**
Sedan 4D EX (V6)	CE666	3285	**4000**	**5450**	**6275**
Wagon 5D LX	CE1()2	3142	**3350**	**4600**	**5450**
Wagon 5D EX	CE189	3197	**3800**	**5100**	**5900**
1995 PRELUDE-4 Cyl.					
Veh. Ident.: JHM(Model)()SC000001 Up.					
Coupe 2D S	BA8()4	2866	**4100**	**5575**	**6425**
Coupe 2D Si	BB2()5	2921	**4400**	**5900**	**6775**
Coupe 2D SE	BB2()7	2963	**4700**	**6225**	**7100**
Coupe 2D VTEC	BB117	2932	**4800**	**6325**	**7200**

HYUNDAI

BODY TYPE	Model No.	Weight	Trade-In	Retail	High Retail
HYUNDAI					
2004 ACCENT-4 Cyl.					
Veh. Ident.: KMH(Model)()4()000001 Up.					
Hatchback 3D (5 Spd.)	CF35C	2255	**5900**	**7450**	**8250**
Hatchback 3D GL	CG35C	2280	**6775**	**8375**	**9125**
Hatchback 3D GT	CG35C	2280	**7275**	**8950**	**9725**
Sedan 4D GL	CG45C	2290	**7275**	**8950**	**9725**

BODY TYPE	Model No.	Weight	Trade-In	Retail	High Retail
2004 ELANTRA-4 Cyl.					
Veh. Ident.: KMH(Model)()D()4()000001 Up.					
Sedan 4D GLS	DN4	2635	**8675**	**10525**	**11250**
Sedan 4D GT	DN4	2635	**9600**	**11575**	**12300**
Hatchback 5D GT	DN5	2635	**10400**	**12450**	**13175**
2004 TIBURON-4 Cyl.					
Veh. Ident.: KMH(Model)5()()4()000001 Up.					
Coupe 2D	HM6	2940	**11575**	**13700**	**14450**
Coupe 2D GT (V6)	HN6	3015	**12925**	**15125**	**15925**
2004 SONATA-V6					
Veh. Ident.: KMH(Model)()4()000001 Up.					
Sedan 4D (4 Cyl.)	WF25S	3181	**10675**	**12725**	**13450**
Sedan 4D	WF25H	3212	**11525**	**13650**	**14400**
Sedan 4D GLS	WF35H	3254	**11875**	**14025**	**14800**
Sedan 4D LX	WF35H	3254	**12650**	**14825**	**15600**
ACCENT/ELANTRA/TIBURON/SONATA OPTIONS					
Add Aluminum/Alloy Wheels (Std. Accent/Elan GT, Tiburon, Sonata GLS/LX)			**300**	**350**	**350**
Add CD Player (Std. Elan GT, Tiburon, Sonata)			**100**	**125**	**125**
Add Cruise Control (Elantra GLS)			**175**	**200**	**200**
Add Infinity Stereo System			**250**	**300**	**300**
Add Leather Seats (Std. Elantra GT, Sonata LX)			**350**	**400**	**400**
Add Power Door Locks (Accent)			**150**	**175**	**175**
Add Power Sunroof			**525**	**600**	**600**
Add Power Windows (Accent)			**175**	**200**	**200**
Add Theft Recovery System			**100**	**125**	**125**
Deduct W/out Air Conditioning			**575**	**575**	**575**
Ded W/out Automatic Trans. (Ex. Accent Base)			**475**	**475**	**475**
2004 XG350-V6					
Veh. Ident.: KMHFU45E()4()000001 Up.					
Sedan 4D	FU45E	3651	**14600**	**17075**	**18100**
Sedan 4D L	FU45E	3651	**15700**	**18250**	**19300**
Add Theft Recovery System			**100**	**125**	**125**
HYUNDAI					
2003 ACCENT-4 Cyl.					
Veh. Ident.: KMH(Model)()3()000001 Up.					
Hatchback 3D (5 Spd.)	CF35C	2255	**4425**	**5825**	**6600**
Hatchback 3D GL	CG35C	2280	**5250**	**6750**	**7575**
Sedan 4D GL	CG45C	2290	**5700**	**7225**	**8000**
2003 ELANTRA-4 Cyl.					
Veh. Ident.: KMH(Model)5D()3()000001 Up.					
Sedan 4D GLS	DN4	2635	**7150**	**8825**	**9600**
Sedan 4D GT	DN4	2635	**7925**	**9675**	**10400**
Hatchback 5D GT	DN5	2635	**8675**	**10525**	**11250**
2003 TIBURON-4 Cyl.					
Veh. Ident.: KMH(Model)5()()3()000001 Up.					
Coupe 2D	HM6	2940	**9575**	**11525**	**12250**
Coupe 2D GT (V6)	HN6	3015	**11050**	**13150**	**13900**
2003 SONATA-V6					
Veh. Ident.: KMH(Model)()3()000001 Up.					
Sedan 4D (4 Cyl.)	WF25S	3181	**9200**	**11125**	**11850**
Sedan 4D	WF25H	3181	**9975**	**11950**	**12700**
Sedan 4D GLS	WF35H	3223	**10425**	**12450**	**13175**
Sedan 4D LX	WF35H	3223	**10950**	**13025**	**13775**

PASSENGER CARS

BODY TYPE	Model No.	Weight	Trade-In	Retail	High Retail
ACCENT/ELANTRA/TIBURON/SONATA OPTIONS					
Add Aluminum/Alloy Wheels .... (Std. Elan GT, Tiburon, Sonata GLS/LX)			250	300	300
Add CD Player (Std. Elan GT, Tiburon, Sonata)			75	100	100
Add Cruise Control (Elantra GLS)			150	175	175
Add Infinity Stereo System (Std. Tiburon GT)			200	225	225
Add Leather Seats (Std. Elantra GT, Sonata LX)			300	350	350
Add Power Door Locks (Accent)			125	150	150
Add Power Sunroof			475	550	550
Add Power Windows (Accent)			150	175	175
Add Theft Recovery System			75	100	100
Deduct W/out Air Conditioning			525	525	525
Ded W/out Automatic Trans. (Ex. Accent Base)			425	425	425
2003 XG350-V6					
Veh. Ident.: KMHFU45E()3()000001 Up.					
Sedan 4D........................	FU45E	3651	12425	14775	15750
Sedan 4D L......................	FU45E	3651	13175	15575	16575
Add Theft Recovery System			75	100	100
HYUNDAI					
2002 ACCENT-4 Cyl.					
Veh. Ident.: KMH(Model)()2()000001 Up.					
Hatchback 3D L (5 Spd.)	CF35G	2255	3050	4275	5000
Hatchback 3D GS	CG35C	2280	3775	5075	5800
Sedan 4D GL.....................	CG45C	2290	4175	5550	6300
2002 ELANTRA-4 Cyl.					
Veh. Ident.: KMH(Model)5D()2()000001 Up.					
Sedan 4D GLS......................	DN4	2635	5375	6875	7700
Hatchback 5D GT	DN5	2635	6725	8350	9100
2002 SONATA-V6					
Veh. Ident.: KMH(Model)()2()000001 Up.					
Sedan 4D (4 Cyl.)	WF25S	3181	6750	8350	9100
Sedan 4D........................	WF25H	3181	7450	9150	9850
Sedan 4D GLS....................	WF35H	3223	7850	9575	10300
Sedan 4D LX.....................	WF35H	3223	8275	10075	10800
ACCENT/ELANTRA/SONATA OPTIONS					
Add A/A Wheels (Std. Elan GT, Sonata GLS/LX)			200	225	225
Add CD Player (Std. Elan GT, Sonata) . . .			75	100	100
Add Cruise Control (Std. Elan GT, Sonata)			125	150	150
Add Power Door Locks (Accent)			100	125	125
Add Power Sunroof			425	475	475
Add Power Windows (Accent)			125	150	150
Add Theft Recovery System			75	100	100
Deduct W/out Air Conditioning			475	475	475
Deduct W/out Automatic Trans. (Ex. Accent L)			375	375	375
2002 XG350-V6					
Veh. Ident.: KMHFU45E()2()000001 Up.					
Sedan 4D........................	FU45E	3651	9400	11450	12350
Sedan 4D L......................	FU45E	3651	10100	12225	13125
Add Theft Recovery System			75	100	100

BODY TYPE	Model No.	Weight	Trade-In	Retail	High Retail
HYUNDAI					
2001 ACCENT-4 Cyl.					
Veh. Ident.: KMH(Model)()1()000001 Up.					
Hatchback 3D L (5 Spd.)	CF3()G	2255	**2100**	**3225**	**3850**
Hatchback 3D GS	CG3()C	2280	**2675**	**3875**	**4575**
Sedan 4D GL	CG4()C	2290	**3025**	**4250**	**4975**
2001 ELANTRA-4 Cyl.					
Veh. Ident.: KMH(Model)()D()1()000001 Up.					
Sedan 4D GLS	DN4	2635	**4050**	**5400**	**6150**
Hatchback 5D GT	DN5	2635	**5200**	**6675**	**7500**
2001 TIBURON-4 Cyl.					
Veh. Ident.: KMHJG1()F()1()000001 Up.					
Coupe 2D	JG1	2633	**6050**	**7600**	**8400**
2001 SONATA-4 Cyl.					
Veh. Ident.: KMH(Model)()1()000001 Up.					
Sedan 4D	WF25S	3072	**4375**	**5750**	**6525**
Sedan 4D GLS (V6)	WF35V	3069	**5150**	**6625**	**7450**
ACCENT/ELANTRA/TIBURON/SONATA OPTIONS					
Add A/A Wheels (Std. Elan GT, Tiburon, Sonata)			**150**	**175**	**175**
Add CD Player (Std. Elan GT, Sonata GLS)			**50**	**75**	**75**
Add Cruise Control (Std. Elan GT, Tiburon, Sonata)			**100**	**125**	**125**
Add Leather Seats (Std. Elantra GT)			**200**	**225**	**225**
Add Power Door Locks (Accent)			**75**	**100**	**100**
Add Power Seat			**100**	**125**	**125**
Add Power Sunroof			**375**	**425**	**425**
Add Power Windows (Accent)			**100**	**125**	**125**
Add Theft Recovery System			**50**	**75**	**75**
Deduct W/out Air Conditioning			**425**	**425**	**425**
Deduct W/out Automatic Trans. (Ex. Accent L)			**325**	**325**	**325**
2001 XG300-V6					
Veh. Ident.: KMHFU44D()1()000001 Up.					
Sedan 4D	FU44D	3604	**6825**	**8450**	**9325**
Sedan 4D L	FU44D	3604	**7475**	**9175**	**10050**
Add Power Sunroof (Std. L)			**425**	**475**	**475**
Add Theft Recovery System			**50**	**75**	**75**
HYUNDAI					
2000 ACCENT-4 Cyl.					
Veh. Ident.: KMH(Model)()G()YU000001 Up.					
Hatchback 3D L (5 Spd.)	CF3	2239	**1500**	**2550**	**3125**
Hatchback 3D GS	CH3	2239	**1975**	**3100**	**3700**
Sedan 4D GL	CG4	2290	**2275**	**3425**	**4075**
2000 ELANTRA-4 Cyl.					
Veh. Ident.: KMH(Model)()F()Y()000001 Up.					
Sedan 4D GLS	JF3	2626	**3100**	**4325**	**5075**
Wagon 4D GLS	JW3	2681	**3450**	**4725**	**5500**
2000 TIBURON-4 Cyl.					
Veh. Ident.: KMHJG2()()()Y()000001 Up.					
Coupe 2D	JG2	2633	**4775**	**6200**	**6975**
2000 SONATA-4 Cyl.					
Veh. Ident.: KMH(Model)()Y()000001 Up.					
Sedan 4D	WF25S	3072	**3300**	**4575**	**5350**
Sedan 4D GL (V6)	WF25V	3107	**3800**	**5125**	**5850**
Sedan 4D GLS (V6)	WF35V	3107	**3950**	**5300**	**6050**

PASSENGER CARS

BODY TYPE	Model No.	Weight	Trade-In	Retail	High Retail
HYUNDAI OPTIONS					
Add Aluminum/Alloy Wheels (Std. Tiburon, Sonata)			100	125	125
Add Compact Disc Player (Std. Sonata GLS)			50	75	75
Add Cruise Control (Std. Tiburon, Sonata)			75	100	100
Add Leather Seats			150	175	175
Add Power Door Locks (Accent)			50	75	75
Add Power Seat			75	100	100
Add Power Sunroof			325	375	375
Add Power Windows (Accent)			75	100	100
Deduct W/out Air Conditioning			375	375	375
Deduct W/out Automatic Trans. (Ex. Accent L)			300	300	300
HYUNDAI					
1999 ACCENT-4 Cyl.					
Veh. Ident.: KMH(Model)4N()X()000001 Up.					
Hatchback 3D L (5 Spd.)	VD1	2088	1150	2150	2675
Hatchback 3D GS	VD3	2132	1525	2575	3150
Sedan 4D GL	VF2	2119	1775	2850	3475
1999 ELANTRA-4 Cyl.					
Veh. Ident.: KMH(Model)4M()X()000001 Up.					
Sedan 4D	JF2	2560	2250	3400	4050
Sedan 4D GLS	JF3		2400	3550	4225
Wagon 4D	JW2	2648	2550	3725	4400
Wagon 4D GLS	JW3		2700	3900	4600
1999 TIBURON-4 Cyl.					
Veh. Ident.: KMH(Model)4()()X()000001 Up.					
Coupe 2D	JG2	2633	2975	4200	4925
Coupe 2D FX	JG3	2644	3775	5075	5800
1999 SONATA-4 Cyl.					
Veh. Ident.: KMH(Model)()X()000001 Up.					
Sedan 4D	WF25S	3072	2500	3675	4350
Sedan 4D GL (V6)	WF25V	3107	2900	4125	4850
Sedan 4D GLS (V6)	WF35V	3107	3125	4375	5125
HYUNDAI OPTIONS					
Add Aluminum/Alloy Wheels (Std. FX, Sonata GLS)			50	75	75
Add Cruise Control (Std. Sonata GLS)			50	75	75
Add Leather Seats			125	150	150
Add Power Seat			50	75	75
Add Power Sunroof			275	325	325
Add Pwr Wind (Std. Elantra GLS, Tiburon, Sonata)			50	75	75
Add Sunroof			125	150	150
Deduct W/out Air Conditioning			325	325	325
Deduct W/out Automatic Trans. (Ex. Accent L)			250	250	250
HYUNDAI					
1998 ACCENT-4 Cyl.					
Veh. Ident.: KMH(Model)4N()W()000001 Up.					
Hatchback 3D L (5 Spd.)	VD1	2101	850	1775	2225
Hatchback 3D GS	VD3	2101	1100	2100	2625
Hatchback 3D GSi	VD3	2150	1500	2550	3125
Sedan 4D GL	VF2	2105	1300	2325	2875
1998 ELANTRA-4 Cyl.					
Veh. Ident.: KMH(Model)4M()W()000001 Up.					
Sedan 4D	JF2	2458	1600	2650	3250
Sedan 4D GLS	JF3	2668	1750	2825	3450
Wagon 4D	JW2	2619	1850	2925	3550
Wagon 4D GLS	JW3	2718	2000	3100	3700

PASSENGER CARS

BODY TYPE	Model No.	Weight	Trade-In	Retail	High Retail
1998 TIBURON-4 Cyl.					
Veh. Ident.: KMH(Model)4()()W()000001 Up.					
Coupe 2D	JG2	2566	**2250**	**3400**	**4050**
Coupe 2D FX	JG3	2597	**2900**	**4100**	**4825**
1998 SONATA-4 Cyl.					
Veh. Ident.: KMH(Model)()W()000001 Up.					
Sedan 4D	CF24F	2935	**1875**	**2950**	**3600**
Sedan 4D GL	CF24F	2966	**1975**	**3075**	**3675**
Sedan 4D GL (V6)	CF24T	3072	**2275**	**3425**	**4075**
Sedan 4D GLS (V6)	CF34T	3072	**2450**	**3625**	**4300**
HYUNDAI OPTIONS					
Add Cruise Control (Std. Sonata GLS)			**50**	**75**	**75**
Add Leather Seats			**100**	**125**	**125**
Add Power Sunroof			**225**	**275**	**275**
Add Sunroof			**100**	**125**	**125**
Deduct W/out Air Conditioning			**275**	**275**	**275**
Deduct W/out Automatic Trans. (Ex. Accent L)			**200**	**200**	**200**
HYUNDAI					
1997 ACCENT-4 Cyl.					
Veh. Ident.: KMH(Model)4N()V()000001 Up.					
Hatchback 3D L (5 Spd.)	VD1	2101	**800**	**1725**	**2175**
Hatchback 3D GS	VD3	2132	**975**	**1925**	**2400**
Hatchback 3D GT	VD3	2220	**1225**	**2225**	**2750**
Sedan 4D GL	VF2	2119	**1050**	**2025**	**2525**
1997 ELANTRA-4 Cyl.					
Veh. Ident.: KMH(Model)4M()V()000001 Up.					
Sedan 4D	JF2	2458	**1200**	**2200**	**2725**
Sedan 4D GLS	JF3	2668	**1325**	**2350**	**2900**
Wagon 4D	JW2	2619	**1400**	**2425**	**3000**
Wagon 4D GLS	JW3	2718	**1525**	**2575**	**3150**
1997 TIBURON-4 Cyl.					
Veh. Ident.: KMH(Model)4()()V()000001 Up.					
Coupe 2D	JG2	2566	**1625**	**2675**	**3275**
Coupe 2D FX	JG3	2597	**2025**	**3150**	**3775**
1997 SONATA-4 Cyl.					
Veh. Ident.: KMH(Model)()V()000001 Up.					
Sedan 4D	CF24F	2935	**1225**	**2225**	**2750**
Sedan 4D GL	CF24F	2966	**1300**	**2325**	**2875**
Sedan 4D GL (V6)	CF24T	3072	**1550**	**2600**	**3200**
Sedan 4D GLS (V6)	CF34T	3072	**1675**	**2725**	**3325**
HYUNDAI OPTIONS					
Add Leather Seats			**75**	**100**	**100**
Add Power Sunroof			**150**	**175**	**175**
Add Sunroof			**50**	**75**	**75**
Deduct W/out Air Conditioning			**150**	**150**	**150**
Deduct W/out Automatic Trans. (Ex. Accent L)			**125**	**125**	**125**
HYUNDAI					
1996 ACCENT-4 Cyl.					
Veh. Ident.: KMH(Model)4N()T()000001 Up.					
Hatchback 3D L (5 Spd.)	VD1	2101	**675**	**1575**	**2000**
Hatchback 3D	VD1	2101	**800**	**1725**	**2175**
Hatchback 3D GT	VD3	2150	**1000**	**1950**	**2425**
Sedan 4D	VF1	2105	**875**	**1800**	**2250**

P
A
S
S
E
N
G
E
R

C
A
R
S

BODY TYPE	Model No.	Weight	Trade-In	Retail	High Retail
1996 ELANTRA-4 Cyl.					
Veh. Ident.: KMH(Model)4M()T()000001 Up.					
Sedan 4D	JF2	2458	**875**	**1800**	**2250**
Sedan 4D GLS	JF3	2668	**975**	**1925**	**2400**
Wagon 4D	JW2	2619	**975**	**1925**	**2400**
Wagon 4D GLS	JW3	2718	**1075**	**2075**	**2600**
1996 SONATA- 4 Cyl.					
Veh. Ident.: KMH(Model)()T()000001 Up.					
Sedan 4D	CF14F	2864	**975**	**1925**	**2400**
Sedan 4D GL	CF24F	2908	**1025**	**2000**	**2475**
Sedan 4D GL (V6)	CF24T	3108	**1125**	**2125**	**2650**
Sedan 4D GLS (V6)	CF34T	3018	**1225**	**2225**	**2750**
HYUNDAI OPTIONS					
Add Power Sunroof			**100**	**125**	**125**
Deduct W/out Air Conditioning			**100**	**100**	**100**
Deduct W/out Automatic Trans. (Ex. Accent L)			**100**	**100**	**100**
HYUNDAI					
1995 ACCENT-4 Cyl.					
Veh. Ident.: KMH(Model)()()()S()000001 Up.					
Hatchback 3D L	VD1	2101	**600**	**1500**	**1900**
Hatchback 3D	VD1	2101	**700**	**1600**	**2025**
Sedan 4D	VF1	2105	**750**	**1675**	**2125**
1995 SCOUPE-4 Cyl.					
Veh. Ident.: KMH(Model)()()()S()000001 Up.					
Coupe 2D	VE2	2176	**725**	**1625**	**2050**
Coupe 2D LS	VE3	2266	**875**	**1800**	**2250**
Coupe 2D Turbo	VE3	2240	**1075**	**2075**	**2600**
1995 ELANTRA-4 Cyl.					
Veh. Ident.: KMH(Model)()()()S()000001 Up.					
Sedan 4D	JF2	2500	**725**	**1625**	**2050**
Sedan 4D GLS	JF3	2628	**775**	**1700**	**2150**
1995 SONATA-4 Cyl.					
Veh. Ident.: KMH(Model)()S()000001 Up.					
Sedan 4D	CF24F	2864	**825**	**1750**	**2200**
Sedan 4D GL	CF24F	2908	**875**	**1800**	**2250**
Sedan 4D GL (V6)	CF24T	3018	**975**	**1925**	**2400**
Sedan 4D GLS (V6)	CF34T	3018	**1025**	**2000**	**2475**

INFINITI

BODY TYPE	Model No.	Weight	Trade-In	Retail	High Retail
INFINITI					
2004 G35-V6					
Veh. Ident.: JNK(Model)E()4()000001 Up.					
Coupe 2D (AT/6 Spd.)	CV54	3416	**28000**	**31725**	**33300**
Sedan 4D	CV51	3336	**23625**	**27000**	**28475**
Sedan 4D x (AWD)	CV51	3677			
2004 I35-V6					
Veh. Ident.: JNKDA31A()4T000001 Up.					
Sedan 4D	DA31	3306	**21700**	**24825**	**26225**
G35/I35 OPTIONS					
Add Bose Stereo System (Std. I35)			**350**	**400**	**400**
Add Leather Seats (Std. G35x, I35)			**525**	**600**	**600**
Add Navigation System			**650**	**725**	**725**

BODY TYPE	Model No.	Weight	Trade-In	Retail	High Retail
Add Power Seat (G35 Sedan RWD).....			225	250	250
Add Power Sunroof (Std. I35)			625	700	700
Add Theft Recovery System			100	125	125
Deduct W/out Auto. Trans. (Ex. G35 Coupe)			625	625	625
2004 M45-V8					
Veh. Ident.: JNKAY41()()4M000001 Up.					
Sedan 4D..........................	AY41	3851	30200	34425	36375
2004 Q45-V8					
Veh. Ident.: JNKBF01A()4M000001 Up.					
Sedan 4D..........................	BF01	3977	35925	40600	42725
Sedan 4D Premium	BF01	3977			
M45/Q45 OPTIONS					
Add Navigation System (Std. Premium)..			750	850	850
Add Theft Recovery System			100	125	125
Deduct W/out Power Sunroof			725	725	725
INFINITI					
2003 G35-V6					
Veh. Ident.: JNK(Model)E()3M000001 Up.					
Coupe 2D (AT/6 Spd.)	CV54	3416	25150	28650	30150
Sedan 4D..........................	CV51	3336	21275	24375	25775
2003 I35-V6					
Veh. Ident.: JNKDA31A()3T000001 Up.					
Sedan 4D..........................	DA31	3306	19200	22175	23500
G35/I35 OPTIONS					
Add Sport Pkg. (I35).................			875	975	975
Add Bose Stereo System (Std. I35)			300	350	350
Add Leather Seats (Std. I35)			475	550	550
Add Navigation System			550	625	625
Add Power Seat (G35 Sedan)			200	225	225
Add Power Sunroof			575	650	650
Add Theft Recovery System			75	100	100
Deduct W/out Auto. Trans. (Ex. G35 Coupe)			575	575	575
2003 M45-V8					
Veh. Ident.: JNKAY41E()3M000001 Up.					
Sedan 4D..........................	AY41	3851	26700	30600	32425
2003 Q45-V8					
Veh. Ident.: JNKBF01A()3M000001 Up.					
Sedan 4D..........................	BF01	3977	30425	34675	36625
Sedan 4D Premium	BF01	3977	34075	38650	40725
M45/Q45 OPTIONS					
Add Navigation System (Std. Premium)..			650	725	725
Add Theft Recovery System			75	100	100
Deduct W/out Power Sunroof			675	675	675
INFINITI					
2002 G20-4 Cyl.					
Veh. Ident.: JNKCP11A()2T000001 Up.					
Sedan 4D..........................	CP11	2923	12475	14875	16025
2002 I35-V6					
Veh. Ident.: JNKDA31A()2T000001 Up.					
Sedan 4D..........................	DA31	3342	16600	19250	20525
G20/I35 OPTIONS					
Add Sport Pkg.			675	750	750
Add Leather Seats (Std. I35)			425	475	475

BODY TYPE	Model No.	Weight	Trade-In	Retail	High Retail
Add Navigation System			450	500	500
Add Power Sunroof			525	600	600
Add Theft Recovery System			75	100	100
Deduct W/out Automatic Trans.			525	525	525
Deduct W/out Power Seat			175	175	175
2002 Q45-V8					
Veh. Ident.: JNKBF01A()2M000001 Up.					
Sedan 4D	BF01	3801	23750	27450	29175
Sedan 4D Premium	BF01		26300	30175	32000
Add Sport Pkg. (Std. Premium)			675	750	750
Add Navigation System			550	625	625
Add Theft Recovery System			75	100	100
Deduct W/out Power Sunroof			625	625	625
INFINITI					
2001 G20-4 Cyl.					
Veh. Ident.: JNKCP11()()1T000001 Up.					
Sedan 4D	CP11	2923	10475	12700	13775
2001 I30-V6					
Veh. Ident.: JNKCA31()()1T000001 Up.					
Sedan 4D	CA31	3342	13200	15650	16850
G20/I30 OPTIONS					
Add Touring Pkg.			450	500	500
Add Leather Seats (Std. I30)			375	425	425
Add Navigation System			400	450	450
Add Power Sunroof			475	550	550
Add Theft Recovery System			50	75	75
Deduct W/out Automatic Trans.			475	475	475
Deduct W/out Power Seat			150	150	150
2001 Q45-V8					
Veh. Ident.: JNKBY31()()1M000001 Up.					
Sedan 4D	BY31	4007	18175	21375	22900
Add Touring Pkg.			450	500	500
Add Navigation System			500	575	575
Add Theft Recovery System			50	75	75
INFINITI					
2000 G20-4 Cyl.					
Veh. Ident.: JNKCP11()()YT300001 Up.					
Sedan 4D	CP11	2923	8350	10400	11425
2000 I30-V6					
Veh. Ident.: JNKCA31()()YT000001 Up.					
Sedan 4D	CA31	3342	11400	13700	14800
G20/I30 OPTIONS					
Add Touring Pkg.			350	400	400
Add Leather Seats (Std. I30)			325	375	375
Add Navigation System			300	350	350
Add Power Sunroof			425	475	475
Deduct W/out Automatic Trans.			425	425	425
Deduct W/out Power Seat			125	125	125
2000 Q45-V8					
Veh. Ident.: JNKBY31()()YM000001 Up.					
Sedan 4D	BY31	4007	14750	17550	18925

BODY TYPE	Model No.	Weight	Trade-In	Retail	High Retail
Add Touring Pkg.			350	400	400
Add Navigation System			450	500	500
INFINITI					
1999 G20-4 Cyl.					
Veh. Ident.: JNKCP11()()X()000001 Up.					
Sedan 4D	CP11	2913	6825	8750	9800
1999 I30-V6					
Veh. Ident.: JNKCA21()()X()000001 Up.					
Sedan 4D	CA21	3165	7625	9625	10675
G20/I30 OPTIONS					
Add Touring Pkg.			250	300	300
Add Leather Seats			275	325	325
Add Power Sunroof			375	425	425
Deduct W/out Automatic Trans.			375	375	375
Deduct W/out Power Seat			100	100	100
1999 Q45-V8					
Veh. Ident.: JNKBY31()()X()000001 Up.					
Sedan 4D	BY31	4007	11650	14175	15425
Add Touring Pkg.			250	300	300
INFINITI					
1998 I30-V6					
Veh. Ident.: JNKCA21()()W()000001 Up.					
Sedan 4D	CA21	3150	6450	8350	9375
Add Touring Pkg.			200	225	225
Add Leather Seats			225	250	250
Add Power Sunroof			325	375	375
Deduct W/out Automatic Trans.			325	325	325
1998 Q45-V8					
Veh. Ident.: JNKBY31A()WM400001 Up.					
Sedan 4D	BY31	3879	8950	11150	12275
Add Touring Pkg.			200	225	225
INFINITI					
1997 I30-V6					
Veh. Ident.: JNKCA21D()V()000001 Up.					
Sedan 4D	CA21	3090	4725	6425	7425
Add Touring Pkg.			150	175	175
Add Leather Seats			200	225	225
Add Power Sunroof			250	300	300
Deduct W/out Automatic Trans.			250	250	250
1997 J30-V6					
Veh. Ident.: JNKAY21D()V()000001 Up.					
Sedan 4D	AY21	3525	4825	6525	7650
1997 Q45-V8					
Veh. Ident.: JNKBY31D()V()000001 Up.					
Sedan 4D	BY31	3880	7525	9600	10775
J30/Q45 OPTIONS					
Add Touring Pkg.			150	175	175

PASSENGER CARS

BODY TYPE	Model No.	Weight	Trade-In	Retail	High Retail
INFINITI					
1996 G20-4 Cyl.					
Veh. Ident.: JNKCP01D()T()000201 Up.					
Sedan 4D	CP01	2780	**2700**	**4075**	**4925**
1996 I30-V6					
Veh. Ident.: JNKCA21D()T()000001 Up.					
Sedan 4D	CA21	2974	**4025**	**5650**	**6600**
G20/I30 OPTIONS					
Add Power Sunroof			**200**	**225**	**225**
Deduct W/out Automatic Trans.			**150**	**150**	**150**
1996 J30-V6					
Veh. Ident.: JNKAY21D()T()000001 Up.					
Sedan 4D	AY21	3408	**4100**	**5725**	**6800**
1996 Q45-V8					
Veh. Ident.: JNKNG01D()T()000001 Up.					
Sedan 4D	NG01	3882	**4825**	**6600**	**7750**
INFINITI					
1995 G20-4 Cyl.					
Veh. Ident.: JNKCP01D()S()200016 Up.					
Sedan 4D	CP01	2926	**2300**	**3625**	**4475**
1995 J30-V6					
Veh. Ident.: JNKAY21D()S()000001 Up.					
Sedan 4D	AY21	3527	**3475**	**5000**	**6050**
1995 Q45-V8					
Veh. Ident.: JNKNG01D()S()000001 Up.					
Sedan 4D	NG01	4039	**4100**	**5775**	**6850**
Sedan 4D Active	NG01	4259	**4375**	**6100**	**7175**

JAGUAR

BODY TYPE	Model No.	Weight	Trade-In	Retail	High Retail
JAGUAR					
2004 X-TYPE-V6-AWD					
Veh. Ident.: SAJ(Model)()4()()00001 Up.					
Sedan 4D 2.5	E()51D	3461	**20200**	**23225**	**24800**
Sedan 4D 3.0	E()51C	3640	**22850**	**26200**	**27875**
Sedan 4D 3.0 Sport	E()51C	3549	**24225**	**27650**	**29375**
2004 S-TYPE-V6/V8					
Veh. Ident.: SAJ(Model)()4()()00001 Up.					
Sedan 4D 3.0	E()01T	3777	**28575**	**32700**	**34600**
Sedan 4D 3.0 Sport	E()01T	3777	**29900**	**34100**	**36025**
Sedan 4D 4.2	EA01U	3874	**31475**	**35775**	**37750**
Sedan 4D 4.2 Sport	EA01U	3874	**32800**	**37300**	**39325**
Sedan 4D 4.2 R	EA03V	4046	**40700**	**45625**	**47900**
2004 XJ8-V8					
Veh. Ident.: SAJ(Model)()4()G00001 Up.					
Sedan 4D	()A71C	3766	**38600**	**43425**	**45650**
Sedan 4D Vanden Plas	()A74C	3803	**46750**	**52025**	**54500**
Sedan XJR Supercharged	()A73B	3948	**52650**	**58250**	**60900**
2004 XK8-V8					
Veh. Ident.: SAJ(Model)()4()()00001 Up.					
Coupe 2D	DA41C	3779			
Coupe XKR Supercharged	DA41B	3865			

BODY TYPE	Model No.	Weight	Trade-In	Retail	High Retail
Convertible 2D	DA42C	3980	**49125**	**55000**	**57550**
Conv XKR Supercharged	DA42B	4042	**57475**	**63800**	**66625**
JAGUAR OPTIONS					
Add Handling Pkg. (Coupe XKR)					
Add Alpine Premium Stereo System			**425**	**475**	**475**
(Std. X-Type Sport, R, Vanden Plas, XJR, XK)					
Add Navigation System (Std. XKR)			**750**	**850**	**850**
Add Power Sunroof (Std. X-Type 3.0, S-Type V8, XJ)			**725**	**825**	**825**
Add Rear Entertainment System			**600**	**675**	**675**
Add Theft Recovery System			**100**	**125**	**125**
Deduct W/out Automatic Trans.			**675**	**675**	**675**
JAGUAR					
2003 X-TYPE-V6-AWD					
Veh. Ident.: SAJ(Model)()3()()00001 Up.					
Sedan 4D 2.5	E()51D	3428	**17225**	**20350**	**21825**
Sedan 4D 2.5 Sport	E()53D	3428	**18050**	**21225**	**22725**
Sedan 4D 3.0	E()51C	3516	**19075**	**22325**	**23875**
Sedan 4D 3.0 Sport	E()53C	3516	**19900**	**23200**	**24775**
2003 S-TYPE-V6/V8					
Veh. Ident.: SAJ(Model)()3()()00001 Up.					
Sedan 4D 3.0	E()01T	3695	**23650**	**27350**	**29075**
Sedan 4D 3.0 Sport	E()03T	3695	**24775**	**28550**	**30300**
Sedan 4D 4.2	EA01U	3874	**26250**	**30125**	**31950**
Sedan 4D 4.2 Sport	EA03U	3874	**27375**	**31425**	**33275**
Sedan 4D 4.2 R	EA03V	4046	**34100**	**38675**	**40750**
2003 XJ8-V8					
Veh. Ident.: SAJ(Model)()3()()00001 Up.					
Sedan 4D	DA14C	3995	**29600**	**33800**	**35725**
Sedan 4D Sport	DA12C	3995	**30725**	**35000**	**36950**
Sedan 4D Vanden Plas	DA24C	4006	**35725**	**40400**	**42525**
Sedan XJR Supercharged	DA15B	4063	**38600**	**43425**	**45650**
Sedan 4D Super V8	DA25B	4129	**44350**	**49500**	**51900**
2003 XK8-V8					
Veh. Ident.: SAJ(Model)()3()()00001 Up.					
Coupe 2D	DA41C	3779	**40775**	**46200**	**48500**
Coupe XKR Supercharged	DA41B	3865	**48500**	**54350**	**56900**
Convertible 2D	DA42C	3980	**43025**	**48575**	**50950**
Conv XKR Supercharged	DA42B	4042	**50850**	**56825**	**59450**
JAGUAR OPTIONS					
Add Handling Pkg. (Coupe XKR)			**1125**	**1250**	**1250**
Add Alpine Stereo System			**375**	**425**	**425**
(Std. R, Vanden Plas, XJR, Super V8, XK8)					
Add Compact Disc Player (X-Type 2.5)			**150**	**175**	**175**
Add Navigation System (Std. XJR, XKR, Super V8)			**650**	**725**	**725**
Add Power Sunroof (Std. S-Type V8, XJ)			**675**	**775**	**775**
Add Theft Recovery System			**75**	**100**	**100**
Deduct W/out Automatic Trans.			**625**	**625**	**625**
JAGUAR					
2002 X-TYPE-V6-AWD					
Veh. Ident.: SAJ(Model)()2()()00001 Up.					
Sedan 4D 2.5	E()51D	3428	**15425**	**18275**	**19675**
Sedan 4D 2.5 Sport	E()53D	3428	**16125**	**19025**	**20450**
Sedan 4D 3.0	E()51C	3516	**16875**	**19825**	**21275**
Sedan 4D 3.0 Sport	E()53C	3516	**17575**	**20725**	**22225**

PASSENGER CARS

BODY TYPE	Model No.	Weight	Trade-In	Retail	High Retail
2002 S-TYPE-V6/V8					
Veh. Ident.: SAJ(Model)()2()()00001 Up.					
Sedan 4D 3.0	DA01N	3816	**19400**	**22675**	**24225**
Sedan 4D 3.0 Sport	DA03N	3816	**21000**	**24375**	**26000**
Sedan 4D 4.0	DA01P	3903	**21350**	**24750**	**26375**
Sedan 4D 4.0 Sport	DA03P	3903	**22350**	**25975**	**27650**
2002 XJ8-V8					
Veh. Ident.: SAJ(Model)()2()()00001 Up.					
Sedan 4D	DA14C	3995	**24275**	**28025**	**29775**
Sedan 4D Sport	DA12C	3995	**25275**	**29100**	**30875**
Sedan 4D Vanden Plas	DA24C	4006	**28850**	**33000**	**34900**
Sedan XJR Supercharged	DA15B	4063	**31825**	**36175**	**38175**
Sedan 4D Super V8	DA25B	4129	**36075**	**40775**	**42900**
2002 XK8-V8					
Veh. Ident.: SAJ(Model)()2()()00001 Up.					
Coupe 2D	DA41C	3759	**34125**	**39175**	**41275**
Coupe XKR Supercharged	DA41B	3827	**40475**	**45875**	**48175**
Convertible 2D	DA42C	3990	**36275**	**41450**	**43600**
Conv XKR Supercharged	DA42B	4039	**42725**	**48250**	**50600**
JAGUAR OPTIONS					
Add Alpine/Audiophile Stereo (X-Type, 3.0, XJ8 Base/Sport)			**325**	**375**	**375**
Add Compact Disc Player (Std. 4.0, XJ, XK)			**125**	**150**	**150**
Add Navigation System (Std. XJR, XKR, Super V8)			**550**	**625**	**625**
Add Power Sunroof (Std. S-Type Sport, 4.0, XJ)			**625**	**700**	**700**
Add Theft Recovery System			**75**	**100**	**100**
Deduct W/out Automatic Trans.			**575**	**575**	**575**
JAGUAR					
2001 S-TYPE-V6/V8					
Veh. Ident.: SAJ(Model)()1()()00001 Up.					
Sedan 4D 3.0	DA01()	3816	**16925**	**19925**	**21375**
Sedan 4D 4.0	DA01()	3903	**18675**	**21900**	**23450**
2001 XJ8-V8					
Veh. Ident.: SAJ(Model)()1()()00001 Up.					
Sedan 4D	DA14C	3946	**19300**	**22550**	**24100**
Sedan 4D L	DA23C	3988	**19900**	**23200**	**24775**
Sedan 4D Vanden Plas	DA24C	4010	**22600**	**26225**	**27900**
Sedan XJR Supercharged	DA15B	4050	**24800**	**28575**	**30350**
Sed Van Plas Supercharged	DA25B	4079	**28325**	**32450**	**34325**
2001 XK8-V8					
Veh. Ident.: SAJ(Model)()1()()00001 Up.					
Coupe 2D	DA41C	3726	**28200**	**32725**	**34625**
Coupe XKR Supercharged	DA41B	3785	**34175**	**39225**	**41325**
Convertible 2D	DA42C	3962	**30250**	**34900**	**36850**
Conv XKR Supercharged	DA42B	4021	**36325**	**41500**	**43650**
JAGUAR OPTIONS					
Add Alpine/Audiophile Stereo (3.0, XJ8 Base/L)			**275**	**325**	**325**
Add Compact Disc Player (S-Type 3.0)			**125**	**150**	**150**
Add Navigation System (Std. Van Plas SC, XKR)			**500**	**575**	**575**
Add Power Sunroof (S-Type 3.0)			**575**	**650**	**650**
Add Theft Recovery System			**50**	**75**	**75**

BODY TYPE	Model No.	Weight	Trade-In	Retail	High Retail
JAGUAR					
2000 S-TYPE-V6/V8					
Veh. Ident.: SAJ(Model)()Y()000001 Up.					
Sedan 4D 3.0	DA01C	3650	**13725**	**16450**	**17800**
Sedan 4D 4.0	DA01D	3770	**14925**	**17725**	**19100**
2000 XJ8-V8					
Veh. Ident.: SAJ(Model)()Y()000001 Up.					
Sedan 4D	DA14C	3938	**15750**	**18625**	**20025**
Sedan 4D L	DA23C	3967	**16250**	**19175**	**20600**
Sedan 4D Vanden Plas	DA24C	3993	**17875**	**21050**	**22550**
Sedan XJR Supercharged	DA15B	4026	**20750**	**24100**	**25700**
Sed Van Plas Supercharged	DA25B		**22875**	**26525**	**28225**
2000 XK8-V8					
Veh. Ident.: SAJ(Model)()Y()000001 Up.					
Coupe 2D	JA41C	3709	**23875**	**27975**	**29725**
Coupe XKR Supercharged	JA41B	3785	**29350**	**33925**	**35850**
Convertible 2D	JA42C	3943	**25825**	**30050**	**31875**
Conv XKR Supercharged	JA42B	4021	**31400**	**36100**	**38100**
JAGUAR OPTIONS					
Add Alpine/Audiophile Stereo (Std. Van Plas SC/XJR, XKR)			**225**	**250**	**250**
Add Compact Disc Player (Std. Van Plas SC/XJR, XKR)			**100**	**125**	**125**
Add Navigation System			**450**	**500**	**500**
Add Power Sunroof (S-Type 3.0)			**525**	**600**	**600**
JAGUAR					
1999 XJ8-V8					
Veh. Ident.: SAJ(Model)()4()XC000001 Up.					
Sedan 4D	HX1	3996	**13650**	**16375**	**17725**
Sedan 4D L	HX6	4044	**14050**	**16800**	**18175**
Sedan 4D Vanden Plas	KX6	4048	**15175**	**18000**	**19375**
Sedan 4D XJR Supercharged	PX1	4075	**18250**	**21450**	**22975**
1999 XK8-V8					
Veh. Ident: SAJ(Model)04()XC000001 Up.					
Coupe 2D	GX5	3709	**19400**	**23150**	**24725**
Convertible 2D	GX2	3943	**21350**	**25250**	**26900**
JAGUAR OPTIONS					
Add Harman Kardon Stereo (Std. XJR)			**175**	**200**	**200**
Add Traction Control (Std. XJR)			**275**	**325**	**325**
JAGUAR					
1998 XJ8-V8					
Veh. Ident.: SAJ(Model)()4()WC000001 Up.					
Sedan 4D	HX1	3996	**10850**	**13275**	**14475**
Sedan 4D L	HX6	4044	**11150**	**13625**	**14850**
Sedan 4D Vanden Plas	KX6	4048	**12100**	**14725**	**16000**
Sedan 4D XJR Supercharged	PX1	4075	**14850**	**17675**	**19050**
1998 XK8-V8					
Veh. Ident.: SAJ(Model)24()WC000001 Up.					
Coupe 2D	GX5	3673	**16050**	**19450**	**20900**
Convertible 2D	GX2	3867	**17900**	**21550**	**23075**
JAGUAR OPTIONS					
Add Harman Kardon Stereo (Std. XJR)			**150**	**175**	**175**
Add Traction Control (Std. XJR)			**200**	**225**	**225**

BODY TYPE	Model No.	Weight	Trade-In	Retail	High Retail
JAGUAR					
1997 XJ6-I6					
Veh. Ident.: SAJ(Model)()()()VC000001 Up.					
Sedan 4D	HX1	4080	**8425**	**10575**	**11775**
Sedan 4D L	HX6	4110	**8625**	**10800**	**12025**
Sedan 4D Vanden Plas	KX6	4130	**9325**	**11600**	**12750**
Sedan 4D XJR Supercharged	PX1	4125	**11800**	**14325**	**15575**
1997 XK8-V8					
Veh. Ident.: SAJ(Model)()()()VC000001 Up.					
Coupe 2D	GX5	3673	**13925**	**17150**	**18500**
Convertible 2D	GX2	3867	**15675**	**19050**	**20475**
JAGUAR OPTIONS					
Add Harman Kardon Stereo (Std. XJR)			**100**	**125**	**125**
JAGUAR					
1996 XJ6-I6/V12					
Veh. Ident.: SAJ(Model)()()()TC000001 Up.					
Sedan 4D	HX1	4080	**7200**	**9225**	**10375**
Sedan 4D Vanden Plas	KX6	4130	**8000**	**10125**	**11300**
Sedan 4D XJR Supercharged	PX1	4215	**10325**	**12675**	**13850**
Sedan 4D XJ12	MX6	4440	**8500**	**10650**	**11850**
1996 XJS-I6					
Veh. Ident.: SAJNX2()()()TC000001 Up.					
Convertible 2D	NX2	3980	**11750**	**14275**	**15525**
JAGUAR					
1995 XJ6-I6/V12					
Veh. Ident.: SAJ(Model)()()()SC000001 Up.					
Sedan 4D	HX1	4080	**6125**	**8075**	**9275**
Sedan 4D Vanden Plas	KX1	4105	**6825**	**8850**	**10100**
Sedan 4D XJR Supercharged	PX1	4215	**8925**	**11125**	**12250**
Sedan 4D XJ12	MX1	4420	**7225**	**9275**	**10425**
1995 XJS-I6/V12					
Veh. Ident.: SAJ(Model)()()()SC000001 Up.					
Coupe 2D XJS6	NX5	3805	**9325**	**11600**	**12750**
Coupe 2D XJS12	NX5	4053	**10825**	**13225**	**14425**
Convertible 2D XJS6	NX2	3980	**11025**	**13500**	**14725**
Convertible 2D XJS12	NX2	4306	**12325**	**14975**	**16250**

KIA

BODY TYPE	Model No.	Weight	Trade-In	Retail	High Retail
KIA					
2004 RIO-4 Cyl.					
Veh. Ident.: KNA(Model)()46500001 Up.					
Sedan 4D	DC125	2403	**6975**	**8600**	**9375**
Wagon 5D Cinco	DC165	2447	**7775**	**9500**	**10225**
2004 SPECTRA-4 Cyl.					
Veh. Ident.: KNA(Model)()45200001 Up.					
Sedan 4D	FB121	2661	**7075**	**8725**	**9500**
Sedan 4D LS	FB121	2672	**7475**	**9175**	**9875**
Hatchback 4D GS	FB161	2686	**7250**	**8925**	**9700**
Hatchback 4D GSX	FB161	2697	**8000**	**9750**	**10475**

BODY TYPE	Model No.	Weight	Trade-In	Retail	High Retail
2004 NEW SPECTRA-4 Cyl.					
Veh. Ident.: KNA(Model)()45200001 Up.					
Sedan 4D LX	FE12()	2701	8075	9850	10575
Sedan 4D EX	FE12()	2826	8550	10375	11100
2004 OPTIMA-4 Cyl.					
Veh. Ident.: KNA(Model)()45000001 Up.					
Sedan 4D LX	GD126	3281	8900	10775	11525
Sedan 4D EX	GD126		10125	12125	12850
Sedan 4D LX (V6)	GD128	3279	9950	11925	12675
Sedan 4D EX (V6)	GD128		11225	13325	14075
RIO/SPECTRA/NEW SPECTRA/OPTIMA OPTIONS					
Add Aluminum/Alloy Wheels (Std. Rio Cinco, Spectra GSX, Optima EX/V6)			300	350	350
Add Compact Disc Player (Rio Sedan)			100	125	125
Add Cruise Control (Std. Optima)			175	200	200
Add Infinity Stereo System (Std. Optima EX)			250	300	300
Add Leather Seats			350	400	400
Add Power Door Locks (Rio)			150	175	175
Add Power Sunroof (Std. Optima EX)			525	600	600
Add Power Windows (Rio)			175	200	200
Add Theft Recovery System			100	125	125
Deduct W/out Air Conditioning			575	575	575
Deduct W/out Automatic Trans.			475	475	475
Deduct W/out Power Steering			125	125	125
2004 AMANTI-V6					
Veh. Ident.: KNALD124()45000001 Up.					
Sedan 4D	LD124	4021	14475	16950	18000
Add Infinity Stereo System			300	350	350
Add Leather Seats			450	500	500
Add Power Sunroof			575	650	650
Add Theft Recovery System			100	125	125
KIA					
2003 RIO-4 Cyl.					
Veh. Ident.: KNA(Model)()36000001 Up.					
Sedan 4D	DC125	2403	4975	6425	7225
Wagon 5D Cinco	DC165	2447	5425	6925	7775
2003 SPECTRA-4 Cyl.					
Veh. Ident.: KNA(Model)()35000001 Up.					
Sedan 4D	FB121	2661	4950	6375	7175
Sedan 4D LS	FB121	2672	5275	6775	7600
Hatchback 4D GS	FB161	2686	5100	6575	7400
Hatchback 4D GSX	FB161	2697	5725	7250	8025
2003 OPTIMA-4 Cyl.					
Veh. Ident.: KNA(Model)()35000001 Up.					
Sedan 4D LX	GD126	3281	7550	9250	9950
Sedan 4D SE	GD126	3301	8675	10525	11250
Sedan 4D LX (V6)	GD128	3279	8225	10025	10750
Sedan 4D SE (V6)	GD128	3279	9350	11275	12000
KIA OPTIONS					
Add A/A Wheels (Std. Spectra GSX, Optima SE)			250	300	300
Add Compact Disc Player (Rio Sedan)			75	100	100
Add Cruise Control (Std. Optima)			150	175	175
Add Infinity Stereo System (Std. Optima SE)			200	225	225
Add Leather Seats			300	350	350

PASSENGER CARS

BODY TYPE	Model No.	Weight	Trade-In	Retail	High Retail
Add Power Door Locks (Rio)			**125**	**150**	**150**
Add Power Windows (Rio)			**150**	**175**	**175**
Add Theft Recovery System			**75**	**100**	**100**
Deduct W/out Air Conditioning			**525**	**525**	**525**
Deduct W/out Automatic Trans.			**425**	**425**	**425**
Deduct W/out Power Steering			**100**	**100**	**100**
KIA					
2002 RIO-4 Cyl.					
Veh. Ident.: KNA(Model)()26000001 Up.					
Sedan 4D	DC123	2242	**3550**	**4825**	**5625**
Wagon 5D Cinco	DC163	2436	**3950**	**5275**	**6000**
2002 SPECTRA-4 Cyl.					
Veh. Ident.: KNA(Model)()25000001 Up.					
Sedan 4D	FB121	2661	**3725**	**5025**	**5750**
Sedan 4D LS	FB121	2672	**4000**	**5325**	**6075**
Hatchback 4D GS	FB161	2686	**3875**	**5175**	**5900**
Hatchback 4D GSX	FB161	2697	**4375**	**5750**	**6525**
2002 OPTIMA-4 Cyl.					
Veh. Ident.: KNA(Model)()25000001 Up.					
Sedan 4D LX	GD126	3157	**5825**	**7350**	**8150**
Sedan 4D SE	GD126	3157	**6900**	**8525**	**9300**
Sedan 4D LX (V6)	GD128	3223	**6550**	**8125**	**8875**
Sedan 4D SE (V6)	GD128	3223	**7500**	**9200**	**9900**
KIA OPTIONS					
Add A/A Wheels (Std. Spectra GSX, Optima SE)			**200**	**225**	**225**
Add Compact Disc Player (Std. SE)			**75**	**100**	**100**
Add Cruise Control (Std. SE, V6)			**125**	**150**	**150**
Add Leather Seats			**250**	**300**	**300**
Add Power Door Locks (Rio)			**100**	**125**	**125**
Add Theft Recovery System			**75**	**100**	**100**
Deduct W/out Air Conditioning			**475**	**475**	**475**
Deduct W/out Automatic Trans.			**375**	**375**	**375**
Deduct W/out Power Steering			**75**	**75**	**75**
KIA					
2001 RIO-4 Cyl.					
Veh. Ident.: KNADC12()()16500001 Up.					
Sedan 4D	DC12()	2242	**2500**	**3675**	**4350**
2001 SEPHIA-4 Cyl.					
Veh. Ident.: KNAFB121()15900001 Up.					
Sedan 4D	FB121	2478	**2650**	**3850**	**4550**
Sedan 4D LS	FB121	2551	**2925**	**4150**	**4875**
2001 SPECTRA-4 Cyl.					
Veh. Ident.: KNAFB161()15200001 Up.					
Hatchback 4D GS	FB161	2560	**2675**	**3875**	**4575**
Hatchback 4D GSX	FB161	2575	**3075**	**4300**	**5025**
2001 OPTIMA-4 Cyl.					
Veh. Ident.: KNA(Model)()15000001 Up.					
Sedan 4D LX	GD126	3157	**4350**	**5725**	**6500**
Sedan 4D SE	GD126	3157	**5225**	**6700**	**7525**
Sedan 4D LX (V6)	GD124	3190	**4975**	**6425**	**7225**
Sedan 4D SE (V6)	GD124	3190	**5750**	**7275**	**8050**
KIA OPTIONS					
Add A/A Wheels (Std. Spectra GSX, Optima SE)			**150**	**175**	**175**
Add Compact Disc Player (Std. SE)			**50**	**75**	**75**

BODY TYPE	Model No.	Weight	Trade-In	Retail	High Retail
Add Cruise Control (Std. SE, V6)			100	125	125
Add Leather Seats			200	225	225
Add Power Door Locks (Sephia)			75	100	100
Add Power Windows (Sephia)			100	125	125
Add Theft Recovery System			50	75	75
Deduct W/out Air Conditioning			425	425	425
Deduct W/out Automatic Trans.			325	325	325
Deduct W/out Power Steering			75	75	75
KIA					
2000 SEPHIA-4 Cyl.					
Veh. Ident.: KNAFB121()Y5000001 Up.					
Sedan 4D	FB121	2478	1950	3050	3650
Sedan 4D LS	FB121	2478	2200	3350	4000
2000 SPECTRA-4 Cyl.					
Veh. Ident.: KNAFB161()Y5000001 Up.					
Hatchback 4D GS	FB161	2560	1950	3050	3650
Hatchback 4D GSX	FB161	2575	2225	3350	4000
KIA OPTIONS					
Add Aluminum/Alloy Wheels (Std. Spectra GSX)			100	125	125
Add Compact Disc Player			50	75	75
Add Cruise Control			75	100	100
Add Power Door Locks (Sephia)			50	75	75
Add Power Windows (Sephia)			75	100	100
Deduct W/out Air Conditioning			375	375	375
Deduct W/out Automatic Trans.			300	300	300
KIA					
1999 SEPHIA-4 Cyl.					
Veh. Ident.: KNAFB121()X5700001 Up.					
Sedan 4D RS	FB121	2478	1650	2700	3300
Sedan 4D LS	FB121	2551	1775	2850	3475
Add Aluminum/Alloy Wheels			50	75	75
Add Cruise Control			50	75	75
Add Power Windows			50	75	75
Deduct W/out Air Conditioning			325	325	325
Deduct W/out Automatic Trans.			250	250	250
KIA					
1998 SEPHIA-4 Cyl.					
Veh. Ident.: KNAFB121()W5200001 Up.					
Sedan 4D RS	FB121	2534	1275	2275	2825
Sedan 4D LS	FB121	2606	1375	2400	2950
Add Cruise Control			50	75	75
Add Power Windows			50	75	75
Deduct W/out Air Conditioning			275	275	275
Deduct W/out Automatic Trans.			200	200	200
KIA					
1997 SEPHIA-4 Cyl.					
Veh. Ident.: KNAFA125()V5200001 Up.					
Sedan 4D RS	FA125	2476	875	1800	2250
Sedan 4D LS	FA125	2520	900	1850	2325
Sedan 4D GS	FA125	2542	1050	2025	2525
Deduct W/out Air Conditioning			150	150	150
Deduct W/out Automatic Trans.			125	125	125

BODY TYPE	Model No.	Weight	Trade-In	Retail	High Retail
KIA					
1996 SEPHIA-4 Cyl.					
Veh Ident.: KNAFA125()T5000001 Up.					
Sedan 4D RS	FA125		**700**	**1600**	**2025**
Sedan 4D LS	FA125		**725**	**1625**	**2050**
Sedan 4D GS	FA125		**850**	**1775**	**2225**
Deduct W/out Air Conditioning			**100**	**100**	**100**
Deduct W/out Automatic Trans.			**100**	**100**	**100**
KIA					
1995 SEPHIA-4 Cyl.					
Veh. Ident.: FNAFA121()S5000001 Up.					
Sedan 4D RS	FA121	2407	**550**	**1425**	**1825**
Sedan 4D LS	FA121	2452	**575**	**1450**	**1850**
Sedan 4D GS	FA121	2474	**675**	**1575**	**2000**

LEXUS

BODY TYPE	Model No.	Weight	Trade-In	Retail	High Retail
LEXUS					
2004 ES-V6					
Veh. Ident.: JTHBA30G()4()000001 Up.					
Sedan 4D ES330	BA30G	3460	**26275**	**29825**	**31350**
2004 IS-I6					
Veh. Ident.: JTH(Model)()4()000001 Up.					
Sedan 4D IS300	BD192	3255	**24675**	**28450**	**30200**
Sport Wagon 5D IS300	ED192	3410	**24525**	**28275**	**30025**
2004 GS-I6/V8					
Veh. Ident.: JT8(Model)()4()000001 Up.					
Sedan 4D GS300	BD69S	3649	**30150**	**34400**	**36350**
Sedan 4D GS430	BL69S	3715	**37375**	**42150**	**44325**
2004 SC-V8					
Veh. Ident.: JTHFN48Y()4()000001 Up.					
Convertible 2D SC430	FN48Y	3840	**49875**	**55800**	**58375**
2004 LS-V8					
Veh. Ident.: JTHBN36F()4()000001 Up.					
Sedan 4D LS430	BN36F	3990	**46850**	**52600**	**55100**
LEXUS OPTIONS					
Add Levinson Stereo (Std. SC)			**425**	**475**	**475**
Add Navigation System (Std. SC)			**750**	**850**	**850**
Add Power Sunroof (Std. ES, GS, LS)			**725**	**825**	**825**
Add Theft Recovery System			**100**	**125**	**125**
Deduct W/out Automatic Trans.			**675**	**675**	**675**
Deduct W/out Leather Seats			**575**	**575**	**575**
Deduct W/out Power Seat			**275**	**275**	**275**
LEXUS					
2003 ES-V6					
Veh. Ident.: JT()BF30G()3()000001 Up.					
Sedan 4D ES300	BF30G	3439	**23500**	**26900**	**28375**
2003 IS-I6					
Veh. Ident.: JTH(Model)()3()000001 Up.					
Sedan 4D IS300	BD192	3255	**21950**	**25400**	**27050**
Sport Wagon 5D IS300	ED192	3410	**21800**	**25250**	**26900**

PASSENGER CARS

BODY TYPE	Model No.	Weight	Trade-In	Retail	High Retail
2003 GS-I6/V8					
Veh. Ident.: JT8(Model)()3()000001 Up.					
Sedan 4D GS300	BD69S	3649	**26475**	**30375**	**32200**
Sedan 4D GS430	BL69S	3715	**32200**	**36675**	**38700**
2003 SC-V8					
Veh. Ident.: JTHFN48Y()3()000001 Up.					
Convertible 2D SC430	FN48Y	3840	**43725**	**49325**	**51725**
2003 LS-V8					
Veh. Ident.: JTHBN30F()3()000001 Up.					
Sedan 4D LS430	BN30F	3945	**39100**	**44425**	**46675**
LEXUS OPTIONS					
Add Levinson Stereo (Std. SC)			**375**	**425**	**425**
Add Navigation System (Std. SC)			**650**	**725**	**725**
Add Power Sunroof (Std. ES, GS)			**675**	**775**	**775**
Add Theft Recovery System			**75**	**100**	**100**
Deduct W/out Automatic Trans.			**625**	**625**	**625**
Deduct W/out Leather Seats			**525**	**525**	**525**
Deduct W/out Power Seat			**250**	**250**	**250**
LEXUS					
2002 ES-V6					
Veh. Ident.: JTHBF30G()2()000001 Up.					
Sedan 4D ES300	BF30G	3439	**20700**	**23775**	**25150**
2002 IS-I6					
Veh. Ident.: JTH(Model)()2()000001 Up.					
Sedan 4D IS300	BD192	3255	**19250**	**22500**	**24050**
Sport Wagon 5D IS300	ED192	3410	**19100**	**22350**	**23900**
2002 GS-I6/V8					
Veh. Ident.: JT8(Model)()2()000001 Up.					
Sedan 4D GS300	BD69S	3638	**22300**	**25925**	**27600**
Sedan 4D GS430	BL69S	3707	**26525**	**30400**	**32225**
2002 SC-V8					
Veh. Ident.: JTHFN48Y()2()000001 Up.					
Convertible 2D SC430	FN48Y	3840	**37500**	**42750**	**44950**
2002 LS-V8					
Veh. Ident.: JTHBN30F()2()000001 Up.					
Sedan 4D LS430	BN30F	3955	**31475**	**36200**	**38200**
LEXUS OPTIONS					
Add Compact Disc Player (GS)			**125**	**150**	**150**
Add Levinson Stereo (Std. SC)			**325**	**375**	**375**
Add Navigation System (Std. SC)			**550**	**625**	**625**
Add Power Sunroof (Std. ES)			**625**	**700**	**700**
Add Theft Recovery System			**75**	**100**	**100**
Deduct W/out Automatic Trans.			**575**	**575**	**575**
Deduct W/out Leather Seats			**475**	**475**	**475**
Deduct W/out Power Seat			**225**	**225**	**225**
LEXUS					
2001 ES-V6					
Veh. Ident.: JT8BF28G()1()000001 Up.					
Sedan 4D ES300	BF28G	3373	**16075**	**18700**	**19975**
2001 IS-I6					
Veh. Ident.: JTHBD182()1()000001 Up.					
Sedan 4D IS300	BD182	3270	**16950**	**19950**	**21400**

P A S S E N G E R C A R S

BODY TYPE	Model No.	Weight	Trade-In	Retail	High Retail
2001 GS-I6/V8					
Veh. Ident.: JT8(Model)()1()000001 Up.					
Sedan 4D GS300	BD69S	3638	**19475**	**22750**	**24300**
Sedan 4D GS430	BL69S	3707	**22200**	**25800**	**27475**
2001 LS-V8					
Veh. Ident.: JTHBN30F()1()000001 Up.					
Sedan 4D LS430	BN30F	3955	**27775**	**32250**	**34125**
LEXUS OPTIONS					
Add Compact Disc Player (Std. IS, LS)			**125**	**150**	**150**
Add Levinson/Nakamichi Stereo			**275**	**325**	**325**
Add Navigation System			**500**	**575**	**575**
Add Power Sunroof			**575**	**650**	**650**
Add Theft Recovery System			**50**	**75**	**75**
Deduct W/out Leather Seats			**425**	**425**	**425**
Deduct W/out Power Seat			**200**	**200**	**200**
LEXUS					
2000 ES-V6					
Veh. Ident.: JT8BF28G()Y()000001 Up.					
Sedan 4D ES300	BF28G	3373	**13725**	**16200**	**17400**
2000 GS-I6/V8					
Veh. Ident.: JT8(Model)()Y()000001 Up.					
Sedan 4D GS300	BD68S	3638	**16975**	**19975**	**21425**
Sedan 4D GS400	BH68X	3693	**18550**	**21750**	**23275**
2000 SC-I6/V8					
Veh. Ident.: JT8(Model)()Y()000001 Up.					
Coupe 2D SC300	CD32Z	3560	**17325**	**20450**	**21925**
Coupe 2D SC400	CH32Y	3655	**19750**	**23025**	**24600**
2000 LS-V8					
Veh. Ident.: JT8BH28F()Y()000001 Up.					
Sedan 4D LS400	BH28F	3890	**19800**	**23575**	**25150**
LEXUS OPTIONS					
Add Compact Disc Player (Std. SC)			**100**	**125**	**125**
Add Nakamichi Stereo			**225**	**250**	**250**
Add Navigation System			**450**	**500**	**500**
Add Power Sunroof			**525**	**600**	**600**
Add Traction Control (SC)			**350**	**400**	**400**
Deduct W/out Leather Seats			**375**	**375**	**375**
LEXUS					
1999 ES-V6					
Veh. Ident.: JT8BF28G()X()000001 Up.					
Sedan 4D ES300	BF28G	3351	**11200**	**13475**	**14575**
1999 GS-I6/V8					
Veh. Ident.: JT8(Model)()X()000001 Up.					
Sedan 4D GS300	BD68S	3638	**14500**	**17300**	**18100**
Sedan 4D GS400	BH68X	3693	**15875**	**18775**	**19625**
1999 SC-I6/V8					
Veh. Ident.: JT8(Model)()X()000001 Up.					
Coupe 2D SC300	CD32Z	3560	**14400**	**17175**	**18525**
Coupe 2D SC400	CH32Y	3655	**16400**	**19325**	**20750**
1999 LS-V8					
Veh. Ident.: JT8BH28F()X()000001 Up.					
Sedan 4D LS400	BH28F	3890	**17025**	**20550**	**22025**

BODY TYPE	Model No.	Weight	Trade-In	Retail	High Retail
LEXUS OPTIONS					
Add Nakamichi Stereo			175	200	200
Add Power Sunroof			475	550	550
Add Traction Control (SC)			275	325	325
Deduct W/out Leather Seats			325	325	325
LEXUS					
1998 ES-V6					
Veh. Ident.: JT8BF28G()W()000001 Up.					
Sedan 4D ES300	BF28G	3318	9150	11275	12300
1998 GS-I6/V8					
Veh. Ident.: JT8(Model)()W()000001 Up.					
Sedan 4D GS300	BD68S	3635	12050	14675	15950
Sedan 4D GS400	BH68X	3690	13225	15950	17275
1998 SC-I6/V8					
Veh. Ident.: JT8(Model)()W()000001 Up.					
Coupe 2D SC300	CD32Z	3560	11950	14500	15775
Coupe 2D SC400	CH32Y	3655	13425	16150	17500
1998 LS-V8					
Veh. Ident.: JT8BH28F()W()000001 Up.					
Sedan 4D LS400	BH28F	3890	14475	17750	19125
LEXUS OPTIONS					
Add Nakamichi Stereo			150	175	175
Add Power Sunroof			425	475	475
Add Traction Control (SC)			200	225	225
Deduct W/out Automatic Trans.			375	375	375
Deduct W/out Leather Seats			275	275	275
LEXUS					
1997 ES-V6					
Veh. Ident.: JT8BF22G()V()000001 Up.					
Sedan 4D ES300	BF22G	3296	7400	9375	10400
1997 GS-I6					
Veh. Ident.: JT8BD42S()V()000001 Up.					
Sedan 4D GS300	BD42S	3660	10025	12350	13525
1997 SC-I6/V8					
Veh. Ident.: JT8(Model)()V()000001 Up.					
Coupe 2D SC300	CD32Z	3516	10175	12525	13700
Coupe 2D SC400	CH32Y	3605	11200	13700	14925
1997 LS-V8					
Veh. Ident.: JT8BH28F()V()000001 Up.					
Sedan 4D LS400	BH28F	3726	11825	14700	15975
LEXUS OPTIONS					
Add Nakamichi Stereo			100	125	125
Add Power Sunroof			350	400	400
Deduct W/out Automatic Trans.			300	300	300
Deduct W/out Leather Seats			250	250	250
LEXUS					
1996 ES-V6					
Veh. Ident.: JT8BF12G()T()000001 Up.					
Sedan 4D ES300	BF12G	3374	6025	7875	8950
1996 GS-I6					
Veh. Ident.: JT8BD42S()T()000001 Up.					
Sedan 4D GS300	BD42S	3660	8525	10675	11875

PASSENGER CARS

BODY TYPE	Model No.	Weight	Trade-In	Retail	High Retail
1996 SC-I6/V8					
Veh. Ident.: JT8(Model)()T()000001 Up.					
Coupe 2D SC300	CD32Z	3555	**8675**	**10850**	**12075**
Coupe 2D SC400	CH32Y	3625	**9550**	**11850**	**13000**
1996 LS-V8					
Veh. Ident.: JT8BH22F()T()000001 Up.					
Sedan 4D LS400	BH22F	3650	**10050**	**12725**	**13900**
LEXUS OPTIONS					
Add Power Sunroof			**275**	**325**	**325**
Deduct W/out Automatic Trans.			**200**	**200**	**200**
LEXUS					
1995 ES-V6					
Veh. Ident.: JT8()K13()()S0000001 Up.					
Sedan 4D ES300	K13	3374	**5125**	**6875**	**7925**
1995 GS-I6					
Veh. Ident.: JT8()S47()()S0000001 Up.					
Sedan 4D GS300	S47	3660	**7250**	**9300**	**10450**
1995 SC-I6/V8					
Veh. Ident.: JT8()(Model)()()S0000001 Up.					
Coupe 2D SC300	Z31	3565	**7550**	**9625**	**10800**
Coupe 2D SC400	Z30	3625	**8300**	**10425**	**11625**
1995 LS-V8					
Veh. Ident.: JT8()F22()()S0000001 Up.					
Sedan 4D LS400	F22	3650	**8550**	**10700**	**11900**

LINCOLN

BODY TYPE	Model No.	Weight	Trade-In	Retail	High Retail
LINCOLN					
2004 LS-V6					
Veh. Ident.: 1LNHM(Model)()()4Y600001 Up.					
Sedan 4D	86	3681	**19350**	**22625**	**24175**
Sedan 4D Sport (V8)	87	3768	**22600**	**26250**	**27925**
2004 TOWN CAR-V8					
Veh. Ident.: 1LN()M(Model)W()4Y600001 Up.					
Sedan 4D Executive	81	4369	**20775**	**24125**	**25725**
Sedan 4D Signature	81		**22725**	**26375**	**28075**
Sedan 4D Ultimate	83		**25375**	**29200**	**30975**
Sedan 4D Ultimate Limited	83		**25975**	**29825**	**31625**
Sedan 4D Executive L	84	4474	**22825**	**26475**	**28175**
Sedan 4D Ultimate L	85		**27425**	**31500**	**33375**
LINCOLN OPTIONS					
Add LSE Package (LS)			**750**	**850**	**850**
Add Audiophile Stereo System (LS V6)			**425**	**475**	**475**
Add Navigation System			**750**	**850**	**850**
Add Power Sunroof			**725**	**825**	**825**
Add Theft Recovery System			**100**	**125**	**125**
LINCOLN					
2003 LS-V6					
Veh. Ident.: 1LNHM(Model)()()3W600001 Up.					
Sedan 4D	86	3674	**16725**	**19675**	**21125**
Sedan 4D Sport (V8)	87	3755	**19675**	**22950**	**24500**

BODY TYPE	Model No.	Weight	Trade-In	Retail	High Retail
2003 TOWN CAR-V8					
Veh. Ident.: 1LN()M(Model)W()3W600001 Up.					
Sedan 4D Executive	81	4308	**18200**	**21400**	**22925**
Sedan 4D Signature	82	4310	**20000**	**23300**	**24875**
Sedan 4D Signature Limited	82		**20600**	**23950**	**25550**
Sedan 4D Cartier	83	4352	**22550**	**26175**	**27850**
Sedan 4D Executive L	84	4428	**20050**	**23375**	**24950**
Sedan 4D Cartier L	85	4467	**24400**	**28150**	**29900**
LINCOLN OPTIONS					
Add Audiophile Stereo System (LS V6)			**375**	**425**	**425**
Add Navigation System			**650**	**725**	**725**
Add Power Sunroof			**675**	**775**	**775**
Add Theft Recovery System			**75**	**100**	**100**
LINCOLN					
2002 LS-V6					
Veh. Ident.: 1LN()M(Model)()()2()600001 Up.					
Sedan 4D (5 Spd. MT)	86	3598	**14900**	**17725**	**19100**
Sedan 4D	86	3593	**14600**	**17400**	**18750**
Sedan 4D (V8)	87	3692	**16500**	**19425**	**20875**
2002 TOWN CAR-V8					
Veh. Ident.: 1LN()M(Model)()()2()600001 Up.					
Sedan 4D Executive	81	4047	**13950**	**16700**	**18075**
Sedan 4D Signature	82	4075	**15600**	**18475**	**19875**
Sedan 4D Cartier	83	4121	**17800**	**20950**	**22450**
Sedan 4D Executive L	84		**15625**	**18500**	**19900**
Sedan 4D Cartier L	85		**19475**	**22750**	**24300**
2002 CONTINENTAL-V8					
Veh. Ident.: 1LN()M97()()2()600001 Up.					
Sedan 4D	97	3895	**13600**	**16325**	**17675**
LINCOLN OPTIONS					
Add LSE Package (LS)			**650**	**725**	**725**
Add Sport Package (Std. LS 5 Spd. MT)			**550**	**625**	**625**
Add Touring Package			**425**	**475**	**475**
Add Alpine Stereo (Std. LS 5 Spd. MT, Cartier)			**325**	**375**	**375**
Add Compact Disc Player (Std. LS)			**125**	**150**	**150**
Add Power Sunroof			**625**	**700**	**700**
Add Theft Recovery System			**75**	**100**	**100**
LINCOLN					
2001 LS-V6					
Veh. Ident.: 1LN()M(Model)()()1()600001 Up.					
Sedan 4D (5 Spd. MT)	86	3598	**12300**	**14950**	**16225**
Sedan 4D	86	3593	**11975**	**14550**	**15825**
Sedan 4D (V8)	87	3692	**13725**	**16475**	**17825**
2001 TOWN CAR-V8					
Veh. Ident.: 1LN()M(Model)()()1()600001 Up.					
Sedan 4D Executive	81	4047	**11250**	**13725**	**14950**
Sedan 4D Signature	82	4075	**12550**	**15200**	**16500**
Sedan 4D Cartier	83	4121	**14250**	**17025**	**18375**
Sedan 4D Executive L	84		**12850**	**15525**	**16825**
Sedan 4D Cartier L	85		**15850**	**18725**	**20125**
2001 CONTINENTAL-V8					
Veh. Ident.: 1LN()M97()()1()600001 Up.					
Sedan 4D	97	3848	**10700**	**13075**	**14275**

BODY TYPE	Model No.	Weight	Trade-In	Retail	High Retail
LINCOLN OPTIONS					
Add Sport Package (Std. LS 5 Spd. MT) .			**450**	**500**	**500**
Add Alpine Stereo (Std. LS 5 Spd. MT, Cartier)			**275**	**325**	**325**
Add Compact Disc Player (Std. LS 5 Spd. MT)			**125**	**150**	**150**
Add Power Sunroof			**575**	**650**	**650**
Add Theft Recovery System			**50**	**75**	**75**
LINCOLN					
2000 LS-V6					
Veh. Ident.: 1LN()M(Model)()()Y()600001 Up.					
Sedan 4D (5 Spd. MT)	86	3598	**9475**	**11750**	**12900**
Sedan 4D	86	3593	**9575**	**11850**	**13000**
Sedan 4D (V8)	87	3692	**10850**	**13225**	**14425**
2000 TOWN CAR-V8					
Veh. Ident.: 1LN()M(Model)()()Y()600001 Up.					
Sedan 4D Executive	81	4047	**8825**	**11000**	**12225**
Sedan 4D Signature	82	4075	**9950**	**12275**	**13450**
Sedan 4D Cartier	83	4121	**11300**	**13800**	**15025**
Sedan 4D Cartier L	83		**12800**	**15475**	**16775**
2000 CONTINENTAL-V8					
Veh. Ident.: 1LN()M97()()Y()600001 Up.					
Sedan 4D	97	3868	**7975**	**10100**	**11275**
LINCOLN OPTIONS					
Add Sport Package (Std. LS 5 Spd. MT) .			**375**	**425**	**425**
Add Alpine Stereo System (LS, Continental)			**225**	**250**	**250**
Add Compact Disc Player			**100**	**125**	**125**
Add Power Sunroof			**525**	**600**	**600**
LINCOLN					
1999 TOWN CAR-V8					
Veh. Ident.: 1LN()M(Model)()()X()600001 Up.					
Sedan 4D Executive	81	4015	**7150**	**9175**	**10325**
Sedan 4D Signature	82	4020	**7975**	**10075**	**11250**
Sedan 4D Cartier	83	4095	**8900**	**11075**	**12200**
1999 CONTINENTAL-V8					
Veh. Ident.: 1LN()M97()()X()600001 Up.					
Sedan 4D	97	3848	**6400**	**8375**	**9600**
LINCOLN OPTIONS					
Add Alpine Stereo System (Continental) .			**175**	**200**	**200**
Add Power Sunroof			**475**	**550**	**550**
LINCOLN					
1998 TOWN CAR-V8					
Veh. Ident.: 1LN()M(Model)()()W()000001 Up.					
Sedan 4D Executive	81	3860	**6400**	**8375**	**9600**
Sedan 4D Signature	82		**7025**	**9050**	**10200**
Sedan 4D Cartier	83		**7825**	**9925**	**11125**
1998 MARK VIII-V8					
Veh. Ident.: 1LN()M(Model)()()W()000001 Up.					
Coupe 2D	91	3765	**5150**	**6975**	**8150**
Coupe 2D LSC	92		**5450**	**7300**	**8475**
1998 CONTINENTAL-V8					
Veh. Ident.: 1LN()M97()()W()000001 Up.					
Sedan 4D	97	3868	**4925**	**6700**	**7850**

BODY TYPE	Model No.	Weight	Trade-In	Retail	High Retail
LINCOLN OPTIONS					
Add JBL Stereo System (Std. Cartier, Mark)			**150**	**175**	**175**
Add Power Sunroof			**425**	**475**	**475**
Deduct W/out Leather Seats			**275**	**275**	**275**
LINCOLN					
1997 TOWN CAR-V8					
Veh. Ident.: 1LN()M(Model)()()V()000001 Up.					
Sedan 4D Executive	81	3997	**4450**	**6175**	**7275**
Sedan 4D Signature	82	3977	**5000**	**6800**	**7950**
Sedan 4D Cartier	83	3977	**5525**	**7375**	**8550**
1997 MARK VIII-V8					
Veh. Ident.: 1LN()M(Model)()()V()000001 Up.					
Coupe 2D	91	3765	**4200**	**5900**	**7000**
Coupe 2D LSC	92	3785	**4400**	**6125**	**7200**
1997 CONTINENTAL-V8					
Veh. Ident.: 1LN()M97()()V()000001 Up.					
Sedan 4D	97	3884	**3700**	**5350**	**6375**
LINCOLN OPTIONS					
Add JBL Stereo System (Std. Cartier, Mark)			**100**	**125**	**125**
Add Power Sunroof			**350**	**400**	**400**
Deduct W/out Leather Seats			**250**	**250**	**250**
LINCOLN					
1996 TOWN CAR-V8					
Veh. Ident.: 1LN()M(Model)()()T()600001 Up.					
Sedan 4D Executive	81	4040	**3625**	**5250**	**6275**
Sedan 4D Signature	82	4040	**4100**	**5775**	**6850**
Sedan 4D Cartier	83	4103	**4500**	**6225**	**7325**
1996 MARK VIII-V8					
Veh. Ident.: 1LN()M91()()T()600001 Up.					
Coupe 2D	91	3767	**3400**	**5000**	**6050**
1996 CONTINENTAL-V8					
Veh. Ident.: 1LN()M97()()T()600001 Up.					
Sedan 4D	97	3881	**3000**	**4525**	**5525**
LINCOLN OPTIONS					
Add Power Sunroof			**275**	**325**	**325**
LINCOLN					
1995 TOWN CAR-V8					
Veh. Ident.: 1LN()M(Model)()()S()600001 Up.					
Sedan 4D Executive	81	4031	**2975**	**4500**	**5500**
Sedan 4D Signature	82	4057	**3300**	**4875**	**5925**
Sedan 4D Cartier	83	4095	**3650**	**5275**	**6300**
1995 MARK VIII-V8					
Veh. Ident.: 1LN()M91()()S()600001 Up.					
Coupe 2D	91	3768	**2825**	**4325**	**5300**
1995 CONTINENTAL-V8					
Veh. Ident.: 1LN()M97()()S()600001 Up.					
Sedan 4D	97	3972	**2550**	**4000**	**4975**

BODY TYPE	Model No.	Weight	Trade-In	Retail	High Retail

P A S S E N G E R C A R S

MAZDA

MAZDA

2004 MAZDA3-4 Cyl.

Veh. Ident.: JM1(Model)()4()100001 Up.

BODY TYPE	Model No.	Weight	Trade-In	Retail	High Retail
Sedan 4D i	BK()2F	2696	**12500**	**14650**	**15425**
Sedan 4D s	BK()23	2762	**13825**	**16075**	**16900**
Wagon 5D s	BK()43	2826	**13975**	**16225**	**17050**
Add Aluminum/Alloy Wheels (Std. s)			**300**	**350**	**350**
Add Cruise Control (Std. s)			**175**	**200**	**200**
Add Leather Seats			**350**	**400**	**400**
Add Navigation System			**550**	**625**	**625**
Add Power Door Locks (Std. s)			**150**	**175**	**175**
Add Power Sunroof			**525**	**600**	**600**
Add Power Windows (Std. s)			**175**	**200**	**200**
Add Theft Recovery System			**100**	**125**	**125**
Deduct W/out Air Conditioning			**575**	**575**	**575**
Deduct W/out Automatic Trans.			**475**	**475**	**475**

2004 MAZDA6-V6

Veh. Ident.: 1YV(Model)()4()N00001 Up.

BODY TYPE	Model No.	Weight	Trade-In	Retail	High Retail
Hatchback 5D i (4 Cyl.)	()P84C	3166	**14100**	**16550**	**17600**
Hatchback 5D s	()P84D	3336	**16350**	**18925**	**20000**
Sedan 4D i (4 Cyl.)	()P80C	3045	**12850**	**15225**	**16225**
Sedan 4D s	()P80D	3241	**15425**	**17950**	**19000**
Sport Wagon 5D s	()P82D	3389	**14275**	**16725**	**17775**

2004 MX-5 MIATA-4 Cyl.-5/6 Spd.

Veh. Ident.: JM1(Model)()4()100001 Up.

BODY TYPE	Model No.	Weight	Trade-In	Retail	High Retail
Convertible 2D	NB353	2447	**14625**	**17100**	**18125**
Convertible 2D LS	NB353	2447	**16225**	**18800**	**19875**
Convertible MAZDASPEED	NB354	2529	**17525**	**20275**	**21400**
MAZDA6/MX-5 MIATA OPTIONS					
Add Aluminum/Alloy Wheels (Sedan 6i)			**325**	**375**	**375**
Add Automatic Trans. (Miata)			**575**	**650**	**650**
Add Bose Stereo (Std. LS, MAZDASPEED)			**300**	**350**	**350**
Add Detachable Hardtop			**650**	**725**	**725**
Add Leather Seats (Std. Miata LS)			**450**	**500**	**500**
Add Power Seat			**200**	**225**	**225**
Add Power Sunroof			**575**	**650**	**650**
Add Theft Recovery System			**100**	**125**	**125**
Deduct W/out Automatic Trans. (Ex. Miata)			**575**	**575**	**575**
Deduct W/out Cruise (Ex. MAZDASPEED)			**200**	**200**	**200**
Deduct W/out Power Door Locks			**175**	**175**	**175**

2004 RX-8-Rotary

Veh. Ident.: JM1(Model)()4()100001 Up.

BODY TYPE	Model No.	Weight	Trade-In	Retail	High Retail
Coupe 2D	FE17N	3053	**19200**	**22175**	**23500**
Coupe 2D Touring	FE17N		**21375**	**24475**	**25875**
Coupe 2D GT	FE17N		**22125**	**25425**	**26850**
Coupe 2D (6 Spd.)	FE173	3029	**20700**	**23750**	**25125**
Coupe 2D Touring (6 Spd.)	FE173		**21925**	**25075**	**26500**
Coupe 2D GT (6 Spd.)	FE173		**22675**	**26000**	**27450**
Add Sport Pkg (Base AT)			**950**	**1075**	**1075**
Add Navigation System			**650**	**725**	**725**

BODY TYPE	Model No.	Weight	Trade-In	Retail	High Retail
Add Theft Recovery System			100	125	125
MAZDA					
2003 PROTEGE'-4 Cyl.					
Veh. Ident.: JM1(Model)()3()000001 Up.					
Sedan 4D DX	BJ22()	2634	7825	9550	10275
Sedan 4D LX	BJ22()	2634	8500	10350	11075
Sedan 4D ES	BJ22()	2634	8850	10725	11475
Sed 4D MAZDASPEED (5Spd.)	BJ22()	2843	13100	15300	16100
Wagon 5D 5	BJ24()	2716	10400	12450	13175
Add Aluminum/Alloy Wheels (DX)			250	300	300
Add Leather Seats			300	350	350
Add Power Sunroof			475	550	550
Add Theft Recovery System			75	100	100
Deduct W/out Air Conditioning			525	525	525
Deduct W/out AT (Ex. MAZDASPEED)			425	425	425
2003 MAZDA6-V6					
Veh. Ident.: 1YV(Model)()3()000001 Up.					
Sedan 4D i (4 Cyl.)	()P80C	3042	11500	13725	14675
Sedan 4D s	()P80D	3243	13800	16225	17250
2003 MX-5 MIATA-4 Cyl.-5/6 Spd.					
Veh. Ident.: JM1NB353()3()000001 Up.					
Convertible 2D	NB353	2387	13325	15725	16750
Convertible 2D LS	NB353	2387	14700	17175	18200
Convertible 2D SE	NB353	2454	15475	18000	19050
MAZDA6/MX-5 MIATA OPTIONS					
Add Aluminum/Alloy Wheels (6i)			275	325	325
Add Automatic Trans. (Miata)			525	600	600
Add Bose Stereo System (Std. Miata LS/SE)			250	300	300
Add Detachable Hardtop			600	675	675
Add Leather Seats (Std. Miata LS/SE)			400	450	450
Add Power Seat (Std. 6s)			175	200	200
Add Power Sunroof			525	600	600
Add Theft Recovery System			75	100	100
Deduct W/out Automatic Trans. (Ex. Miata)			525	525	525
Deduct W/out Cruise Control			175	175	175
Deduct W/out Power Door Locks			150	150	150
MAZDA					
2002 PROTEGE'-4 Cyl.					
Veh. Ident.: JM1(Model)()2()000001 Up.					
Sedan 4D DX	BJ22()	2634	6900	8525	9300
Sedan 4D LX	BJ22()	2634	7325	9025	9725
Sedan 4D ES	BJ22()	2634	7825	9550	10275
Wagon 5D 5	BJ24()	2716	9350	11300	12025
Add Aluminum/Alloy Wheels (Std. ES, 5)			200	225	225
Add Compact Disc Player (Std. LX, ES, 5)			75	100	100
Add Power Sunroof			425	475	475
Add Theft Recovery System			75	100	100
Deduct W/out Air Conditioning			475	475	475
Deduct W/out Automatic Trans.			375	375	375
2002 626-V6					
Veh. Ident.: 1YV(Model)()2()000001 Up.					
Sedan 4D LX (4 Cyl.)	GF22()	2864	7950	9800	10700
Sedan 4D LX	GF22()	3023	9450	11475	12375

PASSENGER CARS

BODY TYPE	Model No.	Weight	Trade-In	Retail	High Retail
Sedan 4D ES	GF22()	3023	**10175**	**12300**	**13200**
2002 MX-5 MIATA-4 Cyl.-5/6 Spd.					
Veh. Ident.: JM1NB353()2()000001 Up.					
Convertible 2D	NB353	2387	**12000**	**14300**	**15275**
Convertible 2D LS	NB353	2387	**13150**	**15550**	**16550**
Convertible 2D SE	NB353		**13875**	**16325**	**17350**
626/MX-5 MIATA OPTIONS					
Add Aluminum/Alloy Wheels (Std. 626 ES, Miata)			**225**	**250**	**250**
Add Automatic Trans. (Miata)			**475**	**550**	**550**
Add Bose Stereo System (Std. Miata LS/SE)			**200**	**225**	**225**
Add Detachable Hardtop			**550**	**625**	**625**
Add Power Seat (Std. 626 ES)			**150**	**175**	**175**
Add Power Sunroof			**475**	**550**	**550**
Add Theft Recovery System			**75**	**100**	**100**
Deduct W/out Automatic Trans. (Ex. Miata)			**475**	**475**	**475**
Deduct W/out Cruise Control			**150**	**150**	**150**
Deduct W/out Power Door Locks			**125**	**125**	**125**
2002 MILLENIA-V6					
Veh. Ident.: JM1(Model)()2()000001 Up.					
Sedan 4D Premium	TA221	3358	**12300**	**14700**	**15850**
Sedan 4D S Supercharged	TA222	3488	**13600**	**16075**	**17275**
Add Bose Stereo System (Std. S)			**250**	**300**	**300**
Add Theft Recovery System			**75**	**100**	**100**
MAZDA					
2001 PROTEGE'-4 Cyl.					
Veh. Ident.: JM1(Model)()1()100001 Up.					
Sedan 4D DX	BJ222	2493	**5425**	**6925**	**7775**
Sedan 4D LX	BJ222	2493	**5750**	**7275**	**8050**
Sedan 4D LX 2.0	BJ22()	2634	**6100**	**7650**	**8450**
Sedan 4D ES 2.0	BJ22()	2634	**6500**	**8075**	**8825**
Sedan 4D MP3 (5 Spd.)	BJ227	2725	**8750**	**10600**	**11325**
Add Aluminum/Alloy Wheels (Std. ES, MP3)			**150**	**175**	**175**
Add Compact Disc Player (Std. LX, ES, MP3)			**50**	**75**	**75**
Add Power Sunroof			**375**	**425**	**425**
Add Theft Recovery System			**50**	**75**	**75**
Deduct W/out Air Conditioning			**425**	**425**	**425**
Deduct W/out Automatic Trans. (Ex. MP3)			**325**	**325**	**325**
2001 626-4 Cyl.					
Veh. Ident.: 1YV(Model)()1()100001 Up.					
Sedan 4D LX	GF22()	2864	**6400**	**8125**	**8975**
Sedan 4D LX (V6)	GF22()	3023	**7700**	**9525**	**10400**
Sedan 4D ES	GF22()	2864	**6875**	**8625**	**9500**
Sedan 4D ES (V6)	GF22()	3023	**8850**	**10775**	**11725**
2001 MX-5 MIATA-4 Cyl.-5/6 Spd.					
Veh. Ident.: JM1NB353()1()100001 Up.					
Convertible 2D	NB353	2387	**10775**	**12950**	**13875**
Convertible 2D LS	NB353	2387	**11725**	**13975**	**14925**
Convertible 2D SE	NB353	2387	**12400**	**14750**	**15725**
626/MX-5 MIATA OPTIONS					
Add Aluminum/Alloy Wheels (Std. 626 ES, Miata)			**175**	**200**	**200**
Add Automatic Trans. (Miata)			**425**	**475**	**475**
Add Bose Stereo (Std. 626 ES V6, Miata LS/SE)			**150**	**175**	**175**
Add Detachable Hardtop			**450**	**500**	**500**

BODY TYPE	Model No.	Weight	Trade-In	Retail	High Retail
Add Power Seat (Std. 626 ES V6)			125	150	150
Add Power Sunroof (Std. 626 ES V6)			425	475	475
Add Theft Recovery System			50	75	75
Deduct W/out Automatic Trans. (Ex. Miata)			425	425	425
Deduct W/out Cruise Control			125	125	125
Deduct W/out Power Door Locks			100	100	100
2001 MILLENIA-V6					
Veh. Ident.: JM1(Model)()1()100001 Up.					
Sedan 4D Premium	TA221	3358	10375	12600	13675
Sedan 4D S Supercharged	TA222	3488	11475	13775	14900
Add Bose Stereo System (Std. S)			200	225	225
Add Theft Recovery System			50	75	75
MAZDA					
2000 PROTEGE'-4 Cyl.					
Veh. Ident.: JM1(Model)()Y()()00001 Up.					
Sedan 4D DX	BJ222	2434	4300	5675	6450
Sedan 4D LX	BJ22()	2449	4550	5950	6750
Sedan 4D ES	BJ22()	2537	5050	6500	7300
Add Aluminum/Alloy Wheels (Std. ES)			100	125	125
Add Compact Disc Player (Std. LX, ES)			50	75	75
Add Power Sunroof			325	375	375
Deduct W/out Air Conditioning			375	375	375
Deduct W/out Automatic Trans.			300	300	300
2000 626-4 Cyl.					
Veh. Ident.: 1YV(Model)()Y()()00001 Up.					
Sedan 4D LX	GF22()	2864	4975	6525	7425
Sedan 4D LX (V6)	GF22()	2961	6075	7775	8700
Sedan 4D ES	GF22()	3023	5350	6975	7925
Sedan 4D ES (V6)	GF22()	3023	7000	8775	9675
2000 MX-5 MIATA-4 Cyl.-5/6 Spd.					
Veh. Ident.: JM1NB353()Y()000001 Up.					
Convertible 2D	NB353	2332	8975	10925	11875
Convertible 2D LS	NB353	2332	9750	11800	12700
Convertible 2D SE	NB353	2332	10375	12500	13400
626/MX-5 MIATA OPTIONS					
Add Aluminum/Alloy Wheels (Std. 626 ES, Miata)			125	150	150
Add Automatic Trans. (Miata)			375	425	425
Add Bose Stereo (Std. 626 ES V6, Miata LS/SE)			100	125	125
Add Detachable Hardtop			400	450	450
Add Power Seat (Std. 626 ES V6)			100	125	125
Add Power Sunroof (Std. 626 ES V6)			375	425	425
Deduct W/out Automatic Trans. (Ex. Miata)			375	375	375
Deduct W/out Cruise Control			100	100	100
Deduct W/out Power Door Locks			75	75	75
2000 MILLENIA-V6					
Veh. Ident.: JM1(Model)()Y()()00001 Up.					
Sedan 4D	TA221	3241	6900	8825	9875
Sedan 4D Premium	TA221	3241	7700	9700	10750
Sedan 4D S Supercharged	TA222	3355	8600	10675	11725
Add Bose Stereo System (Std. S)			150	175	175

PASSENGER CARS

PASSENGER CARS

BODY TYPE	Model No.	Weight	Trade-In	Retail	High Retail
MAZDA					
1999 PROTEGE'-4 Cyl.					
Veh. Ident.: JM1(Model)()X()()00001 Up.					
Sedan 4D DX	BJ222	2434	**3325**	**4575**	**5350**
Sedan 4D LX	BJ222	2449	**3475**	**4750**	**5525**
Sedan 4D ES	BJ221	2537	**3925**	**5225**	**5950**
Add Aluminum/Alloy Wheels (Std. ES)			**50**	**75**	**75**
Add Power Sunroof			**275**	**325**	**325**
Deduct W/out Air Conditioning			**325**	**325**	**325**
Deduct W/out Automatic Trans.			**250**	**250**	**250**
1999 626-4 Cyl.					
Veh. Ident.: 1YV(Model)()X()()00001 Up.					
Sedan 4D LX	GF22C	2798	**3550**	**4950**	**5850**
Sedan 4D LX (V6)	GF22D	2987	**4450**	**5950**	**6825**
Sedan 4D ES	GF22C	2798	**3775**	**5200**	**6000**
Sedan 4D ES (V6)	GF22D	2987	**5200**	**6825**	**7750**
1999 MX-5 MIATA-4 Cyl.-5/6 Spd.					
Veh. Ident.: JM1NB353()X()()00001 Up.					
Convertible 2D	NB353	2299	**7925**	**9775**	**10675**
Convertible 2D Anniversary	NB353		**8975**	**10950**	**11900**
626/MX-5 MIATA OPTIONS					
Add Aluminum/Alloy Wheels (Std. 626 ES V6, Miata)			**75**	**100**	**100**
Add Automatic Trans. (Miata)			**325**	**375**	**375**
Add Detachable Hardtop			**350**	**400**	**400**
Add Leather Seats (Std. 626 ES, Miata Annv)			**225**	**250**	**250**
Add Power Seat (Std. 626 ES V6)			**75**	**100**	**100**
Add Power Sunroof (Std. 626 ES V6)			**325**	**375**	**375**
Deduct W/out Air Conditioning			**450**	**450**	**450**
Deduct W/out Automatic Trans. (Ex. Miata)			**325**	**325**	**325**
Deduct W/out Cruise Control			**75**	**75**	**75**
Deduct W/out Power Door Locks			**50**	**50**	**50**
Deduct W/out Power Windows			**75**	**75**	**75**
1999 MILLENIA-V6					
Veh. Ident.: JM1(Model)()X()()00001 Up.					
Sedan 4D	TA221	3241	**5875**	**7700**	**8750**
Sedan 4D Premium	TA221	3241	**6550**	**8475**	**9500**
Sedan 4D S Supercharged	TA222	3355	**7250**	**9200**	**10200**
Add Bose Stereo System (Std. S)			**100**	**125**	**125**
MAZDA					
1998 PROTEGE'-4 Cyl.					
Veh. Ident.: JM1(Model)()W()000001 Up.					
Sedan 4D DX	BC141	2385	**2550**	**3725**	**4400**
Sedan 4D LX	BC141	2445	**2700**	**3900**	**4600**
Sedan 4D ES	BC142	2573	**3100**	**4325**	**5075**
Add Power Sunroof			**225**	**275**	**275**
Deduct W/out Air Conditioning			**275**	**275**	**275**
Deduct W/out Automatic Trans.			**200**	**200**	**200**
1998 626-4 Cyl.					
Veh. Ident.: 1YV(Model)()W()000001 Up.					
Sedan 4D DX	GF22C	2798	**2575**	**3850**	**4625**
Sedan 4D LX	GF22C	2798	**2875**	**4175**	**4975**
Sedan 4D LX (V6)	GF22D	2994	**3675**	**5100**	**5900**

BODY TYPE	Model No.	Weight	Trade-In	Retail	High Retail
Sedan 4D ES (V6)	GF22D	2994	**4250**	**5725**	**6575**
Add Aluminum/Alloy Wheels (Std. ES)			**50**	**75**	**75**
Add Leather Seats (Std. ES)			**175**	**200**	**200**
Add Power Seat (Std. ES)			**50**	**75**	**75**
Add Power Sunroof (Std. ES)			**275**	**325**	**325**
Deduct W/out Air Conditioning			**400**	**400**	**400**
Deduct W/out Automatic Trans.			**275**	**275**	**275**
1998 MILLENIA-V6					
Veh. Ident.: JM1(Model)()W()000001 Up.					
Sedan 4D	TA221	3216	**4025**	**5625**	**6575**
Sedan 4D Premium	TA221	3216	**4575**	**6250**	**7225**
Sedan 4D S Supercharged	TA222	3391	**5075**	**6825**	**7875**
Add Bose Stereo System (Std. S)			**75**	**100**	**100**
MAZDA					
1997 PROTEGE'-4 Cyl.					
Veh. Ident.: JM1(Model)()V()000001 Up.					
Sedan 4D DX	BC141	2385	**1725**	**2800**	**3425**
Sedan 4D LX	BC141	2445	**1800**	**2875**	**3500**
Sedan 4D ES	BC142	2573	**1975**	**3075**	**3675**
Add Power Sunroof			**150**	**175**	**175**
Deduct W/out Air Conditioning			**150**	**150**	**150**
Deduct W/out Automatic Trans.			**125**	**125**	**125**
1997 626-4 Cyl.					
Veh. Ident.: 1YV(Model)()V5000001 Up.					
Sedan 4D DX	GE22C	2745	**1825**	**3000**	**3675**
Sedan 4D LX	GE22C	2745	**1975**	**3175**	**3875**
Sedan 4D LX (V6)	GE22D	2899	**2475**	**3725**	**4500**
Sedan 4D ES (V6)	GE22D	2899	**2875**	**4175**	**4975**
1997 MX-6-4 Cyl.					
Veh. Ident.: 1YV(Model)()V5000001 Up.					
Coupe 2D	GE31C	2625	**2900**	**4200**	**5000**
Coupe 2D LS (V6)	GE31D	2800	**3625**	**5050**	**5850**
1997 MX-5 MIATA-4 Cyl.-5 Spd.					
Veh. Ident.: JM1NA353()V()000001 Up.					
Convertible 2D	NA353	2293	**4750**	**6275**	**7150**
Convertible 2D M	NA353		**5575**	**7225**	**8100**
626/MX-6/MX-5 MIATA OPTIONS					
Add Automatic Trans. (Miata)			**175**	**200**	**200**
Add Detachable Hardtop			**250**	**300**	**300**
Add Leather Seats (Std. 626 ES, Miata M)			**150**	**175**	**175**
Add Power Seat (Std. 626 ES)			**50**	**75**	**75**
Add Power Sunroof (Std. MX-6 LS, 626 ES)			**200**	**225**	**225**
Deduct W/out Air Conditioning			**250**	**250**	**250**
Deduct W/out Automatic Trans. (Ex. Miata)			**175**	**175**	**175**
Deduct W/out Cruise Control (Ex. 626)			**50**	**50**	**50**
Deduct W/out Power Windows (Ex. 626)			**50**	**50**	**50**
1997 MILLENIA-V6					
Veh. Ident.: JM1(Model)()V()000001 Up.					
Sedan 4D	TA221	3216	**2625**	**4000**	**4900**
Sedan 4D L	TA221	3216	**3075**	**4550**	**5450**
Sedan 4D S Supercharged	TA222	3319	**3400**	**4900**	**5850**
Add Bose Stereo System (Std. S)			**50**	**75**	**75**

PASSENGER CARS

PASSENGER CARS

BODY TYPE	Model No.	Weight	Trade-In	Retail	High Retail
MAZDA					
1996 PROTEGE'-4 Cyl.					
Veh. Ident.: JM1(Model)()T()000001 Up.					
Sedan 4D DX	BB141	2385	**1450**	**2475**	**3050**
Sedan 4D LX	BB141	2445	**1525**	**2575**	**3150**
Sedan 4D ES	BB142	2573	**1675**	**2725**	**3325**
Add Power Sunroof			**100**	**125**	**125**
Deduct W/out Air Conditioning			**100**	**100**	**100**
Deduct W/out Automatic Trans.			**100**	**100**	**100**
1996 626-4 Cyl.					
Veh. Ident.: 1YV(Model)()T()000001 Up.					
Sedan 4D DX	GE22C	2749	**1600**	**2750**	**3400**
Sedan 4D LX	GE22C	2749	**1700**	**2850**	**3525**
Sedan 4D LX (V6)	GE22D	2899	**2150**	**3375**	**4100**
Sedan 4D ES (V6)	GE22D	2899	**2425**	**3675**	**4425**
1996 MX-6-4 Cyl.					
Veh. Ident.: 1YV(Model)()T()000001 Up.					
Coupe 2D	GE31C	2625	**2375**	**3625**	**4375**
Coupe 2D LS (V6)	GE31D	2800	**2975**	**4300**	**5125**
1996 MX-5 MIATA-4 Cyl.-5 Spd.					
Veh. Ident.: JM1NA353()T()000001 Up.					
Convertible 2D	NA353	2293	**4175**	**5650**	**6500**
Convertible 2D M	NA353		**4875**	**6425**	**7325**
626/MX-6/MX-5 MIATA OPTIONS					
Add Automatic Trans. (Miata)			**125**	**150**	**150**
Add Detachable Hardtop			**200**	**225**	**225**
Add Power Sunroof (Std. MX-6 LS, 626 ES)			**150**	**175**	**175**
Deduct W/out Air Conditioning			**150**	**150**	**150**
Deduct W/out Automatic Trans. (Ex. Miata)			**125**	**125**	**125**
1996 MILLENIA-V6					
Veh. Ident.: JM1(Model)()T()000001 Up.					
Sedan 4D	TA221	3216	**2275**	**3600**	**4425**
Sedan 4D L	TA221	3216	**2625**	**4000**	**4900**
Sedan 4D S Supercharged	TA222	3391	**2925**	**4350**	**5225**
MAZDA					
1995 PROTEGE'-4 Cyl.					
Veh. Ident.: JM1(Model)()S()100001 Up.					
Sedan 4D DX	BA141	2449	**1225**	**2225**	**2750**
Sedan 4D LX	BA141	2511	**1300**	**2325**	**2875**
Sedan 4D ES	BA142	2617	**1400**	**2425**	**3000**
1995 MX-3-4 Cyl.					
Veh. Ident.: JM1EC435()S()100001 Up.					
Coupe 2D	EC435	2507	**1725**	**2900**	**3525**
1995 626-4 Cyl.					
Veh. Ident.: 1YV(Model)()S()100001 Up.					
Sedan 4D DX	GE22C	2822	**1375**	**2500**	**3100**
Sedan 4D LX	GE22C	2822	**1450**	**2575**	**3200**
Sedan 4D LX (V6)	GE22D	2985	**1850**	**3025**	**3700**
Sedan 4D ES (V6)	GE22D	2985	**2100**	**3325**	**4025**
1995 MX-6-4 Cyl.					
Veh. Ident.: 1YV(Model)()S()100001 Up.					
Coupe 2D	GE31C	2700	**1925**	**3125**	**3800**
Coupe 2D LS (V6)	GE31D	2875	**2425**	**3675**	**4425**

BODY TYPE	Model No.	Weight	Trade-In	Retail	High Retail
1995 MX-5 MIATA-4 Cyl.					
Veh. Ident.: JM1NA35()()S()100001 Up.					
Convertible 2D	NA35	2293	**3675**	**5100**	**5900**
Convertible 2D M	NA35		**4325**	**5825**	**6700**
626/MX-6/MX-5 MIATA OPTIONS					
Add Detachable Hardtop			**150**	**175**	**175**
1995 RX-7-Rotary Turbo					
Veh. Ident.: JM1FD333()S()100001 Up.					
Coupe 2D	FD333	2881	**13250**	**15700**	**16900**
1995 MILLENIA-V6					
Veh. Ident.: JM1(Model)()S()100001 Up.					
Sedan 4D	TA221	3216	**1925**	**3200**	**3975**
Sedan 4D L	TA221	3216	**2225**	**3550**	**4375**
Sedan 4D S Supercharged	TA222	3391	**2500**	**3850**	**4725**
1995 929-V6					
Veh. Ident.: JM1HD461()S()100001 Up.					
Sedan 4D	HD461	3627	**2375**	**3725**	**4575**

PASSENGER CARS

MERCEDES-BENZ

BODY TYPE	Model No.	Weight	Trade-In	Retail	High Retail
MERCEDES-BENZ					
2004 C CLASS					
Veh. Ident.: WDB(Model)J()4()000001 Up.					
Sport Coupe C230 S'charged	RN40	3250			
Sport Coupe 2D C320	RN64	3385			
Sedan 4D C240	RF61	3360	**23400**	**27100**	**28800**
Sedan 4D C240 (AWD)	RF81	3520	**24900**	**28675**	**30450**
Sport Sedan C230 S'charged	RF40	3250	**22925**	**26575**	**28275**
Sedan 4D C320	RF64	3450	**25900**	**29750**	**31550**
Sport Sedan 4D C320	RF64	3430	**27225**	**31275**	**33125**
Sedan 4D C320 (AWD)	RF84	3550	**27400**	**31475**	**33350**
Sport Sedan C32 AMG S'chgd	RF65	3540			
Wagon 4D C240	RH61	3470	**23050**	**26725**	**28425**
Wagon 4D C240 (AWD)	RH81	3625	**24550**	**28300**	**30050**
Wagon 4D C320	RH64	3495	**25550**	**29375**	**31175**
Wagon 4D C320 (AWD)	RH84	3660	**27050**	**31075**	**32925**
2004 E CLASS					
Veh. Ident.: WDB(Model)J()4()000001 Up.					
Sedan 4D E320	UF65	3635	**38525**	**43350**	**45575**
Sedan 4D E320 (AWD)	UF82	3835	**40925**	**45875**	**48175**
Sedan 4D E500	UF70	3815	**44500**	**49650**	**52050**
Sedan 4D E500 (AWD)	UF83	4010	**46900**	**52175**	**54650**
Sedan 4D E55 AMG	UF76	3990	**69575**	**76575**	
Wagon 4D E320	UH65	3965	**39125**	**43975**	**46200**
Wagon 4D E320 (AWD)	UH82	4155	**41525**	**46500**	**48800**
Wagon 4D E500 (AWD)	UH83	4230			
2004 S CLASS					
Veh. Ident.: WDB(Model)J()4A000001 Up.					
Sedan 4D S430	NG70	4160	**53250**	**59350**	**62050**
Sedan 4D S430 (AWD)	NG83	4390	**55650**	**61875**	**64650**
Sedan 4D S500	NG75	4165	**60775**	**67300**	**70225**
Sedan 4D S500 (AWD)	NG84	4390	**63175**	**69825**	**72825**
Sedan 4D S55 AMG	NG74	4300			

PASSENGER CARS

BODY TYPE	Model No.	Weight	Trade-In	Retail	High Retail
Sedan 4D S600	NG76	4610			
2004 CLK CLASS					
Veh. Ident.: WDB(Model)()()4()000001 Up.					
Coupe 2D CLK320	TJ65	3515	**34850**	**39475**	**41575**
Coupe 2D CLK500	TJ75	3585	**40375**	**45300**	**47575**
Coupe 2D CLK55 AMG	TJ76	3635			
Convertible 2D CLK320	TK65	3770	**41850**	**46850**	**49175**
Convertible 2D CLK500	TK75	3905	**47475**	**52775**	**55275**
Convertible 2D CLK55 AMG	TK76	3960			
2004 CL CLASS					
Veh. Ident.: WDB(Model)J()4A000001 Up.					
Coupe 2D CL500	PJ75	4085	**64175**	**70875**	**73925**
Coupe 2D CL55 AMG	PJ74	4255			
Coupe 2D CL600	PJ76	4473			
2004 SLK CLASS					
Veh. Ident.: WDB(Model)F()4F000001 Up.					
Rdstr SLK230 Supercharged	KK49	3055	**31825**	**36175**	**38175**
Roadster 2D SLK320	KK65	3120	**35500**	**40175**	**42300**
Rdstr SLK32 AMG S'charged	KK66	3220			
2004 SL CLASS					
Veh. Ident.: WDB(Model)F()4F000001 Up.					
Roadster 2D SL500	SK75	4065	**73500**	**80700**	**84025**
Roadster 2D SL55 AMG	SK74	4235			
Roadster 2D SL600	SK76	4429			
MERCEDES-BENZ OPTIONS					
Add AMG Sport Pkg. (Std. AMG 32/55)			**1775**	**1975**	**1975**
Add Appearance Pkg. (E320)			**1325**	**1475**	**1475**
Add Bose/Harman Kardon Stereo (C230, C240, Sport Cpe, E320/500)			**425**	**475**	**475**
Add CD Player (Std. E/S/CL/SL Class)			**175**	**200**	**200**
Add Navigation System (Std. S/CL/SL Class)			**750**	**850**	**850**
Add Power Sunroof (Std. C32, E/CLK55, S/CL Class)			**725**	**825**	**825**
Add Theft Recovery System			**100**	**125**	**125**
Deduct W/out Automatic Trans.			**675**	**675**	**675**
Deduct W/out Leather Seats			**575**	**575**	**575**
Deduct W/out Power Seat			**275**	**275**	**275**
MERCEDES-BENZ					
2003 C CLASS					
Veh. Ident.: WDB(Model)J()3()000001 Up.					
Sport Coupe C230 S'charged	RN40	3250	**16575**	**19500**	**20950**
Sport Coupe 2D C320	RN64	3385	**18575**	**21775**	**23300**
Sedan 4D C240	RF61	3310	**20650**	**24000**	**25600**
Sedan 4D C240 (AWD)	RF81	3520	**22050**	**25525**	**27175**
Sport Sedan C230 S'charged	RF40	3185	**20375**	**23700**	**25300**
Sedan 4D C320	RF64	3430	**22875**	**26525**	**28225**
Sport Sedan 4D C320	RF64	3440	**24000**	**27725**	**29450**
Sedan 4D C320 (AWD)	RF84	3550	**24275**	**28025**	**29775**
Sport Sedan 4D C320 (AWD)	RF84		**25400**	**29225**	**31000**
Sport Sedan C32 AMG S'chgd	RF65	3540	**32850**	**37350**	**39375**
Wagon 4D C240	RH61	3415	**20300**	**23625**	**25200**
Wagon 4D C240 (AWD)	RH81	3625	**21700**	**25125**	**26775**
Wagon 4D C320	RH64	3465	**22525**	**26150**	**27825**
Wagon 4D C320 (AWD)	RH84	3660	**23925**	**27650**	**29375**

BODY TYPE	Model No.	Weight	Trade-In	Retail	High Retail
2003 E CLASS					
Veh. Ident.: WDB(Model)J()3()000001 Up.					
Sedan 4D E320	UF65	3635	**34450**	**39050**	**41125**
Sedan 4D E500	UF70	3815	**39425**	**44275**	**46525**
Sedan 4D E55 AMG	UF76	3990	**62975**	**69600**	**72600**
Wagon 4D E320	JH65	3770	**34700**	**39300**	**41400**
Wagon 4D E320 (AWD)	JH82	3970	**36900**	**41625**	**43775**
2003 S CLASS					
Veh. Ident.: WDB(Model)J()3A000001 Up.					
Sedan 4D S430	NG70	4160	**45800**	**51500**	**53950**
Sedan 4D S430 (AWD)	NG83	4390	**48000**	**53825**	**56350**
Sedan 4D S500	NG75	4165	**51550**	**57550**	**60200**
Sedan 4D S500 (AWD)	NG84	4390	**53750**	**59875**	**62575**
Sedan 4D S55 AMG	NG74	4300	**73575**	**80800**	**84125**
Sedan 4D S600	NG76	4610	**73375**	**80575**	**83900**
2003 CLK CLASS					
Veh. Ident.: WDB(Model)()()3()000001 Up.					
Coupe 2D CLK320	TJ65	3515	**31275**	**35575**	**37550**
Coupe 2D CLK500	TJ75	3585	**36300**	**41000**	**43150**
Coupe 2D CLK55 AMG	TJ76	3585	**42200**	**47225**	**49550**
Convertible 2D CLK320	LK65	3650	**36000**	**40675**	**42800**
Convertible 2D CLK430	LK70	3745	**41025**	**45975**	**48275**
2003 CL CLASS					
Veh. Ident.: WDB(Model)J()3A000001 Up.					
Coupe 2D CL500	PJ75	4070	**55850**	**62100**	**64875**
Coupe 2D CL55 AMG	PJ74	4255	**72775**	**79950**	**83250**
Coupe 2D CL600	PJ76	4390	**69925**	**76950**	**80175**
2003 SLK CLASS					
Veh. Ident.: WDB(Model)F()3F000001 Up.					
Rdstr SLK230 Supercharged	KK49	3055	**27925**	**32025**	**33900**
Roadster 2D SLK320	KK65	3120	**31150**	**35450**	**37425**
Rdstr SLK32 AMG S'charged	KK66	3220	**36850**	**41600**	**43750**
2003 SL CLASS					
Veh. Ident.: WDB(Model)F()3F000001 Up.					
Roadster 2D SL500	SK75	4045	**67125**	**73975**	**77100**
Roadster 2D SL55 AMG	SK74	4235	**86525**	**94450**	**98200**
MERCEDES-BENZ OPTIONS					
Add Sport Pkg. (Std. C Class Sport Cpe/Sed, E500, AMG)			**1125**	**1250**	**1250**
Add Bose/Harman Kardon Stereo (C230, C240, Sport Cpe, Sed E320/500)			**375**	**425**	**425**
Add CD Player (Std. E Class Sed, S/CL/SL Class)			**150**	**175**	**175**
Add Navigation System (Std. S/CL/SL Class)			**650**	**725**	**725**
Add Power Sunroof (Std. C32, E/CLK55, S/CL Class)			**675**	**775**	**775**
Add Theft Recovery System			**75**	**100**	**100**
Deduct W/out Automatic Trans.			**625**	**625**	**625**
Deduct W/out Leather Seats			**525**	**525**	**525**
Deduct W/out Power Seat			**250**	**250**	**250**
MERCEDES-BENZ					
2002 C CLASS					
Veh. Ident.: WDB(Model)J()2()000001 Up.					
Sport Coupe C230 S'charged	RN47	3305	**14925**	**17750**	**18975**
Sedan 4D C240	RF61	3310	**18575**	**21775**	**23300**
Sedan 4D C320	RF64	3450	**20525**	**23875**	**25475**

PASSENGER CARS

BODY TYPE	Model No.	Weight	Trade-In	Retail	High Retail
Sedan 4D C32 AMG S'charged	RF65	3540	**29500**	**33700**	**35625**
Wagon 4D C320	RH64	3495	**20175**	**23500**	**25075**
2002 E CLASS					
Veh. Ident.: WDB(Model)J()2()000001 Up.					
Sedan 4D E320	JF65	3560	**23825**	**27525**	**29250**
Sedan 4D E320 (AWD)	JF82	3760	**25825**	**29650**	**31450**
Sedan 4D E430	JF70	3695	**25850**	**29700**	**31500**
Sedan 4D E430 (AWD)	JF83	3880	**27850**	**31925**	**33800**
Sedan 4D E55 AMG	JF74	3705	**34675**	**39750**	**41850**
Wagon 4D E320	JH65	3770	**24325**	**28075**	**29825**
Wagon 4D E320 (AWD)	JH82	3970	**26325**	**30200**	**32025**
2002 S CLASS					
Veh. Ident.: WDB(Model)J()2A000001 Up.					
Sedan 4D S430	NG70	4125	**38025**	**43300**	**45500**
Sedan 4D S500	NG75	4135	**42350**	**47850**	**50200**
Sedan 4D S55 AMG	NG73	4100	**54000**	**60150**	**62875**
Sedan 4D S600	NG78	4385	**49750**	**55675**	**58250**
2002 CLK CLASS					
Veh. Ident.: WDB(Model)G()2()000001 Up.					
Coupe 2D CLK320	LJ65	3265	**24650**	**28425**	**30175**
Coupe 2D CLK430	LJ70	3365	**28225**	**32350**	**34225**
Coupe 2D CLK55 AMG	LJ74	3485	**33100**	**37625**	**39675**
Convertible 2D CLK320	LK65	3650	**32975**	**37500**	**39525**
Convertible 2D CLK430	LK70	3745	**36650**	**41375**	**43525**
Convertible 2D CLK55 AMG	LK74	3845	**41525**	**46525**	**48825**
2002 CL CLASS					
Veh. Ident.: WDB(Model)J()2A000001 Up.					
Coupe 2D CL500	PJ75	4070	**47650**	**53450**	**55975**
Coupe 2D CL55 AMG	PJ73	4080	**55150**	**61350**	**64100**
Coupe 2D CL600	PJ78	4300	**53175**	**59275**	**61975**
2002 SLK CLASS					
Veh. Ident.: WDB(Model)F()2F000001 Up.					
Rdstr SLK230 Supercharged	KK49	3055	**24525**	**28300**	**30050**
Roadster 2D SLK320	KK65	3120	**27300**	**31375**	**33225**
Rdstr SLK32 AMG S'charged	KK66	3220	**32650**	**37150**	**39175**
2002 SL CLASS					
Veh. Ident.: WDB(Model)F()2F000001 Up.					
Roadster 2D SL500	FA68	4125	**38950**	**44250**	**46500**
Roadster 2D SL600	FA76	4455	**46275**	**51975**	**54450**
MERCEDES-BENZ OPTIONS					
Add Sport Pkg. (Std. AMG)			**1000**	**1125**	**1125**
Add Bose Stereo System (C230/240, E320)			**325**	**375**	**375**
Add CD Player (Std. S55, CL Class, 600)			**125**	**150**	**150**
Add Navigation System (Std. S/CL Class)			**550**	**625**	**625**
Add Power Sunroof (Std. C32, E/CLK 55, S/CL Class)			**625**	**700**	**700**
Add Theft Recovery System			**75**	**100**	**100**
Deduct W/out Automatic Trans.			**575**	**575**	**575**
Deduct W/out Leather Seats			**475**	**475**	**475**
Deduct W/out Power Seat			**225**	**225**	**225**
MERCEDES-BENZ					
2001 C CLASS					
Veh. Ident.: WDB(Model)J()1F000001 Up.					
Sedan 4D C240	RF61	3310	**16600**	**19525**	**20975**
Sedan 4D C320	RD64	3395	**18275**	**21475**	**23000**

BODY TYPE	Model No.	Weight	Trade-In	Retail	High Retail
2001 E CLASS					
Veh. Ident.: WDB(Model)J()1()000001 Up.					
Sedan 4D E320	JF65	3560	**20050**	**23350**	**24925**
Sedan 4D E320 (AWD)	JF82	3760	**21850**	**25275**	**26925**
Sedan 4D E430	JF70	3695	**21875**	**25300**	**26950**
Sedan 4D E430 (AWD)	JF83	3880	**23675**	**27375**	**29100**
Sedan 4D E55 AMG	JF74	3705	**30550**	**35200**	**37175**
Wagon 4D E320	JH65	3770	**20450**	**23775**	**25375**
Wagon 4D E320 (AWD)	JH82	3970	**22250**	**25850**	**27525**
2001 S CLASS					
Veh. Ident.: WDB(Model)J()1A100001 Up.					
Sedan 4D S430	NG70	4045	**32450**	**37400**	**39425**
Sedan 4D S500	NG75	4055	**35575**	**40700**	**42825**
Sedan 4D S55 AMG	NG73	4100	**45875**	**51575**	**54025**
Sedan 4D S600	NG78	4385	**42975**	**48500**	**50875**
2001 CLK CLASS					
Veh. Ident.: WDB(Model)G()1()000001 Up.					
Coupe 2D CLK320	LJ65	3265	**21125**	**24500**	**26125**
Coupe 2D CLK430	LJ70	3365	**24450**	**28200**	**29950**
Coupe 2D CLK55 AMG	LJ74	3485	**28575**	**32725**	**34625**
Convertible 2D CLK320	LK65	3650	**28800**	**32950**	**34850**
Convertible 2D CLK430	LK70	3745	**32225**	**36700**	**38725**
2001 CL CLASS					
Veh. Ident.: WDB(Model)J()1A000001 Up.					
Coupe 2D CL500	PJ75	4070	**41875**	**47350**	**49675**
Coupe 2D CL55 AMG	PJ73	4080	**48725**	**54575**	**57125**
Coupe 2D CL600	PJ78	4255	**46725**	**52475**	**54950**
2001 SLK CLASS					
Veh. Ident.: WDB(Model)F()1F000001 Up.					
Rdstr SLK230 Supercharged	KK49	3055	**21575**	**24975**	**26600**
Roadster 2D SLK320	KK65	3120	**23900**	**27600**	**29325**
2001 SL CLASS					
Veh. Ident.: WDB(Model)F()1F000001 Up.					
Roadster 2D SL500	FA68	4120	**33575**	**38575**	**40650**
Roadster 2D SL600	FA76	4455	**39750**	**45100**	**47375**
MERCEDES-BENZ OPTIONS					
Add Sport Pkg. (Std. AMG)			**850**	**950**	**950**
Add Bose Stereo System (C240, E320)			**275**	**325**	**325**
Add CD Player (Std. S55, CL Class, 600)			**125**	**150**	**150**
Add Navigation System (Std. S/CL Class)			**500**	**575**	**575**
Add Power Sunroof (Std. AMG, S/CL Class)			**575**	**650**	**650**
Add Theft Recovery System			**50**	**75**	**75**
Deduct W/out Automatic Trans.			**525**	**525**	**525**
Deduct W/out Leather Seats			**425**	**425**	**425**
Deduct W/out Power Seat			**200**	**200**	**200**
MERCEDES-BENZ					
2000 C CLASS					
Veh. Ident.: WDB(Model)G()Y()000001 Up.					
Sedan 4D C230 Supercharged	HA24	3195	**11725**	**14275**	**15525**
Sedan 4D C280	HA29	3265	**12450**	**15125**	**16425**
Sedan 4D C43 AMG	HA33	3400	**19750**	**23050**	**24625**
2000 E CLASS					
Veh. Ident.: WDB(Model)()()Y()000001 Up.					
Sedan 4D E320	JF65	3560	**16975**	**19950**	**21400**

PASSENGER CARS

BODY TYPE	Model No.	Weight	Trade-In	Retail	High Retail
Sedan 4D E320 (AWD)	JF82	3760	**18575**	**21800**	**23325**
Sedan 4D E430	JF70	3695	**18600**	**21825**	**23350**
Sedan 4D E430 (AWD)	JF83	3880	**20200**	**23525**	**25100**
Sedan 4D E55 AMG	JF74	3705	**27150**	**31600**	**33475**
Wagon 4D E320	JH65	3770	**17375**	**20500**	**21975**
Wagon 4D E320 (AWD)	JH82	3970	**18975**	**22225**	**23750**
2000 S CLASS					
Veh. Ident.: WDB(Model)()()Y()000001 Up.					
Sedan 4D S430	NG70	4045	**27400**	**31850**	**33725**
Sedan 4D S500	NG75	4055	**29725**	**34325**	**36275**
2000 CLK CLASS					
Veh. Ident.: WDB(Model)G()Y()000001 Up.					
Coupe 2D CLK320	LJ65	3265	**18275**	**21475**	**23000**
Coupe 2D CLK430	LJ70	3365	**21400**	**24800**	**26425**
Convertible 2D CLK320	LK65	3650	**25300**	**29100**	**30875**
Convertible 2D CLK430	LK70	3750	**28525**	**32650**	**34550**
2000 CL CLASS					
Veh. Ident.: WDBPJ75()()Y()000001 Up.					
Coupe 2D CL500	PJ75	4115	**36025**	**41200**	**43350**
2000 SLK CLASS					
Veh. Ident.: WDBKK47F()YF000001 Up.					
Rdstr SLK230 Supercharged	KK47	3000	**18950**	**22175**	**23700**
2000 SL CLASS					
Veh. Ident.: WDB(Model)F()YF000001 Up.					
Roadster 2D SL500	FA68	4120	**28925**	**33475**	**35400**
Roadster 2D SL600	FA76	4455	**34000**	**39025**	**41100**
MERCEDES-BENZ OPTIONS					
Add Sport Pkg. (Ex. AMG, C Class)			**725**	**825**	**825**
Add Bose Stereo System (C230, E320)			**225**	**250**	**250**
Add Compact Disc Player (Std. SL600)			**100**	**125**	**125**
Add Navigation System (Std. S/CL Class)			**450**	**500**	**500**
Add Power Sunroof (Std. AMG, S/CL Class)			**525**	**600**	**600**
Deduct W/out Automatic Trans.			**475**	**475**	**475**
Deduct W/out Leather Seats			**375**	**375**	**375**
MERCEDES-BENZ					
1999 C CLASS					
Veh. Ident.: WDB(Model)()()X()000001 Up.					
Sedan 4D C230 Supercharged	HA24	3250	**10275**	**12625**	**13350**
Sedan 4D C280	HA29	3316	**10900**	**13300**	**14050**
Sedan 4D C43 AMG	HA33	3400	**17575**	**20725**	**21600**
1999 E CLASS					
Veh. Ident.: WDB(Model)()()X()000001 Up.					
Sedan 4D E300 Turbo Diesel	JF25	3640	**15850**	**18750**	**19575**
Sedan 4D E320	JF65	3460	**14800**	**17625**	**18450**
Sedan 4D E320 (AWD)	JF82	3660	**16200**	**19125**	**19975**
Sedan 4D E430	JF70	3640	**16225**	**19150**	**20000**
Sedan 4D E55 AMG	JF74	3680	**24675**	**28850**	**29850**
Wagon 4D E320	JH65	3670	**15100**	**17950**	**18775**
Wagon 4D E320 (AWD)	JH82	3860	**16500**	**19450**	**20300**
1999 S CLASS					
Veh. Ident.: WDB(Model)G()XA000001 Up.					
Sedan 4D S320W	GA32	4480	**18750**	**22450**	**24000**
Sedan 4D S320V	GA33	4500	**19350**	**23100**	**24675**
Sedan 4D S420	GA43	4650	**19750**	**23525**	**25100**

BODY TYPE	Model No.	Weight	Trade-In	Retail	High Retail
Sedan 4D S500	GA51	4700	**22350**	**26375**	**28075**
Sedan 4D S600	GA57	4960	**30150**	**34775**	**36725**
1999 CLK CLASS					
Veh. Ident.: WDB(Model)G()X()000001 Up.					
Coupe 2D CLK320	LJ65	3265	**15775**	**18650**	**19475**
Coupe 2D CLK430	LJ70	3365	**18650**	**21875**	**22775**
Convertible 2D CLK320	LK65	3715	**22275**	**25900**	**26875**
1999 CL CLASS					
Veh. Ident.: WDB(Model)G0XA4000001 Up.					
Coupe 2D CL500	GA70	4695	**22500**	**26525**	**28225**
Coupe 2D CL600	GA76	4960	**27200**	**31650**	**33525**
1999 SLK CLASS					
Veh. Ident.: WDBKK47F()XF000001 Up.					
Rdstr SLK230 Supercharged	KK47	3000	**16650**	**19575**	**21025**
1999 SL CLASS					
Veh. Ident.: WDB(Model)()()X()000001 Up.					
Roadster 2D SL500	FA68	4120	**24950**	**29125**	**30900**
Roadster 2D SL600	FA76	4455	**29025**	**33575**	**35500**
MERCEDES-BENZ OPTIONS					
Add Sport Pkg. (Ex. C Class, AMG)			**625**	**700**	**700**
Add Bose Stereo System (C230, E300/320)			**175**	**200**	**200**
Add Power Sunroof (Std. AMG, S/CL Class)			**475**	**550**	**550**
Deduct W/out Automatic Trans.			**425**	**425**	**425**
Deduct W/out Leather Seats			**325**	**325**	**325**
MERCEDES-BENZ					
1998 C CLASS					
Veh. Ident.: WDB(Model)G()W()400001 Up.					
Sedan 4D C230	HA23	3250	**8550**	**10700**	**11900**
Sedan 4D C280	HA29	3316	**9500**	**11775**	**12925**
Sedan 4D C43 AMG	HA33	3400	**15575**	**18450**	**19850**
1998 E CLASS					
Veh. Ident.: WDB(Model)F()W()000001 Up.					
Sedan 4D E300 Turbo Diesel	JF25	3640	**13775**	**16525**	**17875**
Sedan 4D E320	JF65	3460	**13075**	**15775**	**17100**
Sedan 4D E320 (AWD)	JF82	3660	**14275**	**17050**	**18400**
Sedan 4D E430	JF70	3640	**14300**	**17075**	**18425**
Wagon 4D E320	JH65	3670	**13375**	**16075**	**17400**
Wagon 4D E320 (AWD)	JH82	3860	**14575**	**17375**	**18725**
1998 S CLASS					
Veh. Ident.: WDB(Model)G()WA370001 Up.					
Sedan 4D S320W	GA32	4480	**16425**	**19850**	**21300**
Sedan 4D S320V	GA33	4500	**16925**	**20375**	**21850**
Sedan 4D S420	GA43	4650	**17425**	**21025**	**22525**
Sedan 4D S500	GA51	4700	**20025**	**23825**	**25425**
Sedan 4D S600	GA57	4960	**27825**	**32325**	**34200**
1998 CLK CLASS					
Veh. Ident.: WDBLJ65G()W()000001 Up.					
Coupe 2D CLK320	LJ65	3240	**13525**	**16250**	**17600**
1998 CL CLASS					
Veh. Ident.: WDB(Model)G()W()000001 Up.					
Coupe 2D CL500	GA70	4695	**20875**	**24725**	**26350**
Coupe 2D CL600	GA76	4960	**25375**	**29575**	**31375**

PASSENGER CARS

BODY TYPE	Model No.	Weight	Trade-In	Retail	High Retail
1998 SLK CLASS					
Veh. Ident.: WDBKK47F()WF000001 Up.					
Rdstr SLK230 Supercharged	KK47	3036	**14625**	**17425**	**18775**
1998 SL CLASS					
Veh. Ident.: WDB(Model)F()WF000001 Up.					
Roadster 2D SL500	FA67	4165	**21950**	**25900**	**27575**
Roadster 2D SL600	FA76	4455	**25125**	**29325**	**31125**
MERCEDES-BENZ OPTIONS					
Add Sport Pkg. (Ex. C Class)			**525**	**600**	**600**
Add Power Sunroof (Std. AMG, S Class, CL500/600)			**425**	**475**	**475**
Add Traction Control (C230)			**200**	**225**	**225**
Deduct W/out Leather Seats			**275**	**275**	**275**
MERCEDES-BENZ					
1997 C CLASS					
Veh. Ident.: WDB(Model)()()V()000001 Up.					
Sedan 4D C230	HA23	3195	**7125**	**9150**	**10300**
Sedan 4D C280	HA28	3350	**7800**	**9900**	**11100**
Sedan 4D C36	HM36	3550	**13125**	**15825**	**17150**
1997 E CLASS					
Veh. Ident.: WDB(Model)()()V()000001 Up.					
Sedan 4D E300 Diesel	JF20	3545	**11375**	**13875**	**15100**
Sedan 4D E320	JF55	3605	**10675**	**13050**	**14250**
Sedan 4D E420	JF72	3745	**11675**	**14200**	**15450**
1997 S CLASS					
Veh. Ident.: WDB(Model)()()V()000001 Up.					
Coupe 2D S500	GA70	4695	**19775**	**23550**	**25125**
Coupe 2D S600	GA76	4960	**23975**	**28100**	**29850**
Sedan 4D S320W	GA32	4480	**13450**	**16650**	**18000**
Sedan 4D S320V	GA33	4500	**13850**	**17075**	**18425**
Sedan 4D S420	GA43	4650	**14350**	**17625**	**19000**
Sedan 4D S500	GA51	4700	**16725**	**20175**	**21650**
Sedan 4D S600	GA57	4960	**24375**	**28525**	**30275**
1997 SL CLASS					
Veh. Ident.: WDB(Model)()()V()000001 Up.					
Roadster 2D SL320	FA63	4010	**17325**	**20925**	**22425**
Roadster 2D SL500	FA67	4165	**19900**	**23675**	**25275**
Roadster 2D SL600	FA76	4455	**22700**	**26750**	**28450**
MERCEDES-BENZ OPTIONS					
Add Sport Pkg. (Ex. C Class)			**425**	**475**	**475**
Add Power Sunroof (Std. C36, S Class)			**350**	**400**	**400**
Deduct W/out Leather Seats			**250**	**250**	**250**
MERCEDES-BENZ					
1996 C CLASS					
Veh. Ident.: WDB(Model)()()T()000001 Up.					
Sedan 4D C220	HA22	3150	**6050**	**7975**	**9200**
Sedan 4D C280	HA28	3350	**6625**	**8625**	**9875**
Sedan 4D C36	HM36	3549	**11275**	**13775**	**15000**
1996 E CLASS					
Veh. Ident.: WDB(Model)()()T()000001 Up.					
Sedan 4D E300 Diesel	JF20	3538	**10100**	**12425**	**13600**
Sedan 4D E320	JF55	3605	**9400**	**11675**	**12825**

BODY TYPE	Model No.	Weight	Trade-In	Retail	High Retail
1996 S CLASS					
Veh. Ident.: WDB(Model)()()T()000001 Up.					
Coupe 2D S500	GA70	4695	**18300**	**21975**	**23525**
Coupe 2D S600	GA76	4960	**22100**	**26100**	**27775**
Sedan 4D S320W	GA32	4480	**12100**	**15200**	**16500**
Sedan 4D S320V	GA33	4500	**12450**	**15575**	**16900**
Sedan 4D S420	GA43	4650	**12900**	**16050**	**17375**
Sedan 4D S500	GA51	4700	**15275**	**18600**	**20000**
Sedan 4D S600	GA57	4960	**22925**	**26975**	**28675**
1996 SL CLASS					
Veh. Ident.: WDB(Model)()()T()000001 Up.					
Roadster 2D SL320	FA63	4010	**16550**	**19975**	**21425**
Roadster 2D SL500	FA67	4165	**18925**	**22650**	**24200**
Roadster 2D SL600	FA76	4455	**21325**	**25200**	**26850**
MERCEDES-BENZ OPTIONS					
Add Sport Pkg. (Std. C36)			**350**	**400**	**400**
Add Power Sunroof (Std. C36, S Class)			**275**	**325**	**325**
MERCEDES-BENZ					
1995 C CLASS					
Veh. Ident.: WDB(Model)()()S()000001 Up.					
Sedan 4D C220	HA22	3150	**5150**	**6975**	**8150**
Sedan 4D C280	HA28	3350	**5625**	**7500**	**8675**
Sedan 4D C36	HA36	3549	**9125**	**11375**	**12500**
1995 E CLASS					
Veh. Ident.: WDB(Model)()()S()000001 Up.					
Coupe 2D E320	EA52	3550	**9900**	**12225**	**13400**
Sedan 4D E300 Diesel	EB31	3485	**8125**	**10250**	**11425**
Sedan 4D E320	EA32	3525	**7425**	**9475**	**10650**
Sedan 4D E420	EA34	3745	**8225**	**10350**	**11525**
Station Wagon 4D E320	EA92	3750	**8175**	**10300**	**11475**
Convertible 2D E320	EA66	3990	**19075**	**22325**	**23875**
1995 S CLASS					
Veh. Ident.: WDB(Model)()()S()000001 Up.					
Coupe 2D S500	GA70	4695	**16925**	**19875**	**21325**
Coupe 2D S600	GA76	4960	**20425**	**23750**	**25350**
Sedan 4D S320W	GA32	4610	**10900**	**13300**	**14500**
Sedan 4D S320V	GA33	4610	**11200**	**13700**	**14925**
Sedan 4D S350 Turbo Diesel	GB34	4610	**12200**	**14825**	**16100**
Sedan 4D S420	GA43	4700	**11600**	**14125**	**15375**
Sedan 4D S500	GA51	4760	**13975**	**16725**	**18100**
Sedan 4D S600	GA57	5030	**21325**	**24725**	**26350**
1995 SL CLASS					
Veh. Ident.: WDB(Model)()()S()000001 Up.					
Roadster 2D SL320	FA63	4090	**15700**	**18575**	**19975**
Roadster 2D SL500	FA67	4165	**17950**	**21125**	**22625**
Roadster 2D SL600	FA76	4455	**19950**	**23250**	**24825**

MERCURY

BODY TYPE	Model No.	Weight	Trade-In	Retail	High Retail
MERCURY					
2004 SABLE-V6					
Veh. Ident.: 1ME()M(Model)()()4()600001 Up.					
Sedan 4D GS	50	3308	**9750**	**11800**	**12700**

PASSENGER CARS

BODY TYPE	Model No.	Weight	Trade-In	Retail	High Retail
Sedan 4D LS Premium	55	3315	11800	14050	15000
Sedan 4D LS Platinum	55		12500	14850	15825
Wagon 4D GS	58	3488	11100	13275	14200
Wagon 4D LS Premium	59	3496	13150	15550	16550
Add Aluminum/Alloy Wheels (Std. LS)			325	375	375
Add Compact Disc Player			100	125	125
Add Leather Seats (Std. Platinum)			450	500	500
Add MACH Stereo System			300	350	350
Add Power Seat (Std. LS)			200	225	225
Add Power Sunroof			575	650	650
Add Theft Recovery System			100	125	125
Deduct W/out Third Seat (Wagon)			275	275	275
2004 GRAND MARQUIS-V8					
Veh. Ident.: 2ME()M(Model)W()4X600001 Up.					
Sedan 4D GS	74	4052	12475	14875	16025
Sedan 4D LS	75		14200	16700	17925
Sedan 4D LS Ultimate	75		14700	17250	18475
Sedan 4D Limited	75		15225	17800	19025
Add Handling Package			425	475	475
Add Aluminum/Alloy Wheels (GS)			375	425	425
Add Leather Seats (Std. Limited)			525	600	600
Add Power Sunroof			625	700	700
Add Theft Recovery System			100	125	125
2004 MARAUDER-V8					
Veh. Ident.: 2MEHM79V()4X600001 Up.					
Sedan 4D	79	4195	20325	23350	24725
Add Power Sunroof			625	700	700
Add Theft Recovery System			100	125	125
MERCURY					
2003 SABLE-V6					
Veh. Ident.: 1ME()M(Model)()()3()600001 Up.					
Sedan 4D GS	50	3344	8000	9875	10775
Sedan 4D LS Premium	55	3324	9800	11875	12775
Sedan 4D LS Platinum	55		10425	12575	13475
Wagon 4D GS	58	3523	9200	11225	12100
Wagon 4D LS Premium	59	3504	11000	13200	14125
Wagon 4D LS Platinum	59		11625	13875	14825
Add Aluminum/Alloy Wheels (Std. LS)			275	325	325
Add Compact Disc Player			75	100	100
Add Leather Seats (Std. Platinum)			400	450	450
Add MACH Stereo System			250	300	300
Add Power Seat (Std. LS)			175	200	200
Add Power Sunroof			525	600	600
Add Theft Recovery System			75	100	100
Deduct W/out Third Seat (Wagon)			250	250	250
2003 GRAND MARQUIS-V8					
Veh. Ident.: 2ME()M(Model)W()3X600001 Up.					
Sedan 4D GS	74	4052	11050	13325	14425
Sedan 4D LS	75		12625	15025	16200
Sedan 4D LS Ultimate	75		13150	15600	16775
Sedan 4D LSE	75		13975	16475	17700
Add Handling Package (Std. LSE)			375	425	425

BODY TYPE	Model No.	Weight	Trade-In	Retail	High Retail
Add Aluminum/Alloy Wheels (GS)			325	375	375
Add Compact Disc Player (Std. Ultimate)			125	150	150
Add Leather Seats (Std. LSE)			475	550	550
Add Theft Recovery System			75	100	100
2003 MARAUDER-V8					
Veh. Ident.: 2MEHM75V()3X600001 Up.					
Sedan 4D	75	4195	17775	20650	21975
Add Theft Recovery System			75	100	100
MERCURY					
2002 COUGAR-V6					
Veh. Ident.: 1ZWFT(Model)()()25600001 Up.					
Coupe 2D (4 Cyl., 5 Spd.)	60	2892	7825	9650	10550
Coupe 2D	61	3013	9100	11100	11975
Add Leather Seats			350	400	400
Add Power Seat			150	175	175
Add Power Sunroof			475	550	550
Add Theft Recovery System			75	100	100
Deduct W/out Automatic Trans. (61)			475	475	475
2002 SABLE-V6					
Veh. Ident.: ()ME()M(Model)()()2()600001 Up.					
Sedan 4D GS	50	3366	6825	8575	9450
Sedan 4D LS Premium	55	3387	8500	10400	11325
Wagon 4D GS	58	3531	7900	9725	10625
Wagon 4D LS Premium	59	3573	9575	11625	12525
Add Aluminum/Alloy Wheels (Std. LS)			225	250	250
Add Compact Disc Player			75	100	100
Add Leather Seats			350	400	400
Add MACH Stereo System			200	225	225
Add Power Seat (Std. LS)			150	175	175
Add Power Sunroof			475	550	550
Add Theft Recovery System			75	100	100
Deduct W/out Third Seat (Wagon)			225	225	225
2002 GRAND MARQUIS-V8					
Veh. Ident.: ()ME()M(Model)()()2()600001 Up.					
Sedan 4D GS	74	3957	9350	11475	12500
Sedan 4D LS	75	3973	10575	12800	13875
Sedan 4D LSE	75		11450	13750	14850
Add Aluminum/Alloy Wheels (GS)			275	325	325
Add Compact Disc Player			100	125	125
Add Leather Seats (Std. LSE)			425	475	475
Add Theft Recovery System			75	100	100
MERCURY					
2001 COUGAR-V6					
Veh. Ident.: 1ZW()T(Model)()()15600001 Up.					
Coupe 2D (4 Cyl., 5 Spd.)	60	2829	6500	8225	9075
Coupe 2D	61	2941	7650	9475	10350
Add Leather Seats			300	350	350
Add Power Seat			125	150	150
Add Power Sunroof			425	475	475
Add Theft Recovery System			50	75	75
Deduct W/out Automatic Trans. (61)			425	425	425
Deduct W/out Cruise Control			125	125	125

PASSENGER CARS

BODY TYPE	Model No.	Weight	Trade-In	Retail	High Retail
2001 SABLE-V6					
Veh. Ident.: ()ME()M(Model)()()1()600001 Up.					
Sedan 4D GS	50	3379	5350	6975	7925
Sedan 4D LS	53	3379	6025	7725	8650
Sedan 4D LS Premium	55	3325	6800	8550	9425
Wagon 4D GS	58	3544	6300	8025	8875
Wagon 4D LS Premium	59	3473	7750	9575	10475
Add 3.0L Duratec V6 Engine (53)			275	325	325
Add Aluminum/Alloy Wheels (Std. LS)			175	200	200
Add Compact Disc Player			50	75	75
Add Leather Seats			300	350	350
Add MACH Stereo System			150	175	175
Add Power Seat (Std. LS)			125	150	150
Add Power Sunroof			425	475	475
Add Theft Recovery System			50	75	75
Deduct W/out Third Seat (Wagon)			200	200	200
2001 GRAND MARQUIS-V8					
Veh. Ident.: ()ME()M(Model)()()1()600001 Up.					
Sedan 4D GS	74	3958	8000	10025	11050
Sedan 4D LS	75	3973	8950	11050	12050
Sedan 4D Limited	75		9850	12025	13075
Sedan 4D LSE	75		9575	11725	12775
Add Aluminum/Alloy Wheels (GS, LS)			225	250	250
Add Compact Disc Player			100	125	125
Add Leather Seats (Std. Limited)			375	425	425
Add Theft Recovery System			50	75	75
MERCURY					
2000 MYSTIQUE-V6					
Veh. Ident.: ()ME()M(Model)()()Y()600001 Up.					
Sedan 4D GS (4 Cyl.)	65	2805	3375	4650	5525
Sedan 4D LS	66	2824	4275	5650	6500
Add Aluminum/Alloy Wheels (Std. LS)			125	150	150
Add Compact Disc Player			50	75	75
Add Power Seat (Std. LS)			100	125	125
Add Power Sunroof			375	425	425
Deduct W/out Automatic Trans.			375	375	375
2000 COUGAR-V6					
Veh. Ident.: 1ZW()T(Model)()()Y5600001 Up.					
Coupe 2D (4 Cyl., 5 Spd.)	60	2829	4925	6475	7375
Coupe 2D	61	2941	5950	7625	8525
Add Compact Disc Player			50	75	75
Add Leather Seats			250	300	300
Add Power Seat			100	125	125
Add Power Sunroof			375	425	425
Deduct W/out Automatic Trans. (61)			375	375	375
Deduct W/out Cruise Control			100	100	100
2000 SABLE-V6					
Veh. Ident.: ()ME()M(Model)()()Y()600001 Up.					
Sedan 4D GS	50	3375	4375	5875	6750
Sedan 4D LS	53	3375	4950	6500	7400
Sedan 4D LS Premium	55		5625	7275	8150
Wagon 4D GS	58	3540	5200	6825	7750

BODY TYPE	Model No.	Weight	Trade-In	Retail	High Retail
Wagon 4D LS Premium	59	3540	**6450**	**8175**	**9025**
Add 3.0L Duratec V6 Engine (53)			**250**	**300**	**300**
Add Aluminum/Alloy Wheels (Std. LS)			**125**	**150**	**150**
Add Compact Disc Player			**50**	**75**	**75**
Add Leather Seats			**250**	**300**	**300**
Add MACH Stereo System			**100**	**125**	**125**
Add Power Seat (Std. LS)			**100**	**125**	**125**
Add Power Sunroof			**375**	**425**	**425**
Deduct W/out Third Seat (Wagon)			**175**	**175**	**175**
2000 GRAND MARQUIS-V8					
Veh. Ident.: ()ME()M(Model)()()Y()600001 Up.					
Sedan 4D GS	74	3958	**6975**	**8925**	**9975**
Sedan 4D LS	75	3973	**7825**	**9825**	**10875**
Add Aluminum/Alloy Wheels			**175**	**200**	**200**
Add Compact Disc Player			**75**	**100**	**100**
Add Leather Seats			**325**	**375**	**375**
MERCURY					
1999 TRACER-4 Cyl.					
Veh. Ident.: ()ME()M(Model)()()X()600001 Up.					
Sedan 4D GS	10	2461	**2500**	**3675**	**4350**
Sedan 4D LS	13	2498	**2625**	**3800**	**4500**
Wagon 4D LS	15	2577	**2775**	**3975**	**4700**
Add Aluminum/Alloy Wheels			**50**	**75**	**75**
Add Cruise Control			**50**	**75**	**75**
Add Leather Seats			**125**	**150**	**150**
Add Power Windows			**50**	**75**	**75**
Deduct W/out Air Conditioning			**325**	**325**	**325**
Deduct W/out Automatic Trans.			**250**	**250**	**250**
1999 MYSTIQUE-V6					
Veh. Ident.: ()ME()M(Model)()()X()600001 Up.					
Sedan 4D GS (4 Cyl.)	65	2805	**2800**	**4000**	**4800**
Sedan 4D LS	66	2824	**3575**	**4850**	**5750**
Add Aluminum/Alloy Wheels (Std. LS)			**75**	**100**	**100**
Add Power Seat (Std. LS)			**75**	**100**	**100**
Add Power Sunroof			**325**	**375**	**375**
Deduct W/out Automatic Trans.			**325**	**325**	**325**
1999 COUGAR-V6					
Veh. Ident.: 1ZW()T(Model)()()X5600001 Up.					
Coupe 2D (4 Cyl.)	60	2827	**4275**	**5750**	**6600**
Coupe 2D	61	2941	**4800**	**6325**	**7200**
Add Leather Seats			**225**	**250**	**250**
Add Power Seat			**75**	**100**	**100**
Add Power Sunroof			**325**	**375**	**375**
Deduct W/out Automatic Trans.			**325**	**325**	**325**
Deduct W/out Cruise Control			**75**	**75**	**75**
1999 SABLE-V6					
Veh. Ident.: ()ME()M(Model)()()X()600001 Up.					
Sedan 4D GS	50	3299	**3425**	**4825**	**5725**
Sedan 4D LS	53	3299	**3825**	**5275**	**6100**
Wagon 4D LS	58	3462	**4175**	**5650**	**6500**
Add Aluminum/Alloy Wheels (Std. LS)			**75**	**100**	**100**

PASSENGER CARS

BODY TYPE	Model No.	Weight	Trade-In	Retail	High Retail
Add Leather Seats			225	250	250
Add MACH Stereo System			75	100	100
Add Power Seat (Std. LS)			75	100	100
Add Power Sunroof			325	375	375
Deduct W/out Third Seat (Wagon)			125	125	125
1999 GRAND MARQUIS-V8					
Veh. Ident.: ()ME()M(Model)()()X()600001 Up.					
Sedan 4D GS	74	3917	6225	8100	9100
Sedan 4D LS	75	3922	6925	8875	9925
Add Aluminum/Alloy Wheels			125	150	150
Add Leather Seats			275	325	325
MERCURY					
1998 TRACER-4 Cyl.					
Veh. Ident.: ()M()()M(Model)()()W()000001 Up.					
Sedan 4D GS	10		2000	3100	3700
Sedan 4D LS	13	2469	2125	3250	3875
Wagon 4D LS	15	2532	2225	3375	4025
Add Cruise Control			50	75	75
Add Leather Seats			100	125	125
Add Power Windows			50	75	75
Deduct W/out Air Conditioning			275	275	275
Deduct W/out Automatic Trans.			200	200	200
1998 MYSTIQUE-V6					
Veh. Ident.: ()M()()M(Model)()()W()000001 Up.					
Sedan 4D GS (4 Cyl.)	65	2808	2175	3300	4000
Sedan 4D LS	66		2775	3975	4775
Add Aluminum/Alloy Wheels (Std. LS)			50	75	75
Add Power Seat (Std. LS)			50	75	75
Add Power Sunroof			275	325	325
Deduct W/out Automatic Trans.			275	275	275
1998 SABLE-V6					
Veh. Ident.: ()M()()M(Model)()()W()000001 Up.					
Sedan 4D GS	50		2825	4125	4925
Sedan 4D LS	53	3299	3150	4500	5350
Wagon 4D LS	55	3462	3400	4775	5650
Add Aluminum/Alloy Wheels (Std. LS)			50	75	75
Add Leather Seats			175	200	200
Add MACH Stereo System			50	75	75
Add Power Seat (Std. LS)			50	75	75
Add Power Sunroof			275	325	325
Deduct W/out Third Seat (Wagon)			75	75	75
1998 GRAND MARQUIS-V8					
Veh. Ident.: ()M()()M(Model)()()W()000001 Up.					
Sedan 4D GS	74		5525	7325	8350
Sedan 4D LS	75		6100	7975	9050
Add Aluminum/Alloy Wheels			100	125	125
Add Leather Seats			225	250	250
MERCURY					
1997 TRACER-4 Cyl.					
Veh. Ident.: ()M()()M(Model)()()V()000001 Up.					
Sedan 4D GS	10	2457	1525	2575	3150

BODY TYPE	Model No.	Weight	Trade-In	Retail	High Retail
Sedan 4D LS	13	2503	1625	2675	3275
Wagon 4D LS	15	2569	1675	2725	3325
Deduct W/out Air Conditioning			150	150	150
Deduct W/out Automatic Trans.			125	125	125
1997 MYSTIQUE-4 Cyl.					
Veh. Ident.: ()M()()M(Model)()()V()000001 Up.					
Sedan 4D	65		1675	2725	3375
Sedan 4D GS	65	2861	1725	2800	3450
Sedan 4D LS	66	2884	1875	2950	3625
1997 MYSTIQUE-V6					
Veh. Ident.: ()M()()M(Model)()()V()000001 Up.					
Sedan 4D GS	65		1850	2925	3600
Sedan 4D LS	66		2000	3100	3775
MYSTIQUE OPTIONS					
Add Leather Seats			150	175	175
Add Power Seat (Std. LS)			50	75	75
Add Power Sunroof			200	225	225
Deduct W/out Air Conditioning			250	250	250
Deduct W/out Automatic Trans.			175	175	175
Deduct W/out Cruise Control			25	25	25
Deduct W/out Power Windows			25	25	25
1997 COUGAR-V6					
Veh. Ident.: ()M()()M62()()V()000001 Up.					
Coupe 2D XR7	62	3528	2425	3675	4425
1997 COUGAR-V8					
Veh. Ident.: ()M()()M62()()V()000001 Up.					
Coupe 2D XR7	62	3666	2675	3950	4750
COUGAR OPTIONS					
Add Leather Seats			150	175	175
Add Power Seat			50	75	75
Add Power Sunroof			200	225	225
Deduct W/out Cruise Control			50	50	50
1997 SABLE-V6					
Veh. Ident.: ()M()()M(Model)()()V()000001 Up.					
Sedan 4D GS	50	3333	2150	3375	4100
Sedan 4D LS	53	3360	2375	3625	4375
Wagon 4D GS	55	3476	2300	3550	4300
Wagon 4D LS	58	3502	2525	3800	4575
Add Leather Seats			150	175	175
Add Power Seat (Std. LS)			50	75	75
Add Power Sunroof			200	225	225
Deduct W/out Cruise Control			25	25	25
1997 GRAND MARQUIS-V8					
Veh. Ident.: ()M()()M(Model)()()V()000001 Up.					
Sedan 4D GS	74	3792	3975	5550	6500
Sedan 4D LS	75	3796	4450	6125	7100
Add Aluminum/Alloy Wheels			50	75	75
Add Leather Seats			200	225	225

BODY TYPE	Model No.	Weight	Trade-In	Retail	High Retail
MERCURY					
1996 TRACER-4 Cyl.					
Veh. Ident.: ()M()()M(Model)()()T()600001 Up.					
Sedan 4D	10	2409	**1175**	**2175**	**2700**
Sedan 4D LTS	14	2460	**1300**	**2325**	**2875**
Wagon 4D	15	2485	**1225**	**2225**	**2750**
Add Power Sunroof			**100**	**125**	**125**
Deduct W/out Air Conditioning			**75**	**75**	**75**
Deduct W/out Automatic Trans.			**75**	**75**	**75**
1996 MYSTIQUE-4 Cyl.					
Veh. Ident.: ()M()()M(Model)()()T()600001 Up.					
Sedan 4D GS	65	2833	**1375**	**2400**	**3000**
Sedan 4D LS	66	2855	**1475**	**2500**	**3100**
1996 MYSTIQUE-V6					
Veh. Ident.: ()M()()M(Model)()()T()600001 Up.					
Sedan 4D GS	65	2946	**1500**	**2550**	**3175**
Sedan 4D LS	66	2952	**1600**	**2650**	**3275**
MYSTIQUE OPTIONS					
Add Power Sunroof			**150**	**175**	**175**
Deduct W/out Air Conditioning			**150**	**150**	**150**
Deduct W/out Automatic Trans.			**125**	**125**	**125**
1996 COUGAR-V6					
Veh. Ident.: ()M()()M62()()T()600001 Up.					
Coupe 2D XR7	62	3559	**2100**	**3325**	**4025**
1996 COUGAR-V8					
Veh. Ident.: ()M()()M62()()T()600001 Up.					
Coupe 2D XR7	62	3687	**2325**	**3575**	**4325**
COUGAR OPTIONS					
Add Power Sunroof			**150**	**175**	**175**
1996 SABLE-V6					
Veh. Ident.: ()M()()M(Model)()()T()600001 Up.					
Sedan 4D G	51		**1625**	**2775**	**3425**
Sedan 4D GS	50	3358	**1700**	**2850**	**3525**
Sedan 4D LS	53	3359	**1875**	**3050**	**3725**
Wagon 4D GS	55	3502	**1800**	**2975**	**3650**
Wagon 4D LS	58	3525	**1975**	**3175**	**3875**
Add Power Sunroof			**150**	**175**	**175**
1996 GRAND MARQUIS-V8					
Veh. Ident.: ()M()()M(Model)()()T()600001 Up.					
Sedan 4D GS	74	3796	**3275**	**4775**	**5700**
Sedan 4D LS	75	3796	**3575**	**5100**	**6000**
MERCURY					
1995 TRACER-4 Cyl.					
Veh. Ident.: ()M()()M(Model)()()S()600001 Up.					
Sedan 4D	10	2418	**975**	**1925**	**2400**
Sedan 4D LTS	14	2472	**1100**	**2100**	**2625**
Wagon 4D	15	2498	**1000**	**1950**	**2425**
1995 MYSTIQUE-4 Cyl.					
Veh. Ident.: ()M()()M(Model)()()S()600001 Up.					
Sedan 4D GS	65	2824	**1075**	**2075**	**2625**
Sedan 4D LS	66	2873	**1175**	**2175**	**2750**

BODY TYPE	Model No.	Weight	Trade-In	Retail	High Retail
1995 MYSTIQUE-V6					
Veh. Ident.: ()M()()M(Model)()()S()600001 Up.					
Sedan 4D GS	65		**1200**	**2200**	**2775**
Sedan 4D LS	66	2959	**1300**	**2325**	**2900**
1995 COUGAR-V6					
Veh. Ident.: ()M()()M62()()S()600001 Up.					
Coupe 2D XR7	62	3533	**1700**	**2850**	**3525**
1995 COUGAR-V8					
Veh. Ident.: ()M()()M62()()S()600001 Up.					
Coupe 2D XR7	62	3673	**1875**	**3050**	**3725**
1995 SABLE-V6					
Veh. Ident.: ()M()()M(Model)()()S()600001 Up.					
Sedan 4D GS	50	3144	**1275**	**2375**	**2975**
Sedan 4D LS	53	3188	**1450**	**2575**	**3200**
Sedan 4D LTS	53	3188	**1475**	**2600**	**3225**
Wagon 4D GS	55	3292	**1375**	**2500**	**3100**
Wagon 4D LS	58	3336	**1550**	**2700**	**3350**
1995 GRAND MARQUIS-V8					
Veh. Ident.: ()M()()M(Model)()()S()600001 Up.					
Sedan 4D GS	74	3761	**2825**	**4225**	**5075**
Sedan 4D LS	75	3796	**3050**	**4525**	**5425**

MINI

BODY TYPE	Model No.	Weight	Trade-In	Retail	High Retail
MINI					
2004 COOPER-4 Cyl.-5 Spd.					
Veh. Ident.: WMW(Model)()4T000001 Up.					
Coupe 2D	RC334	2524	**17300**	**19750**	**20600**
Coupe 2D S (6 Spd.)	RE334	2678	**20625**	**23250**	**24175**
Add Automatic Trans.			**575**	**650**	**650**
Add Harman Kardon Stereo System			**300**	**350**	**350**
Add Leather Seats			**450**	**500**	**500**
Add Navigation System			**600**	**675**	**675**
Add Power Sunroof			**575**	**650**	**650**
Add Theft Recovery System			**100**	**125**	**125**
Deduct W/out Cruise Control			**200**	**200**	**200**
MINI					
2003 COOPER-4 Cyl.-5 Spd.					
Veh. Ident.: WMW(Model)()3T()()0001 Up.					
Coupe 2D	RC334	2524	**15750**	**18100**	**18925**
Coupe 2D S (6 Spd.)	RE334	2678	**18825**	**21350**	**22250**
Add Automatic Trans.			**525**	**600**	**600**
Add Harman Kardon Stereo System			**250**	**300**	**300**
Add Leather Seats			**400**	**450**	**450**
Add Navigation System			**500**	**575**	**575**
Add Power Sunroof			**525**	**600**	**600**
Add Theft Recovery System			**75**	**100**	**100**
Deduct W/out Cruise Control			**175**	**175**	**175**

PASSENGER CARS

BODY TYPE	Model No.	Weight	Trade-In	Retail	High Retail
MINI					
2002 COOPER-4 Cyl.-5 Spd.					
Veh. Ident.: WMW(Model)()2T()()0001 Up.					
Coupe 2D	RC334	2524	**14325**	**16600**	**17425**
Coupe 2D S (6 Spd.)	RE334	2679	**17250**	**19675**	**20525**
Add Automatic Trans.			**475**	**550**	**550**
Add Harman Kardon Stereo System			**200**	**225**	**225**
Add Leather Seats			**350**	**400**	**400**
Add Navigation System			**400**	**450**	**450**
Add Power Sunroof			**475**	**550**	**550**
Add Theft Recovery System			**75**	**100**	**100**
Deduct W/out Cruise Control			**150**	**150**	**150**

MITSUBISHI

BODY TYPE	Model No.	Weight	Trade-In	Retail	High Retail
MITSUBISHI					
2004 LANCER-4 Cyl.					
Veh. Ident.: JA3A(Model)()()4()000001 Up.					
Sedan 4D ES	J26	2656	**9125**	**11050**	**11775**
Sedan 4D LS	J36	2795	**9925**	**11900**	**12650**
Sedan 4D O-Z Rally	J86	2700	**10600**	**12650**	**13375**
Sedan 4D Ralliart	J66	2483	**11625**	**13750**	**14500**
Evolution RS (5 Spd., AWD)	H36	3175	**23450**	**26300**	**27275**
Evolution (5 Spd., AWD)	H86	3263	**24675**	**27600**	**28575**
Wagon Sportback LS	D29	3020	**10300**	**12325**	**13050**
Wagon Sportback Ralliart	D69	3042	**11875**	**14025**	**14800**
Add Aluminum/Alloy Wheels (ES, LS)			**300**	**350**	**350**
Add Cruise Control (Sportback LS)			**175**	**200**	**200**
Add Infinity Stereo System			**250**	**300**	**300**
Add Leather Seats			**350**	**400**	**400**
Add Power Sunroof (Std. Sedan LS)			**525**	**600**	**600**
Add Theft Recovery System			**100**	**125**	**125**
Deduct W/out AT (Ex. Evolution)			**475**	**475**	**475**
2004 GALANT-4 Cyl.					
Veh. Ident.: 4A3A(Model)()4E000001 Up.					
Sedan 4D DE	B26F	3351	**12200**	**14550**	**15525**
Sedan 4D ES	B()6F	3351	**12500**	**14850**	**15825**
Sedan 4D LS (V6)	B()6S	3560	**14350**	**16800**	**17850**
Sedan 4D GTS (V6)	B76S	3649	**16700**	**19300**	**20400**
2004 ECLIPSE-4 Cyl.					
Veh. Ident.: 4A3A(Model)()4E000001 Up.					
Coupe 2D RS	C34G	2910	**11450**	**13675**	**14625**
Coupe 2D GS	C44G	2965	**11875**	**14125**	**15075**
Coupe 2D GT (V6)	C84H	3142	**13775**	**16200**	**17225**
Coupe 2D GTS (V6)	C74H	3241	**15275**	**17775**	**18825**
Convertible 2D GS Spyder	E45G	3097	**15200**	**17700**	**18750**
Convertible 2D GT Spyder (V6)	E55H	3296	**16800**	**19425**	**20525**
Convertible GTS Spyder (V6)	E75H	3329			
GALANT/ECLIPSE OPTIONS					
Add A/A Wheels (Std. Galant GTS, Eclipse)			**325**	**375**	**375**
Add Infinity Stereo (Std. GTS, Spyder)			**300**	**350**	**350**
Add Leather Seats (Std. GTS)			**450**	**500**	**500**

BODY TYPE	Model No.	Weight	Trade-In	Retail	High Retail
Add Power Seat (Std. GTS)			200	225	225
Add Power Sunroof (Std. GTS)			575	650	650
Add Theft Recovery System			100	125	125
Deduct W/out Automatic Trans.			575	575	575
2004 DIAMANTE-V6					
Veh. Ident.: 6MMA(Model)P()4T000001 Up.					
Sedan 4D ES	P57	3505	13600	16075	17275
Sedan 4D VR-X	P87	3560	15225	17800	19025
Sedan 4D LS	P67	3582	15150	17725	18950
Add Leather Seats (Std. LS)			525	600	600
Add Theft Recovery System			100	125	125
MITSUBISHI					
2003 LANCER-4 Cyl.					
Veh. Ident.: JA3A(Model)E()3()000001 Up.					
Sedan 4D ES	J26	2646	7525	9225	9925
Sedan 4D LS	J36	2734	8225	10025	10750
Sedan 4D O-Z Rally	J86	2701	8875	10725	11475
Evolution (5 Spd., AWD)	H86	3263	22375	25175	26125
Add Power Sunroof			475	550	550
Add Theft Recovery System			75	100	100
Deduct W/out AT (Ex. Evolution)			425	425	425
2003 GALANT-4 Cyl.					
Veh. Ident.: 4A3A(Model)()3E000001 Up.					
Sedan 4D DE	A36G	3031	8350	10250	11175
Sedan 4D ES	A46G	3075	8625	10525	11475
Sedan 4D ES (V6)	A46H	3252	10225	12350	13250
Sedan 4D LS	A46G	3108	9650	11700	12600
Sedan 4D LS (V6)	A46H	3274	11250	13450	14375
Sedan 4D GTZ (V6)	A46H	3296	12025	14300	15275
2003 ECLIPSE-4 Cyl.					
Veh. Ident.: 4A3A(Model)()3E000001 Up.					
Coupe 2D RS	C34G	2910	9875	11925	12850
Coupe 2D GS	C44G	2965	10250	12375	13275
Coupe 2D GT (V6)	C84H	3142	11950	14225	15175
Coupe 2D GTS (V6)	C74H	3241	13275	15675	16675
Convertible 2D GS Spyder	E45G	3097	13375	15775	16800
Convertible 2D GT Spyder (V6)	E55H	3296	14875	17375	18400
Convertible GTS Spyder (V6)	E75H	3329	15450	17975	19025
GALANT/ECLIPSE OPTIONS					
Add A/A Wheels (Std. Galant LS/GTZ, Eclipse)			275	325	325
Add Infinity (Std. Galant LS/GTZ, GTS, Spyder)			250	300	300
Add Leather Seats (Std. Galant GTZ, GTS)			400	450	450
Add Power Seat (Std. Galant GTZ, GTS)			175	200	200
Add Power Sunroof (Std. Galant LS/GTZ, GTS)			525	600	600
Add Theft Recovery System			75	100	100
Deduct W/out Automatic Trans.			525	525	525
2003 DIAMANTE-V6					
Veh. Ident.: 6MMA(Model)P()3T000001 Up.					
Sedan 4D ES	P57	3439	11550	13850	14975
Sedan 4D VR-X	P87	3549	13200	15650	16850
Sedan 4D LS	P67	3549	13525	16000	17200
Add Infinity Stereo System (Std. LS)			300	350	350

BODY TYPE	Model No.	Weight	Trade-In	Retail	High Retail
Add Leather Seats (Std. LS)			475	550	550
Add Theft Recovery System			75	100	100
MITSUBISHI					
2002 MIRAGE-4 Cyl.					
Veh. Ident.: JA3A(Model)()()2()000001 Up.					
Coupe 2D DE	Y11	2183	4475	5875	6675
Coupe 2D LS	Y31	2293	5175	6650	7475
2002 LANCER-4 Cyl.					
Veh. Ident.: JA3A(Model)E()2()000001 Up.					
Sedan 4D ES	J26	2646	6175	7725	8550
Sedan 4D LS	J36	2734	6750	8350	9100
Sedan 4D O-Z Rally	J86	2701	7250	8925	9700
MIRAGE/LANCER OPTIONS					
Add Aluminum/Alloy Wheels (Std. Lancer LS/O-Z)			200	225	225
Add Compact Disc Player (Coupe DE)			75	100	100
Add Power Door Locks (Coupe DE)			100	125	125
Add Power Sunroof			425	475	475
Add Power Windows (Coupe DE)			125	150	150
Add Theft Recovery System			75	100	100
Deduct W/out Air Conditioning			475	475	475
Deduct W/out Automatic Trans.			375	375	375
2002 GALANT-4 Cyl.					
Veh. Ident.: 4A3A(Model)()2E000001 Up.					
Sedan 4D DE	A36G	3031	6825	8575	9450
Sedan 4D ES	A46G	3075	7075	8850	9750
Sedan 4D ES (V6)	A46H	3252	8475	10375	11300
Sedan 4D LS	A46G	3108	7950	9800	10700
Sedan 4D LS (V6)	A46H	3274	9350	11375	12275
Sedan 4D GTZ (V6)	A46H	3296	10050	12125	13000
2002 ECLIPSE-4 Cyl.					
Veh. Ident.: 4A3A(Model)()2E000001 Up.					
Coupe 2D RS	C34G	2855	8650	10575	11525
Coupe 2D GS	C44G	2944	8975	10925	11875
Coupe 2D GT (V6)	C()4H	3120	10475	12625	13525
Convertible 2D GS Spyder	E45G	3042	11900	14150	15100
Convertible 2D GT Spyder (V6)	E85H	3241	13300	15700	16700
GALANT/ECLIPSE OPTIONS					
Add A/A Wheels (Std. Galant LS/GTZ, Eclipse)			225	250	250
Add Infinity (Std. Galant LS/GTZ, Spyder)			200	225	225
Add Leather Seats (Std. Galant GTZ)			350	400	400
Add Power Seat (Std. Galant GTZ)			150	175	175
Add Power Sunroof (Std. Galant LS/GTZ)			475	550	550
Add Theft Recovery System			75	100	100
Deduct W/out Automatic Trans.			475	475	475
2002 DIAMANTE-V6					
Veh. Ident.: 6MMA(Model)P()2T000001 Up.					
Sedan 4D ES	P57	3439	9950	12125	13175
Sedan 4D VR-X	P87	3549	11300	13600	14700
Sedan 4D LS	P67	3549	11700	14025	15150
Add Infinity Stereo System (Std. LS)			250	300	300
Add Power Sunroof (Std. LS)			525	600	600
Add Theft Recovery System			75	100	100

PASSENGER CARS

BODY TYPE	Model No.	Weight	Trade-In	Retail	High Retail
MITSUBISHI					
2001 MIRAGE-4 Cyl.					
Veh. Ident.: JA3A(Model)()()1()000001 Up.					
Coupe 2D DE	Y11	2183	3550	4825	5625
Coupe 2D LS	Y31	2293	4100	5450	6200
Sedan 4D ES	Y26	2437	3950	5275	6000
Sedan 4D LS	Y36	2459	4325	5700	6475
Add Aluminum/Alloy Wheels			150	175	175
Add Compact Disc Player (Coupe DE)			50	75	75
Add Power Door Locks (Std. LS)			75	100	100
Add Power Sunroof			375	425	425
Add Power Windows (Std. LS)			100	125	125
Add Theft Recovery System			50	75	75
Deduct W/out Air Conditioning			425	425	425
Deduct W/out Automatic Trans.			325	325	325
2001 GALANT-4 Cyl.					
Veh. Ident.: 4A3A(Model)()1E000001 Up.					
Sedan 4D DE	A36G	3031	5575	7225	8100
Sedan 4D ES	A46G	3075	5800	7475	8375
Sedan 4D ES (V6)	A46H	3252	7000	8775	9675
Sedan 4D LS (V6)	A56H	3296	8150	10025	10950
Sedan 4D GTZ (V6)	A46H	3296	8350	10250	11175
2001 ECLIPSE-4 Cyl.					
Veh. Ident.: 4A3A(Model)()1E000001 Up.					
Coupe 2D RS	C34G	2822	7225	9025	9875
Coupe 2D GS	C44G	2910	7500	9300	10175
Coupe 2D GT (V6)	C()4H	3053	8800	10725	11675
Convertible 2D GS Spyder	E()5G	3042	10100	12225	13125
Convertible 2D GT Spyder (V6)	E()5H	3241	11400	13600	14550
GALANT/ECLIPSE OPTIONS					
Add A/A Wheels (Std. Galant LS/GTZ, Eclipse)			175	200	200
Add Infinity Stereo System (Std. Galant LS/GTZ)			150	175	175
Add Leather Seats (Std. Galant LS/GTZ)			300	350	350
Add Power Seat (Std. Galant LS/GTZ)			125	150	150
Add Power Sunroof (Std. Galant LS/GTZ)			425	475	475
Add Theft Recovery System			50	75	75
Deduct W/out Automatic Trans.			425	425	425
2001 DIAMANTE-V6					
Veh. Ident.: 6MMA(Model)()()1T000001 Up.					
Sedan 4D ES	P57	3461	7550	9525	10550
Sedan 4D LS	P67	3549	9075	11200	12225
Add Theft Recovery System			50	75	75
MITSUBISHI					
2000 MIRAGE-4 Cyl.					
Veh. Ident.: JA3A(Model)()()Y()000001 Up.					
Coupe 2D DE	Y11	2183	2525	3700	4375
Coupe 2D LS	Y31	2293	3000	4225	4950
Sedan 4D DE	Y26	2437	3050	4275	5000
Sedan 4D LS	Y36	2503	3625	4900	5700
Add Aluminum/Alloy Wheels (Std. Sedan LS)			100	125	125
Add Compact Disc Player (Coupe DE)			50	75	75
Add Cruise Control (Std. LS)			75	100	100
Add Power Door Locks (Coupe DE)			50	75	75

PASSENGER CARS

BODY TYPE	Model No.	Weight	Trade-In	Retail	High Retail
Add Power Windows (Coupe DE)			75	100	100
Deduct W/out Air Conditioning			375	375	375
Deduct W/out Automatic Trans.			300	300	300
2000 GALANT-4 Cyl.					
Veh. Ident.: 4A3A(Model)()YE000001 Up.					
Sedan 4D DE	A36G	2976	4575	6075	6925
Sedan 4D ES	A46G	3075	4775	6300	7175
Sedan 4D ES (V6)	A46L	3252	5875	7550	8450
Sedan 4D LS (V6)	A56L	3296	6800	8550	9425
Sedan 4D GTZ (V6)	A46L	3263	7000	8775	9675
2000 ECLIPSE-4 Cyl.					
Veh. Ident.: 4A3A(Model)()YE000001 Up.					
Coupe 2D RS	C34G	2822	6050	7750	8675
Coupe 2D GS	C44G	2910	6275	8000	8925
Coupe 2D GT (V6)	C()4L	3053	7375	9175	10050
GALANT/ECLIPSE OPTIONS					
Add A/A Wheels (Std. Galant LS/GTZ, Eclipse)			125	150	150
Add Infinity Stereo System (Std. Galant LS/GTZ)			100	125	125
Add Leather Seats (Std. Galant LS/GTZ)			250	300	300
Add Power Seat (Std. Galant LS/GTZ)			100	125	125
Add Power Sunroof (Std. Galant LS/GTZ)			375	425	425
Deduct W/out Automatic Trans.			375	375	375
2000 DIAMANTE-V6					
Veh. Ident.: 6MMA(Model)()()Y()000001 Up.					
Sedan 4D ES	P57	3443	5925	7775	8825
Sedan 4D LS	P67	3531	7225	9200	10200
MITSUBISHI					
1999 MIRAGE-4 Cyl.					
Veh. Ident.: JA3A(Model)()()X()000001 Up.					
Coupe 2D DE	Y11	2150	2175	3300	3925
Coupe 2D LS	Y31	2280	2425	3575	4250
Sedan 4D DE	Y26	2250	2375	3525	4175
Sedan 4D LS	Y36	2370	2575	3750	4425
Add Aluminum/Alloy Wheels (Std. Coupe LS)			50	75	75
Add Cruise Control			50	75	75
Add Power Sunroof			275	325	325
Add Power Windows			50	75	75
Deduct W/out Air Conditioning			325	325	325
Deduct W/out Automatic Trans.			250	250	250
1999 GALANT-4 Cyl.					
Veh. Ident.: 4A3A(Model)()XE000001 Up.					
Sedan 4D DE	A36G	2835	3675	5100	5900
Sedan 4D DE (V6)	A36L	2999	4575	6100	6950
Sedan 4D ES	A46G	2935	3850	5300	6125
Sedan 4D ES (V6)	A46L	3140	4750	6275	7150
Sedan 4D LS (V6)	A56L	3185	5500	7150	8025
Sedan 4D GTZ (V6)	A46L	3165	5700	7350	8250
1999 ECLIPSE-4 Cyl.					
Veh. Ident.: 4A3A(Model)()()XE000001 Up.					
Coupe 2D RS	K34	2754	4775	6325	7200
Coupe 2D GS	K44	2855	5775	7450	8350
Coupe 2D GS-T	K54	2970	7325	9125	10000
Coupe 2D GSX Turbo (AWD)	L54	3270	9225	11250	12125

BODY TYPE	Model No.	Weight	Trade-In	Retail	High Retail
Convertible 2D GS Spyder	X35	2888	7250	9050	9900
Convertible 2D GS-T Spyder	X55	3053	8800	10725	11675
GALANT/ECLIPSE OPTIONS					
Add Aluminum/Alloy Wheels (Std. Galant LS/GTZ, Eclipse GS-T/GSX, Spyder)			75	100	100
Add Leather Seats (Std. Galant LS/GTZ, Eclipse GSX/GS-T Spyder)			225	250	250
Add Power Sunroof (Std. Galant LS/GTZ, Eclipse GS-T/GSX)			325	375	375
Deduct W/out Air Conditioning			450	450	450
Deduct W/out Automatic Trans.			325	325	325
Deduct W/out Cruise Control (Ex. Galant)			75	75	75
Deduct W/out Power Door Locks			50	50	50
Deduct W/out Power Windows			75	75	75
1999 DIAMANTE-V6					
Veh. Ident.: 6MMAP()7P()XT000001 Up.					
Sedan 4D	P()7	3440	5550	7350	8375
1999 3000GT-V6-5/6 Spd./AT					
Veh. Ident.: JA3A(Model)()()X()000001 Up.					
Coupe 2D	M44	3131	10000	11975	13025
Coupe 2D SL	M84	3263	14550	16825	18050
Coupe VR-4 Turbo (AWD)	N74	3737	20075	22675	24025
DIAMANTE/3000GT OPTIONS					
Add Aluminum/Alloy Wheels (Std. 3000GT)			125	150	150
Add Infinity Stereo System (Std. 3000GT SL/VR-4)			100	125	125
Add Leather Seats (Std. 3000GT SL/VR-4)			275	325	325
Add Power Sunroof (Std. 3000GT SL/VR-4)			375	425	425
Deduct W/out Power Seat (Ex. 3000GT)			100	100	100
MITSUBISHI					
1998 MIRAGE-4 Cyl.					
Veh. Ident.: JA3A(Model)()()W()000001 Up.					
Coupe 2D DE	Y11	2125	1700	2750	3350
Coupe 2D LS	Y31	2260	1950	3050	3650
Sedan 4D DE	Y26	2225	1900	2975	3625
Sedan 4D LS	Y36	2350	2100	3225	3850
Add Cruise Control			50	75	75
Add Power Sunroof			225	275	275
Add Power Windows			50	75	75
Deduct W/out Air Conditioning			275	275	275
Deduct W/out Automatic Trans.			200	200	200
1998 GALANT-4 Cyl.					
Veh. Ident.: 4A3A(Model)G()WE000001 Up.					
Sedan 4D DE	J46	2778	2375	3625	4375
Sedan 4D ES	J56	2877	2500	3750	4525
Sedan 4D LS	J56	2998	3075	4425	5275
1998 ECLIPSE-4 Cyl.					
Veh. Ident.: 4A3A(Model)()()WE000001 Up.					
Coupe 2D RS	K34	2754	3975	5425	6250
Coupe 2D GS	K44	2842	4775	6300	7175
Coupe 2D GS-T	K54	2921	5900	7575	8475
Coupe 2D GSX Turbo (AWD)	L54	3157	7775	9600	10500
Convertible 2D GS Spyder	X35	2888	6150	7850	8775
Convertible 2D GS-T Spyder	X55	3053	7500	9300	10175

PASSENGER CARS

P A S S E N G E R C A R S

BODY TYPE	Model No.	Weight	Trade-In	Retail	High Retail
GALANT/ECLIPSE OPTIONS					
Add Aluminum/Alloy Wheels (Std. Galant LS, Eclipse GS-T/GSX, Spyder)			50	75	75
Add Leather Seats (Std. Galant LS, Eclipse GSX/GS-T Spyder)			175	200	200
Add Power Sunroof (Std. Galant LS, Eclipse GSX)			275	325	325
Deduct W/out Air Conditioning			400	400	400
Deduct W/out Automatic Trans.			275	275	275
Deduct W/out Cruise Control (Ex. Galant)			50	50	50
Deduct W/out Power Windows (Ex. Galant)			50	50	50
1998 DIAMANTE-V6					
Veh. Ident.: 6MMA(Model)P()WT000001 Up.					
Sedan 4D ES	P37	3417	4475	6150	7125
Sedan 4D LS	P()7	3494	5225	7000	8050
1998 3000GT-V6-5/6 Spd./AT					
Veh. Ident.: JA3A(Model)()()W()000001 Up.					
Coupe 2D	M44	3131	8575	10425	11450
Coupe 2D SL	M84	3263	12025	14175	15300
Coupe VR-4 Turbo (AWD)	N74	3737	16975	19400	20700
DIAMANTE/3000GT OPTIONS					
Add Aluminum/Alloy Wheels (Std. Diamante LS, 3000GT)			100	125	125
Add Leather Seats (Std. Diamante LS, 3000GT SL/VR-4).			225	250	250
Add Power Sunroof (Std. Diamante LS, 3000GT SL/VR-4).			325	375	375
Deduct W/out Power Seat (Ex. 3000GT)			75	75	75
MITSUBISHI					
1997 MIRAGE-4 Cyl.					
Veh. Ident.: JA3A(Model)()()V()000001 Up.					
Coupe 2D DE	Y11	2127	1325	2350	2900
Coupe 2D LS	Y31	2260	1550	2600	3200
Sedan 4D DE	Y26	2227	1450	2475	3050
Sedan 4D LS	Y36	2348	1650	2700	3300
Add Power Sunroof			150	175	175
Deduct W/out Air Conditioning			150	150	150
Deduct W/out Automatic Trans.			125	125	125
1997 GALANT-4 Cyl.					
Veh. Ident.: 4A3A(Model)G()VE000001 Up.					
Sedan 4D DE	J46	2777	1750	2925	3600
Sedan 4D ES	J56	2943	1875	3050	3725
Sedan 4D LS	J56	2998	2325	3575	4325
1997 ECLIPSE-4 Cyl.					
Veh. Ident.: 4A3A(Model)()()VE000001 Up.					
Coupe 2D	K24	2725	2775	4075	4875
Coupe 2D RS	K34	2767	2875	4175	4975
Coupe 2D GS	K44	2855	3400	4800	5675
Coupe 2D GS-T	K54	2899	4375	5875	6750
Coupe 2D GSX Turbo (AWD)	L54	3130	5375	7000	7950
Convertible 2D GS Spyder	X35	2888	4500	6000	6875
Convertible 2D GS-T Spyder	X55	3053	5375	7000	7950

BODY TYPE	Model No.	Weight	Trade-In	Retail	High Retail
GALANT/ECLIPSE OPTIONS					
Add Leather Seats (Std. Galant LS, Eclipse GS-T Spyder)			150	175	175
Add Power Sunroof (Std. Galant LS)			200	225	225
Deduct W/out Air Conditioning			250	250	250
Deduct W/out Automatic Trans.			175	175	175
Deduct W/out Cruise Control (Ex. Galant)			50	50	50
Deduct W/out Power Windows (Ex. Galant)			50	50	50
1997 DIAMANTE-V6					
Veh. Ident.: 6MMA(Model)P()VT000001 Up.					
Sedan 4D ES	P37	3363	3200	4700	5625
Sedan 4D LS	P()7	3385	3500	5025	5925
1997 3000GT-V6-5/6 Spd./AT					
Veh. Ident.: JA3A(Model)()()V()000001 Up.					
Coupe 2D	M44	3131	6550	8150	9150
Coupe 2D SL	M84	3263	8650	10500	11550
Coupe VR-4 Turbo (AWD)	N74	3737	13800	16050	17250
DIAMANTE/3000GT OPTIONS					
Add Aluminum/Alloy Wheels (Std. Diamante LS, 3000GT)			50	75	75
Add Leather Seats (Std. Diamante LS, 3000GT SL/VR-4).			200	225	225
Add Power Sunroof			250	300	300
Deduct W/out Power Seat (Ex. 3000GT)			75	75	75
MITSUBISHI					
1996 MIRAGE-4 Cyl.					
Veh. Ident.: JA3()(Model)()()T()000001 Up.					
Coupe 2D S	A11	2085	975	1925	2400
Coupe 2D LS	A31	2250	1075	2075	2600
Sedan 4D S	A26	2225	1100	2100	2625
Deduct W/out Air Conditioning			100	100	100
Deduct W/out Automatic Trans.			100	100	100
1996 GALANT-4 Cyl.					
Veh. Ident.: 4A3()(Model)()()T()000001 Up.					
Sedan 4D S	J46	2755	1425	2550	3175
Sedan 4D ES	J56	2866	1550	2700	3350
Sedan 4D LS	J56	2976	1825	3000	3675
1996 ECLIPSE-4 Cyl.					
Veh. Ident.: 4A3()(Model)()()T()000001 Up.					
Coupe 2D RS	K34	2767	2375	3625	4375
Coupe 2D GS	K44	2855	2825	4125	4925
Coupe 2D GS-T	K54	2899	3650	5075	5875
Coupe 2D GSX Turbo (AWD)	L54	3130	4450	5950	6825
Convertible 2D GS Spyder	X35	2833	3900	5350	6175
Convertible 2D GS-T Spyder	X55	3530	4650	6175	7050
GALANT/ECLIPSE OPTIONS					
Add Power Sunroof (Std. Galant LS)			150	175	175
Deduct W/out Air Conditioning			150	150	150
Deduct W/out Automatic Trans.			125	125	125
1996 DIAMANTE-V6					
Veh. Ident.: JA3()P47()()T()000001 Up.					
Sedan 4D ES	P47	3483	2625	4000	4900

PASSENGER CARS

PASSENGER CARS

BODY TYPE	Model No.	Weight	Trade-In	Retail	High Retail
1996 3000GT-V6-5/6 Spd./AT					
Veh. Ident.: JA3()(Model)()()T()000001 Up.					
Coupe 2D	M84	3252	**5550**	**7075**	**8075**
Coupe 2D SL	M54	3329	**7250**	**8925**	**9975**
Coupe 2D VR-4 Turbo (AWD)	N74	3759	**11475**	**13600**	**14700**
Spyder 2D SL	V65	3781	**16300**	**18700**	**19975**
Spyder 2D VR-4 Turbo (AWD)	W75	4123	**20725**	**23350**	**24725**
DIAMANTE/3000GT OPTIONS					
Add Power Sunroof			**200**	**225**	**225**
MITSUBISHI					
1995 MIRAGE-4 Cyl.					
Veh. Ident.: JA3()(Model)()()S()000001 Up.					
Coupe 2D S	A11	2105	**850**	**1775**	**2225**
Coupe 2D ES	A21	2140	**875**	**1800**	**2250**
Coupe 2D LS	A31	2160	**950**	**1900**	**2375**
Sedan 4D S	A26	2225	**975**	**1925**	**2400**
Sedan 4D ES	A36	2295	**1000**	**1950**	**2425**
1995 EXPO-4 Cyl.					
Veh. Ident.: JA4()(Model)()()S()000001 Up.					
Wagon 4D	D59	3064	**1300**	**2325**	**2875**
Wagon 4D (AWD)	E59	3285	**1550**	**2600**	**3200**
1995 GALANT-4 Cyl.					
Veh. Ident.: 4A3()(Model)()()SE000001 Up.					
Sedan 4D S	J46	2822	**1225**	**2325**	**2900**
Sedan 4D ES	J56	2866	**1350**	**2475**	**3075**
Sedan 4D LS	J56	2976	**1450**	**2575**	**3200**
1995 ECLIPSE-4 Cyl.					
Veh. Ident.: 4A3()(Model)()()SE000001 Up.					
Coupe 2D RS	K34	2800	**2025**	**3225**	**3925**
Coupe 2D GS	K44	2899	**2425**	**3675**	**4425**
Coupe 2D GS Turbo	K54	2954	**3225**	**4600**	**5450**
Coupe 2D GSX Turbo (AWD)	L54	3197	**3825**	**5250**	**6050**
1995 DIAMANTE-V6					
Veh. Ident.: ()()()A(Model)()()S()000001 Up.					
Sedan 4D ES	P47	3483	**1975**	**3250**	**4025**
Sedan 4D LS	P57	3605	**2125**	**3425**	**4225**
Station Wagon 4D ES	P49	3638	**1775**	**3025**	**3775**
1995 3000GT-V6					
Veh. Ident.: JA3()(Model)()()S()000001 Up.					
Coupe 2D	M84	3390	**4725**	**6150**	**7125**
Coupe 2D SL	M54	3439	**6125**	**7675**	**8725**
Coupe VR-4 Turbo (AWD)	N74	3781	**9800**	**11775**	**12825**
Spyder 2D SL	V65	3719	**14625**	**16925**	**18175**
Spyder 2D VR-4 Turbo (AWD)	W75	3781	**18900**	**21425**	**22775**

NISSAN

BODY TYPE	Model No.	Weight	Trade-In	Retail	High Retail
NISSAN					
2004 SENTRA-4 Cyl.					
Veh. Ident.: 3N1(Model)()()4L000001 Up.					
Sedan 4D 1.8	CB51	2513	**9350**	**11275**	**12000**
Sedan 4D 1.8 S	CB51	2580	**9775**	**11750**	**12500**

BODY TYPE	Model No.	Weight	Trade-In	Retail	High Retail
Sedan 4D 2.5 S	AB51	2763	**10900**	**12975**	**13700**
Sedan 4D SE-R	AB51	2714	**12075**	**14225**	**15000**
Sedan SE-R Spec V (6 Spd.)	AB51	2710	**12475**	**14625**	**15400**
Add Aluminum/Alloy Wheels (Std. 2.5, SE-R)			**300**	**350**	**350**
Add Compact Disc Player (1.8 Base)			**100**	**125**	**125**
Add Cruise Control (Std. 2.5, SE-R)			**175**	**200**	**200**
Add Power Sunroof			**525**	**600**	**600**
Add Rockford Fosgate Stereo			**250**	**300**	**300**
Add Theft Recovery System			**100**	**125**	**125**
Deduct W/out Air Conditioning			**575**	**575**	**575**
Deduct W/out Automatic Trans. (Ex. Spec V)			**475**	**475**	**475**
2004 ALTIMA-4 Cyl.					
Veh. Ident.: 1N4(Model)()()4C000001 Up.					
Sedan 4D	AL11	3001	**13950**	**16375**	**17400**
Sedan 4D S	AL11	3039	**14525**	**17000**	**18050**
Sedan 4D SL	AL11	3106	**15800**	**18325**	**19375**
Sedan 4D SE (V6)	BL11	3197	**17650**	**20400**	**21525**
Add Aluminum/Alloy Wheels (Std. SL, SE)			**325**	**375**	**375**
Add Bose Stereo System (Std. SL)			**300**	**350**	**350**
Add Leather Seats (Std. SL)			**450**	**500**	**500**
Add Power Seat (Std. SL, SE)			**200**	**225**	**225**
Add Power Sunroof			**575**	**650**	**650**
Add Theft Recovery System			**100**	**125**	**125**
Deduct W/out Air Conditioning			**700**	**700**	**700**
Deduct W/out Automatic Trans.			**575**	**575**	**575**
2004 MAXIMA-V6					
Veh. Ident.: 1N4BA41E()4C000001 Up.					
Sedan 4D SE	A41	3432	**20925**	**23975**	**25350**
Sedan 4D SL	A41	3467	**22600**	**25925**	**27375**
2004 350Z-V6-6 Spd./AT					
Veh. Ident.: JN1(Model)()(4()000001 Up.					
Coupe 2D	AZ34	3188	**21750**	**24850**	**26250**
Coupe 2D Enthusiast	AZ34	3197	**22525**	**25850**	**27300**
Coupe 2D Performance	AZ34	3217	**23350**	**26725**	**28200**
Coupe 2D Touring	AZ34	3247	**24850**	**28300**	**29800**
Coupe 2D Track	AZ34	3225	**25900**	**29425**	**30950**
Roadster 2D Enthusiast	AZ36	3428	**26875**	**30475**	**32025**
Roadster 2D Touring	AZ36	3462	**28975**	**32750**	**34375**
MAXIMA/350Z OPTIONS					
Add Bose Stereo System (Std. SL, Touring)			**350**	**400**	**400**
Add Leather Seats (Std. SL, Touring)			**525**	**600**	**600**
Add Navigation System			**650**	**725**	**725**
Add Power Sunroof			**625**	**700**	**700**
Add Theft Recovery System			**100**	**125**	**125**
Deduct W/out Automatic Trans. (Ex. 350Z)			**625**	**625**	**625**
NISSAN					
2003 SENTRA-4 Cyl.					
Veh. Ident.: 3N1(Model)()()3L000001 Up.					
Sedan 4D XE	CB51	2513	**8300**	**10125**	**10850**
Sedan 4D GXE	CB51	2581	**8575**	**10400**	**11125**
Sedan 4D Limited Edition	AB51	2764	**9525**	**11475**	**12200**
Sedan 4D SE-R	AB51	2712	**10600**	**12650**	**13375**
Sedan SE-R Spec V (6 Spd.)	AB51	2708	**10950**	**13025**	**13775**

BODY TYPE	Model No.	Weight	Trade-In	Retail	High Retail
Add Aluminum/Alloy Wheels (Std. Ltd. Ed., SE-R)			250	300	300
Add Cruise Control (Std. Ltd. Ed., SE-R)			150	175	175
Add Power Sunroof			475	550	550
Add Rockford Fosgate Stereo			200	225	225
Add Theft Recovery System			75	100	100
Deduct W/out Automatic Trans. (Ex. Spec V)			425	425	425
2003 ALTIMA-4 Cyl.					
Veh. Ident.: 1N4(Model)()()3C000001 Up.					
Sedan 4D	AL11	2983	12825	15200	16200
Sedan 4D S	AL11	3020	13250	15650	16650
Sedan 4D SL	AL11	3106	14350	16800	17850
Sedan 4D SE (V6)	BL11	3197	16000	18550	19625
Add Aluminum/Alloy Wheels (Std. SL, SE)			275	325	325
Add Bose Stereo System (Std. SL)			250	300	300
Add Leather Seats (Std. SL)			400	450	450
Add Power Seat (Std. SL, SE)			175	200	200
Add Power Sunroof			525	600	600
Add Theft Recovery System			75	100	100
Deduct W/out Air Conditioning			650	650	650
Deduct W/out Automatic Trans.			525	525	525
2003 MAXIMA-V6					
Veh. Ident.: JN1DA31()()3T000001 Up.					
Sedan 4D GXE	A31	3233	13950	16425	17650
Sedan 4D SE	A31	3239	15475	18050	19300
Sedan 4D GLE	A31	3289	16050	18650	19925
2003 350Z-V6-6 Spd./AT					
Veh. Ident.: JN1AZ34()()3T000001 Up.					
Coupe 2D	AZ34	3188	19050	22000	23375
Coupe 2D Enthusiast	AZ34	3197	19725	22700	24050
Coupe 2D Performance	AZ34	3217	20500	23525	24900
Coupe 2D Touring	AZ34	3247	21875	25000	26400
Coupe 2D Track	AZ34	3225	22900	26225	27675
MAXIMA/350Z OPTIONS					
Add Bose Stereo System (Std. GLE, Touring)			300	350	350
Add Leather Seats (Std. GLE, Touring)			475	550	550
Add Navigation System			550	625	625
Add Power Sunroof			575	650	650
Add Theft Recovery System			75	100	100
Deduct W/out Automatic Trans. (Ex. 350Z)			575	575	575
NISSAN					
2002 SENTRA-4 Cyl.					
Veh. Ident.: 3N1(Model)()()2()000001 Up.					
Sedan 4D XE	CB51	2548	6875	8475	9225
Sedan 4D GXE	CB51	2593	7175	8850	9625
Sedan 4D SE-R	AB51	2731	8925	10775	11525
Sedan SE-R Spec V (6 Spd.)	AB51	2771	9225	11150	11875
Add Aluminum/Alloy Wheels (Std. SE-R)			200	225	225
Add Compact Disc Player (Std. GXE, SE-R)			75	100	100
Add Cruise Control (Std. SE-R)			125	150	150
Add Power Sunroof			425	475	475
Add Rockford Fosgate Stereo			150	175	175
Add Theft Recovery System			75	100	100
Deduct W/out Air Conditioning			475	475	475

BODY TYPE	Model No.	Weight	Trade-In	Retail	High Retail
Deduct W/out Automatic Trans. (Ex. Spec V)			375	375	375
2002 ALTIMA-4 Cyl.					
Veh. Ident.: 1N4(Model)()()2C000001 Up.					
Sedan 4D	AL11	2983	11775	14025	14975
Sedan 4D S	AL11	3020	12050	14375	15350
Sedan 4D SL	AL11	3028	12975	15350	16350
Sedan 4D SE (V6)	BL11	3178	14425	16900	17950
Add Aluminum/Alloy Wheels (Std. SL, SE)			225	250	250
Add Bose Stereo System (Std. SL)			200	225	225
Add Leather Seats (Std. SL)			350	400	400
Add Power Seat (Std. SL, SE)			150	175	175
Add Power Sunroof			475	550	550
Add Theft Recovery System			75	100	100
Deduct W/out Air Conditioning			600	600	600
Deduct W/out Automatic Trans.			475	475	475
2002 MAXIMA-V6					
Veh. Ident.: JN1DA31()()2()000001 Up.					
Sedan 4D GXE	A31	3218	12375	14750	15900
Sedan 4D SE	A31	3224	13775	16250	17450
Sedan 4D GLE	A31	3275	14225	16725	17950
Add Bose Stereo System (Std. GLE)			250	300	300
Add Leather Seats (Std. GLE)			425	475	475
Add Navigation System			450	500	500
Add Power Sunroof			525	600	600
Add Theft Recovery System			75	100	100
Deduct W/out Automatic Trans.			525	525	525
NISSAN					
2001 SENTRA-4 Cyl.					
Veh. Ident.: 3N1(Model)()()1()000001 Up.					
Sedan 4D XE	CB51	2548	5625	7150	7925
Sedan 4D GXE	CB51	2593	5950	7500	8300
Sedan 4D SE	BB51	2674	6500	8075	8825
Add Aluminum/Alloy Wheels (Std. SE)			150	175	175
Add Compact Disc Player (Std. GXE, SE)			50	75	75
Add Power Sunroof			375	425	425
Add Theft Recovery System			50	75	75
Deduct W/out Air Conditioning			425	425	425
Deduct W/out Automatic Trans.			325	325	325
2001 ALTIMA-4 Cyl.					
Veh. Ident.: 1N4DL01()()1()000001 Up.					
Sedan 4D XE	L01	2851	7875	9700	10600
Sedan 4D GXE	L01	2945	8000	9850	10750
Sedan 4D SE	L01	2962	8625	10525	11475
Sedan 4D GLE	L01	3057	8950	10900	11850
Add Aluminum/Alloy Wheels (Std. SE, GLE)			175	200	200
Add Compact Disc Player (Std. SE, GLE)			50	75	75
Add Leather Seats (Std. GLE)			300	350	350
Add Power Seat (Std. GLE)			125	150	150
Add Power Sunroof			425	475	475
Add Theft Recovery System			50	75	75
Deduct W/out Air Conditioning			550	550	550
Deduct W/out Automatic Trans.			425	425	425

PASSENGER CARS

BODY TYPE	Model No.	Weight	Trade-In	Retail	High Retail
Deduct W/out Cruise Control			125	125	125
Deduct W/out Power Door Locks (Ex. XE)			100	100	100
2001 MAXIMA-V6					
Veh. Ident.: JN1CA31()()1()000001 Up.					
Sedan 4D GXE	A31	3186	10000	12175	13225
Sedan 4D SE	A31	3199	11625	13925	15050
Sedan 4D SE 20th Anniv	A31	3199	12875	15275	16450
Sedan 4D GLE	A31	3294	12025	14375	15500
Add Aluminum/Alloy Wheels (GXE)			225	250	250
Add Bose Stereo System (Std. GLE)			200	225	225
Add Compact Disc Player (Std. SE, GLE)			100	125	125
Add Leather Seats (Std. GLE)			375	425	425
Add Power Sunroof (Std. Anniv)			475	550	550
Add Theft Recovery System			50	75	75
Deduct W/out Automatic Trans.			475	475	475
Deduct W/out Power Seat			150	150	150
NISSAN					
2000 SENTRA-4 Cyl.					
Veh. Ident.: 3N1(Model)()()Y()000001 Up.					
Sedan 4D XE	CB51	2548	4700	6100	6875
Sedan 4D GXE	CB51	2593	4950	6375	7175
Sedan 4D SE	BB51	2674	5400	6900	7750
Add Aluminum/Alloy Wheels (Std. SE)			100	125	125
Add Compact Disc Player (Std. GXE, SE)			50	75	75
Add Power Sunroof			325	375	375
Deduct W/out Air Conditioning			375	375	375
Deduct W/out Automatic Trans.			300	300	300
2000 ALTIMA-4 Cyl.					
Veh. Ident.: 1N4DL01()()Y()000001 Up.					
Sedan 4D XE	L01	2851	6475	8225	9075
Sedan 4D GXE	L01	2945	6575	8325	9175
Sedan 4D SE	L01	2962	7100	8900	9800
Sedan 4D GLE	L01	3057	7375	9175	10050
Add Aluminum/Alloy Wheels (Std. SE, GLE)			125	150	150
Add Compact Disc Player (Std. SE, GLE)			50	75	75
Add Leather Seats (Std. GLE)			250	300	300
Add Power Seat (Std. GLE)			100	125	125
Add Power Sunroof			375	425	425
Deduct W/out Air Conditioning			500	500	500
Deduct W/out Automatic Trans.			375	375	375
Deduct W/out Cruise Control			100	100	100
Deduct W/out Power Door Locks (Ex. XE)			75	75	75
2000 MAXIMA-V6					
Veh. Ident.: JN1CA31()()Y()000001 Up.					
Sedan 4D GXE	A31	3186	8050	10075	11100
Sedan 4D SE	A31	3199	9500	11650	12675
Sedan 4D GLE	A31	3294	9850	12025	13075
Add Aluminum/Alloy Wheels (GXE)			175	200	200
Add Bose Stereo System (Std. GLE)			150	175	175
Add Compact Disc Player (Std. SE, GLE)			75	100	100
Add Leather Seats (Std. GLE)			325	375	375
Add Power Sunroof			425	475	475

BODY TYPE	Model No.	Weight	Trade-In	Retail	High Retail
Deduct W/out Automatic Trans.			425	425	425
Deduct W/out Power Seat			125	125	125
NISSAN					
1999 SENTRA-4 Cyl.					
Veh. Ident: 1N4(Model)D()XC000001 Up.					
Sedan 4D XE	AB41	2376	3575	4850	5650
Sedan 4D GXE	AB41	2438	3700	5000	5800
Sedan 4D SE	BB41	2593	4100	5450	6200
Add Aluminum/Alloy Wheels (Std. SE)			50	75	75
Add Power Sunroof			275	325	325
Deduct W/out Air Conditioning			325	325	325
Deduct W/out Automatic Trans.			250	250	250
1999 ALTIMA-4 Cyl.					
Veh. Ident.: 1N4DL01D()XC000001 Up.					
Sedan 4D XE	L01	2859	5025	6600	7500
Sedan 4D GXE	L01	2919	5125	6750	7675
Sedan 4D SE	L01	2921	5525	7175	8050
Sedan 4D GLE	L01	3012	5775	7450	8350
Add Aluminum/Alloy Wheels (Std. SE, GLE)			75	100	100
Add Leather Seats (Std. GLE)			225	250	250
Add Power Seat (Std. GLE)			75	100	100
Add Power Sunroof			325	375	375
Deduct W/out Air Conditioning			450	450	450
Deduct W/out Automatic Trans.			325	325	325
Deduct W/out Cruise Control			75	75	75
1999 MAXIMA-V6					
Veh. Ident.: JN1CA21()()X()000001 Up.					
Sedan 4D GXE	A21	3012	5725	7525	8575
Sedan 4D SE	A21	3014	7000	8950	10000
Sedan 4D GLE	A21	3085	7300	9250	10275
Add Aluminum/Alloy Wheels (GXE)			125	150	150
Add Bose Stereo System (Std. GLE)			100	125	125
Add Leather Seats (Std. GLE)			275	325	325
Add Power Sunroof			375	425	425
Deduct W/out Automatic Trans.			375	375	375
Deduct W/out Power Seat			100	100	100
NISSAN					
1998 SENTRA-4 Cyl.					
Veh. Ident.: 1N4(Model)D()W()000001 Up.					
Sedan 4D (5 Spd.)	AB41	2315	2450	3625	4300
Sedan 4D XE	AB41	2360	2675	3875	4575
Sedan 4D GXE	AB41	2379	2800	4000	4725
Sedan 4D GLE	AB41	2398	2950	4175	4900
Sedan 4D SE	BB41	2481	3150	4400	5150
1998 200SX-4 Cyl.					
Veh. Ident.: 1N4(Model)D()WC500001 Up.					
Coupe 2D	AB42	2363	2800	4000	4725
Coupe 2D SE	AB42	2418	3200	4450	5200
Coupe 2D SE-R	BB42	2586	3825	5125	5850
SENTRA/200SX OPTIONS					
Add Power Sunroof			225	275	275
Deduct W/out Air Conditioning			275	275	275

PASSENGER CARS

PASSENGER CARS

BODY TYPE	Model No.	Weight	Trade-In	Retail	High Retail
Ded W/out Automatic Trans. (Ex. Sentra Base)			**200**	**200**	**200**
1998 ALTIMA-4 Cyl.					
Veh. Ident.: 1N4DL01D()WC100002 Up.					
Sedan 4D XE	L01	2859	**3900**	**5350**	**6175**
Sedan 4D GXE	L01	2919	**3975**	**5425**	**6250**
Sedan 4D SE	L01	2921	**4275**	**5750**	**6600**
Sedan 4D GLE	L01	3012	**4425**	**5925**	**6800**
1998 240SX-4 Cyl.					
Veh. Ident.: JN1AS44D()WW105101 Up.					
Coupe 2D	S44	2800	**5325**	**6950**	**7900**
Coupe 2D SE	S44	2862	**5950**	**7625**	**8525**
Coupe 2D LE	S44	2862	**6650**	**8400**	**9275**
ALTIMA/240SX OPTIONS					
Add Aluminum/Alloy Wheels (Std. SE, 240SX LE)			**50**	**75**	**75**
Add Leather Seats (Std. Altima GLE, 240SX LE)			**175**	**200**	**200**
Add Power Seat (Std. Altima GLE)			**50**	**75**	**75**
Add Power Sunroof (Std. 240SX LE)			**275**	**325**	**325**
Deduct W/out Air Conditioning			**400**	**400**	**400**
Deduct W/out Automatic Trans.			**275**	**275**	**275**
Deduct W/out Cruise Control			**50**	**50**	**50**
1998 MAXIMA-V6					
Veh. Ident.: JN1CA21()()W()000001 Up.					
Sedan 4D GXE	A21	3012	**4650**	**6325**	**7325**
Sedan 4D SE	A21	3014	**5725**	**7525**	**8575**
Sedan 4D GLE	A21	3085	**5975**	**7825**	**8900**
Add Aluminum/Alloy Wheels (GXE)			**100**	**125**	**125**
Add Bose Stereo System (Std. GLE)			**75**	**100**	**100**
Add Leather Seats (Std. GLE)			**225**	**250**	**250**
Add Power Sunroof			**325**	**375**	**375**
Deduct W/out Automatic Trans.			**325**	**325**	**325**
Deduct W/out Power Seat			**75**	**75**	**75**
NISSAN					
1997 SENTRA-4 Cyl.					
Veh. Ident.: 1N4AB41D()V()000001 Up.					
Sedan 4D (5 Spd.)	B41	2315	**2050**	**3175**	**3800**
Sedan 4D XE	B41	2360	**2200**	**3350**	**4000**
Sedan 4D GXE	B41	2379	**2275**	**3425**	**4075**
Sedan 4D GLE	B41	2398	**2425**	**3600**	**4275**
1997 200SX-4 Cyl.					
Veh. Ident.: 1N4(Model)D()V()000001 Up.					
Coupe 2D	AB42	2330	**2375**	**3525**	**4175**
Coupe 2D SE	AB42	2348	**2625**	**3800**	**4500**
Coupe 2D SE-R	BB42	2419	**3025**	**4250**	**4975**
SENTRA/200SX OPTIONS					
Add Power Sunroof			**150**	**175**	**175**
Deduct W/out Air Conditioning			**150**	**150**	**150**
Ded W/out Automatic Trans. (Ex. Sentra Base)			**125**	**125**	**125**
1997 ALTIMA-4 Cyl.					
Veh. Ident.: 1N4BU31D()V()000001 Up.					
Sedan 4D XE	U31	2850	**2450**	**3700**	**4450**
Sedan 4D GXE	U31	2908	**2550**	**3825**	**4600**
Sedan 4D SE	U31	2882	**2750**	**4050**	**4850**
Sedan 4D GLE	U31	3032	**2700**	**4000**	**4800**

BODY TYPE	Model No.	Weight	Trade-In	Retail	High Retail
1997 240SX-4 Cyl.					
Veh. Ident.: JN1AS44D()V()000001 Up.					
Coupe 2D	S44	2800	**3975**	**5425**	**6250**
Coupe 2D SE	S44	2862	**4450**	**5950**	**6825**
Coupe 2D LE	S44	2862	**5050**	**6650**	**7550**
ALTIMA/240SX OPTIONS					
Add Leather Seats (Std. 240SX LE)			**150**	**175**	**175**
Add Power Sunroof (Std. 240SX LE)			**200**	**225**	**225**
Deduct W/out Air Conditioning			**250**	**250**	**250**
Deduct W/out Automatic Trans.			**175**	**175**	**175**
Deduct W/out Cruise Control			**50**	**50**	**50**
1997 MAXIMA-V6					
Veh. Ident.: JN1CA21D()V()000001 Up.					
Sedan 4D GXE	A21	3000	**4200**	**5850**	**6825**
Sedan 4D SE	A21	3010	**4875**	**6575**	**7600**
Sedan 4D GLE	A21	3097	**5075**	**6825**	**7875**
Add Aluminum/Alloy Wheels (GXE)			**50**	**75**	**75**
Add Bose Stereo System (Std. GLE)			**50**	**75**	**75**
Add Leather Seats (Std. GLE)			**200**	**225**	**225**
Add Power Sunroof			**250**	**300**	**300**
Deduct W/out Automatic Trans.			**250**	**250**	**250**
Deduct W/out Power Seat			**75**	**75**	**75**
NISSAN					
1996 SENTRA-4 Cyl.					
Veh. Ident.: 1N4AB41D()T()700001 Up.					
Sedan 4D (5 Spd.)	B41	2191	**1775**	**2850**	**3475**
Sedan 4D XE	B41	2282	**1875**	**2950**	**3600**
Sedan 4D GXE	B41	2301	**1950**	**3050**	**3650**
Sedan 4D GLE	B41	2320	**2100**	**3225**	**3850**
1996 200SX-4 Cyl.					
Veh. Ident.: 1N4(Model)D()T()500001 Up.					
Coupe 2D	AB42	2252	**1925**	**3025**	**3625**
Coupe 2D SE	AB42	2270	**2125**	**3250**	**3875**
Coupe 2D SE-R	BB42	2413	**2475**	**3650**	**4325**
SENTRA/200SX OPTIONS					
Add Power Sunroof (Std. Sentra GLE)			**100**	**125**	**125**
Deduct W/out Air Conditioning			**100**	**100**	**100**
Ded W/out Automatic Trans. (Ex. Sentra Base)			**100**	**100**	**100**
1996 ALTIMA-4 Cyl.					
Veh. Ident.: 1N4BU31D()TC100001 Up.					
Sedan 4D XE	U31	2756	**2025**	**3225**	**3925**
Sedan 4D GXE	U31	2811	**2100**	**3325**	**4025**
Sedan 4D SE	U31	2822	**2150**	**3375**	**4100**
Sedan 4D GLE	U31	2935	**2250**	**3475**	**4200**
1996 240SX-4 Cyl.					
Veh. Ident.: JN1AS44D()T()000056 Up.					
Coupe 2D	S44	2647	**3175**	**4550**	**5400**
Coupe 2D SE	S44	2654	**3575**	**4975**	**5875**
ALTIMA/240SX OPTIONS					
Add Power Sunroof (Std. Altima GLE)			**150**	**175**	**175**
Deduct W/out Air Conditioning			**150**	**150**	**150**
Deduct W/out Automatic Trans.			**125**	**125**	**125**

PASSENGER CARS

BODY TYPE	Model No.	Weight	Trade-In	Retail	High Retail
1996 MAXIMA-V6					
Veh. Ident.: JN1CA21D()T()000201 Up.					
Sedan 4D GXE	A21	2886	**3675**	**5225**	**6125**
Sedan 4D SE	A21	2895	**4000**	**5575**	**6525**
Sedan 4D GLE	A21	2982	**4150**	**5775**	**6750**
1996 300ZX-V6-5 Spd./AT					
Veh. Ident.: JN1(Model)D()T()040001 Up.					
Coupe 2D	RZ24	3170	**9425**	**11575**	**12600**
Coupe 2D 2+2	RZ26	3284	**10025**	**12225**	**13275**
Coupe 2D Turbo	CZ24	3385	**12675**	**15100**	**16275**
Convertible 2D	RZ27	3284	**12475**	**14875**	**16025**
MAXIMA/300ZX OPTIONS					
Add Power Sunroof			**200**	**225**	**225**
Add T-Top (300ZX Base)			**300**	**350**	**350**
Deduct W/out Automatic Trans. (Ex. 300ZX)			**150**	**150**	**150**
NISSAN					
1995 SENTRA-4 Cyl.					
Veh. Ident.: 1N4AB41D()SC700001 Up.					
Sedan 4D E	B41	2300	**1475**	**2500**	**3075**
Sedan 4D XE	B41	2410	**1575**	**2625**	**3225**
Sedan 4D GXE	B41	2460	**1650**	**2700**	**3300**
Sedan 4D GLE	B41	2500	**1750**	**2825**	**3450**
1995 200SX-4 Cyl.					
Veh. Ident.: 1N4(Model)D()S()700001 Up.					
Coupe 2D	AB42	2381	**1700**	**2775**	**3400**
Coupe 2D SE	AB42	2427	**1900**	**3000**	**3650**
Coupe 2D SE-R	BB42	2594	**2250**	**3400**	**4050**
1995 ALTIMA-4 Cyl.					
Veh. Ident.: 1N4BU31D()S()100003 Up.					
Sedan 4D XE	U31	2924	**1700**	**2850**	**3525**
Sedan 4D GXE	U31	2972	**1775**	**2950**	**3625**
Sedan 4D SE	U31	2968	**1925**	**3125**	**3800**
Sedan 4D GLE	U31	3032	**1875**	**3050**	**3725**
1995 240SX-4 Cyl.					
Veh. Ident.: JN1AS44D()S()000056 Up.					
Coupe 2D	S44	2815	**2750**	**4050**	**4850**
Coupe 2D SE	S44	2821	**3100**	**4450**	**5300**
1995 MAXIMA-V6					
Veh. Ident.: JN1CA21D()S()000301 Up.					
Sedan 4D GXE	A21	3063	**3125**	**4600**	**5500**
Sedan 4D SE	A21	3072	**3350**	**4850**	**5800**
Sedan 4D GLE	A21	3097	**3475**	**5000**	**5950**
1995 300ZX-V6					
Veh. Ident.: JN1(Model)D()SX030002 Up.					
Coupe 2D	RZ24	3379	**8050**	**10075**	**11100**
Coupe 2D 2+2	RZ26	3443	**8550**	**10625**	**11675**
Coupe 2D Turbo	CZ24	3556	**10575**	**12800**	**13875**
Convertible 2D	RZ27	3475	**10450**	**12675**	**13750**
MAXIMA/300ZX OPTIONS					
Add T-Top (300ZX Base)			**250**	**300**	**300**

BODY TYPE	Model No.	Weight	Trade-In	Retail	High Retail
OLDSMOBILE					
OLDSMOBILE					
2004 ALERO-4 Cyl.					
Veh. Ident.: 1G3(Model)2F()4()000001 Up.					
Coupe 2D GX	NK1	2946	**8000**	**9875**	**10775**
Coupe 2D GL	NL1	2961	**9050**	**11050**	**11925**
Sedan 4D GX	NK5	3021	**7950**	**9800**	**10700**
Sedan 4D GL	NL5	3016	**9000**	**10975**	**11925**
2004 ALERO-V6					
Veh. Ident.: 1G3(Model)2E()4()000001 Up.					
Coupe 2D GL	NL1		**9600**	**11650**	**12550**
Coupe 2D GLS	NF1	3085	**11750**	**14000**	**14950**
Sedan 4D GL	NL5		**9550**	**11600**	**12500**
Sedan 4D GLS	NF5	3147	**11700**	**13950**	**14900**
ALERO OPTIONS					
Add Aluminum/Alloy Wheels (GX)			**325**	**375**	**375**
Add Power Seat (Std. GLS)			**200**	**225**	**225**
Add Power Sunroof			**575**	**650**	**650**
Add Theft Recovery System			**100**	**125**	**125**
Deduct W/out Automatic Trans.			**575**	**575**	**575**
OLDSMOBILE					
2003 ALERO-4 Cyl.					
Veh. Ident.: 1G3(Model)2F()3()000001 Up.					
Coupe 2D GX	NK1	2946	**6800**	**8550**	**9425**
Coupe 2D GL	NL1	2961	**7725**	**9550**	**10450**
Sedan 4D GX	NK5	3021	**6750**	**8500**	**9375**
Sedan 4D GL	NL5	3016	**7675**	**9500**	**10375**
2003 ALERO-V6					
Veh. Ident.: 1G3(Model)2E()3()000001 Up.					
Coupe 2D GL	NL1		**8225**	**10100**	**11025**
Coupe 2D GLS	NF1	3085	**10175**	**12300**	**13200**
Sedan 4D GL	NL5		**8175**	**10050**	**10975**
Sedan 4D GLS	NF5	3147	**10125**	**12250**	**13150**
ALERO OPTIONS					
Add Aluminum/Alloy Wheels (GX)			**275**	**325**	**325**
Add Power Seat (Std. GLS)			**175**	**200**	**200**
Add Power Sunroof			**525**	**600**	**600**
Add Theft Recovery System			**75**	**100**	**100**
Deduct W/out Automatic Trans.			**525**	**525**	**525**
2003 AURORA-V8					
Veh. Ident.: 1G3GS64C()34000001 Up.					
Sedan 4D 4.0L	GS6	3802	**17200**	**20325**	**21800**
Add Bose Stereo System			**375**	**425**	**425**
Add Navigation System			**650**	**725**	**725**
Add Power Sunroof			**675**	**775**	**775**
Add Theft Recovery System			**75**	**100**	**100**
OLDSMOBILE					
2002 ALERO-4 Cyl.					
Veh. Ident.: 1G3(Model)()()()2()000001 Up.					
Coupe 2D GX	NK1	2973	**5875**	**7550**	**8450**

PASSENGER CARS

BODY TYPE	Model No.	Weight	Trade-In	Retail	High Retail
Coupe 2D GL	NL1	2997	6700	8450	9325
Sedan 4D GX	NK5	3026	5825	7500	8400
Sedan 4D GL	NL5	3046	6650	8400	9275
2002 ALERO-V6					
Veh. Ident.: 1G3(Model)()()()2()000001 Up.					
Coupe 2D GL	NL1		7100	8875	9775
Coupe 2D GLS	NF1	3060	8825	10750	11700
Sedan 4D GL	NL5		7050	8825	9725
Sedan 4D GLS	NF5	3108	8775	10700	11650
ALERO OPTIONS					
Add Aluminum/Alloy Wheels (GX)			225	250	250
Add Power Seat (Std. GLS)			150	175	175
Add Power Sunroof			475	550	550
Add Theft Recovery System			75	100	100
Deduct W/out Automatic Trans.			475	475	475
2002 INTRIGUE-V6					
Veh. Ident.: 1G3(Model)()()()2F000001 Up.					
Sedan 4D GX	WH5	3434	7700	9525	10400
Sedan 4D GL	WS5		9125	11150	12025
Sedan 4D GLS	WX5		10750	12925	13850
Add Bose Stereo System			200	225	225
Add Leather Seats (Std. GLS)			350	400	400
Add Power Seat (Std. GL, GLS)			150	175	175
Add Power Sunroof (Std. GLS)			475	550	550
Add Theft Recovery System			75	100	100
2002 AURORA-V8					
Veh. Ident.: 1G3(Model)()()()24000001 Up.					
Sedan 4D 3.5L (V6)	GR6	3686	11825	14350	15600
Sedan 4D 4.0L	GS6	3803	13925	16675	18050
Add Bose Stereo System			325	375	375
Add Navigation System			550	625	625
Add Power Sunroof			625	700	700
Add Theft Recovery System			75	100	100
OLDSMOBILE					
2001 ALERO-4 Cyl.					
Veh. Ident.: ()G3(Model)()()()1()000001 Up.					
Coupe 2D GX	NK1	2973	4975	6550	7450
Coupe 2D GL	NL1	2997	5700	7375	8275
Sedan 4D GX	NK5	3026	4925	6475	7375
Sedan 4D GL	NL5	3046	5650	7300	8175
2001 ALERO-V6					
Veh. Ident.: ()G3(Model)()()()1()000001 Up.					
Coupe 2D GL	NL1		6025	7725	8650
Coupe 2D GLS	NF1	3060	7300	9100	9975
Sedan 4D GL	NL5		5975	7675	8600
Sedan 4D GLS	NF5	3108	7250	9050	9900
ALERO OPTIONS					
Add Aluminum/Alloy Wheels (GX)			175	200	200
Add Leather Seats (Std. GLS)			300	350	350
Add Power Seat (Std. GLS)			125	150	150
Add Power Sunroof			425	475	475
Add Theft Recovery System			50	75	75
Deduct W/out Automatic Trans.			425	425	425

BODY TYPE	Model No.	Weight	Trade-In	Retail	High Retail
2001 INTRIGUE-V6					
Veh. Ident.: ()G3(Model)()()()1()000001 Up.					
Sedan 4D GX	WH5	3455	6400	8125	8975
Sedan 4D GL	WS5		7325	9125	10000
Sedan 4D GLS	WX5		8525	10425	11350
Add Bose Stereo System			150	175	175
Add Compact Disc Player (Std. GL, GLS)			50	75	75
Add Leather Seats (Std. GLS)			300	350	350
Add Power Seat (Std. GL, GLS)			125	150	150
Add Power Sunroof			425	475	475
Add Theft Recovery System			50	75	75
2001 AURORA-V8					
Veh. Ident.: ()G3(Model)()()()1()000001 Up.					
Sedan 4D 3.5L (V6)	GR6	3686	9100	11350	12475
Sedan 4D 4.0L	GS6	3803	10650	13025	14225
Add Bose Stereo System			275	325	325
Add Power Sunroof			575	650	650
Add Theft Recovery System			50	75	75
OLDSMOBILE					
2000 ALERO-4 Cyl.					
Veh. Ident.: ()G3(Model)()()()Y()000001 Up.					
Coupe 2D GX	NK1	2958	4025	5475	6300
Coupe 2D GL	NL1		4375	5875	6750
Sedan 4D GX	NK5	3022	3975	5425	6250
Sedan 4D GL	NL5		4325	5825	6700
2000 ALERO-V6					
Veh. Ident.: ()G3(Model)()()()Y()000001 Up.					
Coupe 2D GL	NL1		4675	6200	7075
Coupe 2D GLS	NF1		5750	7425	8325
Sedan 4D GL	NL5		4625	6150	7025
Sedan 4D GLS	NF5		5700	7350	8250
ALERO OPTIONS					
Add Aluminum/Alloy Wheels (Std. GLS)			125	150	150
Add Compact Disc Player (Std. GLS)			50	75	75
Add Leather Seats (Std. GLS)			250	300	300
Add Power Seat (Std. GLS)			100	125	125
Add Power Sunroof			375	425	425
Deduct W/out Automatic Trans.			375	375	375
Deduct W/out Cruise Control			100	100	100
2000 INTRIGUE-V6					
Veh. Ident.: ()G3(Model)()()()Y()000001 Up.					
Sedan 4D GX	WH5	3455	5025	6600	7500
Sedan 4D GL	WS5		5675	7325	8200
Sedan 4D GLS	WX5		6475	8200	9050
Add Bose Stereo System			100	125	125
Add Compact Disc Player (Std. GLS)			50	75	75
Add Leather Seats (Std. GLS)			250	300	300
Add Power Seat (Std. GL, GLS)			100	125	125
Add Power Sunroof			375	425	425

BODY TYPE	Model No.	Weight	Trade-In	Retail	High Retail
OLDSMOBILE					
1999 ALERO-4 Cyl.					
Veh. Ident.: ()G3(Model)()()()X()000001 Up.					
Coupe 2D GX	NK1	2958	3350	4725	5600
Coupe 2D GL	NL1		3675	5100	5900
Sedan 4D GX	NK5	3022	3300	4675	5550
Sedan 4D GL	NL5		3625	5050	5850
1999 ALERO-V6					
Veh. Ident.: ()G3(Model)()()()X()000001 Up.					
Coupe 2D GL	NL1		3975	5425	6250
Coupe 2D GLS	NF1		4750	6275	7150
Sedan 4D GL	NL5		3925	5375	6200
Sedan 4D GLS	NF5		4700	6225	7100
ALERO OPTIONS					
Add Aluminum/Alloy Wheels (Std. GLS)			75	100	100
Add Leather Seats (Std. GLS)			225	250	250
Add Power Seat (Std. GLS)			75	100	100
Add Power Sunroof			325	375	375
Deduct W/out Cruise Control			75	75	75
1999 CUTLASS-V6					
Veh. Ident.: ()G3(Model)()()()X()000001 Up.					
Sedan 4D GL	NB5	3102	3575	4975	5875
Sedan 4D GLS	NG5		4150	5625	6475
Add Aluminum/Alloy Wheels (Std. GLS)			75	100	100
Add Power Seat (Std. GLS)			75	100	100
Add Power Sunroof			325	375	375
Deduct W/out Power Windows			75	75	75
1999 INTRIGUE-V6					
Veh. Ident.: ()G3(Model)()()()X()000001 Up.					
Sedan 4D GX	WH5	3467	4275	5750	6600
Sedan 4D GL	WS5	3467	4700	6225	7100
Sedan 4D GLS	WX5	3434	5175	6800	7725
Add Bose Stereo System			75	100	100
Add Leather Seats (Std. GLS)			225	250	250
Add Power Seat (Std. GL, GLS)			75	100	100
Add Power Sunroof			325	375	375
1999 EIGHTY EIGHT-V6					
Veh. Ident.: ()G3HN5()()()X()000001 Up.					
Sedan 4D	HN5	3455	4225	5850	6825
Sedan 4D LS	HN5		4625	6300	7300
Add Aluminum/Alloy Wheels (Std. LS)			125	150	150
Add Leather Seats			275	325	325
Add Power Sunroof			375	425	425
1999 LSS-V6					
Veh. Ident.: ()G3HY5()()()X()000001 Up.					
Sedan 4D	HY5	3547	5075	6800	7850
Add Power Sunroof			375	425	425
Add Supercharged V6 Engine			200	225	225
1999 AURORA-V8					
Veh. Ident.: ()G3GR6()()()X()000001 Up.					
Sedan 4D	GR6	3967	5175	7000	8175

DEDUCT FOR RECONDITIONING

BODY TYPE	Model No.	Weight	Trade-In	Retail	High Retail
Add Bose Stereo System			175	200	200
Add Power Sunroof			475	550	550
OLDSMOBILE					
1998 ACHIEVA-V6					
Veh Ident.:()G3NL1()()()W()000001 Up.					
Sedan 4D SL	NL5		2150	3375	4100
1998 CUTLASS-V6					
Veh. Ident.: ()G3(Model)()()()W()000001 Up.					
Sedan 4D GL	NB5	3102	3075	4425	5275
Sedan 4D GLS	NG5	3102	3500	4900	5800
CUTLASS OPTIONS					
Add Aluminum/Alloy Wheels (Std. GLS)			50	75	75
Add Power Seat (Std. GLS)			50	75	75
Add Power Sunroof			275	325	325
Deduct W/out Power Windows			50	50	50
1998 INTRIGUE-V6					
Veh. Ident.: ()G3(Model)()()()W()000001 Up.					
Sedan 4D	WH5	3455	3525	4925	5825
Sedan 4D GL	WS5	3455	3850	5300	6125
Sedan 4D GLS	WX5		4200	5675	6525
Add Leather Seats (Std. GLS)			175	200	200
Add Power Seat (Std. GL, GLS)			50	75	75
Add Power Sunroof			275	325	325
1998 EIGHTY EIGHT-V6					
Veh. Ident.: ()G3HN5()()()W()000001 Up.					
Sedan 4D	HN5	3455	3500	5025	5925
Sedan 4D LS	HN5	3455	3850	5425	6350
Add Aluminum/Alloy Wheels (Std. LS)			100	125	125
Add Leather Seats			225	250	250
1998 LSS-V6					
Veh. Ident.: ()G3HY5()()()W()000001 Up.					
Sedan 4D	HY5	3547	4200	5850	6825
Add Power Sunroof			325	375	375
Add Supercharged V6 Engine			200	225	225
1998 REGENCY-V6					
Veh. Ident.: ()G3HC5()()()W()000001 Up.					
Sedan 4D	HC5	3501	4225	5925	7025
Add Power Sunroof			425	475	475
1998 AURORA-V8					
Veh. Ident.: ()G3GR6()()()W()000001 Up.					
Sedan 4D	GR6	3967	4225	5925	7025
Add Bose Stereo System			150	175	175
Add Power Sunroof			425	475	475
OLDSMOBILE					
1997 ACHIEVA-L4					
Veh. Ident.: 1G3(Model)()()()VM300001 Up.					
Coupe 2D SC	NL1	2751	1675	2825	3475
Sedan 4D SL	NL5	2813	1675	2825	3475

BODY TYPE	Model No.	Weight	Trade-In	Retail	High Retail
1997 ACHIEVA-V6					
Veh. Ident.: 1G3(Model)()()()VM300001 Up.					
Coupe 2D SC	NL1		1825	3000	3675
Sedan 4D SL	NL5		1825	3000	3675
ACHIEVA OPTIONS					
Add Power Seat			50	75	75
Add Power Sunroof			200	225	225
Deduct W/out Automatic Trans.			175	175	175
Deduct W/out Cruise Control			25	25	25
Deduct W/out Power Windows			25	25	25
1997 CUTLASS-V6					
Veh. Ident.: 1G3(Model)()()()V6300001 Up.					
Sedan 4D	NB5	2982	2575	3850	4625
Sedan 4D GLS	NG5	3102	2900	4200	5000
Add Power Seat (Std. GLS)			50	75	75
Add Power Sunroof			200	225	225
Deduct W/out Power Windows			25	25	25
1997 CUTLASS SUPREME-V6					
Veh. Ident.: 1G3(Model)()()()VF300001 Up.					
Coupe 2D SL	WH1	3305	2550	3825	4600
Sedan 4D SL	WH5	3424	2550	3825	4600
Add Leather Seats			150	175	175
Add Power Seat			50	75	75
Add Power Sunroof			200	225	225
1997 EIGHTY EIGHT-V6					
Veh. Ident.: 1G3HN5()()()V4800001 Up.					
Sedan 4D	HN5	3465	3000	4425	5325
Sedan 4D LS	HN5	3465	3225	4725	5650
Add Aluminum/Alloy Wheels (Std. LS)			50	75	75
Add Leather Seats			200	225	225
1997 LSS-V6					
Veh. Ident.: 1G3HY5()()()V4800001 Up.					
Sedan 4D	HY5	3547	3550	5075	5975
Add Power Sunroof			250	300	300
Add Supercharged V6 Engine			200	225	225
1997 REGENCY-V6					
Veh. Ident.: 1G3HC5()()()V4800001 Up.					
Sedan 4D	HC5	3501	3550	5175	6175
Add Power Sunroof			350	400	400
1997 AURORA-V8					
Veh. Ident.: 1G3GR6()()()V4100001 Up.					
Sedan 4D	GR6	3967	3725	5375	6400
Add Bose Stereo System			100	125	125
Add Power Sunroof			350	400	400
OLDSMOBILE					
1996 ACHIEVA-L4					
Veh. Ident.: ()G3(Model)()()()T()000001 Up.					
Coupe 2D SC	NL1	2751	1400	2525	3150
Sedan 4D SL	NL5	2813	1400	2525	3150

PASSENGER CARS

BODY TYPE	Model No.	Weight	Trade-In	Retail	High Retail
1996 ACHIEVA-V6					
Veh. Ident.: ()G3(Model)()()()T()000001 Up.					
Coupe 2D SC	NL1		1500	2625	3250
Sedan 4D SL	NL5		1500	2625	3250
ACHIEVA OPTIONS					
Add Power Sunroof			150	175	175
Deduct W/out Automatic Trans.			125	125	125
1996 CIERA-V6					
Veh. Ident.: ()G3(Model)()()()T()000001 Up.					
Sedan 4D SL (L4)	AJ5	2924	1775	2950	3625
Sedan 4D SL	AJ5	3058	1875	3050	3725
Wagon 4D SL	AJ8	3229	1925	3125	3800
1996 CUTLASS SUPREME-V6					
Veh. Ident.: ()G3(Model)()()()T()000001 Up.					
Coupe 2D SL	WH1	3283	2200	3425	4150
Sedan 4D SL	WH5	3388	2200	3425	4150
Add 3.4L V6 Engine			75	100	100
Add Power Sunroof			150	175	175
1996 EIGHTY-EIGHT-V6					
Veh. Ident.: ()G3HN5()()()T()000001 Up.					
Sedan 4D	HN5	3455	2550	3925	4800
Sedan 4D LS	HN5	3459	2725	4125	4975
1996 LSS-V6					
Veh. Ident.: ()G3HY5()()()T()000001 Up.					
Sedan 4D	HY5	3502	2850	4250	5125
Add Power Sunroof			200	225	225
Add Supercharged V6 Engine			150	175	175
1996 NINETY-EIGHT-V6					
Veh. Ident.: ()G3CX5()()()T()000001 Up.					
Sedan 4D Regency Elite	CX5	3515	2950	4475	5450
Add Power Sunroof			275	325	325
1996 AURORA-V8					
Veh. Ident.: ()G3GR6()()()T()000001 Up.					
Sedan 4D	GR6	3967	3200	4775	5800
Add Power Sunroof			275	325	325
OLDSMOBILE					
1995 ACHIEVA-Quad 4					
Veh. Ident.: ()G3(Model)()()()S()000001 Up.					
Coupe 2D S	NL1	2716	1175	2275	2850
Sedan 4D S	NL5	2779	1175	2275	2850
1995 ACHIEVA-V6					
Veh. Ident.: ()G3(Model)()()()S()000001 Up.					
Coupe 2D S	NL1	2735	1275	2375	2975
Sedan 4D S	NL5	2798	1275	2375	2975
1995 CUTLASS CIERA-V6					
Veh. Ident.: ()G3(Model)()()()S()000001 Up.					
Sedan 4D SL (L4)	AJ5	2733	1500	2625	3250
Sedan 4D SL	AJ5	2836	1600	2750	3400
Cruiser Wagon 4D SL	AJ8	2986	1650	2800	3450

BODY TYPE	Model No.	Weight	Trade-In	Retail	High Retail
1995 CUTLASS SUPREME-V6					
Veh. Ident.: ()G3(Model)()()()S()000001 Up.					
Coupe 2D SL	WH1	3243	**1875**	**3050**	**3725**
Sedan 4D SL	WH5	3354	**1875**	**3050**	**3725**
Convertible 2D	WT3	3651	**3100**	**4450**	**5300**
Add 3.4L V6 Engine			**75**	**100**	**100**
1995 EIGHTY-EIGHT ROYALE-V6					
Veh. Ident.: ()G3(Model)()()()S()000001 Up.					
Sedan 4D	HN5	3439	**2050**	**3350**	**4150**
Sedan 4D LS	HY5	3439	**2225**	**3550**	**4375**
Add Supercharged V6 Engine			**150**	**175**	**175**
1995 NINETY-EIGHT-V6					
Veh. Ident.: ()G3CX5()()()S()000001 Up.					
Sedan 4D Regency Elite	CX5	3593	**2500**	**3950**	**4925**
Add Supercharged V6 Engine			**150**	**175**	**175**
1995 AURORA-V8					
Veh. Ident.: ()G3GR5()()()S()000001 Up.					
Sedan 4D	GR5	3967	**2600**	**4050**	**4975**

PLYMOUTH

BODY TYPE	Model No.	Weight	Trade-In	Retail	High Retail
PLYMOUTH					
2001 NEON-4 Cyl.					
Veh. Ident.: ()P3()S46()()1()100001 Up.					
Sedan 4D	S46	2567	**4100**	**5450**	**6200**
Sedan 4D LX	S46		**4475**	**5875**	**6675**
Add Aluminum/Alloy Wheels			**150**	**175**	**175**
Add Compact Disc Player			**50**	**75**	**75**
Add Cruise Control			**100**	**125**	**125**
Add Leather Seats			**200**	**225**	**225**
Add Power Door Locks (Std. LX)			**75**	**100**	**100**
Add Power Sunroof			**375**	**425**	**425**
Add Power Windows (Std. LX)			**100**	**125**	**125**
Add Theft Recovery System			**50**	**75**	**75**
Deduct W/out Air Conditioning			**425**	**425**	**425**
Deduct W/out Automatic Trans.			**325**	**325**	**325**
PLYMOUTH					
2000 NEON-4 Cyl.					
Veh. Ident.: ()P3()S46()()Y()100001 Up.					
Sedan 4D	S46	2567	**3400**	**4675**	**5450**
Sedan 4D LX	S46	2567	**3725**	**5025**	**5750**
Add Aluminum/Alloy Wheels			**100**	**125**	**125**
Add Compact Disc Player			**50**	**75**	**75**
Add Cruise Control			**75**	**100**	**100**
Add Power Door Locks (Std. LX)			**50**	**75**	**75**
Add Power Sunroof			**325**	**375**	**375**
Add Power Windows (Std. LX)			**75**	**100**	**100**
Deduct W/out Air Conditioning			**375**	**375**	**375**
Deduct W/out Automatic Trans.			**300**	**300**	**300**

BODY TYPE	Model No.	Weight	Trade-In	Retail	High Retail
2000 BREEZE-4 Cyl.					
Veh. Ident.: ()P3()J46()()Y()100001 Up.					
Sedan 4D	J46	2942	3700	5125	5925
Add Aluminum/Alloy Wheels			125	150	150
Add Compact Disc Player			50	75	75
Add Power Seat			100	125	125
Add Power Sunroof			375	425	425
Deduct W/out Automatic Trans.			375	375	375
Deduct W/out Cruise Control			100	100	100
Deduct W/out Power Door Locks			75	75	75
Deduct W/out Power Windows			100	100	100
PLYMOUTH					
1999 NEON-4 Cyl.					
Veh. Ident.: ()P3()(Model)()()X()100001 Up.					
Coupe 2D Highline	S42	2389	2500	3675	4350
Sedan 4D Highline	S47	2399	2500	3675	4350
Add Expresso Package			175	200	200
Add Aluminum/Alloy Wheels			50	75	75
Add Cruise Control			50	75	75
Add Power Sunroof			275	325	325
Add Power Windows			50	75	75
Deduct W/out Air Conditioning			325	325	325
Deduct W/out Automatic Trans.			250	250	250
1999 BREEZE-4 Cyl.					
Veh. Ident.: ()P3()J46()()X()100001 Up.					
Sedan 4D	J46	2942	3125	4475	5325
Add Aluminum/Alloy Wheels			75	100	100
Add Power Seat			75	100	100
Add Power Sunroof			325	375	375
Deduct W/out Automatic Trans.			325	325	325
Deduct W/out Cruise Control			75	75	75
Deduct W/out Power Door Locks			50	50	50
Deduct W/out Power Windows			75	75	75
PLYMOUTH					
1998 NEON-4 Cyl.					
Veh. Ident.: ()P3()(Model)()()W()000001 Up.					
Coupe 2D Highline	S42		2025	3125	3725
Sedan 4D Highline	S47		2025	3125	3725
Add Expresso Package			125	150	150
Add Cruise Control			50	75	75
Add Power Sunroof			225	275	275
Add Power Windows			50	75	75
Deduct W/out Air Conditioning			275	275	275
Deduct W/out Automatic Trans.			200	200	200
1998 BREEZE-4 Cyl.					
Veh.Ident.:()P3()J46()()W()000001 Up.					
Sedan 4D	J46	2929	2400	3650	4400
Add Aluminum/Alloy Wheels			50	75	75
Add Power Sunroof			275	325	325
Deduct W/out Automatic Trans.			275	275	275
Deduct W/out Power Windows			50	50	50

BODY TYPE	Model No.	Weight	Trade-In	Retail	High Retail
PLYMOUTH					
1997 NEON-4 Cyl.					
Veh. Ident.: ()P3()(Model)()()V()000001 Up.					
Coupe 2D	S22	2389	**1475**	**2500**	**3075**
Coupe 2D Highline	S42	2416	**1500**	**2550**	**3125**
Sedan 4D	S27	2399	**1475**	**2500**	**3075**
Sedan 4D Highline	S47	2459	**1500**	**2550**	**3125**
Add Expresso Package			**75**	**100**	**100**
Add Power Sunroof			**150**	**175**	**175**
Deduct W/out Air Conditioning			**150**	**150**	**150**
Deduct W/out Automatic Trans.			**125**	**125**	**125**
1997 BREEZE-4 Cyl.					
Veh. Ident.: ()P3()J46()()V()000001 Up.					
Sedan 4D	J46	2931	**1950**	**3150**	**3850**
Deduct W/out Automatic Trans.			**175**	**175**	**175**
Deduct W/out Power Windows			**25**	**25**	**25**
PLYMOUTH					
1996 NEON-4 Cyl.					
Veh. Ident.: ()P3()(Model)()()T()000001 Up.					
Coupe 2D	S22		**1175**	**2175**	**2700**
Coupe 2D Highline	S42	2385	**1200**	**2200**	**2725**
Coupe 2D Sport	S62	2469	**1275**	**2300**	**2850**
Sedan 4D	S27	2343	**1175**	**2175**	**2700**
Sedan 4D Highline	S47	2416	**1200**	**2200**	**2725**
Sedan 4D Sport	S67	2456	**1275**	**2300**	**2850**
Add Power Sunroof			**100**	**125**	**125**
Deduct W/out Air Conditioning			**75**	**75**	**75**
Deduct W/out Automatic Trans.			**75**	**75**	**75**
1996 BREEZE-4 Cyl.					
Veh. Ident.: ()P3()J46()()T()000001 Up.					
Sedan 4D	J46	2931	**1625**	**2775**	**3425**
Add Power Sunroof			**150**	**175**	**175**
Deduct W/out Automatic Trans.			**125**	**125**	**125**
PLYMOUTH					
1995 NEON-4 Cyl.					
Veh. Ident.: ()B3()(Model)()()S()000001 Up.					
Coupe 2D Highline	S42	2377	**1000**	**1950**	**2425**
Coupe 2D Sport	S62	2473	**1075**	**2075**	**2600**
Sedan 4D	S27	2320	**975**	**1925**	**2400**
Sedan 4D Highline	S47	2388	**1000**	**1950**	**2425**
Sedan 4D Sport	S67	2449	**1075**	**2075**	**2600**
1995 ACCLAIM-4 Cyl.					
Veh. Ident.: 1P3()A46()()S()000001 Up.					
Sedan 4D	A46	2771	**1050**	**2125**	**2675**
Sedan 4D (V6)	A46	2795	**1125**	**2200**	**2775**

BODY TYPE	Model No.	Weight	Trade-In	Retail	High Retail

PONTIAC

PONTIAC

2004 SUNFIRE-L4

BODY TYPE	Model No.	Weight	Trade-In	Retail	High Retail
Veh. Ident.: ()G2JB1()F()4()000001 Up.					
Coupe 2D	JB1	2771	**8050**	**9850**	**10575**
Add Aluminum/Alloy Wheels			**300**	**350**	**350**
Add Compact Disc Player			**100**	**125**	**125**
Add Cruise Control			**175**	**200**	**200**
Add Monsoon Stereo System			**250**	**300**	**300**
Add Power Door Locks			**150**	**175**	**175**
Add Power Sunroof			**525**	**600**	**600**
Add Power Windows			**175**	**200**	**200**
Add Theft Recovery System			**100**	**125**	**125**
Add Tilt Steering Wheel			**125**	**150**	**150**
Deduct W/out Automatic Trans.			**475**	**475**	**475**

2004 VIBE-L4

BODY TYPE	Model No.	Weight	Trade-In	Retail	High Retail
Veh. Ident.: 5Y2(Model)()()()4Z000001 Up.					
Wagon 4D	SL6	2701	**11825**	**14075**	**15025**
Wagon 4D GT (6 Spd.)	SN6	2800	**12550**	**14925**	**15900**
Wagon 4D (AWD)	SM6	2976	**13250**	**15650**	**16650**
Add Aluminum/Alloy Wheels (Std. GT)			**325**	**375**	**375**
Add Navigation System			**600**	**675**	**675**
Add Power Sunroof			**575**	**650**	**650**
Add Theft Recovery System			**100**	**125**	**125**
Deduct W/out Automatic Trans. (Ex. GT)			**575**	**575**	**575**
Deduct W/out Cruise Control			**200**	**200**	**200**
Deduct W/out Power Door Locks			**175**	**175**	**175**
Deduct W/out Power Windows			**200**	**200**	**200**

2004 GRAND AM-V6

BODY TYPE	Model No.	Weight	Trade-In	Retail	High Retail
Veh. Ident.: 1G2(Model)2()()4()000001 Up.					
Coupe 2D GT	NV/W1	3168	**12225**	**14575**	**15550**
Sedan 4D SE (4 Cyl.)	NE/F5	3066	**9350**	**11375**	**12275**
Sedan 4D SE	NF/G5		**9900**	**11950**	**12875**
Sedan 4D GT	NV/W5	3091	**12125**	**14450**	**15425**
Add SC/T Appearance Pkg. (GT)			**475**	**550**	**550**
Add Aluminum/Alloy Wheels (Std. GT)			**325**	**375**	**375**
Add Leather Seats			**450**	**500**	**500**
Add Monsoon Stereo System (Std. GT)			**300**	**350**	**350**
Add Power Seat			**200**	**225**	**225**
Add Power Sunroof			**575**	**650**	**650**
Add Theft Recovery System			**100**	**125**	**125**
Deduct W/out Automatic Trans.			**575**	**575**	**575**
Deduct W/out Cruise Control			**200**	**200**	**200**
Deduct W/out Power Windows			**200**	**200**	**200**

2004 BONNEVILLE-V6

BODY TYPE	Model No.	Weight	Trade-In	Retail	High Retail
Veh. Ident.: 1G2(Model)()()()4U000001 Up.					
Sedan 4D SE	HX5	3590	**13575**	**16050**	**17250**
Sedan 4D SLE	HY5	3650	**17700**	**20575**	**21900**
Sedan 4D GXP (V8)	HZ5	3790	**22275**	**25575**	**27000**
Add Aluminum/Alloy Wheels (SE)			**375**	**425**	**425**

PASSENGER CARS

PASSENGER CARS

BODY TYPE	Model No.	Weight	Trade-In	Retail	High Retail
Add Leather Seats (Std. GXP)			525	600	600
Add Power Sunroof			625	700	700
Add Theft Recovery System			100	125	125
2004 GRAND PRIX-V6					
Veh. Ident.: 2G2(Model)()()()41000001 Up.					
Sedan 4D GT1	WP5	3477	12600	14950	15925
Sedan 4D GT2	WS5	3484	14125	16575	17625
Sedan 4D GTP	WR5	3583	15225	17725	18775
Add Comp G Pkg. (GTP)			600	675	675
Add Aluminum/Alloy Wheels (GT1)			325	375	375
Add Leather Seats			450	500	500
Add Monsoon Stereo System			300	350	350
Add Power Seat (GT1)			200	225	225
Add Power Sunroof			575	650	650
Add Theft Recovery System			100	125	125
2004 GTO-V8-6 Spd./AT					
Veh. Ident.: 6G2VX1()G()4L000001 Up.					
Coupe 2D	VX1	3725	20800	23850	25225
Add Theft Recovery System			100	125	125
PONTIAC					
2003 SUNFIRE-L4					
Veh. Ident.: ()G2JB1()F()3()000001 Up.					
Coupe 2D	JB1	2606	7100	8775	9550
Add Aluminum/Alloy Wheels			250	300	300
Add Compact Disc Player			75	100	100
Add Cruise Control			150	175	175
Add Monsoon Stereo System			200	225	225
Add Power Door Locks			125	150	150
Add Power Sunroof			475	550	550
Add Power Windows			150	175	175
Add Theft Recovery System			75	100	100
Add Tilt Steering Wheel			100	125	125
Deduct W/out Automatic Trans.			425	425	425
2003 VIBE-L4					
Veh. Ident.: 5Y2(Model)()()()3Z000001 Up.					
Wagon 4D	SL6	2701	10625	12775	13675
Wagon 4D GT (6 Spd.)	SN6	2800	11300	13525	14450
Wagon 4D (AWD)	SM6	2976	11950	14200	15150
Add Aluminum/Alloy Wheels (Std. GT)			275	325	325
Add Navigation System			500	575	575
Add Power Sunroof			525	600	600
Add Theft Recovery System			75	100	100
Deduct W/out Automatic Trans. (Ex. GT)			525	525	525
Deduct W/out Cruise Control			175	175	175
Deduct W/out Power Door Locks			150	150	150
Deduct W/out Power Windows			175	175	175
2003 GRAND AM-V6					
Veh. Ident.: 1G2(Model)2()()3()000001 Up.					
Coupe 2D GT	NV/W1	3099	10775	12950	13875
Sedan 4D SE (4 Cyl.)	NE/F5	3116	8050	9925	10825
Sedan 4D SE	NE/F/G5		8550	10450	11375
Sedan 4D GT	NV/W5	3118	10675	12850	13750

BODY TYPE	Model No.	Weight	Trade-In	Retail	High Retail
Add SC/T Appearance Pkg. (GT)			450	500	500
Add Aluminum/Alloy Wheels (Std. GT)			275	325	325
Add Leather Seats			400	450	450
Add Monsoon Stereo System (Std. GT)			250	300	300
Add Power Seat			175	200	200
Add Power Sunroof			525	600	600
Add Theft Recovery System			75	100	100
Deduct W/out Automatic Trans.			525	525	525
Deduct W/out Cruise Control			175	175	175
Deduct W/out Power Windows			175	175	175
2003 BONNEVILLE-V6					
Veh. Ident.: 1G2(Model)()()()34000001 Up.					
Sedan 4D SE	HX5	3590	11375	13675	14775
Sedan 4D SLE	HY5	3650	14900	17450	18675
Sedan 4D SSEi	HZ5	3790	16825	19475	20775
Add Aluminum/Alloy Wheels (SE)			325	375	375
Add Leather Seats (Std. SSEi)			475	550	550
Add Power Sunroof			575	650	650
Add Theft Recovery System			75	100	100
2003 GRAND PRIX-V6					
Veh. Ident.: 1G2(Model)2()()3F000001 Up.					
Sedan 4D SE	WJ/K5	3384	9050	11025	11900
Sedan 4D GT	WP5	3496	11500	13725	14675
Sedan 4D GT Limited	WP5		12250	14600	15575
Sedan 4D GTP	WR5	3559	13500	15900	16925
Sedan 4D GTP Limited	WR5		14250	16700	17750
Add Aluminum/Alloy Wheels (Std. GT, GTP)			275	325	325
Add Bose Stereo System			250	300	300
Add Leather Seats (Std. Limited)			400	450	450
Add Power Seat (Std. GT, GTP)			175	200	200
Add Power Sunroof			525	600	600
Add Theft Recovery System			75	100	100
PONTIAC					
2002 SUNFIRE-L4					
Veh. Ident.: 1G2(Model)()()()27000001 Up.					
Coupe 2D SE	JB1	2606	5725	7250	8025
Coupe 2D GT	JD1	2771	6950	8575	9350
Sedan 4D SE	JB5	2644	5700	7225	8000
Add Aluminum/Alloy Wheels (Std. GT)			200	225	225
Add Compact Disc Player (Std. GT)			75	100	100
Add Cruise Control			125	150	150
Add Power Door Locks			100	125	125
Add Power Sunroof			425	475	475
Add Power Windows			125	150	150
Add Theft Recovery System			75	100	100
Deduct W/out Automatic Trans.			375	375	375
2002 GRAND AM-4 Cyl.					
Veh. Ident.: 1G2(Model)()()()2()000001 Up.					
Coupe 2D SE	NE/F1	3066	7150	8925	9825
Sedan 4D SE	NE/F5	3116	7050	8825	9725
2002 GRAND AM-V6					
Veh. Ident.: 1G2(Model)()()()2()000001 Up.					
Coupe 2D SE	NF1		7550	9350	10225

PASSENGER CARS

BODY TYPE	Model No.	Weight	Trade-In	Retail	High Retail
Coupe 2D GT	NV/W1	3091	**9450**	**11475**	**12375**
Sedan 4D SE	NF5		**7450**	**9250**	**10125**
Sedan 4D GT	NV/W5	3168	**9350**	**11375**	**12275**
GRAND AM OPTIONS					
Add Aluminum/Alloy Wheels (Std. GT)			**225**	**250**	**250**
Add Compact Disc Player (Std. GT)			**75**	**100**	**100**
Add Leather Seats			**350**	**400**	**400**
Add Power Seat			**150**	**175**	**175**
Add Power Sunroof			**475**	**550**	**550**
Add Theft Recovery System			**75**	**100**	**100**
Deduct W/out Automatic Trans.			**475**	**475**	**475**
Deduct W/out Cruise Control			**150**	**150**	**150**
Deduct W/out Power Windows			**150**	**150**	**150**
2002 FIREBIRD-V6					
Veh. Ident.: 2G2(Model)()()()22000001 Up.					
Coupe 2D	FS2	3327	**10550**	**12700**	**13600**
Convertible 2D	FS3	3535	**13000**	**15400**	**16400**
2002 FIREBIRD-V8-6 Spd./AT					
Veh. Ident.: 2G2(Model)()()()22000001 Up.					
Coupe 2D Formula	FV2	3452	**15450**	**17975**	**19025**
Coupe 2D Trans Am	FV2	3499	**16750**	**19350**	**20450**
Coupe 2D Trans Am WS6	FV2		**18600**	**21400**	**22550**
Convertible 2D Trans Am	FV3	3623	**18250**	**21050**	**22200**
Convertible 2D Trans Am WS6	FV3		**20100**	**23000**	**24200**
FIREBIRD OPTIONS					
Add Leather Seats (Std. Trans Am)			**350**	**400**	**400**
Add Monsoon Stereo (Base Coupe)			**200**	**225**	**225**
Add Power Seat (Base Coupe)			**150**	**175**	**175**
Add T-Top (Std. Formula, Trans Am)			**625**	**700**	**700**
Add Theft Recovery System			**75**	**100**	**100**
Deduct W/out Automatic Trans. (V6)			**475**	**475**	**475**
2002 BONNEVILLE-V6					
Veh. Ident.: 1G2(Model)()()()24000001 Up.					
Sedan 4D SE	HX5	3633	**9675**	**11825**	**12875**
Sedan 4D SLE	HY5	3678	**12750**	**15175**	**16350**
Sedan 4D SSEi	HZ5	3716	**14325**	**16850**	**18075**
Add Aluminum/Alloy Wheels (SE)			**275**	**325**	**325**
Add Leather Seats (Std. SSEi)			**425**	**475**	**475**
Add Power Sunroof			**525**	**600**	**600**
Add Theft Recovery System			**75**	**100**	**100**
2002 GRAND PRIX-V6					
Veh. Ident.: 1G2(Model)()()()2F000001 Up.					
Coupe 2D GT	WP1	3429	**9800**	**11850**	**12750**
Coupe 2D GTP	WR1	3494	**11950**	**14200**	**15150**
Sedan 4D SE	WJ/K5	3384	**7600**	**9425**	**10300**
Sedan 4D GT	WP5	3496	**9800**	**11850**	**12750**
Sedan 4D GTP	WR5	3559	**11950**	**14200**	**15150**
Add Aluminum/Alloy Wheels (Std. GT, GTP)			**225**	**250**	**250**
Add Bose Stereo System			**200**	**225**	**225**
Add Compact Disc Player (Std. GT, GTP)			**75**	**100**	**100**
Add Leather Seats			**350**	**400**	**400**
Add Power Seat (Std. GT, GTP)			**150**	**175**	**175**
Add Power Sunroof			**475**	**550**	**550**

BODY TYPE	Model No.	Weight	Trade-In	Retail	High Retail
Add Theft Recovery System			75	100	100
PONTIAC					
2001 SUNFIRE-L4					
Veh. Ident.: ()G2(Model)()()()1()000001 Up.					
Coupe 2D SE	JB1	2606	4650	6050	6825
Coupe 2D GT	JD1	2771	5875	7400	8200
Sedan 4D SE	JB5	2644	4625	6025	6800
Add Aluminum/Alloy Wheels (Std. GT)			150	175	175
Add Compact Disc Player (Std. GT)			50	75	75
Add Cruise Control			100	125	125
Add Power Door Locks			75	100	100
Add Power Sunroof			375	425	425
Add Power Windows			100	125	125
Add Theft Recovery System			50	75	75
Add Tilt Steering Wheel (Std. GT)			75	100	100
Deduct W/out Automatic Trans.			325	325	325
2001 GRAND AM-4 Cyl.					
Veh. Ident.: ()G2(Model)()()()1()000001 Up.					
Coupe 2D SE	NE/F1	3066	5975	7675	8600
Sedan 4D SE	NE/F5	3116	5875	7550	8450
2001 GRAND AM-V6					
Veh. Ident.: ()G2(Model)()()()1()000001 Up.					
Coupe 2D SE	NF1		6300	8025	8875
Coupe 2D GT	NV/W1	3091	7875	9725	10625
Sedan 4D SE	NF5		6200	7925	8850
Sedan 4D GT	NV/W5	3168	7775	9600	10500
GRAND AM OPTIONS					
Add Aluminum/Alloy Wheels (Std. GT)			175	200	200
Add Compact Disc Player (Std. GT)			50	75	75
Add Leather Seats			300	350	350
Add Power Seat			125	150	150
Add Power Sunroof			425	475	475
Add Theft Recovery System			50	75	75
Deduct W/out Automatic Trans.			425	425	425
Deduct W/out Cruise Control			125	125	125
Deduct W/out Power Windows			125	125	125
2001 FIREBIRD-V6					
Veh. Ident.: ()G2(Model)()()()1()000001 Up.					
Coupe 2D	FS2	3327	8875	10800	11750
Convertible 2D	FS3	3490	10850	13050	13975
2001 FIREBIRD-V8-6 Spd./AT					
Veh. Ident.: ()G2(Model)()()()1()000001 Up.					
Coupe 2D Formula	FV2	3452	12625	15000	15975
Coupe 2D Trans Am	FV2	3499	14500	16975	18025
Coupe 2D Trans Am WS6	FV2		16150	18700	19775
Convertible 2D Trans Am	FV3	3623	15800	18350	19425
Convertible 2D Trans Am WS6	FV3		17450	20200	21325
FIREBIRD OPTIONS					
Add Leather Seats (Std. Trans Am)			300	350	350
Add Power Seat (Std. Trans Am, Conv)			125	150	150
Add T-Top (Std. Trans Am)			600	675	675
Add Theft Recovery System			50	75	75
Deduct W/out Automatic Trans. (V6)			425	425	425

BODY TYPE	Model No.	Weight	Trade-In	Retail	High Retail
Deduct W/out Power Door Locks			100	100	100
Deduct W/out Power Windows			125	125	125
2001 BONNEVILLE-V6					
Veh. Ident.: ()G2(Model)()()()1()000001 Up.					
Sedan 4D SE	HX5	3633	8350	10400	11425
Sedan 4D SLE	HY5	3678	10575	12800	13875
Sedan 4D SSEi	HZ5	3716	12050	14400	15550
Add Aluminum/Alloy Wheels (SE)			225	250	250
Add Compact Disc Player (Std. SSEi)			100	125	125
Add Leather Seats (Std. SSEi)			375	425	425
Add Power Sunroof			475	550	550
Add Theft Recovery System			50	75	75
2001 GRAND PRIX-V6					
Veh. Ident.: ()G2(Model)()()()1()000001 Up.					
Coupe 2D GT	WP1	3429	8050	9925	10825
Coupe 2D GTP	WR1	3494	10050	12150	13050
Sedan 4D SE	WJ/K5	3384	6375	8100	8950
Sedan 4D GT	WP5	3496	8050	9925	10825
Sedan 4D GTP	WR5	3559	10050	12150	13050
Add Aluminum/Alloy Wheels (Std. GT, GTP)			175	200	200
Add Bose Stereo System			150	175	175
Add Compact Disc Player (Std. GTP)			50	75	75
Add Leather Seats			300	350	350
Add Power Seat (Std. GTP)			125	150	150
Add Power Sunroof			425	475	475
Add Theft Recovery System			50	75	75
Deduct W/out Cruise Control			125	125	125
PONTIAC					
2000 SUNFIRE-L4					
Veh. Ident.: ()G2(Model)()()()Y()000001 Up.					
Coupe 2D SE	JB1	2606	3750	5050	5775
Coupe 2D GT	JD1	2771	4800	6225	7000
Sedan 4D SE	JB5	2644	3725	5025	5750
Convertible 2D GT	JB3	2906	6025	7575	8375
Add Aluminum/Alloy Wheels (Std. GT)			100	125	125
Add Compact Disc Player (Std. GT)			50	75	75
Add Cruise Control (Std. Conv)			75	100	100
Add Power Door Locks (Std. Conv)			50	75	75
Add Power Sunroof			325	375	375
Add Power Windows (Std. Conv)			75	100	100
Add Tilt Steering Wheel (Std. GT)			50	75	75
Deduct W/out Automatic Trans.			300	300	300
2000 GRAND AM-4 Cyl.					
Veh. Ident.: ()G2(Model)()()()Y()000001 Up.					
Coupe 2D SE	NE/F1	3066	4850	6400	7300
Sedan 4D SE	NE/F5	3116	4750	6275	7150
2000 GRAND AM-V6					
Veh. Ident.: ()G2(Model)()()()Y()000001 Up.					
Coupe 2D SE	NF/G1	3066	5150	6775	7700
Coupe 2D GT	NV/W1	3091	6300	8025	8875
Sedan 4D SE	NF/G5	3168	5050	6625	7525
Sedan 4D GT	NV/W5	3168	6200	7900	8825

BODY TYPE	Model No.	Weight	Trade-In	Retail	High Retail
GRAND AM OPTIONS					
Add Aluminum/Alloy Wheels (Std. GT)			125	150	150
Add Compact Disc Player			50	75	75
Add Leather Seats			250	300	300
Add Power Seat			100	125	125
Add Power Sunroof			375	425	425
Deduct W/out Automatic Trans.			375	375	375
Deduct W/out Cruise Control			100	100	100
Deduct W/out Power Windows			100	100	100
2000 FIREBIRD-V6					
Veh. Ident.: ()G2(Model)()()()Y()000001 Up.					
Coupe 2D	FS2	3338	7275	9075	9925
Convertible 2D	FS3	3461	9100	11050	11925
2000 FIREBIRD-V8-6 Spd./AT					
Veh. Ident.: ()G2(Model)()()()Y()000001 Up.					
Coupe 2D Formula	FV2	3441	10775	12950	13875
Coupe 2D Formula WS6	FV2		12225	14575	15550
Coupe 2D Trans Am	FV2	3474	12475	14850	15825
Coupe 2D Trans Am WS6	FV2		13925	16375	17400
Convertible 2D Trans Am	FV3	3567	13700	16125	17150
Convertible 2D Trans Am WS6	FV3		15150	17650	18700
FIREBIRD OPTIONS					
Add Leather Seats (Std. Trans Am)			250	300	300
Add Power Seat (Std. Trans Am, Conv)			100	125	125
Add T-Top (Std. Trans Am)			525	600	600
Deduct W/out Automatic Trans. (V6)			375	375	375
Deduct W/out Power Door Locks			75	75	75
Deduct W/out Power Windows			100	100	100
2000 BONNEVILLE-V6					
Veh. Ident.: ()G2(Model)()()()Y()000001 Up.					
Sedan 4D SE	HX5	3633	6675	8600	9625
Sedan 4D SLE	HY5	3678	8350	10400	11425
Sedan 4D SSEi	HZ5	3691	9675	11825	12875
Add Aluminum/Alloy Wheels (SE)			175	200	200
Add Compact Disc Player (Std. SSEi)			75	100	100
Add Leather Seats (Std. SSEi)			325	375	375
Add Power Sunroof			425	475	475
Deduct W/out Power Seat			125	125	125
2000 GRAND PRIX-V6					
Veh. Ident.: ()G2(Model)()()()Y()000001 Up.					
Coupe 2D GT	WP1	3386	6525	8275	9125
Coupe 2D GTP	WR1	3455	7950	9800	10700
Sedan 4D SE	WJ/K5	3386	5100	6725	7650
Sedan 4D GT	WP5	3955	6525	8275	9125
Sedan 4D GTP	WR5	3523	7950	9800	10700
Add Aluminum/Alloy Wheels (Std. GT, GTP)			125	150	150
Add Bose Stereo System			100	125	125
Add Compact Disc Player (Std. GTP)			50	75	75
Add Leather Seats			250	300	300
Add Power Seat (Std. GTP)			100	125	125
Add Power Sunroof			375	425	425
Deduct W/out Cruise Control			100	100	100

P A S S E N G E R   C A R S

BODY TYPE	Model No.	Weight	Trade-In	Retail	High Retail
PONTIAC					
1999 SUNFIRE-L4					
Veh. Ident.: ()G2(Model)()()()X()000001 Up.					
Coupe 2D SE	JB1	2630	**3025**	**4250**	**4975**
Coupe 2D GT	JD1	2822	**3775**	**5075**	**5800**
Sedan 4D SE	JB5	2670	**3000**	**4225**	**4950**
Convertible 2D GT	JB3	2892	**4800**	**6250**	**7025**
Add Aluminum/Alloy Wheels (Std. GT)			**50**	**75**	**75**
Add Cruise Control (Std. Conv.)			**50**	**75**	**75**
Add Power Sunroof			**275**	**325**	**325**
Add Power Windows (Std. Conv.)			**50**	**75**	**75**
Deduct W/out Air Conditioning			**325**	**325**	**325**
Deduct W/out Automatic Trans.			**250**	**250**	**250**
1999 GRAND AM-4 Cyl.					
Veh. Ident.: ()G2(Model)()()()X()000001 Up.					
Coupe 2D SE	NE1		**3900**	**5350**	**6175**
Sedan 4D SE	NE5		**3800**	**5225**	**6025**
1999 GRAND AM-V6					
Veh. Ident.: ()G2(Model)()()()X()000001 Up.					
Coupe 2D SE	NE1		**4200**	**5675**	**6525**
Coupe 2D GT	NW1	3168	**5075**	**6650**	**7550**
Sedan 4D SE	NE5		**4100**	**5575**	**6425**
Sedan 4D GT	NW5	3168	**4975**	**6525**	**7425**
GRAND AM OPTIONS					
Add Aluminum/Alloy Wheels (Std. GT)			**75**	**100**	**100**
Add Leather Seats			**225**	**250**	**250**
Add Power Seat			**75**	**100**	**100**
Add Power Sunroof			**325**	**375**	**375**
Deduct W/out Cruise Control			**75**	**75**	**75**
Deduct W/out Power Windows			**75**	**75**	**75**
1999 FIREBIRD-V6					
Veh. Ident.: ()G2(Model)()()()X()000001 Up.					
Coupe 2D	FS2	3340	**5900**	**7575**	**8475**
Convertible 2D	FS3	3492	**7550**	**9350**	**10225**
1999 FIREBIRD-V8-6 Spd./AT					
Veh. Ident.: ()G2(Model)()()()X()000001 Up.					
Coupe 2D Formula	FV2	3455	**8950**	**10875**	**11825**
Coupe 2D Formula WS6	FV2		**10250**	**12375**	**13275**
Coupe 2D Trans Am	FV2	3477	**10500**	**12650**	**13550**
Coupe 2D Trans Am WS6	FV2		**11800**	**14050**	**15000**
Convertible 2D Trans Am	FV3	3605	**11625**	**13850**	**14800**
Convertible 2D Trans Am WS6	FV3		**12925**	**15300**	**16300**
FIREBIRD OPTIONS					
Add Leather Seats (Std. Trans Am)			**225**	**250**	**250**
Add Power Seat (Std. Trans Am, Conv.)			**75**	**100**	**100**
Add T-Top (Std. Trans Am)			**475**	**550**	**550**
Deduct W/out Automatic Trans. (V6)			**325**	**325**	**325**
Deduct W/out Power Door Locks			**50**	**50**	**50**
Deduct W/out Power Windows			**75**	**75**	**75**
1999 BONNEVILLE-V6					
Veh. Ident.: ()G2(Model)()()()X()000001 Up.					
Sedan 4D SE	HX5	3446	**4725**	**6425**	**7425**
Sedan 4D SSE	HZ5	3587	**5875**	**7700**	**8750**

BODY TYPE	Model No.	Weight	Trade-In	Retail	High Retail
Sedan 4D SSEi	HZ5		6175	8050	9050
Add Aluminum/Alloy Wheels (SE)			125	150	150
Add Leather Seats (SE)			275	325	325
Add Power Sunroof			375	425	425
Deduct W/out Power Seat			100	100	100
1999 GRAND PRIX-V6					
Veh. Ident.: ()G2(Model)()()()X()000001 Up.					
Coupe 2D GT	WP1	3396	5300	6925	7850
Coupe 2D GTP	WR1		6175	7875	8800
Sedan 4D SE	WJ5	3414	4275	5750	6600
Sedan 4D GT	WP5		5300	6925	7850
Sedan 4D GTP	WR5		6175	7875	8800
Add Aluminum/Alloy Wheels (Std. GT, GTP)			75	100	100
Add Bose Stereo System			75	100	100
Add Leather Seats			225	250	250
Add Power Seat (Std. GTP)			75	100	100
Add Power Sunroof			325	375	375
Deduct W/out Cruise Control			75	75	75
PONTIAC					
1998 SUNFIRE-L4					
Veh. Ident.: ()G2(Model)()()()W()000001 Up.					
Coupe 2D SE	JB1	2637	2425	3575	4250
Coupe 2D GT	JD1	2822	3050	4275	5000
Sedan 4D SE	JB5	2674	2400	3550	4225
Convertible 2D SE	JB3	2870	3350	4600	5375
Add Cruise Control (Std. Conv.)			50	75	75
Add Power Sunroof			225	275	275
Add Power Windows			50	75	75
Deduct W/out Air Conditioning			275	275	275
Deduct W/out Automatic Trans.			200	200	200
1998 GRAND AM-4 Cyl.					
Veh. Ident.: ()G2(Model)()()()W()000001 Up.					
Coupe 2D SE	NE1	2835	2800	4100	4900
Coupe 2D GT	NW1	2945	3350	4725	5600
Sedan 4D SE	NE5	2877	2700	4000	4800
Sedan 4D GT	NW5	2987	3250	4625	5500
1998 GRAND AM-V6					
Veh. Ident.: ()G2(Model)()()()W()000001 Up.					
Coupe 2D SE	NE1		3050	4400	5225
Coupe 2D GT	NW1		3600	5000	5900
Sedan 4D SE	NE5		2950	4275	5100
Sedan 4D GT	NW5		3500	4900	5800
GRAND AM OPTIONS					
Add Aluminum/Alloy Wheels (Std. GT)			50	75	75
Add Leather Seats			175	200	200
Add Power Seat			50	75	75
Add Power Sunroof			275	325	325
Deduct W/out Automatic Trans.			275	275	275
Deduct W/out Cruise Control			50	50	50
Deduct W/out Power Windows			50	50	50

PASSENGER CARS

BODY TYPE	Model No.	Weight	Trade-In	Retail	High Retail
1998 FIREBIRD-V6					
Veh. Ident.: ()G2(Model)()()()W()000001 Up.					
Coupe 2D	FS2	3340	**4675**	**6200**	**7075**
Convertible 2D	FS3	3492	**6175**	**7875**	**8800**
1998 FIREBIRD-V8-6 Spd./AT					
Veh. Ident.: ()G2(Model)()()()W()000001 Up.					
Coupe 2D Formula	FV2	3455	**7325**	**9125**	**10000**
Coupe 2D Formula WS6	FV2	3448	**8550**	**10450**	**11375**
Coupe 2D Trans Am	FV2	3477	**8675**	**10600**	**11550**
Coupe 2D Trans Am WS6	FV2	3479	**9900**	**11975**	**12900**
Convertible 2D Trans Am	FV3	3605	**9725**	**11775**	**12675**
Convertible 2D Trans Am WS6	FV3	3573	**10950**	**13125**	**14050**
FIREBIRD OPTIONS					
Add Leather Seats (Std. Trans Am)			**175**	**200**	**200**
Add Power Seat (Std. Trans Am, Conv.)			**50**	**75**	**75**
Add T-Top (Std. Trans Am)			**425**	**475**	**475**
Deduct W/out Automatic Trans. (V6)			**275**	**275**	**275**
Deduct W/out Power Windows			**50**	**50**	**50**
1998 BONNEVILLE-V6					
Veh. Ident.: ()G2(Model)()()()W()000001 Up.					
Sedan 4D SE	HX5	3446	**3950**	**5525**	**6475**
Sedan 4D SSE	HZ5	3587	**4950**	**6675**	**7700**
Sedan 4D SSEi	HZ5		**5250**	**7025**	**8025**
Add Aluminum/Alloy Wheels (SE)			**100**	**125**	**125**
Add Leather Seats (SE)			**225**	**250**	**250**
Add Power Sunroof			**325**	**375**	**375**
Deduct W/out Power Seat			**75**	**75**	**75**
1998 GRAND PRIX-V6					
Veh. Ident.: ()G2(Model)()()()W()000001 Up.					
Coupe 2D GT	WP1	3396	**4450**	**5950**	**6825**
Coupe 2D GTP	WP1		**4950**	**6500**	**7400**
Sedan 4D SE	WJ5	3373	**3600**	**5025**	**5825**
Sedan 4D GT	WP5	3414	**4450**	**5950**	**6825**
Sedan 4D GTP	WP5		**4950**	**6500**	**7400**
Add Aluminum/Alloy Wheels (Std. GT, GTP)			**50**	**75**	**75**
Add Leather Seats			**175**	**200**	**200**
Add Power Seat (Std. GTP)			**50**	**75**	**75**
Add Power Sunroof			**275**	**325**	**325**
Deduct W/out Cruise Control			**50**	**50**	**50**
PONTIAC					
1997 SUNFIRE-L4					
Veh. Ident.: ()G2(Model)()()()V()000001 Up.					
Coupe 2D SE	JB1	2637	**1975**	**3075**	**3675**
Coupe 2D GT	JD1	2822	**2475**	**3650**	**4325**
Sedan 4D SE	JB5	2674	**1975**	**3075**	**3675**
Convertible 2D SE	JB3	2870	**2675**	**3875**	**4575**
Add Power Sunroof			**150**	**175**	**175**
Deduct W/out Air Conditioning			**150**	**150**	**150**
Deduct W/out Automatic Trans.			**125**	**125**	**125**
1997 GRAND AM-4 Cyl.					
Veh. Ident.: ()G2(Model)()()()V()000001 Up.					
Coupe 2D SE	NE1	2830	**2225**	**3450**	**4175**

BODY TYPE	Model No.	Weight	Trade-In	Retail	High Retail
Coupe 2D GT	NW1	2943	**2675**	**3950**	**4750**
Sedan 4D SE	NE5	2873	**2175**	**3400**	**4125**
Sedan 4D GT	NW5	2985	**2625**	**3900**	**4700**
1997 GRAND AM-V6					
Veh. Ident.: ()G2(Model)()()()V()000001 Up.					
Coupe 2D SE	NE1		**2375**	**3625**	**4375**
Coupe 2D GT	NW1		**2825**	**4125**	**4925**
Sedan 4D SE	NE5		**2325**	**3575**	**4325**
Sedan 4D GT	NW5		**2775**	**4075**	**4875**
GRAND AM OPTIONS					
Add Leather Seats			**150**	**175**	**175**
Add Power Seat			**50**	**75**	**75**
Add Power Sunroof			**200**	**225**	**225**
Deduct W/out Automatic Trans.			**175**	**175**	**175**
Deduct W/out Cruise Control			**25**	**25**	**25**
Deduct W/out Power Windows			**25**	**25**	**25**
1997 FIREBIRD-V6					
Veh. Ident.: ()G2(Model)()()()V()000001 Up.					
Coupe 2D	FS2	3274	**3925**	**5375**	**6200**
Convertible 2D	FS3	3479	**5150**	**6775**	**7700**
1997 FIREBIRD-V8-6 Spd./AT					
Veh. Ident.: ()G2(Model)()()()V()000001 Up.					
Coupe 2D Formula	FV2	3437	**6100**	**7800**	**8725**
Coupe 2D Trans Am	FV2	3477	**6575**	**8325**	**9175**
Convertible 2D Formula	FV3	3607	**7325**	**9125**	**10000**
Convertible 2D Trans Am	FV3	3605	**7800**	**9625**	**10525**
FIREBIRD OPTIONS					
Add Leather Seats			**150**	**175**	**175**
Add Power Seat			**50**	**75**	**75**
Add T-Top			**250**	**300**	**300**
Deduct W/out Automatic Trans. (V6)			**175**	**175**	**175**
Deduct W/out Cruise Control			**25**	**25**	**25**
Deduct W/out Power Windows			**25**	**25**	**25**
1997 BONNEVILLE-V6					
Veh. Ident.: ()G2(Model)()()()V()000001 Up.					
Sedan 4D SE	HX5	3446	**3250**	**4750**	**5675**
Sedan 4D SSE	HZ5	3587	**3850**	**5425**	**6350**
Sedan 4D SSEi	HZ5		**4225**	**5875**	**6850**
Add Aluminum/Alloy Wheels (SE)			**50**	**75**	**75**
Add Leather Seats			**200**	**225**	**225**
Add Power Sunroof			**250**	**300**	**300**
Add Supercharged V6 Engine (Std. SSEi)			**200**	**225**	**225**
Deduct W/out Power Seat			**75**	**75**	**75**
1997 GRAND PRIX-V6					
Veh. Ident.: ()G2(Model)()()()V()000001 Up.					
Coupe 2D GT	WP1	3396	**3700**	**5125**	**5925**
Coupe 2D GTP	WP1		**4000**	**5450**	**6275**
Sedan 4D SE	WJ5	3355	**3100**	**4450**	**5300**
Sedan 4D GT	WP5	3414	**3700**	**5125**	**5925**
Sedan 4D GTP	WP5		**4000**	**5450**	**6275**
Add Leather Seats			**150**	**175**	**175**
Add Power Seat (Std. GTP)			**50**	**75**	**75**
Add Power Sunroof			**200**	**225**	**225**

BODY TYPE	*Model No.*	*Weight*	*Trade-In*	*Retail*	*High Retail*
Deduct W/out Cruise Control			**25**	**25**	**25**
PONTIAC					
1996 SUNFIRE-L4					
Veh. Ident.: ()G2(Model)()()()T()000001 Up.					
Coupe 2D SE	JB1	2679	**1750**	**2825**	**3450**
Coupe 2D GT	JD1	2829	**2200**	**3350**	**4000**
Sedan 4D SE	JB5	2723	**1750**	**2825**	**3450**
Convertible 2D SE	JB3	2835	**2350**	**3500**	**4150**
Add Power Sunroof			**100**	**125**	**125**
Deduct W/out Air Conditioning			**75**	**75**	**75**
Deduct W/out Automatic Trans.			**75**	**75**	**75**
1996 GRAND AM-4 Cyl.					
Veh. Ident.: ()G2(Model)()()()T()000001 Up.					
Coupe 2D SE	NE1	2802	**1825**	**3000**	**3675**
Coupe 2D GT	NW1	2879	**2200**	**3425**	**4150**
Sedan 4D SE	NE5	2855	**1775**	**2950**	**3625**
Sedan 4D GT	NW5	2928	**2150**	**3375**	**4100**
1996 GRAND AM-V6					
Veh. Ident.: ()G2(Model)()()()T()000001 Up.					
Coupe 2D SE	NE1	2781	**1925**	**3125**	**3800**
Coupe 2D GT	NW1	2890	**2300**	**3550**	**4300**
Sedan 4D SE	NE5	2834	**1875**	**3050**	**3725**
Sedan 4D GT	NW5	2907	**2250**	**3475**	**4200**
GRAND AM OPTIONS					
Add Power Sunroof			**150**	**175**	**175**
Deduct W/out Air Conditioning			**150**	**150**	**150**
Deduct W/out Automatic Trans.			**125**	**125**	**125**
1996 FIREBIRD-V6					
Veh. Ident.: ()G2(Model)()()()T()000001 Up.					
Coupe 2D	FS2	3230	**3425**	**4825**	**5725**
Convertible 2D	FS3	3346	**4575**	**6100**	**6950**
1996 FIREBIRD-V8-6 Spd./AT					
Veh. Ident.: ()G2(Model)()()()T()000001 Up.					
Coupe 2D Formula	FV2	3373	**5325**	**6950**	**7900**
Coupe 2D Trans Am	FV2	3445	**5800**	**7475**	**8375**
Convertible 2D Formula	FV3	3489	**6475**	**8200**	**9050**
Convertible 2D Trans Am	FV3	3610	**6950**	**8725**	**9600**
FIREBIRD OPTIONS					
Add T-Top			**200**	**225**	**225**
Deduct W/out Air Conditioning			**150**	**150**	**150**
Deduct W/out Automatic Trans. (V6)			**125**	**125**	**125**
1996 BONNEVILLE-V6					
Veh. Ident.: ()G2(Model)()()()T()000001 Up.					
Sedan 4D SE	HX5	3446	**2600**	**3975**	**4875**
Sedan 4D SSE	HZ5	3582	**3100**	**4575**	**5475**
Sedan 4D SSEi	HZ5		**3425**	**4950**	**5900**
Add Power Sunroof			**200**	**225**	**225**
Add Supercharged V6 Engine (Std. SSEi)			**150**	**175**	**175**
1996 GRAND PRIX-V6					
Veh. Ident.: ()G2(Model)()()()T()000001 Up.					
Coupe 2D SE	WJ1	3284	**2075**	**3300**	**4000**
Coupe 2D GTP	WJ1		**2475**	**3725**	**4500**

BODY TYPE	Model No.	Weight	Trade-In	Retail	High Retail
Sedan 4D SE	WJ5	3358	**2075**	**3300**	**4000**
Sedan 4D GT	WJ5		**2475**	**3725**	**4500**
Add Power Sunroof			**150**	**175**	**175**
PONTIAC					
1995 SUNFIRE-L4					
Veh. Ident.: ()G2(Model)()()()S()000001 Up.					
Coupe 2D SE	JB1	2679	**1425**	**2450**	**3025**
Sedan 4D SE	JB5	2723	**1425**	**2450**	**3025**
Convertible 2D SE	JB3	2835	**2000**	**3100**	**3700**
1995 SUNFIRE-Quad 4					
Veh. Ident.: ()G2JD1()()()S()000001 Up.					
Coupe 2D GT	JD1	2829	**1800**	**2875**	**3500**
1995 GRAND AM-Quad 4					
Veh. Ident.: ()G2(Model)()()()S()000001 Up.					
Coupe 2D SE	NE1	2736	**1400**	**2525**	**3150**
Coupe 2D GT	NW1	2882	**1725**	**2900**	**3575**
Sedan 4D SE	NE5	2793	**1350**	**2475**	**3075**
Sedan 4D GT	NW5	2882	**1675**	**2825**	**3475**
1995 GRAND AM-V6					
Veh. Ident.: ()G2(Model)()()()S()000001 Up.					
Coupe 2D SE	NE1	2769	**1500**	**2625**	**3250**
Coupe 2D GT	NW1	2855	**1825**	**3000**	**3675**
Sedan 4D SE	NE5	2826	**1450**	**2575**	**3200**
Sedan 4D GT	NW5	2915	**1775**	**2950**	**3625**
1995 FIREBIRD-V6					
Veh. Ident.: ()G2(Model)()()()S()000001 Up.					
Coupe 2D	FS2	3230	**2975**	**4300**	**5125**
Convertible 2D	FS3	3346	**4050**	**5525**	**6375**
1995 FIREBIRD-V8					
Veh. Ident.: ()G2(Model)()()()S()000001 Up.					
Coupe 2D Formula	FV2	3373	**4600**	**6125**	**7000**
Coupe 2D Trans Am	FV2	3445	**5075**	**6675**	**7600**
Convertible 2D Formula	FV3	3489	**5675**	**7325**	**8200**
Convertible 2D Trans Am	FV3	3610	**6150**	**7850**	**8775**
FIREBIRD OPTIONS					
Add T-Top			**150**	**175**	**175**
1995 BONNEVILLE-V6					
Veh. Ident.: ()G2(Model)()()()S()000001 Up.					
Sedan 4D SE	HX5	3446	**2150**	**3450**	**4275**
Sedan 4D SSE	HZ5	3587	**2575**	**3950**	**4825**
Sedan 4D SSEi	HZ5		**2900**	**4325**	**5200**
Add Supercharged V6 Engine (Std. SSEi)			**150**	**175**	**175**
1995 GRAND PRIX-V6					
Veh. Ident.: ()G2(Model)()()()S()000001 Up.					
Coupe 2D SE	WJ1	3275	**1675**	**2825**	**3475**
Coupe 2D GTP	WJ1		**2050**	**3250**	**3950**
Sedan 4D SE	WJ5	3370	**1675**	**2825**	**3475**
Sedan 4D GT	WJ5		**2050**	**3250**	**3950**

P A S S E N G E R C A R S

BODY TYPE	Model No.	Weight	Trade-In	Retail	High Retail
PORSCHE					
PORSCHE					
2004 BOXSTER-6 Cyl.-5/6 Spd.					
Veh. Ident.: WP0(Model)()4()600001 Up.					
Roadster 2D	CA298	2811	**33675**	**38225**	**40275**
Roadster 2D S	CB298	2911	**39250**	**44100**	**46325**
Roadster 2D S 50th Annv.	CB298				
2004 911-6 Cyl.-6 Spd.					
Veh. Ident.: WP0(Model)()4S600001 Up.					
Coupe 2D Carrera	AA299	2959			
Coupe 2D Carrera Targa	BA299	3119			
Coupe 2D Carrera 40th Annv.	AA299				
Coupe 2D Carrera Cabriolet	CA299	3135			
Coupe 2D Carrera 4S	AA299	3240			
Coupe 2D Carrera 4 Cabriolet	CA299	3267	**74200**	**81450**	**84800**
Coupe Carrera 4S Cabriolet	CA299	3296			
Coupe 2D Turbo (AWD)	AB299	3388	**93550**	**101875**	**105850**
Coupe Turbo Cabriolet (AWD)	CB299	3660			
PORSCHE OPTIONS					
Add Bose Stereo System (Std. 911 Turbo)			**425**	**475**	**475**
Add Detachable Hardtop			**1050**	**1175**	**1175**
Add Navigation System (Std. 911 Turbo)			**750**	**850**	**850**
Add Theft Recovery System			**100**	**125**	**125**
Add Tiptronic Trans.			**1325**	**1475**	**1475**
Add Traction Control (Std. Annv, 911 4, Turbo)			**650**	**725**	**725**
Deduct W/out Cruise Control			**250**	**250**	**250**
Deduct W/out Leather Seats			**575**	**575**	**575**
Deduct W/out Power Seat			**275**	**275**	**275**
Deduct W/out Power Sunroof			**725**	**725**	**725**
PORSCHE					
2003 BOXSTER-6 Cyl.-5/6 Spd.					
Veh. Ident.: WP0(Model)()3()620001 Up.					
Roadster 2D	CA298	2811	**29625**	**33800**	**35725**
Roadster 2D S	CB298	2911	**34800**	**39400**	**41500**
2003 911-6 Cyl.-6 Spd.					
Veh. Ident.: WP0(Model)()3S600001 Up.					
Coupe 2D Carrera	AA299	2959	**54825**	**61025**	**63775**
Coupe 2D Carrera Targa	BA299	3119	**57675**	**64025**	**66850**
Coupe 2D Carrera Cabriolet	CA299	3135	**60075**	**66550**	**69450**
Coupe 2D Carrera 4S	AA299	3240	**60575**	**67075**	**70000**
Coupe 2D Carrera 4 Cabriolet	CA299	3267	**63575**	**70225**	**73250**
Coupe 2D Turbo (AWD)	AB299	3388	**83225**	**90975**	**94625**
PORSCHE OPTIONS					
Add Bose Stereo System (Std. 911 Turbo)			**375**	**425**	**425**
Add Detachable Hardtop			**975**	**1100**	**1100**
Add Navigation System			**650**	**725**	**725**
Add Theft Recovery System			**75**	**100**	**100**
Add Tiptronic Trans.			**1225**	**1375**	**1375**
Add Traction Control (Std. 911 4, Turbo)			**575**	**650**	**650**
Deduct W/out Cruise Control			**225**	**225**	**225**
Deduct W/out Leather Seats			**525**	**525**	**525**
Deduct W/out Power Sunroof			**675**	**675**	**675**

BODY TYPE	Model No.	Weight	Trade-In	Retail	High Retail
PORSCHE					
2002 BOXSTER-6 Cyl.-5/6 Spd.					
Veh. Ident.: WP0(Model)()2()620001 Up.					
Roadster 2D	CA298	2778	**25725**	**29575**	**31375**
Roadster 2D S	CB298	2855	**30500**	**34775**	**36725**
2002 911-6 Cyl.-6 Spd.					
Veh. Ident.: WP0(Model)()2S600001 Up.					
Coupe 2D Carrera	AA299	2910	**46050**	**51750**	**54225**
Coupe 2D Carrera Targa	BA299	3114	**48950**	**54800**	**57350**
Coupe 2D Carrera Cabriolet	CA299	3075	**50950**	**56925**	**59550**
Coupe 2D Carrera 4S	AA299	3395	**51600**	**57625**	**60275**
Coupe 2D Carrera 4 Cabriolet	CA299	3197	**54250**	**60400**	**63125**
Coupe 2D Turbo (AWD)	AB299	3395	**74250**	**81500**	**84850**
PORSCHE OPTIONS					
Add Bose Stereo System (Std. 911 Turbo)			**325**	**375**	**375**
Add Compact Disc Player			**125**	**150**	**150**
Add Detachable Hardtop			**900**	**1000**	**1000**
Add Navigation System			**550**	**625**	**625**
Add Theft Recovery System			**75**	**100**	**100**
Add Tiptronic Trans.			**1125**	**1250**	**1250**
Add Traction Control (Std. 911 4, Turbo)			**500**	**575**	**575**
Deduct W/out Cruise Control			**200**	**200**	**200**
Deduct W/out Leather Seats			**475**	**475**	**475**
Deduct W/out Power Sunroof			**625**	**625**	**625**
PORSCHE					
2001 BOXSTER-6 Cyl.-5/6 Spd.					
Veh. Ident.: WP0(Model)()1()620001 Up.					
Roadster 2D	CA298	2778	**22675**	**26300**	**27975**
Roadster 2D S	CB298	2855	**27050**	**31025**	**32875**
2001 911-6 Cyl.-6 Spd.					
Veh. Ident.: WP0(Model)()1S6()0001 Up.					
Coupe 2D Carrera	AA299	2910	**39525**	**44875**	**47125**
Coupe 2D Carrera Cabriolet	CA299	3075	**44075**	**49675**	**52075**
Coupe 2D Carrera 4	AA299	3032	**42625**	**48150**	**50500**
Coupe 2D Carrera 4 Cabriolet	CA299	3197	**47175**	**52925**	**55425**
Coupe 2D Turbo (AWD)	AB299	3395	**65500**	**72275**	**75350**
PORSCHE OPTIONS					
Add Compact Disc Player			**125**	**150**	**150**
Add Detachable Hardtop			**825**	**925**	**925**
Add Navigation System			**500**	**575**	**575**
Add Theft Recovery System			**50**	**75**	**75**
Add Tiptronic Trans.			**1025**	**1150**	**1150**
Add Traction Control (Std. 911 4, Turbo)			**425**	**475**	**475**
Deduct W/out Cruise Control			**175**	**175**	**175**
Deduct W/out Leather Seats			**425**	**425**	**425**
Deduct W/out Power Sunroof			**575**	**575**	**575**
PORSCHE					
2000 BOXSTER-6 Cyl.-5/6 Spd.					
Veh. Ident.: WP0(Model)()YS620001 Up.					
Roadster 2D	CA298	2778	**20550**	**23875**	**25475**
Roadster 2D S	CB298	2855	**24525**	**28275**	**30025**
2000 911-6 Cyl.-6 Spd.					
Veh. Ident.: WP0(Model)()YS6()0001 Up.					
Coupe 2D Carrera	AA299	2910	**33625**	**38650**	**40725**

PASSENGER CARS

PASSENGER CARS

BODY TYPE	Model No.	Weight	Trade-In	Retail	High Retail
Coupe 2D Carrera Cabriolet	CA299	3075	**37825**	**43075**	**45275**
Coupe 2D Carrera 4	AA299	3031	**36525**	**41700**	**43875**
Coupe 2D Carrera 4 Cabriolet	CA299	3197	**40725**	**46125**	**48425**
PORSCHE OPTIONS					
Add Compact Disc Player			**100**	**125**	**125**
Add Detachable Hardtop			**750**	**850**	**850**
Add Navigation System			**450**	**500**	**500**
Add Tiptronic Trans.			**925**	**1050**	**1050**
Add Traction Control (Std. 911 4)			**350**	**400**	**400**
Deduct W/out Cruise Control			**150**	**150**	**150**
Deduct W/out Leather Seats			**375**	**375**	**375**
Deduct W/out Power Sunroof			**525**	**525**	**525**

PORSCHE

1999 BOXSTER-6 Cyl.-5 Spd.

Veh. Ident.: WP0CA298()XS620001 Up.

BODY TYPE	Model No.	Weight	Trade-In	Retail	High Retail
Roadster 2D	CA298	2822	**18050**	**21250**	**22125**

1999 911-6 Cyl.-6 Spd.

Veh. Ident.: WP0(Model)()XS6()0001 Up.

BODY TYPE	Model No.	Weight	Trade-In	Retail	High Retail
Coupe 2D Carrera	AA299	2901	**28425**	**32950**	**34025**
Coupe 2D Carrera Cabriolet	CA299	2901	**32275**	**37225**	**38350**
Coupe 2D Carrera 4	AA299	3031	**31175**	**35875**	**36975**
Coupe 2D Carrera 4 Cabriolet	CA299	3197	**35025**	**40125**	**41300**
PORSCHE OPTIONS					
Add Detachable Hardtop (Std. 911 Cabriolet)			**675**	**750**	**750**
Add Tiptronic Trans.			**800**	**900**	**900**
Add Traction Control (Std. 911 4)			**275**	**325**	**325**
Deduct W/out Cruise Control			**125**	**125**	**125**
Deduct W/out Leather Seats			**325**	**325**	**325**
Deduct W/out Power Sunroof			**475**	**475**	**475**

PORSCHE

1998 BOXSTER-6 Cyl.-5 Spd.

Veh. Ident.: WP0CA298()WS000001 Up.

BODY TYPE	Model No.	Weight	Trade-In	Retail	High Retail
Roadster 2D	CA298	2822	**15850**	**18750**	**19575**

1998 911-6 Cyl.-6 Spd.

Veh. Ident.: WP0(Model)()WS300001 Up.

BODY TYPE	Model No.	Weight	Trade-In	Retail	High Retail
Coupe 2D Carrera S	AA299	3064	**27400**	**31875**	**32925**
Coupe 2D Carrera Targa	DA299	3130	**29475**	**34050**	**35150**
Coupe 2D Carrera Cabriolet	CA299	3064	**30925**	**35600**	**36700**
Coupe 2D Carrera 4S	AA299	3197	**33100**	**38100**	**39250**
Coupe 2D Carrera 4 Cabriolet	CA299	3175	**33525**	**38525**	**39675**
PORSCHE OPTIONS					
Add Detachable Hardtop			**600**	**675**	**675**
Add Tiptronic Trans.			**700**	**800**	**800**
Add Traction Control (Std. 911 4)			**200**	**225**	**225**
Deduct W/out Cruise Control			**100**	**100**	**100**
Deduct W/out Leather Seats			**275**	**275**	**275**

PORSCHE

1997 BOXSTER-6 Cyl.-5 Spd.

Veh. Ident.: WP0CA298()VS()()0001 Up.

BODY TYPE	Model No.	Weight	Trade-In	Retail	High Retail
Roadster 2D	CA298	2756	**14150**	**16925**	**17750**

1997 911-6 Cyl.-6 Spd.

Veh. Ident.: WP0(Model)()V()()()0001 Up.

BODY TYPE	Model No.	Weight	Trade-In	Retail	High Retail
Coupe 2D Carrera	AA299	3064	**27275**	**31725**	**32775**
Coupe 2D Carrera Targa	DA299	3130	**28875**	**33425**	**34500**

BODY TYPE	Model No.	Weight	Trade-In	Retail	High Retail
Coupe 2D Carrera Cabriolet	CA299	3064	**30325**	**34975**	**36075**
Coupe 2D Carrera 4S	AA299	3197	**32175**	**37125**	**38250**
Coupe 2D Carrera 4 Cabriolet	CA299	3175	**32825**	**37800**	**38925**
Coupe 2D Turbo 4	AC299	3307	**62075**	**68675**	**70200**
PORSCHE OPTIONS					
Add Detachable Hardtop			**550**	**625**	**625**
Add Tiptronic Trans.			**600**	**675**	**675**
Deduct W/out Cruise Control			**100**	**100**	**100**
Deduct W/out Leather Seats			**250**	**250**	**250**
PORSCHE					
1996 911-6 Cyl.-6 Spd.					
Veh. Ident.: WP0(Model)()TS()()0001 Up.					
Coupe 2D Carrera	AA299	3064	**25550**	**29775**	**30775**
Coupe 2D Carrera Targa	DA299	3130	**27100**	**31550**	**32575**
Coupe 2D Carrera Cabriolet	CA299	3064	**28500**	**33025**	**34100**
Coupe 2D Carrera 4	AA299	3175	**27750**	**32225**	**33300**
Coupe 2D Carrera 4S	AA299	3197	**30050**	**34675**	**35775**
Coupe 2D Carrera 4 Cabriolet	CA299	3175	**30700**	**35375**	**36475**
Coupe 2D Turbo 4	AC299	3307	**55275**	**61500**	**62925**
Add Tiptronic Trans.			**450**	**500**	**500**
PORSCHE					
1995 968-4 Cyl.					
Veh. Ident.: WP0(Model)()SS()()0001 Up.					
Coupe 2D	AA296	3086	**14300**	**17075**	**18425**
Coupe 2D Cabriolet	CA296	3240	**17350**	**20475**	**21950**
1995 911-6 Cyl.					
Veh. Ident.: WP0(Model)()SS()()0001 Up.					
Coupe 2D Carrera 2	AA299	3064	**23775**	**27500**	**28475**
Coupe 2D Carrera 2 Cabriolet	CA299	3064	**26625**	**30525**	**31550**
Coupe 2D Carrera 4	AA299	3173	**25675**	**29500**	**30500**
Coupe 2D Carrera 4 Cabriolet	CA299	3173	**28525**	**32650**	**33725**
1995 928GTS-V8					
Veh. Ident.: WP0AA292()SS()()0001 Up.					
Coupe 2D	AA292	3638	**24550**	**28325**	**30075**
PORSCHE OPTIONS					
Add Tiptronic Trans.			**250**	**300**	**300**

SAAB

BODY TYPE	Model No.	Weight	Trade-In	Retail	High Retail
SAAB					
2004 9-3-4 Cyl. Turbo					
Veh. Ident.: YS3(Model)()()()4()000001 Up.					
Sedan 4D Linear	FB4	3175	**17500**	**20375**	**21700**
Sedan 4D Arc	FD4	3175	**20950**	**24025**	**25400**
Sedan 4D Aero	FH4	3175	**23325**	**26700**	**28175**
Convertible 2D Arc	FD7	3480	**30900**	**34800**	**36475**
Convertible 2D Aero	FH7	3480	**33275**	**37475**	**39225**
Add Power Sunroof			**625**	**700**	**700**
Add Theft Recovery System			**100**	**125**	**125**
Deduct W/out Automatic Trans.			**625**	**625**	**625**
Deduct W/out Power Seat			**225**	**225**	**225**

PASSENGER CARS

PASSENGER CARS

BODY TYPE	Model No.	Weight	Trade-In	Retail	High Retail
2004 9-5-4 Cyl. Turbo					
Veh. Ident.: YS3(Model)()()()43000001 Up.					
Sedan 4D Arc	ED4	3470	**21650**	**25075**	**26725**
Sedan 4D Aero	EH4	3470	**27500**	**31575**	**33450**
Wagon 5D Linear	EB5	3620	**21000**	**24375**	**26000**
Wagon 5D Arc	ED5	3620	**23150**	**26825**	**28525**
Wagon 5D Aero	EH5	3620	**29000**	**33175**	**35075**
Add Harman Kardon Stereo (Std. Aero)			**425**	**475**	**475**
Add Power Sunroof (Std. Arc, Aero)			**725**	**825**	**825**
Add Theft Recovery System			**100**	**125**	**125**
Deduct W/out Automatic Trans.			**675**	**675**	**675**
SAAB					
2003 9-3-4 Cyl. Turbo					
Veh. Ident.: YS3(Model)()()()3()000001 Up.					
Sedan 4D Linear	FB4	3175	**16150**	**18775**	**20050**
Sedan 4D Arc	FD4	3175	**18975**	**21925**	**23300**
Sedan 4D Vector	FF4	3175	**20275**	**23300**	**24650**
Convertible 2D SE	DF7	3200	**21975**	**25175**	**26600**
Add Power Sunroof			**575**	**650**	**650**
Add Theft Recovery System			**75**	**100**	**100**
Deduct W/out Automatic Trans.			**575**	**575**	**575**
Deduct W/out Power Seat			**200**	**200**	**200**
2003 9-5-4 Cyl. Turbo					
Veh. Ident.: YS3(Model)()()()33000001 Up.					
Sedan 4D Linear	EB4	3470	**17425**	**20575**	**22050**
Sedan 4D Arc (V6)	ED4	3580	**19250**	**22525**	**24075**
Sedan 4D Aero	EH4	3470	**21950**	**25450**	**27100**
Wagon 5D Linear	EB5	3620	**18925**	**22175**	**23700**
Wagon 5D Arc (V6)	ED5	3730	**20750**	**24100**	**25700**
Wagon 5D Aero	EH5	3620	**23450**	**27150**	**28875**
Add Harman Kardon Stereo (Std. Arc, Aero)			**375**	**425**	**425**
Add Theft Recovery System			**75**	**100**	**100**
Deduct W/out Automatic Trans.			**625**	**625**	**625**
SAAB					
2002 9-3-4 Cyl. Turbo					
Veh. Ident.: YS3(Model)()()()2()000001 Up.					
Coupe 3D Viggen (5 Spd.)	DP3	3130	**16400**	**19050**	**20325**
Sedan 5D SE	DF5	3060	**13175**	**15625**	**16800**
Sedan 5D Viggen (5 Spd.)	DP5	3170	**16500**	**19150**	**20425**
Convertible 2D SE	DF7	3200	**18125**	**21025**	**22375**
Convertible 2D Viggen (5 Spd.)	DP7	3250	**20950**	**24025**	**25400**
Add Theft Recovery System			**75**	**100**	**100**
Deduct W/out Automatic Trans. (Ex. Viggen)			**525**	**525**	**525**
2002 9-5-4 Cyl. Turbo					
Veh. Ident.: YS3(Model)()()()23000001 Up.					
Sedan 4D Linear	EB4	3470	**13800**	**16550**	**17900**
Sedan 4D Arc (V6)	ED4	3580	**15375**	**18225**	**19625**
Sedan 4D Aero	EH4	3470	**17125**	**20225**	**21700**
Wagon 5D Linear	EB5	3620	**15300**	**18150**	**19550**
Wagon 5D Arc (V6)	ED5	3730	**16875**	**19825**	**21275**
Wagon 5D Aero	EH5	3620	**18625**	**21850**	**23375**
Add Harman Kardon Stereo (Std. Arc, Aero)			**325**	**375**	**375**

BODY TYPE	Model No.	Weight	Trade-In	Retail	High Retail
Add Theft Recovery System			75	100	100
Deduct W/out Automatic Trans.			575	575	575
SAAB					
2001 9-3-4 Cyl. Turbo					
Veh. Ident.: YS3(Model)()()()1()000001 Up.					
Coupe 3D	DD3	2980	10025	12200	13250
Coupe 3D Viggen (5 Spd.)	DP3	3130	14650	17175	18400
Sedan 5D	DD5	3020	10125	12325	13375
Sedan 5D SE	DF5	3060	11600	13900	15025
Sedan 5D Viggen (5 Spd.)	DP5	3170	14750	17275	18500
Convertible 2D SE	DF7	3200	15850	18450	19700
Convertible 2D Viggen (5 Spd.)	DP7	3250	18500	21425	22775
Add Leather Seats (Std. Viggen, SE)			375	425	425
Add Power Sunroof (Std. Viggen, SE)			475	550	550
Add Theft Recovery System			50	75	75
Deduct W/out Automatic Trans. (Ex. Viggen)			475	475	475
2001 9-5-4 Cyl. Turbo					
Veh. Ident.: YS3(Model)()()()13000001 Up.					
Sedan 4D	ED4	3470	10725	13125	14325
Sedan 4D SE Turbo (V6)	EF4	3580	12050	14650	15925
Sedan 4D Aero	EH4	3470	13275	15975	17300
Wagon 5D	ED5	3620	12225	14875	16150
Wagon 5D SE Turbo (V6)	EF5	3730	13550	16275	17625
Wagon 5D Aero	EH5	3620	14775	17600	18975
Add Harman Kardon Stereo (Std. SE, Aero)			275	325	325
Add Theft Recovery System			50	75	75
Deduct W/out Automatic Trans.			525	525	525
Deduct W/out Leather Seats			425	425	425
SAAB					
2000 9-3-4 Cyl. Turbo					
Veh. Ident.: YS3(Model)()()()Y()000001 Up.					
Coupe 3D	DD3	2990	7550	9525	10550
Coupe 3D Viggen (5 Spd.)	DP3	3090	11725	14050	15175
Sedan 5D	DD5	3030	7650	9650	10700
Sedan 5D SE	DF5	3150	8800	10900	11950
Sedan 5D Viggen (5 Spd.)	DP5	3140	11825	14150	15275
Convertible 2D	DD7	3130	11825	14150	15275
Convertible 2D SE	DF7	3160	12400	14800	15950
Convertible 2D Viggen (5 Spd.)	DP7	3220	14925	17475	18700
Add Leather Seats (Std. Viggen, SE, Convertibles)			325	375	375
Add Power Sunroof (Std. Viggen, SE)			425	475	475
Deduct W/out Automatic Trans. (Ex. Viggen)			425	425	425
2000 9-5-4 Cyl. Turbo					
Veh. Ident.: YS3(Model)()()()Y()000001 Up.					
Sedan 4D	ED4	3360	8700	10875	12100
Sedan 4D SE Turbo (V6)	EF4	3520	9775	12100	13250
Sedan 4D Aero	EH4		10925	13350	14575
Wagon 5D	ED5	3470	10200	12550	13725
Wagon 5D SE Turbo (V6)	EF5	3730	11275	13775	15000
Wagon 5D Aero	EH5		12425	15075	16375
Add Harman Kardon Stereo (Std. SE, Aero)			225	250	250
Deduct W/out Automatic Trans.			475	475	475

BODY TYPE	Model No.	Weight	Trade-In	Retail	High Retail
Deduct W/out Leather Seats			375	375	375
SAAB					
1999 9-3-4 Cyl. Turbo					
Veh. Ident.: YS3(Model)()()()X()000001 Up.					
Coupe 3D	DD3	2990	6425	8325	9325
Coupe 3D Viggen (5 Spd.)	DP3	2900	10225	12425	13475
Sedan 5D	DD5	2990	6525	8425	9450
Sedan 5D SE	DF5	3120	7350	9300	10325
Convertible 2D	DD7	3180	10025	12200	13250
Convertible 2D SE	DF7	3200	10375	12600	13675
Add Leather Seats (Std. Viggen, SE, Convertibles)			275	325	325
Add Power Sunroof (Std. Viggen, SE)			375	425	425
Deduct W/out Automatic Trans. (Ex. Viggen)			375	375	375
1999 9-5-4 Cyl. Turbo					
Veh. Ident.: YS3(Model)()X()000001 Up.					
Sedan 4D	ED4()E	3280	6825	8825	10075
Sedan 4D SE	EF4()E	3410	7550	9625	10800
Sedan 4D SE Turbo (V6)	EF48Z	3410	8575	10725	11925
Wagon 5D	ED5()E	3590	9050	11275	12400
Wagon 5D Turbo (V6)	ED58Z	3810	10075	12400	13575
Add Power Sunroof (Std. SE, Wagons)			475	550	550
Deduct W/out Automatic Trans.			425	425	425
Deduct W/out Leather Seats			325	325	325
SAAB					
1998 900-4 Cyl.					
Veh. Ident.: YS3(Model)()()()W()000001 Up.					
Coupe 3D S Turbo	DD3	2980	4750	6450	7450
Coupe 3D SE Turbo	DF3	3020	5350	7125	8125
Sedan 5D S	DD5	2990	4100	5725	6700
Sedan 5D SE Turbo	DF5	3060	5450	7225	8250
Convertible 2D S	DD7	3090	7150	9100	10100
Convertible 2D SE Turbo	DF7	3190	7900	9900	10950
Add Leather Seats (Std. S Convertible, SE)			225	250	250
Add Power Sunroof (Std. SE Coupe/Sedan)			325	375	375
Deduct W/out Automatic Trans.			325	325	325
1998 9000-4 Cyl. Turbo					
Veh. Ident.: YS3CF6()()()W()000001 Up.					
Sedan 5D CSE	CF6	3250	6300	8175	9375
Deduct W/out Automatic Trans.			375	375	375
SAAB					
1997 900-4 Cyl.					
Veh. Ident.: YS3(Model)()()()V()000001 Up.					
Coupe 3D S	DD3	2940	3225	4725	5650
Coupe 3D SE Turbo	DF3	3020	4275	5925	6925
Sedan 5D S	DD5	2990	3325	4825	5775
Sedan 5D SE Turbo	DF5	3060	4375	6025	7000
Sedan 5D SE (V6)	DF5	3170	4075	5700	6675
Convertible 2D S	DD7	3090	6000	7850	8925
Convertible 2D SE Turbo	DF7	3190	6625	8550	9575
Convertible 2D SE (V6)	DF7	3300	6325	8225	9225
Add Leather Seats (Std. S Convertible, SE)			200	225	225
Add Power Sunroof (Std. SE Coupe/Sedan)			250	300	300

BODY TYPE	Model No.	Weight	Trade-In	Retail	High Retail
Deduct W/out Automatic Trans.			250	250	250
1997 9000-4 Cyl.					
Veh. Ident.: YS3(Model)()()()V()000001 Up.					
Sedan 5D CS Turbo	CD6	3130	4125	5750	6825
Sedan 5D CSE Turbo	CF6	3250	4575	6250	7350
Sedan 5D CSE (V6)	CF6	3340	4275	5925	7025
Sedan 5D Aero Turbo	CH6	3250	6150	8025	9200
Add Power Sunroof (Std. CSE/Aero)			350	400	400
Deduct W/out Automatic Trans.			300	300	300
Deduct W/out Leather Seats			250	250	250
Deduct W/out Power Seat			100	100	100
SAAB					
1996 900-4 Cyl.					
Veh. Ident.: YS3(Model)()()()T()000001 Up.					
Coupe 3D S	DD3	2940	2750	4150	5000
Coupe 3D SE Turbo	DF3	3020	3625	5175	6075
Sedan 5D S	DD5	2900	2850	4250	5125
Sedan 5D SE Turbo	DF5	3060	3725	5275	6200
Sedan 5D SE (V6)	DF5	3170	3425	4950	5900
Convertible 2D S	DD7	3080	5150	6900	7950
Convertible 2D SE Turbo	DF7	3160	5700	7500	8525
Convertible 2D SE (V6)	DF7	3260	5400	7175	8175
Add Power Sunroof (Std. SE Coupe/Sedan)			200	225	225
Deduct W/out Automatic Trans.			150	150	150
1996 9000-4 Cyl.					
Veh. Ident.: YS3(Model)()()()T()000001 Up.					
Sedan 5D CS Turbo	CD6	3110	3525	5050	6050
Sedan 5D CSE Turbo	CF6	3220	3925	5500	6550
Sedan 5D CSE (V6)	CF6	3320	3650	5200	6200
Sedan 5D Aero Turbo	CH6	3240	5250	7025	8175
Add Power Sunroof (Std. CSE/Aero)			275	325	325
Deduct W/out Automatic Trans.			200	200	200
SAAB					
1995 900-4 Cyl.					
Veh. Ident.: YS3(Model)()()()S()000001 Up.					
Coupe 3D S	DD3	3000	2325	3650	4500
Coupe 3D SE Turbo	DF3	3060	3100	4575	5475
Sedan 5D S	DD5	3030	2425	3775	4625
Sedan 5D SE (V6)	DF5	3160	3000	4425	5325
Convertible 2D S	DD7	3190	4550	6225	7200
Convertible SE Turbo	DF7	3160	4975	6700	7725
Convertible 2D SE (V6)	DF7	3230	4775	6475	7475
1995 9000-4 Cyl.					
Veh. Ident.: YS3(Model)()()()S()000001 Up.					
Sedan 4D CDE (V6)	CF4	3260	3225	4725	5750
Sedan 5D CS Turbo	CD6	3230	3000	4425	5400
Sedan Super CS Turbo	CD6		3300	4800	5825
Sedan 5D CSE Turbo	CF6	3270	3375	4875	5925
Sedan 5D CSE (V6)	CF6	3310	3125	4600	5600
Sedan 5D Aero Turbo	CH6	3310	4425	6100	7175

PASSENGER CARS

BODY TYPE	Model No.	Weight	Trade-In	Retail	High Retail
SATURN					
SATURN					
2004 ION-4 Cyl.					
Veh. Ident.: 1G8(Model)()()()4Z000001 Up.					
Quad Coupe 4D ION-2	AM/N1	2751	**10325**	**12350**	**13075**
Quad Coupe 4D ION-3	AV/W1		**11625**	**13750**	**14500**
Quad Coupe Red Line (5 Spd.)	AY1	2930	**13450**	**15875**	**16675**
Sedan 4D ION-1	AF/G5	2692	**8225**	**10050**	**10775**
Sedan 4D ION-2	AJ/Z5		**9475**	**11425**	**12150**
Sedan 4D ION-3	AK/L5		**10775**	**12850**	**13575**
Add Alum/Alloy Wheels (Std. ION-3, Red Line)			**300**	**350**	**350**
Add Compact Disc Player (ION-1)			**100**	**125**	**125**
Add Cruise Control (ION-2)			**175**	**200**	**200**
Add Leather Seats (Std. Red Line)			**350**	**400**	**400**
Add Power Sunroof			**525**	**600**	**600**
Add Power Windows (ION-2)			**175**	**200**	**200**
Add Theft Recovery System			**100**	**125**	**125**
Deduct W/out Air Conditioning			**575**	**575**	**575**
Deduct W/out Automatic Trans. (Ex. Red Line)			**475**	**475**	**475**
2004 L SERIES-4 Cyl.					
Veh. Ident.: 1G8(Model)()F()4Y000001 Up.					
Sedan 4D L300-1	JC5	3033	**10425**	**12575**	**13475**
Wagon 4D L300-1	JC8	3107	**11425**	**13650**	**14600**
2004 L SERIES-V6					
Veh. Ident.: 1G8(Model)()R()4Y000001 Up.					
Sedan 4D L300-2	JD5	3197	**12350**	**14700**	**15675**
Sedan 4D L300-3	JL5		**14000**	**16450**	**17500**
Wagon 4D L300-2	JD8	3272	**13350**	**15750**	**16775**
Wagon 4D L300-3	JL8		**15000**	**17500**	**18525**
L SERIES OPTIONS					
Add Aluminum/Alloy Wheels (Std. V6)			**325**	**375**	**375**
Add Leather Seats			**450**	**500**	**500**
Add Power Seat (Std. L300-3)			**200**	**225**	**225**
Add Power Sunroof			**575**	**650**	**650**
Add Rear Entertainment System			**600**	**675**	**675**
Add Theft Recovery System			**100**	**125**	**125**
SATURN					
2003 ION-4 Cyl.					
Veh. Ident.: 1G8(Model)()F()32000001 Up.					
Quad Coupe 4D ION-2	AM/N1	2775	**8700**	**10550**	**11275**
Quad Coupe 4D ION-3	AV/W1		**9825**	**11800**	**12550**
Sedan 4D ION-1	AF/G5	2750	**6975**	**8600**	**9375**
Sedan 4D ION-2	AJ/Z5		**7925**	**9650**	**10375**
Sedan 4D ION-3	AK/L5		**9050**	**10950**	**11700**
Add Aluminum/Alloy Wheels (Std. ION-3)			**250**	**300**	**300**
Add Compact Disc Player (ION-1)			**75**	**100**	**100**
Add Cruise Control (Std. ION-3)			**150**	**175**	**175**
Add Leather Seats			**300**	**350**	**350**
Add Power Sunroof			**475**	**550**	**550**
Add Power Windows (Std. ION-3)			**150**	**175**	**175**
Add Theft Recovery System			**75**	**100**	**100**

BODY TYPE	Model No.	Weight	Trade-In	Retail	High Retail
Deduct W/out Air Conditioning			525	525	525
Deduct W/out Automatic Trans.			425	425	425
2003 L SERIES-4 Cyl.					
Veh. Ident.: 1G8(Model)4F()3Y000001 Up.					
Sedan 4D L200	JT/U5	2989	8875	10800	11750
Wagon 4D LW200	JT/U8	3070	9775	11825	12725
2003 L SERIES-V6					
Veh. Ident.: 1G8(Model)4R()3Y000001 Up.					
Sedan 4D L300	JW5	3198	10750	12925	13850
Wagon 4D LW300	JW8	3272	11650	13875	14825
L SERIES OPTIONS					
Add Aluminum/Alloy Wheels (Std. V6)			275	325	325
Add Leather Seats			400	450	450
Add Power Seat			175	200	200
Add Power Sunroof			525	600	600
Add Rear Entertainment System			500	575	575
Add Theft Recovery System			75	100	100
Deduct W/out Automatic Trans.			525	525	525
SATURN					
2002 S SERIES-4 Cyl.					
Veh. Ident.: 1G8(Model)()()()2Z000001 Up.					
Coupe 3D SC1	ZN/P1	2412	6050	7600	8400
Coupe 3D SC2	ZR/Y1	2465	7375	9075	9775
Sedan 4D SL (5 Spd.)	ZF/S5	2351	4650	6050	6825
Sedan 4D SL1	ZG/H5	2377	5200	6675	7500
Sedan 4D SL2	ZJ/K5	2431	5825	7350	8150
Add Aluminum/Alloy Wheels			200	225	225
Add Compact Disc Player (Std. SC)			75	100	100
Add Cruise Control (Std. SC2)			125	150	150
Add Leather Seats			250	300	300
Add Power Door Locks (Std. SC2)			100	125	125
Add Power Sunroof			425	475	475
Add Power Windows (Std. SC2)			125	150	150
Add Theft Recovery System			75	100	100
Deduct W/out Air Conditioning			475	475	475
Deduct W/out Automatic Trans. (Ex. ZF/S5)			375	375	375
2002 L SERIES-4 Cyl.					
Veh. Ident.: 1G8(Model)()()()2Y000001 Up.					
Sedan 4D L100	JR/S5	2945	6800	8550	9425
Sedan 4D L200	JT/U5	2965	7450	9250	10125
Wagon 4D LW200	JT/U8	3083	8250	10125	11050
2002 L SERIES-V6					
Veh. Ident.: 1G8(Model)()()()2Y000001 Up.					
Sedan 4D L300	JW5	3183	8975	10925	11875
Wagon 4D LW300	JW8	3257	9775	11825	12725
L SERIES OPTIONS					
Add Aluminum/Alloy Wheels (Std. V6)			225	250	250
Add Compact Disc Player (L100)			75	100	100
Add Leather Seats			350	400	400
Add Power Seat			150	175	175
Add Power Sunroof			475	550	550
Add Rear Entertainment System			400	450	450
Add Theft Recovery System			75	100	100

P A S S E N G E R C A R S

BODY TYPE	Model No.	Weight	Trade-In	Retail	High Retail
Deduct W/out Automatic Trans.			475	475	475
Deduct W/out Cruise Control			150	150	150
Deduct W/out Power Door Locks			125	125	125
Deduct W/out Power Windows			150	150	150
SATURN					
2001 S SERIES-4 Cyl.					
Veh. Ident.: 1G8(Model)()()()1()000001 Up.					
Coupe 3D SC1	ZN/P1	2396	5025	6475	7275
Coupe 3D SC2	ZR/Y1	2464	6125	7675	8475
Sedan 4D SL (5 Spd.)	ZF5	2332	3775	5075	5800
Sedan 4D SL1	ZG/H5	2360	4250	5625	6400
Sedan 4D SL2	ZJ/K5	2426	4800	6225	7000
Wagon 4D SW2	ZJ/N8	2480	5375	6875	7700
Add Aluminum/Alloy Wheels			150	175	175
Add Compact Disc Player (Std. SC)			50	75	75
Add Cruise Control (Std. SC2)			100	125	125
Add Leather Seats			200	225	225
Add Power Door Locks (Std. SC2)			75	100	100
Add Power Sunroof			375	425	425
Add Power Windows (Std. SC2)			100	125	125
Add Theft Recovery System			50	75	75
Deduct W/out Air Conditioning			425	425	425
Deduct W/out Automatic Trans. (Ex. ZF5)			325	325	325
2001 L SERIES-4 Cyl.					
Veh. Ident.: 1G8(Model)()()()1()000001 Up.					
Sedan 4D L100	JR/S5	2945	4975	6525	7425
Sedan 4D L200	JT/U5	2995	5850	7525	8425
Wagon 4D LW200	JU8	3082	6500	8225	9075
2001 L SERIES-V6					
Veh. Ident.: 1G8(Model)()()()1()000001 Up.					
Sedan 4D L300	JW5	3183	7075	8850	9750
Wagon 4D LW300	JW8	3258	7725	9550	10450
L SERIES OPTIONS					
Add Aluminum/Alloy Wheels (Std. V6)			175	200	200
Add Compact Disc Player (L100)			50	75	75
Add Leather Seats			300	350	350
Add Power Seat			125	150	150
Add Power Sunroof			425	475	475
Add Theft Recovery System			50	75	75
Deduct W/out Automatic Trans.			425	425	425
SATURN					
2000 S SERIES-4 Cyl.					
Veh. Ident.: 1G8(Model)()()()Y()000001 Up.					
Coupe 3D SC1	ZN/P1	2396	4250	5625	6400
Coupe 3D SC2	ZR/Y1	2463	4750	6175	6950
Sedan 4D SL (5 Spd.)	ZF5	2332	3075	4300	5025
Sedan 4D SL1	ZG/H5	2332	3525	4800	5600
Sedan 4D SL2	ZJ/K5	2425	4025	5350	6100
Wagon 4D SW2	Z(J/K/N)8	2479	4475	5875	6675
Add Aluminum/Alloy Wheels			100	125	125
Add Compact Disc Player			50	75	75
Add Cruise Control			75	100	100
Add Leather Seats			150	175	175

BODY TYPE	Model No.	Weight	Trade-In	Retail	High Retail
Add Power Door Locks			50	75	75
Add Power Sunroof			325	375	375
Add Power Windows			75	100	100
Deduct W/out Air Conditioning			375	375	375
Deduct W/out Automatic Trans. (Ex. ZF5)			300	300	300
2000 L SERIES-4 Cyl.					
Veh. Ident.: 1G8(Model)()()()Y()000001 Up.					
Sedan 4D LS	JR/S5	2910	3975	5425	6250
Sedan 4D LS1	JT/U5	2998	4800	6325	7200
Wagon 4D LW1	JU8	3075	5300	6925	7850
2000 L SERIES-V6					
Veh. Ident.: 1G8(Model)()()()Y()000001 Up.					
Sedan 4D LS2	JW5	3152	5650	7300	8175
Wagon 4D LW2	JW8	3230	6150	7850	8775
L SERIES OPTIONS					
Add Aluminum/Alloy Wheels (Std. V6)			125	150	150
Add Compact Disc Player (LS)			50	75	75
Add Leather Seats			250	300	300
Add Power Seat			100	125	125
Add Power Sunroof			375	425	425
Deduct W/out Automatic Trans.			375	375	375
SATURN					
1999 S SERIES-4 Cyl.					
Veh. Ident.: ()G8(Model)()()()X()000001 Up.					
Coupe 2D SC1	ZE/F1	2350	3425	4700	5475
Coupe 2D SC2	ZG/H1	2419	3825	5125	5850
Coupe 3D SC1	ZN/P1	2288	3600	4900	5700
Coupe 3D SC2	ZR/Y1	2359	4000	5350	6100
Sedan 4D SL (5 Spd.)	ZF5	2326	2550	3725	4400
Sedan 4D SL1	ZG/H5	2355	2925	4150	4875
Sedan 4D SL2	ZJ/K5	2418	3325	4600	5375
Wagon 4D SW1	ZG/H8	2420	3275	4525	5275
Wagon 4D SW2	ZJ/K8	2478	3675	4975	5775
Add Aluminum/Alloy Wheels			50	75	75
Add Cruise Control			50	75	75
Add Leather Seats			125	150	150
Add Power Sunroof			275	325	325
Add Power Windows			50	75	75
Deduct W/out Air Conditioning			325	325	325
Deduct W/out Automatic Trans. (Ex. ZF5)			250	250	250
SATURN					
1998 S SERIES-4 Cyl.					
Veh. Ident.: 1G8(Model)()()()W()000001 Up.					
Coupe 2D SC1	ZE/F1	2338	2850	4050	4750
Coupe 2D SC2	ZG/H1	2410	3175	4425	5175
Sedan 4D SL (5 Spd.)	ZF5	2326	2175	3300	3925
Sedan 4D SL1	ZG/H5	2355	2475	3650	4325
Sedan 4D SL2	ZJ/K5	2422	2800	4000	4725
Wagon 4D SW1	ZG/H8	2420	2725	3925	4625
Wagon 4D SW2	ZJ/K8	2482	3050	4275	5000
Add Cruise Control			50	75	75
Add Leather Seats			100	125	125
Add Power Sunroof			225	275	275

PASSENGER CARS

BODY TYPE	Model No.	Weight	Trade-In	Retail	High Retail
Add Power Windows			50	75	75
Deduct W/out Air Conditioning			275	275	275
Deduct W/out Automatic Trans. (Ex. ZF5)			200	200	200
SATURN					
1997 S SERIES-4 Cyl.					
Veh Ident.: 1G8(Model)()()()V()100001 Up.					
Coupe 2D SC1	ZE/F1	2338	2250	3400	4050
Coupe 2D SC2	ZG/H1	2415	2500	3675	4350
Sedan 4D SL (5 Spd.)	ZF5	2321	1850	2925	3550
Sedan 4D SL1	ZG/H5	2350	2000	3100	3700
Sedan 4D SL2	ZJ/K5	2419	2250	3400	4050
Wagon 4D SW1	ZG/H8	2420	2150	3275	3900
Wagon 4D SW2	ZJ/K8	2484	2400	3550	4225
Add Leather Seats			75	100	100
Add Power Sunroof			150	175	175
Deduct W/out Air Conditioning			150	150	150
Deduct W/out Automatic Trans. (Ex. ZF5)			125	125	125
SATURN					
1996 S SERIES-4 Cyl.					
Veh. Ident.: 1G8(Model)()()()T()000001 Up.					
Coupe 2D SC1	ZE/F1	2312	1900	3000	3650
Coupe 2D SC2	ZG/H1	2392	2075	3200	3825
Sedan 4D SL (5 Spd.)	ZF5	2377	1600	2650	3250
Sedan 4D SL1	ZG/H5	2377	1700	2775	3400
Sedan 4D SL2	ZJ/K5	2451	1875	2950	3600
Wagon 4D SW1	ZG/H8	2468	1850	2925	3550
Wagon 4D SW2	ZJ/K8	2537	2025	3150	3775
Add Power Sunroof			100	125	125
Deduct W/out Air Conditioning			75	75	75
Deduct W/out Automatic Trans. (Ex. ZF5)			75	75	75
SATURN					
1995 S SERIES-4 Cyl.					
Veh. Ident.: 1G8(Model)()()()S()000001 Up.					
Coupe 2D SC1	ZE/F1	2312	1600	2650	3250
Coupe 2D SC2	ZG/H1	2388	1725	2800	3425
Sedan 4D SL	ZF5	2353	1400	2425	3000
Sedan 4D SL1	ZG/H5	2353	1425	2450	3025
Sedan 4D SL2	ZJ/K5	2434	1550	2600	3200
Wagon 4D SW1	ZG/H8	2402	1575	2625	3225
Wagon 4D SW2	ZJ/K8	2477	1700	2775	3400

SCION

BODY TYPE	Model No.	Weight	Trade-In	Retail	High Retail
SCION					
2004 xA-4 Cyl.					
Veh. Ident.: JTKKT6()4()4()000001 Up.					
Hatchback 5D	KT6()4	2340	11325	13425	
2004 xB-4 Cyl.					
Veh. Ident.: JTLKT3()4()4()000001 Up.					
Wagon 5D	KT3()4	2425	12900	15100	
SCION OPTIONS					
Add Aluminum/Alloy Wheels			300	350	

DEDUCT FOR RECONDITIONING

BODY TYPE	Model No.	Weight	Trade-In	Retail	High Retail
Add Theft Recovery System			100	125	
Deduct W/out Automatic Trans.			475	475	

SUBARU

* Model can be identified by VIN. Please refer to the VIN Explanation Section.

SUBARU

2004 IMPREZA-4 Cyl.-AWD

Veh. Ident.: JF1G(Model)()()4()()00001 Up.

BODY TYPE	Model No.	Weight	Trade-In	Retail	High Retail
Sedan 4D RS	D67	2965	14950	17250	18050
Sedan 4D WRX (5 Spd./AT)	D29	3085	18675	21175	22050
Sedan 4D WRX STi (6 Spd.)	D70	3263	24775	27700	28675
Wagon 5D TS	G65	3045	13700	15925	16725
Wagon 5D Outback	G68	3050	15550	17900	18725
Wagon 5D WRX (5 Spd./AT)	G29	3165	18275	20775	21650
Add Aluminum/Alloy Wheels (TS)			300	350	350
Add Power Sunroof			525	600	600
Add Subaru Stereo System (STi)			250	300	300
Add Theft Recovery System			100	125	125
Deduct W/out Automatic Trans. (Ex. WRX)			475	475	475

2004 LEGACY-4 Cyl.-AWD

Veh. Ident.: 4S3B(Model)()()4()()00001 Up.

BODY TYPE	Model No.	Weight	Trade-In	Retail	High Retail
Sedan 4D L	E63	3225	13900	16325	17350
Sedan 4D L Anniversary	E62	3285	14975	17475	18500
Sedan 4D GT	E64	3365	17025	19675	20775
Sedan 4D Outback Ltd.	E68	3495	17975	20725	21850
Sedan Outback 3.0 (6 Cyl.)	E89	3610	19825	22675	23850
Sedan Outback VDC (6 Cyl.)	E89	3630	21425	24375	25600
Wagon 5D L	H63	3350	14900	17375	18400
Wagon 5D L Anniversary	H62	3410	16175	18725	19800
Wagon 5D GT	H64	3470	18225	21000	22150
Wagon 5D Outback	H6()	3430	17075	19725	20825
Wagon 5D Outback Ltd.	H68	3510	19175	22000	23175
Wagon Outback Annv (6 Cyl.)	H81	3655	18975	21800	22975
Wgn Outback L.L. Bean (6 Cyl.)	H80	3715	21725	24700	25950
Wagon Outback VDC (6 Cyl.)	H89	3735	22625	25725	27000

2004 FORESTER-4 Cyl.-AWD

Veh. Ident.: JF1S(Model)()()4()700001 Up.

BODY TYPE	Model No.	Weight	Trade-In	Retail	High Retail
Wagon 5D X	G63	3090	16325	18900	19975
Wagon 5D XS	G65	3095	18475	21275	22425
Wagon 5D XT	G69	3210	19600	22475	23650

2004 BAJA-4 Cyl.-AWD

Veh. Ident.: 4S4B(Model)()()4()100001 Up.

BODY TYPE	Model No.	Weight	Trade-In	Retail	High Retail
Utility 4D Sport	T62	3480	16850	19450	20550
Utility 4D Turbo	T63	3605	18075	20850	22000

LEGACY/FORESTER/BAJA OPTIONS

Option	Trade-In	Retail	High Retail
Add Aluminum/Alloy Wheels (Legacy Base L)	325	375	375
Add Leather (Forester XS/XT, Baja Turbo)	450	500	500
Add Power Seat (Baja Turbo)	200	225	225
Add Power Sunroof (Forester XS/XT)	575	650	650
Add Theft Recovery System	100	125	125
Deduct W/out Automatic Trans.	575	575	575

PASSENGER CARS

BODY TYPE	Model No.	Weight	Trade-In	Retail	High Retail
SUBARU					
2003 IMPREZA-4 Cyl.-AWD					
Veh. Ident.: JF1G(Model)()()3()()00001 Up.					
Sedan 4D RS	D67	2965	**13025**	**15225**	**16025**
Sedan 4D WRX (5 Spd./AT)	D29	3085	**16300**	**18700**	**19525**
Wagon 5D TS	G65	3045	**12025**	**14175**	**14950**
Wagon 5D Outback	G68	3035	**13475**	**15700**	**16500**
Wagon 5D WRX (5 Spd./AT)	G29	3165	**16000**	**18375**	**19200**
Add Aluminum/Alloy Wheels (TS)			**250**	**300**	**300**
Add Theft Recovery System			**75**	**100**	**100**
Deduct W/out Automatic Trans. (Ex. WRX)			**425**	**425**	**425**
2003 LEGACY-4 Cyl.-AWD					
Veh. Ident.: 4S3B(Model)()()3()()00001 Up.					
Sedan 4D L	E63	3225	**12800**	**15175**	**16175**
Sedan 4D GT	E64	3365	**15550**	**18075**	**19125**
Sedan 4D Outback Ltd.	E68	3495	**16425**	**19000**	**20075**
Sedan Outback 3.0 (6 Cyl.)	E89	3610	**18025**	**20800**	**21925**
Sedan Outback VDC (6 Cyl.)	E89	3630	**19475**	**22325**	**23500**
Wagon 5D L	H63	3335	**13800**	**16225**	**17250**
Wagon 5D GT	H64	3470	**16750**	**19350**	**20450**
Wagon 5D Outback	H6()	3430	**15725**	**18250**	**19300**
Wagon 5D Outback Ltd.	H68	3510	**17625**	**20375**	**21500**
Wgn Outback L.L. Bean (6 Cyl.)	H80	3715	**19775**	**22625**	**23800**
Wagon Outback VDC (6 Cyl.)	H89	3735	**20675**	**23575**	**24775**
2003 FORESTER-4 Cyl.-AWD					
Veh. Ident.: JF1S(Model)6()3()700001 Up.					
Wagon 5D X	G63	3090	**14625**	**17100**	**18125**
Wagon 5D XS	G65	3095	**16225**	**18775**	**19850**
2003 BAJA-4 Cyl.-AWD					
Veh. Ident.: 4S4B(Model)C()3()100001 Up.					
Utility 4D Sport	T62	3485	**14250**	**16700**	**17750**
Utility 4D	T61	3485	**14825**	**17300**	**18325**
LEGACY/FORESTER/BAJA OPTIONS					
Add Aluminum/Alloy Wheels (Legacy L)			**275**	**325**	**325**
Add Leather Seats (Std. Legacy GT/Ltd./6 Cyl., Baja Model T61)			**400**	**450**	**450**
Add Power Dual Sunroof (Std. Wagon GT/Ltd./6 Cyl.)			**725**	**825**	**825**
Add Power Sunroof (Std. Sedan GT/Ltd./6 Cyl., Baja)			**525**	**600**	**600**
Add Theft Recovery System			**75**	**100**	**100**
Deduct W/out Automatic Trans.			**525**	**525**	**525**
SUBARU					
2002 IMPREZA-4 Cyl.-AWD					
Veh. Ident.: JF1G(Model)()()2()()00001 Up.					
Sedan 4D RS	D67	2965	**11575**	**13700**	**14450**
Sedan 4D WRX (5 Spd./AT)	D29	3085	**14500**	**16775**	**17600**
Wagon 5D TS	G65	3045	**10700**	**12750**	**13475**
Wagon 5D Outback	G68	3050	**11925**	**14075**	**14850**
Wagon 5D WRX (5 Spd./AT)	G29	3165	**14300**	**16575**	**17400**
Add Aluminum/Alloy Wheels (TS)			**200**	**225**	**225**
Add Theft Recovery System			**75**	**100**	**100**
Deduct W/out Automatic Trans. (Ex. WRX)			**375**	**375**	**375**

BODY TYPE	Model No.	Weight	Trade-In	Retail	High Retail
2002 LEGACY-4 Cyl.-AWD					
Veh. Ident.: 4S3B(Model)()()2()()00001 Up.					
Sedan 4D L	E63	3255	**11300**	**13500**	**14425**
Sedan 4D GT	E64	3345	**13275**	**15675**	**16675**
Sedan 4D GT Ltd.	E65	3370	**14350**	**16800**	**17850**
Sedan 4D Outback Ltd.	E68	3495	**14775**	**17250**	**18275**
Sedan Outback 3.0 (6 Cyl.)	E89	3610	**16025**	**18575**	**19650**
Sedan Outback VDC (6 Cyl.)	E89	3630	**17325**	**20050**	**21175**
Wagon 5D L	H63	3345	**12300**	**14650**	**15625**
Wagon 5D GT	H64	3450	**14475**	**16950**	**18000**
Wagon 5D Outback	H6()	3425	**14150**	**16600**	**17650**
Wagon 5D Outback Ltd.	H68	3510	**15975**	**18525**	**19600**
Wgn Outback L.L. Bean (6 Cyl.)	H80	3715	**17725**	**20475**	**21600**
Wagon Outback VDC (6 Cyl.)	H89	3715	**18525**	**21325**	**22475**
2002 FORESTER-4 Cyl.-AWD					
Veh. Ident.: JF1S(Model)()()2()700001 Up.					
Wagon 5D L	F63	3140	**12475**	**14850**	**15825**
Wagon 5D S	F65	3140	**14025**	**16475**	**17525**
LEGACY/FORESTER OPTIONS					
Add Aluminum/Alloy Wheels (Legacy L)			**225**	**250**	**250**
Add Compact Disc Player (Std. Ltd., 6 Cyl., S)			**75**	**100**	**100**
Add Leather Seats (Std. Ltd., 6 Cyl.)			**350**	**400**	**400**
Add Power Sunroof (Std. Sedan GT/Ltd./6 Cyl.)			**475**	**550**	**550**
Add Theft Recovery System			**75**	**100**	**100**
Deduct W/out Automatic Trans.			**475**	**475**	**475**
SUBARU					
2001 IMPREZA-4 Cyl.-AWD					
Veh. Ident.: JF1G(Model)5()1()()00001 Up.					
Coupe 2D L	M43	2730	**7975**	**9825**	**10550**
Coupe 2D RS	M67	2820	**10300**	**12425**	**13150**
Sedan 4D L	C43	2735	**8075**	**9925**	**10650**
Sedan 4D RS	C67	2825	**10400**	**12550**	**13275**
Wagon 5D L	F43	2835	**8575**	**10475**	**11200**
Wagon 5D Outback	F48	2860	**10050**	**12125**	**12850**
Add Aluminum/Alloy Wheels (Std. RS, Outback)			**150**	**175**	**175**
Add Compact Disc Player (Std. RS)			**50**	**75**	**75**
Add Leather Seats			**200**	**225**	**225**
Add Theft Recovery System			**50**	**75**	**75**
Deduct W/out Automatic Trans.			**325**	**325**	**325**
2001 LEGACY-4 Cyl.-AWD					
Veh. Ident.: 4S3B(Model)()()1()()00001 Up.					
Sedan 4D L	E63	3255	**9525**	**11550**	**12450**
Sedan 4D GT	E64	3345	**11175**	**13375**	**14300**
Sedan 4D GT Ltd.	E65	3370	**12050**	**14325**	**15300**
Sedan 4D Outback Ltd.	E68	3495	**12700**	**15075**	**16075**
Wagon 5D L	H63	3345	**10525**	**12675**	**13575**
Wagon 5D GT	H64	3450	**12375**	**14725**	**15700**
Wagon 5D Outback	H6()	3425	**12300**	**14650**	**15625**
Wagon 5D Outback Ltd.	H68	3510	**13900**	**16325**	**17350**
Wgn Outback L.L. Bean (6 Cyl.)	H80	3715	**15225**	**17725**	**18775**
Wagon Outback VDC (6 Cyl.)	H89	3735	**16000**	**18550**	**19625**
2001 FORESTER-4 Cyl.-AWD					
Veh. Ident.: JF1S(Model)()()1()700001 Up.					
Wagon 5D L	F63	3140	**10975**	**13175**	**14100**

PASSENGER CARS

BODY TYPE	Model No.	Weight	Trade-In	Retail	High Retail
Wagon 5D S	F65	3140	**12275**	**14625**	**15600**
LEGACY/FORESTER OPTIONS					
Add Aluminum/Alloy Wheels (Legacy L)			**175**	**200**	**200**
Add Compact Disc Player (Std. Ltd., 6 Cyl., S)			**50**	**75**	**75**
Add Leather Seats (Std. Ltd., 6 Cyl.)			**300**	**350**	**350**
Add Power Sunroof (Std. Sedan GT/Ltd.)			**425**	**475**	**475**
Add Theft Recovery System			**50**	**75**	**75**
Deduct W/out Automatic Trans.			**425**	**425**	**425**
SUBARU					
2000 IMPREZA-4 Cyl.-AWD					
Veh. Ident.: JF1G(Model)5()Y()400001 Up.					
Coupe 2D L	M43	2730	**6050**	**7725**	**8550**
Coupe 2D RS	M67	2820	**8050**	**9900**	**10625**
Sedan 4D L	C43	2735	**6150**	**7850**	**8675**
Sedan 4D RS	C67	2825	**8150**	**10025**	**10750**
Wagon 5D L	F43	2835	**6650**	**8400**	**9150**
Wagon 5D Outback	F48	2860	**7850**	**9675**	**10400**
Add Aluminum/Alloy Wheels (Std. RS)			**100**	**125**	**125**
Add Compact Disc Player			**50**	**75**	**75**
Deduct W/out Automatic Trans.			**300**	**300**	**300**
2000 LEGACY-4 Cyl.-AWD					
Veh. Ident.: 4S3B(Model)5()Y()200001 Up.					
Sedan 4D L	E63	3245	**7725**	**9550**	**10450**
Sedan 4D GT	E64	3335	**9200**	**11225**	**12100**
Sedan 4D GT Ltd.	E65	3360	**9925**	**12000**	**12925**
Sedan 4D Outback Ltd.	E68	3485	**10600**	**12750**	**13650**
Wagon 5D Brighton	H62	3265	**6725**	**8475**	**9350**
Wagon 5D L	H63	3335	**8725**	**10650**	**11600**
Wagon 5D GT	H64	3440	**10400**	**12550**	**13450**
Wagon 5D Outback	H6()	3415	**10425**	**12575**	**13475**
Wagon 5D Outback Ltd.	H68	3500	**11800**	**14050**	**15000**
2000 FORESTER-4 Cyl.-AWD					
Veh. Ident.: JF1S(Model)5()Y()700001 Up.					
Wagon 5D L	F63	3125	**8475**	**10375**	**11300**
Wagon 5D S	F65	3125	**9500**	**11550**	**12450**
LEGACY/FORESTER OPTIONS					
Add Aluminum/Alloy Wheels (Std. Leg GT/Outback/Ltd., Forester)			**125**	**150**	**150**
Add Compact Disc Player (Std. Ltd.)			**50**	**75**	**75**
Add Leather Seats (Std. Ltd.)			**250**	**300**	**300**
Deduct W/out Automatic Trans.			**375**	**375**	**375**
SUBARU					
1999 IMPREZA-4 Cyl.-AWD					
Veh. Ident.: JF1G(Model)5()X()400001 Up.					
Coupe 2D L	M43	2730	**4500**	**6025**	**6800**
Coupe 2D RS	M67	2840	**6275**	**8000**	**8825**
Sedan 4D L	C43	2735	**4600**	**6125**	**6900**
Wagon 5D L	F43	2835	**5100**	**6725**	**7550**
Wagon 5D Outback	F48	2860	**6100**	**7825**	**8650**
Add Aluminum/Alloy Wheels (Std. RS)			**50**	**75**	**75**
Add Cruise Control			**50**	**75**	**75**
Deduct W/out Automatic Trans.			**250**	**250**	**250**

BODY TYPE	Model No.	Weight	Trade-In	Retail	High Retail
1999 LEGACY-4 Cyl.-AWD					
Veh. Ident.: 4S3B(Model)5()X()240001 Up.					
Sedan 4D L	D43	2885	**5050**	**6625**	**7525**
Sedan 4D L Anniversary	D43	2885	**5425**	**7075**	**7950**
Sedan 4D GT	D67	3125	**6275**	**8000**	**8925**
Sedan 4D GT Ltd.	D67	3130	**6850**	**8625**	**9500**
Sedan 4D Outback	D68	3160	**6375**	**8100**	**8950**
Sedan 4D Outback Ltd.	D68	3200	**7275**	**9075**	**9925**
Wagon 5D Brighton	K42	2905	**4375**	**5875**	**6750**
Wagon 5D L	K43	2975	**6050**	**7750**	**8675**
Wagon 5D L Anniversary	K43	2975	**6425**	**8150**	**9000**
Wagon 5D GT	K67	3200	**7275**	**9075**	**9925**
Wagon 5D Outback	G68	3175	**7375**	**9175**	**10050**
Wagon 5D Outback Ltd.	G68	3190	**7975**	**9850**	**10750**
1999 FORESTER-4 Cyl.-AWD					
Veh. Ident.: JF1S(Model)5()X()700001 Up.					
Wagon 5D (5 Spd.)	F61	3100	**6125**	**7825**	**8750**
Wagon 5D L	F63	3125	**6650**	**8400**	**9275**
Wagon 5D S	F65	3130	**7525**	**9325**	**10200**
LEGACY/FORESTER OPTIONS					
Add Aluminum/Alloy Wheels (Std. Leg Anniv/GT/Outback/Ltd., Forester)			**75**	**100**	**100**
Add Leather Seats (Std. Ltd.)			**225**	**250**	**250**
Add Power Dual Sunroof			**525**	**600**	**600**
Ded W/out Automatic Trans. (Ex. Forester Base)			**325**	**325**	**325**
Deduct W/out Cruise Control			**75**	**75**	**75**
SUBARU					
1998 IMPREZA-4 Cyl.-AWD					
Veh. Ident.: JF1G(Model)5()W()500001 Up.					
Coupe 2D L	M43	2720	**3200**	**4575**	**5350**
Coupe 2D RS	M67	2825	**4850**	**6400**	**7200**
Sedan 4D L	C43	2690	**3300**	**4675**	**5450**
Wagon 5D L	F43	2795	**3800**	**5225**	**5950**
Wagon 5D Outback	F48	2835	**4700**	**6225**	**7000**
Add Cruise Control			**50**	**75**	**75**
Deduct W/out Automatic Trans.			**200**	**200**	**200**
1998 LEGACY-4 Cyl.-AWD					
Veh. Ident.: 4S3B(Model)5()W()500001 Up.					
Sedan 4D L	D43	2885	**3800**	**5225**	**6025**
Sedan 4D GT	D67	3090	**4900**	**6450**	**7350**
Sedan 4D GT Ltd.	D67	3165	**5275**	**6900**	**7825**
Wagon 5D Brighton	K42	2905	**3300**	**4675**	**5550**
Wagon 5D L	K43	2975	**4800**	**6325**	**7200**
Wagon 5D GT	K67	3180	**5900**	**7575**	**8475**
Wagon 5D Outback	G68	3155	**6000**	**7675**	**8600**
Wagon 5D Outback Ltd.	G68	3170	**6400**	**8125**	**8975**
1998 FORESTER-4 Cyl.-AWD					
Veh. Ident.: JF1S(Model)5()W()700001 Up.					
Wagon 5D (5 Spd.)	F61	3020	**4675**	**6200**	**7075**
Wagon 5D L	F63	3040	**5150**	**6775**	**7700**
Wagon 5D S	F65	3040	**5925**	**7600**	**8500**

PASSENGER CARS

BODY TYPE	Model No.	Weight	Trade-In	Retail	High Retail
LEGACY/FORESTER OPTIONS					
Add Aluminum/Alloy Wheels .... (Std. Legacy GT/Outback/Ltd., Forester)			50	75	75
Add Leather Seats (Std. Ltd.)..........			175	200	200
Add Power Dual Sunroof			475	550	550
Ded W/out Automatic Trans. (Ex. Forester Base)			275	275	275
Deduct W/out Cruise Control			50	50	50
SUBARU					
1997 IMPREZA-4 Cyl.-AWD					
Veh. Ident.: JF1G(Model)5()V()400001 Up.					
Coupe 2D Brighton	M()2	2770	1800	2975	3625
Coupe 2D L	M43	2795	2200	3425	4075
Sedan 4D L	C43	2770	2300	3550	4225
Wagon 5D L..........................	F43	2875	2800	4100	4825
Wagon 5D Outback	F48	2915	3525	4925	5725
Deduct W/out Automatic Trans.			125	125	125
1997 LEGACY-4 Cyl.-AWD					
Veh. Ident.: 4S3B(Model)5()V()200001 Up.					
Sedan 4D L	D43	2965	2975	4300	5125
Sedan 4D GT..........................	D67	3160	3775	5200	6000
Sedan 4D LSi.........................	D66	3130	4425	5925	6800
Wagon 5D Brighton	K42	2995	2400	3650	4400
Wagon 5D L..........................	K43	3065	3675	5100	5900
Wagon 5D GT	K67	3250	4475	5975	6850
Wagon 5D Outback	G68	3220	4525	6025	6875
Wagon 5D Outback Ltd..	G68	3230	4775	6300	7175
Wagon 5D LSi	K66	3210	5125	6750	7675
Deduct W/out Automatic Trans.			175	175	175
Deduct W/out Cruise Control			50	50	50
1997 SVX-6 Cyl.-AWD					
Veh. Ident.: JF1C(Model)5()VH100001 Up.					
Coupe 2D L..........................	X83	3525	4550	6225	7200
Coupe 2D LSi	X86	3580	6825	8750	9800
SUBARU					
1996 IMPREZA-4 Cyl.-AWD					
Veh Ident.: JF1G(Model)()()T()410001 Up.					
Coupe 2D Brighton (5 Spd.)	M22	2665	1350	2475	3050
Coupe 2D L...........................	M()3	2715	1800	2975	3625
Coupe 2D LX.........................	M45	2700	2300	3550	4225
Sedan 4D L	C()3	2685	1900	3100	3700
Sedan 4D LX.........................	C45	2835	2400	3650	4325
Wagon 5D L (5 Spd.)	F43	2795	2300	3550	4225
Wagon 5D Outback	F48	2810	3000	4325	5075
Wagon 5D LX.........................	F45	2925	2900	4200	4925
Ded W/out Automatic Trans. (Ex. Brighton/Wagon L)			100	100	100
Deduct W/out AWD			500	500	500
1996 LEGACY-4 Cyl.-AWD					
Veh. Ident.: 4S3B(Model)()()T()202001 Up.					
Sedan 4D L	D()3	2825	2425	3675	4425
Sedan 4D LS	D45	3030	2925	4250	5075
Sedan 4D 2.5 GT......................	D67	3115	2925	4250	5075
Sedan 4D LSi.........................	D66	3125	3425	4825	5725
Wagon 5D Brighton	K42	2895	2050	3250	3950

BODY TYPE	Model No.	Weight	Trade-In	Retail	High Retail
Wagon 5D L	K()3	2915	**3075**	**4425**	**5275**
Wagon 5D Outback	G()8	3080	**3850**	**5300**	**6125**
Wagon 5D LS	K45	3120	**3575**	**4975**	**5875**
Wagon 5D 2.5 GT	K67	3190	**3575**	**4975**	**5875**
Wagon 5D LSi	K66	3200	**4075**	**5550**	**6400**
Deduct W/out Automatic Trans.			**125**	**125**	**125**
Deduct W/out AWD			**500**	**500**	**500**
1996 SVX-6 Cyl.-AWD					
Veh. Ident.: JF1C(Model)()()T()100001 Up.					
Coupe 2D L	X83	3225	**3300**	**4800**	**5725**
Coupe 2D LSi	X86	3580	**5200**	**6975**	**8025**
SUBARU					
1995 IMPREZA-4 Cyl.					
Veh. Ident.: JF1G(Model)()()S()401001 Up.					
Coupe 2D	M21	2400	**825**	**1800**	**2250**
Coupe 2D (AWD)	M21	2555	**1275**	**2375**	**2925**
Coupe 2D L	M23	2565	**1075**	**2150**	**2675**
Coupe 2D L (AWD)	M()3	2690	**1525**	**2650**	**3250**
Coupe 2D LX (AWD)	M65	2840	**1975**	**3175**	**3800**
Sedan 4D	C21	2420	**925**	**1925**	**2400**
Sedan 4D (AWD)	C21	2575	**1375**	**2500**	**3075**
Sedan 4D L	C23	2590	**1175**	**2275**	**2825**
Sedan 4D L (AWD)	C()3	2705	**1625**	**2775**	**3400**
Sedan 4D LX (AWD)	C65	2835	**2075**	**3300**	**3925**
Wagon 5D L (AWD)	F()()	2795	**2125**	**3350**	**4000**
Wagon 5D LX (AWD)	F65	2925	**2575**	**3850**	**4550**
1995 LEGACY-4 Cyl.					
Veh. Ident.: 4S3B(Model)()()S()210001 Up.					
Sedan 4D	D62	2570	**1025**	**2100**	**2650**
Sedan 4D L	D63	2755	**1400**	**2525**	**3150**
Sedan 4D L (AWD)	D63	2905	**1850**	**3025**	**3700**
Sedan 4D LS (AWD)	D65	3030	**2300**	**3550**	**4300**
Sedan 4D LSi (AWD)	D65	3084	**2750**	**4050**	**4850**
Wagon 5D Brighton (AWD)	K62	2980	**1600**	**2750**	**3400**
Wagon 5D L	K63	2850	**2000**	**3200**	**3900**
Wagon 5D L (AWD)	K63	3005	**2450**	**3700**	**4450**
Wagon 5D Outback (AWD)	K63	3080	**2650**	**3925**	**4725**
Wagon 5D LS (AWD)	K65	3120	**2900**	**4200**	**5000**
Wagon 5D LSi (AWD)	K65	3135	**3350**	**4725**	**5600**
1995 SVX-6 Cyl.					
Veh. Ident.: JF1C(Model)()()S()100001 Up.					
Coupe 2D L	X33	3375	**2300**	**3625**	**4475**
Coupe 2D L (AWD)	X33	3525	**2750**	**4150**	**5000**
Coupe 2D LSi (AWD)	X35	3580	**4250**	**5900**	**6875**

SUZUKI

BODY TYPE	Model No.	Weight	Trade-In	Retail	High Retail
SUZUKI					
2004 FORENZA-4 Cyl.					
Veh. Ident.: KL5(Model)52Z()4K000001 Up.					
Sedan 4D S	JD	2701	**7950**	**9675**	**10400**
Sedan 4D LX	JJ	2701	**8925**	**10775**	**11525**

PASSENGER CARS

BODY TYPE	Model No.	Weight	Trade-In	Retail	High Retail
Sedan 4D EX	JJ	2756	9275	11200	11925
2004 AERIO-4 Cyl.					
Veh. Ident.: JS2(Model)()452()0001 Up.					
Sedan 4D S	RA61S	2676	8025	9800	10525
Sedan 4D LX	RA61S	2676	8650	10500	11225
Sedan 4D LX (AWD)	RB61S	2875	9650	11625	12350
Wagon 4D SX	RC61H	2734	9225	11150	11875
Wagon 4D SX (AWD)	RD61H	2932	10225	12250	12975
2004 VERONA-I6					
Veh. Ident.: KL5(Model)52L()4B000001 Up.					
Sedan 4D S	VJ	3380	10350	12375	13100
Sedan 4D LX	VJ	3380	10850	12900	13625
Sedan 4D EX	VM	3380	11875	14000	14750
SUZUKI OPTIONS					
Add Aluminum/Alloy Wheels (S)			300	350	350
Add Theft Recovery System			100	125	125
Deduct W/out Automatic Trans.			475	475	475
SUZUKI					
2003 AERIO-4 Cyl.					
Veh. Ident.: JS2(Model)()35()()0001 Up.					
Sedan 4D S	RA41S	2641	6475	8075	8825
Sedan 4D GS	RA41S	2628	7000	8650	9425
Sedan 4D GS (AWD)	RB41S	2805	7900	9650	10375
Wagon 4D SX	RC41H	2630	7550	9275	9975
Wagon 4D SX (AWD)	RD41H	2807	8450	10275	11000
Add Aluminum/Alloy Wheels (S)			250	300	300
Add Theft Recovery System			75	100	100
Deduct W/out Automatic Trans.			425	425	425
SUZUKI					
2002 ESTEEM-4 Cyl.-5 Spd.					
Veh. Ident.: JS2(Model)()25400001 Up.					
Sedan 4D GL	GB41S	2271	3825	5125	5850
Sedan 4D GLX	GB41S	2293	4225	5600	6375
Wagon 4D GL	GB41W	2403	4225	5600	6375
Wagon 4D GLX	GB41W	2425	4625	6025	6800
2002 AERIO-4 Cyl.					
Veh. Ident.: JS2(Model)()25100001 Up.					
Sedan 4D S	RA41S	2604	5075	6550	7350
Sedan 4D GS	RA41S	2604	5500	7000	7850
Wagon 4D SX	RC41H	2668	6025	7575	8375
SUZUKI OPTIONS					
Add Aluminum/Alloy Wheels (Esteem GL, Aerio S)			200	225	225
Add Automatic Trans. (Esteem)			375	425	425
Add Power Sunroof			425	475	475
Add Theft Recovery System			75	100	100
Deduct W/out Automatic Trans. (Ex. Esteem)			375	375	375
SUZUKI					
2001 SWIFT-4 Cyl.-5 Spd.					
Veh. Ident.: JS2AB21H()16000001 Up.					
Hatchback 3D GA	AB21H	1895	2325	3475	4125
Hatchback 3D GL	AB21H	1895	2525	3700	4375

BODY TYPE	Model No.	Weight	Trade-In	Retail	High Retail
2001 ESTEEM-4 Cyl.-5 Spd.					
Veh. Ident.: ()S2(Model)()1()100001 Up.					
Sedan 4D GL	GB41S	2271	**3150**	**4375**	**5125**
Sedan 4D GLX	GB41S	2293	**3450**	**4725**	**5500**
Wagon 4D GL	GB41W	2403	**3550**	**4825**	**5625**
Wagon 4D GLX	GB41W	2425	**3850**	**5150**	**5875**
SUZUKI OPTIONS					
Add Aluminum/Alloy Wheels (Std. Esteem GLX)			**150**	**175**	**175**
Add Automatic Trans.			**325**	**375**	**375**
Add Compact Disc Player (Std. Esteem)			**50**	**75**	**75**
Add Cruise Control			**100**	**125**	**125**
Add Power Sunroof			**375**	**425**	**425**
Add Theft Recovery System			**50**	**75**	**75**
Deduct W/out Air Conditioning			**425**	**425**	**425**
SUZUKI					
2000 SWIFT-4 Cyl.-5 Spd.					
Veh. Ident.: JS2AB21H()Y()000001 Up.					
Hatchback 3D GA	AB21H	1895	**1850**	**2925**	**3550**
Hatchback 3D GL	AB21H	1895	**2050**	**3175**	**3800**
2000 ESTEEM-4 Cyl.-5 Spd.					
Veh. Ident.: ()S2(Model)()Y()000001 Up.					
Sedan 4D GL	GB31S	2227	**2575**	**3750**	**4425**
Sedan 4D GLX	GB31S	2249	**2825**	**4025**	**4725**
Wagon 4D GL	GB41W	2359	**2975**	**4200**	**4925**
Wagon 4D GLX	GB41W	2381	**3225**	**4475**	**5225**
SUZUKI OPTIONS					
Add Aluminum/Alloy Wheels (Std. Esteem GLX)			**100**	**125**	**125**
Add Automatic Trans.			**300**	**350**	**350**
Add Compact Disc Player			**50**	**75**	**75**
Add Cruise Control			**75**	**100**	**100**
Add Power Sunroof			**325**	**375**	**375**
Deduct W/out Air Conditioning			**375**	**375**	**375**
SUZUKI					
1999 SWIFT-4 Cyl.-5 Spd.					
Veh. Ident.: 2S2AB21H()X()000001 Up.					
Hatchback 3D	AB21H	1895	**1475**	**2500**	**3075**
1999 ESTEEM-4 Cyl.-5 Spd.					
Veh. Ident.: ()S2(Model)()X()000001 Up.					
Sedan 4D GL	GB()1S	2227	**2025**	**3125**	**3725**
Sedan 4D GLX	GB()1S	2249	**2275**	**3425**	**4075**
Wagon 4D GL	GB()1W	2359	**2425**	**3575**	**4250**
Wagon 4D GLX	GB()1W	2381	**2675**	**3850**	**4550**
SUZUKI OPTIONS					
Add Aluminum/Alloy Wheels			**50**	**75**	**75**
Add Automatic Trans.			**250**	**300**	**300**
Add Cruise Control			**50**	**75**	**75**
Add Power Sunroof			**275**	**325**	**325**
Deduct W/out Air Conditioning			**325**	**325**	**325**
SUZUKI					
1998 SWIFT-4 Cyl.-5 Spd.					
Veh. Ident.: 2S2AB21H()W()000001 Up.					
Hatchback 3D	AB21H	1895	**1175**	**2175**	**2700**

PASSENGER CARS

PASSENGER CARS

BODY TYPE	Model No.	Weight	Trade-In	Retail	High Retail
1998 ESTEEM-4 Cyl.-5 Spd.					
Veh. Ident.: ()S2(Model)()W()000001 Up.					
Sedan 4D GL	GB31S	2227	**1650**	**2700**	**3300**
Sedan 4D GLX	GB31S	2249	**1800**	**2875**	**3500**
Wagon 4D GL	GB31W	2359	**2050**	**3175**	**3800**
Wagon 4D GLX	GB31W	2381	**2200**	**3325**	**3950**
SUZUKI OPTIONS					
Add Automatic Trans.			**200**	**225**	**225**
Add Cruise Control			**50**	**75**	**75**
Add Power Sunroof			**225**	**275**	**275**
Deduct W/out Air Conditioning			**275**	**275**	**275**
SUZUKI					
1997 SWIFT-4 Cyl.-5 Spd.					
Veh. Ident.: 2S2AB21H()V()000001 Up.					
Hatchback 3D	AB21H	1878	**950**	**1900**	**2375**
1997 ESTEEM-4 Cyl.-5 Spd.					
Veh. Ident.: ()S2GB31S()V()000001 Up.					
Sedan 4D GL	GB31S	2183	**1200**	**2200**	**2725**
Sedan 4D GLX	GB31S	2213	**1300**	**2325**	**2875**
SUZUKI OPTIONS					
Add Automatic Trans.			**125**	**150**	**150**
Deduct W/out Air Conditioning			**150**	**150**	**150**
SUZUKI					
1996 SWIFT-4 Cyl.-5 Spd.					
Veh. Ident.: 2S2AB21H()T6600001 Up.					
Hatchback 3D	AB21H	1878	**850**	**1775**	**2225**
1996 ESTEEM-4 Cyl.-5 Spd.					
Veh. Ident.: ()S2GB31H()T6600001 Up.					
Sedan 4D GL	GB31S	2240	**950**	**1900**	**2375**
Sedan 4D GLX	GB31S	2273	**1050**	**2025**	**2525**
SUZUKI OPTIONS					
Add Automatic Trans.			**100**	**125**	**125**
Deduct W/out Air Conditioning			**100**	**100**	**100**
SUZUKI					
1995 SWIFT-4 Cyl.					
Veh. Ident.: 2S2AB21H()S6600001 Up.					
Hatchback 3D	AB21H	1856	**750**	**1675**	**2125**
1995 ESTEEM-4 Cyl.					
Veh. Ident.: ()S2GB31S()S()100001 Up.					
Sedan 4D GL	GB31S	2240	**750**	**1675**	**2125**
Sedan 4D GLX	GB31S	2240	**850**	**1775**	**2225**

TOYOTA

BODY TYPE	Model No.	Weight	Trade-In	Retail	High Retail
TOYOTA					
2004 ECHO-4 Cyl.					
Veh. Ident.: JTD(Model)()4()000001 Up.					
Coupe 2D	AT1()3	2035	**9925**	**11900**	**12650**
Sedan 4D	BT1()3	2055	**10425**	**12450**	**13175**
2004 COROLLA-4 Cyl.					
Veh. Ident.: ()()()BR3()E()4()000001 Up.					
Sedan 4D CE	BR3()E	2505	**11400**	**13525**	**14275**

BODY TYPE	Model No.	Weight	Trade-In	Retail	High Retail
Sedan 4D S	BR3()E	2525	**12125**	**14275**	**15050**
Sedan 4D LE	BR3()E	2525	**12150**	**14300**	**15075**
2004 PRIUS-4 Cyl.					
Veh. Ident.: JTDKB2()U()4()000001 Up.					
Liftback 5D	KB2()U	2890	**19300**	**21850**	
ECHO/COROLLA/PRIUS OPTIONS					
Add Aluminum/Alloy Wheels (Std. Prius)			**300**	**350**	**350**
Add CD Player (Std. Corolla, Prius)			**100**	**125**	**125**
Add Cruise Control (Std. Prius)			**175**	**200**	**200**
Add Leather Seats			**350**	**400**	**400**
Add Navigation System			**550**	**625**	**625**
Add Power Door Locks (Std. Corolla S/LE, Prius)			**150**	**175**	**175**
Add Power Sunroof			**525**	**600**	**600**
Add Power Windows (Std. Corolla LE, Prius)			**175**	**200**	**200**
Add Theft Recovery System			**100**	**125**	**125**
Deduct W/out Air Conditioning			**575**	**575**	**575**
Deduct W/out Automatic Trans.			**475**	**475**	**475**
Deduct W/out Power Steering			**125**	**125**	**125**
2004 MATRIX-4 Cyl.					
Veh. Ident.: 2T1(Model)()4C000001 Up.					
Wagon 5D	KR3()E	2679	**12575**	**14750**	**15725**
Wagon 5D (4WD)	LR3()E	2943	**13975**	**16225**	**17250**
Wagon 5D XR	KR3()E	2701	**13225**	**15425**	**16425**
Wagon 5D XR (4WD)	LR3()E	2965	**14625**	**16925**	**17975**
Wagon 5D XRS (6 Spd.)	KY3()E	2800	**14700**	**17000**	**18050**
2004 CELICA-4 Cyl.					
Veh. Ident.: JTD(Model)()4()000001 Up.					
Coupe 2D GT	DR3()T	2425	**15875**	**18425**	**19500**
Coupe 2D GT-S	DY3()T	2500	**18350**	**21125**	**22275**
2004 MR2 SPYDER-4 Cyl.-5 Spd.					
Veh. Ident.: JTDFR320()4()000001 Up.					
Convertible 2D	FR320	2195	**18550**	**21350**	**22500**
2004 CAMRY-4 Cyl.					
Veh. Ident.: ()T()(Model)()4()000001 Up.					
Sedan 4D Standard	BE3()K		**14600**	**17075**	**18100**
Sedan 4D LE	BE3()K	3086	**14800**	**17300**	**18325**
Sedan 4D LE (V6)	BF3()K	3296	**16775**	**19375**	**20475**
Sedan 4D SE	BE3()K	3142	**15500**	**18025**	**19075**
Sedan 4D SE (V6)	BA3()K	3351	**18025**	**20800**	**21925**
Sedan 4D XLE	BE3()K	3219	**16400**	**18975**	**20050**
Sedan 4D XLE (V6)	BF3()K	3362	**18925**	**21750**	**22925**
2004 CAMRY SOLARA-V6					
Veh. Ident.: ()T()(Model)()4()000001 Up.					
Coupe 2D SE (4 Cyl.)	CE3()P	3175	**15325**	**17850**	**18900**
Coupe 2D SE Sport (4 Cyl.)	CE3()P	3175	**16025**	**18575**	**19650**
Coupe 2D SLE (4 Cyl.)	CE3()P	3241	**16850**	**19450**	**20550**
Coupe 2D SE	CA3()P	3417	**17025**	**19700**	**20800**
Coupe 2D SE Sport	CA3()P	3425	**17725**	**20475**	**21600**
Coupe 2D SLE	CA3()P	3439	**19050**	**21875**	**23050**
Convertible 2D SE	FA3()P		**23725**	**26900**	**28200**
Convertible 2D SLE	FA3()P		**25100**	**28350**	**29675**
MATRIX/CELICA/MR2/CAMRY/CAMRY SOLARA OPTIONS					
Add Aluminum/Alloy Wheels (Std. XRS, GT-S, MR2, Camry V6, Solara)			**325**	**375**	**375**

PASSENGER CARS

BODY TYPE	Model No.	Weight	Trade-In	Retail	High Retail
Add Leather Seats (Std. Solara SLE V6) .			**450**	**500**	**500**
Add Navigation System			**600**	**675**	**675**
Add Power Seat (Std. Camry, Solara SLE)			**200**	**225**	**225**
Add Power Sunroof . . . . (Std. Camry SE/XLE V6, Solara SLE) .			**575**	**650**	**650**
Add Sequential Manual Trans. (MR2) . . .			**575**	**650**	**650**
Add Theft Recovery System			**100**	**125**	**125**
Ded W/out Auto Trans. (Ex. Matrix XRS, MR2)			**575**	**575**	**575**
Deduct W/out Cruise Control			**200**	**200**	**200**
Deduct W/out Power Door Locks			**175**	**175**	**175**
Deduct W/out Power Windows			**200**	**200**	**200**
2004 AVALON-V6					
Veh. Ident.: 4T1BF28B()4U000001 Up.					
Sedan 4D XL	BF28B	3417	**20350**	**23400**	**24775**
Sedan 4D XLS	BF28B	3428	**22575**	**25900**	**27350**
Add Aluminum/Alloy Wheels (Std. XLS). .			**375**	**425**	**425**
Add Leather Seats			**525**	**600**	**600**
Add Navigation System			**650**	**725**	**725**
Add Power Sunroof			**625**	**700**	**700**
Add Theft Recovery System			**100**	**125**	**125**
Deduct W/out Power Seat			**225**	**225**	**225**
TOYOTA					
2003 ECHO-4 Cyl.					
Veh. Ident.: JTD(Model)()3()000001 Up.					
Coupe 2D.	AT1()3	2035	**8150**	**9950**	**10675**
Sedan 4D.	BT1()3	2055	**8650**	**10500**	**11225**
2003 COROLLA-4 Cyl.					
Veh. Ident.: ()()()(Model)()3()000001 Up.					
Sedan 4D CE.	BR3()E	2502	**10100**	**12100**	**12825**
Sedan 4D S	BR3()E	2524	**10600**	**12625**	**13350**
Sedan 4D LE	BR3()E	2524	**10675**	**12725**	**13450**
2003 PRIUS-4 Cyl.					
Veh. Ident.: JT2BK1()U()3()000001 Up.					
Sedan 4D.	BK1()U	2765	**16150**	**18525**	**19350**
ECHO/COROLLA/PRIUS OPTIONS					
Add Aluminum/Alloy Wheels (Std. Prius) .			**250**	**300**	**300**
Add Compact Disc Player (Std. Corolla) .			**75**	**100**	**100**
Add Cruise Control			**150**	**175**	**175**
Add Leather Seats			**300**	**350**	**350**
Add Navigation System			**450**	**500**	**500**
Add Power Door Locks (Std. Corolla S/LE, Prius)			**125**	**150**	**150**
Add Power Sunroof			**475**	**550**	**550**
Add Power Windows (Std. Corolla LE, Prius)			**150**	**175**	**175**
Add Theft Recovery System			**75**	**100**	**100**
Deduct W/out Air Conditioning			**525**	**525**	**525**
Deduct W/out Automatic Trans.			**425**	**425**	**425**
Deduct W/out Power Steering			**100**	**100**	**100**
2003 MATRIX-4 Cyl.					
Veh. Ident.: 2T1(Model)()3()000001 Up.					
Wagon 5D	KR3()E	2679	**11325**	**13425**	**14350**
Wagon 5D (4WD).	LR3()E	2943	**12575**	**14750**	**15725**
Wagon 5D XR	KR3()E	2701	**11775**	**13900**	**14850**
Wagon 5D XR (4WD).	LR3()E	2965	**13025**	**15225**	**16225**
Wagon 5D XRS (AT/6 Spd.)	KY3()E	2800	**13250**	**15450**	**16450**

BODY TYPE	Model No.	Weight	Trade-In	Retail	High Retail
2003 CELICA-4 Cyl.					
Veh. Ident.: JTD(Model)()3()000001 Up.					
Coupe 2D GT	DR3()T	2425	**13525**	**15950**	**16975**
Coupe 2D GT-S	DY3()T	2500	**15825**	**18375**	**19450**
2003 MR2 SPYDER-4 Cyl.-5 Spd.					
Veh. Ident.: JTDFR320()3()000001 Up.					
Convertible 2D	FR320	2195	**16275**	**18850**	**19925**
2003 CAMRY-4 Cyl.					
Veh. Ident.: ()T()(Model)()3()000001 Up.					
Sedan 4D LE	BE3()K	3086	**13500**	**15900**	**16925**
Sedan 4D LE (V6)	BF3()K	3296	**15225**	**17725**	**18775**
Sedan 4D SE	BE3()K	3142	**14100**	**16550**	**17600**
Sedan 4D SE (V6)	BF3()K	3351	**15825**	**18375**	**19450**
Sedan 4D XLE	BE3()K	3219	**15025**	**17525**	**18575**
Sedan 4D XLE (V6)	BF3()K	3362	**16750**	**19350**	**20450**
2003 CAMRY SOLARA-V6					
Veh. Ident.: 2T1(Model)()3()000001 Up.					
Coupe 2D SE (4 Cyl.)	CE2()P	3075	**12550**	**14900**	**15875**
Coupe 2D SE	CF2()P	3241	**14050**	**16500**	**17550**
Coupe 2D SLE	CF2()P	3241	**15300**	**17800**	**18850**
Convertible 2D SE (4 Cyl.)	FE2()P	3362	**19525**	**22375**	**23550**
Convertible 2D SE	FF2()P	3472	**21025**	**23950**	**25175**
Convertible 2D SLE	FF2()P	3472	**22275**	**25350**	**26600**
MATRIX/CELICA/MR2/CAMRY/CAMRY SOLARA OPTIONS					
Add Aluminum/Alloy Wheels (Std. XRS, GT-S, MR2, Camry V6, Solara SLE/Conv.)			**275**	**325**	**325**
Add Leather Seats (Std. Solara SLE)			**400**	**450**	**450**
Add Navigation System			**500**	**575**	**575**
Add Power Seat (Std. Camry XLE, Solara SLE)			**175**	**200**	**200**
Add Power Sunroof			**525**	**600**	**600**
Add Sequential Manual Trans. (MR2)			**525**	**600**	**600**
Add Theft Recovery System			**75**	**100**	**100**
Ded W/out Auto Trans. (Ex. Matrix XRS, MR2)			**525**	**525**	**525**
Deduct W/out Cruise Control			**175**	**175**	**175**
Deduct W/out Power Door Locks			**150**	**150**	**150**
Deduct W/out Power Windows			**175**	**175**	**175**
2003 AVALON-V6					
Veh. Ident.: 4T1BF28B()3()000001 Up.					
Sedan 4D XL	BF28B	3417	**17550**	**20425**	**21750**
Sedan 4D XLS	BF28B	3439	**19575**	**22575**	**23925**
Add Aluminum/Alloy Wheels (Std. XLS)			**325**	**375**	**375**
Add Leather Seats			**475**	**550**	**550**
Add Navigation System			**550**	**625**	**625**
Add Power Sunroof			**575**	**650**	**650**
Add Theft Recovery System			**75**	**100**	**100**
Deduct W/out Power Seat			**200**	**200**	**200**
TOYOTA					
2002 ECHO-4 Cyl.					
Veh. Ident.: JTD(Model)()2()000001 Up.					
Coupe 2D	AT1()3	2035	**6675**	**8275**	**9025**
Sedan 4D	BT1()3	2055	**7175**	**8850**	**9625**
2002 COROLLA-4 Cyl.					
Veh. Ident.: ()()()(Model)()2()000001 Up.					
Sedan 4D CE	BR1()E	2410	**7850**	**9575**	**10300**

PASSENGER CARS

BODY TYPE	Model No.	Weight	Trade-In	Retail	High Retail
Sedan 4D S	BR1()E	2405	**8075**	**9850**	**10575**
Sedan 4D LE	BR1()E	2445	**8150**	**9950**	**10675**
2002 PRIUS-4 Cyl.					
Veh. Ident.: JT2BK1()U()2()000001 Up.					
Sedan 4D	BK1()U	2765	**13800**	**16050**	**16875**
ECHO/COROLLA/PRIUS OPTIONS					
Add Aluminum/Alloy Wheels (Std. Prius)			**200**	**225**	**225**
Add Compact Disc Player			**75**	**100**	**100**
Add Cruise Control			**125**	**150**	**150**
Add Navigation System			**350**	**400**	**400**
Add Power Door Locks (Std. Prius)			**100**	**125**	**125**
Add Power Sunroof			**425**	**475**	**475**
Add Power Windows (Std. Prius)			**125**	**150**	**150**
Add Theft Recovery System			**75**	**100**	**100**
Deduct W/out Air Conditioning			**475**	**475**	**475**
Deduct W/out Automatic Trans.			**375**	**375**	**375**
Deduct W/out Power Steering			**75**	**75**	**75**
2002 CELICA-4 Cyl.					
Veh. Ident.: JTD(Model)()2()000001 Up.					
Coupe 2D GT	DR3()T	2425	**11675**	**13925**	**14875**
Coupe 2D GT-S	DY3()T	2500	**13825**	**16275**	**17300**
2002 MR2 SPYDER-4 Cyl.-5 Spd.					
Veh. Ident.: JTDFR320()2()000001 Up.					
Convertible 2D	FR320	2195	**14225**	**16675**	**17725**
2002 CAMRY-4 Cyl.					
Veh. Ident.: ()T()(Model)()2()000001 Up.					
Sedan 4D LE	BE3()K	3086	**12300**	**14650**	**15625**
Sedan 4D LE (V6)	BF3()K	3296	**13550**	**15975**	**17000**
Sedan 4D SE	BE3()K	3142	**12800**	**15175**	**16175**
Sedan 4D SE (V6)	BF3()K	3351	**14275**	**16725**	**17775**
Sedan 4D XLE	BE3()K	3219	**13650**	**16075**	**17100**
Sedan 4D XLE (V6)	BF3()K	3362	**15125**	**17625**	**18675**
2002 CAMRY SOLARA-V6					
Veh. Ident.: 2T1(Model)()2()000001 Up.					
Coupe 2D SE (4 Cyl.)	CE2()P	3075	**11100**	**13300**	**14225**
Coupe 2D SE	CF2()P	3208	**12400**	**14750**	**15725**
Coupe 2D SLE	CF2()P	3241	**13775**	**16200**	**17225**
Convertible 2D SE (4 Cyl.)	FE2()P	3362	**16875**	**19500**	**20600**
Convertible 2D SE	FF2()P	3472	**18175**	**20950**	**22100**
Convertible 2D SLE	FF2()P	3472	**19550**	**22400**	**23575**
CELICA/MR2/CAMRY/CAMRY SOLARA OPTIONS					
Add Aluminum/Alloy Wheels (Std. GT-S, MR2, Camry SE/XLE V6, SLE)			**225**	**250**	**250**
Add Leather Seats (Std. Solara SLE)			**350**	**400**	**400**
Add Navigation System			**400**	**450**	**450**
Add Power Seat (Std. Camry XLE, Solara SLE)			**150**	**175**	**175**
Add Power Sunroof			**475**	**550**	**550**
Add Sequential Manual Trans. (MR2)			**475**	**550**	**550**
Add Theft Recovery System			**75**	**100**	**100**
Deduct W/out Automatic Trans. (Ex. MR2)			**475**	**475**	**475**
Deduct W/out Cruise Control			**150**	**150**	**150**
Deduct W/out Power Door Locks			**125**	**125**	**125**
Deduct W/out Power Windows			**150**	**150**	**150**

BODY TYPE	Model No.	Weight	Trade-In	Retail	High Retail
2002 AVALON-V6					
Veh. Ident.: 4T1BF28B()2()000001 Up.					
Sedan 4D XL	BF28B	3417	**14400**	**16925**	**18175**
Sedan 4D XLS	BF28B	3439	**16225**	**18850**	**20125**
Add Aluminum/Alloy Wheels (Std. XLS)			**275**	**325**	**325**
Add Leather Seats			**425**	**475**	**475**
Add Power Sunroof			**525**	**600**	**600**
Add Theft Recovery System			**75**	**100**	**100**
Deduct W/out Power Seat			**175**	**175**	**175**
TOYOTA					
2001 ECHO-4 Cyl.					
Veh. Ident.: JTD(Model)()1()000001 Up.					
Coupe 2D	AT1()3	2020	**5750**	**7275**	**8050**
Sedan 4D	BT1()3	2030	**6250**	**7800**	**8625**
2001 COROLLA-4 Cyl.					
Veh. Ident.: ()()()(Model)()1()000001 Up.					
Sedan 4D CE	BR1()E	2410	**6625**	**8225**	**8975**
Sedan 4D S	BR1()E	2405	**6825**	**8450**	**9200**
Sedan 4D LE	BR1()E	2445	**6900**	**8525**	**9300**
2001 PRIUS-4 Cyl.					
Veh. Ident.: JT2BK12U()1()000001 Up.					
Sedan 4D	BK12U	2765	**11825**	**13975**	**14725**
ECHO/COROLLA/PRIUS OPTIONS					
Add Aluminum/Alloy Wheels (Std. Prius)			**150**	**175**	**175**
Add Compact Disc Player			**50**	**75**	**75**
Add Cruise Control			**100**	**125**	**125**
Add Power Door Locks (Std. Prius)			**75**	**100**	**100**
Add Power Sunroof			**375**	**425**	**425**
Add Power Windows (Std. Prius)			**100**	**125**	**125**
Add Theft Recovery System			**50**	**75**	**75**
Deduct W/out Air Conditioning			**425**	**425**	**425**
Deduct W/out Automatic Trans.			**325**	**325**	**325**
Deduct W/out Power Steering			**75**	**75**	**75**
2001 CELICA-4 Cyl.					
Veh. Ident.: JTD(Model)()1()000001 Up.					
Coupe 2D GT	DR3()T	2425	**9900**	**11975**	**12900**
Coupe 2D GT-S	DY3()T	2500	**11775**	**14025**	**14975**
2001 MR2 SPYDER-4 Cyl.-5 Spd.					
Veh. Ident.: JTDFR320()1()000001 Up.					
Convertible 2D	FR320	2195	**12450**	**14600**	**15575**
2001 CAMRY-4 Cyl.					
Veh. Ident.: ()T()(Model)()1()000001 Up.					
Sedan 4D CE	BG2()K	2998	**8950**	**10900**	**11850**
Sedan 4D LE	BG2()K	3120	**9800**	**11850**	**12750**
Sedan 4D LE (V6)	BF2()K	3175	**10850**	**13025**	**13950**
Sedan 4D XLE	BG2()K	3131	**11175**	**13375**	**14300**
Sedan 4D XLE (V6)	BF2()K	3252	**12225**	**14575**	**15550**
2001 CAMRY SOLARA-V6					
Veh. Ident.: 2T1(Model)()1()000001 Up.					
Coupe 2D SE (4 Cyl.)	CG2()P	3120	**9650**	**11700**	**12600**
Coupe 2D SE	CF2()P	3230	**10750**	**12925**	**13850**
Coupe 2D SLE	CF2()P	3291	**11950**	**14225**	**15175**
Convertible 2D SE (4 Cyl.)	FG2()P	3395	**14875**	**17375**	**18400**

PASSENGER CARS

PASSENGER CARS

BODY TYPE	Model No.	Weight	Trade-In	Retail	High Retail
Convertible 2D SE	FF2()P	3485	**15975**	**18525**	**19600**
Convertible 2D SLE	FF2()P	3485	**17175**	**19900**	**21000**
CELICA/MR2/CAMRY/CAMRY SOLARA OPTIONS					
Add Aluminum/Alloy Wheels (Std. Celica GT-S, MR2, Camry XLE, Solara SLE)			**175**	**200**	**200**
Add Leather Seats (Std. Solara SLE)			**300**	**350**	**350**
Add Power Seat (Std. Camry XLE, Solara SLE)			**125**	**150**	**150**
Add Power Sunroof			**425**	**475**	**475**
Add Theft Recovery System			**50**	**75**	**75**
Deduct W/out Air Conditioning			**550**	**550**	**550**
Deduct W/out Automatic Trans. (Ex. MR2)			**425**	**425**	**425**
Deduct W/out Cruise Control (Ex. MR2 Spyder)			**125**	**125**	**125**
Deduct W/out Power Door Locks			**100**	**100**	**100**
Deduct W/out Power Windows			**125**	**125**	**125**
2001 AVALON-V6					
Veh. Ident.: 4T1BF28B()1()000001 Up.					
Sedan 4D XL	BF28B	3417	**12775**	**15200**	**16375**
Sedan 4D XLS	BF28B	3439	**14400**	**16925**	**18175**
Add Aluminum/Alloy Wheels (Std. XLS)			**225**	**250**	**250**
Add Leather Seats			**375**	**425**	**425**
Add Power Sunroof			**475**	**550**	**550**
Add Theft Recovery System			**50**	**75**	**75**
Deduct W/out Power Seat			**150**	**150**	**150**
TOYOTA					
2000 ECHO-4 Cyl.					
Veh. Ident.: JTD(Model)()Y()000001 Up.					
Coupe 2D	AT123	2020	**4650**	**6050**	**6825**
Sedan 4D	BT123	2030	**5150**	**6625**	**7450**
2000 COROLLA-4 Cyl.					
Veh. Ident.: ()()()(Model)()Y()000001 Up.					
Sedan 4D VE	BR1()E	2403	**5300**	**6800**	**7625**
Sedan 4D CE	BR1()E	2426	**5550**	**7075**	**7850**
Sedan 4D LE	BR1()E	2459	**5875**	**7425**	**8225**
ECHO/COROLLA OPTIONS					
Add Aluminum/Alloy Wheels			**100**	**125**	**125**
Add Compact Disc Player			**50**	**75**	**75**
Add Cruise Control			**75**	**100**	**100**
Add Power Door Locks (Std. LE)			**50**	**75**	**75**
Add Power Sunroof			**325**	**375**	**375**
Add Power Windows (Std. LE)			**75**	**100**	**100**
Deduct W/out Air Conditioning			**375**	**375**	**375**
Deduct W/out Automatic Trans.			**300**	**300**	**300**
Deduct W/out Power Steering			**50**	**50**	**50**
2000 CELICA-4 Cyl.					
Veh. Ident.: JTD(Model)()Y()000001 Up.					
Coupe 2D GT	DR32T	2425	**8400**	**10300**	**11225**
Coupe 2D GT-S	DY32T	2500	**10000**	**12100**	**12975**
2000 MR2 SPYDER-4 Cyl.-5 Spd.					
Veh. Ident.: JTDFR320()Y()000001 Up.					
Convertible 2D	FR320	2210	**10850**	**12900**	**13825**
2000 CAMRY-4 Cyl.					
Veh. Ident.: ()T()(Model)()Y()000001 Up.					
Sedan 4D CE	BG2()K	2998	**7550**	**9350**	**10225**

BODY TYPE	Model No.	Weight	Trade-In	Retail	High Retail
Sedan 4D LE	BG2()K	3120	**8150**	**10025**	**10950**
Sedan 4D LE (V6)	BF2()K	3175	**9000**	**10950**	**11900**
Sedan 4D XLE	BG2()K	3131	**9375**	**11400**	**12300**
Sedan 4D XLE (V6)	BF2()K	3252	**10225**	**12350**	**13250**
2000 CAMRY SOLARA-V6					
Veh. Ident.: 2T1(Model)()Y()000001 Up.					
Coupe 2D SE (4 Cyl.)	CG2()P	3120	**7925**	**9775**	**10675**
Coupe 2D SE	CF2()P	3230	**8925**	**10850**	**11800**
Coupe 2D SLE	CF2()P	3291	**9900**	**11975**	**12900**
Convertible 2D SE (4 Cyl.)	FN2()P	3395	**12925**	**15300**	**16300**
Convertible 2D SE	FF2()P	3485	**13925**	**16350**	**17375**
Convertible 2D SLE	FF2()P	3485	**14900**	**17375**	**18400**
CELICA/MR2/CAMRY/CAMRY SOLARA OPTIONS					
Add Aluminum/Alloy Wheels (Std. Celica GT-S, MR2, Camry XLE, Solara SLE)			**125**	**150**	**150**
Add Leather Seats (Std. Solara SLE)			**250**	**300**	**300**
Add Power Seat (Std. Camry XLE, Solara SLE)			**100**	**125**	**125**
Add Power Sunroof			**375**	**425**	**425**
Deduct W/out Air Conditioning			**500**	**500**	**500**
Deduct W/out Automatic Trans. (Ex. MR2)			**375**	**375**	**375**
Deduct W/out Cruise Control (Ex. MR2 Spyder)			**100**	**100**	**100**
Deduct W/out Power Door Locks			**75**	**75**	**75**
Deduct W/out Power Windows			**100**	**100**	**100**
2000 AVALON-V6					
Veh. Ident.: 4T1BF28B()Y()000001 Up.					
Sedan 4D XL	BF28B	3417	**11050**	**13325**	**14425**
Sedan 4D XLS	BF28B	3428	**12325**	**14725**	**15875**
Add Aluminum/Alloy Wheels (Std. XLS)			**175**	**200**	**200**
Add Leather Seats			**325**	**375**	**375**
Add Power Sunroof			**425**	**475**	**475**
Deduct W/out Power Seat			**125**	**125**	**125**
TOYOTA					
1999 COROLLA-4 Cyl.					
Veh. Ident.: ()()2BR12E()X()000001 Up.					
Sedan 4D VE	BR1()E	2409	**4425**	**5825**	**6600**
Sedan 4D CE	BR1()E	2420	**4650**	**6050**	**6825**
Sedan 4D LE	BR1()E	2453	**4900**	**6325**	**7125**
Add Aluminum/Alloy Wheels			**50**	**75**	**75**
Add Cruise Control			**50**	**75**	**75**
Add Power Sunroof			**275**	**325**	**325**
Add Power Windows (Std. LE)			**50**	**75**	**75**
Deduct W/out Air Conditioning			**325**	**325**	**325**
Deduct W/out Automatic Trans.			**250**	**250**	**250**
1999 CELICA-4 Cyl.					
Veh. Ident.: JT2(Model)()X()000001 Up.					
Liftback 3D GT	DG02T	2580	**8050**	**9925**	**10825**
Convertible 2D GT	FG02T	2755	**9650**	**11700**	**12600**
1999 CAMRY-4 Cyl.					
Veh. Ident.: ()()2(Model)()X()000001 Up.					
Sedan 4D CE	BG2()K	2998	**6225**	**7925**	**8850**
Sedan 4D LE	BG2()K	3120	**6675**	**8425**	**9300**
Sedan 4D LE (V6)	BF2()K	3175	**7425**	**9225**	**10100**
Sedan 4D XLE	BG2()K	3131	**7625**	**9450**	**10325**

PASSENGER CARS

BODY TYPE	Model No.	Weight	Trade-In	Retail	High Retail
Sedan 4D XLE (V6)	BF2()K	3252	**8375**	**10275**	**11200**
1999 CAMRY SOLARA-V6					
Veh. Ident.: ()()2(Model)()X()000001 Up.					
Coupe 2D SE (4 Cyl.)	CG2()P	3120	**7025**	**8800**	**9575**
Coupe 2D SE	CF2()P	3230	**7925**	**9775**	**10500**
Coupe 2D SLE	CF2()P	3230	**8750**	**10675**	**11400**
CELICA/CAMRY/CAMRY SOLARA OPTIONS					
Add Aluminum/Alloy Wheels (Std. Convertible, Camry XLE, Solara SLE)			**75**	**100**	**100**
Add Leather Seats (Std. Solara SLE)			**225**	**250**	**250**
Add Power Seat (Std. Camry XLE, Solara SLE)			**75**	**100**	**100**
Add Power Sunroof			**325**	**375**	**375**
Deduct W/out Air Conditioning			**450**	**450**	**450**
Deduct W/out Automatic Trans.			**325**	**325**	**325**
Deduct W/out Cruise Control			**75**	**75**	**75**
Deduct W/out Power Door Locks			**50**	**50**	**50**
Deduct W/out Power Windows			**75**	**75**	**75**
1999 AVALON-V6					
Veh. Ident.: 1N()BF1()B()X()000001 Up.					
Sedan 4D XL	BF1()B	3340	**7175**	**9125**	**10125**
Sedan 4D XLS	BF1()B	3340	**8350**	**10400**	**11425**
Add Aluminum/Alloy Wheels (Std. XLS)			**125**	**150**	**150**
Add Leather Seats			**275**	**325**	**325**
Add Power Sunroof			**375**	**425**	**425**
Deduct W/out Power Seat			**100**	**100**	**100**
TOYOTA					
1998 TERCEL-4 Cyl.					
Veh. Ident.: JT2AC52L()W()000001 Up.					
Sedan 2D CE	AC52L	1975	**3075**	**4300**	**5025**
1998 COROLLA-4 Cyl.					
Veh. Ident.: ()()2BR1()E()W()000001 Up.					
Sedan 4D VE	BR1()E	2343	**3675**	**4975**	**5775**
Sedan 4D CE	BR1()E	2355	**3875**	**5175**	**5900**
Sedan 4D LE	BR1()E	2388	**4125**	**5475**	**6225**
TERCEL/COROLLA OPTIONS					
Add Cruise Control			**50**	**75**	**75**
Add Power Sunroof			**225**	**275**	**275**
Add Power Windows (Std. Corolla LE)			**50**	**75**	**75**
Deduct W/out Air Conditioning			**275**	**275**	**275**
Deduct W/out Automatic Trans.			**200**	**200**	**200**
1998 CELICA-4 Cyl.					
Veh. Ident.: JT2(Model)()W()000001 Up.					
Coupe 2D GT	CG02T	2475	**6825**	**8575**	**9450**
Liftback 3D GT	DG02T	2495	**7175**	**8975**	**9875**
Convertible 2D GT	FG02T	2670	**8575**	**10475**	**11400**
1998 CAMRY-4 Cyl.					
Veh. Ident.: ()()2(Model)()W()000001 Up.					
Sedan 4D CE	BG2()K	2906	**5025**	**6600**	**7500**
Sedan 4D CE (V6, 5 Spd.)	BF2()K	2994	**5400**	**7050**	**7925**
Sedan 4D LE	BG2()K	3028	**5425**	**7075**	**7950**
Sedan 4D LE (V6)	BF2()K	3149	**6075**	**7775**	**8700**
Sedan 4D XLE	BG2()K	3039	**6250**	**7975**	**8900**
Sedan 4D XLE (V6)	BF2()K	3160	**6900**	**8675**	**9550**

BODY TYPE	Model No.	Weight	Trade-In	Retail	High Retail
CELICA/CAMRY OPTIONS					
Add Aluminum/Alloy Wheels .... (Std. Celica Convertible, Camry XLE) .			50	75	75
Add Leather Seats			175	200	200
Add Power Seat (Std. Camry XLE)......			50	75	75
Add Power Sunroof			275	325	325
Deduct W/out Air Conditioning			400	400	400
Ded W/out Automatic Trans. (Ex. Camry CE V6)			275	275	275
Ded W/out Cruise Control (Ex. Celica GT Coupe)			50	50	50
Deduct W/out Power Windows			50	50	50
1998 AVALON-V6					
Veh. Ident.: 1N()BF1()B()W()000001 Up.					
Sedan 4D XL	BF1()B	3236	6275	8150	9150
Sedan 4D XLS	BF1()B	3236	7300	9250	10275
1998 SUPRA-I6-5/6 Spd./AT					
Veh. Ident.: JT2(Model)()W()000001 Up.					
Liftback 3D	DD8()A	3162	19400	22375	23700
Liftback 3D Turbo	DE8()A	3412	25000	28475	29975
AVALON/SUPRA OPTIONS					
Add Aluminum/Alloy Wheels (Std. Avalon XLS, Supra)			100	125	125
Add Leather Seats (Std. Supra Turbo) . . .			225	250	250
Add Power Sunroof			325	375	375
Add Removable Roof (Std. Supra Turbo).			450	525	525
Deduct W/out Power Seat			75	75	75
TOYOTA					
1997 TERCEL-4 Cyl.					
Veh. Ident.: JT2(Model)()V()000001 Up.					
Sedan 2D CE	AC52L	2010	2325	3475	4125
Sedan 4D CE	BC52L	2035	2400	3550	4225
1997 COROLLA-4 Cyl.					
Veh. Ident.: ()()2(Model)()V()000001 Up.					
Sedan 4D	BA02E	2337	3275	4525	5275
Sedan 4D CE	BA02E	2441	3325	4575	5350
Sedan 4D DX	BB02E	2403	3500	4775	5575
1997 PASEO-4 Cyl.					
Veh. Ident.: JT2(Model)()V()000001 Up.					
Coupe 2D	CC52H	2025	2925	4150	4875
Convertible 2D	FC52H	2160	3950	5275	6000
TERCEL/COROLLA/PASEO OPTIONS					
Add Power Sunroof			150	175	175
Add Sunroof			50	75	75
Deduct W/out Air Conditioning			150	150	150
Deduct W/out Automatic Trans.			125	125	125
1997 CELICA-4 Cyl.					
Veh. Ident.: JT2(Model)()V()000001 Up.					
Coupe 2D ST	CB02T	2395	4375	5875	6750
Liftback 3D ST	DB02T	2415	4525	6025	6875
Liftback 3D GT	DG02T	2850	5175	6800	7725
Convertible 2D GT	FG02T	2775	6375	8100	8950
1997 CAMRY-4 Cyl.					
Veh. Ident.: ()()2(Model)()V()000001 Up.					
Sedan 4D CE	BG22K	2976	3850	5300	6125
Sedan 4D CE (V6, 5 Spd.)	BF22K	3086	4275	5750	6600

PASSENGER CARS

PASSENGER CARS

BODY TYPE	Model No.	Weight	Trade-In	Retail	High Retail
Sedan 4D LE	BG22K	3086	**4200**	**5675**	**6525**
Sedan 4D LE (V6)	BF22K	3219	**4800**	**6325**	**7200**
Sedan 4D XLE	BG22K		**4800**	**6325**	**7200**
Sedan 4D XLE (V6)	BF22K	3230	**5400**	**7025**	**7900**
CELICA/CAMRY OPTIONS					
Add Leather Seats			**150**	**175**	**175**
Add Power Seat (Std. Camry XLE)			**50**	**75**	**75**
Add Power Sunroof			**200**	**225**	**225**
Deduct W/out Air Conditioning			**250**	**250**	**250**
Ded W/out Automatic Trans. (Ex. Camry CE V6)			**175**	**175**	**175**
Deduct W/out Cruise Control			**50**	**50**	**50**
Deduct W/out Power Windows			**50**	**50**	**50**
1997 AVALON-V6					
Veh. Ident.: 1N()BF12B()V()000001 Up.					
Sedan 4D XL	BF12B	3263	**4900**	**6625**	**7650**
Sedan 4D XLS	BF12B	3287	**5550**	**7350**	**8375**
1997 SUPRA-I6-5/6 Spd./AT					
Veh. Ident.: JT2(Model)()V()000001 Up.					
Liftback 3D	DD82A	3210	**17725**	**20600**	**21925**
Liftback 3D Turbo	DE82A	3445	**22725**	**26050**	**27500**
AVALON/SUPRA OPTIONS					
Add Aluminum/Alloy Wheels (Std. Avalon XLS, Supra)			**50**	**75**	**75**
Add Leather Seats (Std. Supra Turbo)			**200**	**225**	**225**
Add Power Sunroof			**250**	**300**	**300**
Add Removable Roof (Std. Supra Turbo)			**350**	**400**	**400**
Deduct W/out Power Seat			**75**	**75**	**75**
TOYOTA					
1996 TERCEL-4 Cyl.					
Veh. Ident.: JT2(Model)()T()000001 Up.					
Sedan 2D	AC52L	1950	**1825**	**2900**	**3525**
Sedan 2D DX	AC52L	1975	**1950**	**3050**	**3650**
Sedan 4D DX	BC52L	2005	**2025**	**3150**	**3775**
1996 COROLLA-4 Cyl.					
Veh. Ident.: ()()2(Model)()T()000001 Up.					
Sedan 4D	BA02E	2315	**2650**	**3850**	**4550**
Sedan 4D DX	BB02E	2381	**2750**	**3950**	**4650**
Station Wagon 5D DX	EB02E	2403	**3250**	**4500**	**5250**
1996 PASEO-4 Cyl.					
Veh. Ident.: JT2CC52H()T()000001 Up.					
Coupe 2D	CC52H	2025	**2475**	**3650**	**4325**
TERCEL/COROLLA/PASEO OPTIONS					
Add Power Sunroof			**100**	**125**	**125**
Deduct W/out Air Conditioning			**100**	**100**	**100**
Deduct W/out Automatic Trans.			**100**	**100**	**100**
1996 CELICA-4 Cyl.					
Veh. Ident.: JT2(Model)()T()000001 Up.					
Coupe 2D ST	CB02T	2395	**3775**	**5200**	**6000**
Coupe 2D GT	CG02T	2560	**4375**	**5875**	**6750**
Liftback 3D ST	DB02T	2415	**3875**	**5325**	**6150**
Liftback 3D GT	DG02T	2580	**4475**	**5975**	**6850**
Convertible 2D GT	FG02T	2755	**5525**	**7175**	**8050**

BODY TYPE	Model No.	Weight	Trade-In	Retail	High Retail
1996 CAMRY-4 Cyl.					
Veh. Ident.: ()()2(Model)()T()000001 Up.					
Coupe 2D DX	CG12K	2910	**3100**	**4450**	**5300**
Coupe 2D LE	CG12K	3064	**3200**	**4575**	**5425**
Coupe 2D LE (V6)	CF12K	3219	**3700**	**5125**	**5925**
Coupe 2D SE (V6)	CF12K	3164	**4150**	**5625**	**6475**
Sedan 4D DX	BG12K	2932	**3250**	**4625**	**5500**
Sedan 4D LE	BG12K	3086	**3350**	**4725**	**5600**
Sedan 4D LE (V6)	BF12K	3241	**3850**	**5300**	**6125**
Sedan 4D SE (V6)	BF12K	3186	**4300**	**5800**	**6675**
Sedan 4D XLE	BG12K	3131	**3900**	**5350**	**6175**
Sedan 4D XLE (V6)	BF12K	3274	**4400**	**5900**	**6775**
Station Wagon 5D LE	EG12K	3263	**3475**	**4875**	**5775**
Station Wagon 5D LE (V6)	EF12K	3406	**3975**	**5425**	**6250**
CELICA/CAMRY OPTIONS					
Add Power Sunroof			**150**	**175**	**175**
Deduct W/out Air Conditioning			**150**	**150**	**150**
Deduct W/out Automatic Trans.			**125**	**125**	**125**
1996 AVALON-V6					
Veh. Ident.: 1N()BF12B()T()000001 Up.					
Sedan 4D XL	BF12B	3263	**4275**	**5925**	**6925**
Sedan 4D XLS	BF12B	3287	**4725**	**6425**	**7425**
1996 SUPRA-I6-5 Spd./AT					
Veh. Ident.: JT2(Model)()T()000001 Up.					
Liftback 3D	DD82A	3210	**15075**	**17625**	**18850**
Liftback 3D Turbo	DE82A	3460	**19275**	**22250**	**23575**
AVALON/SUPRA OPTIONS					
Add Power Sunroof			**200**	**225**	**225**
Add Removable Roof (Std. Supra Turbo)			**300**	**350**	**350**
TOYOTA					
1995 TERCEL-4 Cyl.					
Veh. Ident.: JT2()(Model)()S()000001 Up.					
Sedan 2D	L55D	1950	**1525**	**2575**	**3150**
Sedan 2D DX	L56D	2070	**1650**	**2700**	**3300**
Sedan 4D DX	L56E	2100	**1725**	**2800**	**3425**
1995 COROLLA-4 Cyl.					
Veh. Ident.: ()()()()(Model)()S()000001 Up.					
Sedan 4D	E04B	2359	**2275**	**3425**	**4075**
Sedan 4D DX	E09B	2458	**2375**	**3525**	**4175**
Sedan 4D LE	E00B	2524	**2700**	**3900**	**4600**
Station Wagon 5D DX	E09V	2480	**2825**	**4025**	**4725**
1995 PASEO-4 Cyl.					
Veh. Ident.: JT2()L45U()S()000001 Up.					
Coupe 2D	L45U	2160	**1925**	**3025**	**3625**
1995 CELICA-4 Cyl.					
Veh. Ident.: JT2()(Model)()S()000001 Up.					
Coupe 2D ST	T00F	2475	**3225**	**4600**	**5450**
Coupe 2D GT	T07F	2620	**3775**	**5200**	**6000**
Liftback 3D ST	T00N	2495	**3325**	**4700**	**5575**
Liftback 3D GT	T07N	2640	**3875**	**5325**	**6150**
Convertible 2D GT	T07K	2815	**4875**	**6425**	**7325**
1995 CAMRY-4 Cyl.					
Veh. Ident.: ()()()(Model)()S()000001 Up.					
Coupe 2D DX	SK11C	2954	**2650**	**3925**	**4725**

BODY TYPE	Model No.	Weight	Trade-In	Retail	High Retail
Coupe 2D LE	SK12C	3064	**2750**	**4050**	**4850**
Coupe 2D LE (V6)	GK12C	3219	**3150**	**4525**	**5375**
Coupe 2D SE (V6)	GK14C	3164	**3575**	**4975**	**5875**
Sedan 4D DX	SK11E	2976	**2750**	**4050**	**4850**
Sedan 4D LE	SK12E	3086	**2850**	**4150**	**4950**
Sedan 4D LE (V6)	GK12E	3241	**3250**	**4625**	**5500**
Sedan 4D SE (V6)	GK14E	3186	**3675**	**5100**	**5900**
Sedan 4D XLE	SK13E	3274	**3375**	**4775**	**5650**
Sedan 4D XLE (V6)	GK13E	3274	**3775**	**5200**	**6000**
Station Wagon 5D LE	SK12W	3263	**2950**	**4275**	**5100**
Station Wagon 5D LE (V6)	GK12W	3406	**3350**	**4725**	**5600**

1995 MR2-4 Cyl.

Veh. Ident.: JT2()(Model)()S()000001 Up.

BODY TYPE	Model No.	Weight	Trade-In	Retail	High Retail
Coupe 2D	W21M	2723	**4525**	**6025**	**6875**
Coupe 2D Turbo	W22N	2888	**6825**	**8575**	**9450**
CELICA/CAMRY/MR2 OPTIONS					
Add T-Top (Std. MR2 Turbo)			**250**	**300**	**300**

1995 AVALON-V6

Veh. Ident.: 1N()()(Model)()S()000001 Up.

BODY TYPE	Model No.	Weight	Trade-In	Retail	High Retail
Sedan 4D XL	B10E	3285	**3650**	**5200**	**6100**
Sedan 4D XLS	B11E	3298	**4000**	**5575**	**6525**

1995 SUPRA-I6

Veh. Ident.: JT2()(Model)()S()000001 Up.

BODY TYPE	Model No.	Weight	Trade-In	Retail	High Retail
Liftback 3D	A81L	3265	**13250**	**15700**	**16900**
Liftback 3D Turbo	A82L	3515	**16500**	**19150**	**20425**
AVALON/SUPRA OPTIONS					
Add Removable Roof			**250**	**300**	**300**

VOLKSWAGEN

* Model can be identified by VIN. Please refer to the VIN Explanation Section.

VOLKSWAGEN

2004 GOLF-4 Cyl.-5 Spd.

Veh. Ident.: ()()W(Model)61J()4()000001 Up.

BODY TYPE	Model No.	Weight	Trade-In	Retail	High Retail
Hatchback 2D GL	BL	2771	**12675**	**14850**	**15625**
Hatchback 2D GTI 1.8T	DE	2934	**15500**	**17850**	**18675**
Hatchback 2D GTI VR6 (6 Spd.)	DH	3036	**16825**	**19250**	**20100**
H'back 2D R32 4Motion (6 Spd.)	KG	3409	**26525**	**29550**	
Hatchback 4D GL	FL	2857	**12925**	**15100**	**15900**
Hatchback 4D GL TDI	FR	2934	**14925**	**17225**	**18025**
Hatchback 4D GLS	GL	2897	**14075**	**16325**	**17150**
Hatchback 4D GLS TDI	GR	2972	**16075**	**18450**	**19275**
Add Aluminum/Alloy Wheels (Std. GTI, R32, GLS)			**300**	**350**	**350**
Add Automatic Trans.			**475**	**550**	**550**
Add Leather Seats			**350**	**400**	**400**
Add Power Sunroof (Std. R32, GLS)			**525**	**600**	**600**
Add Theft Recovery System			**100**	**125**	**125**

2004 NEW BEETLE-4 Cyl.-5 Spd.

Veh. Ident.: 3VW(Model)()4M000001 Up.

BODY TYPE	Model No.	Weight	Trade-In	Retail	High Retail
Coupe 2D GL	BK21C	2743	**12750**	**15125**	**15925**
Coupe 2D GL TDI	BR21C	2899	**13750**	**16175**	**17200**
Coupe 2D GLS	CK21C	2743	**14350**	**16825**	**17650**

BODY TYPE	Model No.	Weight	Trade-In	Retail	High Retail
Coupe 2D GLS TDI	CR21C	3018	**15350**	**17875**	**18700**
Coupe 2D GLS Turbo	CD21C	2820	**15350**	**17875**	**18700**
Coupe 2D Turbo S (6 Spd.)	FE21C	3005	**16575**	**19175**	**20275**
Convertible 2D GL	B()21Y	3075	**18000**	**20775**	
Convertible 2D GLS	C()21Y	3082	**18875**	**21700**	
Convertible 2D GLS Turbo	CD21Y	3166	**19975**	**22850**	
2004 JETTA-4 Cyl.-5 Spd.					
Veh. Ident.: ()VW(Model)()4()000001 Up.					
Sedan 4D GL	R()69M	2895	**13250**	**15650**	**16650**
Sedan 4D GL TDI	RR69M	2970	**15250**	**17750**	**18800**
Sedan 4D GL 1.8T	RE69M	2974	**14650**	**17125**	**18150**
Sedan 4D GLS	S()69M	2934	**15075**	**17575**	**18625**
Sedan 4D GLS TDI	SR69M	3003	**17075**	**19775**	**20875**
Sedan 4D GLS 1.8T	SE69M	3038	**16475**	**19050**	**20125**
Sedan 4D GLI 1.8T (6 Spd.)	SE69M	3106	**17825**	**20575**	**21700**
Sedan 4D GLI VR6 (6 Spd.)	VH69M	3179	**17875**	**20625**	**21750**
Wagon 4D GL	R()61J	3034			
Wagon 4D GL TDI	RR61J	3053			
Wagon 4D GLS	S()61J	2934	**15175**	**17675**	**18725**
Wagon 4D GLS TDI	SR61J	3095			
Wagon 4D GLS 1.8T	SE61J	3175	**16575**	**19150**	**20225**
NEW BEETLE/JETTA OPTIONS					
Add Sport Pkg. (Jetta GLS 1.8T)			**700**	**800**	**800**
Add Aluminum/Alloy Wheels (Beetle/Jetta GL)			**325**	**375**	**375**
Add Automatic Trans.			**575**	**650**	**650**
Add Compact Disc Player (Std. Jetta)			**100**	**125**	**125**
Add Leather Seats (Std. Beetle Turbo S)			**450**	**500**	**500**
Add Power Sunroof (Std. GLS, GLI 1.8T, Beetle Turbo S)			**575**	**650**	**650**
Add Theft Recovery System			**100**	**125**	**125**
2004 PASSAT-4 Cyl. Turbo					
Veh. Ident.: WVW(Model)63B()4()000001 Up.					
Sedan 4D GL	MD	3212			
Sedan 4D GL TDI	ME	3422			
Sedan 4D GLS	PD	3241	**17900**	**20775**	**22125**
Sedan 4D GLS 4Motion	PD	3491	**19400**	**22375**	**23700**
Sedan 4D GLS TDI	PE	3450			
Wagon 4D GL	ND	3307			
Wagon 4D GL TDI	NE	3492			
Wagon 4D GLS	VD	3338	**18650**	**21575**	**22950**
Wagon 4D GLS 4Motion	VD	3590	**20150**	**23175**	**24525**
Wagon 4D GLS TDI	VE	3519			
2004 PASSAT-V6					
Veh. Ident.: WVW(Model)()63B()4()000001 Up.					
Sedan 4D GLX	R	3413	**20875**	**23925**	**25300**
Sedan 4D GLX 4Motion	T	3721	**22375**	**25675**	**27100**
Sedan 4D W8 4Motion	U/K	3847			
Wagon 4D GLX	W	3499	**21625**	**24725**	**26125**
Wagon 4D GLX 4Motion	Y	3840	**23125**	**26475**	**27925**
Wagon 4D W8 4Motion	Z/L	3982			
PASSAT OPTIONS					
Add Sport Pkg.					
Add Aluminum/Alloy Wheels (GL)					
Add Leather Seats (Std. GLX, W8)			**525**	**600**	**600**
Add Theft Recovery System			**100**	**125**	**125**

ADJUST FOR MILEAGE

BODY TYPE	Model No.	Weight	Trade-In	Retail	High Retail
Deduct W/out Automatic Trans.			625	625	625
2004 PHAETON-4MOTION					
Veh. Ident.: WVW(Model)63D()4()000001 Up.					
Sedan 4D V8	()F	5194	43800	48925	51300
Sedan 4D W12	()H	5399	55100	60850	63600
Add Comfort/Four Seat Pkg.					
Add Theft Recovery System			100	125	125
VOLKSWAGEN					
2003 GOLF-4 Cyl.-5 Spd.					
Veh. Ident.: ()()W(Model)61J()3()000001 Up.					
Hatchback 2D GL	BK	2771	10825	12875	13600
Hatchback 2D GL TDI	BP	2853	12425	14575	15350
Hatchback 2D GTI 1.8T	DE	2932	13625	15850	16650
Hatchback GTI 20th Annv (6 Spd.)	KE	2916	17325	19750	20600
Hatchback 2D GTI VR6 (6 Spd.)	DH	3036	14725	17025	17825
Hatchback 4D GL	FK	2857	11050	13125	13875
Hatchback 4D GL TDI	FP	2937	12650	14825	15600
Hatchback 4D GLS	GK	2897	12125	14275	15050
Hatchback 4D GLS TDI	GP	2976	13725	15950	16750
Add Aluminum/Alloy Wheels (Std. GTI, GLS)			250	300	300
Add Automatic Trans.			425	475	475
Add Leather Seats			300	350	350
Add Power Sunroof (Std. Annv, GLS)			475	550	550
Add Theft Recovery System			75	100	100
2003 NEW BEETLE-4 Cyl.-5 Spd.					
Veh. Ident.: 3VW(Model)()3M000001 Up.					
Coupe 2D GL	BK21C	2817	11325	13550	14300
Coupe 2D GL TDI	BP21C	2899	12225	14575	15550
Coupe 2D GL Turbo	BD21C	2820	12175	14525	15500
Coupe 2D GLS	CK21C	2855	12500	14850	15625
Coupe 2D GLS TDI	CP21C	3018	13400	15800	16600
Coupe 2D GLS Turbo	CD21C	2954	13350	15750	16550
Coupe 2D GLX Turbo	DD21C	2958	14275	16725	17550
Coupe 2D Turbo S (6 Spd.)	FE21C	3005	14775	17250	18275
Convertible 2D GL	BK21Y	3075	16400	18975	20050
Convertible 2D GLS	CK21Y	3082	17025	19700	20800
Convertible 2D GLS Turbo	CD21Y	3166	17975	20750	21875
Convertible 2D GLX Turbo	DD21Y	3170	18900	21725	22900
2003 JETTA-4 Cyl.-5 Spd.					
Veh. Ident.: ()VW(Model)()3()000001 Up.					
Sedan 4D GL	RK69M	2892	11575	13800	14750
Sedan 4D GL TDI	RP69M	2974	13375	15775	16800
Sedan 4D GL 1.8T	RE69M	2974	12825	15200	16200
Sedan 4D GLS	SK69M	2934	13125	15525	16525
Sedan 4D GLS TDI	SP69M	3009	14925	17425	18450
Sedan 4D GLS 1.8T	SE69M	3037	14375	16850	17900
Sedan 4D Wolfsburg	PE69M	2974	14225	16675	17725
Sedan 4D GLI VR6 (6 Spd.)	VH69M	3179	15700	18225	19275
Sedan 4D GLX VR6 (AT)	TH69M	3274	16425	19000	20075
Wagon 4D GL	RK61J	3034	11675	13900	14850
Wagon 4D GL TDI	RP61J	3122	13475	15900	16925
Wagon 4D GL 1.8T	RE61J	3130	12925	15300	16300
Wagon 4D GLS	SK61J	3078	13225	15625	16625
Wagon 4D GLS TDI	SP61J	3161	15025	17525	18575

BODY TYPE	Model No.	Weight	Trade-In	Retail	High Retail
Wagon 4D GLS 1.8T	SE61J	3175	14475	16950	18000
Wagon 4D GLS 1.8T Premium	TE61J		15400	17925	18975
NEW BEETLE/JETTA OPTIONS					
Add Sport Pkg. (Jetta GLS 1.8T)			600	675	675
Add Aluminum/Alloy Wheels (Beetle/Jetta GL)			275	325	325
Add Automatic Trans. (Std. Jetta GLX)			525	600	600
Add Compact Disc Player (Std. Jetta)			75	100	100
Add Leather Seats (Std. Jetta GLX/Prem., Beetle GLX/Turbo S)			400	450	450
Add Power Sunroof (Jetta Wolfsburg/GLI)			525	600	600
Add Theft Recovery System			75	100	100
2003 PASSAT-4 Cyl. Turbo					
Veh. Ident.: WVW(Model)()63B()3()000001 Up.					
Sedan 4D GL	M	3212	13875	16350	17575
Sedan 4D GLS	P	3240	15125	17675	18900
Wagon 4D GL	N	3307	14525	17050	18250
Wagon 4D GLS	V	3338	15775	18375	19625
2003 PASSAT-V6					
Veh. Ident.: WVW(Model)()63B()3()000001 Up.					
Sedan 4D GLS	P	3373	16575	19225	20500
Sedan 4D GLX	R	3413	18050	20950	22300
Sedan 4D GLX 4Motion	T	3721	19450	22425	23750
Sedan 4D W8 4Motion	U	3953	22425	25725	27150
Wagon 4D GLS	V	3461	17225	20075	21400
Wagon 4D GLX	W	3499	18700	21625	23000
Wagon 4D GLX 4Motion	Y	3840	20100	23125	24475
Wagon 4D W8 4Motion	Z	4067	23075	26425	27875
PASSAT OPTIONS					
Add Sport Pkg.			825	925	925
Add Aluminum/Alloy Wheels (GL)			325	375	375
Add Leather Seats (Std. GLX, W8)			475	550	550
Add Theft Recovery System			75	100	100
Deduct W/out Automatic Trans.			575	575	575
VOLKSWAGEN					
2002 GOLF-4 Cyl.-5 Spd.					
Veh. Ident.: ()()W(Model)61J()2()000001 Up.					
Hatchback 2D GL	B()	2771	8950	10825	11575
Hatchback 2D GL TDI	BP	2853	10675	12725	13450
Hatchback 2D GTI 1.8T	DE	2932	11700	13825	14575
Hatchback 2D GTI 337 (6 Spd.)	DE		13600	15825	16625
Hatchback 2D GTI VR6	PG	3011	12500	14650	15425
Hatchback GTI VR6 24V (6 Spd.)	PH	3036	12825	15000	15775
Hatchback 4D GL	F()	2857	9150	11075	11800
Hatchback 4D GL TDI	FP	2936	10875	12925	13650
Hatchback 4D GLS	G()	2897	9800	11775	12525
Hatchback 4D GLS TDI	GP	2976	11400	13500	14250
Add Aluminum/Alloy Wheels (Std. GTI)			200	225	225
Add Automatic Trans.			375	425	425
Add Compact Disc Player (Std. GTI 337/VR6 24V)			75	100	100
Add Leather Seats			250	300	300
Add Power Sunroof			425	475	475
Add Theft Recovery System			75	100	100

BODY TYPE	Model No.	Weight	Trade-In	Retail	High Retail
2002 NEW BEETLE-4 Cyl.-5 Spd.					
Veh. Ident.: 3VW(Model)21C()2M000001 Up.					
Coupe 2D GL	B()	2817	**9750**	**11800**	**12550**
Coupe 2D GLS	C()	2855	**10400**	**12550**	**13275**
Coupe 2D GLS TDI	CP	2899	**11200**	**13400**	**14150**
Coupe 2D GLS Turbo	CD	2954	**11325**	**13550**	**14300**
Coupe 2D Sport	ED		**12325**	**14675**	**15650**
Coupe 2D GLX Turbo	DD	2958	**12550**	**14925**	**15700**
Coupe 2D Turbo S (6 Spd.)	FE	3005	**13100**	**15500**	**16500**
2002 JETTA-4 Cyl.-5 Spd.					
Veh. Ident.: ()VW(Model)()2()000001 Up.					
Sedan 4D GL	R()69M	2893	**9600**	**11650**	**12550**
Sedan 4D GL TDI	RP69M	2975	**11375**	**13600**	**14550**
Sedan 4D GLS	S()69M	2908	**10500**	**12650**	**13550**
Sedan 4D GLS TDI	SP69M	2983	**12100**	**14425**	**15400**
Sedan 4D GLS 1.8T	SE69M	2952	**11600**	**13825**	**14775**
Sedan 4D GLS VR6	SG69M	3054	**11900**	**14150**	**15100**
Sedan 4D GLI VR6 (6 Spd.)	VH69M	3179	**13425**	**15825**	**16850**
Sedan 4D GLX VR6	TG69M	3144	**13450**	**15850**	**16875**
Sedan GLX VR6 24V (AT)	TH69M	3263	**14275**	**16725**	**17775**
Wagon 4D GL	R()61J	3034	**9700**	**11750**	**12650**
Wagon 4D GL TDI	RP61J	3121	**11475**	**13700**	**14650**
Wagon 4D GLS	S()61J	3078	**10600**	**12750**	**13650**
Wagon 4D GLS TDI	SP61J	3161	**12200**	**14550**	**15525**
Wagon 4D GLS 1.8T	SE61J	3175	**11700**	**13925**	**14875**
Wagon 4D GLS VR6	SG61J	3127	**12000**	**14275**	**15225**
Wagon 4D GLX VR6	TG61J	3280	**13550**	**15975**	**17000**
2002 CABRIO-4 Cyl.-5 Spd.					
Veh. Ident.: 3VW(Model)C21V()2M000001 Up.					
Convertible 2D GL	B	2824	**10925**	**13100**	**14025**
Convertible 2D GLS	C	2833	**12125**	**14425**	**15400**
Convertible 2D GLX	D	2857	**12775**	**15150**	**16150**
NEW BEETLE/JETTA/CABRIO OPTIONS					
Add Aluminum/Alloy Wheels (Std. Beetle GLS Turbo/Sport/S, Jetta GLI, GLX)			**225**	**250**	**250**
Add Automatic Trans. (Std. GLX 24V)			**475**	**550**	**550**
Add Compact Disc Player (Std. Jetta GLI/GLX 24V)			**75**	**100**	**100**
Add Leather Seats (Std. Sport, GLX, Turbo S)			**350**	**400**	**400**
Add Power Sunroof (Std. Sport, Turbo S, Beetle/Jetta GLX)			**475**	**550**	**550**
Add Theft Recovery System			**75**	**100**	**100**
2002 PASSAT-4 Cyl. Turbo					
Veh. Ident.: WVW(Model)D63B()2()000001 Up.					
Sedan 4D GLS	P	3225	**12800**	**15225**	**16400**
Wagon 4D GLS	V	3322	**13350**	**15800**	**17000**
2002 PASSAT-V6					
Veh. Ident.: WVW(Model)()63B()2()000001 Up.					
Sedan 4D GLS	P	3291	**14050**	**16550**	**17775**
Sedan 4D GLS 4Motion	S	3602	**15350**	**17925**	**19175**
Sedan 4D GLX	R	3336	**16150**	**18775**	**20050**
Sedan 4D GLX 4Motion	T	3644	**17450**	**20300**	**21625**
Sedan 4D W8 4Motion	U	3907	**19800**	**22800**	**24150**
Wagon 4D GLS	V	3388	**14600**	**17125**	**18325**
Wagon 4D GLS 4Motion	X	3717	**15900**	**18500**	**19750**
Wagon 4D GLX	W	3428	**16700**	**19350**	**20650**

BODY TYPE	Model No.	Weight	Trade-In	Retail	High Retail
Wagon 4D GLX 4Motion	Y	3757	18000	20900	22250
Wagon 4D W8 4Motion	Z	4035	20350	23375	24750
PASSAT OPTIONS					
Add Aluminum/Alloy Wheels (Std. GLX, W8)			275	325	325
Add Leather Seats (Std. GLX, W8)			425	475	475
Add Power Sunroof (Std. GLX, W8)			525	600	600
Add Theft Recovery System			75	100	100
Deduct W/out Automatic Trans.			525	525	525
VOLKSWAGEN					
2001 GOLF-4 Cyl.-5 Spd.					
Veh. Ident.: 3VW(Model)()1J()1()000001 Up.					
Hatchback 2D GL	B()	2767	7375	9050	9750
Hatchback 2D GL TDI	BP	2847	8875	10725	11475
Hatchback 2D GTI GLS 1.8T	D()	2860	10025	12000	12750
Hatchback 2D GTI GLX VR6	PG	2999	11175	13250	14000
Hatchback 4D GLS	G()*	2864	8175	9975	10700
Hatchback 4D GLS TDI	GP	2944	9575	11525	12250
Hatchback 4D GLS 1.8T	G()*	2906	8975	10850	11600
Add Aluminum/Alloy Wheels (Std. GTI)			150	175	175
Add Automatic Trans.			325	375	375
Add Compact Disc Player			50	75	75
Add Leather Seats (Std. GTI GLX)			200	225	225
Add Power Sunroof (Std. GTI)			375	425	425
Add Theft Recovery System			50	75	75
2001 NEW BEETLE-4 Cyl.-5 Spd.					
Veh. Ident.: 3VW(Model)()1C()1()000001 Up.					
Coupe 2D GL	B()	2769	7950	9800	10525
Coupe 2D GLS	C()*	2785	8550	10450	11175
Coupe 2D GLS TDI	CP	2867	9250	11275	12000
Coupe 2D GLS Turbo	C()*	2921	9150	11175	11900
Coupe 2D Sport	ED		10175	12300	13200
Coupe 2D GLX Turbo	D()	2959	10400	12550	13275
2001 JETTA-4 Cyl.-5 Spd.					
Veh. Ident.: 3VW(Model)()1()000001 Up.					
Sedan 4D GL	R()()9M	2893	8225	10125	11050
Sedan 4D GL TDI	RP()9M	2975	9775	11850	12750
Sedan 4D GLS	S()()9M*	2908	8975	10925	11875
Sedan 4D GLS TDI	SP()9M	2983	10375	12525	13425
Sedan 4D GLS 1.8T	S()()9M*	2952	9775	11850	12750
Sedan 4D Wolfsburg	P()()9M	2952	10075	12200	13100
Sedan 4D GLS VR6	SG()9M	3045	10175	12300	13200
Sedan 4D GLX VR6	TG()9M	3144	11500	13725	14675
Wagon 4D GLS	S()()1J	3079	9075	11075	11950
Wagon 4D GLS VR6	SG()1J	3202	10275	12425	13325
Wagon 4D GLX VR6	TG()1J	3281	11600	13825	14775
2001 CABRIO-4 Cyl.-5 Spd.					
Veh. Ident.: 3VW(Model)C()1V()1()000001 Up.					
Convertible 2D GL	B	2825	8575	10400	11325
Convertible 2D GLS	C	2834	9675	11625	12525
Convertible 2D GLX	D	2857	10325	12350	13250
NEW BEETLE/JETTA/CABRIO OPTIONS					
Add Aluminum/Alloy Wheels (Std. Beetle Sport, Jetta Wolfsburg, GLX)			175	200	200
Add Automatic Trans.			425	475	475

PASSENGER CARS

PASSENGER CARS

BODY TYPE	Model No.	Weight	Trade-In	Retail	High Retail
Add Compact Disc Player (Std. Beetle GLX)			50	75	75
Add Leather Seats (Std. Sport, GLX)			300	350	350
Add Power Sunroof (Std. Sport, Beetle/Jetta GLX)			425	475	475
Add Theft Recovery System			50	75	75
2001 PASSAT-4 Cyl. Turbo					
Veh. Ident.: WVW(Model)C()3B()1()000001 Up.					
Sedan 4D GLS	A	3043	9550	11700	12750
Wagon 4D GLS	H	3136	10000	12175	13225
2001 PASSAT-V6					
Veh. Ident.: WVW(Model)H()3B()1()000001 Up.					
Sedan 4D GLS	A	3151	10600	12825	13900
Sedan 4D GLS 4Motion	D	3473	11800	14125	15250
Sedan 4D GLX	B	3180	12400	14800	15950
Sedan 4D GLX 4Motion	E	3502	13600	16075	17275
Wagon 4D GLS	H	3244	11050	13300	14400
Wagon 4D GLS 4Motion	K	3574	12250	14625	15775
Wagon 4D GLX	J	3272	12850	15275	16450
Wagon 4D GLX 4Motion	L	3603	14050	16550	17775
2001 NEW PASSAT-4 Cyl. Turbo					
Veh. Ident.: WVW(Model)D()3B()1()000001 Up.					
Sedan 4D GLS	P	3199	10650	12700	13775
Wagon 4D GLS	V	3296	11100	13175	14275
2001 NEW PASSAT-V6					
Veh. Ident.: WVW(Model)H()3B()1()000001 Up.					
Sedan 4D GLS	P	3289	11700	13825	14950
Sedan 4D GLS 4Motion	S	3600	12900	15075	16250
Sedan 4D GLX	R	3333	13500	15725	16925
Sedan 4D GLX 4Motion	T	3642	14700	17000	18250
Wagon 4D GLS	V	3386	12150	14300	15425
Wagon 4D GLS 4Motion	X	3714	13350	15550	16725
Wagon 4D GLX	W	3426	13950	16200	17400
Wagon 4D GLX 4Motion	Y	3502	15150	17475	18700
PASSAT/NEW PASSAT OPTIONS					
Add Aluminum/Alloy Wheels (Std. GLX)			225	250	250
Add Compact Disc Player (Std. GLX)			100	125	125
Add Leather Seats (Std. GLX)			375	425	425
Add Power Sunroof (Std. GLX)			475	550	550
Add Theft Recovery System			50	75	75
Deduct W/out Automatic Trans.			475	475	475
VOLKSWAGEN					
2000 GOLF-4 Cyl.-5 Spd.					
Veh. Ident.: WVW(Model)()1J()Y()000001 Up.					
Hatchback 2D GL	B()	2767	6000	7550	8350
Hatchback 2D GL TDI	BF	2847	7275	8950	9725
Hatchback 2D GTI GLS	D()	2762	7600	9300	10000
Hatchback 2D GTI GLS 1.8T	DH	2811	8300	10125	10850
Hatchback 2D GTI GLX VR6	DE	2890	9250	11175	11900
Hatchback 4D GLS	G()	2864	6750	8350	9100
Hatchback 4D GLS TDI	GF	2944	7950	9700	10425
Hatchback 4D GLS 1.8T	GH	2906	7450	9150	9850
Add Aluminum/Alloy Wheels (Std. GTI)			100	125	125
Add Automatic Trans.			300	350	350
Add Compact Disc Player			50	75	75
Add Leather Seats (Std. GTI GLX)			150	175	175

BODY TYPE	Model No.	Weight	Trade-In	Retail	High Retail
Add Power Sunroof (Std. GTI)			325	375	375
2000 NEW BEETLE-4 Cyl.-5 Spd.					
Veh. Ident.: 3VW(Model)()1C()YM000001 Up.					
Coupe 2D GL	B()	2769	6475	8200	8950
Coupe 2D GLS	C()	2825	7025	8800	9575
Coupe 2D GLS TDI	CF	2867	7625	9450	10175
Coupe 2D GLS Turbo	CD	2785	7525	9325	10025
Coupe 2D GLX Turbo	DD	2964	8425	10325	11050
2000 JETTA-4 Cyl.-5 Spd.					
Veh. Ident.: 3VW(Model)()1H()Y()000001 Up.					
Sedan 4D GL	R()	2884	6500	8225	9075
Sedan 4D GL TDI	RF	2974	7825	9650	10550
Sedan 4D GLS	S()	2934	7150	8925	9825
Sedan 4D GLS TDI	SF	3036	8350	10250	11175
Sedan 4D GLS 1.8T	SD	2922	7850	9675	10575
Sedan 4D GLS VR6	SE	3086	8150	10025	10950
Sedan 4D GLX VR6	TE	3106	9250	11275	12175
2000 CABRIO-4 Cyl.-5 Spd.					
Veh. Ident.: 3VW(Model)C()1E()Y()000001 Up.					
Convertible 2D GL	C	2831	6625	8200	9050
Convertible 2D GLS	D	2853	8275	10075	11000
NEW BEETLE/JETTA/CABRIO OPTIONS					
Add A/A Wheels (Std. Beetle/Jetta GLX, Cabrio GLS)			125	150	150
Add Automatic Trans.			375	425	425
Add Compact Disc Player (Std. Cabrio)			50	75	75
Add Leather Seats (Std. Beetle/Jetta GLX, Cabrio GLS)			250	300	300
Add Power Sunroof (Std. Beetle/Jetta GLX)			375	425	425
Ded W/out Cruise Control (Ex. Beetle/Jetta GL)			100	100	100
Ded W/out Power Windows (Ex. Beetle/Jetta GL)			100	100	100
2000 PASSAT-4 Cyl. Turbo					
Veh. Ident.: WVW(Model)()3B()Y()000001 Up.					
Sedan 4D GLS	MA	3043	7900	9900	10950
Wagon 4D GLS	NA	3136	8300	10350	11375
2000 PASSAT-V6					
Veh. Ident.: WVW(Model)()3B()Y()000001 Up.					
Sedan 4D GLS	MD	3151	8750	10825	11875
Sedan 4D GLS 4Motion	TH	3532	9850	12025	13075
Sedan 4D GLX	PD	3180	10275	12475	13525
Sedan 4D GLX 4Motion	UH	3532	11375	13650	14750
Wagon 4D GLS	ND	3244	9150	11275	12300
Wagon 4D GLS 4Motion	RH	3655	10250	12450	13500
Wagon 4D GLX	WD	3269	10675	12900	13975
Wagon 4D GLX 4Motion	WH	3655	11775	14100	15225
PASSAT OPTIONS					
Add Aluminum/Alloy Wheels (Std. GLX)			175	200	200
Add Compact Disc Player			75	100	100
Add Leather Seats (Std. GLX)			325	375	375
Add Power Sunroof (Std. GLX)			425	475	475
Deduct W/out Automatic Trans.			425	425	425

PASSENGER CARS

BODY TYPE	Model No.	Weight	Trade-In	Retail	High Retail
VOLKSWAGEN					
1999 GOLF-4 Cyl.-5 Spd.					
Veh. Ident.: 3VW(Model)()()1H()X()000001 Up.					
Hatchback 2D GTI VR6	H	2800	7175	8850	9625
Hatchback 4D GL	F	2544	3875	5175	5900
Hatchback 4D Wolfsburg	J		4475	5875	6675
1999 NEW GOLF-4 Cyl.-5 Spd.					
Veh. Ident.: WVW(Model)()1J()X()000001 Up.					
Hatchback 2D GL	B()	2723	4975	6425	7225
Hatchback 2D GL TDI	BF	2791	6125	7675	8475
Hatchback 2D GTI GLS	D()	2762	6275	7850	8675
Hatchback 2D GTI GLX VR6	DE	2890	7700	9425	10150
Hatchback 4D GLS	G()	2820	5675	7200	7975
Hatchback 4D GLS TDI	GF	2875	6775	8375	9125
GOLF/NEW GOLF OPTIONS					
Add Aluminum/Alloy Wheels (Std. GTI, Wolfsburg)			50	75	75
Add Automatic Trans.			250	300	300
Add Leather Seats (Std. New Golf GLX)			125	150	150
Add Power Sunroof (Std. Golf/New Golf GTI)			275	325	325
Deduct W/out Air Conditioning			325	325	325
1999 NEW BEETLE-4 Cyl.-5 Spd.					
Veh. Ident.: 3VW(Model)()1C()XM000001 Up.					
Coupe 2D GL	B()	2769	5525	7175	7950
Coupe 2D GLS	C()	2785	5850	7525	8325
Coupe 2D GLS TDI	CF	2867	6350	8075	8825
Coupe 2D GLS Turbo	CD	2921	6250	7975	8800
Coupe 2D GLX Turbo	DD	2959	7000	8775	9550
1999 JETTA-4 Cyl.-5 Spd.					
Veh. Ident.: ()VW(Model)()1H()X()000001 Up.					
Sedan 4D GL	R()	2590	4075	5525	6375
Sedan 4D TDI	RF	2525	5175	6775	7700
Sedan 4D Wolfsburg	P()		4800	6325	7200
Sedan 4D GLX VR6	TD	2927	5975	7650	8550
1999 NEW JETTA-4 Cyl.-5 Spd.					
Veh. Ident.: WVW(Model)()9M()X()000001 Up.					
Sedan 4D GL	R()	2853	5300	6925	7850
Sedan 4D GL TDI	RF	2873	6500	8225	9075
Sedan 4D GLS	S()	2862	5875	7550	8450
Sedan 4D GLS TDI	SF	2891	6975	8750	9625
Sedan 4D GLS VR6	SE	2994	6775	8525	9400
Sedan 4D GLX VR6	TE	3019	7575	9375	10250
1999 CABRIO-4 Cyl.-5 Spd.					
Veh. Ident.: 3VW(Model)B()1E()X()000001 Up.					
Convertible 2D	A	3079	5350	6850	7675
Convertible 2D GLS	B		6600	8200	8950
1999 NEW CABRIO-4 Cyl.-5 Spd.					
Veh. Ident.: 3VW(Model)()()()()X()000001 Up.					
Convertible 2D GL	C		5850	7400	8200
Convertible 2D GLS	D		7100	8775	9550
BEETLE/JETTA/CABRIO OPTIONS					
Add Aluminum/Alloy Wheels (Std. GLX, Jetta Wolfsburg, Cabrio/New Cabrio GLS)			75	100	100
Add Automatic Trans.			325	375	375

BODY TYPE	Model No.	Weight	Trade-In	Retail	High Retail
Add Leather Seats (Std. Beetle/New Jetta GLX, Cabrio/New Cabrio GLS)			225	250	250
Add Power Sunroof (Std. Beetle/Jetta/New Jetta GLX)			325	375	375
Deduct W/out Air Conditioning			450	450	450
Ded W/out Cruise (Ex. Beetle/New Jetta GL)			75	75	75
Ded W/out Power Windows (Ex. Beetle/New Jetta GL)			75	75	75
1999 PASSAT-4 Cyl. Turbo					
Veh. Ident.: WVW(Model)()3B()X()000001 Up.					
Sedan 4D GLS	MA	3122	6275	8175	8925
Wagon 4D GLS	NA	3194	6625	8550	9325
1999 PASSAT-V6					
Veh. Ident.: WVW(Model)()3B()X()000001 Up.					
Sedan 4D GLS	MD	3245	7025	8975	9750
Sedan 4D GLX	UD	3380	8150	10200	10925
PASSAT OPTIONS					
Add Aluminum/Alloy Wheels (Std. GLX)			125	150	150
Add Leather Seats (Std. GLX)			275	325	325
Add Power Sunroof (Std. GLX)			375	425	425
Deduct W/out Automatic Trans.			375	375	375
VOLKSWAGEN					
1998 GOLF-4 Cyl.-5 Spd.					
Veh. Ident.: 3VW(Model)()81H()W()000001 Up.					
Hatchback 2D GTI	D	2565	4725	6150	6925
Hatchback 2D GTI VR6	H	2800	6175	7750	8575
Hatchback 4D GL	()	2544	3425	4700	5475
Add Automatic Trans.			200	225	225
Add Leather Seats			100	125	125
Add Power Sunroof (Std. VR6/GTI)			225	275	275
Deduct W/out Air Conditioning			275	275	275
1998 NEW BEETLE-4 Cyl.-5 Spd.					
Veh. Ident.: 3VW(Model)81C()W()000001 Up.					
Coupe 2D	BB	2712	4775	6300	7100
Coupe 2D TDI	BF	2712	5175	6800	7625
1998 JETTA-4 Cyl.-5 Spd.					
Veh. Ident.: ()VW(Model)81H()W()000001 Up.					
Sedan 4D GL	R()	2590	3325	4725	5600
Sedan 4D GT	V()	2590	3625	5050	5850
Sedan 4D TDI	RF	2525	4275	5775	6650
Sedan 4D Wolfsburg	P()	2678	3900	5350	6175
Sedan 4D GLS	S()	2729	3900	5350	6175
Sedan 4D GLX VR6	TD	2927	4925	6475	7375
1998 CABRIO-4 Cyl.-5 Spd.					
Veh. Ident.: 3VW(Model)()81E()W()000001 Up.					
Convertible 2D GL	A	2771	4425	5800	6575
Convertible 2D GLS	B	2771	5300	6775	7600
NEW BEETLE/JETTA/CABRIO OPTIONS					
Add A/A Wheels (Std. Jetta GT/Wolfsburg/GLX, GLS)			50	75	75
Add Automatic Trans.			275	325	325
Add Leather Seats (Std. Cabrio GLS)			175	200	200
Add Power Sunroof (Std. Jetta GLX)			275	325	325
Deduct W/out Air Conditioning			400	400	400
Deduct W/out Cruise Control			50	50	50
Deduct W/out Power Windows (Ex. Jetta GL/GT)			50	50	50

PASSENGER CARS

PASSENGER CARS

BODY TYPE	Model No.	Weight	Trade-In	Retail	High Retail
1998 PASSAT-4 Cyl.					
Veh. Ident.: WVW(Model)83B()W()000001 Up.					
Sedan 4D GLS Turbo	MA	3120	**5175**	**6925**	**7775**
Sedan 4D GLS TDI	MG	3133	**5775**	**7600**	**8400**
Wagon 4D GLS Turbo	NA	3194	**5525**	**7325**	**8125**
1998 PASSAT-V6					
Veh. Ident.: WVW(Model)83B()W()000001 Up.					
Sedan 4D GLS	MD	3243	**5825**	**7650**	**8450**
Sedan 4D GLX	PD	3250	**6725**	**8650**	**9425**
PASSAT OPTIONS					
Add Aluminum/Alloy Wheels (Std. GLX)			**100**	**125**	**125**
Add Leather Seats (Std. GLX)			**225**	**250**	**250**
Add Power Sunroof (Std. GLX)			**325**	**375**	**375**
Deduct W/out Automatic Trans.			**325**	**325**	**325**
VOLKSWAGEN					
1997 GOLF-4 Cyl.-5 Spd.					
Veh. Ident.: 3VW(Model)()81H()V()000001 Up.					
Hatchback 2D GTI	D	2564	**3650**	**4950**	**5750**
Hatchback 2D GTI VR6	H	2800	**4350**	**5725**	**6500**
Hatchback 4D GL	()	2525	**2550**	**3725**	**4400**
Add Automatic Trans.			**125**	**150**	**150**
Add Leather Seats			**75**	**100**	**100**
Add Power Sunroof (Std. VR6/GTI)			**150**	**175**	**175**
Deduct W/out Air Conditioning			**150**	**150**	**150**
1997 JETTA-4 Cyl.-5 Spd.					
Veh. Ident.: ()VW(Model)81H()V()000001 Up.					
Sedan 4D GL	R()	2591	**2750**	**4050**	**4850**
Sedan 4D GT	V()	2591	**2900**	**4200**	**5000**
Sedan 4D TDI	RF	2525	**3500**	**4900**	**5800**
Sedan 4D GLS	S()	2675	**3050**	**4400**	**5225**
Sedan 4D GLX VR6	TD	2928	**3950**	**5400**	**6225**
1997 CABRIO-4 Cyl.-5 Spd.					
Veh. Ident.: 3VW(Model)()81E()V()000001 Up.					
Convertible 2D	A	2701	**4025**	**5375**	**6125**
Convertible 2D Highline	B	2701	**4650**	**6050**	**6825**
JETTA/CABRIO OPTIONS					
Add Automatic Trans.			**175**	**200**	**200**
Add Leather Seats (Std. Cabrio Highline)			**150**	**175**	**175**
Add Power Sunroof (Std. Jetta GLX)			**200**	**225**	**225**
Deduct W/out Air Conditioning			**250**	**250**	**250**
Deduct W/out Cruise Control			**50**	**50**	**50**
Deduct W/out Power Windows (Ex. Jetta)			**50**	**50**	**50**
1997 PASSAT-4 Cyl.-5 Spd.					
Veh. Ident.: WVW(Model)83A()V()000001 Up.					
Sedan 4D TDI	GG	3009	**3050**	**4525**	**5425**
Wagon 4D TDI	HG	3075	**3350**	**4850**	**5800**
1997 PASSAT-V6					
Veh. Ident.: WVW(Model)83A()V()000001 Up.					
Sedan 4D GLX VR6	EE	3097	**3400**	**4900**	**5850**
Wagon 4D GLX VR6	FE	3175	**3700**	**5250**	**6175**
PASSAT OPTIONS					
Add Aluminum/Alloy Wheels (Std. GLX)			**50**	**75**	**75**

BODY TYPE	Model No.	Weight	Trade-In	Retail	High Retail
Add Leather Seats			200	225	225
Add Power Sunroof			250	300	300
Deduct W/out Automatic Trans. (Ex. TDI)			250	250	250
VOLKSWAGEN					
1996 GOLF-4 Cyl.-5 Spd.					
Veh. Ident.: 3VW(Model)()81H()T()000001 Up.					
Hatchback 2D GTI	D	2557	2875	4075	4775
Hatchback 2D GTI VR6	H	2811	3475	4750	5525
Hatchback 4D GL	F	2529	2175	3300	3925
Add Automatic Trans.			100	125	125
Add Power Sunroof (Std. VR6/GTI)			100	125	125
Deduct W/out Air Conditioning			100	100	100
1996 JETTA-4 Cyl.-5 Spd.					
Veh. Ident.: ()VW(Model)()81H()T()000001 Up.					
Sedan 4D GL	()	2657	2325	3575	4325
Sedan 4D GLS	S	2723	2525	3800	4575
Sedan 4D GLX VR6	T	2954	3325	4700	5575
1996 CABRIO-4 Cyl.-5 Spd.					
Veh. Ident.: 3VWBB81E()T()000001 Up.					
Convertible 2D	B	2701	3625	4900	5800
JETTA/CABRIO OPTIONS					
Add Automatic Trans.			125	150	150
Add Power Sunroof (Std. Jetta GLX)			150	175	175
Deduct W/out Air Conditioning			150	150	150
1996 PASSAT-4 Cyl.					
Veh. Ident.: WVW(Model)83A()T()000001 Up.					
Sedan 4D GLS	GC	2890	2075	3375	4175
Sedan 4D TDI (5 Spd.)	GG	3009	2675	4050	4900
Wagon 4D TDI (5 Spd.)	HG	3075	2925	4350	5225
1996 PASSAT-V6					
Veh. Ident.: WVW(Model)83A()T()000001 Up.					
Sedan 4D GLX VR6	EE	3097	2900	4325	5200
Wagon 4D GLX VR6	FE	3175	3150	4625	5550
PASSAT OPTIONS					
Add Power Sunroof			200	225	225
Deduct W/out Automatic Trans. (Ex. TDI)			150	150	150
VOLKSWAGEN					
1995 GOLF III-4 Cyl.					
Veh. Ident.: 3VW(Model)()81H()S()000001 Up.					
Hatchback 2D GL	B	2599	1750	2825	3450
Hatchback 2D Sport	B	2599	2150	3275	3900
Hatchback 2D GTI VR6	H	2818	2950	4175	4900
Hatchback 4D	()	2577	1550	2600	3200
Hatchback 4D GL	F	2665	1850	2925	3550
1995 JETTA III-4 Cyl.					
Veh. Ident.: ()V()(Model)()81H()S()000001 Up.					
Sedan 4D	()	2647	1725	2900	3575
Sedan 4D GL	R	2735	1975	3175	3875
Sedan 4D GLS	S	2735	2125	3350	4075
Sedan 4D GLX VR6	T	2980	2775	4075	4875
1995 CABRIO-4 Cyl.					
Veh. Ident.: WVWB()81E()S()000001 Up.					
Convertible 2D	B	2762	3050	4275	5100

BODY TYPE	Model No.	Weight	Trade-In	Retail	High Retail
1995 PASSAT-4 Cyl.					
Veh. Ident.: WVW(Model)()83A()S()000001 Up.					
Sedan 4D GLS	C	2919	**1750**	**3000**	**3750**
Sedan 4D GLX VR6	E	3197	**2425**	**3775**	**4625**
Wagon 4D GLX VR6	F	3267	**2650**	**4025**	**4850**

VOLVO

BODY TYPE	Model No.	Weight	Trade-In	Retail	High Retail
VOLVO					
2004 S40-4 Cyl. Turbo					
Veh. Ident.: YV1VS275()4F000001 Up.					
Sedan 4D	S27	2767	**16550**	**19200**	**20475**
2004 V40-4 Cyl. Turbo					
Veh. Ident.: YV1VW275()4F000001 Up.					
Wagon 4D	W27	2822	**17550**	**20400**	**21725**
2004.5 S40-5 Cyl.					
Veh. Ident.: YV1M(Model)()()42000001 Up.					
Sedan 4D 2.4i	S38	3082			
Sedan 4D Turbo T5	S68	3126			
2004 S60-5 Cyl.					
Veh. Ident.: YV1R(Model)()()42000001 Up.					
Sedan 4D	S6()	3276	**20000**	**23000**	**24350**
Sedan 4D Turbo 2.5T	S59	3400	**22025**	**25200**	**26625**
Sedan 4D Turbo 2.5T (AWD)	H59	3571	**23525**	**26900**	**28375**
Sedan 4D Turbo T5	S53	3446	**23225**	**26575**	**28025**
Sedan 4D R (AWD, AT/6 Spd.)	H52	3571	**28125**	**31875**	**33475**
2004 V70-5 Cyl.					
Veh. Ident.: YV1S(Model)()()4()000001 Up.					
Wagon 4D	W6()	3448	**20825**	**23875**	**25250**
Wagon 4D Turbo 2.5T	W59	3609	**22875**	**26200**	**27650**
Wagon 4D Turbo 2.5T (AWD)	J59	3809	**24375**	**27800**	**29275**
Wagon 4D Turbo T5	W53	3590	**24550**	**27975**	**29450**
Wagon 4D XC Turbo (AWD)	Z59	3832	**26250**	**29775**	**31300**
Wagon 4D R (AWD, AT/6 Spd.)	J52	3757	**29350**	**33150**	**34800**
S40/V40/S60/V70 OPTIONS					
Add Sport Pkg. (2004.5 S40, S60 T5)			**950**	**1075**	**1075**
Add Leather Seats (Std. R)			**525**	**600**	**600**
Add Navigation System			**650**	**725**	**725**
Add Power Sunroof			**625**	**700**	**700**
Add Theft Recovery System			**100**	**125**	**125**
Deduct W/out Automatic Trans. (Ex. R)			**625**	**625**	**625**
Deduct W/out Power Seat			**225**	**225**	**225**
2004 S80-5 Cyl./I6					
Veh. Ident.: YV1T(Model)()()41000001 Up.					
Sedan 4D 2.5T	S59	3583			
Sedan 4D 2.5T (AWD)	H59	3703	**23275**	**26975**	**28675**
Sedan 4D	S92	3576	**22575**	**26225**	**27900**
Sedan 4D T-6	S91	3653	**26325**	**30225**	**32050**
2004 C70-5 Cyl. Turbo					
Veh. Ident.:YV1N(Model)()()4()000001 Up.					
Convertible 2D LT	C63	3450	**28350**	**32475**	**34350**
Convertible 2D HT	C62	3450			

PASSENGER CARS

BODY TYPE	Model No.	Weight	Trade-In	Retail	High Retail
S80/C70 OPTIONS					
Add Navigation System			750	850	850
Add Power Sunroof (Std. T-6)			725	825	825
Add Theft Recovery System			100	125	125
Deduct W/out Automatic Trans.					
Deduct W/out Leather Seats			575	575	575
VOLVO					
2003 S40-4 Cyl. Turbo					
Veh. Ident.: YV1VS2()5()3()000001 Up.					
Sedan 4D	S2()	2767	13575	16050	17250
2003 V40-4 Cyl. Turbo					
Veh. Ident.: YV1VW2()5()3()000001 Up.					
Wagon 4D	W2()	2822	14525	17050	18250
2003 S60-5 Cyl.					
Veh. Ident.: YV1R(Model)()()3()000001 Up.					
Sedan 4D	S6()	3276	16775	19425	20725
Sedan 4D Turbo 2.4T	S58	3400	18500	21425	22775
Sedan 4D Turbo 2.5T (AWD)	H59	3571	19900	22900	24250
Sedan 4D Turbo T5	S53	3446	19500	22475	23800
2003 V70-5 Cyl.					
Veh. Ident.: YV1S(Model)()()3()000001 Up.					
Wagon 4D	W6()	3525	17500	20375	21700
Wagon 4D Turbo 2.4T	W58	3565	19250	22225	23550
Wagon 4D Turbo 2.5T (AWD)	J59	3757	20650	23700	25075
Wagon 4D Turbo T5	W53	3587	20925	24000	25375
Wagon 4D XC Turbo (AWD)	Z59	3827	22175	25450	26875
S40/V40/S60/V70 OPTIONS					
Add Sport Pkg. (S60 T5)			825	925	925
Add Leather Seats			475	550	550
Add Navigation System			550	625	625
Add Power Sunroof			575	650	650
Add Theft Recovery System			75	100	100
Deduct W/out Automatic Trans.			575	575	575
Deduct W/out Power Seat			200	200	200
2003 S80-I6					
Veh. Ident.: YV1T(Model)()()3()000001 Up.					
Sedan 4D	S92	3576	20325	23675	25275
Sedan 4D T-6	S91	3653	23700	27425	29150
2003 C70-5 Cyl. Turbo					
Veh. Ident.: YV1N(Model)D()3()000001 Up.					
Convertible 2D LT	C63	3450	25700	29550	31350
Convertible 2D HT	C62	3450	27475	31550	33425
S80/C70 OPTIONS					
Add Navigation System			650	725	725
Add Power Sunroof (Std. T-6)			675	775	775
Add Theft Recovery System			75	100	100
Deduct W/out Automatic Trans.			625	625	625
Deduct W/out Leather Seats			525	525	525
VOLVO					
2002 S40-4 Cyl. Turbo					
Veh. Ident.: YV1VS295()2()000001 Up.					
Sedan 4D	S29	3068	12125	14500	15650

BODY TYPE	Model No.	Weight	Trade-In	Retail	High Retail
2002 V40-4 Cyl. Turbo					
Veh. Ident.: YV1VW295()2()000001 Up.					
Wagon 4D	W29	3118	**13025**	**15450**	**16625**
2002 S60-5 Cyl.					
Veh. Ident.: YV1R(Model)()()2()000001 Up.					
Sedan 4D	S61	3278	**14400**	**16925**	**18175**
Sedan 4D Turbo 2.4T	S58	3397	**16325**	**18950**	**20225**
Sedan 4D Turbo 2.4T (AWD)	H58	3549	**17625**	**20500**	**21825**
Sedan 4D Turbo T5	S53	3382	**17450**	**20300**	**21625**
2002 V70-5 Cyl.					
Veh. Ident.: YV1S(Model)()()2()000001 Up.					
Wagon 4D	W61	3426	**15325**	**17900**	**19150**
Wagon 4D Turbo 2.4T	W58	3594	**17325**	**20175**	**21500**
Wagon 4D Turbo 2.4T (AWD)	J58	3761	**18625**	**21550**	**22925**
Wagon 4D Turbo T5	W53	3576	**18575**	**21500**	**22875**
Wagon 4D XC Turbo (AWD)	Z58	3807	**19850**	**22850**	**24200**
S40/V40/S60/V70 OPTIONS					
Add Compact Disc Player (Std. T5)			**100**	**125**	**125**
Add Leather Seats			**425**	**475**	**475**
Add Navigation System			**450**	**500**	**500**
Add Power Sunroof (Std. 2.4T, T5, XC)			**525**	**600**	**600**
Add Theft Recovery System			**75**	**100**	**100**
Deduct W/out Automatic Trans.			**525**	**525**	**525**
Deduct W/out Power Seat			**175**	**175**	**175**
2002 S80-I6					
Veh. Ident.: YV1T(Model)D()2()000001 Up.					
Sedan 4D	S92	3589	**17450**	**20600**	**22075**
Sedan 4D T-6	S91	3655	**19825**	**23125**	**24700**
2002 C70-5 Cyl. Turbo					
Veh. Ident.: YV1N(Model)D()2()000001 Up.					
Coupe 2D HT	K53	3395	**19875**	**23175**	**24750**
Convertible 2D LT	C56	3691	**22775**	**26425**	**28125**
Convertible 2D HT	C53	3668	**24075**	**27825**	**29550**
S80/C70 OPTIONS					
Add Navigation System			**550**	**625**	**625**
Add Theft Recovery System			**75**	**100**	**100**
Deduct W/out Automatic Trans.			**575**	**575**	**575**
VOLVO					
2001 S40-4 Cyl. Turbo					
Veh. Ident.: YV1VS295()1()000001 Up.					
Sedan 4D	S29	2767	**9975**	**12175**	**13225**
2001 V40-4 Cyl. Turbo					
Veh. Ident.: YV1VW295()1()000001 Up.					
Wagon 4D	W29	2822	**10825**	**13075**	**14150**
2001 S60-5 Cyl.					
Veh. Ident.: YV1R(Model)()()1()000001 Up.					
Sedan 4D	S61	3146	**12325**	**14725**	**15875**
Sedan 4D Turbo 2.4T	S58	3146	**13575**	**16050**	**17250**
Sedan 4D Turbo T5	S53	3146	**14450**	**16975**	**18225**
2001 V70-5 Cyl.					
Veh. Ident.: YV1S(Model)D()1()000001 Up.					
Wagon 4D	W61	3368	**12925**	**15350**	**16525**
Wagon 4D Turbo 2.4T	W58	3368	**14075**	**16575**	**17800**

BODY TYPE	Model No.	Weight	Trade-In	Retail	High Retail
Wagon 4D Turbo T5	W53	3368	**15600**	**18200**	**19450**
Wagon 4D XC Turbo (AWD)	Z58	3699	**16700**	**19350**	**20650**
S40/V40/S60/V70 OPTIONS					
Add Compact Disc Player (Std. T5)			**100**	**125**	**125**
Add Leather Seats			**375**	**425**	**425**
Add Navigation System			**400**	**450**	**450**
Add Power Sunroof			**475**	**550**	**550**
Add Theft Recovery System			**50**	**75**	**75**
Deduct W/out Automatic Trans.			**475**	**475**	**475**
Deduct W/out Power Seat			**150**	**150**	**150**
2001 S80-I6					
Veh. Ident.: YV1T(Model)D()1()000001 Up.					
Sedan 4D 2.9	S94	3600	**14050**	**16800**	**18175**
Sedan 4D 2.8 T-6	S90	3600	**16225**	**19150**	**20575**
2001 C70-5 Cyl. Turbo					
Veh. Ident.: YV1N(Model)D()1()000001 Up.					
Coupe 2D HT	K53	3200	**15025**	**17850**	**19225**
Convertible 2D LT	C56	3450	**18425**	**21625**	**23150**
Convertible 2D HT	C53	3450	**19625**	**22900**	**24450**
S80/C70 OPTIONS					
Add Navigation System			**500**	**575**	**575**
Add Power Sunroof			**575**	**650**	**650**
Add Theft Recovery System			**50**	**75**	**75**
Deduct W/out Automatic Trans.			**525**	**525**	**525**
Deduct W/out Leather Seats			**425**	**425**	**425**
VOLVO					
2000 S40-4 Cyl. Turbo					
Veh. Ident.: YV1VS255()Y()000001 Up.					
Sedan 4D	S25	3030	**8400**	**10450**	**11475**
2000 V40-4 Cyl. Turbo					
Veh. Ident.: YV1VW255()Y()000001 Up.					
Wagon 4D	W25	3081	**9200**	**11325**	**12350**
2000 S70-5 Cyl.					
Veh. Ident.: YV1T(Model)()()Y()000001 Up.					
Sedan 4D	S61	3155	**9650**	**11800**	**12850**
Sedan 4D GLT Turbo	S56	3245	**10600**	**12825**	**13900**
Sedan 4D Turbo (AWD)	T56	3580	**11700**	**14025**	**15150**
Sedan 4D Turbo T5	S53	3245	**11300**	**13575**	**14675**
2000 V70-5 Cyl.					
Veh. Ident.: YV1L(Model)()()Y()000001 Up.					
Wagon 4D	W61	3254	**10750**	**13000**	**14075**
Wagon 4D GLT Turbo	W56	3342	**11700**	**14025**	**15150**
Wagon 4D XC Turbo (AWD)	Z56	3699	**13500**	**15950**	**17150**
Wagon 4D Turbo R (AWD)	V60	3706	**15225**	**17800**	**19025**
S40/V40/S70/V70 OPTIONS					
Add Compact Disc Player (Std. T5/R)			**75**	**100**	**100**
Add Leather Seats (Std. R)			**325**	**375**	**375**
Add Power Sunroof (Std. R)			**425**	**475**	**475**
Deduct W/out Automatic Trans.			**425**	**425**	**425**
Deduct W/out Power Seat			**125**	**125**	**125**
2000 S80-I6					
Veh. Ident.: YV1T(Model)D()Y()000001 Up.					
Sedan 4D 2.9	S94	3589	**10700**	**13075**	**14275**

PASSENGER CARS

PASSENGER CARS

BODY TYPE	Model No.	Weight	Trade-In	Retail	High Retail
Sedan 4D 2.8 T-6	S90	3695	**12575**	**15225**	**16525**
2000 C70-5 Cyl. Turbo					
Veh. Ident.: YV1N(Model)()()Y()000001 Up.					
Coupe 2D LT	K56	3336	**10925**	**13325**	**14525**
Coupe 2D HT	K53	3347	**12525**	**15175**	**16475**
Convertible 2D LT	C56	3653	**15325**	**18175**	**19575**
Convertible 2D HT	C53	3616	**16425**	**19350**	**20775**
S80/C70 OPTIONS					
Add Navigation System			**450**	**500**	**500**
Add Power Sunroof (Std. C70 HT)			**525**	**600**	**600**
Deduct W/out Automatic Trans.			**475**	**475**	**475**
Deduct W/out Leather Seats			**375**	**375**	**375**
VOLVO					
1999 S70-5 Cyl.					
Veh. Ident.: YV1L(Model)()()X()000001 Up.					
Sedan 4D	S55	3146	**7875**	**9875**	**10925**
Sedan 4D GLT Turbo	S56	3252	**8750**	**10850**	**11900**
Sedan 4D Turbo (AWD)	T56	3642	**9750**	**11925**	**12975**
Sedan 4D Turbo T5	S53	3247	**9550**	**11700**	**12750**
1999 V70-5 Cyl.					
Veh. Ident.: YV1L(Model)()()X()000001 Up.					
Wagon 4D	W55	3243	**8975**	**11075**	**12075**
Wagon 4D GLT Turbo	W56	3349	**9850**	**12025**	**13075**
Wagon 4D Turbo (AWD)	V56	3735	**10850**	**13100**	**14175**
Wagon 4D XC Turbo (AWD)	Z56	3715	**11475**	**13775**	**14900**
Wagon 4D Turbo T5	W53	3344	**10650**	**12900**	**13975**
Wagon 4D Turbo R (AWD)	V62	3741	**12825**	**15250**	**16425**
S70/V70 OPTIONS					
Add Aluminum/Alloy Wheels (Std. Turbos)			**125**	**150**	**150**
Add Leather Seats (Std. R)			**275**	**325**	**325**
Add Power Sunroof (Std. R)			**375**	**425**	**425**
Deduct W/out Automatic Trans.			**375**	**375**	**375**
Deduct W/out Power Seat			**100**	**100**	**100**
1999 S80-I6					
Veh. Ident.: YV1T(Model)D()X()000001 Up.					
Sedan 4D 2.9	S97	3569	**9425**	**11700**	**12850**
Sedan 4D 2.8 T-6	S90	3648	**11050**	**13475**	**14700**
1999 C70-5 Cyl. Turbo					
Veh. Ident.: YV1N(Model)D()X()000001 Up.					
Coupe 2D LT	K56	3601	**9000**	**11200**	**12325**
Coupe 2D HT	K53	3365	**10450**	**12800**	**14000**
Convertible 2D	C56	3601	**12850**	**15525**	**16825**
S80/C70 OPTIONS					
Add Power Sunroof (Std. C70 HT)			**475**	**550**	**550**
Deduct W/out Automatic Trans.			**425**	**425**	**425**
Deduct W/out Leather Seats			**325**	**325**	**325**
VOLVO					
1998 S70-5 Cyl.					
Veh. Ident.: YV1L(Model)()()W()000001 Up.					
Sedan 4D	S55	3152	**5800**	**7625**	**8675**
Sedan 4D GLT Turbo	S56	3300	**6850**	**8775**	**9825**
Sedan 4D Turbo T5	S53	3272	**7650**	**9650**	**10700**

BODY TYPE	Model No.	Weight	Trade-In	Retail	High Retail
1998 V70-5 Cyl.					
Veh. Ident.: YV1L(Model)()()W()000001 Up.					
Wagon 4D	W55	3259	**6900**	**8850**	**9900**
Wagon 4D GLT Turbo	W56	3402	**7950**	**9975**	**11025**
Wagon 4D Turbo (AWD)	W56	3735	**8850**	**10950**	**12025**
Wagon 4D XC Turbo (AWD)	Z56	3768	**9400**	**11550**	**12575**
Wagon 4D Turbo T5	W53	3371	**8750**	**10825**	**11875**
Wagon 4D Turbo R (AWD)	W52	3788	**10275**	**12475**	**13525**
S70/V70 OPTIONS					
Add Aluminum/Alloy Wheels (Std. Turbos)			**100**	**125**	**125**
Add Leather Seats (Std. R)			**225**	**250**	**250**
Add Power Sunroof (Std. Turbos)			**325**	**375**	**375**
Deduct W/out Automatic Trans.			**325**	**325**	**325**
Deduct W/out Power Seat			**75**	**75**	**75**
1998 S90-I6					
Veh. Ident.: YV1KS96()()W()000001 Up.					
Sedan 4D	S96	3541	**6675**	**8675**	**9925**
1998 V90-I6					
Veh. Ident.: YV1KW96()()W()000001 Up.					
Station Wagon 4D	W96	3609	**7575**	**9650**	**10825**
1998 C70-5 Cyl. Turbo					
Veh. Ident.: YV1N(Model)()()W()000001 Up.					
Coupe 2D	K53	3364	**8350**	**10500**	**11700**
Convertible 2D	C56	3649	**10550**	**12900**	**14100**
S90/V90/C70 OPTIONS					
Deduct W/out Automatic Trans.			**375**	**375**	**375**
VOLVO					
1997 850-5 Cyl.					
Veh. Ident.: YV1(Model)()()V()000001 Up.					
Sedan 4D	LS55	3183	**4825**	**6525**	**7550**
Sedan 4D GLT Turbo	LS56	3267	**5425**	**7200**	**8200**
Sedan 4D Turbo T-5	LS57	3272	**6275**	**8150**	**9150**
Sedan 4D Turbo R	LS58	3336	**7500**	**9475**	**10500**
Station Wagon 4D	LW55	3289	**5525**	**7325**	**8350**
Station Wagon GLT Turbo	LW56	3371	**6125**	**8000**	**9075**
Station Wagon 4D Turbo T-5	LW57	3375	**6975**	**8925**	**9975**
Station Wagon 4D Turbo R	LW58	3439	**8200**	**10250**	**11275**
Add Aluminum/Alloy Wheels (Std. Turbos)			**50**	**75**	**75**
Add Leather Seats (Std. R)			**200**	**225**	**225**
Add Power Sunroof (Std. Turbos)			**250**	**300**	**300**
Deduct W/out Automatic Trans.			**250**	**250**	**250**
Deduct W/out Power Seat			**75**	**75**	**75**
1997 960-I6					
Veh. Ident.: YV1(Model)0()V()000001 Up.					
Sedan 4D	KS96	3541	**5125**	**6950**	**8125**
Station Wagon 4D	KW96	3619	**5650**	**7525**	**8725**
VOLVO					
1996 850-5 Cyl.					
Veh. Ident.: YV1(Model)()()T()000001 Up.					
Sedan 4D	LS55	3128	**3925**	**5500**	**6450**
Sedan 4D GLT	LS55	3179	**4325**	**5975**	**6975**
Sedan 4D Turbo	LS57	3278	**4625**	**6300**	**7300**

PASSENGER CARS

PASSENGER CARS

BODY TYPE	Model No.	Weight	Trade-In	Retail	High Retail
Sedan 4D Turbo R	LS58	3278	**6275**	**8150**	**9150**
Station Wagon 4D	LW55	3232	**4525**	**6200**	**7175**
Station Wagon 4D GLT	LW55	3280	**4925**	**6650**	**7675**
Station Wagon 4D Turbo	LW57	3387	**5225**	**7000**	**8050**
Station Wagon 4D Turbo R	LW58	3387	**6875**	**8825**	**9875**
Add Power Sunroof (Std. GLT/Turbo/R)			**200**	**225**	**225**
Deduct W/out Automatic Trans.			**150**	**150**	**150**
1996 960-I6					
Veh. Ident: YV1(Model)()()T()000001 Up.					
Sedan 4D	KS96	3530	**4350**	**6050**	**7125**
Station Wagon 4D	KW96	3601	**4800**	**6575**	**7700**
VOLVO					
1995 850-5 Cyl.					
Veh. Ident.: YV1(Model)()()S()000001 Up.					
Sedan 4D	LS55	3175	**3350**	**4850**	**5800**
Sedan 4D GLT	LS55	3232	**3650**	**5200**	**6100**
Sedan 4D Turbo	LS57	3278	**3925**	**5500**	**6450**
Sedan 4D Turbo T-5R	LS58	3278	**5500**	**7300**	**8325**
Station Wagon 4D	LW55	3285	**3850**	**5425**	**6350**
Station Wagon 4D GLT	LW55	3342	**4150**	**5775**	**6750**
Station Wagon 4D Turbo	LW57	3387	**4425**	**6100**	**7075**
Station Wagon 4D Turbo T-5R	LW58	3387	**6000**	**7850**	**8925**
1995 940-4 Cyl.					
Veh. Ident.: YV1(Model)()()S()000001 Up.					
Sedan 4D	JS83	3234	**3250**	**4825**	**5850**
Sedan 4D Turbo	JS86	3277	**3850**	**5500**	**6550**
Station Wagon 4D	JW83	3316	**3650**	**5275**	**6300**
Station Wagon 4D Turbo	JW86	3361	**4250**	**5950**	**7050**
1995 960-I6					
Veh. Ident.: YV1(Model)()()S()000001 Up.					
Sedan 4D	KS96	3531	**3700**	**5350**	**6375**
Station Wagon 4D	KW96	3621	**4075**	**5750**	**6825**

Optional Equipment

The most popular optional equipment will be listed with each series of Light-Duty Truck. Additional optional equipment can be found in table form on page 2 of this section.

In order to determine the N.A.D.A. value for Light-Duty Truck trims and packages, users should add for the trim level and then add for any additional options listed with that vehicle, EVEN IF a particular option is standard in the trim level being valued (unless otherwise noted). For example:

To determine the N.A.D.A. value for a Chevrolet Silverado C1500 2WD Extended Cab LT one would:
Begin with the base vehicle value...

Fleetside Extended Cab C19* 4413 **12825** **15375** **16550**

add LT Trim...

Add LT Trim **1150** **1300** **1300**

as well as any option standard from the factory on that trim level...

Add Compact Disc Player **100** **125** **125**
Add Leather Seats **375** **425** **425**
Add Power Seat **150** **175** **175**

Work Truck Package

Certain manufacturers offer an optional Work Truck Package on full-size, and to a lesser extent compact, pickup trucks. Work truck package names and acronyms, which include "W/T", "WS", "Special", etc., will vary by manufacturer. For the purposes of our vehicle valuation products, we have chosen to apply generic "Work Truck Pkg." terminology to these packages, regardless of the name or acronym given by the manufacturer. Vehicles outfitted with a given work truck package tend to be similar in look and equipment, which generally consists of a grey colored grille/front fascia, grey bumpers, grey steel wheels, vinyl bench seating surfaces, and may lack certain optional equipment.

Please read your Guide carefully when determining the value of optional equipment. N.A.D.A.'s editors believe that most optional equipment has little or no value on older vehicles. This is especially true of options that cost relatively little when new and which deteriorate with age or use.

Only the more popular vehicle options are listed in the Guide. As such, this guide makes little attempt at addressing non-OEM optional equipment. However, exclusion does not necessarily mean that only OEM-sourced optional equipment should be considered when arriving at a valuation.

VALUES SHOWN BELOW ARE TO BE ADDED TO TRUCK'S GUIDEBOOK VALUE.
TRIM LEVEL VALUES DO NOT INCLUDE THE FOLLOWING EQUIPMENT.

		2004	2003	2002	2001	2000	1999	1998
Auxiliary Fuel Tank	***Trade-In***	150	125	100	75	50	50	
	Retail	175	150	125	100	75	75	
Roll Bar (Pickups)	***Trade-In***	225	200	175	150	125	100	
	Retail	250	225	200	175	150	125	
Bed Liner	***Trade-In***	125	100	75	75	50	50	
	Retail	150	125	100	100	75	75	
Bed Liner-Spray On	***Trade-In***	125	100	75	75	50	50	
	Retail	150	125	100	100	75	75	
Luggage Rack	***Trade-In***	75	50	50				
	Retail	100	75	75				
Fiberglass Cap (Pickups)	***Trade-In***	550	500	450	400	350	300	250
	Retail	625	575	500	450	400	350	300
Towing/Camper Pkg.	***Trade-In***	200	175	150	125	100	75	
	Retail	225	200	175	150	125	100	
Winch	***Trade-In***	350	300	250	200	150	125	100
	Retail	400	350	300	225	175	150	125
Snow Plow Pkg./Plow	***Trade-In***	1075	975	900	800	700	625	525
	Retail	1200	1100	1000	900	800	700	600

Model numbers may vary with AWD, 4WD and/or DRW. See below for variations.

CHEVROLET - GMC - OLDSMOBILE - PONTIAC

4WD/AWD models have the following letter as the 1st position of the Model #:

ASTRO/SAFARI	**L**
C SERIES/SILVERADO/SIERRA	**K**
S10/SONOMA	**T**
COLORADO/CANYON	**T**
MINIVANS	**V**
G SERIES VANS	**H**

CHRYSLER - DODGE - PLYMOUTH

4WD/AWD models have the following letter as the 1st position of the Model #:

DAKOTA	**G**
RAM PICKUP	**F** or **U**
MINIVANS	**T**

FORD

4WD/AWD/DRW models have the following numbers:

AEROSTAR	**4** as the 2nd position of the Model #
RANGER	**1** or **5** as the 3rd position of the Model #
F SERIES (1998-1995)	**4, 6 or 8** as the 3rd position of the Model #
F SERIES (2004-1999)	**1, 4** or **8** as the 3rd position of the Model #
F 350 2WD **DRW** (2004-1999)	**2** as the 3rd position of the Model #
F 350 4WD **DRW** (2004-1999)	**3** as the 3rd position of the Model #

TOYOTA

AWD models have the following letter as the 1st position of the Model #:

SIENNA	**B**

BODY TYPE	Model No.	Weight	Trade-In	Retail	High Retail

ACURA

BODY TYPE	Model No.	Weight	Trade-In	Retail	High Retail
ACURA					
2004 MDX-V6-4WD					
Utility 4D	D182	4451	**28750**	**32575**	**34475**
Utility 4D Touring	D186	4510	**30750**	**34700**	**36650**
Utility 4D Touring DVD	D187		**31350**	**35325**	**37300**
Utility 4D Touring Nav	D188		**31500**	**35500**	**37475**
Utility 4D Touring DVD Nav	D189		**32100**	**36275**	**38275**
Add Running Boards			**150**	**175**	**175**
Add Theft Recovery System			**100**	**125**	**125**
ACURA					
2003 MDX-V6-4WD					
Utility 4D	D182	4420	**25225**	**28700**	**30475**
Utility 4D Touring	D186	4473	**27025**	**30650**	**32475**
Utility 4D Touring DVD	D187		**27525**	**31275**	**33125**
Utility 4D Touring Nav	D188		**27675**	**31425**	**33275**
Utility 4D Touring DVD Nav	D189		**28175**	**31950**	**33825**
Add Theft Recovery System			**75**	**100**	**100**
ACURA					
2002 MDX-V6-4WD					
Utility 4D	D182	4328	**21975**	**25275**	**26925**
Utility 4D Nav	D184		**22525**	**25850**	**27525**
Utility 4D Touring	D186	4387	**23275**	**26650**	**28350**
Utility 4D Touring Nav	D188		**23825**	**27250**	**28975**
Add Theft Recovery System			**75**	**100**	**100**
ACURA					
2001 MDX-V6-4WD					
Utility 4D	D182	4328	**18800**	**21875**	**23400**
Utility 4D Nav	D184		**19200**	**22300**	**23850**
Utility 4D Touring	D186	4387	**19500**	**22600**	**24150**
Utility 4D Touring Nav	D188		**20000**	**23150**	**24725**
Add Theft Recovery System			**50**	**75**	**75**
ACURA					
1999 SLX-V6-4WD					
Utility 4D	DJ58	4615	**8400**	**10500**	**11700**
ACURA					
1998 SLX-V6-4WD					
Utility 4D	DJ58	4540	**6525**	**8450**	**9675**
ACURA					
1997 SLX-V6-4WD					
Utility 4D	DJ58	4315	**5225**	**7000**	**8175**
Utility 4D Premium	DJ58	4640	**6025**	**7900**	**9125**
ACURA					
1996 SLX-V6-4WD					
Utility 4D	DJ58	4315	**4175**	**5850**	**6950**
Utility 4D Premium	DJ58	4640	**4875**	**6625**	**7775**

BODY TYPE	Model No.	Weight	Trade-In	Retail	High Retail
BMW					
BMW					
2004 X3-I6-AWD					
Utility 4D 2.5i	PA73	4001	**27000**	**30625**	**32450**
Utility 4D 3.0i	PA93	4023	**29000**	**32825**	**34725**
2004 X5-I6/V8-AWD					
Utility 4D 3.0i	FA13	4652	**34725**	**39075**	**41150**
Utility 4D 4.4i	FB53	4927	**41525**	**46250**	**48550**
2004 X5-V8-AWD					
Utility 4D 4.8is	FA93	5016	**57025**	**62875**	**65675**
BMW OPTIONS					
Add Sport Pkg. (Std. 4.8is)			**1075**	**1200**	**1200**
Add BMW Premium Stereo System (Std. 4.8is)			**425**	**475**	**475**
Add Navigation System			**750**	**850**	**850**
Add Power Sunroof (Std. 4.8is)			**725**	**825**	**825**
Add Rear Air Conditioning (X5 3.0i)			**200**	**225**	**225**
Add Theft Recovery System			**100**	**125**	**125**
Deduct W/out Automatic Trans.			**675**	**675**	**675**
Deduct W/out Cruise Control			**250**	**250**	**250**
Deduct W/out Leather Seats			**575**	**575**	**575**
Deduct W/out Power Seat			**275**	**275**	**275**
BMW					
2003 X5-I6/V8-4WD					
Utility 4D 3.0i	FA53	4533	**29200**	**33075**	**34975**
Utility 4D 4.4i	FB33	4824	**34800**	**39150**	**41225**
2003 X5-V8-4WD					
Utility 4D 4.6is	FB93	4824	**44800**	**49975**	**52375**
BMW OPTIONS					
Add Sport Pkg. (Std. 4.6is)			**975**	**1100**	**1100**
Add BMW Premium Stereo System (Std. 4.6is)			**375**	**425**	**425**
Add Navigation System			**650**	**725**	**725**
Add Power Sunroof (Std. 4.6is)			**675**	**775**	**775**
Add Rear Air Conditioning (3.0i)			**150**	**175**	**175**
Add Theft Recovery System			**75**	**100**	**100**
Deduct W/out Automatic Trans.			**625**	**625**	**625**
Deduct W/out Leather Seats			**525**	**525**	**525**
BMW					
2002 X5-I6/V8-4WD					
Utility 4D 3.0i	FA53	4533	**26275**	**30150**	**31975**
Utility 4D 4.4i	FB33	4824	**30075**	**34325**	**36275**
2002 X5-V8-4WD					
Utility 4D 4.6is	FB93	4824	**39375**	**44250**	**46500**
BMW OPTIONS					
Add Sport Pkg. (Std. 4.6is)			**900**	**1000**	**1000**
Add BMW Premium Stereo System (Std. 4.6is)			**325**	**375**	**375**
Add Navigation System			**550**	**625**	**625**
Add Power Sunroof (Std. 4.6is)			**625**	**700**	**700**
Add Rear Air Conditioning (3.0i)			**150**	**175**	**175**
Add Theft Recovery System			**75**	**100**	**100**
Deduct W/out Automatic Trans.			**575**	**575**	**575**
Deduct W/out Leather Seats			**475**	**475**	**475**

TRUCKS

SEE TRUCK OPTION PAGE FOR ADDITIONAL OPTIONS

BODY TYPE	Model No.	Weight	Trade-In	Retail	High Retail
BMW					
2001 X5-I6/V8-4WD					
Utility 4D 3.0i	FA53	4519	**22700**	**26325**	**28000**
Utility 4D 4.4i	FB33	4828	**25400**	**29200**	**30975**
Add Sport Pkg			**850**	**950**	**950**
Add BMW Premium Stereo System			**275**	**325**	**325**
Add Compact Disc Player			**125**	**150**	**150**
Add Navigation System			**500**	**575**	**575**
Add Power Sunroof			**575**	**650**	**650**
Add Rear Air Conditioning (Std. 4.4i)			**125**	**150**	**150**
Add Theft Recovery System			**50**	**75**	**75**
Deduct W/out Automatic Trans.			**525**	**525**	**525**
Deduct W/out Leather Seats			**425**	**425**	**425**
BMW					
2000 X5-V8-4WD					
Utility 4D 4.4i	FB33	4828	**22200**	**25775**	**27450**
Add Sport Pkg			**800**	**900**	**900**
Add BMW Premium Stereo System			**225**	**250**	**250**
Add Compact Disc Player			**100**	**125**	**125**
Add Navigation System			**450**	**500**	**500**
Add Power Sunroof			**525**	**600**	**600**

BUICK

BODY TYPE	Model No.	Weight	Trade-In	Retail	High Retail
BUICK					
2004 RENDEZVOUS-V6					
Utility 4D CX	A03	4024	**13900**	**16525**	**17575**
Utility 4D CXL	A03	4250	**16200**	**18975**	**20050**
Utility 4D CX (AWD)	B03		**14975**	**17650**	**18700**
Utility 4D CXL (AWD)	B03		**17275**	**20250**	**21375**
Utility 4D Ultra (AWD)	B03		**20275**	**23425**	**24625**
Add 3.6L V6 Engine (Std. Ultra)			**650**	**725**	**725**
Add 3rd Row Seat (Std. Ultra)			**200**	**225**	**225**
Add Aluminum/Alloy Wheels (Std. CXL, Ultra)			**325**	**375**	**375**
Add Leather Seats (Std. CXL, Ultra)			**450**	**500**	**500**
Add Navigation System			**600**	**675**	**675**
Add Power Seat (Std. CXL, Ultra)			**200**	**225**	**225**
Add Power Sunroof			**575**	**650**	**650**
Add Rear Bucket Seats (Std. Ultra)			**200**	**225**	**225**
Add Rear Entertainment System			**600**	**675**	**675**
Add Theft Recovery System			**100**	**125**	**125**
2004 RAINIER-I6					
Utility 4D CXL	S13S	4442	**20275**	**23425**	**24625**
Utility 4D CXL (V8)	S13P		**21175**	**24375**	**25600**
Utility 4D CXL (AWD)	T13S	4628	**21600**	**24850**	**26100**
Utility 4D CXL (AWD, V8)	T13P		**22500**	**25825**	**27100**
Add Bose Stereo System			**300**	**350**	**350**
Add Navigation System			**600**	**675**	**675**
Add Power Sunroof			**575**	**650**	**650**
Add Rear Entertainment System			**600**	**675**	**675**
Add Running Boards			**150**	**175**	**175**
Add Theft Recovery System			**100**	**125**	**125**

TRUCKS

BODY TYPE	Model No.	Weight	Trade-In	Retail	High Retail
BUICK					
2003 RENDEZVOUS-V6					
Utility 4D CX	A03	4024	**12850**	**15400**	**16400**
Utility 4D CXL	A03	4250	**14750**	**17425**	**18450**
Utility 4D CX (AWD)	B03		**13825**	**16425**	**17450**
Utility 4D CXL (AWD)	B03		**15725**	**18450**	**19525**
Add 3rd Row Seat			**175**	**200**	**200**
Add Aluminum/Alloy Wheels (Std. CXL)			**275**	**325**	**325**
Add Leather Seats (Std. CXL)			**400**	**450**	**450**
Add Power Seat (Std. CXL)			**175**	**200**	**200**
Add Power Sunroof			**525**	**600**	**600**
Add Rear Bucket Seats			**175**	**200**	**200**
Add Rear Entertainment System			**500**	**575**	**575**
Add Theft Recovery System			**75**	**100**	**100**
BUICK					
2002 RENDEZVOUS-V6					
Utility 4D CX	A03	4024	**12075**	**14550**	**15525**
Utility 4D CX (AWD)	B03		**13050**	**15600**	**16600**
Utility 4D CXL (AWD)	B03	4250	**14150**	**16775**	**17825**
Add 3rd Row Seat			**150**	**175**	**175**
Add Aluminum/Alloy Wheels (Std. CXL)			**225**	**250**	**250**
Add Leather Seats (Std. CXL)			**350**	**400**	**400**
Add Power Seat (Std. CXL)			**150**	**175**	**175**
Add Power Sunroof			**475**	**550**	**550**
Add Rear Bucket Seats			**150**	**175**	**175**
Add Theft Recovery System			**75**	**100**	**100**

CADILLAC

BODY TYPE	Model No.	Weight	Trade-In	Retail	High Retail
CADILLAC					
2004 SRX-V6/V8					
Utility 4D 3.6L	E637	4164	**25725**	**29250**	**31025**
Utility 4D 3.6L Luxury	E637		**27225**	**30900**	**32750**
Utility 4D 4.6L Luxury	E63A	4302	**29625**	**33500**	**35425**
Utility 4D 3.6L (AWD)	E637	4320	**26800**	**30375**	**32200**
Utility 4D 3.6L Luxury (AWD)	E637		**28300**	**32100**	**33975**
Utility 4D 4.6L Luxury (AWD)	E63A	4442	**30700**	**34650**	**36600**
Add Bose Stereo System			**425**	**475**	**475**
Add Magnetic Ride Control			**800**	**900**	**900**
Add Navigation System			**750**	**850**	**850**
Add Power 3rd Row Seat			**400**	**450**	**450**
Add Power Sunroof			**725**	**825**	**825**
Add Rear Entertainment System			**600**	**675**	**675**
Add Theft Recovery System			**100**	**125**	**125**
2004 ESCALADE-V8-AWD					
EXT 4D	K62	5879	**37200**	**41675**	**43850**
Utility 4D (2WD)	C63	5367	**35275**	**39650**	**41750**
Utility 4D	K63	5571	**37000**	**41475**	**43625**
ESV 4D	K66	5820	**39150**	**43750**	**45975**
ESV 4D Platinum	K66		**42450**	**47225**	**49550**
Add Navigation System (Std. Platinum)			**750**	**850**	**850**

TRUCKS

SEE TRUCK OPTION PAGE FOR ADDITIONAL OPTIONS

BODY TYPE	Model No.	Weight	Trade-In	Retail	High Retail
Add Power Sunroof (Std. Platinum)			**725**	**825**	**825**
Add Rear Bucket Seats (Std. Platinum)			**200**	**225**	**225**
Add Rear Entertainment System (Std. Platinum)			**600**	**675**	**675**
Add Theft Recovery System			**100**	**125**	**125**
CADILLAC					
2003 ESCALADE-V8-AWD					
EXT 4D	K63	5752	**33000**	**37275**	**39300**
Utility 4D (2WD)	C63	5553	**30850**	**34800**	**36750**
Utility 4D	K63	5809	**32425**	**36650**	**38650**
ESV 4D	K66	5839	**34175**	**38500**	**40575**
Add Navigation System			**650**	**725**	**725**
Add Power Sunroof			**675**	**775**	**775**
Add Rear Bucket Seats			**175**	**200**	**200**
Add Rear Entertainment System			**500**	**575**	**575**
Add Theft Recovery System			**75**	**100**	**100**
CADILLAC					
2002 ESCALADE-V8-AWD					
EXT 4D	K63	5752	**28450**	**32250**	**34125**
Utility 4D (2WD)	C63	5306	**25650**	**29150**	**30925**
Utility 4D	K63	5554	**27225**	**30950**	**32800**
Add Power Sunroof			**625**	**700**	**700**
Add Theft Recovery System			**75**	**100**	**100**
CADILLAC					
2000 ESCALADE-V8-4WD					
Utility 4D	K1/63	5573	**15575**	**18325**	**19725**
CADILLAC					
1999 ESCALADE-V8-4WD					
Utility 4D	K13	5573	**13775**	**16375**	**17725**

CHEVROLET

BODY TYPE	Model No.	Weight	Trade-In	Retail	High Retail
CHEVROLET					
2004 TRACKER-V6-4WD					
Hardtop 4D (2WD)	E13	2866	**10425**	**12700**	**13425**
Hardtop 4D LT (2WD)	E63		**11525**	**13950**	**14700**
Hardtop 4D	J13	2987	**11375**	**13800**	**14550**
Hardtop 4D ZR2	J73		**12425**	**14950**	**15725**
Hardtop 4D LT	J63		**12475**	**15000**	**15775**
Add Cruise Control (Std. ZR2, LT)			**175**	**200**	**200**
Add Leather Seats			**350**	**400**	**400**
Add Power Door Locks (Std. ZR2, LT)			**150**	**175**	**175**
Add Power Windows (Std. ZR2, LT)			**175**	**200**	**200**
Add Theft Recovery System			**100**	**125**	**125**
Add Tilt Steering Wheel (Std. ZR2, LT)			**125**	**150**	**150**
2004 BLAZER-1/2 Ton-V6					
Tailgate 2D LS	S18	3591	**12275**	**14800**	**15775**
Tailgate 2D Xtreme	S18		**14025**	**16650**	**17700**
Tailgate 4D LS	S13	3734	**13275**	**15850**	**16875**
Tailgate 2D LS (4WD)	T18	3866	**13350**	**15950**	**16975**
Tailgate 4D LS (4WD)	T13	4215	**14350**	**17000**	**18050**

TRUCKS

BODY TYPE	Model No.	Weight	Trade-In	Retail	High Retail
Add ZR2 Wide Stance Pkg.			1600	1800	1800
Add Power Seat			200	225	225
Add Power Sunroof			575	650	650
Add Theft Recovery System			100	125	125
Deduct W/out Automatic Trans.			575	575	575
Deduct W/out Cruise Control			200	200	200
Deduct W/out Power Door Locks			175	175	175
Deduct W/out Power Windows			200	200	200
Deduct W/out Tilt Steering Wheel			150	150	150
2004 TRAILBLAZER-1/2 Ton-I6					
Utility 4D LS	S13S	4425	15550	18275	19325
Utility 4D LT	S13S		16850	19675	20775
Utility 4D LS (4WD)	T13S	4612	16650	19450	20550
Utility 4D LT (4WD)	T13S		17950	20950	22100
2004 TRAILBLAZER EXT-1/2 Ton-I6					
Utility 4D EXT LS	S16S	4773	16900	19750	20850
Utility 4D EXT LS (V8)	S16P	4822	17800	20800	21925
Utility 4D EXT LT	S16S		18200	21250	22400
Utility 4D EXT LT (V8)	S16P		19100	22200	23375
Utility 4D EXT LS (4WD)	T16S	4954	18000	21000	22150
Utility 4D EXT LS (4WD, V8)	T16P	5077	18900	21975	23150
Utility 4D EXT LT (4WD)	T16S		19300	22400	23575
Utility 4D EXT LT (4WD, V8)	T16P		20200	23350	24550
TRAILBLAZER/EXT OPTIONS					
Add Bose Stereo System			300	350	350
Add Leather Seats			450	500	500
Add Navigation System			600	675	675
Add Power Seat (Std. LT)			200	225	225
Add Power Sunroof			575	650	650
Add Rear Entertainment System			600	675	675
Add Running Boards			150	175	175
Add Theft Recovery System			100	125	125
Deduct W/out Cruise Control			200	200	200
2004 TAHOE-1/2 Ton-V8					
Utility 4D LS	C13	4828	23975	27375	28850
Utility 4D LS (4WD)	K13	5050	25700	29200	30725
Add LT Trim			1925	2150	2150
Add Z71 Off-Road Pkg			2225	2450	2450
Add Bose Stereo System			350	400	400
Add Leather Seats			525	600	600
Add Power Sunroof			625	700	700
Add Rear Bucket Seats			200	225	225
Add Rear Entertainment System			600	675	675
Add Theft Recovery System			100	125	125
Deduct W/out 3rd Row Seat			200	200	200
2004 AVALANCHE-1/2-3/4 Ton-V8-4WD					
Avalanche 1500 (2WD)	C12	5437	22250	25550	26975
Avalanche 1500	K12	5678	24575	28025	29500
Avalanche 2500	K22	6642	25275	28775	30275
Add Z71 Off-Road Pkg.			600	675	675
Add Bose Stereo System			350	400	400
Add Leather Seats			525	600	600
Add Power Sunroof			625	700	700

TRUCKS

SEE TRUCK OPTION PAGE FOR ADDITIONAL OPTIONS

BODY TYPE	Model No.	Weight	Trade-In	Retail	High Retail
Add Rear Entertainment System			600	675	675
Add Running Boards			150	175	175
Add Theft Recovery System			100	125	125
2004 SUBURBAN-1/2-3/4 Ton-V8					
Utility C1500 LS	C16	4947	24125	27550	29025
Utility C1500 LT	C16		26925	30525	32075
Utility C2500 LS	C26	5520	24925	28375	29875
Utility C2500 LT	C26		27725	31475	33050
Utility K1500 LS (4WD)	K16	5219	25850	29375	30900
Utility K1500 LT (4WD)	K16		28650	32475	34100
Utility K2500 LS (4WD)	K26	5796	26650	30225	31775
Utility K2500 LT (4WD)	K26		29450	33325	34975
Add Z71 Off-Road Pkg. (LS 4WD)			3100	3325	3325
Add 8.1L V8 Engine			450	500	500
Add Bose Stereo System (Std. LT, Z71)			350	400	400
Add Leather Seats (Std. LT, Z71)			525	600	600
Add Power Sunroof			625	700	700
Add Quadrasteer System			1050	1175	1175
Add Rear Bucket Seats			200	225	225
Add Rear Entertainment System			600	675	675
Add Theft Recovery System			100	125	125
2004 SSR-V8					
SSR	S14P	4760	28600	32425	34050
Add Bose Stereo System			425	475	475
Add Running Boards			150	175	175
Add Theft Recovery System			100	125	125
2004 VENTURE-V6					
Extended Cargo Van 4D	X0/23	3838	10750	13050	13975
Van 4D	U0/23	3699	11325	13725	14675
Extended Van 4D	X0/13*	3838	12675	15200	16200
Add LS Trim			475	550	550
Add LT Trim			1150	1300	1300
Add All Wheel Drive			1100	1225	1225
Add Aluminum/Alloy Wheels			325	375	375
Add Compact Disc Player			100	125	125
Add Leather Seats			450	500	500
Add Left Power Sliding Door			300	350	350
Add Power Seat			200	225	225
Add Rear Air Conditioning			200	225	225
Add Rear Bucket Seats			200	225	225
Add Rear Entertainment System			600	675	675
Add Right Power Sliding Door			300	350	350
Add Theft Recovery System			100	125	125
Deduct W/out Cruise Control			200	200	200
* V as the 1st position of the model # denotes AWD					
2004 ASTRO-1/2 Ton-V6					
Cargo Van	M19*	3964	11150	13550	14475
Van	M19*	4321	12150	14650	15625
Van LS	M19*		12850	15400	16400
Van LT	M19*		13800	16400	17425
Add All Wheel Drive			1100	1225	1225
Add Aluminum/Alloy Wheels (Cargo)			325	375	375
Add Compact Disc Player (Std. LS, LT)			100	125	125

TRUCKS

BODY TYPE	Model No.	Weight	Trade-In	Retail	High Retail
Add Leather Seats			450	500	500
Add Power Seat (Std. LT)			200	225	225
Add Rear Air Conditioning (Std. LT)			200	225	225
Add Rear Bucket Seats			200	225	225
Add Running Boards (LS, LT)			150	175	175
Add Theft Recovery System			100	125	125
Deduct W/out Cruise Control			200	200	200
Deduct W/out Power Door Locks			175	175	175
Deduct W/out Power Windows			200	200	200
Deduct W/out Tilt Steering Wheel			150	150	150
* L as the 1st position of the model # denotes AWD					
2004 G1500-1/2 Ton-V8					
Cargo Van 135"	G15*	4845	14150	16800	18025
Express Van 135"	G15*	5258	15500	18225	19475
2004 G2500-3/4 Ton-V8					
Cargo Van 135"	G25*	5017	14800	17475	18700
Extended Cargo Van 155"	G29	5179	15500	18225	19475
Express Van 135"	G25	5877	16700	19500	20800
2004 G3500-1 Ton-V8					
Cargo Van 135"	G35	5427	16000	18750	20025
Extended Cargo Van 155"	G39	5625	16700	19500	20800
Express Van 135"	G35	6015	17350	20325	21650
Extended Express Van 155"	G39	6333	18250	21300	22650
G SERIES VAN OPTIONS					
Add LS Trim			650	725	725
Add Left Access Door (Ex. Extended)			250	300	300
Add 15 Passenger Seating			200	225	225
Add 6.0L V8 Engine (2500 Cargo)			550	625	625
Add All Wheel Drive			1400	1575	1575
Add Aluminum/Alloy Wheels			375	425	425
Add Compact Disc Player			150	175	175
Add Power Seat			225	250	250
Add Rear Air Cond. (Std. Ext. Express)			200	225	225
Add Theft Recovery System			100	125	125
Deduct V6 Engine			750	750	750
Deduct W/out Air Conditioning			750	750	750
Deduct W/out Cruise Control			225	225	225
Deduct W/out Power Door Locks			200	200	200
Deduct W/out Power Windows			225	225	225
Deduct W/out Tilt Steering Wheel			175	175	175
* H as the 1st position of the model # denotes AWD					
2004 S10 PICKUP-1/2 Ton-V6					
Crew Cab LS (4WD)	T13	4083	16150	18900	19750
Add ZR5 Sport Pkg.			500	575	575
Add Leather Seats			450	500	500
Add Power Seat			200	225	225
Add Running Boards			150	175	175
Add Theft Recovery System			100	125	125
2004 COLORADO PICKUP-1/2 Ton-5 Cyl.					
Regular Cab Z85	S14*	3351	11000	13350	14100
Regular Cab Sport	S14		12325	14850	15625
Regular Cab Z71	S14*		12525	15050	15850
Extended Cab Z85	S19*	3607	13150	15725	16525
Extended Cab Sport	S19		14475	17125	17925

TRUCKS

SEE TRUCK OPTION PAGE FOR ADDITIONAL OPTIONS

BODY TYPE	Model No.	Weight	Trade-In	Retail	High Retail
Extended Cab Z71	S19*		**14675**	**17350**	**18150**
Crew Cab Z85 LS	S13*	3752	**14775**	**17450**	**18250**
Crew Cab Sport LS	S13		**15775**	**18525**	**19350**
Crew Cab Z71 LS	S13*		**15975**	**18725**	**19550**
Add LS Trim (Std. Crew)			**500**	**575**	**575**
Add 4 Wheel Drive			**2600**	**2825**	**2825**
Add Alum/Alloy Wheels (Std. Sport, Z71, Crew)			**325**	**375**	**375**
Add Compact Disc Player (Std. Crew)			**100**	**125**	**125**
Add Leather Seats			**450**	**500**	**500**
Add Power Seat			**200**	**225**	**225**
Add Running Boards			**150**	**175**	**175**
Add Theft Recovery System			**100**	**125**	**125**
Deduct 4 Cyl. Engine			**700**	**700**	**700**
Deduct W/out Air Conditioning			**700**	**700**	**700**
Deduct W/out Automatic Trans.			**575**	**575**	**575**
Deduct W/out Cruise Control			**200**	**200**	**200**
Deduct W/out Power Door Locks (LS)			**175**	**175**	**175**
Deduct W/out Power Windows (LS)			**200**	**200**	**200**
Deduct W/out Tilt Steering Wheel			**150**	**150**	**150**
* T as the 1st position of the model # denotes 4WD					
2004 SILVERADO C1500 PICKUP-1/2 Ton-V8					
Fleetside	C14*	4142	**14275**	**16925**	**18175**
Sportside	C14*		**14925**	**17625**	**18850**
Fleetside Extended Cab	C19*	4555	**16375**	**19175**	**20450**
Sportside Extended Cab	C19*		**17025**	**19925**	**21225**
Extended Cab SS (AWD)	K19N		**24650**	**28100**	**29575**
Fleetside Crew Cab LS	C13*	4946	**18725**	**21800**	**23175**
Fleetside Crew Cab LT	C13*		**20675**	**23875**	**25250**
2004 SILVERADO C2500 LD PICKUP-3/4 Ton-V8					
Fleetside	C24	5059	**15175**	**17875**	**19125**
Fleet Extended Cab (4WD)	K29	5524	**19975**	**23125**	**24475**
Fleetside Crew Cab LS	C23*	5506	**19625**	**22750**	**24100**
Fleetside Crew Cab LT	C23*		**21575**	**24825**	**26225**
2004 SILVERADO C2500 HD PICKUP-3/4 Ton-V8					
Fleetside	C24*	5153	**16175**	**18950**	**20225**
Fleetside Extended Cab	C29*	5402	**19575**	**22700**	**24050**
Fleetside Crew Cab	C23*	5614	**20975**	**24200**	**25600**
2004 SILVERADO C3500 PICKUP-1 Ton-V8-Dual Rear Wheels					
RC Fleetside (4WD)	K34	5841	**19675**	**22800**	**24150**
Fleetside Extended Cab	C39*	5951	**20175**	**23350**	**24725**
Fleetside Crew Cab	C33*	6168	**21575**	**24825**	**26225**
SILVERADO PICKUP OPTIONS					
Add LS Trim (Ex. 1500/2500LD Crew, SS)			**700**	**800**	**800**
Add LT Trim (Ex. 1500/2500LD Crew, SS)			**1500**	**1675**	**1675**
Add Z71 Off-Road Pkg. (4WD)			**350**	**400**	**400**
Add 4WD (Std. SS, 2500 LD Ext., 3500 RC)			**2800**	**3025**	**3025**
Add 6.6L V8 Turbo Diesel Engine			**5000**	**5225**	**5225**
Add 8.1L V8 Engine			**1075**	**1200**	**1200**
Add A/A Wheels (Std. 1500/2500LD Crew, SS)			**375**	**425**	**425**
Add Bose Stereo (Std. 1500/2500LD Crew LT, SS)			**350**	**400**	**400**
Add Leather Seats (Std. 1500/2500LD Crew LT, SS)			**525**	**600**	**600**
Add Power Seat (Std. 1500/2500LD Crew LT, SS)			**225**	**250**	**250**
Add Quadrasteer System			**1050**	**1175**	**1175**
Add Rear Entertainment System			**600**	**675**	**675**

BODY TYPE	Model No.	Weight	Trade-In	Retail	High Retail
Add Running Boards			150	175	175
Add Theft Recovery System			100	125	125
Deduct Work Truck Pkg.			1100	1100	1100
Deduct V6 Engine			750	750	750
Deduct W/out Air Conditioning			750	750	750
Deduct W/out Automatic Trans.			625	625	625
Deduct W/out Compact Disc Player			150	150	150
Deduct W/out Cruise Control			225	225	225
Deduct W/out Power Door Locks			200	200	200

* K as the 1st position of the model # denotes 4WD

CHEVROLET

2003 TRACKER-4 Cyl.-4WD

BODY TYPE	Model No.	Weight	Trade-In	Retail	High Retail
Convertible 2D (2WD)	E18	2690	7550	9575	10300
Convertible 2D	J18	2811	8650	10775	11525
Convertible 2D ZR2	J78		9725	11950	12700
Hardtop 4D (2WD)	E13	2866	8500	10625	11350
Hardtop 4D (2WD, V6)	E13		9925	12175	12900
Hardtop 4D LT (2WD, V6)	E63		10275	12550	13275
Hardtop 4D	J13	2987	9600	11825	12575
Hardtop 4D (V6)	J13		11025	13375	14125
Hardtop 4D ZR2 (V6)	J73		11325	13725	14475
Hardtop 4D LT (V6)	J63		11375	13800	14550
Add Alum/Alloy Wheels (Std. Base V6, ZR2, LT)			250	300	300
Add Cruise Control (Std. Base V6, ZR2, LT)			150	175	175
Add Leather Seats			300	350	350
Add Power Door Locks (Std. Base V6, ZR2, LT)			125	150	150
Add Power Windows (Std. Base V6, ZR2, LT)			150	175	175
Add Theft Recovery System			75	100	100
Add Tilt Steering Wheel (Std. Base V6, ZR2, LT)			100	125	125
Deduct W/out Automatic Trans.			425	425	425

2003 BLAZER-1/2 Ton-V6

BODY TYPE	Model No.	Weight	Trade-In	Retail	High Retail
Tailgate 2D LS	S18	3518	10700	12975	13900
Tailgate 2D Xtreme	S18		12350	14850	15825
Tailgate 4D LS	S13	3671	11400	13800	14750
Tailgate 2D LS (4WD)	T18	3848	11725	14150	15100
Tailgate 4D LS (4WD)	T13	4049	12425	14950	15925
Add ZR2 Wide Stance Pkg.			1250	1400	1400
Add Power Seat			175	200	200
Add Power Sunroof			525	600	600
Add Theft Recovery System			75	100	100
Deduct W/out Automatic Trans.			525	525	525
Deduct W/out Cruise Control			175	175	175
Deduct W/out Power Door Locks			150	150	150
Deduct W/out Power Windows			175	175	175
Deduct W/out Tilt Steering Wheel			125	125	125

2003 TRAILBLAZER-1/2 Ton-I6

BODY TYPE	Model No.	Weight	Trade-In	Retail	High Retail
Utility 4D LS	S13S	4432	14325	16975	18025
Utility 4D LT	S13S		15425	18150	19200
Utility 4D LTZ	S13S		17000	19875	20975
Utility 4D LS (4WD)	T13S	4616	15350	18075	19125
Utility 4D LT (4WD)	T13S		16450	19250	20350
Utility 4D LTZ (4WD)	T13S		18150	21175	22325

2003 TRAILBLAZER EXT-1/2 Ton-I6

BODY TYPE	Model No.	Weight	Trade-In	Retail	High Retail
Utility 4D EXT LS	S16S	4787	15625	18350	19425

TRUCKS

SEE TRUCK OPTION PAGE FOR ADDITIONAL OPTIONS

BODY TYPE	Model No.	Weight	Trade-In	Retail	High Retail
Utility 4D EXT LS (V8)	S16P	4670	16375	19150	20225
Utility 4D EXT LT	S16S		16725	19525	20625
Utility 4D EXT LT (V8)	S16P		17475	20450	21575
Utility 4D EXT LS (4WD)	T16S	4968	16650	19450	20550
Utility 4D EXT LS (4WD, V8)	T16P		17400	20375	21500
Utility 4D EXT LT (4WD)	T16S	4968	17750	20750	21875
Utility 4D EXT LT (4WD, V8)	T16P		18500	21550	22700
TRAILBLAZER/EXT OPTIONS					
Add Bose Stereo System			250	300	300
Add Leather Seats (Std. LTZ)			400	450	450
Add Power Sunroof			525	600	600
Add Rear Entertainment System			500	575	575
Add Running Boards			125	150	150
Add Theft Recovery System			75	100	100
Deduct W/out Cruise Control			175	175	175
2003 TAHOE-1/2 Ton-V8					
Utility 4D LS	C13	4828	20925	24150	25525
Utility 4D LS (4WD)	K13	5050	22675	26000	27450
Add LT Trim			1225	1375	1375
Add Z71 Off-Road Pkg			1525	1700	1700
Add Bose Stereo System			300	350	350
Add Leather Seats			475	550	550
Add Power Sunroof			575	650	650
Add Rear Bucket Seats			175	200	200
Add Rear Entertainment System			500	575	575
Add Theft Recovery System			75	100	100
Deduct W/out 3rd Row Seat			175	175	175
2003 AVALANCHE-1/2-3/4 Ton-V8-4WD					
Avalanche 1500 (2WD)	C13	5437	19350	22450	23775
Avalanche 1500	K13	5678	21325	24550	25950
Avalanche 2500 (2WD)	C23	6353	19950	23075	24425
Avalanche 2500	K23	6642	21925	25200	26625
Add Z71 Off-Road Pkg.			400	450	450
Add Bose Stereo System			300	350	350
Add Leather Seats			475	550	550
Add Power Sunroof			575	650	650
Add Rear Entertainment System			500	575	575
Add Running Boards			125	150	150
Add Theft Recovery System			75	100	100
2003 SUBURBAN-1/2-3/4 Ton-V8					
Utility C1500 LS	C16	4947	21075	24300	25700
Utility C1500 LT	C16		23075	26450	27900
Utility C2500 LS	C26	5520	21875	25150	26575
Utility C2500 LT	C26		23875	27300	28775
Utility K1500 LS (4WD)	K16	5219	22825	26150	27600
Utility K1500 LT (4WD)	K16		24825	28275	29775
Utility K2500 LS (4WD)	K26	5796	23625	27000	28475
Utility K2500 LT (4WD)	K26		25625	29125	30650
Add Z71 Off-Road Pkg. (LS 4WD)			2350	2575	2575
Add 8.1L V8 Engine			425	475	475
Add Bose Stereo System (Std. LT, Z71)			300	350	350
Add Leather Seats (Std. LT, Z71)			475	550	550
Add Power Sunroof			575	650	650

TRUCKS

BODY TYPE	Model No.	Weight	Trade-In	Retail	High Retail
Add Quadrasteer System			1000	1125	1125
Add Rear Bucket Seats			175	200	200
Add Rear Entertainment System			500	575	575
Add Theft Recovery System			75	100	100
2003 SSR-V8					
SSR	S14P	4760	26425	29975	31775
Add Bose Stereo System			375	425	425
Add Running Boards			125	150	150
Add Theft Recovery System			75	100	100
2003 VENTURE-V6					
Extended Cargo Van 4D	X0/23		8850	11000	11950
Van 4D	U0/23	3699	9575	11775	12675
Extended Van 4D	X03*	3838	10775	13075	14000
Extended Van 4D Warner Bros.	X13*		14425	17075	18100
Add LS Trim (Ex. Warner Bros.)			450	500	500
Add LT Trim (Ex. Warner Bros.)			1100	1225	1225
Add All Wheel Drive			1000	1125	1125
Add Aluminum/Alloy Wheels (Std. WB)			275	325	325
Add Compact Disc Player (Cargo, Van 4D)			75	100	100
Add Leather Seats (Std. Warner Bros.)			400	450	450
Add Left Power Sliding Door			250	300	300
Add Power Seat (Std. Warner Bros.)			175	200	200
Add Rear Air Cond. (Std. Warner Bros.)			150	175	175
Add Rear Bucket Seats (Std. WB)			175	200	200
Add Rear Entertainment System (Std. WB)			500	575	575
Add Right Power Door (Std. WB)			250	300	300
Add Theft Recovery System			75	100	100
Deduct W/out Cruise Control			175	175	175
Deduct W/out Power Windows			175	175	175

* V as the 1st position of the model # denotes AWD

BODY TYPE	Model No.	Weight	Trade-In	Retail	High Retail
2003 ASTRO-1/2 Ton-V6					
Cargo Van	M19*	3964	9050	11200	12075
Van	M19*	4321	9900	12125	13000
Van LS	M19*		10550	12825	13725
Van LT	M19*		11375	13775	14725
Add All Wheel Drive			1000	1125	1125
Add Aluminum/Alloy Wheels (Cargo)			275	325	325
Add Compact Disc Player (Std. LS, LT)			75	100	100
Add Leather Seats			400	450	450
Add Power Seat (Std. LT)			175	200	200
Add Rear Air Conditioning (Std. LT)			150	175	175
Add Rear Bucket Seats			175	200	200
Add Running Boards (LS, LT)			125	150	150
Add Theft Recovery System			75	100	100
Deduct W/out Cruise Control			175	175	175
Deduct W/out Power Door Locks			150	150	150
Deduct W/out Power Windows			175	175	175
Deduct W/out Tilt Steering Wheel			125	125	125

* L as the 1st position of the model # denotes AWD

BODY TYPE	Model No.	Weight	Trade-In	Retail	High Retail
2003 G1500-1/2 Ton-V8					
Cargo Van 135"	G15*	4596	12475	15000	16150
Express Van 135"	G15*	5015	13775	16400	17625

SEE TRUCK OPTION PAGE FOR ADDITIONAL OPTIONS

BODY TYPE	Model No.	Weight	Trade-In	Retail	High Retail
2003 G2500-3/4 Ton-V8					
Cargo Van 135"	G25*	4711	**13075**	**15650**	**16850**
Extended Cargo Van 155"	G29	4885	**13725**	**16350**	**17575**
Express Van 135"	G25	5645	**14925**	**17625**	**18850**
Extended Express Van 155"	G29	5985	**15725**	**18475**	**19725**
2003 G3500-1 Ton-V8					
Cargo Van 135"	G35	5021	**14225**	**16875**	**18100**
Extended Cargo Van 155"	G39	5462	**14875**	**17550**	**18775**
Express Van 135"	G35	5780	**15525**	**18250**	**19500**
Extended Express Van 155"	G39	6122	**16325**	**19100**	**20375**
G SERIES VAN OPTIONS					
Add LS Trim			**625**	**700**	**700**
Add Left Access Door (Ex. Extended)			**225**	**250**	**250**
Add 15 Passenger Seating			**175**	**200**	**200**
Add 6.0L V8 Engine (2500 Cargo)			**550**	**625**	**625**
Add All Wheel Drive			**1300**	**1450**	**1450**
Add Aluminum/Alloy Wheels			**325**	**375**	**375**
Add Compact Disc Player			**125**	**150**	**150**
Add Power Seat			**200**	**225**	**225**
Add Rear Air Cond. (Std. Ext. Express)			**150**	**175**	**175**
Add Theft Recovery System			**75**	**100**	**100**
Deduct V6 Engine			**725**	**725**	**725**
Deduct W/out Air Conditioning			**700**	**700**	**700**
Deduct W/out Cruise Control			**200**	**200**	**200**
Deduct W/out Power Door Locks			**175**	**175**	**175**
Deduct W/out Power Windows			**200**	**200**	**200**
Deduct W/out Tilt Steering Wheel			**150**	**150**	**150**

* H as the 1st position of the model # denotes AWD

BODY TYPE	Model No.	Weight	Trade-In	Retail	High Retail
2003 S10 PICKUP-1/2 Ton-V6					
Fleetside	S14	3042	**8775**	**10900**	**11650**
Sportside	S14		**9075**	**11225**	**11950**
Fleetside Extended Cab	S19*	3212	**10525**	**12800**	**13525**
Sportside Extended Cab	S19*		**10825**	**13125**	**13875**
Crew Cab LS (4WD)	T13	4039	**14775**	**17450**	**18250**
Add LS Trim (Std. Crew)			**500**	**575**	**575**
Add Xtreme Pkg.			**1200**	**1350**	**1350**
Add ZR2 Wide Stance Pkg.			**1100**	**1225**	**1225**
Add ZR5 Sport Pkg. (Crew)			**425**	**475**	**475**
Add 4 Wheel Drive (Std. Crew)			**2550**	**2775**	**2775**
Add Aluminum/Alloy Wheels (Std. Crew)			**275**	**325**	**325**
Add Compact Disc Player (Std. Crew)			**75**	**100**	**100**
Add Cruise Control (Std. Crew)			**175**	**200**	**200**
Add Leather Seats			**400**	**450**	**450**
Add Power Door Locks (Std. Crew)			**150**	**175**	**175**
Add Power Seat			**175**	**200**	**200**
Add Power Sunroof			**525**	**600**	**600**
Add Power Windows (Std. Crew)			**175**	**200**	**200**
Add Running Boards			**125**	**150**	**150**
Add Theft Recovery System			**75**	**100**	**100**
Add Tilt Steering Wheel (Std. Crew)			**125**	**150**	**150**
Deduct 4 Cyl. Engine			**650**	**650**	**650**
Deduct W/out Air Conditioning			**650**	**650**	**650**
Deduct W/out Automatic Trans.			**525**	**525**	**525**

* T as the 1st position of the model # denotes 4WD

BODY TYPE	Model No.	Weight	Trade-In	Retail	High Retail
2003 SILVERADO C1500 PICKUP-1/2 Ton-V8					
Fleetside	C14*	4142	**12925**	**15475**	**16650**
Sportside	C14*		**13525**	**16125**	**17325**
Fleetside Extended Cab	C19*	4548	**15025**	**17700**	**18925**
Sportside Extended Cab	C19*		**15625**	**18350**	**19600**
Extended Cab SS (AWD)	K19N	5298	**22925**	**26275**	**27725**
2003 SILVERADO C1500 HD PICKUP-1/2 Ton-V8					
Fleetside Crew Cab LS	C13*	5506	**18175**	**21200**	**22550**
Fleetside Crew Cab LT	C13*		**19700**	**22825**	**24175**
2003 SILVERADO C2500 LD PICKUP-3/4 Ton-V8					
Fleetside	C24	5059	**13825**	**16425**	**17650**
Fleet Extended Cab (4WD)	K29	5524	**18625**	**21675**	**23050**
2003 SILVERADO C2500 HD PICKUP-3/4 Ton-V8					
Fleetside	C24*	5153	**14825**	**17500**	**18725**
Fleetside Extended Cab	C29*	5402	**18025**	**21050**	**22400**
Fleetside Crew Cab	C23*	5615	**19425**	**22525**	**23875**
2003 SILVERADO C3500 PICKUP-1 Ton-V8-Dual Rear Wheels					
RC Fleetside (4WD)	K34	5841	**18175**	**21200**	**22550**
Fleetside Extended Cab	C39*	5951	**18675**	**21725**	**23100**
Fleetside Crew Cab	C33*	6168	**20075**	**23225**	**24575**
SILVERADO PICKUP OPTIONS					
Add LS Trim (Ex. 1500 HD, SS)			**650**	**725**	**725**
Add LT Trim (Ex. 1500 HD, SS)			**1400**	**1575**	**1575**
Add Z71 Off-Road Pkg. (4WD)			**300**	**350**	**350**
Add 4WD (Std. SS, 2500 LD Ext., 3500 RC)			**2700**	**2925**	**2925**
Add 6.6L V8 Turbo Diesel Engine			**4800**	**5025**	**5025**
Add 8.1L V8 Engine			**1000**	**1125**	**1125**
Add A/A Wheels (Std. 1500 HD, SS)			**325**	**375**	**375**
Add Bose Stereo System (Std. SS)			**300**	**350**	**350**
Add Compact Disc Player (Std. 1500 HD, SS)			**125**	**150**	**150**
Add Leather Seats (Std. 1500 HD LT, SS)			**475**	**550**	**550**
Add Power Seat (Std. 1500 HD LT, SS)			**200**	**225**	**225**
Add Quadrasteer System			**1000**	**1125**	**1125**
Add Rear Entertainment System			**500**	**575**	**575**
Add Running Boards			**125**	**150**	**150**
Add Theft Recovery System			**75**	**100**	**100**
Deduct Work Truck Pkg.			**1100**	**1100**	**1100**
Deduct V6 Engine			**725**	**725**	**725**
Deduct W/out Air Conditioning			**700**	**700**	**700**
Deduct W/out Automatic Trans.			**575**	**575**	**575**
Deduct W/out Cruise Control			**200**	**200**	**200**
Deduct W/out Power Door Locks			**175**	**175**	**175**

* K as the 1st position of the model # denotes 4WD

CHEVROLET

BODY TYPE	Model No.	Weight	Trade-In	Retail	High Retail
2002 TRACKER-4 Cyl.-4WD					
Convertible 2D (2WD)	E18	2690	**6100**	**7950**	**8775**
Convertible 2D	J18	2811	**7050**	**9025**	**9725**
Convertible 2D ZR2	J78		**7950**	**10000**	**10725**
Hardtop 4D (2WD)	E13	2866	**7000**	**8950**	**9725**
Hardtop 4D LT (2WD, V6)	E63		**8550**	**10650**	**11375**
Hardtop 4D	J13	2987	**7950**	**10000**	**10725**
Hardtop 4D ZR2 (V6)	J73		**9450**	**11650**	**12375**
Hardtop 4D LT (V6)	J63		**9500**	**11700**	**12450**
Add Aluminum/Alloy Wheels (Std. ZR2, LT)			**200**	**225**	**225**

SEE TRUCK OPTION PAGE FOR ADDITIONAL OPTIONS

BODY TYPE	Model No.	Weight	Trade-In	Retail	High Retail
Add Cruise Control (Std. ZR2, LT)			125	150	150
Add Leather Seats			250	300	300
Add Power Door Locks (Std. ZR2, LT)			100	125	125
Add Power Windows (Std. ZR2, LT)			125	150	150
Add Theft Recovery System			75	100	100
Add Tilt Steering Wheel (Std. ZR2, LT)			75	100	100
Deduct W/out Automatic Trans.			375	375	375
2002 BLAZER-1/2 Ton-V6					
Tailgate 2D LS	S18	3603	9600	11825	12725
Tailgate 2D Xtreme	S18	3603	11150	13550	14475
Tailgate 4D LS	S13	3718	10200	12475	13375
Tailgate 2D LS (4WD)	T18	3869	10600	12900	13825
Tailgate 4D LS (4WD)	T13	4114	11200	13625	14575
Add ZR2 Wide Stance Pkg.			900	1000	1000
Add Bose Stereo System			200	225	225
Add Compact Disc Player			75	100	100
Add Leather Seats			350	400	400
Add Power Seat			150	175	175
Add Power Sunroof			475	550	550
Add Theft Recovery System			75	100	100
Deduct W/out Automatic Trans.			475	475	475
Deduct W/out Cruise Control			150	150	150
Deduct W/out Power Door Locks			125	125	125
Deduct W/out Power Windows			150	150	150
Deduct W/out Tilt Steering Wheel			100	100	100
2002 TRAILBLAZER-1/2 Ton-I6					
Utility 4D LS	S13S	4442	12750	15275	16275
Utility 4D LT	S13S		13550	16150	17175
Utility 4D LTZ	S13S		14950	17625	18675
Utility 4D LS (4WD)	T13S	4628	13750	16350	17375
Utility 4D LT (4WD)	T13S		14550	17200	18225
Utility 4D LTZ (4WD)	T13S		15950	18700	19775
2002 TRAILBLAZER EXT-1/2 Ton-I6					
Utility 4D EXT LT	S16S	4836	14850	17525	18575
Utility 4D EXT LT (4WD)	T16S	5020	15850	18600	19675
TRAILBLAZER/EXT OPTIONS					
Add Bose Stereo System			200	225	225
Add Leather Seats (Std. LTZ)			350	400	400
Add Power Sunroof			475	550	550
Add Rear Entertainment System			400	450	450
Add Running Boards (LT, LTZ)			100	125	125
Add Theft Recovery System			75	100	100
Deduct W/out Cruise Control			150	150	150
2002 TAHOE-1/2 Ton-V8					
Utility 4D LS	C13	4828	18000	21025	22375
Utility 4D LS (4WD)	K13	5050	19575	22700	24050
Add LT Trim			1175	1325	1325
Add Z71 Off-Road Pkg			1375	1550	1550
Add Leather Seats			425	475	475
Add Power Sunroof			525	600	600
Add Theft Recovery System			75	100	100
Deduct W/out 3rd Row Seat			150	150	150

BODY TYPE	Model No.	Weight	Trade-In	Retail	High Retail
2002 AVALANCHE-1/2-3/4 Ton-V8-4WD					
Avalanche 1500 (2WD)	C13/6	5400	**16900**	**19725**	**21025**
Avalanche 1500	K13/6	5652	**18675**	**21725**	**23100**
Avalanche 2500 (2WD)	C23	6353	**17400**	**20375**	**21700**
Avalanche 2500	K23	6642	**19175**	**22275**	**23600**
Add Z71 Off-Road Pkg.			**350**	**400**	**400**
Add Leather Seats			**425**	**475**	**475**
Add Power Sunroof			**525**	**600**	**600**
Add Running Boards			**100**	**125**	**125**
Add Theft Recovery System			**75**	**100**	**100**
2002 SUBURBAN-1/2-3/4 Ton-V8					
Utility C1500 LS	C16	4914	**18125**	**21150**	**22500**
Utility C1500 LT	C16		**19725**	**22850**	**24200**
Utility C2500 LS	C26	5447	**18925**	**22000**	**23375**
Utility C2500 LT	C26		**20525**	**23700**	**25075**
Utility K1500 LS (4WD)	K16	5219	**19700**	**22825**	**24175**
Utility K1500 LT (4WD)	K16		**21300**	**24550**	**25950**
Utility K2500 LS (4WD)	K26	5796	**20500**	**23700**	**25075**
Utility K2500 LT (4WD)	K26		**22100**	**25400**	**26825**
Add Z71 Off-Road Pkg. (LS 4WD)			**1825**	**2050**	**2050**
Add 8.1L V8 Engine			**400**	**450**	**450**
Add Leather Seats (Std. LT, Z71)			**425**	**475**	**475**
Add Power Sunroof			**525**	**600**	**600**
Add Rear Bucket Seats			**150**	**175**	**175**
Add Theft Recovery System			**75**	**100**	**100**
2002 VENTURE-V6					
Van 4D	U0/23	3699	**8075**	**10150**	**11075**
Extended Van 4D	X03*	3838	**9175**	**11350**	**12250**
Extended Van 4D Warner Bros.	X13*		**12825**	**15375**	**16375**
Add LS Trim (Ex. Warner Bros.)			**450**	**500**	**500**
Add LT Trim (Ex. Warner Bros.)			**1050**	**1175**	**1175**
Add All Wheel Drive			**900**	**1000**	**1000**
Add Aluminum/Alloy Wheels (Std. WB)			**225**	**250**	**250**
Add Compact Disc Player (Van 4D)			**75**	**100**	**100**
Add Left Power Sliding Door			**250**	**300**	**300**
Add Power Seat (Std. Warner Bros.)			**150**	**175**	**175**
Add Rear Air Cond. (Std. Warner Bros.)			**150**	**175**	**175**
Add Rear Bucket Seats (Std. WB)			**150**	**175**	**175**
Add Right Power Door (Std. WB)			**250**	**300**	**300**
Add Theft Recovery System			**75**	**100**	**100**
Deduct W/out Cruise Control			**150**	**150**	**150**
Deduct W/out Power Windows			**150**	**150**	**150**

* V as the 1st position of the model # denotes AWD

BODY TYPE	Model No.	Weight	Trade-In	Retail	High Retail
2002 ASTRO-1/2 Ton-V6					
Cargo Van	M19*	3915	**7325**	**9325**	**10200**
Van LS	M19*	4323	**8825**	**10975**	**11925**
Van LT	M19*		**9800**	**12025**	**12900**
Add All Wheel Drive			**900**	**1000**	**1000**
Add Aluminum/Alloy Wheels (Std. LT)			**225**	**250**	**250**
Add Compact Disc Player (Std. LS, LT)			**75**	**100**	**100**
Add Leather Seats			**350**	**400**	**400**
Add Power Seat (Std. LT)			**150**	**175**	**175**
Add Rear Air Conditioning (Std. LT)			**150**	**175**	**175**

TRUCKS

SEE TRUCK OPTION PAGE FOR ADDITIONAL OPTIONS

BODY TYPE	Model No.	Weight	Trade-In	Retail	High Retail
Add Rear Bucket Seats			150	175	175
Add Running Boards (LS, LT)			100	125	125
Add Theft Recovery System			75	100	100
Deduct W/out Cruise Control			150	150	150
Deduct W/out Power Door Locks			125	125	125
Deduct W/out Power Windows			150	150	150
Deduct W/out Tilt Steering Wheel			100	100	100
* L as the 1st position of the model # denotes AWD					
2002 G1500-1/2 Ton-V8					
Cargo Van 135"	G15	4639	11000	13350	14450
Express Van 135"	G15	5062	12250	14775	15925
Express Van 135" LT	G65		15250	17975	19225
2002 G2500-3/4 Ton-V8					
Cargo Van 135"	G25	4816	11550	13975	15100
Extended Cargo Van 155"	G29	5000	12150	14675	15825
Express Van 135"	G25	5808	12800	15350	16525
Extended Express Van 155"	G29	6018	13550	16150	17350
2002 G3500-1 Ton-V8					
Cargo Van 135"	G35	5345	12100	14600	15750
Extended Cargo Van 155"	G39	5539	12700	15250	16425
Express Van 135"	G35	5947	13350	15950	17150
Extended Express Van 155"	G39	6158	14100	16750	17975
G SERIES VAN OPTIONS					
Add LS Trim (Ex. LT)			600	675	675
Add 15 Passenger Seating			150	175	175
Add 6.5L V8 Turbo Diesel Engine			1100	1225	1225
Add 8.1L V8 Engine			400	450	450
Add Aluminum/Alloy Wheels (Std. LT)			275	325	325
Add Compact Disc Player (Std. LT)			100	125	125
Add Leather Seats			425	475	475
Add Power Seat (Std. LT)			175	200	200
Add Rear Air Cond. (Std. LT, Ext. Express)			150	175	175
Add Theft Recovery System			75	100	100
Deduct V6 Engine			700	700	700
Deduct W/out Air Conditioning			650	650	650
Deduct W/out Cruise Control			175	175	175
Deduct W/out Power Door Locks			150	150	150
Deduct W/out Power Windows			175	175	175
Deduct W/out Tilt Steering Wheel			125	125	125
2002 S10 PICKUP-1/2 Ton-V6					
Fleetside	S14	3016	7300	9300	10000
Sportside	S14		7575	9600	10325
Fleetside Extended Cab	S19*	3198	9000	11150	11875
Sportside Extended Cab	S19*		9275	11450	12175
Crew Cab LS (4WD)	T13	4039	13300	15875	16675
Add LS Trim (Std. Crew)			400	450	450
Add Xtreme Pkg.			1100	1225	1225
Add ZR2 Wide Stance Pkg.			900	1000	1000
Add ZR5 Sport Pkg. (Crew)			350	400	400
Add 4 Wheel Drive (Std. Crew)			2450	2675	2675
Add Aluminum/Alloy Wheels (Std. Crew)			225	250	250
Add Compact Disc Player (Std. Crew)			75	100	100
Add Cruise Control (Std. Crew)			150	175	175
Add Leather Seats			350	400	400

TRUCKS

BODY TYPE	Model No.	Weight	Trade-In	Retail	High Retail
Add Power Door Locks (Std. Crew)			125	150	150
Add Power Seat			150	175	175
Add Power Windows (Std. Crew)			150	175	175
Add Running Boards			100	125	125
Add Theft Recovery System			75	100	100
Add Tilt Steering Wheel (Std. Crew)			100	125	125
Deduct 4 Cyl. Engine			600	600	600
Deduct W/out Air Conditioning			600	600	600
Deduct W/out Automatic Trans.			475	475	475
* T as the 1st position of the model # denotes 4WD					
2002 SILVERADO C1500 PICKUP-1/2 Ton-V8					
Fleetside	C14*	4073	11225	13625	14725
Sportside	C14*		11775	14225	15350
Fleetside Extended Cab	C19*	4534	13325	15925	17125
Sportside Extended Cab	C19*		13875	16500	17725
2002 SILVERADO C1500 HD PICKUP-1/2 Ton-V8					
Fleetside Crew Cab LS	C13*	5461	15925	18675	19950
Fleetside Crew Cab LT	C13*		17125	20100	21425
2002 SILVERADO C2500 LD PICKUP-3/4 Ton-V8					
Fleetside	C24	4995	12025	14500	15650
Fleet Extended Cab (4WD)	K29	5497	16675	19475	20775
2002 SILVERADO C2500 HD PICKUP-3/4 Ton-V8					
Fleetside	C24*	5126	13025	15600	16775
Fleetside Extended Cab	C29*	5393	16125	18900	20175
Fleetside Crew Cab	C23*	5605	17425	20425	21750
2002 SILVERADO C3500 PICKUP-1 Ton-V8-Dual Rear Wheels					
RC Fleetside (4WD)	K34	5845	16275	19050	20325
Fleetside Extended Cab	C39*	5935	16725	19525	20825
Fleetside Crew Cab	C33*	6103	18025	21050	22400
SILVERADO PICKUP OPTIONS					
Add LS Trim (Ex. 1500 HD)			600	675	675
Add LT Trim (Ex. 1500 HD)			1200	1350	1350
Add Z71 Off-Road Pkg. (4WD)			225	250	250
Add 4WD (Std. 2500 LD Ext., 3500 RC)			2550	2775	2775
Add 6.6L V8 Turbo Diesel Engine			4475	4700	4700
Add 8.1L V8 Engine			925	1050	1050
Add Aluminum/Alloy Wheels (Std. 1500 HD)			275	325	325
Add Compact Disc Player (Std. 1500 HD)			100	125	125
Add Leather Seats (Std. 1500 HD LT)			425	475	475
Add Power Seat (Std. 1500 HD LT)			175	200	200
Add Running Boards			100	125	125
Add Theft Recovery System			75	100	100
Deduct Work Truck Pkg.			1050	1050	1050
Deduct V6 Engine			700	700	700
Deduct W/out Air Conditioning			650	650	650
Deduct W/out Automatic Trans.			525	525	525
Deduct W/out Cruise Control			175	175	175
Deduct W/out Power Door Locks			150	150	150
* K as the 1st position of the model # denotes 4WD					
CHEVROLET					
2001 TRACKER-4 Cyl.-4WD					
Convertible 2D (2WD)	E18	2602	4725	6425	7225
Convertible 2D	J18	2602	5675	7500	8300
Convertible 2D ZR2	J78	2639	6425	8350	9100

TRUCKS

SEE TRUCK OPTION PAGE FOR ADDITIONAL OPTIONS

BODY TYPE	Model No.	Weight	Trade-In	Retail	High Retail
Hardtop 4D (2WD)	E13	2866	**5575**	**7375**	**8175**
Hardtop 4D LT (2WD, V6)	E63	2866	**6975**	**8925**	**9700**
Hardtop 4D	J13	2639	**6525**	**8450**	**9200**
Hardtop 4D ZR2 (V6)	J73	2987	**7825**	**9875**	**10600**
Hardtop 4D LT (V6)	J63	2987	**7925**	**10000**	**10725**
Add Aluminum/Alloy Wheels (Std. ZR2, LT)			**150**	**175**	**175**
Add Compact Disc Player (Std. LT)			**50**	**75**	**75**
Add Cruise Control (Std. ZR2, LT)			**100**	**125**	**125**
Add Leather Seats			**200**	**225**	**225**
Add Power Door Locks (Std. ZR2, LT)			**75**	**100**	**100**
Add Power Windows (Std. ZR2, LT)			**100**	**125**	**125**
Add Theft Recovery System			**50**	**75**	**75**
Add Tilt Steering Wheel (Std. ZR2, LT)			**75**	**100**	**100**
Deduct W/out Automatic Trans.			**325**	**325**	**325**
2001 BLAZER-1/2 Ton-V6					
Tailgate 2D LS	S18	3536	**7400**	**9425**	**10300**
Tailgate 2D Xtreme	S18		**8850**	**11000**	**11950**
Tailgate 4D LS	S13	3692	**8025**	**10100**	**11025**
Tailgate 2D LS (4WD)	T18	3814	**8300**	**10400**	**11325**
Tailgate 4D LS (4WD)	T13	4023	**8925**	**11100**	**11975**
Add LT Trim (LS)			**600**	**675**	**675**
Add TrailBlazer Trim			**650**	**725**	**725**
Add ZR2 Wide Stance Pkg.			**700**	**800**	**800**
Add Bose Stereo System			**150**	**175**	**175**
Add Compact Disc Player			**50**	**75**	**75**
Add Leather Seats			**300**	**350**	**350**
Add Power Seat			**125**	**150**	**150**
Add Power Sunroof			**425**	**475**	**475**
Add Theft Recovery System			**50**	**75**	**75**
Deduct W/out Automatic Trans.			**425**	**425**	**425**
Deduct W/out Cruise Control			**125**	**125**	**125**
Deduct W/out Power Door Locks			**100**	**100**	**100**
Deduct W/out Power Windows			**125**	**125**	**125**
Deduct W/out Tilt Steering Wheel			**100**	**100**	**100**
2001 TAHOE-1/2 Ton-V8					
Utility 4D	C13	4828	**10475**	**12750**	**13825**
Utility 4D LS	C13		**14775**	**17450**	**18675**
Utility 4D (4WD)	K13	5050	**11650**	**14075**	**15200**
Utility 4D LS (4WD)	K13		**15950**	**18700**	**19975**
Add LT Trim (LS)			**900**	**1000**	**1000**
Add Z71 Off-Road Pkg (LS)			**1050**	**1175**	**1175**
Add Aluminum/Alloy Wheels (Base)			**225**	**250**	**250**
Add Compact Disc Player (Std. LS, LT)			**100**	**125**	**125**
Add Leather Seats			**375**	**425**	**425**
Add Power Sunroof			**475**	**550**	**550**
Add Theft Recovery System			**50**	**75**	**75**
Deduct W/out 3rd Row Seat (Ex. Base)			**125**	**125**	**125**
Deduct W/out Air Conditioning			**600**	**600**	**600**
Deduct W/out Cruise Control			**150**	**150**	**150**
Deduct W/out Power Seat (Ex. Base)			**150**	**150**	**150**
Deduct W/out Running Boards (Ex. Base)			**75**	**75**	**75**
2001 SUBURBAN-1/2-3/4 Ton-V8					
Utility C1500	C16	4914	**11600**	**14025**	**15150**

TRUCKS

BODY TYPE	Model No.	Weight	Trade-In	Retail	High Retail
Utility C1500 LS	C16		**14900**	**17575**	**18800**
Utility C1500 LT	C16		**16175**	**18950**	**20225**
Utility C2500	C26	5447	**12400**	**14925**	**16075**
Utility C2500 LS	C26		**15700**	**18425**	**19675**
Utility C2500 LT	C26		**16975**	**19850**	**21150**
Utility K1500 (4WD)	K16	5123	**12775**	**15325**	**16500**
Utility K1500 LS (4WD)	K16		**16075**	**18825**	**20100**
Utility K1500 LT (4WD)	K16		**17350**	**20325**	**21650**
Utility K2500 (4WD)	K26	5760	**13575**	**16175**	**17375**
Utility K2500 LS (4WD)	K26		**16875**	**19700**	**21000**
Utility K2500 LT (4WD)	K26		**18150**	**21175**	**22525**
Add Z71 Off-Road Pkg. (LS 4WD)			**1450**	**1625**	**1625**
Add 8.1L V8 Engine			**375**	**425**	**425**
Add Aluminum/Alloy Wheels (Base)			**225**	**250**	**250**
Add Compact Disc Player (Std. LS, LT)			**100**	**125**	**125**
Add Leather Seats (Std. LT, Z71)			**375**	**425**	**425**
Add Power Sunroof			**475**	**550**	**550**
Add Rear Bucket Seats			**125**	**150**	**150**
Add Theft Recovery System			**50**	**75**	**75**
Deduct W/out 3rd Row Seat			**125**	**125**	**125**
Deduct W/out Air Conditioning			**600**	**600**	**600**
Deduct W/out Cruise Control			**150**	**150**	**150**
Deduct W/out Power Seat (Ex. Base)			**150**	**150**	**150**
Deduct W/out Running Boards (Ex. Base)			**75**	**75**	**75**
2001 VENTURE-V6					
Van 4D	U0/23	3746	**6100**	**7975**	**8900**
Extended Van 4D	X03	3900	**7050**	**9025**	**9875**
Extended Van 4D Warner Bros.	X13		**9750**	**11975**	**12900**
Add LS Trim (Ex. Warner Bros.)			**425**	**475**	**475**
Add LT Trim (Ex. Warner Bros.)			**975**	**1100**	**1100**
Add Aluminum/Alloy Wheels (Std. WB)			**175**	**200**	**200**
Add Compact Disc Player (Std. Warner Bros.)			**50**	**75**	**75**
Add Power Seat (Std. Warner Bros.)			**125**	**150**	**150**
Add Power Sliding Door (Std. Warner Bros.)			**225**	**250**	**250**
Add Rear Air Cond. (Std. Warner Bros.)			**125**	**150**	**150**
Add Rear Bucket Seats (Std. WB)			**125**	**150**	**150**
Add Theft Recovery System			**50**	**75**	**75**
Deduct W/out Cruise Control			**125**	**125**	**125**
Deduct W/out Power Windows			**125**	**125**	**125**
2001 ASTRO-1/2 Ton-V6					
Cargo Van	M19*	3915	**5875**	**7725**	**8650**
Van LS	M19*	4323	**7325**	**9350**	**10225**
Van LT	M19*	4323	**8150**	**10250**	**11175**
Add All Wheel Drive			**800**	**900**	**900**
Add Aluminum/Alloy Wheels (Std. LT)			**175**	**200**	**200**
Add Compact Disc Player (Std. LS, LT)			**50**	**75**	**75**
Add Leather Seats			**300**	**350**	**350**
Add Power Seat (Std. LT)			**125**	**150**	**150**
Add Rear Air Conditioning (Std. LT)			**125**	**150**	**150**
Add Rear Bucket Seats			**125**	**150**	**150**
Add Running Boards (LS, LT)			**75**	**100**	**100**
Add Theft Recovery System			**50**	**75**	**75**
Deduct W/out Cruise Control			**125**	**125**	**125**
Deduct W/out Power Door Locks			**100**	**100**	**100**

TRUCKS

SEE TRUCK OPTION PAGE FOR ADDITIONAL OPTIONS

BODY TYPE	Model No.	Weight	Trade-In	Retail	High Retail
Deduct W/out Power Windows			125	125	125
Deduct W/out Tilt Steering Wheel			100	100	100
* L as the 1st position of the model # denotes AWD					
2001 G1500-1/2 Ton-V8					
Cargo Van 135"	G15	4660	9250	11425	12450
Express Van 135"	G15	5062	10450	12725	13800
Express Van 135" LT	G65		13150	15725	16925
2001 G2500-3/4 Ton-V8					
Cargo Van 135"	G25	4850	9750	11975	13025
Extended Cargo Van 155"	G29	5052	10325	12575	13650
Express Van 135"	G25	5808	10950	13250	14350
Extended Express Van 155"	G29	6019	11650	14075	15200
2001 G3500-1 Ton-V8					
Cargo Van 135"	G35	5387	10250	12500	13550
Extended Cargo Van 155"	G39	5589	10825	13125	14200
Express Van 135"	G35	5947	11450	13875	15000
Extended Express Van 155"	G39	6158	12150	14650	15800
G SERIES VAN OPTIONS					
Add LS Trim (Ex. LT)			575	650	650
Add 15 Passenger Seating			125	150	150
Add 6.5L V8 Turbo Diesel Engine			1000	1125	1125
Add 8.1L V8 Engine			375	425	425
Add Aluminum/Alloy Wheels (Std. LT)			225	250	250
Add Compact Disc Player (Std. LT)			100	125	125
Add Leather Seats			375	425	425
Add Power Seat (Std. LT)			150	175	175
Add Rear Air Cond. (Std. LT, Ext. Express)			125	150	150
Add Theft Recovery System			50	75	75
Deduct V6 Engine			675	675	675
Deduct W/out Air Conditioning			600	600	600
Deduct W/out Cruise Control			150	150	150
Deduct W/out Power Door Locks			125	125	125
Deduct W/out Power Windows			150	150	150
Deduct W/out Tilt Steering Wheel			100	100	100
2001 S10 PICKUP-1/2 Ton-V6					
Fleetside	S14	3016	6050	7925	8750
Sportside	S14	3016	6300	8200	8950
Fleetside Extended Cab	S19*	3198	7650	9675	10400
Sportside Extended Cab	S19*	3198	7900	9950	10675
Crew Cab LS (4WD)	T13	4039	11950	14425	15200
Add LS Trim (Std. Crew)			400	450	450
Add Xtreme Pkg.			1000	1125	1125
Add ZR2 Wide Stance Pkg.			700	800	800
Add 4 Wheel Drive (Std. Crew)			2350	2575	2575
Add Aluminum/Alloy Wheels (Std. Crew)			175	200	200
Add Compact Disc Player (Std. Crew)			50	75	75
Add Cruise Control (Std. Crew)			125	150	150
Add Power Door Locks (Std. Crew)			100	125	125
Add Power Windows (Std. Crew)			125	150	150
Add Running Boards			75	100	100
Add Theft Recovery System			50	75	75
Add Tilt Steering Wheel (Std. Crew)			100	125	125
Deduct 4 Cyl. Engine			550	550	550
Deduct W/out 3rd Door (Ext. Cab)			200	200	200

TRUCKS

BODY TYPE	Model No.	Weight	Trade-In	Retail	High Retail
Deduct W/out Air Conditioning			550	550	550
Deduct W/out Automatic Trans.			425	425	425

* T as the 1st position of the model # denotes 4WD

2001 SILVERADO C1500 PICKUP-1/2 Ton-V8

BODY TYPE	Model No.	Weight	Trade-In	Retail	High Retail
Fleetside	C14*	4058	9925	12150	13200
Sportside	C14*	4058	10425	12700	13775
Fleetside Extended Cab	C19*	4413	12025	14500	15650
Sportside Extended Cab	C19*	4413	12525	15050	16225
2001 SILVERADO C1500 HD PICKUP-1/2 Ton-V8					
Fleetside Crew Cab LS	C13*		14625	17275	18500
Fleetside Crew Cab LT	C13*		15700	18425	19675
2001 SILVERADO C2500 LD PICKUP-3/4 Ton-V8					
Fleetside	C24*	4995	10725	13025	14100
Fleet Extended Cab (4WD)	K29	5508	15175	17875	19125
2001 SILVERADO C2500 HD PICKUP-3/4 Ton-V8					
Fleetside	C24*	5171	11725	14150	15275
Fleetside Extended Cab	C29*	5236	14575	17225	18450
Fleetside Crew Cab	C23*	5585	15975	18725	20000
2001 SILVERADO C3500 PICKUP-1 Ton-V8-Dual Rear Wheels					
Fleetside	C34*	5647	12325	14825	15975
Fleetside Extended Cab	C39*	5997	15175	17875	19125
Fleetside Crew Cab	C33*	6216	16575	19375	20675
SILVERADO PICKUP OPTIONS					
Add LS Trim (Ex. 1500 HD)			600	675	675
Add LT Trim (Ex. 1500 HD)			1100	1225	1225
Add Z71 Off-Road Pkg. (4WD)			200	225	225
Add 4 Wheel Drive (Std. 2500 LD Extended)			2350	2575	2575
Add 6.6L V8 Turbo Diesel Engine			4300	4525	4525
Add 8.1L V8 Engine			850	950	950
Add Aluminum/Alloy Wheels (Std. 1500 HD)			225	250	250
Add Compact Disc Player (Std. 1500 HD)			100	125	125
Add Leather Seats (Std. 1500 HD LT)			375	425	425
Add Power Seat (Std. 1500 HD LT)			150	175	175
Add Running Boards			75	100	100
Add Theft Recovery System			50	75	75
Deduct V6 Engine			675	675	675
Deduct W/out Air Conditioning			600	600	600
Deduct W/out Automatic Trans.			475	475	475
Deduct W/out Cruise Control			150	150	150
Deduct W/out Power Door Locks			125	125	125

* K as the 1st position of the model # denotes 4WD

CHEVROLET

2000 TRACKER-4 Cyl.-4WD

BODY TYPE	Model No.	Weight	Trade-In	Retail	High Retail
Convertible 2D (2WD)	E18	2602	3775	5375	6125
Convertible 2D	J18	2723	4775	6525	7325
Hardtop 4D (2WD)	E13	2866	4575	6275	7075
Hardtop 4D	J13	2987	5575	7400	8200
Add Aluminum/Alloy Wheels			100	125	125
Add Compact Disc Player			50	75	75
Add Cruise Control			75	100	100
Add Power Door Locks			50	75	75
Add Power Windows			75	100	100
Add Tilt Steering Wheel			50	75	75
Deduct 1.6L Engine			150	150	150

SEE TRUCK OPTION PAGE FOR ADDITIONAL OPTIONS

Yes! Sign me up for a one-year subscription, 4 quarterly issues, of the Consumer Edition of the N.A.D.A. Official Used Car Guide® for just $29.95*.

____
Name

____
Company

____
Address

____
City/State/Zip

____
Email

____
Phone

____
Fax

Please begin my subscription with the:

❑ Winter ❑ Spring ❑ Summer ❑ Fall

*29.95 offer for new subscribers

PAYMENT INFORMATION ⟶

PAYMENT OPTIONS

❑ Check or Money Order Enclosed for $29.95

CREDIT CARD

❑ Visa ❑ MasterCard
❑ American Express ❑ Discover

Card No.

Expiration Date

Name on Card

Signature

Complete this form and mail to:

N.A.D.A. Official Used Car Guide® Company
c/o Consumer Guide
8400 Westpark Drive
McLean, VA 22102

For immediate service call toll-free:

(1-866-GET-NADA) / 1-866-438-6232
Fax: 703-821-7269

BODY TYPE	Model No.	Weight	Trade-In	Retail	High Retail
Deduct W/out Air Conditioning			375	375	375
Deduct W/out Automatic Trans.			300	300	300
2000 BLAZER-1/2 Ton-V6					
Tailgate 2D LS	S18	3518	5575	7375	8275
Tailgate 4D LS	S13	3671	6025	7875	8800
Tailgate 2D LS (4WD)	T18	3848	6375	8300	9150
Tailgate 4D LS (4WD)	T13	4049	6825	8775	9675
Add LT Trim			500	575	575
Add TrailBlazer Trim			550	625	625
Add ZR2 Wide Stance Pkg.			625	700	700
Add Bose Stereo System			100	125	125
Add Compact Disc Player			50	75	75
Add Leather Seats			250	300	300
Add Power Seat			100	125	125
Add Power Sunroof			375	425	425
Deduct W/out Automatic Trans.			375	375	375
Deduct W/out Cruise Control			100	100	100
Deduct W/out Power Door Locks			75	75	75
Deduct W/out Power Windows			100	100	100
Deduct W/out Tilt Steering Wheel			75	75	75
2000 TAHOE-1/2 Ton-V8					
Utility 4D Limited	C13	4828	11900	14350	15475
Utility 4D Z71 (4WD)	K13	5250	13175	15725	16925
2000 NEW TAHOE-1/2 Ton-V8					
Utility 4D	C13	4828	9150	11300	12325
Utility 4D LS	C13		12950	15500	16675
Utility 4D (4WD)	K13	5050	10150	12400	13450
Utility 4D LS (4WD)	K13		13950	16575	17800
NEW TAHOE OPTIONS					
Add LT Trim (LS)			700	800	800
Add Aluminum/Alloy Wheels (Base)			175	200	200
Add Compact Disc Player (Std. LS, LT)			75	100	100
Add Leather Seats			325	375	375
Add Power Sunroof			425	475	475
Deduct W/out 3rd Row Seat (Ex. Base)			100	100	100
Deduct W/out Air Conditioning			550	550	550
Deduct W/out Cruise Control			125	125	125
Deduct W/out Power Seat (Ex. Base)			125	125	125
Deduct W/out Running Boards (Ex. Base)			50	50	50
2000 SUBURBAN-1/2-3/4 Ton-V8					
Utility C1500	C16	4934	10275	12525	13600
Utility C1500 LS	C16		13075	15625	16800
Utility C1500 LT	C16		14200	16825	18050
Utility C2500	C26	5447	11025	13375	14475
Utility C2500 LS	C26		13825	16425	17650
Utility C2500 LT	C26		14950	17625	18850
Utility K1500 (4WD)	K16	5123	11275	13675	14775
Utility K1500 LS (4WD)	K16		14075	16700	17925
Utility K1500 LT (4WD)	K16		15200	17900	19150
Utility K2500 (4WD)	K26	5760	12025	14475	15625
Utility K2500 LS (4WD)	K26		14825	17500	18725
Utility K2500 LT (4WD)	K26		15950	18700	19975
Add Aluminum/Alloy Wheels (Base)			175	200	200

TRUCKS

BODY TYPE	Model No.	Weight	Trade-In	Retail	High Retail
Add Compact Disc Player (Std. LS, LT)			75	100	100
Add Leather Seats (Std. LT)			325	375	375
Add Power Sunroof			425	475	475
Add Rear Bucket Seats			100	125	125
Deduct W/out 3rd Row Seat			100	100	100
Deduct W/out Air Conditioning			550	550	550
Deduct W/out Cruise Control			125	125	125
Deduct W/out Power Seat (Ex. Base)			125	125	125
Deduct W/out Running Boards (Ex. Base)			50	50	50
2000 VENTURE-V6					
Extended Cargo Van 4D	X03	3688	4100	5750	6600
Van 4D	U0/23	3699	4650	6375	7250
Extended Van 4D	X03	3838	5500	7300	8175
Extended Van 4D Warner Bros.	X13		7300	9300	10175
Add LS Trim (Ex. Warner Bros.)			400	450	450
Add LT Trim (Ex. Warner Bros.)			875	975	975
Add Aluminum/Alloy Wheels (Std. WB)			125	150	150
Add Compact Disc Player (Std. Warner Bros.)			50	75	75
Add Power Seat (Std. Warner Bros.)			100	125	125
Add Power Sliding Door			200	225	225
Add Rear Air Cond. (Std. Warner Bros.)			100	125	125
Add Rear Bucket Seats (Std. WB)			100	125	125
Deduct W/out Cruise Control			100	100	100
Deduct W/out Power Windows			100	100	100
2000 ASTRO-1/2 Ton-V6					
Cargo Van	M19*	3887	4950	6700	7625
Van	M19*	4186	6075	7950	8875
Add LS Trim			500	575	575
Add LT Trim			850	950	950
Add All Wheel Drive			700	800	800
Add Aluminum/Alloy Wheels			125	150	150
Add Compact Disc Player			50	75	75
Add Leather Seats			250	300	300
Add Power Seat			100	125	125
Add Rear Air Conditioning			100	125	125
Add Rear Bucket Seats			100	125	125
Add Running Boards (Ex. Cargo)			50	75	75
Deduct W/out Air Conditioning			500	500	500
Deduct W/out Cruise Control			100	100	100
Deduct W/out Power Door Locks			75	75	75
Deduct W/out Power Windows			100	100	100
Deduct W/out Tilt Steering Wheel			75	75	75
* L as the 1st position of the model # denotes AWD					
2000 G1500-1/2 Ton-V8					
Cargo Van 135"	G15	4660	7725	9775	10825
Express Van 135"	G15	5142	8875	11025	12025
2000 G2500-3/4 Ton-V8					
Cargo Van 135"	G25	4850	8175	10275	11300
Extended Cargo Van 155"	G29	5052	8725	10875	11925
Express Van 135"	G25	5823	9325	11525	12550
Extended Express Van 155"	G29	6045	9975	12225	13275
2000 G3500-1 Ton-V8					
Cargo Van 135"	G35	5387	8625	10750	11800
Extended Cargo Van 155"	G39	5589	9175	11350	12375

TRUCKS

SEE TRUCK OPTION PAGE FOR ADDITIONAL OPTIONS

BODY TYPE	Model No.	Weight	Trade-In	Retail	High Retail
Express Van 135"	G35	5987	**9775**	**12000**	**13050**
Extended Express Van 155"	G39	6208	**10425**	**12700**	**13775**
G SERIES VAN OPTIONS					
Add LS Trim			**550**	**625**	**625**
Add 15 Passenger Seating			**100**	**125**	**125**
Add 6.5L V8 Turbo Diesel Engine			**900**	**1000**	**1000**
Add 7.4L V8 Engine			**300**	**350**	**350**
Add Aluminum/Alloy Wheels			**175**	**200**	**200**
Add Compact Disc Player			**75**	**100**	**100**
Add Power Seat			**125**	**150**	**150**
Add Rear Air Cond. (Std. Ext. Express)			**100**	**125**	**125**
Deduct V6 Engine			**600**	**600**	**600**
Deduct W/out Air Conditioning			**550**	**550**	**550**
Deduct W/out Cruise Control			**125**	**125**	**125**
Deduct W/out Power Door Locks			**100**	**100**	**100**
Deduct W/out Power Windows			**125**	**125**	**125**
Deduct W/out Tilt Steering Wheel			**75**	**75**	**75**
2000 S10 PICKUP-1/2 Ton-V6					
Fleetside	S14*	3015	**5050**	**6800**	**7625**
Sportside	S14*	3015	**5275**	**7050**	**7825**
Fleetside Extended Cab	S19*	3216	**6550**	**8475**	**9225**
Sportside Extended Cab	S19*	3216	**6775**	**8725**	**9500**
Add LS Trim			**350**	**400**	**400**
Add Xtreme Pkg.			**800**	**900**	**900**
Add ZR2 Wide Stance Pkg.			**625**	**700**	**700**
Add 4 Wheel Drive			**2000**	**2225**	**2225**
Add Aluminum/Alloy Wheels			**125**	**150**	**150**
Add Compact Disc Player			**50**	**75**	**75**
Add Cruise Control			**100**	**125**	**125**
Add Power Door Locks			**75**	**100**	**100**
Add Power Windows			**100**	**125**	**125**
Add Running Boards			**50**	**75**	**75**
Add Tilt Steering Wheel			**75**	**100**	**100**
Deduct 4 Cyl. Engine			**500**	**500**	**500**
Deduct W/out 3rd Door (Ext. Cab)			**175**	**175**	**175**
Deduct W/out Air Conditioning			**500**	**500**	**500**
Deduct W/out Automatic Trans.			**375**	**375**	**375**
* T as the 1st position of the model # denotes 4WD					
2000 CLASSIC C2500 PICKUP-3/4 Ton-V8					
Fleetside	C24*	4292	**8475**	**10575**	**11625**
Fleetside Extended Cab	C29*		**10275**	**12525**	**13600**
Fleetside Crew Cab	C23*	5416	**10875**	**13175**	**14275**
2000 C3500 PICKUP-1 Ton-5.7L V8					
Fleetside	C34*	4870	**9175**	**11350**	**12375**
Fleetside Extended Cab	C39*	5458	**11550**	**13975**	**15100**
Fleetside Crew Cab	C33*		**11575**	**14000**	**15125**
2000 SILVERADO C1500 PICKUP-1/2 Ton-V8					
Fleetside	C14*	3923	**8475**	**10575**	**11625**
Sportside	C14*	3923	**8925**	**11075**	**12075**
Fleetside Extended Cab	C19*	4235	**10525**	**12800**	**13875**
Sportside Extended Cab	C19*	4235	**10975**	**13300**	**14400**
2000 SILVERADO C2500 PICKUP-3/4 Ton-6.0L V8					
Fleetside	C24*	4586	**9175**	**11350**	**12375**
HD Fleetside	C24*		**9375**	**11550**	**12575**

TRUCKS

BODY TYPE	Model No.	Weight	Trade-In	Retail	High Retail
Fleetside Extended Cab	C29*	4766	**11225**	**13625**	**14725**
C SERIES/SILVERADO PICKUP OPTIONS					
Add LS Trim			**550**	**625**	**625**
Add LT Trim			**950**	**1075**	**1075**
Add Z71 Off-Road Pkg. (4WD)			**150**	**175**	**175**
Add 4 Wheel Drive			**2000**	**2225**	**2225**
Add 6.5L V8 Turbo Diesel Engine			**900**	**1000**	**1000**
Add 7.4L V8 Engine			**300**	**350**	**350**
Add Aluminum/Alloy Wheels			**175**	**200**	**200**
Add Compact Disc Player			**75**	**100**	**100**
Add Dual Rear Whls (Std. 3500 Extended)			**575**	**650**	**650**
Add Leather Seats			**325**	**375**	**375**
Add Power Seat			**125**	**150**	**150**
Add Running Boards			**50**	**75**	**75**
Deduct V6 Engine			**600**	**600**	**600**
Deduct W/out 4th Door (Silverado Ext.)			**275**	**275**	**275**
Deduct W/out 6.0L V8 (Silverado 2500)			**450**	**450**	**450**
Deduct W/out Air Conditioning			**550**	**550**	**550**
Deduct W/out Automatic Trans.			**425**	**425**	**425**
Deduct W/out Cruise Control			**125**	**125**	**125**
Deduct W/out Power Door Locks			**100**	**100**	**100**
Deduct W/out Tilt Steering Wheel			**75**	**75**	**75**

* K as the 1st position of the model # denotes 4WD

CHEVROLET

1999 TRACKER-4 Cyl.-4WD

BODY TYPE	Model No.	Weight	Trade-In	Retail	High Retail
Convertible 2D (2WD)	E18	2596	**2875**	**4350**	**5100**
Convertible 2D	J18	2717	**3950**	**5600**	**6375**
Hardtop 4D (2WD)	E13	2860	**3625**	**5200**	**5925**
Hardtop 4D	J13	2891	**4700**	**6425**	**7225**
Add Aluminum/Alloy Wheels			**50**	**75**	**75**
Add Cruise Control			**50**	**75**	**75**
Add Power Windows			**50**	**75**	**75**
Deduct 1.6L Engine			**125**	**125**	**125**
Deduct W/out Air Conditioning			**325**	**325**	**325**
Deduct W/out Automatic Trans.			**250**	**250**	**250**

1999 BLAZER-1/2 Ton-V6

BODY TYPE	Model No.	Weight	Trade-In	Retail	High Retail
Tailgate 2D	S18	3518	**4350**	**6025**	**6875**
Tailgate 4D	S13	3671	**4875**	**6625**	**7525**
Tailgate 2D (4WD)	T18	3848	**5125**	**6875**	**7800**
Tailgate 4D (4WD)	T13	4049	**5650**	**7450**	**8350**
Add LS Trim			**475**	**550**	**550**
Add LT Trim			**825**	**925**	**925**
Add TrailBlazer Trim			**875**	**975**	**975**
Add ZR2 Wide Stance Pkg.			**525**	**600**	**600**
Add Aluminum/Alloy Wheels			**75**	**100**	**100**
Add Bose Stereo System			**75**	**100**	**100**
Add Leather Seats			**225**	**250**	**250**
Add Power Seat			**75**	**100**	**100**
Add Power Sunroof			**325**	**375**	**375**
Deduct W/out Automatic Trans.			**325**	**325**	**325**
Deduct W/out Cruise Control			**75**	**75**	**75**
Deduct W/out Power Door Locks			**50**	**50**	**50**
Deduct W/out Power Windows			**75**	**75**	**75**
Deduct W/out Tilt Steering Wheel			**50**	**50**	**50**

TRUCKS

SEE TRUCK OPTION PAGE FOR ADDITIONAL OPTIONS

BODY TYPE	Model No.	Weight	Trade-In	Retail	High Retail
1999 TAHOE-1/2 Ton-V8					
Utility 2D	C18	4525	6825	8775	9825
Utility 2D LS	C18		7625	9675	10725
Utility 4D LS	C13	4876	8175	10275	11300
Utility 2D (4WD)	K18	4869	7650	9700	10750
Utility 2D LS (4WD)	K18		8450	10575	11625
Utility 4D LS (4WD)	K13	5279	9000	11175	12200
Add Limited Trim (4D 2WD)			675	750	750
Add LT Trim (LS)			600	675	675
Add Z71 Off-Road (4D 4WD)			850	950	950
Add 6.5L V8 Turbo Diesel Engine			800	900	900
Add Aluminum/Alloy Wheels (Base)			125	150	150
Add Leather Seats			275	325	325
Add Rear Air Conditioning			75	100	100
Deduct W/out Air Conditioning			500	500	500
Deduct W/out Cruise Control			100	100	100
Deduct W/out Tilt Steering Wheel			50	50	50
1999 SUBURBAN-1/2-3/4 Ton-V8					
Utility C1500	C16	4825	6950	8925	9975
Utility C1500 LS	C16		8300	10425	11450
Utility C1500 LT	C16		9175	11375	12400
Utility C2500	C26	5249	7500	9525	10550
Utility C2500 LS	C26		8850	11000	12075
Utility C2500 LT	C26		9725	11950	13000
Utility K1500 (4WD)	K16	5297	7775	9825	10875
Utility K1500 LS (4WD)	K16		9125	11300	12325
Utility K1500 LT (4WD)	K16		10000	12250	13300
Utility K2500 (4WD)	K26	5574	8325	10425	11450
Utility K2500 LS (4WD)	K26		9675	11900	12950
Utility K2500 LT (4WD)	K26		10550	12825	13900
Add 6.5L V8 Turbo Diesel Engine			800	900	900
Add 7.4L V8 Engine			275	325	325
Add Aluminum/Alloy Wheels (Base)			125	150	150
Add Rear Air Cond. (Std. LS, LT)			75	100	100
Deduct W/out 3rd Row Seat			100	100	100
Deduct W/out Air Conditioning			500	500	500
Deduct W/out Cruise Control			100	100	100
Deduct W/out Tilt Steering Wheel			50	50	50
1999 VENTURE-V6					
Extended Cargo Van 4D	X03	3688	3325	4875	5775
Van 3D	U06	3699	3650	5225	6025
Van 4D	U03	3699	3875	5475	6300
Extended Van 4D	X03	3838	4675	6375	7250
Add LS Trim			375	425	425
Add LT Trim			825	925	925
Add Aluminum/Alloy Wheels			75	100	100
Add Power Seat			75	100	100
Add Power Sliding Door			175	200	200
Add Rear Air Conditioning			75	100	100
Add Rear Bucket Seats			75	100	100
Deduct W/out Cruise Control			75	75	75
Deduct W/out Power Windows			75	75	75
1999 ASTRO-1/2 Ton-V6					
Cargo Van	M19*	3887	4075	5725	6575

TRUCKS

BODY TYPE	Model No.	Weight	Trade-In	Retail	High Retail
Van	M19*	4186	**5200**	**6975**	**7925**
Add LS Trim			**450**	**500**	**500**
Add LT Trim			**750**	**850**	**850**
Add All Wheel Drive			**600**	**675**	**675**
Add Aluminum/Alloy Wheels			**75**	**100**	**100**
Add Leather Seats			**225**	**250**	**250**
Add Power Seat			**75**	**100**	**100**
Add Rear Air Conditioning			**75**	**100**	**100**
Add Rear Bucket Seats			**75**	**100**	**100**
Deduct W/out Air Conditioning			**450**	**450**	**450**
Deduct W/out Cruise Control			**75**	**75**	**75**
Deduct W/out Power Door Locks			**50**	**50**	**50**
Deduct W/out Power Windows			**75**	**75**	**75**
Deduct W/out Tilt Steering Wheel			**50**	**50**	**50**
* L as the 1st position of the model # denotes AWD					
1999 G1500-1/2 Ton-V8					
Cargo Van 135"	G15	4660	**6825**	**8775**	**9825**
Express Van 135"	G15	5142	**7925**	**9975**	**11025**
1999 G2500-3/4 Ton-V8					
Cargo Van 135"	G25	4850	**7225**	**9225**	**10225**
Extended Cargo Van 155"	G29	5052	**7750**	**9800**	**10850**
Express Van 135"	G25	5823	**8325**	**10425**	**11450**
Extended Express Van 155"	G29	6045	**8925**	**11075**	**12075**
1999 G3500-1 Ton-V8					
Cargo Van 135"	G35	5387	**7625**	**9650**	**10700**
Extended Cargo Van 155"	G39	5589	**8150**	**10225**	**11250**
Express Van 135"	G35	5987	**8725**	**10850**	**11900**
Extended Express Van 155"	G39	6208	**9325**	**11500**	**12525**
G SERIES VAN OPTIONS					
Add LS Trim			**525**	**600**	**600**
Add 15 Passenger Seating			**100**	**125**	**125**
Add 6.5L V8 Turbo Diesel Engine			**800**	**900**	**900**
Add 7.4L V8 Engine			**275**	**325**	**325**
Add Aluminum/Alloy Wheels			**125**	**150**	**150**
Add Power Seat			**100**	**125**	**125**
Add Rear Air Cond. (Std. Ext. Express)			**75**	**100**	**100**
Deduct V6 Engine			**500**	**500**	**500**
Deduct W/out Air Conditioning			**500**	**500**	**500**
Deduct W/out Cruise Control			**100**	**100**	**100**
Deduct W/out Power Door Locks			**75**	**75**	**75**
Deduct W/out Power Windows			**100**	**100**	**100**
Deduct W/out Tilt Steering Wheel			**50**	**50**	**50**
1999 S10 PICKUP-1/2 Ton-V6					
Fleetside	S14*	3031	**4275**	**5950**	**6750**
Sportside	S14*	3031	**4475**	**6175**	**6950**
Fleetside Extended Cab	S19*	3240	**5700**	**7525**	**8325**
Sportside Extended Cab	S19*	3240	**5900**	**7725**	**8550**
Add LS Trim (Std. S19)			**300**	**350**	**350**
Add Xtreme Pkg.			**600**	**675**	**675**
Add ZR2 Wide Stance Pkg.			**525**	**600**	**600**
Add 4 Wheel Drive			**1800**	**2000**	**2000**
Add Aluminum/Alloy Wheels			**75**	**100**	**100**
Add Cruise Control			**75**	**100**	**100**
Add Power Door Locks			**50**	**75**	**75**

TRUCKS

SEE TRUCK OPTION PAGE FOR ADDITIONAL OPTIONS

BODY TYPE	Model No.	Weight	Trade-In	Retail	High Retail
Add Power Windows			75	100	100
Add Tilt Steering Wheel			50	75	75
Deduct 4 Cyl. Engine			450	450	450
Deduct W/out 3rd Door (Ext. Cab)			100	100	100
Deduct W/out Air Conditioning			450	450	450
Deduct W/out Automatic Trans.			325	325	325
* T as the 1st position of the model # denotes 4WD					
1999 CLASSIC C1500 PICKUP-1/2 Ton-V8					
Fleetside Extended Cab LS	C19*	4145	8550	10675	11725
1999 CLASSIC C2500 PICKUP-3/4 Ton-V8					
Fleetside	C24*		7150	9150	10150
Fleetside Extended Cab	C29*		8650	10775	11825
Fleetside Crew Cab	C23*		9350	11550	12575
1999 C3500 PICKUP-1 Ton-5.7L V8					
Fleetside	C34*		7850	9900	10950
Fleetside Extended Cab	C39*		9875	12100	13150
Fleetside Crew Cab	C33*	5509	10050	12300	13350
1999 SILVERADO C1500 PICKUP-1/2 Ton-V8					
Fleetside	C14*	3923	7650	9700	10750
Sportside	C14*		8050	10125	11150
Fleetside Extended Cab	C19*	4235	9600	11825	12875
Sportside Extended Cab	C19*		10000	12250	13300
1999 SILVERADO C2500 PICKUP-3/4 Ton-6.0L V8					
Fleetside	C24*	4586	8350	10475	11525
HD Fleetside	C24*	4911	8500	10625	11675
Fleetside Extended Cab	C29*	4766	10300	12575	13650
C SERIES/SILVERADO PICKUP OPTIONS					
Add LS Trim (Std. Classic C1500)			500	575	575
Add LT Trim			850	950	950
Add Z71 Off-Road Pkg. (4WD)			100	125	125
Add 4 Wheel Drive			1800	2000	2000
Add 6.5L V8 Turbo Diesel Engine			800	900	900
Add 7.4L V8 Engine			275	325	325
Add Aluminum/Alloy Wheels			125	150	150
Add Dual Rear Whls (Std. 3500 Extended)			525	600	600
Add Leather Seats			275	325	325
Add Power Seat			100	125	125
Deduct V6 Engine			500	500	500
Deduct W/out 6.0L V8 (Silverado 2500)			400	400	400
Deduct W/out Air Conditioning			500	500	500
Deduct W/out Automatic Trans.			375	375	375
Deduct W/out Cruise Control			100	100	100
Deduct W/out Power Door Locks			75	75	75
Deduct W/out Tilt Steering Wheel			50	50	50
* K as the 1st position of the model # denotes 4WD					
CHEVROLET					
1998 TRACKER-4 Cyl.-5 Spd.-4WD					
Convertible 2D (2WD)	E18	2339	2150	3525	4175
Convertible 2D	J18	2555	3150	4675	5450
Hardtop 4D (2WD)	E13	2747	2650	4100	4825
Hardtop 4D	J13	2747	3650	5250	5975
Add Automatic Trans.			200	225	225
Add Cruise Control			50	75	75
Add Power Windows			50	75	75

TRUCKS

BODY TYPE	Model No.	Weight	Trade-In	Retail	High Retail
Deduct W/out Air Conditioning			**275**	**275**	**275**
1998 BLAZER-1/2 Ton-V6					
Tailgate 2D	S18	3515	**3625**	**5225**	**6025**
Tailgate 4D	S13	3685	**4225**	**5900**	**6775**
Tailgate 2D (4WD)	T18	3874	**4325**	**6000**	**6875**
Tailgate 4D (4WD)	T13	4046	**4925**	**6675**	**7600**
Add LS Trim			**400**	**450**	**450**
Add LT Trim			**700**	**800**	**800**
Add ZR2 Wide Stance Pkg.			**450**	**500**	**500**
Add Aluminum/Alloy Wheels			**50**	**75**	**75**
Add Leather Seats			**175**	**200**	**200**
Add Power Seat			**50**	**75**	**75**
Add Power Sunroof			**275**	**325**	**325**
Deduct W/out Automatic Trans.			**275**	**275**	**275**
Deduct W/out Cruise Control			**50**	**50**	**50**
Deduct W/out Power Windows			**50**	**50**	**50**
1998 TAHOE-1/2 Ton-V8					
Utility 2D	C18	4632	**5925**	**7750**	**8800**
Utility 2D LS	C18		**6750**	**8675**	**9725**
Utility 4D LS	C13	4423	**7150**	**9125**	**10125**
Utility 2D (4WD)	K18	4952	**6600**	**8525**	**9550**
Utility 2D LS (4WD)	K18		**7425**	**9450**	**10475**
Utility 4D LS (4WD)	K13	4865	**7825**	**9875**	**10925**
Add LT Trim (LS)			**550**	**625**	**625**
Add 6.5L V8 Turbo Diesel Engine			**700**	**800**	**800**
Add Aluminum/Alloy Wheels (Base)			**100**	**125**	**125**
Add Leather Seats			**225**	**250**	**250**
Add Rear Air Conditioning			**50**	**75**	**75**
Deduct W/out Air Conditioning			**450**	**450**	**450**
Deduct W/out Cruise Control			**75**	**75**	**75**
Deduct W/out Tilt Steering Wheel			**50**	**50**	**50**
1998 SUBURBAN-1/2-3/4 Ton-V8					
Utility C1500	C16	4825	**6600**	**8525**	**9550**
Utility C1500 LS	C16		**7275**	**9275**	**10300**
Utility C1500 LT	C16		**8050**	**10100**	**11125**
Utility C2500	C26	5249	**7150**	**9125**	**10125**
Utility C2500 LS	C26		**7825**	**9875**	**10925**
Utility C2500 LT	C26		**8600**	**10725**	**11775**
Utility K1500 (4WD)	K16	5293	**7275**	**9275**	**10300**
Utility K1500 LS (4WD)	K16		**7950**	**10025**	**11050**
Utility K1500 LT (4WD)	K16		**8725**	**10875**	**11925**
Utility K2500 (4WD)	K26	5694	**7825**	**9875**	**10925**
Utility K2500 LS (4WD)	K26		**8500**	**10625**	**11675**
Utility K2500 LT (4WD)	K26		**9275**	**11475**	**12500**
Add 6.5L V8 Turbo Diesel Engine			**700**	**800**	**800**
Add 7.4L V8 Engine			**250**	**300**	**300**
Add Aluminum/Alloy Wheels (Base)			**100**	**125**	**125**
Add Rear Air Cond. (Std. LS, LT)			**50**	**75**	**75**
Deduct W/out 3rd Row Seat			**100**	**100**	**100**
Deduct W/out Air Conditioning			**450**	**450**	**450**
Deduct W/out Cruise Control			**75**	**75**	**75**
Deduct W/out Tilt Steering Wheel			**50**	**50**	**50**

TRUCKS

SEE TRUCK OPTION PAGE FOR ADDITIONAL OPTIONS

BODY TYPE	Model No.	Weight	Trade-In	Retail	High Retail
1998 VENTURE-V6					
Extended Cargo Van 3D	X06	3688	2650	4075	4875
Extended Cargo Van 4D	X03	3688	2850	4325	5150
Van 3D	U06	3699	3275	4825	5725
Van 4D	U03	3699	3475	5050	5850
Extended Van 3D	X06	3838	3875	5500	6325
Extended Van 4D	X03	3838	4075	5725	6575
Add LS Trim			350	400	400
Add Aluminum/Alloy Wheels			50	75	75
Add Power Seat			50	75	75
Add Power Sliding Door			150	175	175
Add Rear Air Conditioning			50	75	75
Add Rear Bucket Seats			50	75	75
Deduct W/out Cruise Control			50	50	50
Deduct W/out Power Windows			50	50	50
1998 ASTRO-1/2 Ton-V6					
Cargo Van	M19*	4197	3575	5175	5975
Van	M19*	4427	4650	6375	7250
Add LS Trim			350	400	400
Add LT Trim			600	675	675
Add 3rd Row Seat			100	125	125
Add All Wheel Drive			500	575	575
Add Aluminum/Alloy Wheels			50	75	75
Add Leather Seats			175	200	200
Add Power Seat			50	75	75
Add Rear Air Conditioning			50	75	75
Add Rear Bucket Seats			50	75	75
Deduct W/out Air Conditioning			400	400	400
Deduct W/out Cruise Control			50	50	50
Deduct W/out Power Windows			50	50	50
* L as the 1st position of the model # denotes AWD					
1998 G1500-1/2 Ton-V8					
Chevy Van 135"	G15	4654	5925	7775	8825
Express Van 135"	G15	5075	7025	9000	10050
1998 G2500-3/4 Ton-V8					
Chevy Van 135"	G25	4829	6275	8175	9175
Extended Chevy Van 155"	G29	4983	6775	8725	9775
Express Van 135"	G25	5803	7375	9375	10400
Extended Express Van 155"	G29	6008	7875	9925	10975
1998 G3500-1 Ton-V8					
Chevy Van 135"	G35	5434	6625	8550	9575
Extended Chevy Van 155"	G39	5609	7125	9125	10125
Express Van 135"	G35	5937	7725	9775	10825
Extended Express Van 155"	G39	6142	8225	10325	11350
G SERIES VAN OPTIONS					
Add LS Trim			500	575	575
Add 15 Passenger Seating			100	125	125
Add 6.5L V8 Turbo Diesel Engine			700	800	800
Add 7.4L V8 Engine			250	300	300
Add Aluminum/Alloy Wheels			100	125	125
Add Power Seat			75	100	100
Add Rear Air Conditioning			50	75	75
Deduct V6 Engine			400	400	400
Deduct W/out Air Conditioning			450	450	450

TRUCKS

BODY TYPE	Model No.	Weight	Trade-In	Retail	High Retail
Deduct W/out Cruise Control			75	75	75
Deduct W/out Power Door Locks			50	50	50
Deduct W/out Power Windows			75	75	75
Deduct W/out Tilt Steering Wheel			50	50	50
1998 S10 PICKUP-1/2 Ton-V6					
Fleetside	S14*	3003	3725	5325	6075
Sportside	S14*	3003	3900	5525	6275
Fleetside Extended Cab	S19*	3222	5125	6900	7750
Sportside Extended Cab	S19*	3222	5300	7075	7850
Add LS Trim (Std. S19)			250	300	300
Add SS Trim			300	350	350
Add ZR2 Wide Stance Pkg.			450	500	500
Add 4 Wheel Drive			1600	1800	1800
Add Aluminum/Alloy Wheels			50	75	75
Add Cruise Control			50	75	75
Add Power Windows			50	75	75
Deduct 4 Cyl. Engine			350	350	350
Deduct W/out 3rd Door (Ext. Cab)			75	75	75
Deduct W/out Air Conditioning			400	400	400
Deduct W/out Automatic Trans.			275	275	275
* T as the 1st position of the model # denotes 4WD					
1998 C1500 PICKUP-1/2 Ton-V8					
Sportside	C14*	3876	6550	8475	9500
Fleetside	C14*	3876	6200	8075	9075
Fleetside Extended Cab	C19*	4145	7475	9500	10525
Sportside Extended Cab	C19*	4145	8025	10100	11125
1998 C2500 PICKUP-3/4 Ton-V8					
Fleetside	C24*	4292	6800	8750	9800
HD Fleetside	C24*	5107	6925	8875	9925
Fleetside Extended Cab	C29*	4432	8075	10150	11175
HD Fleetside Extended Cab	C29*	5107	8200	10300	11325
1998 C3500 PICKUP-1 Ton-V8					
Fleetside	C34*	4681	7500	9525	10550
Fleetside Extended Cab	C39*	5458	9250	11425	12450
Fleetside Crew Cab	C33*	5488	9325	11500	12525
C SERIES PICKUP OPTIONS					
Add Silverado Trim			400	450	450
Add 4 Wheel Drive			1600	1800	1800
Add 6.5L V8 Turbo Diesel Engine			700	800	800
Add 7.4L V8 Engine			250	300	300
Add Aluminum/Alloy Wheels			100	125	125
Add Dual Rear Wheels (Std. 3500 Ext.)			475	550	550
Add Leather Seats			225	250	250
Add Power Seat			75	100	100
Add Third Door (Std. Sportside)			200	225	225
Deduct Work Truck Pkg.			1375	1375	1375
Deduct V6 Engine (Ex. WT)			400	400	400
Deduct W/out Air Conditioning			450	450	450
Deduct W/out Automatic Trans.			325	325	325
Deduct W/out Cruise Control (Ex. WT)			75	75	75
Deduct W/out Power Door Locks (Ex. WT)			50	50	50
Deduct W/out Tilt Steering Wheel (Ex. WT)			50	50	50
* K as the 1st position of the model # denotes 4WD					

TRUCKS

SEE TRUCK OPTION PAGE FOR ADDITIONAL OPTIONS

BODY TYPE	Model No.	Weight	Trade-In	Retail	High Retail
CHEVROLET					
1997 BLAZER-1/2 Ton-V6					
Tailgate 2D	S18	3515	**3100**	**4625**	**5500**
Tailgate 4D	S13	3686	**3400**	**4950**	**5850**
Tailgate 2D (4WD)	T18	3880	**3700**	**5300**	**6125**
Tailgate 4D (4WD)	T13	4046	**4000**	**5625**	**6475**
Add LS Trim			**350**	**400**	**400**
Add LT Trim			**600**	**675**	**675**
Add ZR2 Wide Stance Pkg.			**350**	**400**	**400**
Add Leather Seats			**150**	**175**	**175**
Add Power Seat			**50**	**75**	**75**
Add Power Sunroof			**200**	**225**	**225**
Deduct W/out Automatic Trans.			**175**	**175**	**175**
Deduct W/out Cruise Control			**50**	**50**	**50**
Deduct W/out Power Windows			**50**	**50**	**50**
1997 TAHOE-1/2 Ton-V8					
Utility 2D	C18	4471	**5750**	**7575**	**8625**
Utility 2D LS	C18		**6150**	**8025**	**9025**
Utility 4D LS	C13	4816	**6350**	**8250**	**9250**
Utility 2D (4WD)	K18	4827	**6350**	**8250**	**9250**
Utility 2D LS (4WD)	K18		**6750**	**8700**	**9750**
Utility 4D LS (4WD)	K13	5225	**6950**	**8900**	**9950**
Add LT Trim (LS)			**500**	**575**	**575**
Add 6.5L V8 Turbo Diesel Engine			**525**	**600**	**600**
Add Aluminum/Alloy Wheels (Base)			**50**	**75**	**75**
Add Leather Seats			**200**	**225**	**225**
Deduct W/out Air Conditioning			**350**	**350**	**350**
Deduct W/out Cruise Control			**75**	**75**	**75**
Deduct W/out Power Seat (Ex. Base)			**75**	**75**	**75**
1997 SUBURBAN-1/2-3/4 Ton-V8					
Utility C1500	C16	4802	**6050**	**7925**	**9000**
Utility C1500 LS	C16		**6450**	**8350**	**9375**
Utility C1500 LT	C16		**7150**	**9150**	**10150**
Utility C2500	C26	5243	**6450**	**8350**	**9375**
Utility C2500 LS	C26		**6850**	**8800**	**9850**
Utility C2500 LT	C26		**7550**	**9575**	**10600**
Utility K1500 (4WD)	K16	5234	**6650**	**8575**	**9600**
Utility K1500 LS (4WD)	K16		**7050**	**9025**	**10025**
Utility K1500 LT (4WD)	K16		**7750**	**9800**	**10850**
Utility K2500 (4WD)	K26	5687	**7050**	**9025**	**10025**
Utility K2500 LS (4WD)	K26		**7450**	**9475**	**10500**
Utility K2500 LT (4WD)	K26		**8150**	**10250**	**11275**
Add 6.5L V8 Turbo Diesel Engine			**525**	**600**	**600**
Add 7.4L V8 Engine			**250**	**300**	**300**
Add Aluminum/Alloy Wheels (Base)			**50**	**75**	**75**
Deduct W/out Air Conditioning			**350**	**350**	**350**
Deduct W/out Cruise Control			**75**	**75**	**75**
Deduct W/out Power Seat (Ex. Base)			**75**	**75**	**75**
1997 VENTURE-V6					
Van 3D	U06	3935	**2850**	**4325**	**5150**
Van 4D	U03		**3000**	**4500**	**5350**
Extended Van 3D	X06	4056	**3250**	**4800**	**5675**
Extended Van 4D	X03	3913	**3400**	**4950**	**5850**

TRUCKS

BODY TYPE	Model No.	Weight	Trade-In	Retail	High Retail
Add LS Trim			325	375	375
Add Power Seat			50	75	75
Add Power Sliding Door			125	150	150
Deduct W/out Cruise Control			50	50	50
Deduct W/out Power Windows			50	50	50
1997 ASTRO-1/2 Ton-V6					
Cargo Van	M19*	3913	3400	4950	5850
Van	M19*	4187	4000	5625	6475
Add LS Trim			250	300	300
Add LT Trim			450	500	500
Add All Wheel Drive			400	450	450
Add Leather Seats			150	175	175
Add Power Seat			50	75	75
Deduct W/out Air Conditioning			250	250	250
Deduct W/out Cruise Control			50	50	50
Deduct W/out Power Windows			50	50	50
* L as the 1st position of the model # denotes AWD					
1997 G10-1/2 Ton-V8					
Chevy Van 135"	G15	4654	4950	6700	7725
Express Van 135"	G15	5075	5750	7575	8625
1997 G20-3/4 Ton-V8					
Chevy Van 135"	G25	4829	5150	6925	7975
Extended Chevy Van 155"	G29	4989	5550	7350	8375
Express Van 135"	G25	5802	5950	7800	8875
Extended Express Van 155"	G29	6008	6350	8250	9250
1997 G30-1 Ton-V8					
Chevy Van 135"	G35	5434	5350	7125	8125
Extended Chevy Van 155"	G39	5609	5750	7575	8625
Express Van 135"	G35	5937	6150	8025	9025
Extended Express Van 155"	G39	6142	6550	8475	9500
G SERIES VAN OPTIONS					
Add LS Trim			350	400	400
Add 6.5L V8 Turbo Diesel Engine			525	600	600
Add 7.4L V8 Engine			250	300	300
Add Aluminum/Alloy Wheels			50	75	75
Add Power Seat			75	100	100
Deduct V6 Engine			300	300	300
Deduct W/out Air Conditioning			350	350	350
Deduct W/out Cruise Control			75	75	75
Deduct W/out Power Windows			75	75	75
1997 S10 PICKUP-1/2 Ton-V6					
Fleetside	S14*	3062	3200	4725	5500
Sportside	S14*	3062	3350	4900	5700
Fleetside Extended Cab	S19*	3246	4200	5875	6675
Sportside Extended Cab	S19*	3246	4350	6025	6800
Add LS Trim (Std. S19)			200	225	225
Add SS Trim			200	225	225
Add ZR2 Wide Stance Pkg.			350	400	400
Add 4 Wheel Drive			1300	1450	1450
Add Cruise Control			50	75	75
Add Power Windows			50	75	75
Deduct 4 Cyl. Engine			200	200	200
Deduct W/out 3rd Door (Ext. Cab)			50	50	50

TRUCKS

SEE TRUCK OPTION PAGE FOR ADDITIONAL OPTIONS

BODY TYPE	Model No.	Weight	Trade-In	Retail	High Retail
Deduct W/out Air Conditioning			250	250	250
Deduct W/out Automatic Trans.			175	175	175
* T as the 1st position of the model # denotes 4WD					
1997 C1500 PICKUP-1/2 Ton-V8					
Sportside	C14*	3879	5750	7575	8625
Fleetside	C14*	3869	5500	7300	8325
Fleetside Extended Cab	C19*	4160	6650	8575	9600
Sportside Extended Cab	C19*	4170	6900	8850	9900
1997 C2500 PICKUP-3/4 Ton-V8					
Fleetside	C24*	4294	5900	7750	8800
HD Fleetside	C24*	4699	6000	7850	8925
Fleetside Extended Cab	C29*	4445	7050	9025	10025
HD Fleetside Extended Cab	C29*	5442	7150	9150	10150
1997 C3500 PICKUP-1 Ton-V8					
Fleetside	C34*	4845	6500	8425	9450
Fleetside Extended Cab	C39*	5395	8025	10100	11125
Fleetside Crew Cab	C33*	5504	8050	10125	11150
C SERIES PICKUP OPTIONS					
Add Silverado Trim			350	400	400
Add 4 Wheel Drive			1300	1450	1450
Add 6.5L V8 Turbo Diesel Engine			525	600	600
Add 7.4L V8 Engine			250	300	300
Add Aluminum/Alloy Wheels			50	75	75
Add Dual Rear Wheels (Std. 3500 Ext.)			375	425	425
Add Leather Seats			200	225	225
Add Power Seat			75	100	100
Add Third Door			100	125	125
Deduct Work Truck Pkg.			1250	1250	1250
Deduct V6 Engine (Ex. WT)			300	300	300
Deduct W/out Air Conditioning			350	350	350
Deduct W/out Automatic Trans.			250	250	250
Deduct W/out Cruise Control (Ex. WT)			75	75	75
Deduct W/out Power Windows (Ex. WT)			75	75	75
* K as the 1st position of the model # denotes 4WD					
CHEVROLET					
1996 BLAZER-1/2 Ton-V6					
Tailgate 2D	S18	3535	2500	3925	4725
Tailgate 4D	S13	3691	2800	4275	5100
Tailgate 2D (4WD)	T18	3814	3100	4625	5500
Tailgate 4D (4WD)	T13	4023	3400	4950	5850
Add LS Trim			325	375	375
Add LT Trim			550	625	625
Deduct W/out Automatic Trans.			125	125	125
1996 TAHOE-1/2 Ton-V8					
Utility 2D	C18	4463	5000	6750	7775
Utility 2D LS	C18		5400	7200	8200
Utility 4D LS	C13	4765	5600	7400	8425
Utility 2D (4WD)	K18	4727	5600	7400	8425
Utility 2D LS (4WD)	K18		6000	7850	8925
Utility 4D LS (4WD)	K13	5175	6200	8075	9075
Add LT Trim (LS)			425	475	475
Add 6.5L V8 Turbo Diesel Engine			500	575	575
Deduct W/out Air Conditioning			250	250	250

TRUCKS

BODY TYPE	Model No.	Weight	Trade-In	Retail	High Retail
1996 SUBURBAN-1/2-3/4 Ton-V8					
Utility C1500	C16	4752	**5400**	**7200**	**8200**
Utility C1500 LS	C16		**5800**	**7625**	**8675**
Utility C1500 LT	C16		**6225**	**8125**	**9125**
Utility C2500	C26	5210	**5800**	**7625**	**8675**
Utility C2500 LS	C26		**6200**	**8075**	**9075**
Utility C2500 LT	C26		**6625**	**8550**	**9575**
Utility K1500 (4WD)	K16		**6000**	**7850**	**8925**
Utility K1500 LS (4WD)	K16		**6400**	**8300**	**9300**
Utility K1500 LT (4WD)	K16		**6825**	**8775**	**9825**
Utility K2500 (4WD)	K26		**6400**	**8300**	**9300**
Utility K2500 LS (4WD)	K26		**6800**	**8750**	**9800**
Utility K2500 LT (4WD)	K26		**7225**	**9225**	**10225**
Add 6.5L V8 Turbo Diesel Engine			**500**	**575**	**575**
Add 7.4L V8 Engine			**225**	**250**	**250**
Deduct W/out Air Conditioning			**250**	**250**	**250**
1996 LUMINA-V6					
Cargo Van	U05	3366	**1150**	**2325**	**2900**
Wagon	U06	3686	**1800**	**3100**	**3775**
Deduct W/out Air Conditioning			**150**	**150**	**150**
1996 ASTRO-1/2 Ton-V6					
Cargo Van	M19*	3398	**2825**	**4300**	**5125**
Van	M19*	3885	**3350**	**4900**	**5800**
Add LS Trim			**200**	**225**	**225**
Add LT Trim			**350**	**400**	**400**
Add All Wheel Drive			**400**	**450**	**450**
Deduct W/out Air Conditioning			**150**	**150**	**150**
* L as the 1st position of the model # denotes AWD					
1996 G10-1/2 Ton-V8					
Chevy Van 135"	G15	4642	**3925**	**5550**	**6500**
Express Van 135"	G15	5066	**4725**	**6450**	**7450**
1996 G20-3/4 Ton-V8					
Chevy Van 135"	G25	4817	**4125**	**5775**	**6750**
Extended Chevy Van 155"	G29	4969	**4525**	**6225**	**7200**
Express Van 135"	G25	5793	**4925**	**6675**	**7700**
Extended Express Van 155"	G29	5998	**5325**	**7100**	**8100**
1996 G30-1 Ton-V8					
Chevy Van 125"	G35	4791	**4225**	**5900**	**6875**
Chevy Van 135"	G35	5422	**4325**	**6000**	**7000**
Extended Chevy Van 146"	G39	5109	**4625**	**6350**	**7350**
Extended Chevy Van 155"	G39	5596	**4725**	**6450**	**7450**
Sportvan 125"	G35	5248	**5025**	**6775**	**7825**
Extended Sportvan 146"	G39	5635	**5425**	**7225**	**8250**
Express Van 135"	G35	5928	**5125**	**6875**	**7925**
Extended Express Van 155"	G39	6132	**5525**	**7325**	**8350**
G SERIES VAN OPTIONS					
Add Beauville Trim			**300**	**350**	**350**
Add LS Trim			**300**	**350**	**350**
Add 6.5L V8 Diesel Engine			**150**	**175**	**175**
Add 6.5L V8 Turbo Diesel Engine			**500**	**575**	**575**
Add 7.4L V8 Engine			**225**	**250**	**250**
Deduct V6 Engine			**200**	**200**	**200**
Deduct W/out Air Conditioning			**250**	**250**	**250**

SEE TRUCK OPTION PAGE FOR ADDITIONAL OPTIONS

BODY TYPE	Model No.	Weight	Trade-In	Retail	High Retail
1996 S10 PICKUP-1/2 Ton-V6					
Fleetside	S14*	2822	2700	4150	4875
Sportside	S14*	3070	2825	4300	5025
Fleetside Extended Cab	S19*	3081	3600	5175	5900
Sportside Extended Cab	S19*	3246	3725	5325	6075
Add LS Trim (Std. S19)			200	225	225
Add SS Trim			200	225	225
Add ZR2 Wide Stance Pkg.			300	350	350
Add 4 Wheel Drive			1200	1350	1350
Deduct 4 Cyl. Engine			175	175	175
Deduct W/out Air Conditioning			150	150	150
Deduct W/out Automatic Trans.			125	125	125
* T as the 1st position of the model # denotes 4WD					
1996 C1500 PICKUP-1/2 Ton-V8					
Sportside	C14*	3840	5050	6800	7850
Fleetside	C14*	3851	4800	6525	7550
Fleetside Extended Cab	C19*	4121	5850	7675	8725
Sportside Extended Cab	C19*	4121	6100	7975	9050
1996 C2500 PICKUP-3/4 Ton-V8					
Fleetside	C24*	4269	5200	6975	8025
HD Fleetside	C24*	4269	5275	7050	8050
Fleetside Extended Cab	C29*	4400	6250	8150	9150
1996 C3500 PICKUP-1 Ton-V8					
Fleetside	C34*	4798	5800	7625	8675
Fleetside Extended Cab	C39*	5074	7200	9200	10200
Fleetside Crew Cab	C33*	5475	7250	9250	10275
C SERIES PICKUP OPTIONS					
Add Silverado Trim			300	350	350
Add 4 Wheel Drive			1200	1350	1350
Add 6.5L V8 Turbo Diesel Engine			500	575	575
Add 7.4L V8 Engine			225	250	250
Add Dual Rear Wheels (Std. 3500 Ext.)			350	400	400
Deduct Work Truck Pkg.			1000	1000	1000
Deduct V6 Engine (Ex. WT)			200	200	200
Deduct W/out Air Conditioning			250	250	250
Deduct W/out Automatic Trans.			150	150	150
* K as the 1st position of the model # denotes 4WD					
CHEVROLET					
1995 BLAZER-1/2 Ton-V6					
Tailgate 2D	S18	3533	2150	3525	4275
Tailgate 4D	S13	3689	2375	3775	4550
Tailgate 2D (4WD)	T18	3812	2750	4200	5000
Tailgate 4D (4WD)	T13	4020	2975	4475	5325
Add LS Trim			300	350	350
Add LT Trim			500	575	575
1995 TAHOE-1/2 Ton-V8					
Utility 4D LS	C13	4769	4825	6550	7575
Utility 2D (4WD)	K18	4747	4925	6675	7700
Utility 2D LS (4WD)	K18		5225	7000	8050
Utility 4D LS (4WD)	K13	5124	5425	7225	8250
Add LT Trim (LS)			350	400	400
Add 6.5L V8 Turbo Diesel Engine			475	550	550

TRUCKS

BODY TYPE	Model No.	Weight	Trade-In	Retail	High Retail
1995 SUBURBAN-1/2-3/4 Ton-V8					
Utility C1500	C16	4692	**4700**	**6425**	**7425**
Utility C1500 LS	C16		**5000**	**6750**	**7775**
Utility C1500 LT	C16		**5350**	**7125**	**8125**
Utility C2500	C26	5176	**5100**	**6850**	**7900**
Utility C2500 LS	C26		**5400**	**7200**	**8200**
Utility C2500 LT	C26		**5750**	**7575**	**8625**
Utility K1500 (4WD)	K16		**5300**	**7075**	**8075**
Utility K1500 LS (4WD)	K16		**5600**	**7400**	**8425**
Utility K1500 LT (4WD)	K16		**5950**	**7800**	**8875**
Utility K2500 (4WD)	K26		**5700**	**7525**	**8575**
Utility K2500 LS (4WD)	K26		**6000**	**7850**	**8925**
Utility K2500 LT (4WD)	K26		**6350**	**8250**	**9250**
Add 6.5L V8 Turbo Diesel Engine			**475**	**550**	**550**
Add 7.4L V8 Engine			**200**	**225**	**225**
1995 LUMINA-V6					
Cargo Van	U05	3342	**875**	**2000**	**2525**
Wagon	U06	3516	**1525**	**2775**	**3425**
Add LS Trim			**150**	**175**	**175**
1995 ASTRO-1/2 Ton-V6					
Cargo Van	M19*	3804	**2000**	**3350**	**4075**
Van CS	M19*	4083	**2500**	**3925**	**4725**
Add CL Trim			**150**	**175**	**175**
Add LT Trim			**300**	**350**	**350**
Add All Wheel Drive			**350**	**400**	**400**
* L as the 1st position of the model # denotes AWD					
1995 G10-1/2 Ton-V8					
Chevy Van 110"	G15	4069	**2650**	**4100**	**4950**
1995 G20-3/4 Ton-V8					
Chevy Van 110"	G25	4052	**2850**	**4325**	**5200**
Sportvan 125"	G25	4770	**3450**	**5025**	**5925**
1995 G30-1 Ton-V8					
Chevy Van 125"	G35	4811	**3050**	**4575**	**5475**
Extended Chevy Van 146"	G39	5154	**3450**	**5025**	**5925**
Sportvan 125"	G35	5326	**3650**	**5250**	**6175**
Extended Sportvan 146"	G39	5661	**4050**	**5700**	**6675**
G SERIES VAN OPTIONS					
Add Beauville Trim			**300**	**350**	**350**
Add 7.4L V8 Engine			**200**	**225**	**225**
Deduct V6 Engine			**150**	**150**	**150**
1995 S10 PICKUP-1/2 Ton-V6					
Fleetside	S14*	2983	**2250**	**3625**	**4300**
Fleetside Extended Cab	S19*	3185	**3150**	**4675**	**5450**
Add LS Trim (Std. S19)			**200**	**225**	**225**
Add SS Trim			**200**	**225**	**225**
Add ZR2 Wide Stance Pkg.			**250**	**300**	**300**
Add 4 Wheel Drive			**1100**	**1225**	**1225**
Deduct 4 Cyl. Engine			**125**	**125**	**125**
* T as the 1st position of the model # denotes 4WD					
1995 C1500 PICKUP-1/2 Ton-V8					
Sportside	C14*	3814	**4350**	**6025**	**7000**
Fleetside	C14*	3803	**4150**	**5800**	**6775**

TRUCKS

SEE TRUCK OPTION PAGE FOR ADDITIONAL OPTIONS

BODY TYPE	Model No.	Weight	Trade-In	Retail	High Retail
Fleetside Extended Cab	C19*	4071	5150	6925	7975
Sportside Extended Cab	C19*	4082	5350	7125	8125
1995 C2500 PICKUP-3/4 Ton-V8					
Fleetside	C24*	4119	4550	6250	7225
Fleetside Extended Cab	C29*	4339	5550	7350	8375
1995 C3500 PICKUP-1 Ton-V8					
Fleetside	C34*	4772	5050	6800	7850
Fleetside Extended Cab	C39*	5048	6375	8275	9275
Fleetside Crew Cab	C33*	5397	6450	8350	9375
C SERIES PICKUP OPTIONS					
Add Silverado Trim			250	300	300
Add 4 Wheel Drive			1100	1225	1225
Add 6.5L V8 Turbo Diesel Engine			475	550	550
Add 7.4L V8 Engine			200	225	225
Add Dual Rear Wheels (Std. 3500 Ext. Cab)			325	375	375
Deduct Work Truck Pkg.			950	950	950
Deduct V6 Engine (Ex. WT)			150	150	150

* K as the 1st position of the model # denotes 4WD

CHRYSLER

**See Passenger Car Section for All PT Cruiser Models.

CHRYSLER

BODY TYPE	Model No.	Weight	Trade-In	Retail	High Retail
2004 PACIFICA-V6					
Wagon 4D	M68	4442	17900	20900	22050
Wagon 4D (AWD)	F68	4675	20100	23250	24450
Add Infinity Intermezzo Stereo System			300	350	350
Add Leather Seats			450	500	500
Add Navigation System			600	675	675
Add Power Sunroof			575	650	650
Add Rear Entertainment System			600	675	675
Add Theft Recovery System			100	125	125
2004 TOWN & COUNTRY-V6					
Wagon	P45	4025	12325	14825	15800
Wagon LX	P44	4068	13775	16375	17400
Wagon EX	P74	4228	16675	19475	20575
Wagon Touring	P54*	4299	17675	20675	21800
Wagon Touring Platinum	P54	4254	19825	22950	24150
Wagon Limited	P64*	4331	22050	25325	26575
Add All Wheel Drive			1100	1225	1225
Add Aluminum/Alloy Wheels (LX)			325	375	375
Add Leather Seats (Std. Platinum, Ltd.)			450	500	500
Add Navigation System (Std. Limited)			600	675	675
Add Power Seat (Base, LX)			200	225	225
Add Power Sunroof			575	650	650
Add Rear Air Conditioning (LX)			200	225	225
Add Rear Bucket Seats (LX)			200	225	225
Add Rear Entertainment System (Std. Platinum)			600	675	675
Add Right Power Sliding Door (Base, LX)			300	350	350
Add Theft Recovery System			100	125	125

* T as the 1st position of the model # denotes AWD

BODY TYPE	Model No.	Weight	Trade-In	Retail	High Retail
CHRYSLER					
2003 TOWN & COUNTRY-V6					
Wagon	P24		**12350**	**14875**	**15850**
Wagon eL	P34	4165	**12350**	**14875**	**15850**
Wagon LX	P44	4068	**12175**	**14675**	**15650**
Wagon EX	P74	4228	**13775**	**16375**	**17400**
Wagon LXi	P54*	4299	**16075**	**18825**	**19900**
Wagon Limited	P64*	4331	**18075**	**21100**	**22250**
Add All Wheel Drive			**1000**	**1125**	**1125**
Add Aluminum/Alloy Wheels (LX)			**275**	**325**	**325**
Add Compact Disc Player (Base, LX)			**75**	**100**	**100**
Add Leather Seats (EX)			**400**	**450**	**450**
Add Power Seat (LX)			**175**	**200**	**200**
Add Power Sunroof			**525**	**600**	**600**
Add Rear Air Conditioning (Base, LX)			**150**	**175**	**175**
Add Rear Bucket Seats (LX)			**175**	**200**	**200**
Add Rear Entertainment System			**500**	**575**	**575**
Add Right Power Sliding Door (eL, LX)			**250**	**300**	**300**
Add Theft Recovery System			**75**	**100**	**100**
* T as the 1st position of the model # denotes AWD					
2003 VOYAGER-V6					
Voyager LX Base	J25	3886	**9950**	**12175**	**13075**
Voyager LX	J45	3989	**10875**	**13175**	**14100**
Add Compact Disc Player			**75**	**100**	**100**
Add Power Seat			**175**	**200**	**200**
Add Rear Bucket Seats			**175**	**200**	**200**
Add Theft Recovery System			**75**	**100**	**100**
Deduct 4 Cyl. Engine			**650**	**650**	**650**
Deduct W/out Cruise Control			**175**	**175**	**175**
Deduct W/out Power Door Locks			**150**	**150**	**150**
Deduct W/out Power Windows			**175**	**175**	**175**
Deduct W/out Tilt Steering Wheel			**125**	**125**	**125**
CHRYSLER					
2002 TOWN & COUNTRY-V6					
Wagon eL	P34		**10350**	**12625**	**13525**
Wagon LX	P44*	4107	**10200**	**12450**	**13350**
Wagon EX	P74	4275	**11900**	**14350**	**15325**
Wagon LXi	P54*	4265	**13700**	**16300**	**17325**
Wagon Limited	P64*	4358	**15200**	**17900**	**18950**
Add All Wheel Drive			**900**	**1000**	**1000**
Add Aluminum/Alloy Wheels (LX)			**225**	**250**	**250**
Add Compact Disc Player (Std. EX, Ltd.)			**75**	**100**	**100**
Add Leather Seats (Std. Limited)			**350**	**400**	**400**
Add Left Power Sliding Door (EX)			**250**	**300**	**300**
Add Power Seat (LX)			**150**	**175**	**175**
Add Rear Air Conditioning (LX)			**150**	**175**	**175**
Add Rear Bucket Seats (LX)			**150**	**175**	**175**
Add Right Power Sliding Door (eL, LX)			**250**	**300**	**300**
Add Theft Recovery System			**75**	**100**	**100**
* T as the 1st position of the model # denotes AWD					
2002 VOYAGER-V6					
Voyager eC (4 Cyl.)	J15		**6325**	**8225**	**9075**
Voyager	J25	3869	**7725**	**9750**	**10650**

TRUCKS

SEE TRUCK OPTION PAGE FOR ADDITIONAL OPTIONS

BODY TYPE	Model No.	Weight	Trade-In	Retail	High Retail
Voyager LX	J45	4038	**8625**	**10750**	**11700**
Add Compact Disc Player			**75**	**100**	**100**
Add Power Seat			**150**	**175**	**175**
Add Power Sliding Door			**250**	**300**	**300**
Add Rear Bucket Seats			**150**	**175**	**175**
Add Theft Recovery System			**75**	**100**	**100**
Deduct 4 Cyl. Engine (Ex. eC)			**600**	**600**	**600**
Deduct W/out Cruise Control (Ex. eC)			**150**	**150**	**150**
Deduct W/out Power Door Locks			**125**	**125**	**125**
Deduct W/out Power Windows (Ex. eC)			**150**	**150**	**150**
Deduct W/out Tilt Steering Wheel (Ex. eC)			**100**	**100**	**100**
CHRYSLER					
2001 TOWN & COUNTRY-V6					
Wagon LX	P44*	4098	**8425**	**10550**	**11500**
Wagon EX	P74		**10275**	**12550**	**13450**
Wagon LXi	P54*		**11325**	**13750**	**14700**
Wagon Limited	P64*		**12525**	**15050**	**16050**
Add All Wheel Drive			**800**	**900**	**900**
Add Aluminum/Alloy Wheels (LX)			**175**	**200**	**200**
Add Compact Disc Player (Std. EX, Ltd.)			**50**	**75**	**75**
Add Leather Seats (Std. Limited)			**300**	**350**	**350**
Add Power Seat (LX)			**125**	**150**	**150**
Add Power Sliding Door (LX)			**225**	**250**	**250**
Add Rear Air Conditioning (LX)			**125**	**150**	**150**
Add Rear Bucket Seats			**125**	**150**	**150**
Add Theft Recovery System			**50**	**75**	**75**
* T as the 1st position of the model # denotes AWD					
2001 VOYAGER-V6					
Voyager	J25	3920	**6825**	**8775**	**9675**
Voyager LX	J45	4061	**7525**	**9550**	**10450**
Add Compact Disc Player			**50**	**75**	**75**
Add Power Seat			**125**	**150**	**150**
Add Power Sliding Door			**225**	**250**	**250**
Add Rear Bucket Seats			**125**	**150**	**150**
Add Theft Recovery System			**50**	**75**	**75**
Deduct 4 Cyl. Engine			**500**	**500**	**500**
Deduct W/out Cruise Control			**125**	**125**	**125**
Deduct W/out Power Door Locks			**100**	**100**	**100**
Deduct W/out Power Windows			**125**	**125**	**125**
Deduct W/out Tilt Steering Wheel			**100**	**100**	**100**
CHRYSLER					
2000 TOWN & COUNTRY-V6					
Wagon LX	P44*	4045	**6875**	**8825**	**9725**
Wagon LXi	P54*	4065	**7475**	**9500**	**10375**
Wagon Limited	P64*	4065	**8325**	**10425**	**11350**
Add All Wheel Drive			**700**	**800**	**800**
Add Aluminum/Alloy Wheels (Std. Ltd.)			**125**	**150**	**150**
Add Compact Disc Player (Std. Ltd.)			**50**	**75**	**75**
Add Leather Seats (Std. Limited)			**250**	**300**	**300**
Add Rear Air Conditioning (Std. Limited)			**100**	**125**	**125**
* T as the 1st position of the model # denotes AWD					
2000 VOYAGER-V6					
Voyager	J25	3536	**3950**	**5575**	**6425**

TRUCKS

BODY TYPE	Model No.	Weight	Trade-In	Retail	High Retail
Voyager SE	J45		5000	6750	7675
Grand Voyager	J24	3836	5325	7100	7975
Grand Voyager SE	J44		6025	7875	8800
Add 3rd Row Seat (Base Voyager)			100	125	125
Add Aluminum/Alloy Wheels (SE)			125	150	150
Add Compact Disc Player			50	75	75
Add Left Sliding Door (Base Voyager)			250	300	300
Add Power Seat			100	125	125
Add Rear Air Conditioning			100	125	125
Add Rear Bucket Seats			100	125	125
Deduct 4 Cyl. Engine			400	400	400
Deduct W/out Air Conditioning			500	500	500
Deduct W/out Cruise Control			100	100	100
Deduct W/out Power Door Locks			75	75	75
Deduct W/out Power Windows			100	100	100
Deduct W/out Tilt Steering Wheel			75	75	75
CHRYSLER 1999 TOWN & COUNTRY-V6					
Wagon SX	P55	3958	4925	6675	7600
Wagon LX	P54*	4082	5625	7450	8350
Wagon LXi	P54*		6275	8175	9025
Wagon Limited	P64*	4168	6775	8725	9600
Add All Wheel Drive			600	675	675
Add Aluminum/Alloy Wheels (LX)			75	100	100
Add Leather Seats (Std. LXi, Ltd.)			225	250	250
Add Rear Air Conditioning (Std. LXi, Ltd.)			75	100	100
* T as the 1st position of the model # denotes AWD					
CHRYSLER 1998 TOWN & COUNTRY-V6					
Wagon SX	P55	3959	4600	6300	7175
Wagon LX	P54*	4042	5100	6850	7775
Wagon LXi	P64*	4042	5700	7525	8425
Add All Wheel Drive			500	575	575
Add Aluminum/Alloy Wheels (LX)			50	75	75
Add Leather Seats (Std. LXi)			175	200	200
Add Power Seat (Std. LXi)			50	75	75
Add Rear Air Conditioning (Std. LXi)			50	75	75
* T as the 1st position of the model # denotes AWD					
CHRYSLER 1997 TOWN & COUNTRY-V6					
Wagon SX	P55	3879	3800	5400	6225
Wagon LX	P54	4262	4100	5750	6600
Wagon LXi	P64	4262	4500	6200	7075
Add All Wheel Drive			400	450	450
Add Leather Seats (Std. LXi)			150	175	175
Add Power Seat (Std. LXi)			50	75	75
CHRYSLER 1996 TOWN & COUNTRY-V6					
Wagon LX	P55	3863	3100	4625	5500
Wagon	P54	3951	3350	4900	5800
Wagon LXi	P64	4154	3650	5250	6050

TRUCKS

SEE TRUCK OPTION PAGE FOR ADDITIONAL OPTIONS

BODY TYPE	Model No.	Weight	Trade-In	Retail	High Retail
CHRYSLER					
1995 TOWN & COUNTRY-V6					
Wagon	H54	3980	**2050**	**3400**	**4125**
Add All Wheel Drive			**350**	**400**	**400**

DODGE

BODY TYPE	Model No.	Weight	Trade-In	Retail	High Retail
DODGE					
2004 CARAVAN-V6					
Caravan C/V	P21	3764	**11825**	**14275**	**15225**
Grand Caravan C/V	P23	3838	**13325**	**15900**	**16925**
Caravan SE	P25	3862	**11975**	**14450**	**15425**
Caravan SXT	P45	3999	**13175**	**15750**	**16775**
Grand Caravan SE	P24	3991	**13475**	**16050**	**17075**
Grand Caravan EX	P74	4218	**15775**	**18500**	**19575**
Grand Caravan SXT	P44*	4093	**15775**	**18500**	**19575**
Grand Caravan Anniversary	P44	4186	**17925**	**20925**	**22075**
Add All Wheel Drive			**1100**	**1225**	**1225**
Add Infinity Stereo System			**300**	**350**	**350**
Add Leather Seats (Std. Annv)			**450**	**500**	**500**
Add Power Seat (Caravan SXT)			**200**	**225**	**225**
Add Power Sunroof			**575**	**650**	**650**
Add Rear Air Conditioning (SE)			**200**	**225**	**225**
Add Rear Bucket Seats (SE)			**200**	**225**	**225**
Add Rear Entertainment System (Std. Annv)			**600**	**675**	**675**
Add Right Pwr Sliding Door (Caravan SXT)			**300**	**350**	**350**
Add Theft Recovery System			**100**	**125**	**125**
Deduct 4 Cyl. Engine			**700**	**700**	**700**
Deduct W/out Cruise Control			**200**	**200**	**200**
Deduct W/out Power Door Locks			**175**	**175**	**175**
Deduct W/out Power Windows			**200**	**200**	**200**
Deduct W/out Tilt Steering Wheel			**150**	**150**	**150**

*T as the 1st position of the model # denotes AWD

BODY TYPE	Model No.	Weight	Trade-In	Retail	High Retail
2004 DURANGO-1/2 Ton-V8-4WD					
Wagon 4D ST (2WD)	D38	4671	**15950**	**18700**	**19775**
Wagon 4D SLT (2WD)	D48	4676	**17450**	**20425**	**21550**
Wagon 4D SLT HEMI (2WD)	D48D	4896	**18450**	**21475**	**22625**
Wagon 4D Limited (2WD)	D58	4888	**19800**	**22925**	**24125**
Wagon 4D Limited HEMI (2WD)	D58D	4898	**20800**	**23975**	**25200**
Wagon 4D ST	B38	4981	**17025**	**19900**	**21000**
Wagon 4D SLT	B48	4987	**18525**	**21575**	**22725**
Wagon 4D SLT HEMI	B48D	5076	**19525**	**22625**	**23800**
Wagon 4D Limited	B58	5045	**20875**	**24075**	**25300**
Wagon 4D Limited HEMI	B58D	5079	**21875**	**25150**	**26400**
Add Aluminum/Alloy Wheels (Std. Limited)			**325**	**375**	**375**
Add Leather Seats (Std. Limited)			**450**	**500**	**500**
Add Power Sunroof			**575**	**650**	**650**
Add Rear Entertainment System			**600**	**675**	**675**
Add Running Boards (SLT, Limited)			**150**	**175**	**175**
Add Theft Recovery System			**100**	**125**	**125**
Deduct V6 Engine			**800**	**800**	**800**

BODY TYPE	Model No.	Weight	Trade-In	Retail	High Retail
2004 DAKOTA PICKUP-1/2 Ton-V6					
Sweptline Base	L16*	3714	9925	12150	12875
Sweptline SXT	L16*		10350	12600	13500
Sweptline Sport	L36*	3714	10625	12900	13625
Sweptline SLT	L46*	3714	10625	12900	13625
Club Cab Base	L12*	3829	12075	14575	15350
Club Cab SXT	L12*		12500	15025	15825
Club Cab Sport	L32*	3829	12775	15325	16125
Club Cab SLT	L42*	3829	12775	15325	16125
Quad Cab SXT	L18*		14250	16900	17950
Quad Cab Sport	L38*	4208	14175	16800	17850
Quad Cab SLT	L48*	4208	14175	16800	17625
Add 4 Wheel Drive			2600	2825	2825
Add Aluminum/Alloy Wheels (Base)			325	375	375
Add CD Player (Std. SXT)			100	125	125
Add Cruise Control (Std. Quad SXT)			200	225	225
Add Leather Seats			450	500	500
Add Power Door Locks			175	200	200
Add Power Seat			200	225	225
Add Power Windows			200	225	225
Add Running Boards			150	175	175
Add Theft Recovery System			100	125	125
Add Tilt Steering Wheel (Std. Quad SXT)			150	175	175
Add V8 Engine			500	575	575
Deduct W/out Automatic Trans.			575	575	575

* G as the 1st position of the model # denotes 4WD

BODY TYPE	Model No.	Weight	Trade-In	Retail	High Retail
2004 RAM 1500 PICKUP-1/2 Ton-V8					
Sweptline	A16*	4542	14025	16650	17875
Swept SRT-10 (V10, 6 Spd.)	A16H	5000	32825	37075	38825
Quad Cab	A18*	4877	16025	18775	20050
2004 RAM 2500 PICKUP-3/4 Ton-V8					
Sweptline	A26*	5413	15925	18675	19950
Quad Cab	A28*	5566	19925	23075	24425
2004 RAM 3500 PICKUP-1 Ton-I6/V8					
Sweptline DRW 5.7L HEMI	A46D*	5919	17325	20300	21625
Quad Cab SRW TD	A386*	6482	24950	28425	29925
Quad Cab SRW H.O. TD	A38C*	6452	25350	28850	30350
Quad DRW 5.7L HEMI	A48D*	6348	21325	24550	25950
Quad Cab DRW T-Diesel	A486*	6922	25725	29225	30750
Quad Cab DRW H.O. TD	A48C*	7062	26125	29650	31175
RAM PICKUP OPTIONS					
Add Laramie Trim			1400	1575	1575
Add SLT Trim			700	800	800
Add Sport Trim			325	375	375
Add Off-Road Pkg.			350	400	400
Add 4 Wheel Drive			2800	3025	3025
Add 5.7L HEMI V8 Eng. (1500)			700	800	800
Add 5.9L H.O. T-Diesel Eng. (2500, 3500 Swept)			4800	5025	5025
Add 5.9L T-Diesel Eng. (2500, 3500 Swept)			4400	4625	4625
Add Aluminum/Alloy Wheels (Std. SRT-10)			375	425	425
Add Compact Disc Player (Std. SRT-10)			150	175	175
Add Leather Seats (Std. SRT-10)			525	600	600
Add Navigation System			650	725	725
Add Power Seat			225	250	250
Add Running Boards			150	175	175

SEE TRUCK OPTION PAGE FOR ADDITIONAL OPTIONS

BODY TYPE	Model No.	Weight	Trade-In	Retail	High Retail
Add Theft Recovery System			100	125	125
Deduct Work Truck Pkg.			1100	1100	1100
Deduct V6 Engine			750	750	750
Deduct W/out AT (Ex. SRT-10)			625	625	625
Deduct W/out Cruise Control			225	225	225

* U as the 1st position of the model # denotes 4WD

DODGE

2003 CARAVAN-V6

BODY TYPE	Model No.	Weight	Trade-In	Retail	High Retail
Caravan C/V	P21	3764	9200	11375	12275
Grand Caravan C/V	P23	3838	10525	12800	13700
Caravan SE	P25	3862	9850	12075	12950
Caravan SXT	P25	3946	10200	12450	13350
Caravan Sport	P45	3999	10775	13075	14000
Grand Caravan SE	P24	3991	11175	13575	14525
Grand Caravan eL	P34	4163	12100	14600	15575
Grand Caravan Sport	P44*	4093	12100	14600	15575
Grand Caravan EX	P74	4218	13700	16300	17325
Grand Caravan ES	P54*	4258	15500	18225	19275
Add All Wheel Drive			1000	1125	1125
Add Aluminum/Alloy Wheels (Sport)			275	325	325
Add Compact Disc Player (Std. EX, ES)			75	100	100
Add Leather Seats			400	450	450
Add Left Power Sliding Door (EX)			250	300	300
Add Power Seat (Std. EX, ES)			175	200	200
Add Power Sunroof			525	600	600
Add Rear Air Conditioning (SE)			150	175	175
Add Rear Bucket Seats (Caravan Sport)			175	200	200
Add Rear Entertainment System			500	575	575
Add Right Pwr Sliding Door (Std. EX, ES)			250	300	300
Add Theft Recovery System			75	100	100
Deduct 4 Cyl. Engine			650	650	650
Deduct W/out Cruise Control			175	175	175
Deduct W/out Power Door Locks			150	150	150
Deduct W/out Power Windows			175	175	175
Deduct W/out Tilt Steering Wheel			125	125	125

* T as the 1st position of the model # denotes AWD

2003 DURANGO-1/2 Ton-V8-4WD

BODY TYPE	Model No.	Weight	Trade-In	Retail	High Retail
Wagon 4D Sport (2WD)	R38	4379	12400	14925	15900
Wagon 4D SXT (2WD)	R38		12650	15200	16200
Wagon 4D SLT (2WD)	R48		14400	17050	18075
Wagon 4D SLT Plus (2WD)	R58		15600	18325	19375
Wagon 4D Sport	S38	4629	13425	16025	17050
Wagon 4D SXT	S38		13675	16300	17325
Wagon 4D SLT	S48		15425	18150	19200
Wagon 4D SLT Plus	S58		16625	19425	20525
Wagon 4D R/T Sport	S78	4726	18350	21400	22550
Add Compact Disc Player (Sport)			75	100	100
Add Leather Seats (Std. Plus, R/T)			400	450	450
Add Rear Entertainment System			500	575	575
Add Running Boards (SXT, Base SLT)			125	150	150
Add Theft Recovery System			75	100	100

2003 RAM VAN 1500-1/2 Ton-V8

BODY TYPE	Model No.	Weight	Trade-In	Retail	High Retail
Van 109.6"	B11	4192	11700	14125	15250
Van 127.6"	B11	4405	11800	14250	15375

TRUCKS

BODY TYPE	Model No.	Weight	Trade-In	Retail	High Retail
Maxivan 127.6"	B11	4507	**12500**	**15025**	**16200**
2003 RAM VAN 2500-3/4 Ton-V8					
Van 127.6"	B21	4733	**12500**	**15025**	**16200**
Maxivan 127.6"	B21	4902	**13200**	**15775**	**16975**
2003 RAM VAN 3500-1 Ton-V8					
Van 127.6"	B31	4733	**13200**	**15775**	**16975**
Maxivan 127.6"	B31	4636	**13900**	**16525**	**17750**
RAM VAN OPTIONS					
Add Aluminum/Alloy Wheels			**325**	**375**	**375**
Add Compact Disc Player			**125**	**150**	**150**
Add Theft Recovery System			**75**	**100**	**100**
Deduct V6 Engine			**725**	**725**	**725**
Deduct W/out Air Conditioning			**700**	**700**	**700**
Deduct W/out Cruise Control			**200**	**200**	**200**
Deduct W/out Power Door Locks			**175**	**175**	**175**
Deduct W/out Power Windows			**200**	**200**	**200**
Deduct W/out Tilt Steering Wheel			**150**	**150**	**150**
2003 DAKOTA PICKUP-1/2 Ton-V6					
Sweptline Base	L16*	3641	**8375**	**10475**	**11200**
Sweptline SXT	L16*		**8725**	**10850**	**11600**
Sweptline Sport	L36*		**9025**	**11175**	**11900**
Sweptline SLT	L46*		**9025**	**11175**	**11900**
Sweptline R/T Sport	L76Z	3940	**11775**	**14200**	**14975**
Club Cab Base	L12*	3871	**10575**	**12850**	**13575**
Club Cab SXT	L12*		**10925**	**13225**	**13975**
Club Cab Sport	L32*		**11225**	**13625**	**14375**
Club Cab SLT	L42*		**11225**	**13625**	**14375**
Club Cab R/T Sport	L72Z	4123	**13975**	**16600**	**17425**
Quad Cab Sport	L38*	4244	**12525**	**15050**	**15850**
Quad Cab SLT	L48*		**12525**	**15050**	**15850**
Add 4 Wheel Drive			**2550**	**2775**	**2775**
Add Aluminum/Alloy Wheels (Base)			**275**	**325**	**325**
Add CD Player (Std. SXT)			**75**	**100**	**100**
Add Cruise Control (Std. R/T)			**175**	**200**	**200**
Add Leather Seats			**400**	**450**	**450**
Add Power Door Locks			**150**	**175**	**175**
Add Power Seat			**175**	**200**	**200**
Add Power Windows			**175**	**200**	**200**
Add Running Boards			**125**	**150**	**150**
Add Theft Recovery System			**75**	**100**	**100**
Add Tilt Steering Wheel (Std. R/T)			**125**	**150**	**150**
Add V8 Engine (Std. R/T Sport)			**500**	**575**	**575**
Deduct W/out Automatic Trans.			**525**	**525**	**525**

* G as the 1st position of the model # denotes 4WD

BODY TYPE	Model No.	Weight	Trade-In	Retail	High Retail
2003 RAM 1500 PICKUP-1/2 Ton-V8					
Sweptline	A16*	4516	**12575**	**15100**	**16275**
Quad Cab	A18*	4804	**14675**	**17350**	**18575**
2003 RAM 2500 PICKUP-3/4 Ton-V8					
Sweptline	A26*	5414	**14375**	**17025**	**18225**
Quad Cab	A28*	5521	**18175**	**21200**	**22550**
2003 RAM 3500 PICKUP-1 Ton-I6/V8					
Sweptline DRW 5.7L HEMI	A46D*	5858	**15925**	**18675**	**19950**
Quad Cab SRW T-Diesel	A386*	6392	**23400**	**26775**	**28250**
Quad SRW H.O. TD 6 Spd.	A38C*	6528	**23500**	**26875**	**28350**

TRUCKS

SEE TRUCK OPTION PAGE FOR ADDITIONAL OPTIONS

BODY TYPE	Model No.	Weight	Trade-In	Retail	High Retail
Quad DRW 5.7L HEMI	A48D*	6226	**19625**	**22750**	**24100**
Quad Cab DRW T-Diesel	A486*	6863	**24125**	**27550**	**29025**
Quad DRW H.O. TD 6 Spd.	A48C*	7003	**24225**	**27650**	**29125**
RAM PICKUP OPTIONS					
Add Laramie Trim			**1300**	**1450**	**1450**
Add SLT Trim			**650**	**725**	**725**
Add Sport Trim			**300**	**350**	**350**
Add Off-Road Pkg.			**300**	**350**	**350**
Add 4 Wheel Drive			**2700**	**2925**	**2925**
Add 5.7L HEMI V8 Eng. (1500)			**650**	**725**	**725**
Add 5.9L H.O. T-Diesel Eng. (2500, 3500 Swept)			**4500**	**4725**	**4725**
Add 5.9L T-Diesel Eng. (2500, 3500 Swept)			**4300**	**4525**	**4525**
Add 8.0L V10 Eng. (Ex. T-Diesels)			**200**	**225**	**225**
Add Aluminum/Alloy Wheels			**325**	**375**	**375**
Add Compact Disc Player			**125**	**150**	**150**
Add Leather Seats			**475**	**550**	**550**
Add Power Seat			**200**	**225**	**225**
Add Running Boards			**125**	**150**	**150**
Add Theft Recovery System			**75**	**100**	**100**
Deduct Work Truck Pkg.			**1100**	**1100**	**1100**
Deduct V6 Engine			**725**	**725**	**725**
Deduct W/out Air Conditioning			**700**	**700**	**700**
Deduct W/out AT (Ex. H.O. T-Diesel)			**575**	**575**	**575**
Deduct W/out Cruise Control			**200**	**200**	**200**
Deduct W/out Tilt Steering Wheel			**150**	**150**	**150**

* U as the 1st position of the model # denotes 4WD

DODGE
2002 CARAVAN-V6

BODY TYPE	Model No.	Weight	Trade-In	Retail	High Retail
Caravan eC (4 Cyl.)	P15		**6100**	**7975**	**8900**
Caravan SE	P25	3869	**7450**	**9450**	**10325**
Caravan Sport	P45	4039	**8350**	**10450**	**11375**
Grand Caravan SE	P24	4011	**8700**	**10825**	**11775**
Grand Caravan eL	P34		**9750**	**11975**	**12900**
Grand Caravan Sport	P44*	4106	**9600**	**11800**	**12700**
Grand Caravan EX	P74	4263	**11350**	**13750**	**14700**
Grand Caravan ES	P54*	4238	**12900**	**15450**	**16450**
Add 3rd Row Seat (eC)			**150**	**175**	**175**
Add All Wheel Drive			**900**	**1000**	**1000**
Add Aluminum/Alloy Wheels (Sport)			**225**	**250**	**250**
Add Compact Disc Player (Std. EX)			**75**	**100**	**100**
Add Leather Seats			**350**	**400**	**400**
Add Left Power Sliding Door (EX)			**250**	**300**	**300**
Add Power Seat (Std. EX, ES)			**150**	**175**	**175**
Add Rear Air Conditioning (Sport)			**150**	**175**	**175**
Add Rear Bucket Seats (Sport)			**150**	**175**	**175**
Add Right Pwr Sliding Door (Std. EX, ES)			**250**	**300**	**300**
Add Theft Recovery System			**75**	**100**	**100**
Deduct 4 Cyl. Engine (Ex. eC)			**600**	**600**	**600**
Deduct W/out Cruise Control (Ex. eC)			**150**	**150**	**150**
Deduct W/out Power Door Locks			**125**	**125**	**125**
Deduct W/out Power Windows (Ex. eC)			**150**	**150**	**150**
Deduct W/out Tilt Steering Wheel (Ex. eC)			**100**	**100**	**100**

* T as the 1st position of the model # denotes AWD

TRUCKS

BODY TYPE	Model No.	Weight	Trade-In	Retail	High Retail
2002 DURANGO-1/2 Ton-V8-4WD					
Wagon 4D Sport (2WD)	R38	4379	**10625**	**12925**	**13850**
Wagon 4D SXT (2WD)	R38		**10825**	**13150**	**14075**
Wagon 4D SLT (2WD)	R48		**12425**	**14950**	**15925**
Wagon 4D SLT Plus (2WD)	R58		**13175**	**15750**	**16775**
Wagon 4D Sport	S38	4629	**11625**	**14075**	**15025**
Wagon 4D SXT	S38		**11825**	**14275**	**15225**
Wagon 4D SLT	S48		**13425**	**16025**	**17050**
Wagon 4D SLT Plus	S58		**14175**	**16825**	**17875**
Wagon 4D R/T Sport	S78	4726	**15875**	**18625**	**19700**
Add Compact Disc Player (Sport)			**75**	**100**	**100**
Add Leather Seats (Std. Plus, R/T)			**350**	**400**	**400**
Add Running Boards (Base SLT)			**100**	**125**	**125**
Add Theft Recovery System			**75**	**100**	**100**
2002 RAM VAN 1500-1/2 Ton-V8					
Wagon 109.6"	B15	4566	**11350**	**13750**	**14850**
Van 109.6"	B11	4192	**10100**	**12350**	**13400**
Van 127.6"	B11	4405	**10200**	**12450**	**13500**
Maxivan 127.6"	B11	4507	**10850**	**13150**	**14250**
2002 RAM VAN 2500-3/4 Ton-V8					
Wagon 127.6"	B25	5134	**12100**	**14600**	**15750**
Van 127.6"	B21	4733	**10850**	**13150**	**14250**
Maxivan 127.6"	B21	4902	**11500**	**13925**	**15050**
2002 RAM VAN 3500-1 Ton-V8					
Maxiwagon 127.6"	B35	5570	**13550**	**16150**	**17350**
Van 127.6"	B31	4733	**11500**	**13925**	**15050**
Maxivan 127.6"	B31		**12150**	**14650**	**15800**
RAM VAN OPTIONS					
Add Premium Trim			**600**	**675**	**675**
Add 11/12 Passenger Seating (2500)			**150**	**175**	**175**
Add Aluminum/Alloy Wheels			**275**	**325**	**325**
Add Compact Disc Player			**100**	**125**	**125**
Add Power Seat			**175**	**200**	**200**
Add Rear Air Conditioning			**150**	**175**	**175**
Add Theft Recovery System			**75**	**100**	**100**
Deduct V6 Engine			**700**	**700**	**700**
Deduct W/out Air Conditioning			**650**	**650**	**650**
Deduct W/out Cruise Control			**175**	**175**	**175**
Deduct W/out Power Door Locks			**150**	**150**	**150**
Deduct W/out Power Windows			**175**	**175**	**175**
Deduct W/out Tilt Steering Wheel			**125**	**125**	**125**
2002 DAKOTA PICKUP-1/2 Ton-V6					
Sweptline Base	L16*	3426	**7200**	**9200**	**9900**
Sweptline SXT	L16*		**7500**	**9525**	**10250**
Sweptline Sport	L36*	3426	**7800**	**9850**	**10575**
Sweptline SLT	L46*	3641	**7800**	**9850**	**10575**
Sweptline R/T Sport	L36Z	3940	**10350**	**12625**	**13350**
Club Cab Base	L12*	3645	**9300**	**11500**	**12225**
Club Cab SXT	L12*		**9600**	**11825**	**12575**
Club Cab Sport	L32*	3645	**9900**	**12150**	**12875**
Club Cab SLT	L42*	3871	**9900**	**12150**	**12875**
Club Cab R/T Sport	L32Z	4123	**12450**	**14975**	**15750**
Quad Cab Sport	L38*	4244	**11350**	**13775**	**14525**
Quad Cab SLT	L48*	4244	**11350**	**13775**	**14525**

SEE TRUCK OPTION PAGE FOR ADDITIONAL OPTIONS

BODY TYPE	Model No.	Weight	Trade-In	Retail	High Retail
Add 4 Wheel Drive			2450	2675	2675
Add Aluminum/Alloy Wheels (Base)			225	250	250
Add CD Player (Std. SXT)			75	100	100
Add Cruise Control (Std. R/T)			150	175	175
Add Leather Seats			350	400	400
Add Power Door Locks			125	150	150
Add Power Seat			150	175	175
Add Power Windows			150	175	175
Add Running Boards			100	125	125
Add Theft Recovery System			75	100	100
Add Tilt Steering Wheel (Std. R/T)			100	125	125
Add V8 Engine (Std. R/T Sport)			450	500	500
Deduct 4 Cyl. Engine			600	600	600
Deduct W/out Automatic Trans.			475	475	475
* G as the 1st position of the model # denotes 4WD					
2002 RAM 1500 PICKUP-1/2 Ton-V8					
Sweptline	A16*	4499	10475	12750	13825
Quad Cab	A18*	4884	12575	15100	16275
2002 RAM 2500 PICKUP-3/4 Ton-V8					
Sweptline HD	C26*	5090	11475	13900	15025
Quad Cab HD	C23*	5359	14575	17250	18475
2002 RAM 3500 PICKUP-1 Ton-V8-Dual Rear Wheels					
Sweptline	C36*	5523	12475	15000	16150
Quad Cab	C33*	5897	15575	18300	19550
RAM PICKUP OPTIONS					
Add SLT Plus Trim			1200	1350	1350
Add SLT Trim			600	675	675
Add Sport Trim			300	350	350
Add 4 Wheel Drive			2550	2775	2775
Add 5.9L 6 Cyl. H.O. Turbo Diesel Engine			4500	4725	4725
Add 5.9L 6 Cyl. Turbo Diesel Engine			4300	4525	4525
Add 8.0L V10 Engine			400	450	450
Add Aluminum/Alloy Wheels			275	325	325
Add Compact Disc Player			100	125	125
Add Leather Seats			425	475	475
Add Power Seat			175	200	200
Add Running Boards			100	125	125
Add Theft Recovery System			75	100	100
Deduct V6 Engine			700	700	700
Deduct W/out Air Conditioning			650	650	650
Deduct W/out AT (Ex. H.O. T-Diesel)			525	525	525
Deduct W/out Cruise Control			175	175	175
Deduct W/out Tilt Steering Wheel			125	125	125
* F or U as the 1st position of the model # denotes 4WD					
DODGE					
2001 CARAVAN-V6					
Caravan SE	P25	3920	6475	8400	9275
Caravan Sport	P45	4064	7175	9175	10050
Grand Caravan SE	P24		7375	9400	10275
Grand Caravan Sport	P44*	4093	8075	10150	11075
Grand Caravan EX	P74		9875	12100	12975
Grand Caravan ES	P54*	4252	10625	12925	13850
Add All Wheel Drive			800	900	900
Add Aluminum/Alloy Wheels (Sport)			175	200	200

TRUCKS

BODY TYPE	Model No.	Weight	Trade-In	Retail	High Retail
Add Compact Disc Player (Std. EX)			50	75	75
Add Leather Seats			300	350	350
Add Power Seat (Std. EX, ES)			125	150	150
Add Power Sliding Door (Std. EX, ES)			225	250	250
Add Rear Air Conditioning (Std. EX, ES)			125	150	150
Add Rear Bucket Seats			125	150	150
Add Theft Recovery System			50	75	75
Deduct 4 Cyl. Engine			500	500	500
Deduct W/out Cruise Control			125	125	125
Deduct W/out Power Door Locks			100	100	100
Deduct W/out Power Windows			125	125	125
Deduct W/out Tilt Steering Wheel			100	100	100
* T as the 1st position of the model # denotes AWD					
2001 DURANGO-1/2 Ton-V8-4WD					
Wagon 4D Sport (2WD)	R28	4408	9825	12075	12950
Wagon 4D SLT (2WD)	R28		10825	13150	14075
Wagon 4D SLT Plus (2WD)	R28		11575	14000	14950
Wagon 4D Sport	S28	4648	10725	13025	13950
Wagon 4D SLT	S28		11725	14175	15125
Wagon 4D SLT Plus	S28		12475	15000	15975
Wagon 4D R/T Sport	S28		13425	16025	17050
Add 3rd Row Seat			125	150	150
Add Compact Disc Player (Std. Plus, R/T)			50	75	75
Add Rear Air Conditioning			125	150	150
Add Running Boards (Base SLT)			75	100	100
Add Theft Recovery System			50	75	75
2001 RAM VAN 1500-1/2 Ton-V8					
Wagon 109.6"	B15	4591	9450	11650	12675
Van 109.6"	B11	4195	8250	10350	11375
Van 127.6"	B11	4411	8350	10450	11475
Maxivan 127.6"	B11	4500	8950	11100	12100
2001 RAM VAN 2500-3/4 Ton-V8					
Wagon 127.6"	B25	5173	10150	12400	13450
Van 127.6"	B21	4757	8950	11100	12100
Maxivan 127.6"	B21	4912	9550	11750	12800
2001 RAM VAN 3500-1 Ton-V8					
Maxiwagon 127.6"	B35	5623	11350	13750	14850
Van 127.6"	B31	4779	9550	11750	12800
Maxivan 127.6"	B31	4949	10150	12400	13450
RAM VAN OPTIONS					
Add Premium Trim			550	625	625
Add 11/12 Passenger Seating (2500)			125	150	150
Add Aluminum/Alloy Wheels			225	250	250
Add Compact Disc Player			100	125	125
Add Power Seat			150	175	175
Add Rear Air Conditioning			125	150	150
Add Theft Recovery System			50	75	75
Deduct V6 Engine			675	675	675
Deduct W/out Air Conditioning			600	600	600
Deduct W/out Cruise Control			150	150	150
Deduct W/out Power Door Locks			125	125	125
Deduct W/out Power Windows			150	150	150
Deduct W/out Tilt Steering Wheel			100	100	100

TRUCKS

SEE TRUCK OPTION PAGE FOR ADDITIONAL OPTIONS

BODY TYPE	Model No.	Weight	Trade-In	Retail	High Retail
2001 DAKOTA PICKUP-1/2 Ton-V6					
Sweptline	L26*	3389	6050	7925	8750
Sweptline R/T Sport	L26Z	3850	8750	10900	11650
Club Cab	L22*	3617	8150	10250	10975
Club Cab R/T Sport	L22Z	4075	10850	13150	13900
Quad Cab Sport/SLT	L2A*	4151	9950	12200	12925
Add SLT Trim (Ex. R/T, Quad)			400	450	450
Add Sport Trim (Ex. R/T, Quad)			400	450	450
Add 4 Wheel Drive			2350	2575	2575
Add A/A Wheels (Std. R/T, Quad)			175	200	200
Add Compact Disc Player			50	75	75
Add Cruise Control (Std. R/T)			125	150	150
Add Leather Seats			300	350	350
Add Power Door Locks			100	125	125
Add Power Seat			125	150	150
Add Power Windows			125	150	150
Add Running Boards			75	100	100
Add Theft Recovery System			50	75	75
Add Tilt Steering Wheel (Std. R/T)			100	125	125
Add V8 Engine (Std. R/T Sport)			400	450	450
Deduct 4 Cyl. Engine			550	550	550
Deduct W/out Air Conditioning			550	550	550
Deduct W/out Automatic Trans.			425	425	425
* G as the 1st position of the model # denotes 4WD					
2001 RAM 1500 PICKUP-1/2 Ton-V8					
Sweptline	C16*	4280	7875	9925	10975
Club Cab	C12*	4749	9075	11250	12275
Quad Cab	C13*	4833	9925	12150	13200
2001 RAM 2500 PICKUP-3/4 Ton-V8					
Sweptline HD	C26*	5068	9775	12000	13050
Quad Cab HD	C23*	5369	12575	15100	16275
2001 RAM 3500 PICKUP-1 Ton-V8-Dual Rear Wheels					
Sweptline	C36*	5467	10775	13075	14150
Quad Cab	C33*	5876	13575	16175	17375
RAM PICKUP OPTIONS					
Add SLT Plus Trim			1100	1225	1225
Add SLT Trim			550	625	625
Add Sport Trim			275	325	325
Add 4 Wheel Drive			2350	2575	2575
Add 5.9L 6 Cyl. H.O. Turbo Diesel Engine			4400	4625	4625
Add 5.9L 6 Cyl. Turbo Diesel Engine			4200	4425	4425
Add 8.0L V10 Engine			375	425	425
Add Aluminum/Alloy Wheels			225	250	250
Add Compact Disc Player			100	125	125
Add Leather Seats			375	425	425
Add Power Seat			150	175	175
Add Running Boards			75	100	100
Add Theft Recovery System			50	75	75
Deduct Work Truck Pkg.			1500	1500	1500
Deduct V6 Engine (Ex. WT)			675	675	675
Deduct W/out Air Conditioning			600	600	600
Deduct W/out AT (Ex. H.O. T-Diesel)			475	475	475
Deduct W/out Cruise Control			150	150	150
Deduct W/out Tilt Steering Wheel			100	100	100

* F as the 1st position of the model # denotes 4WD

BODY TYPE	Model No.	Weight	Trade-In	Retail	High Retail
DODGE					
2000 CARAVAN-V6					
Caravan	P25	3514	**3950**	**5575**	**6425**
Caravan SE	P45		**5000**	**6750**	**7675**
Grand Caravan	P24	3916	**5325**	**7100**	**7975**
Grand Caravan SE	P44*		**6025**	**7875**	**8800**
Grand Caravan LE	P54*		**6675**	**8600**	**9475**
Grand Caravan ES	P74*		**7425**	**9425**	**10300**
Add Sport Trim			**325**	**375**	**375**
Add 3rd Row Seat (Base Caravan)			**100**	**125**	**125**
Add All Wheel Drive			**700**	**800**	**800**
Add Aluminum/Alloy Wheels (Std. ES)			**125**	**150**	**150**
Add Compact Disc Player (Std. Grand ES)			**50**	**75**	**75**
Add Leather Seats			**250**	**300**	**300**
Add Left Sliding Door (Base Caravan)			**250**	**300**	**300**
Add Power Seat (Std. LE, ES)			**100**	**125**	**125**
Add Rear Air Conditioning			**100**	**125**	**125**
Add Rear Bucket Seats			**100**	**125**	**125**
Deduct 4 Cyl. Engine			**400**	**400**	**400**
Deduct W/out Air Conditioning			**500**	**500**	**500**
Deduct W/out Cruise Control			**100**	**100**	**100**
Deduct W/out Power Door Locks			**75**	**75**	**75**
Deduct W/out Power Windows			**100**	**100**	**100**
Deduct W/out Tilt Steering Wheel			**75**	**75**	**75**
* T as the 1st position of the model # denotes AWD					
2000 DURANGO-1/2 Ton-V8-4WD					
Wagon 4D Sport (2WD)	R28		**7650**	**9675**	**10575**
Wagon 4D SLT (2WD)	R28	4360	**8550**	**10650**	**11600**
Wagon 4D SLT Plus (2WD)	R28		**9150**	**11300**	**12200**
Wagon 4D Sport	S28		**8450**	**10575**	**11525**
Wagon 4D SLT	S28	4598	**9350**	**11550**	**12450**
Wagon 4D SLT Plus	S28		**9950**	**12200**	**13100**
Wagon 4D R/T Sport	S28		**10650**	**12950**	**13875**
Add 3rd Row Seat			**100**	**125**	**125**
Add Compact Disc Player (Std. Plus, R/T)			**50**	**75**	**75**
Add Rear Air Conditioning			**100**	**125**	**125**
Add Running Boards (SLT, SLT Plus)			**50**	**75**	**75**
2000 RAM VAN 1500-1/2 Ton-V8					
Wagon 109.6"	B15	4797	**7900**	**9950**	**11000**
Van 109.6"	B11	4388	**6750**	**8675**	**9725**
Van 127.6"	B11	4593	**6850**	**8800**	**9850**
Maxivan 127.6"	B11	4677	**7400**	**9400**	**10425**
2000 RAM VAN 2500-3/4 Ton-V8					
Wagon 127.6"	B25	5151	**8550**	**10675**	**11725**
Van 127.6"	B21	4719	**7400**	**9400**	**10425**
Maxivan 127.6"	B21	4857	**7950**	**10000**	**11050**
2000 RAM VAN 3500-1 Ton-V8					
Maxiwagon 127.6"	B35	5586	**9650**	**11875**	**12925**
Van 127.6"	B31	4747	**7950**	**10000**	**11050**
Maxivan 127.6"	B31	4919	**8500**	**10625**	**11675**
RAM VAN OPTIONS					
Add Premium Trim			**500**	**575**	**575**
Add 11/12 Passenger Seating (2500)			**100**	**125**	**125**

TRUCKS

SEE TRUCK OPTION PAGE FOR ADDITIONAL OPTIONS

BODY TYPE	Model No.	Weight	Trade-In	Retail	High Retail
Add Aluminum/Alloy Wheels			175	200	200
Add Compact Disc Player			75	100	100
Add Power Seat			125	150	150
Add Rear Air Conditioning			100	125	125
Deduct V6 Engine			600	600	600
Deduct W/out Air Conditioning			550	550	550
Deduct W/out Cruise Control			125	125	125
Deduct W/out Power Door Locks			100	100	100
Deduct W/out Power Windows			125	125	125
Deduct W/out Tilt Steering Wheel			75	75	75
2000 DAKOTA PICKUP-1/2 Ton-V6					
Sweptline	L26*	3569	5275	7050	7825
Sweptline R/T Sport	L26Z	3875	7875	9925	10650
Club Cab	L22*	3806	7025	9000	9775
Club Cab R/T Sport	L22Z	4101	9625	11825	12575
Quad Cab Sport/SLT	L2A*	4124	8875	11025	11750
Add SLT Trim (Ex. R/T, Quad)			350	400	400
Add Sport Trim (Ex. R/T, Quad)			350	400	400
Add 4 Wheel Drive			2000	2225	2225
Add A/A Wheels (Std. R/T, Quad)			125	150	150
Add Compact Disc Player			50	75	75
Add Cruise Control (Std. R/T)			100	125	125
Add Power Door Locks			75	100	100
Add Power Seat			100	125	125
Add Power Windows			100	125	125
Add Running Boards			50	75	75
Add Tilt Steering Wheel (Std. R/T)			75	100	100
Add V8 Engine (Std. R/T Sport)			400	450	450
Deduct 4 Cyl. Engine			500	500	500
Deduct W/out Air Conditioning			500	500	500
Deduct W/out Automatic Trans.			375	375	375
* G as the 1st position of the model # denotes 4WD					
2000 RAM 1500 PICKUP-1/2 Ton-V8					
Sweptline	C16*	4384	6950	8900	9950
Club Cab	C12*	4721	7950	10000	11050
Quad Cab	C13*	4807	8675	10800	11850
2000 RAM 2500 PICKUP-3/4 Ton-V8					
Sweptline HD	C26*	4966	8750	10875	11925
Quad Cab HD	C23*	5247	11150	13550	14650
2000 RAM 3500 PICKUP-1 Ton-V8-Dual Rear Wheels					
Sweptline	C36*	5387	9750	11975	13025
Quad Cab	C33*	5671	12150	14650	15800
RAM PICKUP OPTIONS					
Add Laramie SLT Trim			500	575	575
Add SLT Plus Trim			950	1075	1075
Add Sport Trim			250	300	300
Add 4 Wheel Drive			2000	2225	2225
Add 5.9L 6 Cyl. Turbo Diesel Engine			4500	4725	4725
Add 8.0L V10 Engine			350	400	400
Add Aluminum/Alloy Wheels			175	200	200
Add Compact Disc Player			75	100	100
Add Leather Seats			325	375	375
Add Power Seat			125	150	150
Add Running Boards			50	75	75

BODY TYPE	Model No.	Weight	Trade-In	Retail	High Retail
Deduct Work Truck Pkg.			1400	1400	1400
Deduct V6 Engine (Ex. WT)			600	600	600
Deduct W/out Air Conditioning			550	550	550
Deduct W/out Automatic Trans.			425	425	425
Deduct W/out Cruise Control			125	125	125
Deduct W/out Tilt Steering Wheel			75	75	75

* F as the 1st position of the model # denotes 4WD

DODGE

1999 CARAVAN-V6

BODY TYPE	Model No.	Weight	Trade-In	Retail	High Retail
Caravan	P25	3517	3050	4575	5425
Caravan SE	P45	3709	4250	5925	6800
Caravan LE	P55	3967	4900	6650	7550
Grand Caravan	P24	3684	4175	5850	6725
Grand Caravan SE	P44*	3811	5050	6800	7725
Grand Caravan LE	P54*	4050	5700	7525	8425
Grand Caravan ES	P74*		6250	8150	9000
Add Sport Trim			300	350	350
Add 3rd Row Seat (Base Caravan)			100	125	125
Add All Wheel Drive			600	675	675
Add Aluminum/Alloy Wheels (Std. ES)			75	100	100
Add Leather Seats			225	250	250
Add Left Sliding Door (Base Caravan)			225	250	250
Add Power Seat (Std. LE, ES)			75	100	100
Add Rear Air Conditioning			75	100	100
Add Rear Bucket Seats			75	100	100
Deduct 4 Cyl. Engine			300	300	300
Deduct W/out Air Conditioning			450	450	450
Deduct W/out Cruise Control			75	75	75
Deduct W/out Power Door Locks			50	50	50
Deduct W/out Power Windows			75	75	75
Deduct W/out Tilt Steering Wheel			50	50	50

* T as the 1st position of the model # denotes AWD

1999 DURANGO-1/2 Ton-V8-4WD

BODY TYPE	Model No.	Weight	Trade-In	Retail	High Retail
Wagon 4D SLT (2WD)	R28	4394	6925	8875	9775
Wagon 4D SLT	S28	4655	7675	9725	10625
Add 3rd Row Seat			100	125	125
Add Leather Seats			225	250	250
Add Power Seat			75	100	100
Add Rear Air Conditioning			75	100	100

1999 RAM VAN 1500-1/2 Ton-V8

BODY TYPE	Model No.	Weight	Trade-In	Retail	High Retail
Wagon 109.6"	B15	4400	7075	9050	10050
Van 109.6"	B11	4379	5975	7825	8900
Van 127.6"	B11	4516	6075	7950	9025
Maxivan 127.6"	B11	4523	6575	8500	9525

1999 RAM VAN 2500-3/4 Ton-V8

BODY TYPE	Model No.	Weight	Trade-In	Retail	High Retail
Wagon 127.6"	B25	4713	7675	9700	10750
Van 127.6"	B21	4710	6575	8500	9525
Maxivan 127.6"	B21	4847	7075	9050	10050

1999 RAM VAN 3500-1 Ton-V8

BODY TYPE	Model No.	Weight	Trade-In	Retail	High Retail
Maxiwagon 127.6"	B35	4737	8675	10800	11850
Van 127.6"	B31	4737	7075	9050	10050
Maxivan 127.6"	B31	4910	7575	9600	10625

SEE TRUCK OPTION PAGE FOR ADDITIONAL OPTIONS

BODY TYPE	Model No.	Weight	Trade-In	Retail	High Retail
RAM VAN OPTIONS					
Add Premium Trim			450	500	500
Add 11/12 Passenger Seating (2500)			100	125	125
Add Aluminum/Alloy Wheels			125	150	150
Add Power Seat			100	125	125
Add Rear Air Conditioning			75	100	100
Deduct V6 Engine			500	500	500
Deduct W/out Air Conditioning			500	500	500
Deduct W/out Cruise Control			100	100	100
Deduct W/out Power Door Locks			75	75	75
Deduct W/out Power Windows			100	100	100
Deduct W/out Tilt Steering Wheel			50	50	50
1999 DAKOTA PICKUP-1/2 Ton-V6					
Sweptline	L26*	3518	4475	6175	6950
Sweptline R/T Sport	L26Z		6625	8550	9325
Club Cab	L22*	3749	6000	7875	8700
Club Cab R/T Sport	L22Z		8150	10250	10975
Add SLT Trim (Ex. R/T Sport)			325	375	375
Add Sport Trim (Ex. R/T Sport)			325	375	375
Add 4 Wheel Drive			1800	2000	2000
Add Aluminum/Alloy Wheels (Std. R/T)			75	100	100
Add Cruise Control (Std. R/T)			75	100	100
Add Power Door Locks			50	75	75
Add Power Windows			75	100	100
Add Tilt Steering Wheel (Std. R/T)			50	75	75
Add V8 Engine (Std. R/T Sport)			375	425	425
Deduct 4 Cyl. Engine			450	450	450
Deduct W/out Air Conditioning			450	450	450
Deduct W/out Automatic Trans.			325	325	325
* G as the 1st position of the model # denotes 4WD					
1999 RAM 1500 PICKUP-1/2 Ton-V8					
Sweptline	C16*	4345	6300	8200	9200
Club Cab	C12*	4666	7150	9125	10125
Quad Cab	C13*	4740	7850	9900	10950
1999 RAM 2500 PICKUP-3/4 Ton-V8					
Sweptline HD	C26*	4923	7900	9950	11000
Club Cab HD	C22*	5224	9200	11375	12400
Quad Cab HD	C23*	5302	10100	12350	13400
1999 RAM 3500 PICKUP-1 Ton-V8-Dual Rear Wheels					
Sweptline	C36*	5492	8900	11050	12050
Quad Cab	C33*	5742	11100	13475	14575
RAM PICKUP OPTIONS					
Add Laramie SLT Trim (Std. Sport)			450	500	500
Add Sport Trim			675	750	750
Add 4 Wheel Drive			1800	2000	2000
Add 5.9L 6 Cyl. Turbo Diesel Engine			4500	4725	4725
Add 8.0L V10 Engine			325	375	375
Add Aluminum/Alloy Wheels			125	150	150
Add Leather Seats			275	325	325
Add Power Seat			100	125	125
Deduct Work Truck Pkg.			1400	1400	1400
Deduct V6 Engine (Ex. WT)			500	500	500
Deduct W/out Air Conditioning			500	500	500
Deduct W/out Automatic Trans.			375	375	375

TRUCKS

BODY TYPE	Model No.	Weight	Trade-In	Retail	High Retail
Deduct W/out Cruise Control			100	100	100
Deduct W/out Tilt Steering Wheel			50	50	50

* F as the 1st position of the model # denotes 4WD

DODGE

1998 CARAVAN-V6

BODY TYPE	Model No.	Weight	Trade-In	Retail	High Retail
Caravan	P25	3533	2300	3675	4425
Caravan SE	P45	3533	3550	5125	5925
Caravan LE	P55	3533	4150	5800	6675
Grand Caravan	P24	3706	3500	5075	5875
Grand Caravan SE	P44*	3706	4450	6150	7025
Grand Caravan LE	P54*	3706	5050	6800	7725
Grand Caravan ES	P54*	3706	5500	7300	8175
Add Sport Trim			275	325	325
Add 3rd Row Seat (Base Caravan)			100	125	125
Add All Wheel Drive			500	575	575
Add Aluminum/Alloy Wheels (Std. ES)			50	75	75
Add Leather Seats			175	200	200
Add Left Sliding Door (Base Caravan)			200	225	225
Add Power Seat (Std. ES)			50	75	75
Add Rear Air Conditioning			50	75	75
Add Rear Bucket Seats			50	75	75
Deduct 4 Cyl. Engine			200	200	200
Deduct W/out Air Conditioning			400	400	400
Deduct W/out Cruise Control			50	50	50
Deduct W/out Power Windows			50	50	50

* T as the 1st position of the model # denotes AWD

1998 DURANGO-1/2 Ton-V8-4WD

BODY TYPE	Model No.	Weight	Trade-In	Retail	High Retail
Wagon 4D SLT	S28	4736	6525	8425	9300
Add 3rd Row Seat			100	125	125
Add Leather Seats			175	200	200
Add Power Seat			50	75	75
Add Rear Air Conditioning			50	75	75

1998 RAM VAN 1500-1/2 Ton-V8

BODY TYPE	Model No.	Weight	Trade-In	Retail	High Retail
Wagon 109.6"	B15	4666	5700	7525	8575
Van 109.6"	B11	4186	4600	6300	7300
Van 127.6"	B11	4397	4700	6425	7425
Maxivan 127.6"	B11	4675	5150	6900	7950

1998 RAM VAN 2500-3/4 Ton-V8

BODY TYPE	Model No.	Weight	Trade-In	Retail	High Retail
Wagon 127.6"	B25	5223	6250	8150	9150
Van 127.6"	B21	4617	5150	6900	7950
Maxivan 127.6"	B21	5291	5600	7400	8425

1998 RAM VAN 3500-1 Ton-V8

BODY TYPE	Model No.	Weight	Trade-In	Retail	High Retail
Maxiwagon 127.6"	B35	5900	7150	9150	10150
Van 127.6"	B31	4621	5600	7400	8425
Maxivan 127.6"	B31	4832	6050	7925	9000

RAM VAN OPTIONS

BODY TYPE	Model No.	Weight	Trade-In	Retail	High Retail
Add Premium Trim			400	450	450
Add 11/12 Passenger Seating (2500)			100	125	125
Add Aluminum/Alloy Wheels			100	125	125
Add Power Seat			75	100	100
Add Rear Air Conditioning			50	75	75
Deduct V6 Engine			400	400	400
Deduct W/out Air Conditioning			450	450	450

SEE TRUCK OPTION PAGE FOR ADDITIONAL OPTIONS

BODY TYPE	Model No.	Weight	Trade-In	Retail	High Retail
Deduct W/out Cruise Control			75	75	75
Deduct W/out Power Door Locks			50	50	50
Deduct W/out Power Windows			75	75	75
Deduct W/out Tilt Steering Wheel			50	50	50
1998 DAKOTA PICKUP-1/2 Ton-V6					
Sweptline	L26*	3273	3900	5525	6275
Sweptline R/T Sport	L26Z		5550	7350	8250
Club Cab	L22*	3762	5100	6875	7700
Club Cab R/T Sport	L22Z		6750	8700	9575
Add SLT Trim (Ex. R/T Sport)			300	350	350
Add Sport Trim (Ex. R/T Sport)			300	350	350
Add 4 Wheel Drive			1600	1800	1800
Add Aluminum/Alloy Wheels (Std. R/T)			50	75	75
Add Cruise Control (Std. R/T)			50	75	75
Add Power Windows			50	75	75
Add V8 Engine (Std. R/T Sport)			350	400	400
Deduct 4 Cyl. Engine			350	350	350
Deduct W/out Air Conditioning			400	400	400
Deduct W/out Automatic Trans.			275	275	275
* G as the 1st position of the model # denotes 4WD					
1998 RAM 1500 PICKUP-1/2 Ton-V8					
Sweptline	C16*	4308	5775	7600	8650
Club Cab	C12*	4751	6625	8550	9575
Quad Cab	C13*	4788	7325	9325	10350
1998 RAM 2500 PICKUP-3/4 Ton-V8					
Sweptline HD	C26*	4860	7075	9050	10050
Club Cab HD	C22*	5040	8275	10375	11400
Quad Cab HD	C23*	5077	9075	11250	12275
1998 RAM 3500 PICKUP-1 Ton-V8-Dual Rear Wheels					
Sweptline	C36*	5699	8075	10150	11175
Quad Cab	C33*	5850	10075	12325	13375
RAM PICKUP OPTIONS					
Add Laramie SLT Trim (Std. Sport, SST)			400	450	450
Add Sport Trim			600	675	675
Add SST Pkg.			800	900	900
Add 4 Wheel Drive			1600	1800	1800
Add 5.9L 6 Cyl. Turbo Diesel Engine			4200	4425	4425
Add 8.0L V10 Engine			300	350	350
Add Aluminum/Alloy Wheels			100	125	125
Add Leather Seats			225	250	250
Add Power Seat			75	100	100
Deduct Work Truck Pkg.			1200	1200	1200
Deduct V6 Engine (Ex. WT)			400	400	400
Deduct W/out Air Conditioning			450	450	450
Deduct W/out Automatic Trans.			325	325	325
Deduct W/out Cruise Control			75	75	75
Deduct W/out Tilt Steering Wheel			50	50	50
* F as the 1st position of the model # denotes 4WD					
DODGE					
1997 CARAVAN-V6					
Caravan	P25	3455	1950	3275	3975
Caravan SE	P45	3689	2900	4375	5200
Caravan LE	P55	3872	3300	4850	5750
Caravan ES	P55	3872	3600	5175	5975

TRUCKS

BODY TYPE	Model No.	Weight	Trade-In	Retail	High Retail
Grand Caravan	P24	3711	**2650**	**4100**	**4900**
Grand Caravan SE	P44	3791	**3600**	**5175**	**5975**
Grand Caravan LE	P54	3955	**4000**	**5625**	**6475**
Grand Caravan ES	P54	3955	**4300**	**5975**	**6850**
Add Sport Trim			**175**	**200**	**200**
Add All Wheel Drive			**400**	**450**	**450**
Add Leather Seats			**150**	**175**	**175**
Add Left Sliding Door (Std. LE, ES)			**150**	**175**	**175**
Add Power Seat			**50**	**75**	**75**
Deduct 4 Cyl. Engine			**150**	**150**	**150**
Deduct W/out Air Conditioning			**250**	**250**	**250**
Deduct W/out Cruise Control			**50**	**50**	**50**
Deduct W/out Power Windows			**50**	**50**	**50**
1997 RAM VAN 1500-1/2 Ton-V8					
Wagon 109.6"	B15	4399	**4250**	**5925**	**6925**
Van 109.6"	B11	3799	**3450**	**5025**	**5925**
Van 127.6"	B11	3992	**3500**	**5075**	**5975**
1997 RAM VAN 2500-3/4 Ton-V8					
Wagon 127.6"	B25	4790	**4550**	**6250**	**7225**
Van 109.6"	B21	3829	**3700**	**5300**	**6225**
Van 127.6"	B21	4032	**3750**	**5350**	**6275**
Maxivan 127.6"	B21	4234	**4100**	**5750**	**6725**
1997 RAM VAN 3500-1 Ton-V8					
Wagon 127.6"	B35	5047	**4800**	**6525**	**7550**
Maxiwagon 127.6"	B35	5343	**5150**	**6925**	**7975**
Van 127.6"	B31	4414	**4000**	**5625**	**6575**
Maxivan 127.6"	B31	4633	**4350**	**6025**	**7000**
RAM VAN OPTIONS					
Add SLT Trim			**300**	**350**	**350**
Add Aluminum/Alloy Wheels			**50**	**75**	**75**
Add Power Seat			**75**	**100**	**100**
Deduct V6 Engine			**300**	**300**	**300**
Deduct W/out Air Conditioning			**350**	**350**	**350**
Deduct W/out Cruise Control			**75**	**75**	**75**
Deduct W/out Power Windows			**75**	**75**	**75**
1997 DAKOTA PICKUP-1/2 Ton-V6					
Sweptline	L26*	3273	**3175**	**4700**	**5475**
Club Cab	L23*	3762	**4275**	**5950**	**6750**
Add SLT Trim			**250**	**300**	**300**
Add Sport Trim			**200**	**225**	**225**
Add 4 Wheel Drive			**1300**	**1450**	**1450**
Add Cruise Control			**50**	**75**	**75**
Add Power Windows			**50**	**75**	**75**
Add V8 Engine			**250**	**300**	**300**
Deduct 4 Cyl. Engine			**200**	**200**	**200**
Deduct W/out Air Conditioning			**250**	**250**	**250**
Deduct W/out Automatic Trans.			**175**	**175**	**175**
* G as the 1st position of the model # denotes 4WD					
1997 RAM 1500 PICKUP-1/2 Ton-V8					
Sweptline	C16*	4028	**4800**	**6525**	**7550**
Club Cab	C13*	4575	**5700**	**7525**	**8575**
1997 RAM 2500 PICKUP-3/4 Ton-V8					
Sweptline HD	C26*	4765	**5700**	**7525**	**8575**

SEE TRUCK OPTION PAGE FOR ADDITIONAL OPTIONS

BODY TYPE	Model No.	Weight	Trade-In	Retail	High Retail
Club Cab HD	C23*	4983	6600	8525	9550
1997 RAM 3500 PICKUP-1 Ton-V8-Dual Rear Wheels					
Sweptline	C36*	5254	6600	8525	9550
Club Cab	C33*	5583	7500	9525	10550
RAM PICKUP OPTIONS					
Add Laramie SLT Trim (Std. SST)			350	400	400
Add Sport Trim			175	200	200
Add SST Pkg.			650	725	725
Add 4 Wheel Drive			1300	1450	1450
Add 5.9L 6 Cyl. Turbo Diesel Engine			4000	4225	4225
Add 8.0L V10 Engine			250	300	300
Add Aluminum/Alloy Wheels			50	75	75
Add Leather Seats			200	225	225
Add Power Seat			75	100	100
Deduct Work Truck Pkg.			1100	1100	1100
Deduct V6 Engine (Ex. WT)			300	300	300
Deduct W/out Air Conditioning			350	350	350
Deduct W/out Automatic Trans.			250	250	250
Deduct W/out Cruise Control			75	75	75

* F as the 1st position of the model # denotes 4WD

DODGE

BODY TYPE	Model No.	Weight	Trade-In	Retail	High Retail
1996 CARAVAN-V6					
Caravan	P25	3528	1700	2975	3650
Caravan SE	P45	3696	2350	3750	4525
Caravan LE	P55	3875	2750	4200	5000
Caravan ES	P55	3875	3000	4500	5350
Grand Caravan	P24	3680	2200	3575	4325
Grand Caravan SE	P44	3766	2850	4325	5150
Grand Caravan LE	P54	3949	3250	4800	5675
Grand Caravan ES	P54	3949	3500	5075	5875
Add Sport Trim			150	175	175
Deduct 4 Cyl. Engine			150	150	150
Deduct W/out Air Conditioning			150	150	150
1996 RAM VAN 1500-1/2 Ton-V8					
Wagon 109.6"	B15	4243	3525	5100	6000
Van 109.6"	B11	3880	2825	4300	5175
1996 RAM VAN 2500-3/4 Ton-V8					
Wagon 127.6"	B25	4257	3750	5350	6275
Van 109.6"	B21	3830	3050	4575	5475
Van 127.6"	B24	3993	3050	4575	5475
Maxivan 127.6"	B24	4159	3400	4950	5900
1996 RAM VAN 3500-1 Ton-V8					
Wagon 127.6"	B35	4643	3975	5600	6550
Maxiwagon 127.6"	B34	4837	4325	6000	7000
Van 127.6"	B31	4112	3275	4825	5775
Maxivan 127.6"	B34	4439	3625	5225	6125
RAM VAN OPTIONS					
Add SLT Trim			250	300	300
Deduct V6 Engine			200	200	200
Deduct W/out Air Conditioning			250	250	250
1996 DAKOTA PICKUP-1/2 Ton-V6					
Sweptline	L26*	3042	2500	3925	4625
Sweptline Sport	L26*	3042	2450	3875	4575
Club Cab	L23*	3528	3300	4850	5650

TRUCKS

BODY TYPE	Model No.	Weight	Trade-In	Retail	High Retail
Club Cab Sport	L23*	3528	**3250**	**4800**	**5600**
Add SLT Trim			**225**	**250**	**250**
Add 4 Wheel Drive			**1200**	**1350**	**1350**
Add V8 Engine			**225**	**250**	**250**
Deduct 4 Cyl. Engine			**175**	**175**	**175**
Deduct W/out Air Conditioning			**150**	**150**	**150**
Deduct W/out Automatic Trans.			**125**	**125**	**125**
* G as the 1st position of the model # denotes 4WD					
1996 RAM 1500 PICKUP-1/2 Ton-V8					
Sweptline	C16*	4028	**4150**	**5800**	**6775**
Club Cab	C13*	4529	**4950**	**6700**	**7725**
1996 RAM 2500 PICKUP-3/4 Ton-V8					
Sweptline	C26*	4612	**4900**	**6650**	**7675**
HD Sweptline	C26*	4760	**4975**	**6725**	**7750**
Club Cab	C23*	4885	**5700**	**7525**	**8575**
1996 RAM 3500 PICKUP-1 Ton-V8-Dual Rear Wheels					
Sweptline	C36*	5160	**5650**	**7475**	**8500**
Club Cab	C33*	5493	**6450**	**8350**	**9375**
RAM PICKUP OPTIONS					
Add Laramie SLT Trim			**325**	**375**	**375**
Add Sport Trim			**150**	**175**	**175**
Add 4 Wheel Drive			**1200**	**1350**	**1350**
Add 5.9L 6 Cyl. Turbo Diesel Engine			**3200**	**3425**	**3425**
Add 8.0L V10 Engine			**225**	**250**	**250**
Deduct Work Truck Pkg.			**1000**	**1000**	**1000**
Deduct V6 Engine (Ex. WT)			**200**	**200**	**200**
Deduct W/out Air Conditioning			**250**	**250**	**250**
Deduct W/out Automatic Trans.			**150**	**150**	**150**
* F as the 1st position of the model # denotes 4WD					
DODGE					
1995 CARAVAN-V6					
Caravan C/V	H11	3134	**875**	**2000**	**2525**
Extended Caravan C/V	H14	3393	**1125**	**2300**	**2875**
Caravan	H25	3287	**1125**	**2300**	**2875**
Caravan SE	H45	3439	**1500**	**2750**	**3400**
Caravan LE	H55	3620	**1750**	**3050**	**3725**
Caravan ES	H55	3620	**1900**	**3225**	**3925**
Grand Caravan	H24	3530	**1375**	**2600**	**3225**
Grand Caravan SE	H44	3638	**1750**	**3050**	**3725**
Grand Caravan LE	H54	3776	**2000**	**3350**	**4075**
Grand Caravan ES	H54	3776	**2150**	**3525**	**4275**
Add Sport Trim			**125**	**150**	**150**
Add All Wheel Drive			**350**	**400**	**400**
Deduct 4 Cyl. Engine			**125**	**125**	**125**
1995 RAM VAN 1500-1/2 Ton-V8					
Wagon 109.6"	B15	4094	**2700**	**4150**	**5000**
Van 109.6"	B11	3795	**2100**	**3450**	**4275**
1995 RAM VAN 2500-3/4 Ton-V8					
Wagon 127.6"	B25	4192	**2900**	**4375**	**5250**
Maxiwagon 127.6"	B24	4581	**3225**	**4775**	**5700**
Van 109.6"	B21	3745	**2300**	**3700**	**4550**
Maxivan 127.6"	B24	4074	**2625**	**4075**	**4925**

TRUCKS

SEE TRUCK OPTION PAGE FOR ADDITIONAL OPTIONS

BODY TYPE	Model No.	Weight	Trade-In	Retail	High Retail
1995 RAM VAN 3500-1 Ton-V8					
Wagon 127.6"	B35	4543	3100	4625	5550
Maxiwagon 127.6"	B34	4737	3425	5000	5950
Van 127.6"	B31	4204	2500	3925	4800
Maxivan 127.6"	B34	4354	2825	4300	5175
RAM VAN OPTIONS					
Add SLT Trim			225	250	250
Deduct V6 Engine			150	150	150
1995 DAKOTA PICKUP-1/2 Ton-V6					
Sweptline	L26*	3051	2025	3375	4025
Sweptline Sport	L26*	3051	2000	3350	4000
Club Cab	L23*	3586	2775	4250	4975
Club Cab Sport	L23*	3586	2750	4200	4925
Add SLT Trim			200	225	225
Add 4 Wheel Drive			1100	1225	1225
Add V8 Engine			200	225	225
Deduct 4 Cyl. Engine			125	125	125
* G as the 1st position of the model # denotes 4WD					
1995 RAM 1500 PICKUP-1/2 Ton-V8					
Sweptline	C16*	4052	3550	5125	6025
Club Cab	C13*	4570	4300	5975	6975
1995 RAM 2500 PICKUP-3/4 Ton-V8					
Sweptline	C26*	4624	4200	5875	6850
Club Cab	C23*	4881	4950	6700	7725
1995 RAM 3500 PICKUP-1 Ton-V8-Dual Rear Wheels					
Sweptline	C36*	5210	4850	6600	7625
Club Cab	C33*	5617	5600	7400	8425
RAM PICKUP OPTIONS					
Add Laramie SLT Trim			300	350	350
Add Sport Trim			125	150	150
Add 4 Wheel Drive			1100	1225	1225
Add 5.9L 6 Cyl. Turbo Diesel Engine			2900	3125	3125
Add 8.0L V10 Engine			200	225	225
Deduct Work Truck Pkg.			950	950	950
Deduct V6 Engine (Ex. WT)			150	150	150
* F as the 1st position of the model # denotes 4WD					

FORD

FORD

BODY TYPE	Model No.	Weight	Trade-In	Retail	High Retail
2004 ESCAPE-V6					
Utility 4D XLS	U02	3019	13150	15725	16750
Utility 4D XLT	U03	3181	15000	17675	18725
Utility 4D Limited	U04		16700	19500	20600
Utility 4D XLS (4WD)	U92	3175	14225	16875	17925
Utility 4D XLT (4WD)	U93	3346	16075	18825	19900
Utility 4D Limited (4WD)	U94		17775	20775	21900
Add Aluminum/Alloy Wheels (XLS)			325	375	375
Add Leather Seats (Std. Limited)			450	500	500
Add MACH Stereo System			300	350	350
Add Power Sunroof			575	650	650
Add Running Boards (XLS, XLT)			150	175	175

BODY TYPE	Model No.	Weight	Trade-In	Retail	High Retail
Add Theft Recovery System			100	125	125
Deduct 4 Cyl. Engine			750	750	750
Deduct W/out Automatic Trans.			575	575	575
Deduct W/out Cruise Control			200	200	200
2004 EXPLORER SPORT TRAC-1/2 Ton-V6					
Utility 4D XLS	U67	4135	17200	20150	21275
Utility 4D XLT	U67		18200	21225	22375
Utility 4D XLS (4WD)	U77	4349	18575	21625	22775
Utility 4D XLT (4WD)	U77		19575	22700	23875
2004 EXPLORER-1/2 Ton-V6					
Wagon 4D XLS	U62	4304	13350	15950	16975
Wagon 4D XLT	U63		15850	18600	19675
Wagon 4D Eddie Bauer	U64		19700	22825	24025
Wagon 4D Limited	U65		20100	23250	24450
Wagon 4D XLS (4WD/AWD)	U72/82	4469	14425	17100	18125
Wagon 4D XLT (4WD/AWD)	U73/83		16925	19775	20875
4D Eddie Bauer (4WD/AWD)	U74/84		20775	23975	25200
4D Limited (4WD/AWD)	U75/85		21175	24425	25650
EXPLORER SPORT TRAC/EXPLORER OPTIONS					
Add Adrenalin Package (Sport Trac XLT)			700	800	800
Add NBX Package (XLT)			500	575	575
Add 3rd Row Seat			200	225	225
Add 4.6L V8 Engine			400	450	450
Add Leather Seats (Std. Eddie Bauer, Ltd.)			450	500	500
Add Pioneer/Audiophile Stereo (Std. Adrenalin, Eddie Bauer, Limited).			300	350	350
Add Power Seat (Std. U63/73/83, E. Bauer, Ltd.)			200	225	225
Add Power Sunroof			575	650	650
Add Rear Air Conditioning			200	225	225
Add Rear Bucket Seats (E. Bauer, Limited)			200	225	225
Add Rear Entertainment System			600	675	675
Add Running Boards (U62/U72/U82, XLT)			150	175	175
Add Theft Recovery System			100	125	125
2004 EXPEDITION-1/2 Ton-V8					
Utility XLS	U13	5218	19125	22200	23525
Utility XLT	U15		20125	23275	24625
Utility Eddie Bauer	U17	5394	24925	28375	29875
Utility XLS (4WD)	U14	5499	20850	24050	25425
Utility XLT (4WD)	U16		21850	25125	26550
Utility Eddie Bauer (4WD)	U18	5671	26650	30225	31775
Add NBX Package (XLT)			400	450	450
Add Leather Seats (XLT)			525	600	600
Add Navigation System			650	725	725
Add Power 3rd Row Seat			200	225	225
Add Power Sunroof			625	700	700
Add Rear Bucket Seats			200	225	225
Add Rear Entertainment System			600	675	675
Add Theft Recovery System			100	125	125
Deduct 4.6L V8 Engine (Ex. XLS)			400	400	400
Deduct W/out 3rd Row Seat			200	200	200
Deduct W/out Rear Air Conditioning (Ex. XLS)			200	200	200
Deduct W/out Running Boards (Ex. XLS)			150	150	150
2004 EXCURSION-3/4 Ton-V10					
Utility XLS	U40	6650	20575	23750	25125

SEE TRUCK OPTION PAGE FOR ADDITIONAL OPTIONS

BODY TYPE	Model No.	Weight	Trade-In	Retail	High Retail
Utility XLS T-Diesel	U40P				
Utility XLT	U40		21175	24400	25800
Utility XLT T-Diesel	U40P		29675	33550	35200
Utility Eddie Bauer	U44		24075	27475	28950
Utility Eddie Bauer T-Diesel	U44P		32575	36800	38525
Utility Limited	U42		24075	27475	28950
Utility Limited T-Diesel	U42P		32575	36800	38525
Utility XLS (4WD)	U41	7087	22450	25775	27200
Utility XLS T-Diesel (4WD)	U41P				
Utility XLT (4WD)	U41		23050	26400	27850
Utility XLT T-Diesel (4WD)	U41P		31550	35550	37250
Utility Eddie Bauer (4WD)	U45	7190	25950	29475	31000
Utility Eddie Bauer TD (4WD)	U45P		34450	38775	40550
Utility Limited (4WD)	U43		25950	29475	31000
Utility Limited T-Diesel (4WD)	U43P		34450	38775	40550
Add Leather Seats (XLT)			525	600	600
Add Rear Bucket Seats			200	225	225
Add Rear Entertainment System			600	675	675
Add Theft Recovery System			100	125	125
Deduct 5.4L V8 Engine			700	700	700
Deduct W/out 3rd Row Seat			200	200	200
Deduct W/out Power Seat			225	225	225
Deduct W/out Rear Air Conditioning			200	200	200
2004 FREESTAR-V6					
Cargo Van	A54	4275	10575	12850	13750
Wagon 4D S	A50		12525	15050	16050
Wagon 4D SE	A51		13075	15625	16625
Wagon 4D SES	A57		14125	16750	17800
Wagon 4D SEL	A52		15175	17875	18925
Wagon 4D Limited	A58		18025	21025	22175
Add Alum/Alloy Wheels (Std. SES, SEL, Ltd.)			325	375	375
Add CD Player (Cargo Van, S)			100	125	125
Add Dual Power Sliding Doors (Std. Ltd.)			600	675	675
Add Leather Seats (Std. Limited)			450	500	500
Add Power Seat (Std. SES, SEL, Ltd.)			200	225	225
Add Rear Air Cond. (Std. SES, SEL, Ltd.)			200	225	225
Add Rear Bucket Seats (Std. SEL, Ltd.)			200	225	225
Add Rear Entertainment System			600	675	675
Add Theft Recovery System			100	125	125
Deduct W/out Cruise Control			200	200	200
2004 ECONOLINE E150-1/2 Ton-V8					
Cargo Van	E14	4834	14325	16975	18225
Club Wagon	E11	5506	15525	18250	19500
2004 ECONOLINE E250-3/4 Ton-V8					
Cargo Van	E24	5146	15025	17725	18950
Extended Cargo Van	S24	5371	15825	18575	19850
2004 ECONOLINE E350-1 Ton-V8					
Super Duty Cargo Van	E34	5423	15525	18250	19500
Super Duty Wagon	E31	5804	16725	19525	20825
Super Duty Ext. Cargo Van	S34	5582	16325	19100	20375
Super Duty Ext. Wagon	S31	6160	17725	20725	22075
ECONOLINE OPTIONS					
Add Chateau Trim			900	1000	1000
Add XLT Trim			700	800	800

TRUCKS

BODY TYPE	Model No.	Weight	Trade-In	Retail	High Retail
Add 6.0L V8 Turbo Diesel Engine			5000	5225	5225
Add 6.8L V10 Engine			425	475	475
Add Aluminum/Alloy Wheels			375	425	425
Add AutoVision Entertainment System			600	675	675
Add Compact Disc Player			150	175	175
Add Leather Seats			525	600	600
Add Power Seat			225	250	250
Add Rear Air Cond. (Std. E350 Ext. Wagon)			200	225	225
Add Rear Bucket Seats			200	225	225
Add Running Boards			150	175	175
Add Theft Recovery System			100	125	125
Deduct W/out Air Conditioning			750	750	750
Deduct W/out Cruise Control			225	225	225
Deduct W/out Power Door Locks			200	200	200
Deduct W/out Power Windows			225	225	225
2004 RANGER PICKUP-1/2 Ton-V6					
Styleside	R10*	3028	9775	12000	12750
Flareside	R10*		10100	12350	13075
Styleside Supercab 2D	R14*	3193	11275	13700	14450
Styleside Supercab 4D	R44*		11775	14225	15000
Flareside Supercab 2D	R14*		11600	14025	14800
Flareside Supercab 4D	R44*		12100	14600	15375
Add Edge Trim (Std. Tremor)			725	825	825
Add FX4 Off-Road Pkg.			300	350	350
Add XLT Trim			650	725	725
Add FX4/Level II Off-Road Pkg.			1100	1225	1225
Add Tremor Pkg.			1025	1150	1150
Add 4 Wheel Drive			2600	2825	2825
Add Aluminum/Alloy Wheels			325	375	375
Add Compact Disc Player			100	125	125
Add Cruise Control			200	225	225
Add Leather Seats			450	500	500
Add Pioneer Stereo System (Ex. Tremor)			300	350	350
Add Power Door Locks			175	200	200
Add Power Windows			200	225	225
Add Running Boards			150	175	175
Add Theft Recovery System			100	125	125
Add Tilt Steering Wheel			150	175	175
Deduct 4 Cyl. Engine			700	700	700
Deduct W/out Air Conditioning			700	700	700
Deduct W/out Automatic Trans.			575	575	575
* 1 or 5 as the 3rd position of the model # denotes 4WD					
2004 F150 HERITAGE PICKUP-1/2 Ton-V8					
Styleside XL	F17*		13825	16450	17675
Flareside XL	F07*		14475	17125	18325
Flareside Lightning	F073	4670	24900	28375	29875
Styleside Supercab XL	X17*		16125	18875	20150
2004 F150 PICKUP-1/2 Ton-V8					
Styleside XL	F12*	4788	14200	16850	18075
Styleside STX	F12*		14825	17500	18725
Styleside XLT	F12*		15425	18150	19400
Styleside FX4 (4WD)	F14		19525	22650	24000
Flareside STX	F02*		15475	18200	19450
Flareside XLT	F02*		16075	18850	20125
Flareside FX4 (4WD)	F04		20175	23350	24725

SEE TRUCK OPTION PAGE FOR ADDITIONAL OPTIONS

TRUCKS

BODY TYPE	Model No.	Weight	Trade-In	Retail	High Retail
2004 F150 SUPERCAB PICKUP-1/2 Ton-V8					
Styleside Supercab XL	X12*	5115	16650	19450	20750
Styleside Supercab STX	X12*	4993	17275	20250	21575
Styleside Supercab XLT	X12*		17875	20900	22250
Style Supercab FX4 (4WD)	X14		21975	25275	26700
Styleside Supercab Lariat	X12*		20125	23300	24650
Flareside Supercab STX	X02*		17925	20950	22300
Flareside Supercab XLT	X02*		18525	21575	22950
Flare Supercab FX4 (4WD)	X04		22625	25975	27425
2004 F150 SUPERCREW PICKUP-1/2 Ton-V8					
SuperCrew XLT	W12*	5210	20225	23400	24775
SuperCrew FX4 (4WD)	W14		24325	27775	29250
SuperCrew Lariat	W12*		22475	25800	27225
2004 F250 SUPER DUTY PICKUP-3/4 Ton-V8					
Styleside XL	F20*	5411	16725	19525	20825
Styleside Supercab XL	X20*	5604	19825	22950	24300
Styleside Crew Cab XL	W20*	5840	21725	24975	26375
2004 F350 SUPER DUTY PICKUP-1 Ton-V8					
Styleside XL	F30*	5405	17725	20725	22075
Styleside Supercab XL	X30*	5598	20825	24025	25400
Styleside Crew Cab XL	W30*	5834	22725	26050	27500
F SERIES PICKUP OPTIONS					
Add FX4 Off-Road Pkg. (Super Duty)			325	375	375
Add Harley Davidson Trim (Super Duty)			4475	4700	4700
Add King Ranch Trim (Super Duty)			3300	3525	3525
Add Lariat Trim (Super Duty)			2675	2900	2900
Add XLT Trim (Heritage, Super Duty)			1225	1375	1375
Add 4 Wheel Drive (Std. F150 FX4)			2800	3025	3025
Add 6.0L V8 Turbo Diesel Engine			5000	5225	5225
Add 6.8L V10 Engine			425	475	475
Add 7700 Payload Pkg. (F150 Heritage)			700	800	800
Add Aluminum/Alloy Wheels (XL)			375	425	425
Add Audiophile Stereo System			350	400	400
Add Compact Disc Player (XL)			150	175	175
Add Dual Rear Wheels			775	875	875
Add Heavy Duty Payload Pkg. (F150)			700	800	800
Add Leather Seats (XLT, FX4)			525	600	600
Add Power Seat (XLT, FX4)			225	250	250
Add Power Sunroof			625	700	700
Add Rear Bucket Seats (Super Duty)			200	225	225
Add Rear Entertainment System			600	675	675
Add Running Boards (Std. Super Duty Harley/K-Ranch/Lariat)			150	175	175
Add Theft Recovery System			100	125	125
Deduct Work Truck Pkg.			1100	1100	1100
Deduct V6 Engine			750	750	750
Deduct W/out Air Conditioning			750	750	750
Deduct W/out Automatic Trans.			625	625	625
Deduct W/out Cruise Control			225	225	225
Deduct W/out Tilt Steering Wheel			175	175	175

* 1, 3, 4, or 8 as the 3rd position of the model # denotes 4WD

FORD

BODY TYPE	Model No.	Weight	Trade-In	Retail	High Retail
2003 ESCAPE-V6					
Utility 4D XLS	U02	3019	11800	14250	15200
Utility 4D XLT	U03	3181	13700	16300	17325

TRUCKS

BODY TYPE	Model No.	Weight	Trade-In	Retail	High Retail
Utility 4D Limited	U04		**15400**	**18125**	**19175**
Utility 4D XLS (4WD)	U92	3175	**12825**	**15375**	**16375**
Utility 4D XLT (4WD)	U93	3346	**14725**	**17400**	**18425**
Utility 4D Limited (4WD)	U94		**16425**	**19200**	**20300**
Add Aluminum/Alloy Wheels (XLS)			**275**	**325**	**325**
Add Leather Seats (Std. Limited)			**400**	**450**	**450**
Add MACH Stereo System (Std. Limited)			**250**	**300**	**300**
Add Power Sunroof			**525**	**600**	**600**
Add Running Boards (XLS, XLT)			**125**	**150**	**150**
Add Theft Recovery System			**75**	**100**	**100**
Deduct 4 Cyl. Engine			**725**	**725**	**725**
Deduct W/out Automatic Trans.			**525**	**525**	**525**
Deduct W/out Cruise Control			**175**	**175**	**175**
2003 EXPLORER SPORT TRAC-1/2 Ton-V6					
Utility 4D XLS	U67	4139	**15500**	**18225**	**19275**
Utility 4D XLT	U67	4128	**16400**	**19175**	**20275**
Utility 4D XLS (4WD)	U77	4352	**16875**	**19675**	**20775**
Utility 4D XLT (4WD)	U77	4342	**17775**	**20775**	**21900**
2003 EXPLORER-1/2 Ton-V6					
Wagon 2D Sport XLS	U60	3898	**12200**	**14700**	**15675**
Wagon 2D Sport XLT	U60	3887	**13100**	**15650**	**16650**
Wagon 4D XLS	U62	4286	**12175**	**14650**	**15625**
Wagon 4D XLT	U63		**14175**	**16800**	**17850**
Wagon 4D Eddie Bauer	U64		**17175**	**20100**	**21225**
Wagon 4D Limited	U65		**17425**	**20400**	**21525**
Wagon 2D Sport XLS (4WD)	U70	4088	**13225**	**15800**	**16825**
Wagon 2D Sport XLT (4WD)	U70	4078	**14125**	**16750**	**17800**
Wagon 4D XLS (4WD/AWD)	U72/82	4434	**13200**	**15775**	**16800**
Wagon 4D XLT (4WD/AWD)	U73/83		**15200**	**17900**	**18950**
4D Eddie Bauer (4WD/AWD)	U74/84		**18200**	**21225**	**22375**
4D Limited (4WD/AWD)	U75/85		**18450**	**21500**	**22650**
EXPLORER SPORT TRAC/EXPLORER OPTIONS					
Add NBX Package (XLT)			**450**	**500**	**500**
Add 3rd Row Seat			**175**	**200**	**200**
Add 4.6L V8 Engine			**350**	**400**	**400**
Add Leather Seats (Std. Eddie Bauer, Ltd.)			**400**	**450**	**450**
Add Pioneer/Audiophile Stereo (Std. E. Bauer, Ltd.)			**250**	**300**	**300**
Add Power Seat (Std. U63/73/83, E. Bauer, Ltd.)			**175**	**200**	**200**
Add Power Sunroof			**525**	**600**	**600**
Add Rear Air Conditioning			**150**	**175**	**175**
Add Rear Entertainment System			**500**	**575**	**575**
Add Running Boards (U62/U72/U82, XLT)			**125**	**150**	**150**
Add Theft Recovery System			**75**	**100**	**100**
Deduct W/out Automatic Trans.			**525**	**525**	**525**
Deduct W/out Cruise Control			**175**	**175**	**175**
Deduct W/out Tilt Steering Wheel			**125**	**125**	**125**
2003 EXPEDITION-1/2 Ton-V8					
Utility XLT	U15	5267	**17825**	**20825**	**22175**
Utility Eddie Bauer	U17		**21125**	**24350**	**25750**
Utility XLT (4WD)	U16	5564	**19400**	**22525**	**23875**
Utility Eddie Bauer (4WD)	U18	5686	**22800**	**26150**	**27600**
Add FX4 Off-Road Pkg. (XLT)			**500**	**575**	**575**
Add Audiophile Stereo (XLT)			**300**	**350**	**350**
Add Leather Seats (XLT)			**475**	**550**	**550**

SEE TRUCK OPTION PAGE FOR ADDITIONAL OPTIONS

BODY TYPE	Model No.	Weight	Trade-In	Retail	High Retail
Add Navigation System			550	625	625
Add Power 3rd Row Seat			175	200	200
Add Power Sunroof			575	650	650
Add Rear Bucket Seats			175	200	200
Add Rear Entertainment System			500	575	575
Add Theft Recovery System			75	100	100
Deduct 4.6L V8 Engine			375	375	375
Deduct W/out 3rd Row Seat			175	175	175
Deduct W/out Rear Air Conditioning			150	150	150
Deduct W/out Running Boards			125	125	125
2003 EXCURSION-3/4 Ton-V10					
Utility XLT	U40	6650	19175	22275	23600
Utility XLT 7.3L T-Diesel	U40F		26475	30050	31600
Utility Eddie Bauer	U44		21975	25275	26700
Utility E. Bauer 7.3L T-Diesel	U44F		29275	33150	34800
Utility Limited	U42		21975	25275	26700
Utility Limited 7.3L T-Diesel	U42F		29275	33150	34800
Utility XLT (4WD)	U41	7087	21050	24275	25675
Utility XLT 7.3L T-Diesel (4WD)	U41F		28350	32175	33800
Utility Eddie Bauer (4WD)	U45		23850	27275	28750
Utility E. Bauer 7.3L TD (4WD)	U45F		31150	35125	36825
Utility Limited (4WD)	U43		23850	27275	28750
Utility Limited 7.3L TD (4WD)	U43F		31150	35125	36825
Add 6.0L V8 Turbo Diesel Engine (7.3L)			300	350	350
Add Leather Seats (XLT)			475	550	550
Add Rear Bucket Seats			175	200	200
Add Rear Entertainment System			500	575	575
Add Theft Recovery System			75	100	100
Deduct 5.4L V8 Engine			650	650	650
Deduct W/out Power Seat			200	200	200
2003 WINDSTAR-V6					
Cargo Van	A54		7150	9150	10025
Wagon 3D	A50	4017	8825	10975	11925
Wagon 4D LX	A51		10575	12850	13750
Wagon SE	A52		12375	14900	15875
Wagon SEL	A53		14925	17600	18650
Wagon Limited	A58		15825	18575	19650
Add Aluminum/Alloy Wheels (LX 4D)			275	325	325
Add AutoVision Entertainment System			500	575	575
Add CD Player (Van, Wagon 3D)			75	100	100
Add Dual Power Doors (Std. SEL, Ltd.)			500	575	575
Add Left Sliding Door (Wagon 3D)			400	450	450
Add Power Seat (LX 4D)			175	200	200
Add Rear Air Cond. (Wgn 3D, LX 4D)			150	175	175
Add Rear Bucket Seats (LX 4D)			175	200	200
Add Theft Recovery System			75	100	100
Deduct W/out Cruise Control			175	175	175
2003 ECONOLINE E150-1/2 Ton-V8					
Cargo Van	E14	4793	12875	15425	16600
Club Wagon	E11	5005	13950	16575	17800
2003 ECONOLINE E250-3/4 Ton-V8					
Cargo Van	E24	5146	13475	16075	17275
Extended Cargo Van	S24	5279	14250	16900	18150

BODY TYPE	Model No.	Weight	Trade-In	Retail	High Retail
2003 ECONOLINE E350-1 Ton-V8					
Super Duty Cargo Van	E34	5483	**14075**	**16700**	**17925**
Super Duty Wagon	E31	5793	**15150**	**17850**	**19075**
Super Duty Ext. Cargo Van	S34	5632	**14850**	**17525**	**18750**
Super Duty Ext. Wagon	S31	6228	**16075**	**18825**	**20100**
ECONOLINE OPTIONS					
Add Chateau Trim			**900**	**1000**	**1000**
Add XLT Trim			**700**	**800**	**800**
Add 6.8L V10 Engine			**400**	**450**	**450**
Add 7.3L V8 Turbo Diesel Engine			**4400**	**4625**	**4625**
Add Aluminum/Alloy Wheels			**325**	**375**	**375**
Add AutoVision Entertainment System			**500**	**575**	**575**
Add Compact Disc Player			**125**	**150**	**150**
Add Leather Seats			**475**	**550**	**550**
Add Power Seat			**200**	**225**	**225**
Add Rear Air Cond. (Std. E350 Ext. Wagon)			**150**	**175**	**175**
Add Rear Bucket Seats			**175**	**200**	**200**
Add Running Boards			**125**	**150**	**150**
Add Theft Recovery System			**75**	**100**	**100**
Deduct V6 Engine			**725**	**725**	**725**
Deduct W/out Air Conditioning			**700**	**700**	**700**
Deduct W/out Cruise Control			**200**	**200**	**200**
Deduct W/out Power Door Locks			**175**	**175**	**175**
Deduct W/out Power Windows			**200**	**200**	**200**
2003 RANGER PICKUP-1/2 Ton-V6					
Styleside	R10*	4360	**8600**	**10725**	**11475**
Flareside	R10*		**8900**	**11050**	**11775**
Styleside Supercab 2D	R14*	4740	**10150**	**12400**	**13125**
Styleside Supercab 4D	R44*		**10650**	**12925**	**13650**
Flareside Supercab 2D	R14*		**10450**	**12725**	**13450**
Flareside Supercab 4D	R44*		**10950**	**13275**	**14025**
Add Edge Trim (Std. Tremor)			**675**	**750**	**750**
Add FX4 Off-Road Pkg.			**275**	**325**	**325**
Add XLT Trim			**600**	**675**	**675**
Add FX4/Level II Off-Road Pkg.			**1000**	**1125**	**1125**
Add Tremor Pkg.			**925**	**1050**	**1050**
Add 4 Wheel Drive			**2550**	**2775**	**2775**
Add Aluminum/Alloy Wheels			**275**	**325**	**325**
Add Compact Disc Player			**75**	**100**	**100**
Add Cruise Control			**175**	**200**	**200**
Add Power Door Locks			**150**	**175**	**175**
Add Power Windows			**175**	**200**	**200**
Add Running Boards			**125**	**150**	**150**
Add Theft Recovery System			**75**	**100**	**100**
Add Tilt Steering Wheel			**125**	**150**	**150**
Deduct 4 Cyl. Engine			**650**	**650**	**650**
Deduct W/out Air Conditioning			**650**	**650**	**650**
Deduct W/out Automatic Trans.			**525**	**525**	**525**

* 1 or 5 as the 3rd position of the model # denotes 4WD

BODY TYPE	Model No.	Weight	Trade-In	Retail	High Retail
2003 F150 PICKUP-1/2 Ton-V8					
Styleside XL	F17*	3990	**12575**	**15100**	**16275**
Flareside XL	F07*	4002	**13175**	**15750**	**16950**
Flareside Lightning	F073	4670	**22775**	**26125**	**27575**
Styleside Supercab XL	X17*	4224	**14875**	**17550**	**18775**

SEE TRUCK OPTION PAGE FOR ADDITIONAL OPTIONS

TRUCKS

BODY TYPE	Model No.	Weight	Trade-In	Retail	High Retail
Flareside Supercab XL	X07*	4236	15475	18200	19450
Flare S-Cab King Ranch	X07*		18350	21400	22750
2003 F150 SUPERCREW PICKUP-1/2 Ton-V8					
SuperCrew XLT	W07*	4655	17475	20450	21775
SuperCrew Lariat	W07*		18850	21925	23300
SuperCrew King Ranch	W07*		19150	22250	23575
SuperCrew Harley Davidson	W073		27225	30975	32550
2003 F250 SUPER DUTY PICKUP-3/4 Ton-V8					
Styleside XL	F20*	5420	15275	17975	19225
Styleside Supercab XL	X20*	5601	18375	21425	22775
Styleside Crew Cab XL	W20*	5841	20075	23225	24575
2003 F350 SUPER DUTY PICKUP-1 Ton-V8					
Styleside XL	F30*	5415	16175	18950	20225
Styleside Supercab XL	X30*	5596	19275	22375	23700
Styleside Crew Cab XL	W30*	5836	20975	24200	25600
F SERIES PICKUP OPTIONS					
Add FX4 Off-Road Pkg.			300	350	350
Add Heritage Trim (Ex. XLT)			1125	1250	1250
Add King Ranch Trim (Super Duty)			1600	1800	1800
Add Lariat Trim (XL)			1350	1500	1500
Add STX Trim			350	400	400
Add XLT Trim (XL)			650	725	725
Add 4 Wheel Drive			2700	2925	2925
Add 6.0L V8 Turbo Diesel Engine			4800	5025	5025
Add 6.8L V10 Engine			400	450	450
Add 7.3L V8 Turbo Diesel Engine			4450	4675	4675
Add 7700 Payload Pkg. (F150)			675	750	750
Add Aluminum/Alloy Wheels (Std. S-Crew, Lightning, K-Ranch)			325	375	375
Add Audiophile Stereo System			300	350	350
Add CD (Std. S-Crew, Lightning, K-Ranch)			125	150	150
Add Dual Rear Wheels			725	825	825
Add Leather Seats**			475	550	550
Add Power Seat**			200	225	225
Add Power Sunroof			575	650	650
Add Rear Bucket Seats (K-Ranch S-Crew, Super Duty)			175	200	200
Add Rear Entertainment System			500	575	575
Add Running Boards (Std. K-Ranch, Harley)			125	150	150
Add Theft Recovery System			75	100	100
Deduct Work Truck Pkg.			1100	1100	1100
Deduct V6 Engine			725	725	725
Deduct W/out Air Conditioning			700	700	700
Deduct W/out Automatic Trans.			575	575	575
Deduct W/out Cruise Control			200	200	200
Deduct W/out Tilt Steering Wheel			150	150	150

**Std. Lightning, SuperCrew Lariat/Harley, K-Ranch

*1,3, or 8 as the 3rd position of the model # denotes 4WD

BODY TYPE	Model No.	Weight	Trade-In	Retail	High Retail
FORD					
2002 ESCAPE-V6					
Utility 4D XLS	U01	2991	10450	12725	13625
Utility 4D XLT	U03		12300	14800	15775
Utility 4D XLS (4WD)	U02	3133	11450	13875	14825
Utility 4D XLT (4WD)	U04		13300	15875	16900
Add Aluminum/Alloy Wheels (XLS)			225	250	250

TRUCKS

BODY TYPE	Model No.	Weight	Trade-In	Retail	High Retail
Add Leather Seats			350	400	400
Add MACH Stereo System			200	225	225
Add Power Sunroof			475	550	550
Add Running Boards			100	125	125
Add Theft Recovery System			75	100	100
Deduct 4 Cyl. Engine			675	675	675
Deduct W/out Automatic Trans.			475	475	475
Deduct W/out Cruise Control			150	150	150
2002 EXPLORER SPORT TRAC-1/2 Ton-V6					
Utility 4D	U67	4091	14325	16975	18025
Utility 4D (4WD)	U77	4310	15625	18350	19425
2002 EXPLORER-1/2 Ton-V6					
Wagon 2D Sport	U60		10250	12500	13400
Wagon 4D XLS	U62	4094	10150	12400	13300
Wagon 4D XLT	U63	4104	12100	14575	15550
Wagon 4D Eddie Bauer	U64		13550	16150	17175
Wagon 4D Limited	U65		13750	16350	17375
Wagon 2D Sport (4WD)	U70		11250	13650	14600
Wagon 4D XLS (4WD)	U72	4334	11150	13550	14475
Wagon 4D XLT (4WD)	U73	4344	13100	15650	16650
Wagon 4D Eddie Bauer (4WD)	U74		14550	17200	18225
Wagon 4D Limited (4WD)	U75		14750	17425	18450
EXPLORER SPORT TRAC/EXPLORER OPTIONS					
Add 3rd Row Seat			150	175	175
Add 4.6L V8 Engine			300	350	350
Add Compact Disc Player (XLS)			75	100	100
Add Leather Seats (Std. Eddie Bauer, Ltd.)			350	400	400
Add Pioneer Stereo System (Sport/Sport Trac)			200	225	225
Add Power Seat (Std. XLT, E. Bauer, Ltd.)			150	175	175
Add Power Sunroof			475	550	550
Add Rear Air Conditioning			150	175	175
Add Running Boards (Std. Eddie Bauer, Ltd.)			100	125	125
Add Theft Recovery System			75	100	100
Deduct W/out Automatic Trans.			475	475	475
Deduct W/out Cruise Control			150	150	150
Deduct W/out Tilt Steering Wheel			100	100	100
2002 EXPEDITION-1/2 Ton-V8					
Utility XLT	U15	4909	14850	17525	18750
Utility Eddie Bauer	U17	5082	16500	19300	20600
Utility XLT (4WD)	U16	5297	16425	19225	20500
Utility Eddie Bauer (4WD)	U18	5449	18025	21050	22400
Add Compact Disc Player (XLT)			100	125	125
Add Leather Seats (XLT)			425	475	475
Add Power Sunroof			525	600	600
Add Rear Bucket Seats			150	175	175
Add Rear Entertainment System			400	450	450
Add Theft Recovery System			75	100	100
Deduct 4.6L V8 Engine			350	350	350
Deduct W/out 3rd Row Seat			150	150	150
Deduct W/out Rear Air Conditioning			150	150	150
Deduct W/out Running Boards			100	100	100
2002 EXCURSION-3/4 Ton-V10					
Utility XLT	U40	6650	15775	18500	19750
Utility XLT T-Diesel	U40F	-	22375	25675	27100

SEE TRUCK OPTION PAGE FOR ADDITIONAL OPTIONS

BODY TYPE	Model No.	Weight	Trade-In	Retail	High Retail
Utility Limited	U42	6734	18375	21425	22775
Utility Limited T-Diesel	U42F		24975	28450	29950
Utility XLT (4WD)	U41	7087	17550	20550	21875
Utility XLT T-Diesel (4WD)	U41F		24150	27575	29050
Utility Limited (4WD)	U43	7190	20150	23300	24650
Utility Limited T-Diesel (4WD)	U43F		26750	30325	31875
Add Leather Seats (XLT)			425	475	475
Add Rear Bucket Seats			150	175	175
Add Rear Entertainment System			400	450	450
Add Theft Recovery System			75	100	100
Deduct 5.4L V8 Engine			600	600	600
Deduct W/out Power Seat			175	175	175
2002 WINDSTAR-V6					
Cargo Van	A54		5750	7575	8475
Wagon 3D LX	A50		7625	9650	10550
Wagon 4D LX	A51		8925	11075	11950
Wagon SE	A52		10975	13300	14225
Wagon SEL	A53		13125	15700	16700
Wagon Limited	A58		14025	16650	17700
Add Aluminum/Alloy Wheels (LX 4D)			225	250	250
Add AutoVision Entertainment System			400	450	450
Add CD Player (Van, LX)			75	100	100
Add Dual Power Doors (Std. SEL, Ltd.)			500	575	575
Add Left Sliding Door (LX 3D)			350	400	400
Add Power Seat (LX 4D)			150	175	175
Add Rear Air Cond. (LX 4D)			150	175	175
Add Rear Bucket Seats (LX 4D)			150	175	175
Add Theft Recovery System			75	100	100
Deduct W/out Cruise Control			150	150	150
Deduct W/out Tilt Steering Wheel			100	100	100
2002 ECONOLINE E150-1/2 Ton-V8					
Cargo Van	E14	4795	11075	13450	14550
Club Wagon	E11	5101	12200	14700	15850
Club Wagon Traveler	E11		14550	17200	18425
2002 ECONOLINE E250-3/4 Ton-V8					
Cargo Van	E24	5169	11575	14000	15125
Extended Cargo Van	S24	5297	12325	14850	16000
2002 ECONOLINE E350-1 Ton-V8					
Super Duty Cargo Van	E34	5472	12075	14575	15725
Super Duty Wagon	E31	5809	13200	15775	16975
Super Duty Ext. Cargo Van	S34	5616	12825	15375	16550
Super Duty Ext. Wagon	S31	6119	13950	16575	17800
Super Duty Wagon Traveler	S31		16300	19075	20350
ECONOLINE OPTIONS					
Add Chateau Trim (Ex. Traveler)			800	900	900
Add XLT Trim (Ex. Traveler)			650	725	725
Add 6.8L V10 Engine			375	425	425
Add 7.3L V8 Turbo Diesel Engine			4050	4275	4275
Add Aluminum/Alloy Wheels (Std. Traveler)			275	325	325
Add Compact Disc Player (Std. Traveler)			100	125	125
Add Power Seat (Std. Traveler)			175	200	200
Add Rear Air Cond. (Std. Traveler)			150	175	175
Add Rear Bucket Seats (Std. Traveler)			150	175	175
Add Running Boards (Std. Traveler)			100	125	125

TRUCKS

BODY TYPE	Model No.	Weight	Trade-In	Retail	High Retail
Add Theft Recovery System			75	100	100
Deduct V6 Engine			700	700	700
Deduct W/out Air Conditioning			650	650	650
Deduct W/out Cruise Control			175	175	175
Deduct W/out Power Door Locks			150	150	150
Deduct W/out Power Windows			175	175	175
2002 RANGER PICKUP-1/2 Ton-V6					
Styleside	R10*	2988	7200	9200	9900
Flareside	R10*		7475	9500	10225
Styleside Supercab 2D	R14*	3159	8800	10950	11700
Styleside Supercab 4D	R44*		9300	11475	12200
Flareside Supercab 2D	R14*		9075	11250	11975
Flareside Supercab 4D	R44*		9575	11775	12525
Add Edge Trim (Std. Tremor)			625	700	700
Add FX4 Off-Road Pkg.			900	1000	1000
Add XLT Trim			550	625	625
Add Tremor Pkg.			825	925	925
Add 4 Wheel Drive			2450	2675	2675
Add Aluminum/Alloy Wheels			225	250	250
Add Compact Disc Player			75	100	100
Add Cruise Control			150	175	175
Add Power Door Locks			125	150	150
Add Power Windows			150	175	175
Add Running Boards			100	125	125
Add Theft Recovery System			75	100	100
Add Tilt Steering Wheel			100	125	125
Deduct 4 Cyl. Engine			600	600	600
Deduct W/out Air Conditioning			600	600	600
Deduct W/out Automatic Trans.			475	475	475
* 1 or 5 as the 3rd position of the model # denotes 4WD					
2002 F150 PICKUP-1/2 Ton-V8					
Styleside XL	F17*	3990	10750	13050	14125
Flareside XL	F07*	4002	11300	13700	14800
Flareside Lightning	F073	4670	20550	23725	25100
Styleside Supercab XL	X17*	4224	13150	15725	16925
Flareside Supercab XL	X07*	4236	13700	16300	17525
Supercab King Ranch	X17*		15475	18200	19450
2002 F150 SUPERCREW PICKUP-1/2 Ton-V8					
SuperCrew XLT	W07*	4655	15650	18375	19625
SuperCrew Lariat	W07*		16750	19550	20850
SuperCrew King Ranch	W07*		17000	19850	21150
SuperCrew Harley Davidson	W073		24250	27675	29150
2002 F250 SUPER DUTY PICKUP-3/4 Ton-V8					
Styleside XL	F20*	5356	13250	15825	17025
Styleside Supercab XL	X20*	5585	16150	18900	20175
Styleside Crew Cab XL	W20*	5870	17950	20950	22300
2002 F350 SUPER DUTY PICKUP-1 Ton-V8					
Styleside XL	F30*	5486	14050	16675	17900
Styleside Supercab XL	X30*	5601	16950	19775	21075
Styleside Crew Cab XL	W30*	5895	18750	21825	23200
F SERIES PICKUP OPTIONS					
Add FX4 Off-Road Pkg.			225	250	250
Add Lariat Trim (XL)			1100	1225	1225
Add XLT Trim (XL)			600	675	675

SEE TRUCK OPTION PAGE FOR ADDITIONAL OPTIONS

TRUCKS

BODY TYPE	Model No.	Weight	Trade-In	Retail	High Retail
Add 4 Wheel Drive			2550	2775	2775
Add 6.3L V10 Engine			375	425	425
Add 7.3L V8 Turbo Diesel Engine			4200	4425	4425
Add 7700 Payload Pkg. (F150)			650	725	725
Add Aluminum/Alloy Wheels (Std. S-Crew, Lightning, K-Ranch)			275	325	325
Add CD (Std. S-Crew, Lightning, K-Ranch)			100	125	125
Add Dual Rear Wheels			675	750	750
Add Leather Seats**			425	475	475
Add Power Seat**			175	200	200
Add Power Sunroof			525	600	600
Add Rear Bucket Seats (K-Ranch S-Crew, Super Duty)			150	175	175
Add Rear Entertainment System			400	450	450
Add Running Boards (Std. K-Ranch, Harley)			100	125	125
Add Theft Recovery System			75	100	100
Deduct Work Truck Pkg.			1050	1050	1050
Deduct V6 Engine			700	700	700
Deduct W/out Air Conditioning			650	650	650
Deduct W/out Automatic Trans.			525	525	525
Deduct W/out Cruise Control			175	175	175
Deduct W/out Tilt Steering Wheel			125	125	125

**Std. Lightning, SuperCrew Lariat/Harley, K-Ranch

* 1,3, or 8 as the 3rd position of the model # denotes 4WD

FORD

2001 ESCAPE-V6

BODY TYPE	Model No.	Weight	Trade-In	Retail	High Retail
Utility 4D XLS	U01	3065	9100	11275	12175
Utility 4D XLT	U03		10750	13050	13975
Utility 4D XLS (4WD)	U02	3238	10000	12225	13125
Utility 4D XLT (4WD)	U04		11650	14075	15025
Add Aluminum/Alloy Wheels (XLS)			175	200	200
Add Leather Seats			300	350	350
Add MACH Stereo System			150	175	175
Add Power Seat			125	150	150
Add Power Sunroof			425	475	475
Add Running Boards			75	100	100
Add Theft Recovery System			50	75	75
Deduct 4 Cyl. Engine			625	625	625
Deduct W/out Automatic Trans.			425	425	425
Deduct W/out Cruise Control			125	125	125

2001 EXPLORER SPORT TRAC-1/2 Ton-V6

BODY TYPE	Model No.	Weight	Trade-In	Retail	High Retail
Utility 4D	U67	4148	11550	13975	14925
Utility 4D (4WD)	U77	4365	12750	15300	16300

2001 EXPLORER-1/2 Ton-V6

BODY TYPE	Model No.	Weight	Trade-In	Retail	High Retail
Wagon 2D Sport	U60	3650	7875	9925	10825
Wagon 4D XLS	U62	3845	7175	9175	10050
Wagon 4D XLT	U63		8425	10550	11500
Wagon 4D Eddie Bauer	U64		9925	12175	13075
Wagon 4D Limited	U65		10075	12325	13225
Wagon 2D Sport (4WD)	U70	3850	8775	10925	11875
Wagon 4D XLS (4WD)	U72	4045	8075	10175	11100
4D XLT (4WD/AWD)	U73/83		9325	11525	12425
4D Eddie Bauer (4WD/AWD)	U74/84		10825	13125	14050
4D Limited (4WD/AWD)	U75/85		10975	13325	14250

TRUCKS

BODY TYPE	Model No.	Weight	Trade-In	Retail	High Retail
EXPLORER SPORT TRAC/EXPLORER OPTIONS					
Add 5.0L V8 Engine			250	300	300
Add Compact Disc Player (XLS)			50	75	75
Add Leather Seats (Std. Eddie Bauer, Ltd.)			300	350	350
Add MACH/Pioneer Stereo (Std. Eddie Bauer, Ltd.)			150	175	175
Add Power Seat (Std. XLT, E. Bauer, Ltd.)			125	150	150
Add Power Sunroof			425	475	475
Add Running Boards (Std. Eddie Bauer, Ltd.)			75	100	100
Add Theft Recovery System			50	75	75
Deduct W/out Automatic Trans.			425	425	425
Deduct W/out Cruise Control			125	125	125
Deduct W/out Tilt Steering Wheel			100	100	100
2001 EXPEDITION-1/2 Ton-V8					
Utility XLT	U15	4891	12275	14800	15950
Utility Eddie Bauer	U17	5045	13875	16500	17725
Utility XLT (4WD)	U16	5345	13475	16050	17250
Utility Eddie Bauer (4WD)	U18	5468	15075	17775	19000
Add Compact Disc Player (XLT)			100	125	125
Add Leather Seats (XLT)			375	425	425
Add Power Sunroof			475	550	550
Add Rear Bucket Seats			125	150	150
Add Rear Entertainment System			350	400	400
Add Theft Recovery System			50	75	75
Deduct 4.6L V8 Engine			325	325	325
Deduct W/out 3rd Row Seat			125	125	125
Deduct W/out Rear Air Conditioning			125	125	125
Deduct W/out Running Boards			75	75	75
2001 EXCURSION-3/4 Ton-V10					
Utility XLT	U40	6650	13525	16125	17325
Utility XLT T-Diesel	U40F		19675	22800	24150
Utility Limited	U42	6734	15825	18575	19850
Utility Limited T-Diesel	U42F		21975	25275	26700
Utility XLT (4WD)	U41	7087	15000	17700	18925
Utility XLT T-Diesel (4WD)	U41F		21150	24375	25775
Utility Limited (4WD)	U43	7190	17300	20275	21600
Utility Limited T-Diesel (4WD)	U43F		23450	26850	28325
Add Leather Seats (XLT)			375	425	425
Add Rear Entertainment System			350	400	400
Add Theft Recovery System			50	75	75
Deduct 5.4L V8 Engine			600	600	600
Deduct W/out Power Seat			150	150	150
2001 WINDSTAR-V6					
Cargo Van	A54	3719	4350	6025	6875
Wagon 3D LX	A50	4058	5875	7700	8625
Wagon 4D LX	A51	4058	6825	8775	9675
Wagon SE Sport	A57	4225	8575	10700	11650
Wagon SE	A52	4223	8775	10925	11875
Wagon SEL	A53	4296	11025	13375	14300
Wagon Limited	A58	4283	11925	14375	15350
Add Aluminum/Alloy Wheels (LX 4D)			175	200	200
Add AutoVision Entertainment System			350	400	400
Add CD Player (Van, LX, SE Spt.)			50	75	75
Add Dual Power Doors (Std. SEL, Ltd.)			450	500	500

TRUCKS

SEE TRUCK OPTION PAGE FOR ADDITIONAL OPTIONS

BODY TYPE	Model No.	Weight	Trade-In	Retail	High Retail
Add Leather Seats (Std. SEL, Ltd.)			300	350	350
Add Left Sliding Door (LX 3D)			300	350	350
Add Power Seat (LX 4D, SE Spt.)			125	150	150
Add Rear Air Cond. (LX 4D)			125	150	150
Add Rear Bucket Seats (LX 4D)			125	150	150
Add Theft Recovery System			50	75	75
Deduct W/out Cruise Control			125	125	125
Deduct W/out Tilt Steering Wheel			100	100	100
2001 ECONOLINE E150-1/2 Ton-V8					
Cargo Van	E14	4778	9350	11550	12575
Club Wagon	E11	5101	10425	12700	13775
Club Wagon Traveler	E11		12700	15250	16425
2001 ECONOLINE E250-3/4 Ton-V8					
Cargo Van	E24	5152	9750	11975	13025
Extended Cargo Van	S24	5280	10475	12750	13825
2001 ECONOLINE E350-1 Ton-V8					
Super Duty Cargo Van	E34	5455	10150	12400	13450
Super Duty Wagon	E31	5809	11225	13625	14725
Super Duty Ext. Cargo Van	S34	5599	10875	13175	14275
Super Duty Ext. Wagon	S31	6105	11950	14425	15575
ECONOLINE OPTIONS					
Add Chateau Trim (Ex. Traveler)			700	800	800
Add XLT Trim (Ex. Traveler)			600	675	675
Add 6.8L V10 Engine			350	400	400
Add 7.3L V8 Turbo Diesel Engine			3650	3875	3875
Add Aluminum/Alloy Wheels (Std. Traveler)			225	250	250
Add Compact Disc Player (Std. Traveler)			100	125	125
Add Power Seat (Std. Traveler)			150	175	175
Add Rear Air Cond. (Std. Traveler)			125	150	150
Add Rear Bucket Seats (Std. Traveler)			125	150	150
Add Running Boards (Std. Traveler)			75	100	100
Add Theft Recovery System			50	75	75
Deduct V6 Engine			675	675	675
Deduct W/out Cruise Control			150	150	150
Deduct W/out Power Door Locks			125	125	125
Deduct W/out Power Windows			150	150	150
Deduct W/out Tilt Steering Wheel			100	100	100
2001 RANGER PICKUP-1/2 Ton-V6					
Styleside	R10*	3085	5800	7625	8425
Flareside	R10*		6050	7925	8750
Styleside Supercab 2D	R14*	3310	7300	9300	10000
Styleside Supercab 4D	R14*		7800	9850	10575
Flareside Supercab 2D	R14*		7550	9575	10300
Flareside Supercab 4D	R14*		8050	10125	10850
Add Edge Trim			575	650	650
Add XLT Trim			500	575	575
Add 4 Wheel Drive			2350	2575	2575
Add Aluminum/Alloy Wheels			175	200	200
Add Compact Disc Player			50	75	75
Add Cruise Control			125	150	150
Add Power Door Locks			100	125	125
Add Power Windows			125	150	150
Add Running Boards			75	100	100
Add Theft Recovery System			50	75	75

TRUCKS

BODY TYPE	Model No.	Weight	Trade-In	Retail	High Retail
Add Tilt Steering Wheel			100	125	125
Deduct 4 Cyl. Engine			550	550	550
Deduct W/out Air Conditioning			550	550	550
Deduct W/out Automatic Trans.			425	425	425
* 1 or 5 as the 3rd position of the model # denotes 4WD					
2001 F150 PICKUP-1/2 Ton-V8					
Styleside XL	F17*	3935	8425	10525	11575
Flareside XL	F07*		8925	11075	12075
Flareside Lightning	F073	4670	18100	21125	22475
Styleside Supercab XL	X17*	4213	10925	13250	14350
Flareside Supercab XL	X07*		11425	13850	14975
2001 F150 SUPERCREW PICKUP-1/2 Ton-V8					
SuperCrew XLT	W07*	4581	13100	15675	16875
SuperCrew Lariat	W07*		14100	16725	17950
SuperCrew King Ranch	W07*		14350	17000	18250
SuperCrew Harley Davidson	W07	4697	17850	20850	22200
2001 F250 SUPER DUTY PICKUP-3/4 Ton-V8					
Styleside XL	F20*	5058	10875	13175	14275
Styleside Supercab XL	X20*	5224	13375	15950	17150
Styleside Crew Cab XL	W20*	5572	15175	17875	19125
2001 F350 SUPER DUTY PICKUP-1 Ton-V8					
Styleside XL	F30*	5182	11675	14100	15225
Styleside Supercab XL	X30*	5243	14175	16800	18025
Styleside Crew Cab XL	W30*	5591	15975	18725	20000
F SERIES PICKUP OPTIONS					
Add Lariat Trim (XL)			1000	1125	1125
Add XLT Trim (XL)			550	625	625
Add 4 Wheel Drive			2350	2575	2575
Add 6.8L V10 Engine			350	400	400
Add 7.3L V8 Turbo Diesel Engine			4150	4375	4375
Add 7700 Payload Pkg. (F150)			650	725	725
Add Aluminum/Alloy Wheels (Std. SuperCrew, Lightning)			225	250	250
Add Compact Disc (Std. SuperCrew, Lightning)			100	125	125
Add Dual Rear Wheels			625	700	700
Add Leather Seats**			375	425	425
Add Power Seat**			150	175	175
Add Power Sunroof			475	550	550
Add Rear Entertainment System			350	400	400
Add Running Boards (Std. K-Ranch, Harley)			75	100	100
Add Theft Recovery System			50	75	75
Deduct Work Truck Pkg.			1000	1000	1000
Deduct V6 Engine			675	675	675
Deduct W/out Air Conditioning			600	600	600
Deduct W/out Automatic Trans.			475	475	475
Deduct W/out Cruise Control			150	150	150
Deduct W/out Tilt Steering Wheel			100	100	100
** Std. Lightning, SuperCrew Lariat/King Ranch/Harley					
* 1,3, or 8 as the 3rd position of the model # denotes 4WD					
FORD					
2000 EXPLORER-1/2 Ton-V6					
Wagon 2D Sport	U60	3650	5675	7500	8400
Wagon 4D XL	U61	3891	5275	7050	7925
Wagon 4D XLS	U62	3875	5775	7600	8500

SEE TRUCK OPTION PAGE FOR ADDITIONAL OPTIONS

BODY TYPE	Model No.	Weight	Trade-In	Retail	High Retail
Wagon 4D XLT	U63	3891	**6325**	**8225**	**9075**
Wagon 4D Eddie Bauer	U64	3891	**7625**	**9675**	**10575**
Wagon 4D Limited	U65	3891	**7825**	**9900**	**10800**
Wagon 2D Sport (4WD)	U70	3903	**6500**	**8425**	**9300**
Wagon 4D XL (4WD)	U71	4113	**6100**	**7975**	**8900**
Wagon 4D XLS (4WD)	U72	4113	**6600**	**8525**	**9400**
4D XLT (4WD/AWD)	U73/83	4113	**7150**	**9150**	**10025**
4D Eddie Bauer (4WD/AWD)	U74/84	4113	**8450**	**10575**	**11525**
4D Limited (4WD/AWD)	U75/85	4113	**8650**	**10775**	**11725**
Add 5.0L V8 Engine			**225**	**250**	**250**
Add Aluminum/Alloy Wheels (XL)			**125**	**150**	**150**
Add Compact Disc Player (XL, Sport, XLS)			**50**	**75**	**75**
Add Leather Seats (Std. Eddie Bauer, Ltd.)			**250**	**300**	**300**
Add MACH Stereo System (Std. Eddie Bauer, Ltd.)			**100**	**125**	**125**
Add Power Seat (Std. XLT, E. Bauer, Ltd).			**100**	**125**	**125**
Add Power Sunroof			**375**	**425**	**425**
Add Running Boards (Std. Eddie Bauer, Ltd.)			**50**	**75**	**75**
Deduct W/out Automatic Trans			**375**	**375**	**375**
Deduct W/out Cruise Control			**100**	**100**	**100**
Deduct W/out Power Door Locks			**75**	**75**	**75**
Deduct W/out Power Windows			**100**	**100**	**100**
Deduct W/out Tilt Steering Wheel			**75**	**75**	**75**
2000 EXPEDITION-1/2 Ton-V8					
Utility XLT	U15	4916	**10000**	**12250**	**13300**
Utility Eddie Bauer	U17	5305	**11500**	**13925**	**15050**
Utility XLT (4WD)	U16	5080	**11000**	**13350**	**14450**
Utility Eddie Bauer (4WD)	U18	5447	**12500**	**15025**	**16200**
Add Compact Disc Player (XLT)			**75**	**100**	**100**
Add Leather Seats (XLT)			**325**	**375**	**375**
Add Power Sunroof			**425**	**475**	**475**
Add Rear Bucket Seats			**100**	**125**	**125**
Deduct 4.6L V8 Engine			**300**	**300**	**300**
Deduct W/out 3rd Row Seat			**100**	**100**	**100**
Deduct W/out Rear Air Conditioning			**100**	**100**	**100**
Deduct W/out Running Boards			**50**	**50**	**50**
2000 EXCURSION-3/4 Ton-V10					
Utility XLT	U40	6734	**11450**	**13875**	**15000**
Utility XLT T-Diesel	U40F		**17450**	**20450**	**21775**
Utility Limited	U42	6734	**13600**	**16200**	**17400**
Utility Limited T-Diesel	U42F		**19600**	**22725**	**24075**
Utility XLT (4WD)	U41	7190	**12750**	**15300**	**16475**
Utility XLT T-Diesel (4WD)	U41F		**18750**	**21825**	**23200**
Utility Limited (4WD)	U43	7190	**14900**	**17575**	**18800**
Utility Limited T-Diesel (4WD)	U43F		**20900**	**24100**	**25475**
Add Leather Seats (XLT)			**325**	**375**	**375**
Deduct 5.4L V8 Engine			**550**	**550**	**550**
Deduct W/out Power Seat			**125**	**125**	**125**
2000 WINDSTAR-V6					
Cargo Van	A54	3709	**3650**	**5225**	**6025**
Wagon	A50	3910	**4450**	**6125**	**7000**
Wagon LX	A51	3910	**5400**	**7175**	**8050**
Wagon SE	A52	3988	**6600**	**8525**	**9400**
Wagon SEL	A53	3988	**8250**	**10350**	**11275**

TRUCKS

BODY TYPE	Model No.	Weight	Trade-In	Retail	High Retail
Wagon Limited	A53	3988	**8850**	**11000**	**11950**
Add Aluminum/Alloy Wheels (LX)			**125**	**150**	**150**
Add Compact Disc Player (Std. SEL, Ltd.)			**50**	**75**	**75**
Add Dual Power Doors (Std. SEL, Ltd.)			**400**	**450**	**450**
Add Leather Seats (Std. SEL, Ltd.)			**250**	**300**	**300**
Add Left Sliding Door (Wagon, LX)			**250**	**300**	**300**
Add Power Seat (Std. SE, SEL, Ltd.)			**100**	**125**	**125**
Add Power Sliding Door (LX, SE)			**200**	**225**	**225**
Add Rear Air Cond (Std. SE, SEL, Ltd.)			**100**	**125**	**125**
Add Rear Bucket Seats (LX)			**100**	**125**	**125**
Add Rear Entertainment System			**250**	**300**	**300**
Deduct W/out Cruise Control			**100**	**100**	**100**
Deduct W/out Tilt Steering Wheel			**75**	**75**	**75**
2000 ECONOLINE E150-1/2 Ton-V8					
Cargo Van	E14	4690	**7925**	**9975**	**11025**
Wagon	E11	5140	**8925**	**11075**	**12075**
2000 ECONOLINE E250-3/4 Ton-V8					
Cargo Van	E24	5080	**8275**	**10375**	**11400**
Extended Cargo Van	S24	5225	**8975**	**11125**	**12150**
2000 ECONOLINE E350-1 Ton-V8					
Super Duty Cargo Van	E34	5340	**8675**	**10800**	**11850**
Super Duty Wagon	E31	5872	**9675**	**11900**	**12950**
Super Duty Ext. Cargo Van	S34	5485	**9375**	**11575**	**12600**
Super Duty Ext. Wagon	S31	6186	**10525**	**12800**	**13875**
ECONOLINE OPTIONS					
Add Chateau Trim			**650**	**725**	**725**
Add XLT Trim			**550**	**625**	**625**
Add 6.8L V10 Engine			**325**	**375**	**375**
Add 7.3L V8 Turbo Diesel Engine			**3450**	**3675**	**3675**
Add Aluminum/Alloy Wheels			**175**	**200**	**200**
Add Compact Disc Player			**75**	**100**	**100**
Add Power Seat			**125**	**150**	**150**
Add Rear Air Conditioning			**100**	**125**	**125**
Add Rear Bucket Seats			**100**	**125**	**125**
Deduct V6 Engine			**600**	**600**	**600**
Deduct W/out Cruise Control			**125**	**125**	**125**
Deduct W/out Power Door Locks			**100**	**100**	**100**
Deduct W/out Power Windows			**125**	**125**	**125**
Deduct W/out Tilt Steering Wheel			**75**	**75**	**75**
2000 RANGER PICKUP-1/2 Ton-V6					
Styleside	R10*	3068	**4775**	**6500**	**7300**
Flareside	R10*	3068	**5000**	**6750**	**7575**
Styleside Supercab 2D	R14*	3599	**6050**	**7900**	**8725**
Styleside Supercab 4D	R14*		**6400**	**8300**	**9050**
Flareside Supercab 2D	R14*	3540	**6275**	**8175**	**8925**
Flareside Supercab 4D	R14*		**6625**	**8550**	**9325**
Add XLT Trim			**450**	**500**	**500**
Add 4 Wheel Drive			**2000**	**2225**	**2225**
Add Aluminum/Alloy Wheels			**125**	**150**	**150**
Add Compact Disc Player			**50**	**75**	**75**
Add Cruise Control			**100**	**125**	**125**
Add Power Door Locks			**75**	**100**	**100**
Add Power Windows			**100**	**125**	**125**
Add Running Boards			**50**	**75**	**75**

SEE TRUCK OPTION PAGE FOR ADDITIONAL OPTIONS

BODY TYPE	Model No.	Weight	Trade-In	Retail	High Retail
Add Tilt Steering Wheel			75	100	100
Deduct 4 Cyl. Engine			500	500	500
Deduct W/out Air Conditioning			500	500	500
Deduct W/out Automatic Trans.			375	375	375

* 1 or 5 as the 3rd position of the model # denotes 4WD

2000 F150 PICKUP-1/2 Ton-V8

BODY TYPE	Model No.	Weight	Trade-In	Retail	High Retail
Styleside XL	F17*	3923	7075	9050	10050
Flareside XL	F07*		7525	9550	10575
Flareside Lightning	F073	4670	16225	19000	20275
Styleside Supercab XL	X17*	4204	9475	11675	12725
Flareside Supercab XL	X07*		9925	12150	13200
Flareside Supercab Harley	X07		15375	18075	19325

2000 F250 SUPER DUTY PICKUP-3/4 Ton-V8

BODY TYPE	Model No.	Weight	Trade-In	Retail	High Retail
Styleside XL	F20*	5260	9625	11825	12875
Styleside Supercab XL	X20*		12125	14625	15775
Styleside Crew Cab XL	W20*	5490	13825	16425	17650

2000 F350 SUPER DUTY PICKUP-1 Ton-V8

BODY TYPE	Model No.	Weight	Trade-In	Retail	High Retail
Styleside XL	F30*	5195	10425	12700	13775
Styleside Supercab XL	X30*	5256	12925	15475	16650
Styleside Crew Cab XL	W30*	5604	14625	17275	18500

F SERIES PICKUP OPTIONS

BODY TYPE	Model No.	Weight	Trade-In	Retail	High Retail
Add Lariat Trim (XL)			900	1000	1000
Add XLT Trim (XL)			500	575	575
Add 4 Wheel Drive			2000	2225	2225
Add 6.8L V10 Engine			325	375	375
Add 7.3L V8 Turbo Diesel Engine			4100	4325	4325
Add 7700 Payload Pkg. (F150)			625	700	700
Add Aluminum/Alloy Wheels (Std. Lightning, Harley)			175	200	200
Add Compact Disc (Std. Lightning, Harley)			75	100	100
Add Dual Rear Wheels			575	650	650
Add Leather Seats (Std. Lightning, Harley)			325	375	375
Add Power Seat (Std. Lightning, Harley)			125	150	150
Add Running Boards			50	75	75
Deduct Work Truck Pkg.			1000	1000	1000
Deduct V6 Engine			600	600	600
Deduct W/out Air Conditioning			550	550	550
Deduct W/out Automatic Trans.			425	425	425
Deduct W/out Cruise Control			125	125	125
Deduct W/out Tilt Steering Wheel			75	75	75

* 1,3, or 8 as the 3rd position of the model # denotes 4WD

FORD

1999 EXPLORER-1/2 Ton-V6

BODY TYPE	Model No.	Weight	Trade-In	Retail	High Retail
Wagon 2D Sport	U22	3680	4350	6025	6875
Wagon 4D	U32	3876	4950	6700	7625
Wagon 2D Sport (4WD)	U24	3903	5125	6875	7800
Wagon 4D (4WD/AWD)	U34/U35	4113	5725	7550	8450
Add Eddie Bauer Trim			1200	1350	1350
Add Limited Trim			1350	1500	1500
Add XLS Trim			350	400	400
Add XLT Trim			500	575	575
Add 5.0L V8 Engine			225	250	250
Add Aluminum/Alloy Wheels (4D)			75	100	100
Add Leather Seats			225	250	250
Add MACH Stereo System			75	100	100

BODY TYPE	Model No.	Weight	Trade-In	Retail	High Retail
Add Power Seat			75	100	100
Add Power Sunroof			325	375	375
Deduct W/out Automatic Trans.			325	325	325
Deduct W/out Cruise Control			75	75	75
Deduct W/out Power Door Locks			50	50	50
Deduct W/out Power Windows			75	75	75
Deduct W/out Tilt Steering Wheel			50	50	50
1999 EXPEDITION-1/2 Ton-V8					
Utility XLT	U17	4980	8900	11075	12075
Utility Eddie Bauer	U17	4980	10250	12525	13600
Utility XLT (4WD)	U18	5350	9725	11950	13000
Utility Eddie Bauer (4WD)	U18	5350	11075	13425	14525
Add Leather Seats (XLT)			275	325	325
Add Power Sunroof			375	425	425
Deduct 4.6L V8 Engine			275	275	275
Deduct W/out 3rd Row Seat			100	100	100
Deduct W/out Rear Air Conditioning			75	75	75
1999 WINDSTAR-V6					
Cargo Van	A54	3719	2875	4375	5200
Wagon 3.0L	A51	3739	3675	5275	6100
Wagon LX	A51	3890	4625	6350	7225
Wagon SE	A52	4194	5625	7450	8350
Wagon SEL	A53	4270	6925	8900	9800
Add Aluminum/Alloy Wheels (LX)			75	100	100
Add Dual Power Sliding Doors (Std. SEL)			350	400	400
Add Leather Seats (Std. SEL)			225	250	250
Add Left Sliding Door (3.0L, LX)			225	250	250
Add Power Seat (Std. SE, SEL)			75	100	100
Add Power Sliding Door (LX, SE)			175	200	200
Add Rear Air Cond (Std. SE, SEL)			75	100	100
Add Rear Bucket Seats (LX)			75	100	100
Deduct W/out Air Conditioning			450	450	450
Deduct W/out Cruise Control			75	75	75
Deduct W/out Power Door Locks			50	50	50
Deduct W/out Power Windows			75	75	75
Deduct W/out Tilt Steering Wheel			50	50	50
1999 ECONOLINE E150-1/2 Ton-V8					
Cargo Van	E14	4650	7025	8975	10025
Wagon	E11	5182	8025	10100	11125
1999 ECONOLINE E250-3/4 Ton-V8					
Cargo Van	E24	5014	7350	9350	10375
Extended Cargo Van	S24	5145	8000	10050	11075
1999 ECONOLINE E350-1 Ton-V8					
Super Duty Cargo Van	E34	5379	7725	9775	10825
Super Duty Wagon	E31	5852	8725	10850	11900
Super Duty Ext. Cargo Van	S34	5518	8375	10475	11525
Super Duty Ext. Wagon	S31	6186	9375	11575	12600
ECONOLINE OPTIONS					
Add Chateau Trim			600	675	675
Add XLT Trim			500	575	575
Add 6.8L V10 Engine			300	350	350
Add 7.3L V8 Turbo Diesel Engine			3200	3425	3425
Add Aluminum/Alloy Wheels			125	150	150

TRUCKS

SEE TRUCK OPTION PAGE FOR ADDITIONAL OPTIONS

BODY TYPE	Model No.	Weight	Trade-In	Retail	High Retail
Add Power Seat			100	125	125
Add Rear Air Conditioning			75	100	100
Add Rear Bucket Seats			75	100	100
Deduct V6 Engine			500	500	500
Deduct W/out Air Conditioning			500	500	500
Deduct W/out Cruise Control			100	100	100
Deduct W/out Power Door Locks			75	75	75
Deduct W/out Power Windows			100	100	100
Deduct W/out Tilt Steering Wheel			50	50	50
1999 RANGER PICKUP-1/2 Ton-V6					
Styleside	R10*	3009	4125	5775	6550
Flareside	R10*		4325	6000	6800
Styleside Supercab 2D	R14*		5250	7025	7800
Styleside Supercab 4D	R14*		5450	7250	8025
Flareside Supercab 2D	R14*		5450	7250	8025
Flareside Supercab 4D	R14*		5650	7450	8250
Add XLT Trim			400	450	450
Add 4 Wheel Drive			1800	2000	2000
Add Aluminum/Alloy Wheels			75	100	100
Add Cruise Control			75	100	100
Add Power Door Locks			50	75	75
Add Power Windows			75	100	100
Add Tilt Steering Wheel			50	75	75
Deduct 4 Cyl. Engine			450	450	450
Deduct W/out Air Conditioning			450	450	450
Deduct W/out Automatic Trans.			325	325	325
* 1 or 5 as the 3rd position of the model # denotes 4WD					
1999 F150 PICKUP-1/2 Ton-V8					
Styleside XL	F17*	3923	6550	8475	9500
Flareside XL	F07*	3949	6950	8900	9950
Flareside Lightning	F073	4670	14850	17525	18750
Styleside Supercab XL	X17*	4216	8700	10825	11875
Flareside Supercab XL	X07*	4241	9100	11275	12300
1999 F250 PICKUP-3/4 Ton-V8					
Styleside XL	F27*	4352	7150	9125	10125
Styleside Supercab XL	X27*	4517	9300	11475	12500
1999 F250 SUPER DUTY PICKUP-3/4 Ton-V8					
Styleside XL	F20*	4956	8950	11100	12100
Styleside Supercab XL	X20*	5189	11400	13800	14925
Styleside Crew Cab XL	W20*	5487	12750	15300	16475
1999 F350 SUPER DUTY PICKUP-1 Ton-V8					
Styleside XL	F30*	4966	9650	11850	12900
Styleside Supercab XL	X30*	5199	12100	14600	15750
Styleside Crew Cab XL	W30*	5497	13450	16025	17225
F SERIES PICKUP OPTIONS					
Add Lariat Trim (XL)			825	925	925
Add XLT Trim (XL)			450	500	500
Add 4 Wheel Drive			1800	2000	2000
Add 6.8L V10 Engine			300	350	350
Add 7.3L V8 Turbo Diesel Engine			4000	4225	4225
Add A/A Wheels (Std. Lightning)			125	150	150
Add Dual Rear Wheels			525	600	600
Add Leather Seats (Std. Lightning)			275	325	325
Add Power Seat (Std. Lightning)			100	125	125

BODY TYPE	Model No.	Weight	Trade-In	Retail	High Retail
Deduct Work Truck Pkg.			900	900	900
Deduct V6 Engine			500	500	500
Deduct W/out Air Conditioning			500	500	500
Deduct W/out Automatic Trans.			375	375	375
Deduct W/out Cruise Control			100	100	100
Deduct W/out Power Door Locks (XLT)			75	75	75
Deduct W/out Power Windows (XLT)			100	100	100
Deduct W/out Tilt Steering Wheel			50	50	50

* 1,3, or 8 as the 3rd position of the model # denotes 4WD

FORD

1998 EXPLORER-1/2 Ton-V6

BODY TYPE	Model No.	Weight	Trade-In	Retail	High Retail
Wagon 2D Sport	U22	3692	3625	5225	6025
Wagon 4D	U32	3911	4275	5975	6850
Wagon 2D Sport (4WD)	U24	3919	4325	6000	6875
Wagon 4D (4WD/AWD)	U34/U35	4146	4975	6725	7650
Add Eddie Bauer Trim			1000	1125	1125
Add Limited Trim			1250	1400	1400
Add XLT Trim			450	500	500
Add 5.0L V8 Engine			200	225	225
Add Aluminum/Alloy Wheels (4D)			50	75	75
Add Leather Seats			175	200	200
Add MACH Stereo System			50	75	75
Add Power Seat			50	75	75
Add Power Sunroof			275	325	325
Deduct W/out Automatic Trans.			275	275	275
Deduct W/out Cruise Control			50	50	50
Deduct W/out Power Windows			50	50	50

1998 EXPEDITION-1/2 Ton-V8

BODY TYPE	Model No.	Weight	Trade-In	Retail	High Retail
Utility XLT	U17	4983	7675	9700	10750
Utility Eddie Bauer	U17	4983	8775	10900	11950
Utility XLT (4WD)	U18	5329	8350	10475	11525
Utility Eddie Bauer (4WD)	U18	5329	9450	11650	12675
Add Leather Seats (XLT)			225	250	250
Add MACH Stereo System			75	100	100
Add Power Sunroof			325	375	375
Deduct 4.6L V8 Engine			250	250	250
Deduct W/out 3rd Row Seat			100	100	100
Deduct W/out Cruise Control			75	75	75
Deduct W/out Power Seat			75	75	75
Deduct W/out Rear Air Conditioning			50	50	50

1998 WINDSTAR-V6

BODY TYPE	Model No.	Weight	Trade-In	Retail	High Retail
Cargo Van	A54	3546	2200	3575	4325
Wagon 3.0L	A51	3710	2700	4150	4950
Wagon GL	A51	3762	3500	5075	5875
Wagon LX	A51	3946	4200	5850	6725
Wagon Limited	A51	4001	4900	6650	7550
Add Aluminum/Alloy Wheels (GL)			50	75	75
Add JBL Premium Stereo System			50	75	75
Add Leather Seats (Std. Limited)			175	200	200
Add Power Seat (Std. LX, Limited)			50	75	75
Add Rear Air Conditioning			50	75	75
Add Rear Bucket Seats (Std. Limited)			50	75	75
Deduct W/out Air Conditioning			400	400	400

TRUCKS

SEE TRUCK OPTION PAGE FOR ADDITIONAL OPTIONS

BODY TYPE	Model No.	Weight	Trade-In	Retail	High Retail
Deduct W/out Cruise Control			50	50	50
Deduct W/out Power Windows			50	50	50
1998 E150 VAN-1/2 Ton-V8					
Cargo Van	E14	4650	5875	7725	8775
Club Wagon	E11	5125	6925	8875	9925
1998 E250 VAN-3/4 Ton-V8					
Cargo Van	E24	5012	6175	8075	9075
Super Cargo Van	S24	5145	6775	8725	9775
1998 E350 VAN-1 Ton-V8					
Cargo Van	E34	5356	6525	8450	9475
Super Cargo Van	S34	5495	7125	9125	10125
Club Wagon HD	E31	5783	7575	9600	10625
Super Club Wagon	S31	6030	8175	10275	11300
E SERIES VAN OPTIONS					
Add Chateau Trim			525	600	600
Add XLT Trim			450	500	500
Add 6.8L V10 Engine			300	350	350
Add 7.3L V8 Turbo Diesel Engine			2600	2825	2825
Add Aluminum/Alloy Wheels			100	125	125
Add Power Seat			75	100	100
Add Rear Air Conditioning			50	75	75
Add Rear Bucket Seats			50	75	75
Deduct V6 Engine			400	400	400
Deduct W/out Air Conditioning			450	450	450
Deduct W/out Cruise Control			75	75	75
Deduct W/out Power Door Locks			50	50	50
Deduct W/out Power Windows			75	75	75
Deduct W/out Tilt Steering Wheel			50	50	50
1998 RANGER PICKUP-1/2 Ton-V6					
Styleside	R10*	3030	3675	5275	6000
Flareside	R10*		3850	5475	6225
Flareside Splash	R10*	3146	4375	6050	6825
Styleside Supercab	R14*	3210	4875	6625	7450
Flareside Supercab	R14*		5050	6800	7625
Flareside Supercab Splash	R14*	3626	5575	7375	8175
Add XLT Trim (Ex. Splash)			350	400	400
Add 4 Wheel Drive			1600	1800	1800
Add A/A Wheels (Std. Splash)			50	75	75
Add Cruise Control			50	75	75
Add Power Seat			50	75	75
Add Power Windows			50	75	75
Deduct 4 Cyl. Engine			350	350	350
Deduct W/out Air Conditioning			400	400	400
Deduct W/out Automatic Trans.			275	275	275
* 1 or 5 as the 3rd position of the model # denotes 4WD					
1998 F150 PICKUP-1/2 Ton-V8					
Styleside XL	F17*	3880	6025	7900	8975
Flareside XL	F07*	3958	6425	8350	9375
Styleside Supercab XL	X17*	4067	7725	9775	10825
Flareside Supercab XL	X07*	4220	8125	10225	11250
1998 F250 PICKUP-3/4 Ton-V8					
Styleside XL	F27*	4300	6625	8575	9600
Styleside Supercab XL	X27*	4364	8325	10450	11475

TRUCKS

BODY TYPE	Model No.	Weight	Trade-In	Retail	High Retail
F SERIES PICKUP OPTIONS					
Add Lariat Trim (XL)			750	850	850
Add STX Trim (XL)			450	500	500
Add XLT Trim (XL)			400	450	450
Add 4 Wheel Drive			1600	1800	1800
Add Aluminum/Alloy Wheels			100	125	125
Add Leather Seats			225	250	250
Add Power Seat			75	100	100
Deduct Work Truck Pkg.			925	925	925
Deduct V6 Engine			400	400	400
Deduct W/out Air Conditioning			450	450	450
Deduct W/out Automatic Trans.			325	325	325
Deduct W/out Cruise Control (Ex. WT)			75	75	75
Deduct W/out Tilt Steering Wheel (Ex. WT)			50	50	50
* 8 as the 3rd position of the model # denotes 4WD					
FORD					
1997 EXPLORER-1/2 Ton-V6					
Wagon 2D	U22	3707	3100	4625	5500
Wagon 4D	U32	3939	3500	5075	5875
Wagon 2D (4WD)	U24	3931	3650	5250	6050
Wagon 4D (4WD/AWD)	U34/U35	4166	4050	5700	6550
Add Eddie Bauer Trim			775	875	875
Add Limited Trim			875	975	975
Add Sport Trim			300	350	350
Add XLT Trim			400	450	450
Add 5.0L V8 Engine			200	225	225
Add Leather Seats			150	175	175
Add Power Seat			50	75	75
Add Power Sunroof			200	225	225
Deduct W/out Automatic Trans.			175	175	175
Deduct W/out Cruise Control			50	50	50
Deduct W/out Power Windows			50	50	50
1997 EXPEDITION-1/2 Ton-V8					
Utility XLT	U17	4827	6500	8425	9450
Utility Eddie Bauer	U17	4827	7400	9425	10450
Utility XLT (4WD)	U18	5212	7100	9075	10075
Utility Eddie Bauer (4WD)	U18	5212	8000	10075	11100
Add Leather Seats (Std. Eddie Bauer)			200	225	225
Add Power Sunroof			250	300	300
Deduct 4.6L V8 Engine			200	200	200
Deduct W/out Cruise Control			75	75	75
Deduct W/out Power Seat			75	75	75
1997 AEROSTAR-1/2 Ton-V6					
Cargo Van	A14	3414	1500	2750	3400
Wagon XLT	A11*	3717	2100	3450	4175
Extended Wagon XLT	A31*	3827	3000	4500	5350
Add All Wheel Drive			400	450	450
Deduct W/out Air Conditioning			250	250	250
Deduct W/out Cruise Control			50	50	50
Deduct W/out Power Windows (Ex. Cargo)			50	50	50
* 4 as the 2nd position of the model # denotes AWD					
1997 WINDSTAR-V6					
Cargo Van	A54		1775	3075	3750

SEE TRUCK OPTION PAGE FOR ADDITIONAL OPTIONS

TRUCKS

BODY TYPE	Model No.	Weight	Trade-In	Retail	High Retail
Wagon	A51		2300	3700	4450
Wagon GL	A51		2850	4325	5150
Wagon LX	A51		3500	5075	5875
Add Leather Seats			150	175	175
Add Power Seat (Std. LX)			50	75	75
Deduct W/out Air Conditioning			250	250	250
Deduct W/out Cruise Control			50	50	50
Deduct W/out Power Windows			50	50	50
1997 E150 VAN-1/2 Ton-V8					
Cargo Van	E14	4660	5000	6750	7775
Club Wagon	E11	5136	5925	7775	8825
1997 E250 VAN-3/4 Ton-V8					
Cargo Van	E24		5250	7025	8025
Super Cargo Van	S24	5221	5650	7475	8500
1997 E350 VAN-1 Ton-V8					
Cargo Van	E34		5500	7300	8325
Super Cargo Van	S34		5900	7750	8800
Club Wagon HD	E31		6425	8325	9325
Super Club Wagon	S31		6825	8775	9825
E SERIES VAN OPTIONS					
Add Chateau Trim			400	450	450
Add XL Trim (Ex. Club Wagon)			100	125	125
Add XLT Trim			300	350	350
Add 6.8L V10 Engine			300	350	350
Add 7.3L V8 Turbo Diesel Engine			2600	2825	2825
Add Aluminum/Alloy Wheels			50	75	75
Add Power Seat			75	100	100
Deduct V6 Engine			300	300	300
Deduct W/out Air Conditioning			350	350	350
Deduct W/out Cruise Control			75	75	75
Deduct W/out Power Windows			75	75	75
1997 RANGER PICKUP-1/2 Ton-V6					
Styleside	R10*	2963	3050	4575	5350
Flareside	R10*		3200	4725	5500
Flareside Splash	R10*		3500	5075	5800
Styleside Supercab	R14*	3240	4050	5700	6475
Flareside Supercab	R14*		4200	5875	6675
Flareside Supercab Splash	R14*		4500	6200	6975
Add STX Trim			275	325	325
Add XLT Trim (Ex. Splash)			300	350	350
Add 4 Wheel Drive			1300	1450	1450
Add Cruise Control			50	75	75
Add Power Seat			50	75	75
Add Power Windows			50	75	75
Deduct 4 Cyl. Engine			200	200	200
Deduct W/out Air Conditioning			250	250	250
Deduct W/out Automatic Trans.			175	175	175

* 1 or 5 as the 3rd position of the model # denotes 4WD

BODY TYPE	Model No.	Weight	Trade-In	Retail	High Retail
1997 F150 PICKUP-1/2 Ton-V8					
Styleside XL	F17*	3850	4900	6650	7675
Flareside XL	F07*		5150	6925	7975
Styleside Supercab XL	X17*	4045	6400	8300	9300
Flareside Supercab XL	X07*		6650	8575	9600

BODY TYPE	Model No.	Weight	Trade-In	Retail	High Retail
1997 F250 PICKUP-3/4 Ton-V8; W25 7.5L V8					
Styleside XL	F27*		5500	7300	8325
Heavy Duty XL	F25*		5650	7475	8500
Styleside Supercab XL	X27*		7000	8975	10025
Heavy Duty Supercab XL	X25*		7150	9150	10150
Heavy Duty Crew Cab XL	W25*		8400	10500	11550
1997 F350 PICKUP-1 Ton-5.8L V8, Supercab 7.5L V8					
Styleside XL	F35*		6650	8575	9600
Styleside Crew Cab XL	W35*		9150	11325	12350
Styleside Supercab XL	X35*		8775	10925	12000
F SERIES PICKUP OPTIONS					
Add Lariat Trim (XL)			700	800	800
Add XLT Trim (XL)			350	400	400
Add 4 Wheel Drive			1300	1450	1450
Add 7.3L V8 Turbo Diesel Engine			3350	3575	3575
Add 7.5L V8 Engine (Std. F250 Crew, F350 Supercab)			250	300	300
Add Aluminum/Alloy Wheels			50	75	75
Add Dual Rear Wheels (Std. 350 Supercab)			375	425	425
Add Leather Seats			200	225	225
Add Power Seat			75	100	100
Deduct Work Truck Pkg.			875	875	875
Deduct 6 Cyl. Engine			300	300	300
Deduct W/out Air Conditioning			350	350	350
Deduct W/out Automatic Trans.			250	250	250
Deduct W/out Cruise Control (Ex. WT)			75	75	75

* 6 or 8 as the 3rd position of the model # denotes 4WD

FORD

BODY TYPE	Model No.	Weight	Trade-In	Retail	High Retail
1996 EXPLORER-1/2 Ton-V6					
Wagon 2D	U22	3733	2500	3925	4725
Wagon 4D	U32	3952	2900	4375	5200
Wagon 2D (4WD)	U24	3981	3050	4575	5425
Wagon 4D (4WD/AWD)	U34/U35	4189	3450	5025	5825
Add Eddie Bauer Trim			725	825	825
Add Limited Trim			825	925	925
Add Sport Trim			250	300	300
Add XLT Trim			350	400	400
Add 5.0L V8 Engine			150	175	175
Add Power Sunroof			150	175	175
Deduct W/out Automatic Trans.			125	125	125
1996 BRONCO-1/2 Ton-V8-4WD					
Wagon	U15	4587	4800	6525	7550
Add Eddie Bauer Trim			700	800	800
Add XLT Trim			350	400	400
Deduct W/out Air Conditioning			250	250	250
Deduct W/out Automatic Trans.			150	150	150
1996 AEROSTAR-1/2 Ton-V6					
Cargo Van	A14	3411	1100	2275	2850
Wagon XLT	A11*	3714	1700	2975	3650
Extended Wagon XLT	A31*	3824	2400	3800	4575
Add All Wheel Drive			400	450	450
Deduct W/out Air Conditioning			150	150	150

* 4 as the 2nd position of the model # denotes AWD

TRUCKS

SEE TRUCK OPTION PAGE FOR ADDITIONAL OPTIONS

BODY TYPE	Model No.	Weight	Trade-In	Retail	High Retail
1996 WINDSTAR-V6					
Cargo Van	A54	3487	**1350**	**2575**	**3200**
Wagon GL	A51	3733	**2200**	**3575**	**4325**
Wagon LX	A51	3920	**2800**	**4275**	**5100**
Deduct W/out Air Conditioning			**150**	**150**	**150**
1996 E150 VAN-1/2 Ton-V8					
Cargo Van	E14	4677	**4000**	**5625**	**6575**
Club Wagon	E11	5121	**4700**	**6425**	**7425**
1996 E250 VAN-3/4 Ton-V8					
Cargo Van	E24	5043	**4250**	**5925**	**6925**
Super Cargo Van	S24	5185	**4650**	**6375**	**7375**
1996 E350 VAN-1 Ton-V8					
Cargo Van	E34	5185	**4500**	**6200**	**7175**
Super Cargo Van	S34	5333	**4900**	**6650**	**7675**
Club Wagon HD	E31	5580	**5200**	**6975**	**8025**
Super Club Wagon	S31	5884	**5600**	**7400**	**8425**
E SERIES VAN OPTIONS					
Add Chateau Trim			**350**	**400**	**400**
Add XL Trim (Ex. Club Wagon)			**100**	**125**	**125**
Add XLT Trim			**250**	**300**	**300**
Add 7.3L V8 Turbo Diesel Engine			**2225**	**2450**	**2450**
Add 7.5L V8 Engine			**225**	**250**	**250**
Deduct 6 Cyl. Engine			**200**	**200**	**200**
Deduct W/out Air Conditioning			**250**	**250**	**250**
1996 RANGER PICKUP-1/2 Ton-V6					
Styleside	R10*	2961	**2500**	**3925**	**4625**
Flareside	R10*		**2650**	**4100**	**4825**
Flareside Splash	R10*	3120	**2925**	**4400**	**5150**
Styleside Supercab	R14*	3260	**3400**	**4950**	**5750**
Flareside Supercab	R14*		**3550**	**5125**	**5850**
Flareside Supercab Splash	R14*	3425	**3825**	**5450**	**6200**
Add STX Trim			**250**	**300**	**300**
Add XLT Trim (Ex. Splash)			**250**	**300**	**300**
Add 4 Wheel Drive			**1200**	**1350**	**1350**
Deduct 4 Cyl. Engine			**175**	**175**	**175**
Deduct W/out Air Conditioning			**150**	**150**	**150**
Deduct W/out Automatic Trans.			**125**	**125**	**125**
* 1 or 5 as the 3rd position of the model # denotes 4WD					
1996 F150 PICKUP-1/2 Ton-V8					
Styleside XL	F15*	3919	**4000**	**5625**	**6575**
Styleside Supercab XL	X15*	4189	**5100**	**6850**	**7900**
1996 F250 PICKUP-3/4 Ton-5.8L V8; W25 7.5L V8					
Styleside XL	F25*	4333	**4600**	**6300**	**7300**
Heavy Duty XL	F25*	4534	**4675**	**6400**	**7400**
Heavy Duty Supercab XL	X25*	4965	**5775**	**7600**	**8650**
Heavy Duty Crew Cab XL	W25*	5286	**7000**	**8975**	**10025**
1996 F350 PICKUP-1 Ton-5.8L V8, Supercab 7.5L V8					
Styleside XL	F35*	4896	**5600**	**7400**	**8425**
Styleside Crew Cab XL	W35*	5229	**7700**	**9750**	**10800**
Styleside Supercab XL	X35*	5333	**7275**	**9275**	**10300**
F SERIES PICKUP OPTIONS					
Add Eddie Bauer Trim (XL)			**500**	**575**	**575**
Add XLT Trim (XL)			**325**	**375**	**375**

TRUCKS

BODY TYPE	Model No.	Weight	Trade-In	Retail	High Retail
Add 4 Wheel Drive			1200	1350	1350
Add 7.3L V8 Turbo Diesel Engine			2550	2775	2775
Add 7.5L V8 Engine (Std. F250 HD Crew, F350 Supercab).			225	250	250
Add Dual Rear Wheels (Std. 350 Supercab)			350	400	400
Deduct Work Truck Pkg.			800	800	800
Deduct 6 Cyl. Engine			200	200	200
Deduct W/out Air Conditioning			250	250	250
Deduct W/out Automatic Trans.			150	150	150

* 4 or 6 as the 3rd position of the model # denotes 4WD

FORD

1995 EXPLORER-1/2 Ton-V6

BODY TYPE	Model No.	Weight	Trade-In	Retail	High Retail
Wagon 2D	U22	3646	2200	3575	4325
Wagon 4D	U32	3844	2500	3925	4725
Wagon 2D (4WD)	U24	3863	2750	4200	5000
Wagon 4D (4WD)	U34	4053	3050	4575	5425
Add Eddie Bauer Trim			650	725	725
Add Expedition Trim			650	725	725
Add Limited Trim			750	850	850
Add Sport Trim			200	225	225
Add XLT Trim			300	350	350

1995 BRONCO-1/2 Ton-V8-4WD

BODY TYPE	Model No.	Weight	Trade-In	Retail	High Retail
Wagon	U15	4587	4000	5625	6575
Add Eddie Bauer Trim			625	700	700
Add XLT Trim			300	350	350

1995 AEROSTAR-1/2 Ton-V6

BODY TYPE	Model No.	Weight	Trade-In	Retail	High Retail
Cargo Van	A14	3402	825	1925	2450
Wagon XLT	A11*	3646	1475	2725	3375
Extended Wagon XLT	A31*	3833	2075	3425	4150
Add All Wheel Drive			350	400	400

* 4 as the 2nd position of the model # denotes AWD

1995 WINDSTAR-V6

BODY TYPE	Model No.	Weight	Trade-In	Retail	High Retail
Cargo Van	A54	3545	1000	2150	2700
Wagon GL	A51	3730	1800	3100	3775
Wagon LX	A51		2350	3750	4525

1995 E150 VAN-1/2 Ton-V8

BODY TYPE	Model No.	Weight	Trade-In	Retail	High Retail
Cargo Van	E14	4677	2900	4375	5250
Club Wagon	E11	5141	3800	5400	6325

1995 E250 VAN-3/4 Ton-V8

BODY TYPE	Model No.	Weight	Trade-In	Retail	High Retail
Cargo Van	E24	5067	3125	4650	5575
Super Cargo Van	S24	5225	3525	5100	6000

1995 E350 VAN-1 Ton-V8

BODY TYPE	Model No.	Weight	Trade-In	Retail	High Retail
Cargo Van	E34	5204	3350	4900	5850
Super Cargo Van	S34	5372	3750	5350	6275
Club Wagon HD	E31	5628	4250	5925	6925
Super Club Wagon	S31	5863	4650	6375	7375

E SERIES VAN OPTIONS

BODY TYPE	Model No.	Weight	Trade-In	Retail	High Retail
Add Chateau Trim			300	350	350
Add XLT Trim			200	225	225
Add 7.3L V8 Turbo Diesel Engine			2100	2325	2325
Add 7.5L V8 Engine			200	225	225
Deduct 6 Cyl. Engine			150	150	150

TRUCKS

SEE TRUCK OPTION PAGE FOR ADDITIONAL OPTIONS

BODY TYPE	Model No.	Weight	Trade-In	Retail	High Retail
1995 RANGER PICKUP-1/2 Ton-V6					
Styleside	R10*	2907	**2050**	**3400**	**4050**
Flareside Splash	R10*		**2400**	**3800**	**4500**
Styleside Supercab	R14*	3209	**2850**	**4325**	**5075**
Flareside Supercab Splash	R14*		**3200**	**4725**	**5500**
Add Sport Trim			**175**	**200**	**200**
Add STX Trim			**225**	**250**	**250**
Add XLT Trim (Ex. Splash)			**225**	**250**	**250**
Add 4 Wheel Drive			**1100**	**1225**	**1225**
Deduct 4 Cyl. Engine			**125**	**125**	**125**
* 1 or 5 as the 3rd position of the model # denotes 4WD					
1995 F150 PICKUP-1/2 Ton-V8					
Styleside XL	F15*	3896	**3500**	**5075**	**5975**
Flareside XL	F15*	3957	**3750**	**5350**	**6275**
Styleside Lightning	F15*	4446	**6350**	**8250**	**9250**
Styleside Supercab XL	X15*	4186	**4500**	**6200**	**7175**
Flareside Supercab XL	X15*	4269	**4750**	**6475**	**7475**
1995 F250 PICKUP-3/4 Ton-V8					
Styleside XL	F25*	4230	**4050**	**5700**	**6675**
Styleside Supercab XL	X25*	4750	**5050**	**6800**	**7850**
1995 F350 PICKUP-1 Ton-5.8L V8, Supercab 7.5L V8					
Styleside XL	F35*	4881	**4700**	**6425**	**7425**
Styleside Crew Cab XL	W35*	5224	**6550**	**8475**	**9500**
Styleside Supercab XL	X35*	5387	**6225**	**8125**	**9125**
F SERIES PICKUP OPTIONS					
Add Eddie Bauer Trim (XL)			**450**	**500**	**500**
Add XLT Trim (XL)			**300**	**350**	**350**
Add 4 Wheel Drive			**1100**	**1225**	**1225**
Add 7.3L V8 Turbo Diesel Engine			**2200**	**2425**	**2425**
Add 7.5L V8 Engine (Std. 350 Supercab).			**200**	**225**	**225**
Add Dual Rear Wheels (Std. 350 Supercab)			**325**	**375**	**375**
Deduct Work Truck Pkg.			**800**	**800**	**800**
Deduct 6 Cyl. Engine			**150**	**150**	**150**
* 4 or 6 as the 3rd position of the model # denotes 4WD					

GEO

BODY TYPE	Model No.	Weight	Trade-In	Retail	High Retail
GEO					
1997 TRACKER-4 Cyl.-5 Spd.-4WD					
Utility 2D Convertible (2WD)	E18	2339	**1650**	**2925**	**3550**
Utility 2D Convertible	J18	2555	**2550**	**3975**	**4700**
Utility 4D Hardtop (2WD)	E13	2619	**2050**	**3400**	**4050**
Utility 4D Hardtop	J13	2747	**2950**	**4450**	**5200**
Add Automatic Trans.			**125**	**150**	**150**
Deduct W/out Air Conditioning			**150**	**150**	**150**
GEO					
1996 TRACKER-4 Cyl.-5 Spd.-4WD					
Utility 2D Convertible (2WD)	E18	2339	**1325**	**2550**	**3125**
Utility 2D Convertible	J18	2555	**2125**	**3500**	**4150**
Utility 4D Hardtop (2WD)	E13	2619	**1675**	**2950**	**3600**
Utility 4D Hardtop	J13	2747	**2475**	**3900**	**4600**
Add Automatic Trans.			**100**	**125**	**125**

TRUCKS

BODY TYPE	Model No.	Weight	Trade-In	Retail	High Retail
Deduct W/out Air Conditioning			**100**	**100**	**100**
GEO					
1995 TRACKER-4 Cyl.-4WD					
Utility Convertible (2WD)	E18	2189	**1175**	**2350**	**2900**
Utility Hardtop	J18	2387	**2225**	**3600**	**4275**
Utility Convertible	J18	2365	**1925**	**3250**	**3875**

GMC

BODY TYPE	Model No.	Weight	Trade-In	Retail	High Retail
GMC					
2004 ENVOY-1/2 Ton-I6					
Utility 4D SLE	S13S	4425	**16850**	**19675**	**20775**
Utility 4D SLT	S13S		**19000**	**22100**	**23275**
Utility 4D SLE (4WD)	T13S	4612	**17950**	**20950**	**22100**
Utility 4D SLT (4WD)	T13S		**20100**	**23250**	**24450**
2004 ENVOY XL-1/2 Ton-I6					
Utility 4D XL SLE	S16S	4773	**18200**	**21250**	**22400**
Utility 4D XL SLE (V8)	S16P	4822	**19100**	**22200**	**23375**
Utility 4D XL SLT	S16S		**20350**	**23525**	**24725**
Utility 4D XL SLT (V8)	S16P		**21250**	**24475**	**25700**
Utility 4D XL SLE (4WD)	T16S	4954	**19300**	**22400**	**23575**
Utility 4D XL SLE (4WD, V8)	T16P	5007	**20200**	**23350**	**24550**
Utility 4D XL SLT (4WD)	T16S		**21450**	**24675**	**25925**
Utility 4D XL SLT (4WD, V8)	T16P		**22350**	**25650**	**26925**
2004 ENVOY XUV-1/2 Ton-I6					
Utility 4D SLE	S12S	4945	**18650**	**21725**	**22900**
Utility 4D SLE (V8)	S12P		**19550**	**22675**	**23850**
Utility 4D SLT	S12S		**20800**	**24000**	**25225**
Utility 4D SLT (V8)	S12P		**21700**	**24975**	**26225**
Utility 4D SLE (4WD)	T12S	5042	**19750**	**22875**	**24075**
Utility 4D SLE (4WD, V8)	T12P		**20650**	**23825**	**25050**
Utility 4D SLT (4WD)	T12S		**21900**	**25175**	**26425**
Utility 4D SLT (4WD, V8)	T12P		**22800**	**26125**	**27400**
ENVOY/ENVOY XL/ENVOY XUV OPTIONS					
Add Bose Stereo System			**300**	**350**	**350**
Add Navigation System			**600**	**675**	**675**
Add Power Seat (Std. SLT)			**200**	**225**	**225**
Add Power Sunroof			**575**	**650**	**650**
Add Rear Entertainment System			**600**	**675**	**675**
Add Running Boards			**150**	**175**	**175**
Add Theft Recovery System			**100**	**125**	**125**
Deduct W/out Cruise Control			**200**	**200**	**200**
2004 YUKON-1/2 Ton-V8					
Utility 4D SLE	C13	5042	**23975**	**27375**	**28850**
Utility 4D SLE (4WD)	K13	5269	**25700**	**29200**	**30725**
Add SLT Trim			**1925**	**2150**	**2150**
Add Z71 Off-Road Pkg.			**300**	**350**	**350**
Add Bose Stereo System			**350**	**400**	**400**
Add Leather Seats			**525**	**600**	**600**
Add Power Sunroof			**625**	**700**	**700**
Add Rear Bucket Seats			**200**	**225**	**225**
Add Rear Entertainment System			**600**	**675**	**675**
Add Theft Recovery System			**100**	**125**	**125**

TRUCKS

SEE TRUCK OPTION PAGE FOR ADDITIONAL OPTIONS

BODY TYPE	Model No.	Weight	Trade-In	Retail	High Retail
Deduct W/out 3rd Row Seat			200	200	200
Deduct W/out Running Boards			150	150	150
2004 DENALI-1/2 Ton-V8-AWD					
Utility 4D	K63	5425	32475	36675	38700
Utility XL 4D	K66	5839	33175	37425	39450
Sierra Ext. Cab 4D	K69	5478	23875	27275	29000
Add Navigation System			750	850	850
Add Power Sunroof			725	825	825
Add Rear Bucket Seats			200	225	225
Add Rear Entertainment System			600	675	675
Add Theft Recovery System			100	125	125
2004 YUKON XL-1/2-3/4 Ton-V8					
Utility C1500 SLE	C16	5323	24125	27550	29025
Utility C1500 SLT	C16		26925	30525	32075
Utility C2500 SLE	C26	5812	24925	28375	29875
Utility C2500 SLT	C26		27725	31475	33050
Utility K1500 SLE (4WD)	K16	5567	25850	29375	30900
Utility K1500 SLT (4WD)	K16		28650	32475	34100
Utility K2500 SLE (4WD)	K26	6113	26650	30225	31775
Utility K2500 SLT (4WD)	K26		29450	33325	34975
Add 8.1L V8 Engine			450	500	500
Add Bose Stereo System (Std. SLT)			350	400	400
Add Power Sunroof			625	700	700
Add Quadrasteer System			1050	1175	1175
Add Rear Bucket Seats			200	225	225
Add Rear Entertainment System			600	675	675
Add Theft Recovery System			100	125	125
Deduct W/out Running Boards			150	150	150
2004 SAFARI-1/2 Ton-V6					
Cargo Van	M19*	3953	11150	13550	14475
Van	M19*	4309	12150	14650	15625
Van SLE	M19*		12850	15400	16400
Van SLT	M19*		13800	16400	17425
Add All Wheel Drive			1100	1225	1225
Add Aluminum/Alloy Wheels (Cargo)			325	375	375
Add Compact Disc Player (Std. SLE, SLT)			100	125	125
Add Leather Seats			450	500	500
Add Power Seat (Std. SLT)			200	225	225
Add Rear Air Conditioning (Std. SLT)			200	225	225
Add Rear Bucket Seats			200	225	225
Add Running Boards (SLE, SLT)			150	175	175
Add Theft Recovery System			100	125	125
Deduct W/out Cruise Control			200	200	200
Deduct W/out Power Door Locks			175	175	175
Deduct W/out Power Windows			200	200	200
Deduct W/out Tilt Steering Wheel			150	150	150

* L as the 1st position of the model # denotes AWD

BODY TYPE	Model No.	Weight	Trade-In	Retail	High Retail
2004 G1500-1/2 Ton-V8					
Cargo Van 135"	G15*	4845	14150	16800	18025
Savana 135"	G15*	5258	15500	18225	19475
2004 G2500-3/4 Ton-V8					
Cargo Van 135"	G25*	5017	14800	17475	18700
Extended Cargo Van 155"	G29	5344	15500	18225	19475

TRUCKS

BODY TYPE	Model No.	Weight	Trade-In	Retail	High Retail
Savana 135"	G25	5877	**16700**	**19500**	**20800**
2004 G3500-1 Ton-V8					
Cargo Van 135"	G35	5427	**16000**	**18750**	**20025**
Extended Cargo Van 155"	G39	5625	**16700**	**19500**	**20800**
Savana 135"	G35	6015	**17350**	**20325**	**21650**
Extended Savana 155"	G39	6333	**18250**	**21300**	**22650**
G SERIES VAN OPTIONS					
Add SLE Trim			**650**	**725**	**725**
Add Left Access Door (Ex. Extended)			**250**	**300**	**300**
Add 15 Passenger Seating			**200**	**225**	**225**
Add 6.0L V8 Engine (2500 Cargo)			**550**	**625**	**625**
Add All Wheel Drive			**1400**	**1575**	**1575**
Add Aluminum/Alloy Wheels			**375**	**425**	**425**
Add Compact Disc Player			**150**	**175**	**175**
Add Power Seat			**225**	**250**	**250**
Add Rear Air Cond. (Std. Ext. Savana)			**200**	**225**	**225**
Add Theft Recovery System			**100**	**125**	**125**
Deduct V6 Engine			**750**	**750**	**750**
Deduct W/out Air Conditioning			**750**	**750**	**750**
Deduct W/out Cruise Control			**225**	**225**	**225**
Deduct W/out Power Door Locks			**200**	**200**	**200**
Deduct W/out Power Windows			**225**	**225**	**225**
Deduct W/out Tilt Steering Wheel			**175**	**175**	**175**
* H as the 1st position of the model # denotes AWD					
2004 SONOMA PICKUP-1/2 Ton-V6					
Crew Cab SLS (4WD)	T13	4083	**16150**	**18900**	**19750**
Add ZR5 Sport Pkg.			**500**	**575**	**575**
Add Leather Seats			**450**	**500**	**500**
Add Power Seat			**200**	**225**	**225**
Add Running Boards			**150**	**175**	**175**
Add Theft Recovery System			**100**	**125**	**125**
2004 CANYON PICKUP-1/2 Ton-5 Cyl.					
Regular Cab Z85	S14*	3351	**11000**	**13350**	**14100**
Regular Cab Z71	S14*		**12525**	**15050**	**15850**
Extended Cab Z85	S19*	3607	**13150**	**15725**	**16525**
Extended Cab Z71	S19*		**14675**	**17350**	**18150**
Crew Cab Z85 SLE	S13*	3752	**14775**	**17450**	**18250**
Crew Cab Z71 SLE	S13*		**15975**	**18725**	**19550**
Add SLE Trim (Std. Crew)			**500**	**575**	**575**
Add 4 Wheel Drive			**2600**	**2825**	**2825**
Add Alum/Alloy Wheels (Std. Z71, Crew)			**325**	**375**	**375**
Add CD Player (Std. Z71, Crew)			**100**	**125**	**125**
Add Leather Seats			**450**	**500**	**500**
Add Power Seat			**200**	**225**	**225**
Add Running Boards			**150**	**175**	**175**
Add Theft Recovery System			**100**	**125**	**125**
Deduct 4 Cyl. Engine			**700**	**700**	**700**
Deduct W/out Air Conditioning			**700**	**700**	**700**
Deduct W/out Automatic Trans.			**575**	**575**	**575**
Deduct W/out Cruise Control			**200**	**200**	**200**
Deduct W/out Power Door Locks (SLE)			**175**	**175**	**175**
Deduct W/out Power Windows (SLE)			**200**	**200**	**200**
Deduct W/out Tilt Steering Wheel			**150**	**150**	**150**

* T as the 1st position of the model # denotes 4WD

TRUCKS

SEE TRUCK OPTION PAGE FOR ADDITIONAL OPTIONS

BODY TYPE	Model No.	Weight	Trade-In	Retail	High Retail
2004 SIERRA 1500 PICKUP-1/2 Ton-V8					
Wideside	C14*	4142	**14275**	**16925**	**18175**
Sportside	C14*		**14925**	**17625**	**18850**
Wideside Extended Cab	C19*	4548	**16375**	**19175**	**20450**
Sportside Extended Cab	C19*		**17025**	**19925**	**21225**
Wideside Crew Cab SLE	C13*	4946	**18725**	**21800**	**23175**
Wideside Crew Cab SLT	C13*		**20675**	**23875**	**25250**
2004 SIERRA 2500 LD PICKUP-3/4 Ton-V8					
Wideside	C24		**15175**	**17875**	**19125**
Wide Extended Cab (4WD)	K29		**19975**	**23125**	**24475**
Wideside Crew Cab SLE	C23*	5506	**19625**	**22750**	**24100**
Wideside Crew Cab SLT	C23*		**21575**	**24825**	**26225**
2004 SIERRA 2500 HD PICKUP-3/4 Ton-V8					
Wideside	C24*	5153	**16175**	**18950**	**20225**
Wideside Extended Cab	C29*	5402	**19575**	**22700**	**24050**
Wideside Crew Cab	C23*	5615	**20975**	**24200**	**25600**
2004 SIERRA 3500 PICKUP-1 Ton-V8-Dual Rear Wheels					
RC Wideside (4WD)	K34	5841	**19675**	**22800**	**24150**
Wideside Extended Cab	C39*	5951	**20175**	**23350**	**24725**
Wideside Crew Cab	C33*	6168	**21575**	**24825**	**26225**
SIERRA PICKUP OPTIONS					
Add SLE Trim (Ex. 1500/2500LD Crew)			**700**	**800**	**800**
Add SLT Trim (Ex. 1500/2500LD Crew)			**1500**	**1675**	**1675**
Add Z71 Off-Road Pkg. (4WD)			**350**	**400**	**400**
Add 4WD (Std. 2500 LD Ext, 3500 RC)			**2800**	**3025**	**3025**
Add 6.6L V8 Turbo Diesel Engine			**5000**	**5225**	**5225**
Add 8.1L V8 Engine			**1075**	**1200**	**1200**
Add A/A Wheels (Std. 1500/2500LD Crew)			**375**	**425**	**425**
Add Bose Stereo (Std. 1500/2500LD Crew SLT)			**350**	**400**	**400**
Add Leather Seats (Std. 1500/2500LD Crew SLT)			**525**	**600**	**600**
Add Power Seat (Std. 1500/2500LD Crew SLT)			**225**	**250**	**250**
Add Quadrasteer System			**1050**	**1175**	**1175**
Add Rear Entertainment System			**600**	**675**	**675**
Add Running Boards			**150**	**175**	**175**
Add Theft Recovery System			**100**	**125**	**125**
Deduct Work Truck Pkg.			**1100**	**1100**	**1100**
Deduct V6 Engine			**750**	**750**	**750**
Deduct W/out Air Conditioning			**750**	**750**	**750**
Deduct W/out Automatic Trans.			**625**	**625**	**625**
Deduct W/out Compact Disc Player			**150**	**150**	**150**
Deduct W/out Cruise Control			**225**	**225**	**225**
Deduct W/out Power Door Locks			**200**	**200**	**200**

* K as the 1st position of the model # denotes 4WD

GMC

BODY TYPE	Model No.	Weight	Trade-In	Retail	High Retail
2003 ENVOY-1/2 Ton-I6					
Utility 4D SLE	S13S	4582	**15550**	**18275**	**19325**
Utility 4D SLT	S13S		**17350**	**20325**	**21450**
Utility 4D SLE (4WD)	T13S	4767	**16575**	**19375**	**20475**
Utility 4D SLT (4WD)	T13S		**18375**	**21425**	**22575**
2003 ENVOY XL-1/2 Ton-I6					
Utility 4D XL SLE	S16S	4938	**16850**	**19675**	**20775**
Utility 4D XL SLE (V8)	S16P	4868	**17600**	**20600**	**21725**
Utility 4D XL SLT	S16S		**18650**	**21700**	**22875**
Utility 4D XL SLT (V8)	S16P		**19400**	**22500**	**23675**
Utility 4D XL SLE (4WD)	T16S	5118	**17875**	**20900**	**22050**

TRUCKS

BODY TYPE	Model No.	Weight	Trade-In	Retail	High Retail
Utility 4D XL SLE (4WD, V8)	T16P	5055	**18625**	**21700**	**22875**
Utility 4D XL SLT (4WD)	T16S		**19675**	**22800**	**24000**
Utility 4D XL SLT (4WD, V8)	T16P		**20425**	**23600**	**24800**
ENVOY/ENVOY XL OPTIONS					
Add Bose Stereo System			**250**	**300**	**300**
Add Power Seat (Std. SLT)			**175**	**200**	**200**
Add Power Sunroof			**525**	**600**	**600**
Add Rear Entertainment System			**500**	**575**	**575**
Add Running Boards			**125**	**150**	**150**
Add Theft Recovery System			**75**	**100**	**100**
Deduct W/out Cruise Control			**175**	**175**	**175**
2003 YUKON-1/2 Ton-V8					
Utility 4D SLE	C13	4828	**20925**	**24150**	**25525**
Utility 4D SLE (4WD)	K13	5050	**22675**	**26000**	**27450**
Add SLT Trim			**1225**	**1375**	**1375**
Add Z71 Off-Road Pkg.			**250**	**300**	**300**
Add Bose Stereo System			**300**	**350**	**350**
Add Leather Seats			**475**	**550**	**550**
Add Power Sunroof			**575**	**650**	**650**
Add Rear Bucket Seats			**175**	**200**	**200**
Add Rear Entertainment System			**500**	**575**	**575**
Add Theft Recovery System			**75**	**100**	**100**
Deduct W/out 3rd Row Seat			**175**	**175**	**175**
Deduct W/out Running Boards			**125**	**125**	**125**
2003 DENALI-1/2 Ton-V8-AWD					
Utility 4D	K63	5425	**28100**	**31900**	**33775**
Utility XL 4D	K66	5839	**28700**	**32550**	**34450**
Sierra Ext. Cab 4D	K69	5478	**21500**	**24750**	**26375**
Add Navigation System			**650**	**725**	**725**
Add Power Sunroof			**675**	**775**	**775**
Add Rear Bucket Seats			**175**	**200**	**200**
Add Rear Entertainment System			**500**	**575**	**575**
Add Theft Recovery System			**75**	**100**	**100**
2003 YUKON XL-1/2-3/4 Ton-V8					
Utility C1500 SLE	C16	4914	**21075**	**24300**	**25700**
Utility C1500 SLT	C16		**23075**	**26450**	**27900**
Utility C2500 SLE	C26	5447	**21875**	**25150**	**26575**
Utility C2500 SLT	C26		**23875**	**27300**	**28775**
Utility K1500 SLE (4WD)	K16	5123	**22825**	**26150**	**27600**
Utility K1500 SLT (4WD)	K16		**24825**	**28275**	**29775**
Utility K2500 SLE (4WD)	K26	5760	**23625**	**27000**	**28475**
Utility K2500 SLT (4WD)	K26		**25625**	**29125**	**30650**
Add 8.1L V8 Engine			**425**	**475**	**475**
Add Bose Stereo System (Std. SLT)			**300**	**350**	**350**
Add Power Sunroof			**575**	**650**	**650**
Add Quadrasteer System			**1000**	**1125**	**1125**
Add Rear Bucket Seats			**175**	**200**	**200**
Add Rear Entertainment System			**500**	**575**	**575**
Add Theft Recovery System			**75**	**100**	**100**
Deduct W/out Running Boards			**125**	**125**	**125**
2003 SAFARI-1/2 Ton-V6					
Cargo Van	M19*	3964	**9050**	**11200**	**12075**
Van	M19*	4321	**9900**	**12125**	**13000**

SEE TRUCK OPTION PAGE FOR ADDITIONAL OPTIONS

BODY TYPE	Model No.	Weight	Trade-In	Retail	High Retail
Van SLE	M19*		10550	12825	13725
Van SLT	M19*		11375	13775	14725
Add All Wheel Drive			1000	1125	1125
Add Aluminum/Alloy Wheels (Cargo)			275	325	325
Add Compact Disc Player (Std. SLE, SLT)			75	100	100
Add Leather Seats			400	450	450
Add Power Seat (Std. SLT)			175	200	200
Add Rear Air Conditioning (Std. SLT)			150	175	175
Add Rear Bucket Seats			175	200	200
Add Running Boards (SLE, SLT)			125	150	150
Add Theft Recovery System			75	100	100
Deduct W/out Cruise Control			175	175	175
Deduct W/out Power Door Locks			150	150	150
Deduct W/out Power Windows			175	175	175
Deduct W/out Tilt Steering Wheel			125	125	125
* L as the 1st position of the model # denotes AWD					
2003 G1500-1/2 Ton-V8					
Cargo Van 135"	G15*	4596	12475	15000	16150
Savana 135"	G15*	5015	13775	16400	17625
2003 G2500-3/4 Ton-V8					
Cargo Van 135"	G25*	4711	13075	15650	16850
Extended Cargo Van 155"	G29	4885	13725	16350	17575
Savana 135"	G25	5645	14925	17625	18850
Extended Savana 155"	G29	5985	15725	18475	19725
2003 G3500-1 Ton-V8					
Cargo Van 135"	G35	5021	14225	16875	18100
Extended Cargo Van 155"	G39	5462	14875	17550	18775
Savana 135"	G35	5780	15525	18250	19500
Extended Savana 155"	G39	6122	16325	19100	20375
G SERIES VAN OPTIONS					
Add SLE Trim			625	700	700
Add Left Access Door (Ex. Extended)			225	250	250
Add 15 Passenger Seating			175	200	200
Add 6.0L V8 Engine (2500 Cargo)			550	625	625
Add All Wheel Drive			1300	1450	1450
Add Aluminum/Alloy Wheels			325	375	375
Add Compact Disc Player			125	150	150
Add Power Seat			200	225	225
Add Rear Air Cond. (Std. Ext. Savana)			150	175	175
Add Theft Recovery System			75	100	100
Deduct V6 Engine			725	725	725
Deduct W/out Air Conditioning			700	700	700
Deduct W/out Cruise Control			200	200	200
Deduct W/out Power Door Locks			175	175	175
Deduct W/out Power Windows			200	200	200
Deduct W/out Tilt Steering Wheel			150	150	150
* H as the 1st position of the model # denotes AWD					
2003 SONOMA PICKUP-1/2 Ton-V6					
Wideside	S14	3042	8775	10900	11650
Sportside	S14		9075	11225	11950
Wideside Extended Cab	S19*	3212	10525	12800	13525
Sportside Extended Cab	S19*		10825	13125	13875
Crew Cab SLS (4WD)	T13	4234	14775	17450	18250
Add SLS Trim (Std. Crew)			500	575	575

TRUCKS

BODY TYPE	Model No.	Weight	Trade-In	Retail	High Retail
Add ZR2 Wide Stance Pkg.			**1100**	**1225**	**1225**
Add ZR5 Sport Pkg. (Crew)			**425**	**475**	**475**
Add ZRX Street Rider Pkg.			**1200**	**1350**	**1350**
Add 4 Wheel Drive (Std. Crew)			**2550**	**2775**	**2775**
Add Aluminum/Alloy Wheels (Std. Crew)			**275**	**325**	**325**
Add Compact Disc Player (Std. Crew)			**75**	**100**	**100**
Add Cruise Control (Std. Crew)			**175**	**200**	**200**
Add Leather Seats			**400**	**450**	**450**
Add Power Door Locks (Std. Crew)			**150**	**175**	**175**
Add Power Seat			**175**	**200**	**200**
Add Power Windows (Std. Crew)			**175**	**200**	**200**
Add Running Boards			**125**	**150**	**150**
Add Theft Recovery System			**75**	**100**	**100**
Add Tilt Steering Wheel (Std. Crew)			**125**	**150**	**150**
Deduct 4 Cyl. Engine			**650**	**650**	**650**
Deduct W/out Air Conditioning			**650**	**650**	**650**
Deduct W/out Automatic Trans.			**525**	**525**	**525**
* T as the 1st position of the model # denotes 4WD					
2003 SIERRA 1500 PICKUP-1/2 Ton-V8					
Wideside	C14*	4142	**12925**	**15475**	**16650**
Sportside	C14*		**13525**	**16125**	**17325**
Wideside Extended Cab	C19*	4548	**15025**	**17700**	**18925**
Sportside Extended Cab	C19*		**15625**	**18350**	**19600**
2003 SIERRA 1500 HD PICKUP-1/2 Ton-V8					
Wideside Crew Cab SLE	C13*	5506	**18175**	**21200**	**22550**
Wideside Crew Cab SLT	C13*		**19700**	**22825**	**24175**
2003 SIERRA 2500 LD PICKUP-3/4 Ton-V8					
Wideside	C24	5059	**13825**	**16425**	**17650**
Wide Extended Cab (4WD)	K29	5524	**18625**	**21675**	**23050**
2003 SIERRA 2500 HD PICKUP-3/4 Ton-V8					
Wideside	C24*	5153	**14825**	**17500**	**18725**
Wideside Extended Cab	C29*	5402	**18025**	**21050**	**22400**
Wideside Crew Cab	C23*	5615	**19425**	**22525**	**23875**
2003 SIERRA 3500 PICKUP-1 Ton-V8-Dual Rear Wheels					
RC Wideside (4WD)	K34	5841	**18175**	**21200**	**22550**
Wideside Extended Cab	C39*	5951	**18675**	**21725**	**23100**
Wideside Crew Cab	C33*	6168	**20075**	**23225**	**24575**
SIERRA PICKUP OPTIONS					
Add SLE Trim (Ex. 1500 HD)			**650**	**725**	**725**
Add SLT Trim (Ex. 1500 HD)			**1400**	**1575**	**1575**
Add Z71 Off-Road Pkg. (4WD)			**300**	**350**	**350**
Add 4WD (Std. 2500 LD Ext, 3500 RC)			**2700**	**2925**	**2925**
Add 6.6L V8 Turbo Diesel Engine			**4800**	**5025**	**5025**
Add 8.1L V8 Engine			**1000**	**1125**	**1125**
Add Aluminum/Alloy Wheels (Std. 1500 HD)			**325**	**375**	**375**
Add Bose Stereo System			**300**	**350**	**350**
Add CD Player (Std. 1500 HD)			**125**	**150**	**150**
Add Leather Seats (Std. 1500 HD SLT)			**475**	**550**	**550**
Add Power Seat (Std. 1500 HD SLT)			**200**	**225**	**225**
Add Quadrasteer System			**1000**	**1125**	**1125**
Add Rear Entertainment System			**500**	**575**	**575**
Add Running Boards			**125**	**150**	**150**
Add Theft Recovery System			**75**	**100**	**100**
Deduct Work Truck Pkg.			**1100**	**1100**	**1100**
Deduct V6 Engine			**725**	**725**	**725**

SEE TRUCK OPTION PAGE FOR ADDITIONAL OPTIONS

BODY TYPE	Model No.	Weight	Trade-In	Retail	High Retail
Deduct W/out Air Conditioning			700	700	700
Deduct W/out Automatic Trans.			575	575	575
Deduct W/out Cruise Control			200	200	200
Deduct W/out Power Door Locks			175	175	175

* K as the 1st position of the model # denotes 4WD

GMC

BODY TYPE	Model No.	Weight	Trade-In	Retail	High Retail
2002 ENVOY-1/2 Ton-I6					
Utility 4D SLE	S13	4442	13925	16550	17600
Utility 4D SLT	S13		15325	18025	19075
Utility 4D SLE (4WD)	T13	4628	14925	17600	18650
Utility 4D SLT (4WD)	T13		16325	19100	20175
2002 ENVOY XL-1/2 Ton-I6					
Utility 4D XL SLE	S16	4836	15225	17925	18975
Utility 4D XL SLT	S16		16625	19425	20525
Utility 4D XL SLE (4WD)	T16	5020	16225	18975	20050
Utility 4D XL SLT (4WD)	T16		17625	20600	21725
ENVOY/ENVOY XL OPTIONS					
Add Bose Stereo System			200	225	225
Add Power Sunroof			475	550	550
Add Rear Entertainment System			400	450	450
Add Running Boards			100	125	125
Add Theft Recovery System			75	100	100
2002 YUKON-1/2 Ton-V8					
Utility 4D SLE	C13	4878	18000	21025	22375
Utility 4D SLE (4WD)	K13	5113	19575	22700	24050
Add SLT Trim			1175	1325	1325
Add Leather Seats			425	475	475
Add Power Sunroof			525	600	600
Add Theft Recovery System			75	100	100
Deduct W/out 3rd Row Seat			150	150	150
Deduct W/out Running Boards			100	100	100
2002 DENALI-1/2 Ton-V8-AWD					
Utility 4D	K63	5425	24050	27450	29175
Utility XL 4D	K66	5709	24450	27875	29625
Sierra Ext. Cab 4D	K69		19200	22300	23850
Add Power Sunroof			625	700	700
Add Rear Bucket Seats			150	175	175
Add Theft Recovery System			75	100	100
2002 YUKON XL-1/2-3/4 Ton-V8					
Utility C1500 SLE	C16	4947	18125	21150	22500
Utility C1500 SLT	C16		19725	22850	24200
Utility C2500 SLE	C26	5521	18925	22000	23375
Utility C2500 SLT	C26		20525	23700	25075
Utility K1500 SLE (4WD)	K16	5123	19700	22825	24175
Utility K1500 SLT (4WD)	K16		21300	24550	25950
Utility K2500 SLE (4WD)	K26	5760	20500	23700	25075
Utility K2500 SLT (4WD)	K26		22100	25400	26825
Add 8.1L V8 Engine			400	450	450
Add Power Sunroof			525	600	600
Add Rear Bucket Seats			150	175	175
Add Theft Recovery System			75	100	100
Deduct W/out Running Boards			100	100	100

BODY TYPE	Model No.	Weight	Trade-In	Retail	High Retail
2002 SAFARI-1/2 Ton-V6					
Cargo Van	M19*	3915	**7325**	**9325**	**10200**
Van SLE	M19*	4323	**8825**	**10975**	**11925**
Van SLT	M19*		**9800**	**12025**	**12900**
Add All Wheel Drive			**900**	**1000**	**1000**
Add Aluminum/Alloy Wheels (Std. SLT)			**225**	**250**	**250**
Add Compact Disc Player (Std. SLE, SLT)			**75**	**100**	**100**
Add Leather Seats			**350**	**400**	**400**
Add Power Seat (Std. SLT)			**150**	**175**	**175**
Add Rear Air Conditioning (Std. SLT)			**150**	**175**	**175**
Add Rear Bucket Seats			**150**	**175**	**175**
Add Running Boards (SLE, SLT)			**100**	**125**	**125**
Add Theft Recovery System			**75**	**100**	**100**
Deduct W/out Cruise Control			**150**	**150**	**150**
Deduct W/out Power Door Locks			**125**	**125**	**125**
Deduct W/out Power Windows			**150**	**150**	**150**
Deduct W/out Tilt Steering Wheel			**100**	**100**	**100**
* L as the 1st position of the model # denotes AWD					
2002 G1500-1/2 Ton-V8					
Cargo Van 135"	G15	4639	**11000**	**13350**	**14450**
Savana 135"	G15	5062	**12250**	**14775**	**15925**
Savana 135" SLT	G65		**15250**	**17975**	**19225**
2002 G2500-3/4 Ton-V8					
Cargo Van 135"	G25	4816	**11550**	**13975**	**15100**
Extended Cargo Van 155"	G29	5000	**12150**	**14675**	**15825**
Savana 135"	G25	5808	**12800**	**15350**	**16525**
Extended Savana 155"	G29	6018	**13550**	**16150**	**17350**
2002 G3500-1 Ton-V8					
Cargo Van 135"	G35	5345	**12100**	**14600**	**15750**
Extended Cargo Van 155"	G39	5539	**12700**	**15250**	**16425**
Savana 135"	G35	5947	**13350**	**15950**	**17150**
Extended Savana 155"	G39	6158	**14100**	**16750**	**17975**
G SERIES VAN OPTIONS					
Add SLE Trim (Ex. SLT)			**600**	**675**	**675**
Add 15 Passenger Seating			**150**	**175**	**175**
Add 6.5L V8 Turbo Diesel Engine			**1100**	**1225**	**1225**
Add 8.1L V8 Engine			**400**	**450**	**450**
Add Aluminum/Alloy Wheels (Std. SLT)			**275**	**325**	**325**
Add Compact Disc Player (Std. SLT)			**100**	**125**	**125**
Add Leather Seats			**425**	**475**	**475**
Add Power Seat (Std. SLT)			**175**	**200**	**200**
Add Rear Air Cond. (Std. SLT, Ext. Savana)			**150**	**175**	**175**
Add Theft Recovery System			**75**	**100**	**100**
Deduct V6 Engine			**700**	**700**	**700**
Deduct W/out Air Conditioning			**650**	**650**	**650**
Deduct W/out Cruise Control			**175**	**175**	**175**
Deduct W/out Power Door Locks			**150**	**150**	**150**
Deduct W/out Power Windows			**175**	**175**	**175**
Deduct W/out Tilt Steering Wheel			**125**	**125**	**125**
2002 SONOMA PICKUP-1/2 Ton-V6					
Wideside	S14	3016	**7300**	**9300**	**10000**
Sportside	S14		**7575**	**9600**	**10325**
Wideside Extended Cab	S19*	3198	**9000**	**11150**	**11875**
Sportside Extended Cab	S19*		**9275**	**11450**	**12175**

TRUCKS

SEE TRUCK OPTION PAGE FOR ADDITIONAL OPTIONS

BODY TYPE	Model No.	Weight	Trade-In	Retail	High Retail
Crew Cab SLS (4WD)	T13	4039	13300	15875	16675
Add SLS Trim (Std. Crew)			400	450	450
Add ZR2 Highrider Pkg.			900	1000	1000
Add ZR5 Sport Pkg. (Crew)			350	400	400
Add 4 Wheel Drive (Std. Crew)			2450	2675	2675
Add Aluminum/Alloy Wheels (Std. Crew)			225	250	250
Add Compact Disc Player (Std. Crew)			75	100	100
Add Cruise Control (Std. Crew)			150	175	175
Add Leather Seats			350	400	400
Add Power Door Locks (Std. Crew)			125	150	150
Add Power Seat			150	175	175
Add Power Windows (Std. Crew)			150	175	175
Add Running Boards			100	125	125
Add Theft Recovery System			75	100	100
Add Tilt Steering Wheel (Std. Crew)			100	125	125
Deduct 4 Cyl. Engine			600	600	600
Deduct W/out Air Conditioning			600	600	600
Deduct W/out Automatic Trans.			475	475	475
* T as the 1st position of the model # denotes 4WD					
2002 SIERRA 1500 PICKUP-1/2 Ton-V8					
Wideside	C14*	4073	11225	13625	14725
Sportside	C14*		11775	14225	15350
Wideside Extended Cab	C19*	4534	13325	15925	17125
Sportside Extended Cab	C19*		13875	16500	17725
2002 SIERRA 1500 HD PICKUP-1/2 Ton-V8					
Wideside Crew Cab SLE	C13*	5461	15925	18675	19950
Wideside Crew Cab SLT	C13*		17125	20100	21425
2002 SIERRA 2500 LD PICKUP-3/4 Ton-V8					
Wideside	C24	4995	12025	14500	15650
Wide Extended Cab (4WD)	K29	5497	16675	19475	20775
2002 SIERRA 2500 HD PICKUP-3/4 Ton-V8					
Wideside	C24*	5126	13025	15600	16775
Wideside Extended Cab	C29*	5393	16125	18900	20175
Wideside Crew Cab	C23*	5605	17425	20425	21750
2002 SIERRA 3500 PICKUP-1 Ton-V8-Dual Rear Wheels					
RC Wideside (4WD)	K34	5845	16275	19050	20325
Wideside Extended Cab	C39*		16725	19525	20825
Wideside Crew Cab	C33*	6103	18025	21050	22400
SIERRA PICKUP OPTIONS					
Add SLE Trim (Ex. 1500 HD)			600	675	675
Add SLT Trim (Ex. 1500 HD)			1200	1350	1350
Add Z71 Off-Road Pkg. (4WD)			225	250	250
Add 4WD (Std. 2500 LD Ext, 3500 RC)			2550	2775	2775
Add 6.6L V8 Turbo Diesel Engine			4475	4700	4700
Add 8.1L V8 Engine			925	1050	1050
Add Aluminum/Alloy Wheels (Std. 1500 HD)			275	325	325
Add CD Player (Std. 1500 HD)			100	125	125
Add Leather Seats (Std. 1500 HD SLT)			425	475	475
Add Power Seat (Std. 1500 HD SLT)			175	200	200
Add Running Boards			100	125	125
Add Theft Recovery System			75	100	100
Deduct Work Truck Pkg.			1050	1050	1050
Deduct V6 Engine			700	700	700
Deduct W/out Air Conditioning			650	650	650

TRUCKS

BODY TYPE	Model No.	Weight	Trade-In	Retail	High Retail
Deduct W/out Automatic Trans.			**525**	**525**	**525**
Deduct W/out Cruise Control			**175**	**175**	**175**
Deduct W/out Power Door Locks			**150**	**150**	**150**

* K as the 1st position of the model # denotes 4WD

GMC

2001 JIMMY-1/2 Ton-V6

BODY TYPE	Model No.	Weight	Trade-In	Retail	High Retail
Tailgate 2D SLS	S18	3518	**7400**	**9425**	**10300**
Tailgate 4D SL	S13		**7250**	**9250**	**10125**
Tailgate 4D SLE	S13	3671	**8025**	**10100**	**11025**
Tailgate 4D Diamond	S63	3887	**9050**	**11225**	**12100**
Tailgate 2D SLS (4WD)	T18	3848	**8300**	**10400**	**11325**
Tailgate 4D SL (4WD)	T13		**8150**	**10250**	**11175**
Tailgate 4D SLE (4WD)	T13	4049	**8925**	**11100**	**11975**
Tailgate 4D Diamond (4WD)	T63		**9950**	**12200**	**13100**
Add SLT Trim (4D SLE)			**950**	**1075**	**1075**
Add Bose Stereo System			**150**	**175**	**175**
Add Compact Disc Player (SL, SLS)			**50**	**75**	**75**
Add Power Seat (2D)			**125**	**150**	**150**
Add Power Sunroof			**425**	**475**	**475**
Add Theft Recovery System			**50**	**75**	**75**
Deduct W/out Automatic Trans.			**425**	**425**	**425**
Deduct W/out Cruise Control			**125**	**125**	**125**
Deduct W/out Power Door Locks			**100**	**100**	**100**
Deduct W/out Power Windows			**125**	**125**	**125**
Deduct W/out Tilt Steering Wheel			**100**	**100**	**100**

2001 YUKON-1/2 Ton-V8

BODY TYPE	Model No.	Weight	Trade-In	Retail	High Retail
Utility 4D SLE	C13	4878	**14775**	**17450**	**18675**
Utility 4D SLE (4WD)	K13	5113	**15950**	**18700**	**19975**
Add SLT Trim			**900**	**1000**	**1000**
Add Leather Seats			**375**	**425**	**425**
Add Power Sunroof			**475**	**550**	**550**
Add Theft Recovery System			**50**	**75**	**75**
Deduct W/out 3rd Row Seat			**125**	**125**	**125**
Deduct W/out Running Boards			**75**	**75**	**75**

2001 DENALI-1/2 Ton-V8-AWD

BODY TYPE	Model No.	Weight	Trade-In	Retail	High Retail
Utility 4D	K63	5425	**20500**	**23675**	**25275**
Utility XL 4D	K66	5839	**20750**	**23950**	**25550**
Add Power Sunroof			**575**	**650**	**650**
Add Rear Bucket Seats			**125**	**150**	**150**
Add Theft Recovery System			**50**	**75**	**75**

2001 YUKON XL-1/2-3/4 Ton-V8

BODY TYPE	Model No.	Weight	Trade-In	Retail	High Retail
Utility C1500 SLE	C16	4947	**14900**	**17575**	**18800**
Utility C1500 SLT	C16		**16175**	**18950**	**20225**
Utility C2500 SLE	C26	5521	**15700**	**18425**	**19675**
Utility C2500 SLT	C26		**16975**	**19850**	**21150**
Utility K1500 SLE (4WD)	K16	5219	**16075**	**18825**	**20100**
Utility K1500 SLT (4WD)	K16		**17350**	**20325**	**21650**
Utility K2500 SLE (4WD)	K26	5796	**16875**	**19700**	**21000**
Utility K2500 SLT (4WD)	K26		**18150**	**21175**	**22525**
Add 8.1L V8 Engine			**375**	**425**	**425**
Add Power Sunroof			**475**	**550**	**550**
Add Rear Bucket Seats			**125**	**150**	**150**
Add Theft Recovery System			**50**	**75**	**75**

TRUCKS

SEE TRUCK OPTION PAGE FOR ADDITIONAL OPTIONS

BODY TYPE	Model No.	Weight	Trade-In	Retail	High Retail
Deduct W/out Running Boards			75	75	75
2001 SAFARI-1/2 Ton-V6					
Cargo Van	M19*	3915	5875	7725	8650
Van SLE	M19*	4323	7325	9350	10225
Van SLT	M19*		8150	10250	11175
Add All Wheel Drive			800	900	900
Add Aluminum/Alloy Wheels (Std. SLT)			175	200	200
Add Compact Disc Player (Std. SLE, SLT)			50	75	75
Add Leather Seats			300	350	350
Add Power Seat (Std. SLT)			125	150	150
Add Rear Air Conditioning (Std. SLT)			125	150	150
Add Rear Bucket Seats			125	150	150
Add Running Boards (SLE, SLT)			75	100	100
Add Theft Recovery System			50	75	75
Deduct W/out Cruise Control			125	125	125
Deduct W/out Power Door Locks			100	100	100
Deduct W/out Power Windows			125	125	125
Deduct W/out Tilt Steering Wheel			100	100	100
* L as the 1st position of the model # denotes AWD					
2001 G1500-1/2 Ton-V8					
Cargo Van 135"	G15	4639	9250	11425	12450
Savana 135"	G15		10450	12725	13800
Savana 135" SLT	G65		13150	15725	16925
2001 G2500-3/4 Ton-V8					
Cargo Van 135"	G25	4816	9750	11975	13025
Extended Cargo Van 155"	G29	5000	10325	12575	13650
Savana 135"	G25		10950	13250	14350
Extended Savana 155"	G29		11650	14075	15200
2001 G3500-1 Ton-V8					
Cargo Van 135"	G35	5345	10250	12500	13550
Extended Cargo Van 155"	G39	5540	10825	13125	14200
Savana 135"	G35		11450	13875	15000
Extended Savana 155"	G39		12150	14650	15800
G SERIES VAN OPTIONS					
Add SLE Trim (Ex. SLT)			575	650	650
Add 15 Passenger Seating			125	150	150
Add 6.5L V8 Turbo Diesel Engine			1000	1125	1125
Add 8.1L V8 Engine			375	425	425
Add Aluminum/Alloy Wheels (Std. SLT)			225	250	250
Add Compact Disc Player (Std. SLT)			100	125	125
Add Leather Seats			375	425	425
Add Power Seat (Std. SLT)			150	175	175
Add Rear Air Cond. (Std. SLT, Ext. Savana)			125	150	150
Add Theft Recovery System			50	75	75
Deduct V6 Engine			675	675	675
Deduct W/out Air Conditioning			600	600	600
Deduct W/out Cruise Control			150	150	150
Deduct W/out Power Door Locks			125	125	125
Deduct W/out Power Windows			150	150	150
Deduct W/out Tilt Steering Wheel			100	100	100
2001 SONOMA PICKUP-1/2 Ton-V6					
Wideside	S14	3016	6050	7925	8750
Sportside	S14		6300	8200	8950
Wideside Extended Cab	S19*	3198	7650	9675	10400

TRUCKS

BODY TYPE	Model No.	Weight	Trade-In	Retail	High Retail
Sportside Extended Cab	S19*		7900	9950	10675
Crew Cab SLS (4WD)	T13	4039	11950	14425	15200
Add SLE Trim			500	575	575
Add SLS Trim (Std. Crew)			400	450	450
Add ZR2 Highrider Pkg.			700	800	800
Add 4 Wheel Drive (Std. Crew)			2350	2575	2575
Add Aluminum/Alloy Wheels (Std. Crew)			175	200	200
Add Compact Disc Player (Std. Crew)			50	75	75
Add Cruise Control (Std. Crew)			125	150	150
Add Power Door Locks (Std. Crew)			100	125	125
Add Power Windows (Std. Crew)			125	150	150
Add Running Boards			75	100	100
Add Theft Recovery System			50	75	75
Add Tilt Steering Wheel (Std. Crew)			100	125	125
Deduct 4 Cyl. Engine			550	550	550
Deduct W/out 3rd Door (Ext. Cab)			200	200	200
Deduct W/out Air Conditioning			550	550	550
Deduct W/out Automatic Trans.			425	425	425
* T as the 1st position of the model # denotes 4WD					
2001 SIERRA 1500 PICKUP-1/2 Ton-V8					
Wideside	C14*	4058	9925	12150	13200
Sportside	C14*	4046	10425	12700	13775
Wideside Extended Cab	C19*	4413	12025	14500	15650
Sportside Extended Cab	C19*	4402	12525	15050	16225
C3 Extended Cab (AWD)	K69	5013	17125	20075	21400
2001 SIERRA 1500 HD PICKUP-1/2 Ton-V8					
Wideside Crew Cab SLE	C13*		14625	17275	18500
Wideside Crew Cab SLT	C13*		15700	18425	19675
2001 SIERRA 2500 LD PICKUP-3/4 Ton-V8					
Wideside	C24*	4995	10725	13025	14100
Wide Extended Cab (4WD)	K29	5508	15175	17875	19125
2001 SIERRA 2500 HD PICKUP-3/4 Ton-V8					
Wideside	C24*	5171	11725	14150	15275
Wideside Extended Cab	C29*	5236	14575	17225	18450
Wideside Crew Cab	C23*	5585	15975	18725	20000
2001 SIERRA 3500 PICKUP-1 Ton-V8-Dual Rear Wheels					
Wideside	C34*	5935	12325	14825	15975
Wideside Extended Cab	C39*	5997	15175	17875	19125
Wideside Crew Cab	C33*	6216	16575	19375	20675
SIERRA PICKUP OPTIONS					
Add SLE Trim (Ex. 1500 HD, C3)			600	675	675
Add SLT Trim (Ex. 1500 HD, C3)			1100	1225	1225
Add Z71 Off-Road Pkg. (4WD)			200	225	225
Add 4WD (Std. 2500 LD Extended, C3)			2350	2575	2575
Add 6.6L V8 Turbo Diesel Engine			4300	4525	4525
Add 8.1L V8 Engine			850	950	950
Add Aluminum/Alloy Wheels (Std. 1500 HD, C3)			225	250	250
Add CD Player (Std. 1500 HD, C3)			100	125	125
Add Leather Seats (Std. 1500 HD SLT, C3)			375	425	425
Add Power Seat (Std. 1500 HD SLT, C3)			150	175	175
Add Running Boards			75	100	100
Add Theft Recovery System			50	75	75
Deduct V6 Engine			675	675	675
Deduct W/out Air Conditioning			600	600	600

TRUCKS

SEE TRUCK OPTION PAGE FOR ADDITIONAL OPTIONS

BODY TYPE	Model No.	Weight	Trade-In	Retail	High Retail
Deduct W/out Automatic Trans.			475	475	475
Deduct W/out Cruise Control			150	150	150
Deduct W/out Power Door Locks			125	125	125
* K as the 1st position of the model # denotes 4WD					
GMC					
2000 JIMMY-1/2 Ton-V6					
Tailgate 2D SLS	S18	3605	5575	7375	8275
Tailgate 4D SLE	S13	3720	6025	7875	8800
Tailgate 4D Diamond	S13		6875	8825	9725
Tailgate 2D SLS (4WD)	T18	3869	6375	8300	9150
Tailgate 4D SLE (4WD)	T13	4116	6825	8775	9675
Tailgate 4D Diamond (4WD)	T13		7675	9725	10625
Tailgate 4D Envoy (4WD)	T13	4157	8475	10600	11550
Add SLT Trim (4D SLE)			800	900	900
Add Bose Stereo System (Std. Envoy)			100	125	125
Add Compact Disc Player (Std. 4D)			50	75	75
Add Power Seat (2D)			100	125	125
Add Power Sunroof			375	425	425
Deduct W/out Automatic Trans.			375	375	375
Deduct W/out Cruise Control			100	100	100
Deduct W/out Power Door Locks			75	75	75
Deduct W/out Power Windows			100	100	100
Deduct W/out Tilt Steering Wheel			75	75	75
2000 YUKON-1/2 Ton-V8					
Utility 4D SLE	C13	4828	12950	15500	16675
Utility 4D SLE (4WD)	K13	5050	13950	16575	17800
Add SLT Trim			700	800	800
Add Leather Seats			325	375	375
Add Power Sunroof			425	475	475
Deduct W/out 3rd Row Seat			100	100	100
Deduct W/out Running Boards			50	50	50
2000 DENALI-1/2 Ton-V8-4WD					
Utility 4D	K1/63	5564	15000	17675	19050
2000 YUKON XL-1/2-3/4 Ton-V8					
Utility C1500 SLE	C16	4914	13075	15625	16800
Utility C1500 SLT	C16		14200	16825	18050
Utility C2500 SLE	C26	5447	13825	16425	17650
Utility C2500 SLT	C26		14950	17625	18850
Utility K1500 SLE (4WD)	K16	5123	14075	16700	17925
Utility K1500 SLT (4WD)	K16		15200	17900	19150
Utility K2500 SLE (4WD)	K26	5810	14825	17500	18725
Utility K2500 SLT (4WD)	K26		15950	18700	19975
YUKON XL OPTIONS					
Add Power Sunroof			425	475	475
Add Rear Bucket Seats			100	125	125
Deduct W/out Running Boards			50	50	50
2000 SAFARI-1/2 Ton-V6					
Cargo Van	M19*	3915	4950	6700	7625
Van SL	M19*	4323	6075	7950	8875
Add SLE Trim			500	575	575
Add SLT Trim			850	950	950
Add All Wheel Drive			700	800	800
Add Aluminum/Alloy Wheels			125	150	150

TRUCKS

BODY TYPE	Model No.	Weight	Trade-In	Retail	High Retail
Add Compact Disc Player			50	75	75
Add Leather Seats			250	300	300
Add Power Seat			100	125	125
Add Rear Air Conditioning			100	125	125
Add Rear Bucket Seats			100	125	125
Add Running Boards (Ex. Cargo)			50	75	75
Deduct W/out Air Conditioning			500	500	500
Deduct W/out Cruise Control			100	100	100
Deduct W/out Power Door Locks			75	75	75
Deduct W/out Power Windows			100	100	100
Deduct W/out Tilt Steering Wheel			75	75	75
* L as the 1st position of the model # denotes AWD					
2000 G1500-1/2 Ton-V8					
Cargo Van 135"	G15	4639	7725	9775	10825
Savana 135"	G15	5062	8875	11025	12025
2000 G2500-3/4 Ton-V8					
Cargo Van 135"	G25	4816	8175	10275	11300
Extended Cargo Van 155"	G29	5000	8725	10875	11925
Savana 135"	G25	5808	9325	11525	12550
Extended Savana 155"	G29	6018	9975	12225	13275
2000 G3500-1 Ton-V8					
Cargo Van 135"	G35	5345	8625	10750	11800
Extended Cargo Van 155"	G39	5539	9175	11350	12375
Savana 135"	G35	5947	9775	12000	13050
Extended Savana 155"	G39	6158	10425	12700	13775
G SERIES VAN OPTIONS					
Add SLE Trim			550	625	625
Add 15 Passenger Seating			100	125	125
Add 6.5L V8 Turbo Diesel Engine			900	1000	1000
Add 7.4L V8 Engine			300	350	350
Add Aluminum/Alloy Wheels			175	200	200
Add Compact Disc Player			75	100	100
Add Power Seat			125	150	150
Add Rear Air Cond. (Std. Ext. Savana)			100	125	125
Deduct V6 Engine			600	600	600
Deduct W/out Air Conditioning			550	550	550
Deduct W/out Cruise Control			125	125	125
Deduct W/out Power Door Locks			100	100	100
Deduct W/out Power Windows			125	125	125
Deduct W/out Tilt Steering Wheel			75	75	75
2000 SONOMA PICKUP-1/2 Ton-V6					
Wideside	S14*	3112	5050	6800	7625
Sportside	S14*		5275	7050	7825
Wideside Extended Cab	S19*	3216	6550	8475	9225
Sportside Extended Cab	S19*		6775	8725	9500
Add SLE Trim			400	450	450
Add SLS Trim			350	400	400
Add ZR2 Highrider Pkg.			625	700	700
Add 4 Wheel Drive			2000	2225	2225
Add Aluminum/Alloy Wheels			125	150	150
Add Compact Disc Player			50	75	75
Add Cruise Control			100	125	125
Add Power Door Locks			75	100	100
Add Power Windows			100	125	125

TRUCKS

SEE TRUCK OPTION PAGE FOR ADDITIONAL OPTIONS

BODY TYPE	Model No.	Weight	Trade-In	Retail	High Retail
Add Running Boards			50	75	75
Add Tilt Steering Wheel			75	100	100
Deduct 4 Cyl. Engine			500	500	500
Deduct W/out 3rd Door (Ext. Cab)			175	175	175
Deduct W/out Air Conditioning			500	500	500
Deduct W/out Automatic Trans.			375	375	375
* T as the 1st position of the model # denotes 4WD					
2000 CLASSIC SIERRA 2500 PICKUP-3/4 Ton-V8					
Wideside	C24*	4883	8475	10575	11625
Wideside Extended Cab	C29*	5188	10275	12525	13600
Wideside Crew Cab	C23*	5370	10875	13175	14275
2000 SIERRA 3500-1 Ton-5.7L V8					
Wideside	C34*	4908	9175	11350	12375
Wideside Extended Cab	C39*	5509	11550	13975	15100
Wideside Crew Cab	C33*	5917	11575	14000	15125
2000 NEW SIERRA 1500 PICKUP-1/2 Ton-V8					
Wideside	C14*	3944	8475	10575	11625
Sportside	C14*	3956	8925	11075	12075
Wideside Extended Cab	C19*	4289	10525	12800	13875
Sportside Extended Cab	C19*	4277	10975	13300	14400
2000 NEW SIERRA 2500 PICKUP-3/4 Ton-6.0L V8					
Wideside	C24*	4588	9175	11350	12375
HD Wideside	C24*	4625	9375	11550	12575
Wideside Extended Cab	C29*		11225	13625	14725
SIERRA PICKUP OPTIONS					
Add SLE Trim			550	625	625
Add SLT Trim			950	1075	1075
Add Z71 Off-Road Pkg. (4WD)			150	175	175
Add 4 Wheel Drive			2000	2225	2225
Add 6.5L V8 Turbo Diesel Engine			900	1000	1000
Add 7.4L V8 Engine			300	350	350
Add Aluminum/Alloy Wheels			175	200	200
Add Compact Disc Player			75	100	100
Add Dual Rear Whls (Std. 3500 Extended)			575	650	650
Add Leather Seats			325	375	375
Add Power Seat			125	150	150
Add Running Boards			50	75	75
Deduct V6 Engine			600	600	600
Deduct W/out 4th Door (New Sierra Ext.)			275	275	275
Deduct W/out 6.0L V8 (New Sierra 2500)			450	450	450
Deduct W/out Air Conditioning			550	550	550
Deduct W/out Automatic Trans.			425	425	425
Deduct W/out Cruise Control			125	125	125
Deduct W/out Power Door Locks			100	100	100
Deduct W/out Tilt Steering Wheel			75	75	75
* K as the 1st position of the model # denotes 4WD					
GMC					
1999 JIMMY-1/2 Ton-V6					
Tailgate 2D	S18	3518	4350	6025	6875
Tailgate 4D	S13	3671	4875	6625	7525
Tailgate 2D (4WD)	T18	3848	5125	6875	7800
Tailgate 4D (4WD)	T13	4049	5650	7450	8350
Tailgate 4D Envoy (4WD)	T13	4049	7725	9750	10650
Add SLE Trim			475	550	550

BODY TYPE	Model No.	Weight	Trade-In	Retail	High Retail
Add SLS Trim			475	550	550
Add SLT Trim			825	925	925
Add Aluminum/Alloy Wheels (Std. Envoy)			75	100	100
Add Bose Stereo System (Std. Envoy)			75	100	100
Add Leather Seats (Std. Envoy)			225	250	250
Add Power Seat (Std. Envoy)			75	100	100
Add Power Sunroof			325	375	375
Deduct W/out Automatic Trans.			325	325	325
Deduct W/out Cruise Control			75	75	75
Deduct W/out Power Door Locks			50	50	50
Deduct W/out Power Windows			75	75	75
Deduct W/out Tilt Steering Wheel			50	50	50
1999 YUKON-1/2 Ton-V8					
Utility 4D SLE	C13	4865	8175	10275	11300
Utility 4D SLE (4WD)	K13	5268	9000	11175	12200
Add SLT Trim			600	675	675
Add Leather Seats			275	325	325
Add Rear Air Conditioning			75	100	100
1999 DENALI-1/2 Ton-V8-4WD					
Utility 4D	K13	5564	12375	14900	16175
1999 SUBURBAN-1/2-3/4 Ton-V8					
Utility C1500	C16	4825	6950	8925	9975
Utility C1500 SLE	C16		8300	10425	11450
Utility C1500 SLT	C16		9175	11375	12400
Utility C2500	C26	5249	7500	9525	10550
Utility C2500 SLE	C26		8850	11000	12075
Utility C2500 SLT	C26		9725	11950	13000
Utility K1500 (4WD)	K16		7775	9825	10875
Utility K1500 SLE (4WD)	K16		9125	11300	12325
Utility K1500 SLT (4WD)	K16		10000	12250	13300
Utility K2500 (4WD)	K26		8325	10425	11450
Utility K2500 SLE (4WD)	K26		9675	11900	12950
Utility K2500 SLT (4WD)	K26		10550	12825	13900
SUBURBAN OPTIONS					
Add 6.5L V8 Turbo Diesel Engine			800	900	900
Add 7.4L V8 Engine			275	325	325
Add Aluminum/Alloy Wheels (Base)			125	150	150
Add Rear Air Cond. (Std. SLE, SLT)			75	100	100
Deduct W/out 3rd Row Seat			100	100	100
Deduct W/out Air Conditioning			500	500	500
Deduct W/out Cruise Control			100	100	100
Deduct W/out Tilt Steering Wheel			50	50	50
1999 SAFARI-1/2 Ton-V6					
Cargo Van	M19*	3925	4075	5725	6575
Van SL	M19*	4200	5200	6975	7925
Add SLE Trim			450	500	500
Add SLT Trim			750	850	850
Add All Wheel Drive			600	675	675
Add Aluminum/Alloy Wheels			75	100	100
Add Leather Seats			225	250	250
Add Power Seat			75	100	100
Add Rear Air Conditioning			75	100	100
Add Rear Bucket Seats			75	100	100
Deduct W/out Air Conditioning			450	450	450

SEE TRUCK OPTION PAGE FOR ADDITIONAL OPTIONS

BODY TYPE	Model No.	Weight	Trade-In	Retail	High Retail
Deduct W/out Cruise Control			75	75	75
Deduct W/out Power Door Locks			50	50	50
Deduct W/out Power Windows			75	75	75
Deduct W/out Tilt Steering Wheel			50	50	50
* L as the 1st position of the model # denotes AWD					
1999 G1500-1/2 Ton-V8					
Cargo Van 135"	G15	4665	6825	8775	9825
Savana 135"	G15	5070	7925	9975	11025
1999 G2500-3/4 Ton-V8					
Cargo Van 135"	G25	4805	7225	9225	10225
Extended Cargo Van 155"	G29	5000	7750	9800	10850
Savana 135"	G25	5717	8325	10425	11450
Extended Savana 155"	G29	5899	8925	11075	12075
1999 G3500-1 Ton-V8					
Cargo Van 135"	G35	5336	7625	9650	10700
Extended Cargo Van 155"	G39	5493	8150	10225	11250
Savana 135"	G35	5905	8725	10850	11900
Extended Savana 155"	G39	6078	9325	11500	12525
G SERIES VAN OPTIONS					
Add SLE Trim			525	600	600
Add 15 Passenger Seating			100	125	125
Add 6.5L V8 Turbo Diesel Engine			800	900	900
Add 7.4L V8 Engine			275	325	325
Add Aluminum/Alloy Wheels			125	150	150
Add Power Seat			100	125	125
Add Rear Air Cond. (Std. Ext. Savana)			75	100	100
Deduct V6 Engine			500	500	500
Deduct W/out Air Conditioning			500	500	500
Deduct W/out Cruise Control			100	100	100
Deduct W/out Power Door Locks			75	75	75
Deduct W/out Power Windows			100	100	100
Deduct W/out Tilt Steering Wheel			50	50	50
1999 SONOMA PICKUP-1/2 Ton-V6					
Wideside	S14*	3029	4275	5950	6750
Sportside	S14*		4475	6175	6950
Wideside Extended Cab	S19*	3232	5700	7525	8325
Sportside Extended Cab	S19*		5900	7725	8550
Add SLE Trim			350	400	400
Add SLS Trim (Std. S19)			300	350	350
Add ZR2 Highrider Pkg.			525	600	600
Add 4 Wheel Drive			1800	2000	2000
Add Aluminum/Alloy Wheels			75	100	100
Add Cruise Control			75	100	100
Add Power Door Locks			50	75	75
Add Power Windows			75	100	100
Add Tilt Steering Wheel			50	75	75
Deduct 4 Cyl. Engine			450	450	450
Deduct W/out 3rd Door (Ext. Cab)			100	100	100
Deduct W/out Air Conditioning			450	450	450
Deduct W/out Automatic Trans.			325	325	325
* T as the 1st position of the model # denotes 4WD					
1999 CLASSIC SIERRA 1500 PICKUP-1/2 Ton-V8					
Wideside Extended Cab SLE	C19*	4145	8550	10675	11725

TRUCKS

BODY TYPE	Model No.	Weight	Trade-In	Retail	High Retail
1999 CLASSIC SIERRA 2500 PICKUP-3/4 Ton-V8					
Wideside	C24*	4821	**7150**	**9150**	**10150**
Wideside Extended Cab	C29*	5301	**8650**	**10775**	**11825**
Wideside Crew Cab	C23*	5416	**9350**	**11550**	**12575**
1999 SIERRA 3500-1 Ton-5.7L V8					
Wideside	C34*	4870	**7850**	**9900**	**10950**
Wideside Extended Cab	C39*	5458	**9875**	**12100**	**13150**
Wideside Crew Cab	C33*	5869	**10050**	**12300**	**13350**
1999 NEW SIERRA 1500 PICKUP-1/2 Ton-V8					
Wideside	C14*	3923	**7650**	**9700**	**10750**
Sportside	C14*	3911	**8050**	**10125**	**11150**
Wideside Extended Cab	C19*	4235	**9600**	**11825**	**12875**
Sportside Extended Cab	C19*	4346	**10000**	**12250**	**13300**
1999 NEW SIERRA 2500 PICKUP-3/4 Ton-6.0L V8					
Wideside	C24*	4586	**8350**	**10475**	**11525**
HD Wideside	C24*	4911	**8500**	**10625**	**11675**
Wideside Extended Cab	C29*	4766	**10300**	**12575**	**13650**
SIERRA PICKUP OPTIONS					
Add SLE Trim (Std. Classic 1500)			**500**	**575**	**575**
Add SLT Trim (Classic 1500)			**400**	**450**	**450**
Add SLT Trim			**850**	**950**	**950**
Add Z71 Off-Road Pkg. (4WD)			**100**	**125**	**125**
Add 4 Wheel Drive			**1800**	**2000**	**2000**
Add 6.5L V8 Turbo Diesel Engine			**800**	**900**	**900**
Add 7.4L V8 Engine			**275**	**325**	**325**
Add Aluminum/Alloy Wheels			**125**	**150**	**150**
Add Dual Rear Whls (Std. 3500 Extended)			**525**	**600**	**600**
Add Leather Seats			**275**	**325**	**325**
Add Power Seat			**100**	**125**	**125**
Deduct V6 Engine			**500**	**500**	**500**
Deduct W/out 6.0L V8 (New Sierra 2500)			**400**	**400**	**400**
Deduct W/out Air Conditioning			**500**	**500**	**500**
Deduct W/out Automatic Trans.			**375**	**375**	**375**
Deduct W/out Cruise Control			**100**	**100**	**100**
Deduct W/out Power Door Locks			**75**	**75**	**75**
Deduct W/out Tilt Steering Wheel			**50**	**50**	**50**

* K as the 1st position of the model # denotes 4WD

GMC

BODY TYPE	Model No.	Weight	Trade-In	Retail	High Retail
1998 JIMMY-1/2 Ton-V6					
Tailgate 2D	S18	3518	**3625**	**5225**	**6025**
Tailgate 4D	S13	3671	**4225**	**5900**	**6775**
Tailgate 2D (4WD)	T18	3848	**4325**	**6000**	**6875**
Tailgate 4D (4WD)	T13	3999	**4925**	**6675**	**7600**
Tailgate 4D Envoy (4WD)	T13	4049	**6550**	**8475**	**9350**
Add SLE Trim			**400**	**450**	**450**
Add SLS Trim			**400**	**450**	**450**
Add SLT Trim			**700**	**800**	**800**
Add Aluminum/Alloy Wheels (Std. Envoy)			**50**	**75**	**75**
Add Leather Seats (Std. Envoy)			**175**	**200**	**200**
Add Power Seat (Std. Envoy)			**50**	**75**	**75**
Add Power Sunroof			**275**	**325**	**325**
Deduct W/out Automatic Trans.			**275**	**275**	**275**
Deduct W/out Cruise Control			**50**	**50**	**50**
Deduct W/out Power Windows			**50**	**50**	**50**

SEE TRUCK OPTION PAGE FOR ADDITIONAL OPTIONS

TRUCKS

BODY TYPE	Model No.	Weight	Trade-In	Retail	High Retail
1998 YUKON-1/2 Ton-V8					
Utility 4D SLE	C13	4911	**7150**	**9125**	**10125**
Utility 4D SLE (4WD)	K13	5331	**7825**	**9875**	**10925**
Add SLT Trim			**550**	**625**	**625**
Add Leather Seats			**225**	**250**	**250**
Add Rear Air Conditioning			**50**	**75**	**75**
1998 SUBURBAN-1/2-3/4 Ton-V8					
Utility C1500	C16	4820	**6600**	**8525**	**9550**
Utility C1500 SLE	C16		**7275**	**9275**	**10300**
Utility C1500 SLT	C16		**8050**	**10100**	**11125**
Utility C2500	C26	5286	**7150**	**9125**	**10125**
Utility C2500 SLE	C26		**7825**	**9875**	**10925**
Utility C2500 SLT	C26		**8600**	**10725**	**11775**
Utility K1500 (4WD)	K16	5297	**7275**	**9275**	**10300**
Utility K1500 SLE (4WD)	K16		**7950**	**10025**	**11050**
Utility K1500 SLT (4WD)	K16		**8725**	**10875**	**11925**
Utility K2500 (4WD)	K26	5750	**7825**	**9875**	**10925**
Utility K2500 SLE (4WD)	K26		**8500**	**10625**	**11675**
Utility K2500 SLT (4WD)	K26		**9275**	**11475**	**12500**
Add 6.5L V8 Turbo Diesel Engine			**700**	**800**	**800**
Add 7.4L V8 Engine			**250**	**300**	**300**
Add Aluminum/Alloy Wheels (Base)			**100**	**125**	**125**
Add Rear Air Cond. (Std. SLE, SLT)			**50**	**75**	**75**
Deduct W/out 3rd Row Seat			**100**	**100**	**100**
Deduct W/out Air Conditioning			**450**	**450**	**450**
Deduct W/out Cruise Control			**75**	**75**	**75**
Deduct W/out Tilt Steering Wheel			**50**	**50**	**50**
1998 SAFARI-1/2 Ton-V6					
Cargo Van	M19*	3887	**3575**	**5175**	**5975**
Van SLX	M19*	4185	**4650**	**6375**	**7250**
Add SLE Trim			**350**	**400**	**400**
Add SLT Trim			**600**	**675**	**675**
Add 3rd Row Seat			**100**	**125**	**125**
Add All Wheel Drive			**500**	**575**	**575**
Add Aluminum/Alloy Wheels			**50**	**75**	**75**
Add Leather Seats			**175**	**200**	**200**
Add Power Seat			**50**	**75**	**75**
Add Rear Air Conditioning			**50**	**75**	**75**
Add Rear Bucket Seats			**50**	**75**	**75**
Deduct W/out Air Conditioning			**400**	**400**	**400**
Deduct W/out Cruise Control			**50**	**50**	**50**
Deduct W/out Power Windows			**50**	**50**	**50**

* L as the 1st position of the model # denotes AWD

BODY TYPE	Model No.	Weight	Trade-In	Retail	High Retail
1998 G1500-1/2 Ton-V8					
Cargo Van 135"	G15	4616	**5925**	**7775**	**8825**
Savana 135"	G15	5075	**7025**	**9000**	**10050**
1998 G2500-3/4 Ton-V8					
Cargo Van 135"	G25	4806	**6275**	**8175**	**9175**
Extended Cargo Van 155"	G29	5000	**6775**	**8725**	**9775**
Savana 135"	G25	5803	**7375**	**9375**	**10400**
Extended Savana 155"	G29	6008	**7875**	**9925**	**10975**
1998 G3500-1 Ton-V8					
Cargo Van 135"	G35	5331	**6625**	**8550**	**9575**
Extended Cargo Van 155"	G39	6078	**7125**	**9125**	**10125**

TRUCKS

BODY TYPE	Model No.	Weight	Trade-In	Retail	High Retail
Savana 135"	G35	5937	**7725**	**9775**	**10825**
Extended Savana 155"	G39	6142	**8225**	**10325**	**11350**
G SERIES VAN OPTIONS					
Add SLE Trim			**500**	**575**	**575**
Add 15 Passenger Seating			**100**	**125**	**125**
Add 6.5L V8 Turbo Diesel Engine			**700**	**800**	**800**
Add 7.4L V8 Engine			**250**	**300**	**300**
Add Aluminum/Alloy Wheels			**100**	**125**	**125**
Add Power Seat			**75**	**100**	**100**
Add Rear Air Conditioning			**50**	**75**	**75**
Deduct V6 Engine			**475**	**475**	**475**
Deduct W/out Air Conditioning			**400**	**400**	**400**
Deduct W/out Cruise Control			**75**	**75**	**75**
Deduct W/out Power Door Locks			**50**	**50**	**50**
Deduct W/out Power Windows			**75**	**75**	**75**
Deduct W/out Tilt Steering Wheel			**50**	**50**	**50**
1998 SONOMA PICKUP-1/2 Ton-V6					
Wideside	S14*	3029	**3725**	**5325**	**6075**
Sportside	S14*	3029	**3900**	**5525**	**6275**
Wideside Extended Cab	S19*	3232	**5125**	**6900**	**7750**
Sportside Extended Cab	S19*	3232	**5300**	**7075**	**7850**
Add SLE Trim			**300**	**350**	**350**
Add SLS Trim (Std. S19)			**250**	**300**	**300**
Add ZR2 Highrider Pkg.			**450**	**500**	**500**
Add 4 Wheel Drive			**1600**	**1800**	**1800**
Add Aluminum/Alloy Wheels			**50**	**75**	**75**
Add Cruise Control			**50**	**75**	**75**
Add Power Windows			**50**	**75**	**75**
Deduct 4 Cyl. Engine			**350**	**350**	**350**
Deduct W/out 3rd Door (Ext. Cab)			**75**	**75**	**75**
Deduct W/out Air Conditioning			**400**	**400**	**400**
Deduct W/out Automatic Trans.			**275**	**275**	**275**
*T as the 1st position of the model # denotes 4WD					
1998 SIERRA 1500 PICKUP-1/2 Ton-V8					
Sportside	C14*	3869	**6550**	**8475**	**9500**
Wideside	C14*	3869	**6200**	**8075**	**9075**
Wideside Extended Cab	C19*	4160	**7475**	**9500**	**10525**
Sportside Extended Cab	C19*	4160	**8025**	**10100**	**11125**
1998 SIERRA 2500 PICKUP-3/4 Ton-V8					
Wideside	C24*	4292	**6800**	**8750**	**9800**
Heavy Duty Wideside	C24*		**6925**	**8875**	**9925**
Wideside Extended Cab	C29*	4432	**8075**	**10150**	**11175**
HD Wideside Extended Cab	C29*	5107	**8200**	**10300**	**11325**
1998 SIERRA 3500 PICKUP-1 Ton-V8					
Wideside	C34*	4870	**7500**	**9525**	**10550**
Wideside Extended Cab	C39*	5458	**9250**	**11425**	**12450**
Wideside Crew Cab	C33*	5488	**9325**	**11500**	**12525**
SIERRA PICKUP OPTIONS					
Add SLE Trim			**400**	**450**	**450**
Add SLT Trim			**800**	**900**	**900**
Add 4 Wheel Drive			**1600**	**1800**	**1800**
Add 6.5L V8 Turbo Diesel Engine			**700**	**800**	**800**
Add 7.4L V8 Engine			**250**	**300**	**300**
Add Aluminum/Alloy Wheels			**100**	**125**	**125**

SEE TRUCK OPTION PAGE FOR ADDITIONAL OPTIONS

TRUCKS

BODY TYPE	Model No.	Weight	Trade-In	Retail	High Retail
Add Dual Rear Wheels (Std. 3500 Ext.)			475	550	550
Add Leather Seats			225	250	250
Add Power Seat			75	100	100
Add Third Door (Std. Sportside)			200	225	225
Deduct Work Truck Pkg.			1375	1375	1375
Deduct V6 Engine (Ex. WT)			400	400	400
Deduct W/out Air Conditioning			450	450	450
Deduct W/out Automatic Trans.			325	325	325
Deduct W/out Cruise Control (Ex. WT)			75	75	75
Deduct W/out Power Door Locks (Ex. WT)			50	50	50
Deduct W/out Tilt Steering Wheel (Ex. WT)			50	50	50

* K as the 1st position of the model # denotes 4WD

GMC

1997 JIMMY-1/2 Ton-V6

BODY TYPE	Model No.	Weight	Trade-In	Retail	High Retail
Tailgate 2D	S18	3515	3100	4625	5500
Tailgate 4D	S13	3686	3400	4950	5850
Tailgate 2D (4WD)	T18	3880	3700	5300	6125
Tailgate 4D (4WD)	T13	4046	4000	5625	6475
Add SLE Trim			350	400	400
Add SLS Trim			350	400	400
Add SLT Trim			600	675	675
Add Leather Seats			150	175	175
Add Power Seat			50	75	75
Add Power Sunroof			200	225	225
Deduct W/out Automatic Trans.			175	175	175
Deduct W/out Cruise Control			50	50	50
Deduct W/out Power Windows			50	50	50

1997 YUKON-1/2 Ton-V8

BODY TYPE	Model No.	Weight	Trade-In	Retail	High Retail
Utility 2D	C18	4471	5750	7575	8625
Utility 2D SLE	C18		6150	8025	9025
Utility 4D SLE	C13	4816	6350	8250	9250
Utility 2D (4WD)	K18	4827	6350	8250	9250
Utility 2D SLE (4WD)	K18		6750	8700	9750
Utility 4D SLE (4WD)	K13	5225	6950	8900	9950
Add SLT Trim (SLE)			500	575	575
Add 6.5L V8 Turbo Diesel Engine			525	600	600
Add Aluminum/Alloy Wheels (Base)			50	75	75
Add Leather Seats			200	225	225
Deduct W/out Air Conditioning			350	350	350
Deduct W/out Cruise Control			75	75	75
Deduct W/out Power Seat (Ex. Base)			75	75	75

1997 SUBURBAN-1/2-3/4 Ton-V8

BODY TYPE	Model No.	Weight	Trade-In	Retail	High Retail
Utility C1500	C16	4802	6050	7925	9000
Utility C1500 SLE	C16		6450	8350	9375
Utility C1500 SLT	C16		7150	9150	10150
Utility C2500	C26	5243	6450	8350	9375
Utility C2500 SLE	C26		6850	8800	9850
Utility C2500 SLT	C26		7550	9575	10600
Utility K1500 (4WD)	K16		6650	8575	9600
Utility K1500 SLE (4WD)	K16		7050	9025	10025
Utility K1500 SLT (4WD)	K16		7750	9800	10850
Utility K2500 (4WD)	K26		7050	9025	10025
Utility K2500 SLE (4WD)	K26		7450	9475	10500
Utility K2500 SLT (4WD)	K26		8150	10250	11275

TRUCKS

BODY TYPE	Model No.	Weight	Trade-In	Retail	High Retail
Add 6.5L V8 Turbo Diesel Engine			**525**	**600**	**600**
Add 7.4L V8 Engine			**250**	**300**	**300**
Add Aluminum/Alloy Wheels (Base)			**50**	**75**	**75**
Deduct W/out Air Conditioning			**350**	**350**	**350**
Deduct W/out Cruise Control			**75**	**75**	**75**
Deduct W/out Power Seat (Ex. Base)			**75**	**75**	**75**
1997 SAFARI-1/2 Ton-V6					
Cargo Van	M19*	3932	**3400**	**4950**	**5850**
Van SLX	M19*	4198	**4000**	**5625**	**6475**
Add SLE Trim			**250**	**300**	**300**
Add SLT Trim			**450**	**500**	**500**
Add All Wheel Drive			**400**	**450**	**450**
Add Leather Seats			**150**	**175**	**175**
Add Power Seat			**50**	**75**	**75**
Deduct W/out Air Conditioning			**250**	**250**	**250**
Deduct W/out Cruise Control			**50**	**50**	**50**
Deduct W/out Power Windows			**50**	**50**	**50**
* L as the 1st position of the model # denotes AWD					
1997 G1500-1/2 Ton-V8					
Cargo Van 135"	G15	4654	**4950**	**6700**	**7725**
Savana 135"	G15	5075	**5750**	**7575**	**8625**
1997 G2500-3/4 Ton-V8					
Cargo Van 135"	G25	4829	**5150**	**6925**	**7975**
Extended Cargo Van 155"	G29	4983	**5550**	**7350**	**8375**
Savana 135"	G25	5803	**5950**	**7800**	**8875**
Extended Savana 155"	G29	6008	**6350**	**8250**	**9250**
1997 G3500-1 Ton-V8					
Cargo Van 135"	G35	5434	**5350**	**7125**	**8125**
Extended Cargo Van 155"	G39	5609	**5750**	**7575**	**8625**
Savana 135"	G35	5937	**6150**	**8025**	**9025**
Extended Savana 155"	G39	6142	**6550**	**8475**	**9500**
G SERIES VAN OPTIONS					
Add SLE Trim			**350**	**400**	**400**
Add 6.5L V8 Turbo Diesel Engine			**525**	**600**	**600**
Add 7.4L V8 Engine			**250**	**300**	**300**
Add Aluminum/Alloy Wheels			**50**	**75**	**75**
Add Power Seat			**75**	**100**	**100**
Deduct V6 Engine			**300**	**300**	**300**
Deduct W/out Air Conditioning			**350**	**350**	**350**
Deduct W/out Cruise Control			**75**	**75**	**75**
Deduct W/out Power Windows			**75**	**75**	**75**
1997 SONOMA PICKUP-1/2 Ton-V6					
Wideside	S14*	2930	**3200**	**4725**	**5500**
Sportside	S14*	3062	**3350**	**4900**	**5700**
Wideside Extended Cab	S19*	3168	**4200**	**5875**	**6675**
Sportside Extended Cab	S19*	3246	**4350**	**6025**	**6800**
Add SLE Trim			**250**	**300**	**300**
Add SLS Trim (Std. S19)			**200**	**225**	**225**
Add ZR2 Highrider Pkg.			**350**	**400**	**400**
Add 4 Wheel Drive			**1300**	**1450**	**1450**
Add Cruise Control			**50**	**75**	**75**
Add Power Windows			**50**	**75**	**75**
Deduct 4 Cyl. Engine			**200**	**200**	**200**

TRUCKS

SEE TRUCK OPTION PAGE FOR ADDITIONAL OPTIONS

BODY TYPE	Model No.	Weight	Trade-In	Retail	High Retail
Deduct W/out 3rd Door (Ext. Cab)			50	50	50
Deduct W/out Air Conditioning			250	250	250
Deduct W/out Automatic Trans.			175	175	175
* T as the 1st position of the model # denotes 4WD					
1997 SIERRA 1500 PICKUP-1/2 Ton-V8					
Sportside	C14*	3879	5750	7575	8625
Wideside	C14*	3869	5500	7300	8325
Wideside Extended Cab	C19*	4160	6650	8575	9600
Sportside Extended Cab	C19*	4170	6900	8850	9900
1997 SIERRA 2500 PICKUP-3/4 Ton-V8					
Wideside	C24*	4299	5900	7750	8800
Heavy Duty Wideside	C24*	4699	6000	7850	8925
Wideside Extended Cab	C29*	4445	7050	9025	10025
HD Wideside Extended Cab	C29*	5013	7150	9150	10150
1997 SIERRA 3500 PICKUP-1 Ton-V8					
Wideside	C34*	4845	6500	8425	9450
Wideside Extended Cab	C39*	5395	8025	10100	11125
Wideside Crew Cab	C33*	5504	8050	10125	11150
SIERRA PICKUP OPTIONS					
Add SLE Trim			350	400	400
Add SLT Trim			700	800	800
Add 4 Wheel Drive			1300	1450	1450
Add 6.5L V8 Turbo Diesel Engine			525	600	600
Add 7.4L V8 Engine			250	300	300
Add Aluminum/Alloy Wheels			50	75	75
Add Dual Rear Wheels (Std. 3500 Ext. Cab)			375	425	425
Add Leather Seats			200	225	225
Add Power Seat			75	100	100
Add Third Door			100	125	125
Deduct Work Truck Pkg.			1250	1250	1250
Deduct V6 Engine (Ex. WT)			300	300	300
Deduct W/out Air Conditioning			350	350	350
Deduct W/out Automatic Trans.			250	250	250
Deduct W/out Cruise Control (Ex. WT)			75	75	75
Deduct W/out Power Windows (Ex. WT)			75	75	75
* K as the 1st position of the model # denotes 4WD					
GMC					
1996 JIMMY-1/2 Ton-V6					
Tailgate 2D	S18	3500	2500	3925	4725
Tailgate 4D	S13	3654	2800	4275	5100
Tailgate 2D (4WD)	T18	3760	3100	4625	5500
Tailgate 4D (4WD)	T13	4007	3400	4950	5850
Add SLE Trim			325	375	375
Add SLS Trim			325	375	375
Add SLT Trim			550	625	625
Deduct W/out Automatic Trans.			125	125	125
1996 YUKON-1/2 Ton-V8					
Utility 2D	C18	4284	5000	6750	7775
Utility 2D SLE	C18		5400	7200	8200
Utility 4D SLE	C13	4779	5600	7400	8425
Utility 2D (4WD)	K18	4731	5600	7400	8425
Utility 2D SLE (4WD)	K18		6000	7850	8925
Utility 4D SLE (4WD)	K13	5134	6200	8075	9075

TRUCKS

BODY TYPE	Model No.	Weight	Trade-In	Retail	High Retail
Add SLT Trim (SLE)			425	475	475
Add 6.5L V8 Turbo Diesel Engine			500	575	575
Deduct W/out Air Conditioning			250	250	250
1996 SUBURBAN-1/2-3/4 Ton-V8					
Utility C1500	C16	4634	5400	7200	8200
Utility C1500 SLE	C16		5800	7625	8675
Utility C1500 SLT	C16		6225	8125	9125
Utility C2500	C26	5120	5800	7625	8675
Utility C2500 SLE	C26		6200	8075	9075
Utility C2500 SLT	C26		6625	8550	9575
Utility K1500 (4WD)	K16		6000	7850	8925
Utility K1500 SLE (4WD)	K16		6400	8300	9300
Utility K1500 SLT (4WD)	K16		6825	8775	9825
Utility K2500 (4WD)	K26	5604	6400	8300	9300
Utility K2500 SLE (4WD)	K26		6800	8750	9800
Utility K2500 SLT (4WD)	K26		7225	9225	10225
Add 6.5L V8 Turbo Diesel Engine			500	575	575
Add 7.4L V8 Engine			225	250	250
Deduct W/out Air Conditioning			250	250	250
1996 SAFARI-1/2 Ton-V6					
Cargo Van	M19*	3885	2825	4300	5125
Van SLX	M19*	4068	3350	4900	5800
Add SLE Trim			200	225	225
Add SLT Trim			350	400	400
Add All Wheel Drive			400	450	450
Deduct W/out Air Conditioning			150	150	150
* L as the 1st position of the model # denotes AWD					
1996 G1500-1/2 Ton-V8					
Cargo Van 135"	G15	4641	3925	5550	6500
Savana 135"	G15	5065	4725	6450	7450
1996 G2500-3/4 Ton-V8					
Cargo Van 135"	G25	4816	4125	5775	6750
Extended Cargo Van 155"	G29		4525	6225	7200
Savana 135"	G25	5792	4925	6675	7700
Extended Savana 155"	G29	5997	5325	7100	8100
1996 G3500-1 Ton-V8					
Cargo Van 135"	G35	5421	4325	6000	7000
Extended Cargo Van 155"	G39		4725	6450	7450
Savana 135"	G35	5927	5125	6875	7925
Extended Savana 155"	G39	6131	5525	7325	8350
Vandura 125"	G35	4752	4225	5900	6875
Extended Vandura 146"	G39	5109	4625	6350	7350
Rally 125"	G35	5248	5025	6775	7825
Extended Rally 146"	G39	5635	5425	7225	8250
G SERIES VAN OPTIONS					
Add SLE Trim			300	350	350
Add STX Trim			300	350	350
Add 6.5L V8 Diesel Engine			150	175	175
Add 6.5L V8 Turbo Diesel Engine			500	575	575
Add 7.4L V8 Engine			225	250	250
Deduct V6 Engine			200	200	200
Deduct W/out Air Conditioning			250	250	250
1996 SONOMA PICKUP-1/2 Ton-V6					
Wideside	S14*	2930	2700	4150	4875

TRUCKS

SEE TRUCK OPTION PAGE FOR ADDITIONAL OPTIONS

BODY TYPE	Model No.	Weight	Trade-In	Retail	High Retail
Wideside Club Coupe	S19*	3168	3600	5175	5900
Add SLE Trim			250	300	300
Add SLS Trim (Std. S19)			200	225	225
Add ZR2 Highrider Pkg.			300	350	350
Add 4 Wheel Drive			1200	1350	1350
Deduct 4 Cyl. Engine			175	175	175
Deduct W/out Air Conditioning			150	150	150
Deduct W/out Automatic Trans.			125	125	125
* T as the 1st position of the model # denotes 4WD					
1996 SIERRA 1500 PICKUP-1/2 Ton-V8					
Sportside	C14*		5050	6800	7850
Wideside	C14*	3688	4800	6525	7550
Wideside Club Coupe	C19*	4057	5850	7675	8725
Sportside Club Coupe	C19*		6100	7975	9050
1996 SIERRA 2500 PICKUP-3/4 Ton-V8					
Wideside	C24*	4269	5200	6975	8025
Heavy Duty Wideside	C24*		5275	7050	8050
Wideside Club Coupe	C29*	4400	6250	8150	9150
1996 SIERRA 3500 PICKUP-1 Ton-V8					
Wideside	C34*	4802	5800	7625	8675
Wideside Club Coupe	C39*		7200	9200	10200
Wideside Crew Cab	C33*	5475	7250	9250	10275
SIERRA PICKUP OPTIONS					
Add SLE Trim			300	350	350
Add SLT Trim			600	675	675
Add 4 Wheel Drive			1200	1350	1350
Add 6.5L V8 Turbo Diesel Engine			500	575	575
Add 7.4L V8 Engine			225	250	250
Add Dual Rear Wheels (Std. 3500 Club Coupe)			350	400	400
Deduct Work Truck Pkg.			1000	1000	1000
Deduct V6 Engine (Ex. WT)			200	200	200
Deduct W/out Air Conditioning			250	250	250
Deduct W/out Automatic Trans.			150	150	150
* K as the 1st position of the model # denotes 4WD					
GMC					
1995 JIMMY-1/2 Ton-V6					
Tailgate 2D	S18	3533	2150	3525	4275
Tailgate 4D	S13	3689	2375	3775	4550
Tailgate 2D (4WD)	T18	3812	2750	4200	5000
Tailgate 4D (4WD)	T13	4020	2975	4475	5325
Add SLE Trim			300	350	350
Add SLS Trim			300	350	350
Add SLT Trim			500	575	575
1995 YUKON-1/2 Ton-V8					
Utility 4D SLE	C13	4768	4825	6550	7575
Utility 2D (4WD)	K18	4748	4925	6675	7700
Utility 2D SLE (4WD)	K18		5225	7000	8050
Utility 4D SLE (4WD)	K13	5024	5425	7225	8250
Add SLT Trim (SLE)			350	400	400
Add 6.5L V8 Turbo Diesel Engine			475	550	550
1995 SUBURBAN-1/2-3/4 Ton-V8					
Utility C1500	C16	4692	4700	6425	7425
Utility C1500 SLE	C16		5000	6750	7775

BODY TYPE	Model No.	Weight	Trade-In	Retail	High Retail
Utility C1500 SLT	C16		**5350**	**7125**	**8125**
Utility C2500	C26	5176	**5100**	**6850**	**7900**
Utility C2500 SLE	C26		**5400**	**7200**	**8200**
Utility C2500 SLT	C26		**5750**	**7575**	**8625**
Utility K1500 (4WD)	K16		**5300**	**7075**	**8075**
Utility K1500 SLE (4WD)	K16		**5600**	**7400**	**8425**
Utility K1500 SLT (4WD)	K16		**5950**	**7800**	**8875**
Utility K2500 (4WD)	K26		**5700**	**7525**	**8575**
Utility K2500 SLE (4WD)	K26		**6000**	**7850**	**8925**
Utility K2500 SLT (4WD)	K26		**6350**	**8250**	**9250**
Add 6.5L V8 Turbo Diesel Engine			**475**	**550**	**550**
Add 7.4L V8 Engine			**200**	**225**	**225**
1995 SAFARI-1/2 Ton-V6					
Cargo Van XT	M19*	3804	**2000**	**3350**	**4075**
Van SLX XT	M19*	4083	**2500**	**3925**	**4725**
Add SLE Trim			**150**	**175**	**175**
Add SLT Trim			**300**	**350**	**350**
Add All Wheel Drive			**350**	**400**	**400**
* L as the 1st position of the model # denotes AWD					
1995 G1500-1/2 Ton-V8					
Vandura 110"	G15	4069	**2650**	**4100**	**4950**
1995 G2500-3/4 Ton-V8					
Vandura 110"	G25	4052	**2850**	**4325**	**5200**
Rally 125"	G25	4770	**3450**	**5025**	**5925**
1995 G3500-1 Ton-V8					
Vandura 125"	G35	4811	**3050**	**4575**	**5475**
Extended Vandura 146"	G39	5154	**3450**	**5025**	**5925**
Rally 125"	G35	5326	**3650**	**5250**	**6175**
Extended Rally 146"	G39	5661	**4050**	**5700**	**6675**
G SERIES VAN OPTIONS					
Add STX Trim			**300**	**350**	**350**
Add 7.4L V8 Engine			**200**	**225**	**225**
Deduct V6 Engine			**150**	**150**	**150**
1995 SONOMA PICKUP-1/2 Ton-V6					
Wideside	S14*	2983	**2250**	**3625**	**4300**
Wideside Club Coupe	S19*	3185	**3150**	**4675**	**5450**
Add SLE Trim			**225**	**250**	**250**
Add SLS Trim (Std. S19)			**200**	**225**	**225**
Add ZR2 Highrider Pkg.			**250**	**300**	**300**
Add 4 Wheel Drive			**1100**	**1225**	**1225**
Deduct 4 Cyl. Engine			**125**	**125**	**125**
* T as the 1st position of the model # denotes 4WD					
1995 SIERRA 1500 PICKUP-1/2 Ton-V8					
Sportside	C14*	3812	**4350**	**6025**	**7000**
Wideside	C14*	3801	**4150**	**5800**	**6775**
Wideside Club Coupe	C19*	4068	**5150**	**6925**	**7975**
Sportside Club Coupe	C19*	4079	**5350**	**7125**	**8125**
1995 SIERRA 2500 PICKUP-3/4 Ton-V8					
Wideside	C24*	4116	**4550**	**6250**	**7225**
Wideside Club Coupe	C29*	4336	**5550**	**7350**	**8375**
1995 SIERRA 3500 PICKUP-1 Ton-V8					
Wideside	C34*	4693	**5050**	**6800**	**7850**
Wideside Club Coupe	C39*	4969	**6375**	**8275**	**9275**

SEE TRUCK OPTION PAGE FOR ADDITIONAL OPTIONS

BODY TYPE	Model No.	Weight	Trade-In	Retail	High Retail
Wideside Crew Cab	C33*	5320	6450	8350	9375
SIERRA PICKUP OPTIONS					
Add SLE Trim			250	300	300
Add SLT Trim			575	650	650
Add 4 Wheel Drive			1100	1225	1225
Add 6.5L V8 Turbo Diesel Engine			475	550	550
Add 7.4L V8 Engine			200	225	225
Add Dual Rear Wheels (Std. 3500 Club Coupe)			325	375	375
Deduct Work Truck Pkg.			950	950	950
Deduct V6 Engine (Ex. WT)			150	150	150

* K as the 1st position of the model # denotes 4WD

HONDA

HONDA

BODY TYPE	Model No.	Weight	Trade-In	Retail	High Retail
2004 CR-V-4 Cyl.-4WD					
Utility 4D LX (2WD)	RD68(4/5)	3201	15450	17975	18800
Utility 4D LX	RD7(7/8)(4/5)	3258	16400	18975	19825
Utility 4D EX	RD7(7/8)8	3287	18000	20775	21650
Add Aluminum/Alloy Wheels (LX)			300	350	350
Add Running Boards			150	175	175
Add Theft Recovery System			100	125	125
Deduct W/out Automatic Trans.			475	475	475
2004 PILOT-V6-4WD					
Utility 4D LX	YF181	4416	21800	24775	26025
Utility 4D EX	YF184	4439	23600	26750	28050
Utility 4D EX-L	YF185		24200	27400	28700
Utility 4D EX-L DVD	YF186		24800	28025	29350
Utility 4D EX-L Nav	YF187		24800	28025	29350
Add Aluminum/Alloy Wheels (LX)			325	375	375
Add Running Boards			150	175	175
Add Theft Recovery System			100	125	125
2004 ODYSSEY-V6					
Wagon 5D LX	RL185	4310	18725	21775	22950
Wagon 5D EX	RL186	4365	20725	23925	25150
Wagon 5D EX DVD	RL188		21325	24550	25800
Wagon 5D EX-L	RL189		21325	24550	25800
Wagon 5D EX-L DVD	RL180		21925	25200	26450
Wagon 5D EX-L Nav	RL187		21925	25200	26450
Add Aluminum/Alloy Wheels (LX)			325	375	375
Add Compact Disc Player (Std. EX)			100	125	125
Add Theft Recovery System			100	125	125
2004 ELEMENT-4 Cyl.					
Utility LX	YH1(7/8)3	3371	14300	16750	17575
Utility EX	YH1(7/8)(5/6)	3391	15475	18000	18825
Utility LX (4WD)	YH2(7/8)3	3508	15250	17750	18575
Utility EX (4WD)	YH2(7/8)(5/6)	3527	16425	19000	19850
Add Aluminum/Alloy Wheels (Std. EX)			300	350	350
Add Running Boards			150	175	175
Add Theft Recovery System			100	125	125
Deduct W/out Automatic Trans.			475	475	475

TRUCKS

BODY TYPE	Model No.	Weight	Trade-In	Retail	High Retail
HONDA					
2003 CR-V-4 Cyl.-4WD					
Utility 4D LX (2WD)	RD68(4/5)	3201	**14225**	**16700**	**17525**
Utility 4D LX	RD7(7/8)(4/5)	3258	**15125**	**17625**	**18450**
Utility 4D EX	RD7(7/8)8	3287	**16625**	**19225**	**20075**
Add Aluminum/Alloy Wheels (LX)			**250**	**300**	**300**
Add Running Boards			**125**	**150**	**150**
Add Theft Recovery System			**75**	**100**	**100**
Deduct W/out Automatic Trans.			**425**	**425**	**425**
2003 PILOT-V6-4WD					
Utility 4D LX	YF181	4416	**19675**	**22525**	**23700**
Utility 4D EX	YF184	4439	**21475**	**24425**	**25650**
Utility 4D EX-L	YF185		**21975**	**24975**	**26225**
Utility 4D EX-L DVD	YF186		**22475**	**25550**	**26825**
Utility 4D EX-L Nav	YF187		**22475**	**25550**	**26825**
Add Aluminum/Alloy Wheels (LX)			**275**	**325**	**325**
Add Running Boards			**125**	**150**	**150**
Add Theft Recovery System			**75**	**100**	**100**
2003 ODYSSEY-V6					
Wagon 5D LX	RL185	4310	**17100**	**19975**	**21075**
Wagon 5D EX	RL186	4365	**18800**	**21875**	**23050**
Wagon 5D EX-L	RL189		**19300**	**22400**	**23575**
Wagon 5D EX-L DVD	RL180		**19800**	**22925**	**24125**
Wagon 5D EX-L Nav	RL187		**19800**	**22925**	**24125**
Add Aluminum/Alloy Wheels (LX)			**275**	**325**	**325**
Add Compact Disc Player (Std. EX)			**75**	**100**	**100**
Add Theft Recovery System			**75**	**100**	**100**
2003 ELEMENT-4 Cyl.					
Utility DX	YH1(7/8)2	3352	**13250**	**15650**	**16450**
Utility EX	YH1(7/8)(5/6)	3414	**14400**	**16850**	**17675**
Utility DX (4WD)	YH282	3456	**14100**	**16550**	**17375**
Utility EX (4WD)	YH28(5/6)	3595	**15250**	**17750**	**18575**
Add Aluminum/Alloy Wheels (Std. EX)			**250**	**300**	**300**
Add Compact Disc Player (Std. EX)			**75**	**100**	**100**
Add Running Boards			**125**	**150**	**150**
Add Theft Recovery System			**75**	**100**	**100**
Deduct W/out Air Conditioning			**525**	**525**	**525**
Deduct W/out Automatic Trans.			**425**	**425**	**425**
HONDA					
2002 CR-V-4 Cyl.-4WD					
Utility 4D LX (2WD)	RD68(4/5)	3201	**13000**	**15400**	**16200**
Utility 4D LX	RD7(7/8)(4/5)	3258	**13950**	**16400**	**17225**
Utility 4D EX	RD7(7/8)8	3287	**15050**	**17550**	**18375**
Add Aluminum/Alloy Wheels (LX)			**200**	**225**	**225**
Add Running Boards			**100**	**125**	**125**
Add Theft Recovery System			**75**	**100**	**100**
Deduct W/out Automatic Trans.			**375**	**375**	**375**
2002 PASSPORT-V6					
Utility 4D LX	CK58	3782	**11425**	**13850**	**14800**
Utility 4D EX	CK58	3842	**12675**	**15225**	**16225**
Utility 4D LX (4WD)	DM58	4013	**12425**	**14950**	**15925**
Utility 4D EX (4WD)	DM58	4088	**13675**	**16300**	**17325**

SEE TRUCK OPTION PAGE FOR ADDITIONAL OPTIONS

BODY TYPE	Model No.	Weight	Trade-In	Retail	High Retail
Add Compact Disc Player			75	100	100
Add Leather Seats			350	400	400
Add Power Seat			150	175	175
Add Theft Recovery System			75	100	100
Deduct W/out Automatic Trans.			475	475	475
2002 ODYSSEY-V6					
Wagon 5D LX	RL185	4299	15100	17800	18850
Wagon 5D EX	RL186	4354	16550	19325	20425
Wagon 5D EX-L	RL189	4376	16950	19775	20875
Wagon 5D EX-L DVD	RL180	4398	17350	20325	21450
Wagon 5D EX-L Nav	RL187		17350	20325	21450
Add Aluminum/Alloy Wheels (LX)			225	250	250
Add Compact Disc Player (Std. EX)			75	100	100
Add Theft Recovery System			75	100	100
HONDA					
2001 CR-V-4 Cyl.-4WD					
Utility 4D LX (2WD)	RD284	3126	10500	12775	13500
Utility 4D LX	RD184	3210	11725	14150	14925
Utility 4D EX	RD186	3219	12625	15150	15950
Utility 4D SE	RD187		13075	15625	16425
Add Aluminum/Alloy Wheels (LX)			150	175	175
Add Compact Disc Player (Std. EX, SE)			50	75	75
Add Theft Recovery System			50	75	75
Deduct W/out Automatic Trans.			325	325	325
2001 PASSPORT-V6					
Utility 4D LX	CK58	3782	9450	11625	12525
Utility 4D EX	CK58	3842	10775	13050	13975
Utility 4D LX (4WD)	DM58	4013	10350	12600	13500
Utility 4D EX (4WD)	DM58	4088	11675	14100	15050
Add Compact Disc Player (Std. EX)			50	75	75
Add Leather Seats			300	350	350
Add Theft Recovery System			50	75	75
Deduct W/out Automatic Trans.			425	425	425
2001 ODYSSEY-V6					
Wagon 5D LX	RL18(1/5)	4248	12975	15550	16550
Wagon 5D EX	RL186	4288	14225	16875	17925
Wagon 5D EX Nav	RL187		14575	17250	18275
Add Aluminum/Alloy Wheels (LX)			175	200	200
Add Compact Disc Player (Std. EX)			50	75	75
Add Theft Recovery System			50	75	75
HONDA					
2000 CR-V-4 Cyl.-4WD					
Utility 4D LX (2WD)	RD284	3126	8875	11025	11750
Utility 4D LX	RD184	3210	9525	11725	12475
Utility 4D EX	RD186	3219	10175	12425	13150
Utility 4D SE	RD187		10575	12850	13575
Add Aluminum/Alloy Wheels (LX)			100	125	125
Add Compact Disc Player (Std. EX, SE)			50	75	75
Deduct W/out Automatic Trans.			300	300	300
2000 PASSPORT-V6					
Utility 4D LX	CK58	3774	7625	9650	10550

BODY TYPE	Model No.	Weight	Trade-In	Retail	High Retail
Utility 4D EX	CK58	3857	**8875**	**11025**	**11900**
Utility 4D LX (4WD)	DM58	4041	**8450**	**10550**	**11500**
Utility 4D EX (4WD)	DM58	4102	**9700**	**11925**	**12850**
Add Compact Disc Player (Std. EX)			**50**	**75**	**75**
Add Leather Seats			**250**	**300**	**300**
Deduct W/out Automatic Trans.			**375**	**375**	**375**
2000 ODYSSEY-V6					
Wagon 5D LX	RL18(4/5)	4233	**10800**	**13100**	**14025**
Wagon 5D EX	RL186	4288	**11800**	**14225**	**15175**
Wagon 5D EX Nav	RL187		**12050**	**14525**	**15500**
Add Aluminum/Alloy Wheels (LX)			**125**	**150**	**150**
Add Compact Disc Player (Std. EX)			**50**	**75**	**75**
HONDA					
1999 CR-V-4 Cyl.-4WD					
Utility 4D LX (2WD)	RD284	3126	**7450**	**9475**	**10200**
Utility 4D LX	RD184	3210	**8350**	**10450**	**11175**
Utility 4D EX	RD186	3219	**8900**	**11050**	**11775**
Add Aluminum/Alloy Wheels (LX)			**50**	**75**	**75**
Deduct W/out Automatic Trans.			**250**	**250**	**250**
1999 PASSPORT-V6					
Utility 4D LX	CK58	3650	**6350**	**8250**	**9100**
Utility 4D EX	CK58	3652	**7450**	**9475**	**10350**
Utility 4D LX (4WD)	CM58	3924	**7125**	**9125**	**10000**
Utility 4D EX (4WD)	CM58	3926	**8225**	**10325**	**11250**
Add Leather Seats			**225**	**250**	**250**
Deduct W/out Automatic Trans.			**325**	**325**	**325**
1999 ODYSSEY-V6					
Wagon 5D LX	RL18(4/5)	4211	**8675**	**10825**	**11775**
Wagon 5D EX	RL18(6/7)	4288	**9675**	**11900**	**12825**
Add Aluminum/Alloy Wheels (LX)			**75**	**100**	**100**
Add Rear Bucket Seats (LX)			**75**	**100**	**100**
HONDA					
1998 CR-V-4 Cyl.-4WD					
Utility 4D LX (2WD)	RD284	3036	**6600**	**8525**	**9300**
Utility 4D LX	RD184	3236	**7325**	**9350**	**10050**
Utility 4D EX	RD186	3245	**7925**	**10000**	**10725**
Deduct W/out Automatic Trans.			**200**	**200**	**200**
1998 PASSPORT-V6					
Utility 4D LX	CK58	3584	**4900**	**6625**	**7525**
Utility 4D EX	CK58	3611	**5900**	**7725**	**8650**
Utility 4D LX (4WD)	CM58	3882	**5575**	**7375**	**8275**
Utility 4D EX (4WD)	CM58	3884	**6575**	**8500**	**9375**
Add Leather Seats			**175**	**200**	**200**
Deduct W/out Automatic Trans.			**275**	**275**	**275**
1998 ODYSSEY-4 Cyl.					
Wagon 5D LX	RA38(4/6)	3450	**6350**	**8250**	**9100**
Wagon 5D EX	RA387	3483	**7050**	**9025**	**9875**
Add Aluminum/Alloy Wheels (LX)			**50**	**75**	**75**
Add Rear Bucket Seats (LX)			**50**	**75**	**75**

SEE TRUCK OPTION PAGE FOR ADDITIONAL OPTIONS

BODY TYPE	Model No.	Weight	Trade-In	Retail	High Retail
HONDA					
1997 CR-V-4 Cyl.-4WD					
Utility 4D	RD184	3164	**6550**	**8475**	**9225**
1997 PASSPORT-V6					
Utility 4D LX	CK58	3883	**3900**	**5525**	**6375**
Utility 4D EX	CK58	3946	**4600**	**6300**	**7175**
Utility 4D LX (4WD)	CM58	4133	**4500**	**6200**	**7075**
Utility 4D EX (4WD)	CM58	4209	**5200**	**6975**	**7925**
PASSPORT OPTIONS					
Deduct W/out Air Conditioning			**250**	**250**	**250**
Deduct W/out Automatic Trans.			**175**	**175**	**175**
1997 ODYSSEY-4 Cyl.					
Wagon 5D LX	RA18(4/6)	3450	**5350**	**7125**	**8000**
Wagon 5D EX	RA187	3483	**5750**	**7575**	**8475**
HONDA					
1996 PASSPORT-V6					
Utility 4D DX (4 Cyl., 5 Spd.)	CK58	3663	**2650**	**4100**	**4900**
Utility 4D LX	CK58	3883	**3200**	**4725**	**5600**
Utility 4D EX	CK58	3946	**3850**	**5475**	**6300**
Utility 4D LX (4WD)	CM58	4133	**3800**	**5400**	**6225**
Utility 4D EX (4WD)	CM58	4209	**4450**	**6150**	**7025**
Deduct W/out Air Conditioning			**150**	**150**	**150**
Deduct W/out Automatic Trans. (Ex. 4D DX)			**125**	**125**	**125**
1996 ODYSSEY-4 Cyl.					
Wagon 5D LX	RA18(4/6)	3450	**4750**	**6475**	**7375**
Wagon 5D EX	RA187	3483	**5100**	**6850**	**7775**
HONDA					
1995 PASSPORT-V6					
Utility 4D DX (4 Cyl.)	CG58	3545	**2075**	**3425**	**4150**
Utility 4D LX	CG58	3810	**2375**	**3775**	**4550**
Utility 4D LX (4WD)	CY58	4013	**2975**	**4475**	**5325**
Utility 4D EX (4WD)	CY58	4057	**3575**	**5150**	**5950**
1995.5 PASSPORT-V6					
Utility 4D DX (4 Cyl.)	CK58	3693	**2325**	**3725**	**4500**
Utility 4D LX	CK58	3823	**2625**	**4075**	**4875**
Utility 4D EX	CK58	3886	**3275**	**4825**	**5725**
Utility 4D LX (4WD)	CM58	4073	**3225**	**4775**	**5650**
Utility 4D EX (4WD)	CM58	4137	**3875**	**5500**	**6325**
1995 ODYSSEY-4 Cyl.					
Wagon 5D LX	RA184/6	3479	**3825**	**5450**	**6275**
Wagon 5D EX	RA187	3490	**4125**	**5775**	**6650**

HUMMER

BODY TYPE	Model No.	Weight	Trade-In	Retail	High Retail
HUMMER					
2004 H2-V8-4WD					
Utility 4D	N23	6400	**38200**	**42725**	**44925**
Utility 4D Adventure	N23		**39000**	**43575**	**45800**
Utility 4D Luxury	N23		**39000**	**43575**	**45800**
Add 3rd Row Seat (Std. Luxury)			**200**	**225**	**225**

TRUCKS

BODY TYPE	Model No.	Weight	Trade-In	Retail	High Retail
Add Air Suspension (Std. Adventure)			500	575	575
Add Navigation System			750	850	850
Add Power Sunroof			725	825	825
Add Running Boards (Std. Luxury)			150	175	175
Add Theft Recovery System			100	125	125
Deduct W/out Leather Seats			575	575	575
HUMMER					
2003 H2-V8-4WD					
Utility 4D	N23	6400	34725	39050	41125
Utility 4D Adventure	N23		35425	39800	41900
Utility 4D Luxury	N23		35225	39600	41700
Add 3rd Row Seat			175	200	200
Add Air Suspension (Std. Adventure)			400	450	450
Add Power Sunroof			675	775	775
Add Running Boards (Std. Luxury)			125	150	150
Add Theft Recovery System			75	100	100
Deduct W/out Leather Seats			525	525	525

HYUNDAI

BODY TYPE	Model No.	Weight	Trade-In	Retail	High Retail
HYUNDAI					
2004 SANTA FE-V6					
Utility 4D (4 Cyl.)	SB1	3494	12925	15475	16275
Utility 4D GLS	SC1	3549	14725	17400	18200
Utility 4D LX	SC1	3737	16075	18850	19700
Utility 4D GLS (4WD)	SC7	3752	15675	18425	19250
Utility 4D LX (4WD)	SC7	3946	17025	19900	20750
Add 3.5L V6 Engine (GLS)			500	575	575
Add Power Sunroof			525	600	600
Add Running Boards			150	175	175
Add Theft Recovery System			100	125	125
Deduct W/out Automatic Trans.			475	475	475
Deduct W/out Cruise Control			175	175	175
HYUNDAI					
2003 SANTA FE-V6					
Utility 4D (4 Cyl.)	SB1	3494	11825	14275	15050
Utility 4D GLS	SC1	3549	13425	16025	16850
Utility 4D LX	SC1		13975	16600	17425
Utility 4D GLS (4WD)	SC7	3752	14275	16925	17750
Utility 4D LX (4WD)	SC7		14825	17500	18300
Add 3.5L V6 Engine (GLS/LX)			450	500	500
Add Power Sunroof			475	550	550
Add Running Boards			125	150	150
Add Theft Recovery System			75	100	100
Deduct W/out Automatic Trans.			425	425	425
Deduct W/out Cruise Control			150	150	150
HYUNDAI					
2002 SANTA FE-V6					
Utility 4D (4 Cyl.)	SB1	3494	9775	12000	12750
Utility 4D GLS	SC1	3549	11375	13775	14525
Utility 4D LX	SC1		11825	14275	15050
Utility 4D GLS (4WD)	SC7	3752	12175	14675	15450

TRUCKS

SEE TRUCK OPTION PAGE FOR ADDITIONAL OPTIONS

BODY TYPE	Model No.	Weight	Trade-In	Retail	High Retail
Utility 4D LX (4WD)	SC7		12625	15150	15950
Add Power Sunroof			425	475	475
Add Theft Recovery System			75	100	100
Deduct W/out Automatic Trans.			375	375	375
Deduct W/out Cruise Control			125	125	125
HYUNDAI					
2001 SANTA FE-V6					
Utility 4D GL	SB	3549	8800	10950	11700
Utility 4D GLS	SC		9250	11450	12175
Utility 4D LX	SC		9500	11725	12475
Utility 4D GL (4WD)	SB	3752	9525	11750	12500
Utility 4D GLS (4WD)	SC		9975	12225	12950
Utility 4D LX (4WD)	SC		10225	12500	13225
Add Theft Recovery System			50	75	75
Deduct 4 Cyl. Engine			625	625	625
Deduct W/out Automatic Trans.			325	325	325
Deduct W/out Cruise Control			100	100	100
Deduct W/out Power Door Locks			75	75	75

INFINITI

BODY TYPE	Model No.	Weight	Trade-In	Retail	High Retail
INFINITI					
2004 FX-V6/V8-AWD					
FX35 (2WD)	AS08U	4056	27100	30775	32625
FX35 Touring (2WD)	AS08U		29500	33375	35300
FX35	AS08W	4215	28175	31975	33850
FX35 Touring	AS08W		30575	34500	36450
FX45	BS08W	4309	32925	37175	39200
FX45 Premium	BS08W		34225	38550	40625
Add Sport Pkg. (FX35 Touring)			700	800	800
Add Technology Pkg. (Touring/Premium)			1950	2175	2175
Add Rear Entertainment System			600	675	675
Add Theft Recovery System			100	125	125
2004 QX56-V8-AWD					
Utility 4D (2WD)	AA08A	5360	37825	42350	44525
Utility 4D	AA08C	5631	39400	44025	46250
Add Power Sunroof			725	825	825
Add Rear Entertainment System			600	675	675
Add Theft Recovery System			100	125	125
Deduct W/out Rear Bucket Seats			200	200	200
INFINITI					
2003 QX4-V6-4WD					
Utility 4D (2WD)	R09X	4074	20975	24175	25775
Utility 4D	R09Y	4352	22000	25275	26925
Add Navigation System			650	725	725
Add Power Sunroof			675	775	775
Add Rear Entertainment System			500	575	575
Add Theft Recovery System			75	100	100
2003 FX-V6/V8-AWD					
FX35 (2WD)	AS08U		24725	28175	29925
FX35 Premium (2WD)	AS08U		27025	30675	32500

TRUCKS

BODY TYPE	Model No.	Weight	Trade-In	Retail	High Retail
FX35	AS08W		25800	29325	31125
FX35 Premium	AS08W		28100	31900	33775
FX45	BS08W		30100	34000	35925
FX45 Premium	BS08W		31250	35225	37200
Add Sport Pkg. (FX35 Premium)			600	675	675
Add Technology Pkg. (Premium)			2500	2725	2725
Add Theft Recovery System			75	100	100
INFINITI					
2002 QX4-V6-4WD					
Utility 4D (2WD)	R09X	4074	18375	21425	22950
Utility 4D	R09Y	4352	19375	22475	24025
Add Navigation System			550	625	625
Add Power Sunroof			625	700	700
Add Rear Entertainment System			400	450	450
Add Theft Recovery System			75	100	100
INFINITI					
2001 QX4-V6-4WD					
Utility 4D (2WD)	R07/9X	4074	15900	18650	20050
Utility 4D	R07/9Y	4352	16800	19625	21075
Add Navigation System			500	575	575
Add Power Sunroof			575	650	650
Add Rear Entertainment System			350	400	400
Add Theft Recovery System			50	75	75
INFINITI					
2000 QX4-V6-4WD					
Utility 4D	R07Y	4320	12975	15525	16825
Add Navigation System			450	500	500
Add Power Sunroof			525	600	600
INFINITI					
1999 QX4-V6-4WD					
Utility 4D	R05Y	4275	10300	12575	13750
1999.5 QX4-V6-4WD					
Utility 4D	R07Y		11100	13475	14700
1999/1999.5 QX4 OPTIONS					
Add Power Sunroof			475	550	550
INFINITI					
1998 QX4-V6-4WD					
Utility 4D	R05Y	4289	8500	10625	11825
Add Power Sunroof			425	475	475
INFINITI					
1997 QX4-V6-4WD					
Utility 4D	R05Y	4275	7650	9675	10875
Add Power Sunroof			350	400	400

ISUZU

BODY TYPE	Model No.	Weight	Trade-In	Retail	High Retail
ISUZU					
2004 RODEO-V6					
Utility 4D S 3.2	K58W	3836	13125	15700	16700

SEE TRUCK OPTION PAGE FOR ADDITIONAL OPTIONS

BODY TYPE	Model No.	Weight	Trade-In	Retail	High Retail
Utility 4D S 3.5	K58Y	3947	13825	16450	17500
Utility 4D S 3.2 (4WD)	M58W	4132	14200	16850	17900
Utility 4D S 3.5 (4WD)	M58Y	4145	14900	17575	18625
Add Aluminum/Alloy Wheels			325	375	375
Add Leather Seats			450	500	500
Add Power Sunroof			575	650	650
Add Running Boards (3.5)			150	175	175
Add Theft Recovery System			100	125	125
Deduct W/out Air Conditioning			700	700	700
Deduct W/out Automatic Trans.			575	575	575
Deduct W/out Power Door Locks			175	175	175
Deduct W/out Power Windows			200	200	200
Deduct W/out Tilt Steering Wheel			150	150	150
2004 AXIOM-V6-4WD					
Utility 4D S (2WD)	E58Y	4004	15700	18425	19500
Utility 4D XS (2WD)	E58Y		17250	20200	21325
Utility 4D S	F58Y	4240	16775	19575	20675
Utility 4D XS	F58Y		18325	21350	22500
Add Compact Disc Player (S 2WD)			100	125	125
Add Power Sunroof (Std. XS)			575	650	650
Add Theft Recovery System			100	125	125
2004 ASCENDER 5-PASSENGER-I6-4WD					
Utility 4D S (2WD)	S13S	4425	15800	18550	19625
Utility 4D LS (2WD)	S13S	4425	17300	20275	21400
Utility 4D Luxury (2WD)	S13S	4425	18500	21550	22700
Utility 4D S	T13S	4612	16875	19700	20800
Utility 4D LS	T13S	4612	18375	21425	22575
Utility 4D Luxury	T13S	4612	19575	22700	23875
2004 ASCENDER 7-PASSENGER-I6-4WD					
Utility 4D S (2WD)	S16S	4790	17150	20075	21200
Utility 4D LS (2WD)	S16S	4790	18650	21725	22900
Utility 4D LS (2WD, V8)	S16P	4835	19650	22775	23975
Utility 4D Limited (2WD, V8)	S16P	4835	20850	24050	25275
Utility 4D S	T16S	4967	18225	21275	22425
Utility 4D LS	T16S	4967	19725	22875	24075
Utility 4D LS (V8)	T16P	5020	20725	23925	25150
Utility 4D Limited (V8)	T16P	5020	21925	25225	26475
ASCENDER OPTIONS					
Add Leather Seats (Std. Luxury, Ltd.)			450	500	500
Add Running Boards (Std. Limited)			150	175	175
Add Theft Recovery System			100	125	125
Deduct W/out Cruise Control			200	200	200
Deduct W/out Power Seat			200	200	200
ISUZU					
2003 RODEO SPORT-4 Cyl.					
Utility 2D Soft Top (5 Spd.)	K57D	3557			
Utility 2D Hard Top	K57D				
Utility 2D Hard Top (V6)	K57W	3776	11250	13650	14400
Utility 2D H'Top (4WD, V6)	M57W	4010			
Add Aluminum/Alloy Wheels			250	300	300
Add Power Door Locks			125	150	150
Add Power Windows			150	175	175
Add Running Boards			125	150	150

TRUCKS

BODY TYPE	Model No.	Weight	Trade-In	Retail	High Retail
Add Theft Recovery System			75	100	100
Deduct W/out Air Conditioning			525	525	525
2003 RODEO-V6					
Utility 4D S (4 Cyl.)	K58D	3750	11025	13350	14275
Utility 4D S	K58W	3966	12025	14500	15475
Utility 4D S (4WD)	M58W	4171	13050	15600	16600
Add Aluminum/Alloy Wheels			275	325	325
Add Leather Seats			400	450	450
Add Power Seat			175	200	200
Add Power Sunroof			525	600	600
Add Running Boards			125	150	150
Add Theft Recovery System			75	100	100
Deduct W/out Air Conditioning			650	650	650
Deduct W/out Automatic Trans.			525	525	525
Deduct W/out Power Door Locks			150	150	150
Deduct W/out Power Windows			175	175	175
2003 AXIOM-V6-4WD					
Utility 4D S (2WD)	E58X	3927	13725	16325	17350
Utility 4D XS (2WD)	E58X		14975	17650	18700
Utility 4D S	F58X	4188	14750	17425	18450
Utility 4D XS	F58X		16000	18750	19825
Add Compact Disc Player (S 2WD)			75	100	100
Add Power Sunroof (Std. XS)			525	600	600
Add Theft Recovery System			75	100	100
2003 ASCENDER 7-PASSENGER-I6-4WD					
Utility 4D S (2WD)	S16S	4790	15625	18350	19425
Utility 4D LS (2WD)	S16S	4790	17300	20275	21400
Utility 4D LS (2WD, V8)	S16P	4835	18100	21125	22275
Utility 4D Limited (2WD, V8)	S16P	4835	19300	22400	23575
Utility 4D S	T16S	4967	16825	19625	20725
Utility 4D LS	T16S	4967	18325	21350	22500
Utility 4D LS (V8)	T16P	5020	19125	22200	23375
Utility 4D Limited (V8)	T16P	5020	20325	23500	24700
Add Power Seat (S 2WD)			175	200	200
Add Running Boards (Std. Limited)			125	150	150
Add Theft Recovery System			75	100	100
ISUZU					
2002 RODEO SPORT-4 Cyl.-5 Spd.					
Utility 2D Soft Top	K57D	3551	7300	9300	10000
Utility 2D Soft Top (V6, AT)	K57W	3686	8825	10975	11725
Utility 2D S'Top (4WD, V6, AT)	M57W	3935	9675	11900	12650
Utility 2D Hard Top	K57D	3617	7400	9400	10125
Utility 2D Hard Top (AT)	K57D	3650	7825	9875	10600
Utility 2D Hard Top (V6, AT)	K57W	3759	8925	11075	11800
Utility 2D H'Top (4WD, V6, AT)	M57W	4002	9775	12000	12750
Add Aluminum/Alloy Wheels			200	225	225
Add Compact Disc Player			75	100	100
Add Power Door Locks			100	125	125
Add Power Windows			125	150	150
Add Running Boards			100	125	125
Add Theft Recovery System			75	100	100
Deduct W/out Air Conditioning			475	475	475

TRUCKS

SEE TRUCK OPTION PAGE FOR ADDITIONAL OPTIONS

BODY TYPE	Model No.	Weight	Trade-In	Retail	High Retail
2002 RODEO-V6					
Utility 4D S (4 Cyl.)	K58D	3701	8525	10650	11600
Utility 4D SE (4 Cyl.)	K58D		8825	10975	11925
Utility 4D S	K58W	3848	9575	11800	12700
Utility 4D SE	K58W		9875	12125	13000
Utility 4D LS	K58W	3923	10775	13100	14025
Utility 4D LSE	K58W		12275	14800	15775
Utility 4D S (4WD)	M58W	4124	10575	12875	13800
Utility 4D SE (4WD)	M58W		10875	13200	14125
Utility 4D LS (4WD)	M58W	4163	11775	14225	15175
Utility 4D LSE (4WD)	M58W		13275	15875	16900
Add A/A Wheels (Std. SE, LSE)			225	250	250
Add Compact Disc Player (S, SE)			75	100	100
Add Power Seat (Std. LSE)			150	175	175
Add Power Sunroof (Std. LSE)			475	550	550
Add Running Boards (Std. SE)			100	125	125
Add Theft Recovery System			75	100	100
Deduct W/out Air Conditioning			600	600	600
Deduct W/out Automatic Trans.			475	475	475
Deduct W/out Power Door Locks			125	125	125
Deduct W/out Power Windows			150	150	150
2002 TROOPER-V6-4WD					
Utility 4D S (2WD)	DS58X	4238	10375	12625	13525
Utility 4D LS (2WD)	DS58X	4273	11875	14325	15300
Utility 4D Limited (2WD)	DS58X	4388	12775	15325	16325
Utility 4D S	DJ58X	4465	11375	13775	14725
Utility 4D LS	DJ58X	4500	12875	15425	16425
Utility 4D Limited	DJ58X	4615	13775	16375	17400
Add Compact Disc Player (S)			75	100	100
Add Running Boards (Std. Limited)			100	125	125
Add Theft Recovery System			75	100	100
Deduct W/out Automatic Trans.			475	475	475
2002 AXIOM-V6-4WD					
Utility 4D (2WD)	E58X	3920	11675	14125	15075
Utility 4D XS (2WD)	E58X	3920	12725	15275	16275
Utility 4D	F58X	4180	12675	15225	16225
Utility 4D XS	F58X	4180	13725	16350	17375
Add Leather Seats (Std. XS)			350	400	400
Add Power Sunroof (Std. XS)			475	550	550
Add Theft Recovery System			75	100	100
ISUZU					
2001 RODEO SPORT-4 Cyl.-5 Spd.					
Utility 2D Soft Top	K57D	3543	5875	7700	8525
Utility 2D Soft Top (AT)	K57D	3587	6200	8075	8825
Utility 2D Soft Top (V6, AT)	K57W	3686	7175	9150	9850
Utility 2D S'Top (4WD, V6)	M57W	3877	7550	9600	10325
Utility 2D S'Top (4WD, V6, AT)	M57W	3920	7875	9950	10675
Utility 2D Hard Top	K57D	3609	5975	7825	8650
Utility 2D Hard Top (AT)	K57D	3653	6300	8175	8925
Utility 2D Hard Top (V6, AT)	K57W	3752	7275	9250	9950
Utility 2D H'Top (4WD, V6, AT)	M57W	3986	7975	10050	10775
Add Aluminum/Alloy Wheels			150	175	175
Add Compact Disc Player			50	75	75

TRUCKS

BODY TYPE	Model No.	Weight	Trade-In	Retail	High Retail
Add Power Door Locks			75	100	100
Add Power Windows			100	125	125
Add Running Boards			75	100	100
Add Theft Recovery System			50	75	75
Deduct W/out Air Conditioning			425	425	425
2001 RODEO-V6					
Utility 4D S (4 Cyl.)	K58D	3701	6550	8450	9325
Utility 4D S	K58W	3848	7525	9525	10400
Utility 4D LS	K58W	3848	8650	10775	11725
Utility 4D Anniversary	K58W		9850	12075	12950
Utility 4D LSE	K58W	3923	10050	12275	13175
Utility 4D S (4WD)	M58W	4124	8425	10525	11475
Utility 4D LS (4WD)	M58W	4124	9550	11750	12650
Utility 4D Anniversary (4WD)	M58W		10750	13025	13950
Utility 4D LSE (4WD)	M58W	4163	10950	13275	14200
Add A/A Wheels (Std. Annv., LSE)			175	200	200
Add Compact Disc Player (Std. Annv., LSE)			50	75	75
Add Power Seat (Std. Annv., LSE)			125	150	150
Add Power Sunroof (Std. Annv., LSE)			425	475	475
Add Running Boards			75	100	100
Add Theft Recovery System			50	75	75
Deduct W/out Air Conditioning			550	550	550
Deduct W/out Automatic Trans.			425	425	425
Deduct W/out Power Door Locks			100	100	100
Deduct W/out Power Windows			125	125	125
2001 TROOPER-V6-4WD					
Utility 4D S (2WD)	DS58X	4238	7850	9900	10800
Utility 4D LS (2WD)	DS58X	4273	8700	10825	11775
Utility 4D Anniversary (2WD)	DS58X		9250	11425	12325
Utility 4D Limited (2WD)	DS58X	4388	9975	12200	13100
Utility 4D S	DJ58X	4455	8750	10875	11825
Utility 4D LS	DJ58X	4500	9600	11800	12700
Utility 4D Anniversary	DJ58X		10150	12400	13300
Utility 4D Limited	DJ58X	4615	10875	13175	14100
Add Compact Disc Player (S)			50	75	75
Add Power Sunroof (Std. Limited)			425	475	475
Add Running Boards			75	100	100
Add Theft Recovery System			50	75	75
Deduct W/out Automatic Trans.			425	425	425
2001 VEHICROSS-V6-4WD					
Utility 2D	CN57X	3955	13600	16200	17400
Add Theft Recovery System			50	75	75
ISUZU					
2000 AMIGO-4 Cyl.-5 Spd.					
Utility 2D Soft Top	K57D	3523	4775	6525	7325
Utility 2D Soft Top (V6, AT)	K57W		5950	7825	8650
Utility 2D S'Top (4WD, V6)	M57W	3675	6250	8150	8900
Utility 2D S'Top (4WD, V6, AT)	M57W		6575	8500	9250
Utility 2D Hard Top	K57D	3589	4875	6625	7450
Utility 2D Hard Top (V6, AT)	K57W		6050	7925	8750
Utility 2D H'Top (4WD, V6, AT)	M57W	3909	6675	8625	9400
Add Aluminum/Alloy Wheels			100	125	125
Add Compact Disc Player			50	75	75

TRUCKS

SEE TRUCK OPTION PAGE FOR ADDITIONAL OPTIONS

BODY TYPE	Model No.	Weight	Trade-In	Retail	High Retail
Add Power Door Locks			50	75	75
Add Power Windows			75	100	100
Add Running Boards			50	75	75
Deduct W/out Air Conditioning			375	375	375
2000 RODEO-V6					
Util 4D S (4 Cyl., 5 Spd.)	K58D	3671	4775	6500	7400
Utility 4D S	K58W	3848	6025	7900	8825
Utility 4D LS	K58W	3848	7075	9050	9900
Utility 4D LSE	K58W	3848	8375	10475	11400
Utility 4D S (4WD)	M58W	4104	6850	8800	9700
Utility 4D LS (4WD)	M58W	4104	7900	9950	10850
Utility 4D LSE (4WD)	M58W	4104	9200	11375	12275
Add Aluminum/Alloy Wheels (Std. LSE)			125	150	150
Add Compact Disc Player (Std. LSE)			50	75	75
Add Power Sunroof (Std. LSE)			375	425	425
Add Running Boards			50	75	75
Deduct W/out Air Conditioning			500	500	500
Deduct W/out AT (Ex. S 4 Cyl.)			375	375	375
2000 TROOPER-V6-4WD					
Utility 4D S (2WD)	DS58X	4238	6625	8550	9425
Utility 4D LS (2WD)	DS58X	4273	7375	9375	10250
Utility 4D Limited (2WD)	DS58X	4388	8425	10525	11475
Utility 4D S	DJ58X	4455	7450	9450	10325
Utility 4D LS	DJ58X	4500	8200	10275	11200
Utility 4D Limited	DJ58X	4615	9250	11425	12325
Add Compact Disc Player (Std. LS, Ltd)			50	75	75
Add Power Sunroof (Std. Limited)			375	425	425
Add Running Boards			50	75	75
Deduct W/out Automatic Trans.			375	375	375
2000 HOMBRE PICKUP-4 Cyl.-5 Spd.					
S	CS144	3067	3225	4750	5525
XS	CS144	3067	3525	5100	5825
Spacecab S	CS194	3231	4650	6375	7175
Spacecab XS	CS194	3231	4950	6700	7525
Add 4 Wheel Drive			2000	2225	2225
Add Aluminum/Alloy Wheels			125	150	150
Add Automatic Trans.			375	425	425
Add Compact Disc Player			50	75	75
Add Cruise Control			100	125	125
Add Power Door Locks			75	100	100
Add Power Windows			100	125	125
Add Running Boards			50	75	75
Add Third Door			175	200	200
Add Tilt Steering Wheel			75	100	100
Add V6 Engine			500	575	575
Deduct W/out Air Conditioning			500	500	500
2000 VEHICROSS-V6-4WD					
Utility 2D	CN57X	3955	12050	14500	15650
ISUZU					
1999 AMIGO-4 Cyl.-5 Spd.					
Utility 2D Soft Top	K57D	3329	4100	5725	6500
Utility 2D Soft Top (V6, AT)	K57W		5150	6900	7750
Utility 2D Soft Top (4WD)	M57D	3583	4800	6550	7350

TRUCKS

BODY TYPE	Model No.	Weight	Trade-In	Retail	High Retail
Utility 2D S'Top (4WD, V6)	M57W	3668	5500	7300	8075
Utility 2D S'Top (4WD, V6, AT)	M57W		5775	7600	8400
Utility 2D Hard Top	K57D	3359	4200	5850	6650
Utility 2D Hard Top (V6, AT)	K57W		5250	7000	7850
Utility 2D H'Top (4WD, V6, AT)	M57W	3762	5875	7725	8550
Add Aluminum/Alloy Wheels			50	75	75
Add Power Windows			50	75	75
Deduct W/out Air Conditioning			325	325	325
1999 OASIS-4 Cyl.					
Wagon S 7-Passenger	RJ286/7	3473	6875	8825	9725
Wagon S 6-Passenger	RJ288/9	3473	7625	9650	10550
Add Aluminum/Alloy Wheels (7-Pass.)			75	100	100
1999 RODEO-V6					
Util 4D S (4 Cyl., 5 Spd.)	K58D	3495	4125	5800	6675
Utility 4D S	K58W	3651	5225	7000	7950
Utility 4D LS	K58W	3651	6025	7900	8825
Utility 4D LSE	K58W		7125	9125	10000
Utility 4D S (4WD)	M58W	3860	5925	7775	8700
Utility 4D LS (4WD)	M58W	3863	6725	8675	9550
Utility 4D LSE (4WD)	M58W	3926	7825	9875	10775
Add Aluminum/Alloy Wheels (Std. LSE)			75	100	100
Add Power Sunroof (Std. LSE)			325	375	375
Deduct W/out Air Conditioning			450	450	450
Deduct W/out AT (Ex. S 4 Cyl.)			325	325	325
1999 TROOPER-V6-4WD					
Utility 4D S	DJ58X	4465	6525	8450	9325
Utility 4D Performance	DJ58X		7075	9075	9925
Utility 4D Luxury	DJ58X		7925	10000	10900
Add Leather Seats (Std. Luxury)			225	250	250
Add Power Seat (Std. Luxury)			75	100	100
Add Power Sunroof (Std. Luxury)			325	375	375
Deduct W/out Automatic Trans.			325	325	325
1999 HOMBRE PICKUP-4 Cyl.-5 Spd.					
S	CS144	3024	2800	4275	5000
XS	CS144	3024	3050	4575	5350
Spacecab XS	CS194	3278	4100	5750	6525
Add 4 Wheel Drive			1800	2000	2000
Add Aluminum/Alloy Wheels			75	100	100
Add Automatic Trans.			325	375	375
Add Cruise Control			75	100	100
Add Power Door Locks			50	75	75
Add Power Windows			75	100	100
Add Tilt Steering Wheel			50	75	75
Add V6 Engine			450	500	500
Deduct W/out Air Conditioning			450	450	450
1999 VEHICROSS-V6-4WD					
Utility 2D	CN57X	3955	10125	12375	13425
ISUZU					
1998 AMIGO-4 Cyl.-5 Spd.					
Utility 2D	K57D	3335	3200	4750	5525
Utility 2D (4WD)	M57D	3588	3850	5475	6225

TRUCKS

SEE TRUCK OPTION PAGE FOR ADDITIONAL OPTIONS

BODY TYPE	Model No.	Weight	Trade-In	Retail	High Retail
Utility 2D (4WD, V6)	M57W	3588	4500	6200	6975
Add Cruise Control			50	75	75
Add Power Windows			50	75	75
Deduct W/out Air Conditioning			275	275	275
1998 OASIS-4 Cyl.					
Wagon S	RJ284/6	3473	5675	7475	8375
Wagon LS	RJ287	3483	6375	8275	9125
Add Aluminum/Alloy Wheels (S)			50	75	75
1998 RODEO-V6					
Util 4D S (4 Cyl., 5 Spd.)	K58D	3471	3675	5250	6050
Utility 4D S	K58W	3626	4550	6250	7125
Utility 4D LS	K58W	3651	5100	6850	7775
Utility 4D S (4WD)	M58W	3924	5225	7000	7950
Utility 4D LS (4WD)	M58W	3926	5775	7600	8500
Add Aluminum/Alloy Wheels (S)			50	75	75
Add Leather Seats			175	200	200
Add Power Sunroof			275	325	325
Deduct W/out Air Conditioning			400	400	400
Deduct W/out AT (Ex. S 4 Cyl.)			275	275	275
Deduct W/out Cruise Control (Ex. S 4 Cyl.)			50	50	50
Deduct W/out Power Windows (Ex. S 4 Cyl.)			50	50	50
1998 TROOPER-V6-4WD					
Utility 4D S	DJ58X	4540	5300	7075	7950
Utility 4D Performance	DJ58X		5750	7575	8475
Utility 4D Luxury	DJ58X		6500	8400	9275
Add Leather Seats (Std. Luxury)			175	200	200
Add Power Seat (Std. Luxury)			50	75	75
Add Power Sunroof (Std. Luxury)			275	325	325
Deduct W/out Automatic Trans.			275	275	275
1998 HOMBRE PICKUP-4 Cyl.-5 Spd.					
S	CS144	3125	2400	3800	4500
XS	CS144	3125	2600	4025	4725
Spacecab XS	CS194	3305	3600	5175	5900
Add 4 Wheel Drive			1600	1800	1800
Add Aluminum/Alloy Wheels			50	75	75
Add Automatic Trans.			275	325	325
Add Cruise Control			50	75	75
Add Power Windows			50	75	75
Add V6 Engine			350	400	400
Deduct W/out Air Conditioning			400	400	400
ISUZU					
1997 OASIS-4 Cyl.					
Wagon S	RJ184/6	3473	4850	6600	7500
Wagon LS	RJ187	3483	5250	7025	7900
Deduct W/out Cruise Control			50	50	50
1997 RODEO-V6					
Util 4D S (4 Cyl., 5 Spd.)	K58E	3705	2725	4175	4975
Utility 4D S	K58V	3890	3350	4900	5800
Utility 4D LS	K58V	3952	3825	5450	6275
Utility 4D S (4WD)	M58V	4110	3950	5575	6425
Utility 4D LS (4WD)	M58V	4115	4425	6125	7000

TRUCKS

BODY TYPE	Model No.	Weight	Trade-In	Retail	High Retail
Add Leather Seats			150	175	175
Add Sunroof			100	125	125
Deduct W/out Air Conditioning			250	250	250
Deduct W/out AT (Ex. S 4 Cyl.)			175	175	175
Deduct W/out Cruise Control (Ex. S 4 Cyl.)			50	50	50
Deduct W/out Power Windows (Ex. S 4 Cyl.)			50	50	50
1997 TROOPER-V6-4WD					
Utility 4D S	DJ58V	4315	4300	5975	6850
Utility 4D LS	DJ58V	4315	4700	6425	7325
Utility 4D Limited	DJ58V	4640	5300	7075	7950
Add Leather Seats (Std. Limited)			150	175	175
Add Power Seat (Std. Limited)			50	75	75
Add Power Sunroof (Std. Limited)			200	225	225
Deduct W/out Air Conditioning			250	250	250
Deduct W/out Automatic Trans.			175	175	175
Deduct W/out Cruise Control			50	50	50
Deduct W/out Power Windows			50	50	50
1997 HOMBRE PICKUP-4 Cyl.-5 Spd.					
S	CS144	3125	2000	3350	4000
XS	CS144	3125	2175	3550	4225
Spacecab XS	CS194	3305	2975	4475	5225
Add Automatic Trans.			175	200	200
Add Cruise Control			50	75	75
Add Power Windows			50	75	75
Add V6 Engine			200	225	225
Deduct W/out Air Conditioning			250	250	250
ISUZU					
1996 OASIS-4 Cyl.					
Wagon S	RJ184/6	3473	4000	5625	6475
Wagon LS	RJ187	3483	4350	6025	6875
1996 RODEO-V6					
Util 4D S (4 Cyl., 5 Spd.)	K58E	3705	2250	3625	4375
Utility 4D S	K58V	3890	2625	4075	4875
Utility 4D LS	K58V	3925	3025	4550	5400
Utility 4D S (4WD)	M58V	4110	3225	4775	5650
Utility 4D LS (4WD)	M58V	4115	3625	5225	6025
RODEO OPTIONS					
Deduct W/out Air Conditioning			150	150	150
Deduct W/out AT (Ex. S 4 Cyl.)			125	125	125
1996 TROOPER-V6-4WD					
Utility 4D S	DJ58V	4275	3700	5300	6125
Utility 4D LS	DJ58V	4315	4075	5725	6575
Utility 4D Limited	DJ58V	4640	4525	6225	7100
Utility 4D SE	DJ58V		4625	6350	7225
Add Power Sunroof (Std. SE, Limited)			150	175	175
Deduct W/out Air Conditioning			150	150	150
Deduct W/out Automatic Trans.			125	125	125
1996 HOMBRE PICKUP-4 Cyl.-5 Spd.					
S	CS144	2822	1750	3050	3650
XS	CS144		1900	3225	3850
Deduct W/out Air Conditioning			150	150	150

TRUCKS

SEE TRUCK OPTION PAGE FOR ADDITIONAL OPTIONS

BODY TYPE	Model No.	Weight	Trade-In	Retail	High Retail
ISUZU					
1995 RODEO-V6					
Utility 4D S (4 Cyl.)	CG58	3545	**1750**	**3050**	**3725**
Utility 4D S	CG58	3755	**1950**	**3275**	**3975**
Utility 4D LS	CG58	3810	**2300**	**3700**	**4450**
Utility 4D S (4WD)	CY58	4050	**2550**	**3975**	**4775**
Utility 4D LS (4WD)	CY58	4025	**2900**	**4375**	**5200**
1995.5 RODEO-V6					
Utility 4D S (4 Cyl.)	CK58E		**2000**	**3350**	**4075**
Utility 4D S	CK58V		**2200**	**3575**	**4325**
Utility 4D LS	CK58V		**2575**	**4000**	**4800**
Utility 4D S (4WD)	CM58V		**2800**	**4275**	**5100**
Utility 4D LS (4WD)	CM58V		**3175**	**4700**	**5575**
1995 TROOPER-V6-4WD					
Utility 4D S	DJ58	4315	**3225**	**4775**	**5650**
Utility 4D LS	DJ58	4315	**3575**	**5150**	**5950**
Utility 4D Limited	DJ58	4510	**4075**	**5725**	**6575**
1995 PICKUPS-4 Cyl.					
S	CL1(1/4)	2855	**1550**	**2800**	**3425**
S (4WD)	CR11	3355	**2650**	**4100**	**4825**

JEEP

BODY TYPE	Model No.	Weight	Trade-In	Retail	High Retail
JEEP					
2004 WRANGLER-6 Cyl.-5 Spd.-4WD					
Jeep SE (4 Cyl.)	A29	3235	**13250**	**15650**	**16450**
Jeep X	A39	3407	**15550**	**18075**	**18900**
Jeep Sport	A49	3450	**16600**	**19175**	**20025**
Jeep Unlimited (AT)	A49	3721	**17850**	**20600**	**21725**
Jeep Sahara	A59	3575	**18750**	**21550**	**22450**
Jeep Rubicon	A69	3716	**20850**	**23775**	**24700**
Add Columbia Pkg. (X)			**300**	**350**	**350**
Add Rocky Mountain Pkg. (X)			**300**	**350**	**350**
Add Aluminum/Alloy Wheels (Std. Unlimited, Sahara, Rubicon)			**325**	**375**	**375**
Add Automatic Trans. (Std. Unlimited)			**575**	**650**	**650**
Add Compact Disc Player (SE)			**100**	**125**	**125**
Add Hard Top			**650**	**725**	**725**
Add Running Boards			**150**	**175**	**175**
Add Theft Recovery System			**100**	**125**	**125**
Deduct W/out Air Conditioning			**700**	**700**	**700**
Deduct W/out Cruise Control			**200**	**200**	**200**
2004 LIBERTY-V6-4WD					
Wagon 4D Sport (2WD)	K48	3648	**13575**	**16175**	**17200**
Wagon 4D Sport	L48	3826	**14650**	**17325**	**18350**
Wagon 4D Renegade (2WD)	K38	3846	**16275**	**19050**	**20125**
Wagon 4D Renegade	L38	4044	**17350**	**20325**	**21450**
Wagon 4D Limited (2WD)	K58	3898	**15525**	**18250**	**19300**
Wagon 4D Limited	L58	4115	**16600**	**19400**	**20500**
Add Columbia Pkg. (Sport)			**300**	**350**	**350**
Add Rocky Mountain Pkg. (Sport)			**300**	**350**	**350**
Add Aluminum/Alloy Wheels (Sport)			**325**	**375**	**375**

TRUCKS

BODY TYPE	Model No.	Weight	Trade-In	Retail	High Retail
Add Leather Seats			450	500	500
Add Power Seat			200	225	225
Add Power Sunroof			575	650	650
Add Running Boards			150	175	175
Add Theft Recovery System			100	125	125
Deduct 4 Cyl. Engine			750	750	750
Deduct W/out Air Conditioning			700	700	700
Deduct W/out Automatic Trans.			575	575	575
Deduct W/out Cruise Control			200	200	200
Deduct W/out Power Door Locks			175	175	175
Deduct W/out Power Windows			200	200	200
Deduct W/out Tilt Steering Wheel			150	150	150
2004 GRAND CHEROKEE-6 Cyl.-4WD					
Station Wgn 4D Laredo (2WD)	X48S	3790	15875	18625	19700
Station Wagon 4D Laredo	W48S	3995	16975	19800	20900
Station Wgn 4D Limited (2WD)	X58S	3910	19475	22600	23775
Station Wagon 4D Limited	W58S	4095	20575	23750	24975
2004 GRAND CHEROKEE-V8-4WD					
Station Wgn 4D Laredo (2WD)	X48N	3880	17025	19925	21025
Station Wagon 4D Laredo	W48N	4084	18125	21150	22300
Station Wgn 4D Limited (2WD)	X58N	3973	20625	23825	25050
Station Wagon 4D Limited	W58N	4155	21725	24975	26225
Station Wgn Limited HO (2WD)	X58J	4000	21375	24625	25875
Station Wgn 4D Limited HO	W58J	4208	22475	25800	27075
Station Wgn Overland HO (2WD)	X68J	4122	22525	25850	27125
Station Wgn 4D Overland HO	W68J	4356	23625	27000	28300
GRAND CHEROKEE OPTIONS					
Add Columbia Pkg. (Laredo)			450	500	500
Add Freedom Pkg. (Laredo)			300	350	350
Add Rocky Mountain Pkg. (Laredo)			400	450	450
Add Special Edition Pkg. (Laredo)			500	575	575
Add 4.7L V8 High Output Engine (Freedom V8)			750	850	850
Add Leather Seats (Laredo)			450	500	500
Add Navigation System			600	675	675
Add Power Sunroof (Std. Overland)			575	650	650
Add Running Boards			150	175	175
Add Theft Recovery System			100	125	125
JEEP					
2003 WRANGLER-6 Cyl.-5 Spd.-4WD					
Jeep SE (4 Cyl.)	A29	3235	12050	14350	15125
Jeep X	A39	3407	14500	16975	17800
Jeep Sport	A49	3450	15400	17925	18750
Jeep Sahara	A59	3575	17400	20125	21000
Jeep Rubicon	A69	3716	19400	22250	23150
Add Freedom Pkg. (X)			300	350	350
Add Aluminum/Alloy Wheels (Std. Sahara, Rubicon)			275	325	325
Add Automatic Trans.			525	600	600
Add Compact Disc Player (Std. Sahara)			75	100	100
Add Hard Top			600	675	675
Add Theft Recovery System			75	100	100
Deduct W/out Air Conditioning			650	650	650
Deduct W/out Cruise Control			175	175	175
Deduct W/out Tilt Steering Wheel			125	125	125

SEE TRUCK OPTION PAGE FOR ADDITIONAL OPTIONS

BODY TYPE	Model No.	Weight	Trade-In	Retail	High Retail
2003 LIBERTY-V6-4WD					
Wagon 4D Sport (2WD)	K48	3648	**12275**	**14800**	**15775**
Wagon 4D Sport	L48	3826	**13300**	**15875**	**16900**
Wagon 4D Renegade (2WD)	K38	3846	**14525**	**17200**	**18225**
Wagon 4D Renegade	L38	4044	**15550**	**18275**	**19325**
Wagon 4D Limited (2WD)	K58	3898	**13575**	**16175**	**17200**
Wagon 4D Limited	L58	4115	**14600**	**17275**	**18300**
Add Freedom Pkg. (Sport)			**250**	**300**	**300**
Add Aluminum/Alloy Wheels (Sport)			**275**	**325**	**325**
Add Compact Disc Player (Sport)			**75**	**100**	**100**
Add Leather Seats			**400**	**450**	**450**
Add Power Seat			**175**	**200**	**200**
Add Power Sunroof			**525**	**600**	**600**
Add Theft Recovery System			**75**	**100**	**100**
Deduct 4 Cyl. Engine			**725**	**725**	**725**
Deduct W/out Air Conditioning			**650**	**650**	**650**
Deduct W/out Automatic Trans.			**525**	**525**	**525**
Deduct W/out Cruise Control			**175**	**175**	**175**
Deduct W/out Power Door Locks			**150**	**150**	**150**
Deduct W/out Power Windows			**175**	**175**	**175**
Deduct W/out Tilt Steering Wheel			**125**	**125**	**125**
2003 GRAND CHEROKEE-6 Cyl.-4WD					
Station Wgn 4D Laredo (2WD)	X48S	3784	**14125**	**16750**	**17800**
Station Wagon 4D Laredo	W48S	3989	**15150**	**17850**	**18900**
Station Wgn 4D Limited (2WD)	X58S	3901	**17375**	**20350**	**21475**
Station Wagon 4D Limited	W58S	4088	**18400**	**21450**	**22600**
2003 GRAND CHEROKEE-V8-4WD					
Station Wgn 4D Laredo (2WD)	X48N	3877	**14975**	**17675**	**18725**
Station Wagon 4D Laredo	W48N	4081	**16000**	**18750**	**19825**
Station Wgn 4D Limited (2WD)	X58N	3968	**18225**	**21250**	**22400**
Station Wagon 4D Limited	W58N	4150	**19250**	**22350**	**23525**
Station Wgn Limited HO (2WD)	X58J	3995	**19275**	**22375**	**23550**
Station Wgn 4D Limited HO	W58J	4203	**20300**	**23475**	**24675**
Station Wgn 4D Overland HO	W68J	4355	**21000**	**24225**	**25450**
GRAND CHEROKEE OPTIONS					
Add Leather Seats (Laredo)			**400**	**450**	**450**
Add Power Sunroof (Std. HO)			**525**	**600**	**600**
Add Theft Recovery System			**75**	**100**	**100**
JEEP					
2002 WRANGLER-6 Cyl.-5 Spd.-4WD					
Jeep SE (4 Cyl.)	A29	3110	**10750**	**12925**	**13650**
Jeep X	A39		**13350**	**15775**	**16575**
Jeep Sport	A49	3360	**14150**	**16600**	**17425**
Jeep Sahara	A59	3454	**15750**	**18300**	**19125**
Add Aluminum/Alloy Wheels (Std. Sahara)			**225**	**250**	**250**
Add Automatic Trans.			**475**	**550**	**550**
Add Compact Disc Player (Std. Sahara)			**75**	**100**	**100**
Add Hard Top			**550**	**625**	**625**
Add Theft Recovery System			**75**	**100**	**100**
Deduct W/out Air Conditioning			**600**	**600**	**600**
Deduct W/out Cruise Control			**150**	**150**	**150**
Deduct W/out Tilt Steering Wheel			**100**	**100**	**100**

TRUCKS

BODY TYPE	Model No.	Weight	Trade-In	Retail	High Retail
2002 LIBERTY-V6-4WD					
Wagon 4D Sport (2WD)	K48	3648	**11125**	**13475**	**14400**
Wagon 4D Sport	L48	3826	**12125**	**14625**	**15600**
Wagon 4D Renegade (2WD)	K38	4003	**13025**	**15575**	**16575**
Wagon 4D Renegade	L38	4251	**14025**	**16650**	**17700**
Wagon 4D Limited (2WD)	K58	3898	**12225**	**14750**	**15725**
Wagon 4D Limited	L58	4115	**13225**	**15800**	**16825**
Add Aluminum/Alloy Wheels (Sport)			**225**	**250**	**250**
Add Compact Disc Player (Sport)			**75**	**100**	**100**
Add Leather Seats			**350**	**400**	**400**
Add Power Seat			**150**	**175**	**175**
Add Power Sunroof			**475**	**550**	**550**
Add Theft Recovery System			**75**	**100**	**100**
Deduct 4 Cyl. Engine			**700**	**700**	**700**
Deduct W/out Air Conditioning			**600**	**600**	**600**
Deduct W/out Automatic Trans.			**475**	**475**	**475**
Deduct W/out Cruise Control			**150**	**150**	**150**
Deduct W/out Power Door Locks			**125**	**125**	**125**
Deduct W/out Power Windows			**150**	**150**	**150**
Deduct W/out Tilt Steering Wheel			**100**	**100**	**100**
2002 GRAND CHEROKEE-6 Cyl.-4WD					
Station Wgn 4D Sport (2WD)	X38S	3689	**13025**	**15575**	**16575**
Station Wagon 4D Sport	W38S	3872	**14000**	**16625**	**17675**
Station Wgn 4D Laredo (2WD)	X48S	3786	**12675**	**15200**	**16200**
Station Wagon 4D Laredo	W48S	3970	**13675**	**16275**	**17300**
Station Wgn 4D Limited (2WD)	X58S	3895	**14975**	**17650**	**18700**
Station Wagon 4D Limited	W58S	4072	**15975**	**18725**	**19800**
2002 GRAND CHEROKEE-V8-4WD					
Station Wgn 4D Sport (2WD)	X38N		**13625**	**16225**	**17250**
Station Wagon 4D Sport	W38N		**14600**	**17250**	**18275**
Station Wgn 4D Laredo (2WD)	X48N	3863	**13275**	**15850**	**16875**
Station Wagon 4D Laredo	W48N	4041	**14275**	**16900**	**17950**
Station Wgn 4D Limited (2WD)	X58N	3964	**15575**	**18300**	**19350**
Station Wagon 4D Limited	W58N	4147	**16575**	**19350**	**20450**
Station Wgn Limited HO (2WD)	X58J	3999	**16575**	**19350**	**20450**
Station Wgn 4D Limited HO	W58J	4206	**17575**	**20550**	**21675**
Station Wgn 4D Overland HO	W68J	4364	**18125**	**21150**	**22300**
GRAND CHEROKEE OPTIONS					
Add Leather Seats (Laredo)			**350**	**400**	**400**
Add Power Sunroof (Std. HO)			**475**	**550**	**550**
Add Theft Recovery System			**75**	**100**	**100**
JEEP					
2001 WRANGLER-6 Cyl.-5 Spd.-4WD					
Jeep SE (4 Cyl.)	A29	3105	**9475**	**11675**	**12425**
Jeep Sport	A49	3316	**12675**	**15200**	**16000**
Jeep Sahara	A59	3362	**14125**	**16750**	**17575**
Add Aluminum/Alloy Wheels (Std. Sahara)			**175**	**200**	**200**
Add Automatic Trans.			**425**	**475**	**475**
Add Compact Disc Player (Std. Sahara)			**50**	**75**	**75**
Add Hard Top			**450**	**500**	**500**
Add Theft Recovery System			**50**	**75**	**75**
Deduct W/out Air Conditioning			**550**	**550**	**550**
Deduct W/out Cruise Control			**125**	**125**	**125**
Deduct W/out Tilt Steering Wheel			**100**	**100**	**100**

TRUCKS

SEE TRUCK OPTION PAGE FOR ADDITIONAL OPTIONS

BODY TYPE	Model No.	Weight	Trade-In	Retail	High Retail
2001 CHEROKEE-6 Cyl.-4WD					
Station Wagon 2D SE (2WD)	T27		6175	8050	8900
Station Wagon 4D SE (2WD)	T28		7475	9500	10375
Station Wagon 2D SE	F27		7125	9100	9975
Station Wagon 4D SE	F28		8425	10525	11475
Station Wagon 2D Sport (2WD)	T47	3150	7125	9100	9975
Station Wagon 4D Sport (2WD)	T48	3190	8425	10550	11500
Station Wagon 2D Sport	F47	3297	8075	10150	11075
Station Wagon 4D Sport	F48	3355	9375	11575	12475
Station Wagon Classic (2WD)	T58		8975	11125	12000
Station Wagon Classic	F58		9925	12150	13050
Station Wagon Limited (2WD)	T5/68		9625	11850	12750
Station Wagon Limited	F5/68		10575	12850	13750
Add A/A Wheels (Std. Classic, Ltd.)			175	200	200
Add Compact Disc Player			50	75	75
Add Leather Seats			300	350	350
Add Power Seat			125	150	150
Add Theft Recovery System			50	75	75
Deduct W/out Air Conditioning			550	550	550
Deduct W/out Automatic Trans.			425	425	425
Deduct W/out Cruise Control			125	125	125
Deduct W/out Power Door Locks			100	100	100
Deduct W/out Power Windows			125	125	125
Deduct W/out Tilt Steering Wheel			100	100	100
2001 GRAND CHEROKEE-6 Cyl.-4WD					
Station Wgn 4D Laredo (2WD)	X48S	3783	10825	13150	14075
Station Wagon 4D Laredo	W48S	3972	11725	14175	15125
Station Wgn 4D Limited (2WD)	X58S	3883	12275	14800	15775
Station Wagon 4D Limited	W58S	4067	13175	15750	16775
2001 GRAND CHEROKEE-V8-4WD					
Station Wgn 4D Laredo (2WD)	X48N	3866	11475	13900	14850
Station Wagon 4D Laredo	W48N	4042	12375	14900	15875
Station Wgn 4D Limited (2WD)	X58N	3955	12925	15500	16500
Station Wagon 4D Limited	W58N	4134	13825	16450	17500
GRAND CHEROKEE OPTIONS					
Add Compact Disc Player (Std. Limited)			50	75	75
Add Leather Seats (Std. Limited)			300	350	350
Add Power Seat (Std. Limited)			125	150	150
Add Power Sunroof			425	475	475
Add Theft Recovery System			50	75	75
JEEP					
2000 WRANGLER-6 Cyl.-5 Spd.-4WD					
Jeep SE (4 Cyl.)	A29	3045	8550	10675	11400
Jeep Sport	A49	3202	11550	13975	14725
Jeep Sahara	A59	3247	12950	15500	16300
Add Aluminum/Alloy Wheels (Std. Sahara)			125	150	150
Add Automatic Trans.			375	425	425
Add Compact Disc Player (Std. Sahara)			50	75	75
Add Hard Top			400	450	450
Deduct W/out Air Conditioning			500	500	500
Deduct W/out Cruise Control			100	100	100
Deduct W/out Tilt Steering Wheel			75	75	75

TRUCKS

BODY TYPE	Model No.	Weight	Trade-In	Retail	High Retail
2000 CHEROKEE-6 Cyl.-4WD					
Station Wagon 2D SE (2WD)	T27	3017	**4625**	**6350**	**7225**
Station Wagon 4D SE (2WD)	T28	3067	**5675**	**7500**	**8400**
Station Wagon 2D SE	F27	3313	**5450**	**7250**	**8125**
Station Wagon 4D SE	F28	3313	**6500**	**8425**	**9300**
Station Wagon 2D Sport (2WD)	T47	3154	**5550**	**7350**	**8250**
Station Wagon 4D Sport (2WD)	T48	3194	**6600**	**8525**	**9400**
Station Wagon 2D Sport	F47	3313	**6375**	**8275**	**9125**
Station Wagon 4D Sport	F48	3360	**7425**	**9450**	**10325**
Station Wagon Classic (2WD)	T58	3218	**6975**	**8950**	**9850**
Station Wagon Classic	F58	3386	**7800**	**9850**	**10750**
Station Wagon Limited (2WD)	T68	3218	**7700**	**9750**	**10650**
Station Wagon Limited	F68	3386	**8525**	**10650**	**11600**
Add A/A Wheels (Std. Classic, Ltd.)			**125**	**150**	**150**
Add Compact Disc Player			**50**	**75**	**75**
Add Power Seat (Std. Limited)			**100**	**125**	**125**
Deduct 4 Cyl. Engine			**625**	**625**	**625**
Deduct W/out Air Conditioning			**500**	**500**	**500**
Deduct W/out Automatic Trans.			**375**	**375**	**375**
Deduct W/out Cruise Control			**100**	**100**	**100**
Deduct W/out Power Door Locks			**75**	**75**	**75**
Deduct W/out Power Windows			**100**	**100**	**100**
Deduct W/out Tilt Steering Wheel			**75**	**75**	**75**
2000 GRAND CHEROKEE-6 Cyl.-4WD					
Station Wgn 4D Laredo (2WD)	248S	3773	**8650**	**10775**	**11725**
Station Wagon 4D Laredo	W48S	3955	**9450**	**11650**	**12550**
Station Wgn 4D Limited (2WD)	258S	3773	**9900**	**12125**	**13000**
Station Wagon 4D Limited	W58S	3955	**10700**	**13000**	**13925**
2000 GRAND CHEROKEE-V8-4WD					
Station Wgn 4D Laredo (2WD)	248N		**9250**	**11425**	**12325**
Station Wagon 4D Laredo	W48N		**10050**	**12300**	**13200**
Station Wgn 4D Limited (2WD)	258N		**10500**	**12775**	**13675**
Station Wagon 4D Limited	W58N		**11300**	**13725**	**14675**
GRAND CHEROKEE OPTIONS					
Add Compact Disc Player (Std. Limited)			**50**	**75**	**75**
Add Leather Seats (Std. Limited)			**250**	**300**	**300**
Add Power Seat (Std. Limited)			**100**	**125**	**125**
Add Power Sunroof			**375**	**425**	**425**
JEEP					
1999 WRANGLER-6 Cyl.-5 Spd.-4WD					
Jeep SE (4 Cyl.)	Y29	3045	**6850**	**8800**	**9575**
Jeep Sport	Y19	3202	**9650**	**11875**	**12625**
Jeep Sahara	Y49	3247	**10950**	**13300**	**14050**
Add Aluminum/Alloy Wheels (Std. Sahara)			**75**	**100**	**100**
Add Automatic Trans.			**325**	**375**	**375**
Add Hard Top			**350**	**400**	**400**
Deduct W/out Air Conditioning			**450**	**450**	**450**
Deduct W/out Cruise Control			**75**	**75**	**75**
Deduct W/out Tilt Steering Wheel			**50**	**50**	**50**
1999 CHEROKEE-6 Cyl.-4WD					
Station Wagon 2D SE (2WD)	T27	3154	**3700**	**5300**	**6125**
Station Wagon 4D SE (2WD)	T28	3194	**4550**	**6250**	**7125**
Station Wagon 2D SE	F27	3313	**4450**	**6150**	**7025**

TRUCKS

SEE TRUCK OPTION PAGE FOR ADDITIONAL OPTIONS

BODY TYPE	Model No.	Weight	Trade-In	Retail	High Retail
Station Wagon 4D SE	F28	3360	5300	7100	7975
Station Wagon 2D Sport (2WD)	T67		4525	6225	7100
Station Wagon 4D Sport (2WD)	T68		5375	7150	8025
Station Wagon 2D Sport	F67		5275	7050	7925
Station Wagon 4D Sport	F68		6125	8025	8875
Station Wagon Classic (2WD)	T68		5625	7425	8325
Station Wagon Classic	F68		6375	8300	9150
Station Wagon Limited (2WD)	T78		6475	8375	9250
Station Wagon Limited	F78		7225	9225	10100
Add A/A Wheels (Std. Classic, Ltd.)			75	100	100
Add Power Seat (Std. Limited)			75	100	100
Deduct 4 Cyl. Engine			575	575	575
Deduct W/out Air Conditioning			450	450	450
Deduct W/out Automatic Trans.			325	325	325
Deduct W/out Cruise Control			75	75	75
Deduct W/out Power Door Locks			50	50	50
Deduct W/out Power Windows			75	75	75
Deduct W/out Tilt Steering Wheel			50	50	50
1999 GRAND CHEROKEE-6 Cyl.-4WD					
Station Wgn 4D Laredo (2WD)	258S	3739	7075	9050	9900
Station Wagon 4D Laredo	W58S	3916	7850	9900	10800
Station Wgn 4D Limited (2WD)	268S	3814	7975	10050	10975
Station Wagon 4D Limited	W68S	3997	8750	10875	11825
1999 GRAND CHEROKEE-V8-4WD					
Station Wagon 4D Laredo	W58N	3969	8300	10400	11325
Station Wagon 4D Limited	W68N	4050	9200	11375	12275
GRAND CHEROKEE OPTIONS					
Add Leather Seats (Std. Limited)			225	250	250
Add Power Seat (Std. Limited)			75	100	100
Add Power Sunroof			325	375	375
JEEP					
1998 WRANGLER-6 Cyl.-5 Spd.-4WD					
Jeep SE (4 Cyl.)	Y29	3045	5900	7750	8575
Jeep Sport	Y19	3202	8500	10625	11350
Jeep Sahara	Y49	3202	9700	11925	12675
Add Aluminum/Alloy Wheels (Std. Sahara)			50	75	75
Add Automatic Trans.			275	325	325
Add Hard Top			300	350	350
Deduct W/out Air Conditioning			400	400	400
Deduct W/out Cruise Control			50	50	50
1998 CHEROKEE-6 Cyl.-4WD					
Station Wagon 2D SE (2WD)	T27		3000	4500	5350
Station Wagon 4D SE (2WD)	T28		3650	5225	6025
Station Wagon 2D SE	J27		3675	5275	6100
Station Wagon 4D SE	J28		4325	6000	6875
Station Wagon 2D Sport (2WD)	T67		3800	5400	6225
Station Wagon 4D Sport (2WD)	T68		4450	6125	7000
Station Wagon 2D Sport	J67		4475	6175	7050
Station Wagon 4D Sport	J68		5125	6900	7825
Station Wagon Classic (2WD)	T68		4550	6250	7125
Station Wagon Classic	J68		5225	7000	7950
Station Wagon Limited (2WD)	T6/78		5350	7125	8000
Station Wagon Limited	J6/78		6025	7900	8825

BODY TYPE	Model No.	Weight	Trade-In	Retail	High Retail
Add A/A Wheels (Std. Classic, Ltd.)			50	75	75
Add Power Seat			50	75	75
Deduct 4 Cyl. Engine			475	475	475
Deduct W/out Air Conditioning			400	400	400
Deduct W/out Automatic Trans.			275	275	275
Deduct W/out Cruise Control			50	50	50
Deduct W/out Power Windows			50	50	50
1998 GRAND CHEROKEE-6 Cyl.-4WD					
Station Wgn 4D Laredo (2WD)	X58S	3621	4625	6350	7225
Station Wagon 4D Laredo	Z58S	3800	5325	7100	7975
Station Wgn 4D TSi (2WD)	X58S		5100	6850	7775
Station Wagon 4D TSi	Z58S		5800	7625	8525
Station Wagon 4D SE (2WD)	X48S		4925	6675	7600
Station Wagon 4D SE	Z48S		5625	7425	8325
Station Wgn 4D Limited (2WD)	X78S	3621	5325	7100	7975
Station Wagon 4D Limited	Z78S	3800	6025	7875	8800
1998 GRAND CHEROKEE-5.2L V8, 5.9L Ltd. V8					
Station Wgn 4D Laredo (2WD)	X58Y	3755	4975	6725	7650
Station Wagon 4D Laredo	Z58Y	3936	5675	7475	8375
Station Wgn 4D TSi (2WD)	X58Y		5450	7250	8125
Station Wagon 4D TSi	Z58Y		6150	8025	8875
Station Wagon 4D SE (2WD)	X48Y		5275	7050	7925
Station Wagon 4D SE	Z48Y		5975	7825	8750
Station Wgn 4D Limited (2WD)	X78Y	3755	5675	7500	8400
Station Wagon 4D Limited	Z78Y	3936	6375	8275	9125
Station Wagon 5.9 Limited	Z88Z	4261	6800	8725	9600
GRAND CHEROKEE OPTIONS					
Add Leather Seats (Std. TSi, Limited)			175	200	200
Add Power Seat (Std. TSi, SE, Limited)			50	75	75
Add Power Sunroof (Std. 5.9 Limited)			275	325	325
JEEP					
1997 WRANGLER-6 Cyl.-5 Spd.-4WD					
Jeep SE (4 Cyl.)	Y29	3092	4700	6425	7225
Jeep Sport	Y19	3229	7000	8975	9750
Jeep Sahara	Y49	3229	8100	10175	10900
Add Automatic Trans.			175	200	200
Add Hard Top			250	300	300
Deduct W/out Air Conditioning			250	250	250
1997 CHEROKEE-6 Cyl.-4WD					
Station Wagon 2D SE (2WD)	T27	2947	2175	3550	4300
Station Wagon 4D SE (2WD)	T28	2993	2750	4200	5000
Station Wagon 2D SE	J27	3111	3025	4550	5400
Station Wagon 4D SE	J28	3153	3600	5175	5975
Station Wagon 2D Sport (2WD)	T67	2947	2925	4400	5225
Station Wagon 4D Sport (2WD)	T68	2933	3500	5075	5875
Station Wagon 2D Sport	J67	3111	3775	5375	6200
Station Wagon 4D Sport	J68	3153	4350	6025	6875
Station Wagon 4D Cntry (2WD)	T78	2933	4150	5800	6675
Station Wagon 4D Country	J78	3153	5000	6750	7675
Add Leather Seats			150	175	175
Add Power Seat			50	75	75
Deduct 4 Cyl. Engine			300	300	300
Deduct W/out Air Conditioning			250	250	250

TRUCKS

SEE TRUCK OPTION PAGE FOR ADDITIONAL OPTIONS

BODY TYPE	Model No.	Weight	Trade-In	Retail	High Retail
Deduct W/out Automatic Trans.			175	175	175
Deduct W/out Cruise Control			50	50	50
Deduct W/out Power Windows			50	50	50
1997 GRAND CHEROKEE-6 Cyl.-4WD					
Station Wgn 4D Laredo (2WD)	X58S	3614	4150	5800	6675
Station Wagon 4D Laredo	Z58S	3790	4800	6525	7425
Station Wgn 4D TSi (2WD)	X58S	3582	4450	6150	7025
Station Wagon 4D TSi	Z58S	3740	5100	6850	7775
Station Wgn 4D Limited (2WD)	X78S	3614	4900	6650	7550
Station Wagon 4D Limited	Z78S	3790	5550	7350	8250
1997 GRAND CHEROKEE-V8-4WD					
Station Wgn 4D Laredo (2WD)	X58Y	3614	4400	6100	6950
Station Wagon 4D Laredo	Z58Y	3790	5050	6800	7725
Station Wgn 4D TSi (2WD)	X58Y	3582	4700	6425	7325
Station Wagon 4D TSi	Z58Y	3740	5350	7125	8000
Station Wgn 4D Limited (2WD)	X78Y	3614	5150	6925	7850
Station Wagon 4D Limited	Z78Y	3790	5800	7625	8525
GRAND CHEROKEE OPTIONS					
Add Leather Seats (Std. TSi, Limited)			150	175	175
Add Power Seat (Std. Limited)			50	75	75
Add Power Sunroof			200	225	225
JEEP					
1996 CHEROKEE-6 Cyl.-4WD					
Station Wagon 2D SE (2WD)	T27	2891	1650	2925	3600
Station Wagon 4D SE (2WD)	T28	2932	2050	3400	4125
Station Wagon 2D SE	J27	3057	2500	3925	4725
Station Wagon 4D SE	J28	3100	2900	4375	5200
Station Wagon 2D Sport (2WD)	T67	2891	2150	3525	4275
Wagon 4D Sport/Classic (2WD)	T68	2932	2550	3975	4775
Station Wagon 2D Sport	J67	2891	3000	4500	5350
Station Wagon 4D Sport/Classic	J68	3057	3400	4950	5850
Station Wagon 4D Cntry (2WD)	T78	2932	3050	4575	5425
Station Wagon 4D Country	J78	3100	3900	5525	6375
Deduct 4 Cyl. Engine			225	225	225
Deduct W/out Air Conditioning			150	150	150
Deduct W/out Automatic Trans.			125	125	125
1996 GRAND CHEROKEE-6 Cyl.-4WD					
Station Wgn 4D Laredo (2WD)	X58S	3614	3550	5125	5925
Station Wagon 4D Laredo	Z58S	3790	4200	5875	6750
Station Wgn 4D Limited (2WD)	X78S	3582	4250	5925	6800
Station Wagon 4D Limited	Z78S	3740	4900	6650	7550
1996 GRAND CHEROKEE-V8-4WD					
Station Wagon 4D Laredo	Z58Y	3931	4425	6125	7000
Station Wagon 4D Limited	Z78Y		5125	6875	7800
GRAND CHEROKEE OPTIONS					
Add Power Sunroof			150	175	175
JEEP					
1995 WRANGLER-6 Cyl.-4WD					
Jeep S (4 Cyl.)	Y19	2943	3675	5275	6100
Jeep SE	Y29	3085	4875	6625	7525
Jeep Sahara	Y49		5475	7275	8150
Add Rio Grande Trim			225	250	250
Add Sport Trim			250	300	300

TRUCKS

BODY TYPE	Model No.	Weight	Trade-In	Retail	High Retail
Add Hard Top			**300**	**350**	**350**
1995 CHEROKEE-6 Cyl.-4WD					
Station Wagon 2D SE (2WD)	T27		**1000**	**2150**	**2700**
Station Wagon 4D SE (2WD)	T28		**1350**	**2575**	**3200**
Station Wagon 2D SE	J27		**1850**	**3175**	**3875**
Station Wagon 4D SE	J28		**2200**	**3575**	**4325**
Station Wagon 2D Sport (2WD)	T67	2876	**1500**	**2750**	**3400**
Station Wagon 4D Sport (2WD)	T68	2928	**1850**	**3175**	**3875**
Station Wagon 2D Sport	J67	3042	**2350**	**3750**	**4525**
Station Wagon 4D Sport	J68	3090	**2700**	**4150**	**4950**
Station Wagon 4D Cntry (2WD)	T78	2928	**2300**	**3700**	**4450**
Station Wagon 4D Country	J78	3090	**3150**	**4675**	**5550**
Deduct 4 Cyl. Engine			**200**	**200**	**200**
1995 GRAND CHEROKEE-6 Cyl.-4WD					
Station Wgn 4D SE (2WD)	X68S	3569	**2500**	**3925**	**4725**
Station Wagon 4D SE	Z68S	3675	**3150**	**4675**	**5550**
Station Wgn 4D Laredo (2WD)	X58S		**2750**	**4200**	**5000**
Station Wagon 4D Laredo	Z58S		**3400**	**4950**	**5850**
Station Wgn 4D Limited (2WD)	X78S		**3400**	**4950**	**5850**
Station Wagon 4D Limited	Z78S		**4050**	**5700**	**6550**
1995 GRAND CHEROKEE-V8-4WD					
Station Wagon 4D SE	Z68Y	3958	**3350**	**4900**	**5800**
Station Wagon 4D Laredo	Z58Y		**3600**	**5175**	**5975**
Station Wagon 4D Limited	Z78Y		**4250**	**5925**	**6800**

KIA

BODY TYPE	Model No.	Weight	Trade-In	Retail	High Retail
KIA					
2004 SEDONA-V6					
Wagon LX	UP13	4802	**12375**	**14900**	**15875**
Wagon EX	UP13		**13775**	**16375**	**17400**
Add Leather Seats			**450**	**500**	**500**
Add Power Sunroof			**575**	**650**	**650**
Add Rear Entertainment System			**600**	**675**	**675**
Add Theft Recovery System			**100**	**125**	**125**
2004 SORENTO-V6-4WD					
Utility 4D LX (2WD)	JD	4057	**14775**	**17450**	**18475**
Utility 4D EX (2WD)	JD		**16175**	**18950**	**20025**
Utility 4D LX	JC	4255	**15850**	**18600**	**19675**
Utility 4D EX	JC		**17250**	**20225**	**21350**
Add Aluminum/Alloy Wheels (LX)			**325**	**375**	**375**
Add Leather Seats			**450**	**500**	**500**
Add Running Boards			**150**	**175**	**175**
Add Theft Recovery System			**100**	**125**	**125**
Deduct W/out Automatic Trans.			**575**	**575**	**575**
KIA					
2003 SEDONA-V6					
Wagon LX	UP13	4802	**10800**	**13100**	**14025**
Wagon EX	UP13		**12050**	**14525**	**15500**
Add Leather Seats			**400**	**450**	**450**
Add Power Sunroof			**525**	**600**	**600**

TRUCKS

SEE TRUCK OPTION PAGE FOR ADDITIONAL OPTIONS

BODY TYPE	Model No.	Weight	Trade-In	Retail	High Retail
Add Theft Recovery System			75	100	100
2003 SORENTO-V6-4WD					
Utility 4D LX (2WD)	J(C/D)	4057	13550	16150	17175
Utility 4D EX (2WD)	J(C/D)		14750	17425	18450
Utility 4D LX	JC	4255	14575	17225	18250
Utility 4D EX	JC		15775	18500	19575
Add Aluminum/Alloy Wheels (LX)			275	325	325
Add Leather Seats			400	450	450
Add Theft Recovery System			75	100	100
KIA					
2002 SPORTAGE-4 Cyl.-4WD					
Utility 2D Convertible (2WD)	JB62	3108	5175	6950	7800
Utility 2D Convertible (5 Spd.)	JA62	3230	5750	7575	8375
Utility 4D (2WD)	JB72	3186	6750	8700	9475
Utility 4D	JA72	3352	7750	9800	10525
Add Aluminum/Alloy Wheels (2D)			200	225	225
Add Compact Disc Player			75	100	100
Add Cruise Control			125	150	150
Add Theft Recovery System			75	100	100
Deduct W/out Air Conditioning			475	475	475
Ded W/out Automatic Trans. (Ex. Conv. 4WD)			375	375	375
2002 SEDONA-V6					
Wagon LX	UP13	4709	8475	10575	11525
Wagon EX	UP13		9475	11675	12575
Add Compact Disc Player (Std. EX)			75	100	100
Add Leather Seats			350	400	400
Add Power Sunroof			475	550	550
Add Theft Recovery System			75	100	100
KIA					
2001 SPORTAGE-4 Cyl.-4WD					
Utility 2D Convertible (2WD)	JB62	3230	3325	4875	5675
Utility 2D Convertible (5 Spd.)	JA62	3352	4075	5725	6500
Utility 4D (2WD)	JB72		4925	6675	7500
Utility 4D	JA72		6000	7850	8675
Utility 4D EX (2WD)	JB72		5575	7400	8200
Utility 4D EX	JA72		6650	8575	9350
Utility 4D Limited (2WD)	JB72		5725	7550	8350
Utility 4D Limited	JA72		6800	8750	9525
Add Aluminum/Alloy Wheels (2D)			150	175	175
Add Compact Disc Player (Std. EX, Ltd.)			50	75	75
Add Cruise Control (Conv.)			100	125	125
Add Leather Seats			200	225	225
Add Theft Recovery System			50	75	75
Deduct W/out Air Conditioning			425	425	425
Ded W/out Automatic Trans. (Ex. Conv. 4WD)			325	325	325
KIA					
2000 SPORTAGE-4 Cyl.-4WD					
Utility 2D Convertible (2WD)	JB62	3108	2125	3500	4150
Utility 2D Convertible (5 Spd.)	JA62	3230	2925	4425	5175
Utility 4D (2WD)	JB72	3186	3525	5100	5825
Utility 4D	JA72	3352	4700	6425	7225
Utility 4D EX (2WD)	JB72	3186	4225	5900	6700

TRUCKS

BODY TYPE	Model No.	Weight	Trade-In	Retail	High Retail
Utility 4D EX	JA72	3352	**5300**	**7075**	**7850**
Add A/A Wheels (Std. 4D 4WD, EX)			**100**	**125**	**125**
Add Compact Disc Player (Std. EX)			**50**	**75**	**75**
Add Cruise Control (Std. EX)			**75**	**100**	**100**
Add Leather Seats			**150**	**175**	**175**
Deduct W/out Air Conditioning			**375**	**375**	**375**
Ded W/out Automatic Trans. (Ex. Conv. 4WD)			**300**	**300**	**300**
KIA					
1999 SPORTAGE-4 Cyl.-4WD					
Utility 2D Convertible (2WD)	JB62	3102	**1650**	**2900**	**3525**
Utility 2D Convertible (5 Spd.)	JA62	3223	**2275**	**3675**	**4350**
Utility 4D (2WD)	JB72	3186	**3000**	**4500**	**5250**
Utility 4D	JA72	3352	**3925**	**5550**	**6300**
Utility 4D EX (2WD)	JB72	3186	**3600**	**5175**	**5900**
Utility 4D EX	JA72	3352	**4475**	**6175**	**6950**
Add A/A Wheels (Std. 4D 4WD, EX)			**50**	**75**	**75**
Add Cruise Control (Std. EX)			**50**	**75**	**75**
Add Leather Seats			**125**	**150**	**150**
Deduct W/out Air Conditioning			**325**	**325**	**325**
Ded W/out Automatic Trans. (Ex. Conv. 4WD)			**250**	**250**	**250**
KIA					
1998 SPORTAGE-4 Cyl.-4WD					
Utility 4D (2WD)	JB72	3186	**2425**	**3850**	**4550**
Utility 4D	JA72	3352	**3375**	**4925**	**5725**
Utility 4D EX (2WD)	JB72	3186	**2875**	**4375**	**5125**
Utility 4D EX	JA72	3352	**3825**	**5425**	**6175**
Add Leather Seats			**100**	**125**	**125**
Deduct W/out Air Conditioning			**275**	**275**	**275**
Deduct W/out Automatic Trans.			**200**	**200**	**200**
KIA					
1997 SPORTAGE-4 Cyl.-4WD					
Utility 4D (2WD)	JB72	3159	**1800**	**3100**	**3700**
Utility 4D	JA72	3303	**2700**	**4150**	**4875**
Utility 4D EX (2WD)	JB72	3159	**2200**	**3575**	**4250**
Utility 4D EX	JA72	3303	**3100**	**4625**	**5400**
Add Leather Seats			**75**	**100**	**100**
Deduct W/out Air Conditioning			**150**	**150**	**150**
Deduct W/out Automatic Trans.			**125**	**125**	**125**
KIA					
1996 SPORTAGE-4 Cyl.-4WD					
Utility 4D (2WD, 5 Spd.)	JB72	3069	**1225**	**2425**	**3000**
Utility 4D	JA72	3280	**2125**	**3500**	**4150**
Utility 4D EX	JA72	3280	**2475**	**3900**	**4600**
Deduct W/out Air Conditioning			**100**	**100**	**100**
Deduct W/out Automatic Trans. (Ex. 2WD)			**100**	**100**	**100**
KIA					
1995 SPORTAGE-4 Cyl.-4WD					
Utility 4D (2WD)	JB72	3069	**1025**	**2175**	**2700**
Utility 4D	JA72	3280	**1775**	**3075**	**3675**
Utility 4D EX	JA72	3280	**2075**	**3425**	**4075**

TRUCKS

SEE TRUCK OPTION PAGE FOR ADDITIONAL OPTIONS

BODY TYPE	Model No.	Weight	Trade-In	Retail	High Retail
LAND ROVER/RANGE ROVER					
LAND ROVER					
2004 FREELANDER-V6-AWD					
Utility 3D SE3	NY1		18850	21925	23300
Utility 4D SE	NY2	3562	18750	21825	23200
Utility 4D HSE	NE2		20800	24000	25375
Add Harman Kardon Stereo (Std. SE3)			350	400	400
Add Leather Seats (SE3)			525	600	600
Add Power Sunroof (SE)			625	700	700
Add Theft Recovery System			100	125	125
2004 DISCOVERY-V8-4WD					
Utility S	TL/K	4608	23600	26975	28675
Utility SE	TY/W		26050	29575	30925
Utility HSE	TP/R		29450	33300	35200
Add 3rd Row Seat			200	225	225
Add Harman Kardon Stereo (SE)			425	475	475
Add Rear Air Conditioning			200	225	225
Add Rear Entertainment System			600	675	675
Add Theft Recovery System			100	125	125
Deduct W/out Dual Sunroof			875	875	875
2004 RANGE ROVER-V8-4WD					
Utility 4.4 HSE	M(E/F/H)11	5379	56600	62425	65200
Add Theft Recovery System			100	125	125
LAND ROVER					
2003 FREELANDER-V6-4WD					
Utility 4D S	NM2	3562	14525	17200	18425
Utility 3D SE3	NY1	3577	15350	18075	19325
Utility 4D SE	NY2		16125	18900	20175
Utility 4D HSE	NE2		18075	21100	22450
Add Harman Kardon Stereo (Std. SE3, HSE)			300	350	350
Add Leather Seats (SE3)			475	550	550
Add Power Sunroof (SE)			575	650	650
Add Theft Recovery System			75	100	100
2003 DISCOVERY-V8-4WD					
Utility S	TL/K	4576	18975	22075	23600
Utility SE	TY/W		22525	25850	27525
Utility HSE	TP/R		24825	28300	30050
Add Suspension Pkg.			600	675	675
Add 3rd Row Seat			175	200	200
Add Compact Disc Player (S)			150	175	175
Add Harman Kardon Stereo (SE)			375	425	425
Add Rear Air Conditioning			150	175	175
Add Rear Entertainment System			500	575	575
Add Theft Recovery System			75	100	100
Deduct W/out Dual Sunroof			825	825	825
2003 RANGE ROVER-V8-4WD					
Utility 4.4 HSE	MB11	5379	47400	52700	55200
Add Theft Recovery System			75	100	100

TRUCKS

BODY TYPE	Model No.	Weight	Trade-In	Retail	High Retail
LAND ROVER					
2002 FREELANDER-V6-4WD					
Utility 4D S	NM2	3562	12525	15050	16225
Utility 4D SE	NY2		13725	16325	17550
Utility 4D HSE	NE2		15825	18550	19800
Add Harman Kardon Stereo (Std. HSE)			250	300	300
Add Power Sunroof (Std. HSE)			525	600	600
Add Theft Recovery System			75	100	100
2002 DISCOVERY-V8-4WD					
Utility Series II SD	TL/K	4576	14625	17300	18650
Utility Series II SE	TY/W		17775	20775	22275
Add Performance Pkg. (SE)			550	625	625
Add 3rd Row Seat			150	175	175
Add Compact Disc Player (Std. SE)			125	150	150
Add Rear Air Conditioning			150	175	175
Add Theft Recovery System			75	100	100
Deduct W/out Dual Sunroof			775	775	775
2002 RANGE ROVER-V8-4WD					
Utility 4.6 HSE	PM16		25975	29825	31625
Add Theft Recovery System			75	100	100
LAND ROVER					
2001 DISCOVERY-V8-4WD					
Utility Series II SD	TL/K	4576	13075	15625	16950
Utility Series II LE	TH/J		13775	16375	17725
Utility Series II SE	TY/W		15075	17775	19150
Add Performance Pkg. (SE)			500	575	575
Add 3rd Row Seat			125	150	150
Add Compact Disc Player (Std. SE)			125	150	150
Add Rear Air Conditioning			125	150	150
Add Theft Recovery System			50	75	75
Deduct W/out Dual Sunroof			725	725	725
2001 RANGE ROVER-V8-4WD					
Utility 4.6 SE	PL16	4960	18075	21250	22750
Utility 4.6 HSE	PM16		21125	24500	26125
Add Navigation System (Std. HSE)			500	575	575
Add Theft Recovery System			50	75	75
LAND ROVER					
2000 DISCOVERY-V8-4WD					
Utility Series II	TL/Y	4576	11600	14025	15275
Add Performance Pkg.			450	500	500
Add 3rd Row Seat			100	125	125
Add Compact Disc Player			100	125	125
Add Harman Kardon Stereo			225	250	250
Add Rear Air Conditioning			100	125	125
Deduct W/out Dual Sunroof			675	675	675
Deduct W/out Leather Seats			375	375	375
Deduct W/out Power Seat			175	175	175
2000 RANGE ROVER-V8-4WD					
Utility 4.0 SE	PV15	4960	13550	16275	17625
Utility 4.6 HSE	PV16	4960	16550	19500	20950

TRUCKS

SEE TRUCK OPTION PAGE FOR ADDITIONAL OPTIONS

BODY TYPE	Model No.	Weight	Trade-In	Retail	High Retail
Add Navigation System			450	500	500
LAND ROVER					
1999 DISCOVERY-V8-4WD					
Utility Series II	TY12	4575	9950	12175	13325
Utility SD	JY12		8150	10225	11400
Add Performance Pkg.			400	450	450
Add 3rd Row Seat			100	125	125
Add Harman Kardon Stereo			175	200	200
Add Rear Air Conditioning			75	100	100
Deduct W/out Dual Sunroof			625	625	625
Deduct W/out Leather Seats			325	325	325
Deduct W/out Power Seat			150	150	150
1999 RANGE ROVER-V8-4WD					
Utility 4.0 SE	PV12	4960	11975	14550	15825
Utility 4.6 HSE	PV14	4960	14775	17575	18950
LAND ROVER					
1998 DISCOVERY-V8-4WD					
Utility LE	JY12	4465	7350	9350	10525
Utility LSE	JY12	4650	7750	9800	11000
Add 3rd Row Seat			100	125	125
Add Rear Air Conditioning			50	75	75
1998 RANGE ROVER-V8-4WD					
Utility 4.0 SE	PV12	4960	10375	12725	13900
Utility 4.6 HSE	PV14	4960	12675	15325	16625
LAND ROVER					
1997 DISCOVERY-V8-4WD					
Utility 4D	JY12	4465	6400	8300	9500
Deduct W/out Automatic Trans.			300	300	300
Deduct W/out Dual Sunroof			500	500	500
Deduct W/out Leather Seats			250	250	250
Deduct W/out Power Seat			100	100	100
1997 RANGE ROVER-V8-4WD					
Utility 4.0 SE	PV12	4960	9600	11900	13050
Utility 4.6 HSE	PV14	4960	11800	14325	15575
LAND ROVER					
1996 DISCOVERY-V8-4WD					
Utility 4D	JN/Y12	4465	5500	7300	8475
Deduct W/out Automatic Trans.			200	200	200
Deduct W/out Dual Sunroof			400	400	400
1996 RANGE ROVER-V8-4WD					
Utility 4.0 SE	PE/V12	4960	8875	11025	12150
Utility 4.6 HSE	PE/V14	4960	10575	12850	14050
LAND ROVER					
1995 DISCOVERY-V8-4WD					
Utility 4D	JN/Y12	4379	4500	6200	7300
1995 RANGE ROVER-V8-4WD					
Utility 4D County Classic	HE/V12	4401	6500	8425	9650
Utility 4D County LWB	HC/F13	4807	7300	9300	10450
Utility 4D 4.0 SE	PE/V12	4960	7700	9750	10950

BODY TYPE	Model No.	Weight	Trade-In	Retail	High Retail
LEXUS					
LEXUS					
2004 RX330-V6-AWD					
Wagon 4D (2WD)	GA31U	3860	**31700**	**35750**	**37725**
Wagon 4D	HA31U	4065	**32800**	**37025**	**39050**
Add Performance Pkg.			**1500**	**1675**	**1675**
Add Levinson Audio System			**425**	**475**	**475**
Add Navigation System			**750**	**850**	**850**
Add Rear Entertainment System			**600**	**675**	**675**
Add Running Boards			**150**	**175**	**175**
Add Theft Recovery System			**100**	**125**	**125**
Deduct W/out Leather Seats			**575**	**575**	**575**
Deduct W/out Power Sunroof			**725**	**725**	**725**
2004 GX470-V8-4WD					
Wagon	BT20X	4740	**38900**	**43475**	**45700**
Add Kinetic Dynamic Suspension			**750**	**850**	**850**
Add Mark Levinson/Navigation System			**1175**	**1325**	**1325**
Add Rear Entertainment System			**600**	**675**	**675**
Add Theft Recovery System			**100**	**125**	**125**
Deduct W/out 3rd Row Seat			**200**	**200**	**200**
Deduct W/out Rear Air Conditioning			**200**	**200**	**200**
2004 LX470-V8-4WD					
Wagon	HT00W	5590	**48600**	**53975**	**56500**
Add Levinson Audio System			**425**	**475**	**475**
Add Rear Entertainment System			**600**	**675**	**675**
Add Theft Recovery System			**100**	**125**	**125**
LEXUS					
2003 RX300-V6-4WD					
Wagon 4D (2WD)	GF10U	3715	**25550**	**29050**	**30825**
Wagon 4D	HF10U	3924	**26575**	**30150**	**31975**
Add Compact Disc Player			**150**	**175**	**175**
Add Navigation System			**650**	**725**	**725**
Add Theft Recovery System			**75**	**100**	**100**
Deduct W/out Leather Seats			**525**	**525**	**525**
2003 GX470-V8-4WD					
Wagon	BT20X	4675	**36100**	**40500**	**42625**
Add Mark Levinson/Navigation System			**1025**	**1150**	**1150**
Add Rear Entertainment System			**500**	**575**	**575**
Add Theft Recovery System			**75**	**100**	**100**
Deduct W/out 3rd Row Seat			**175**	**175**	**175**
Deduct W/out Power Sunroof			**675**	**675**	**675**
Deduct W/out Rear Air Conditioning			**150**	**150**	**150**
2003 LX470-V8-4WD					
Wagon	HT00W	5590	**43475**	**48575**	**50950**
Add Levinson Audio System			**375**	**425**	**425**
Add Rear Entertainment System			**500**	**575**	**575**
Add Theft Recovery System			**75**	**100**	**100**

TRUCKS

SEE TRUCK OPTION PAGE FOR ADDITIONAL OPTIONS

BODY TYPE	Model No.	Weight	Trade-In	Retail	High Retail
LEXUS					
2002 RX300-V6-4WD					
Wagon 4D (2WD)	GF10U	3715	**21850**	**25125**	**26775**
Wagon 4D	HF10U	3924	**22650**	**26000**	**27675**
Add Compact Disc Player			**125**	**150**	**150**
Add Navigation System			**550**	**625**	**625**
Add Power Sunroof			**625**	**700**	**700**
Add Theft Recovery System			**75**	**100**	**100**
Deduct W/out Leather Seats			**475**	**475**	**475**
2002 LX470-V8-4WD					
Wagon	HT00W	5401	**34775**	**39400**	**41500**
Add Levinson Audio System			**325**	**375**	**375**
Add Theft Recovery System			**75**	**100**	**100**
LEXUS					
2001 RX300-V6-4WD					
Wagon 4D (2WD)	GF10U	3715	**19675**	**22800**	**24350**
Wagon 4D	HF10U	3924	**20475**	**23675**	**25275**
Add Compact Disc Player			**125**	**150**	**150**
Add Nakamichi Stereo System			**275**	**325**	**325**
Add Navigation System			**500**	**575**	**575**
Add Power Sunroof			**575**	**650**	**650**
Add Theft Recovery System			**50**	**75**	**75**
Deduct W/out Leather Seats			**425**	**425**	**425**
2001 LX470-V8-4WD					
Wagon	HT00W	5401	**29000**	**33150**	**35050**
Add Levinson Audio System			**275**	**325**	**325**
Add Navigation System			**500**	**575**	**575**
Add Theft Recovery System			**50**	**75**	**75**
LEXUS					
2000 RX300-V6-4WD					
Wagon 4D (2WD)	GF10U	3692	**16075**	**18825**	**20250**
Wagon 4D	HF10U	3900	**16800**	**19600**	**21050**
Add Compact Disc Player			**100**	**125**	**125**
Add Nakamichi Stereo System			**225**	**250**	**250**
Add Power Sunroof			**525**	**600**	**600**
Deduct W/out Leather Seats			**375**	**375**	**375**
2000 LX470-V8-4WD					
Wagon	HT00W	5401	**24400**	**28150**	**29900**
Add Nakamichi Stereo System			**225**	**250**	**250**
LEXUS					
1999 RX300-V6-4WD					
Wagon 4D (2WD)	GF10U	3692	**13375**	**15950**	**17275**
Wagon 4D	HF10U	3900	**14075**	**16725**	**18100**
Add Nakamichi Stereo System			**175**	**200**	**200**
Add Power Sunroof			**475**	**550**	**550**
Deduct W/out Leather Seats			**325**	**325**	**325**
1999 LX470-V8-4WD					
Wagon	HT00W	5401	**20975**	**24350**	**25975**
Add Nakamichi Stereo System			**175**	**200**	**200**
Add Power Sunroof			**475**	**550**	**550**

BODY TYPE	Model No.	Weight	Trade-In	Retail	High Retail
LEXUS					
1998 LX470-V8-4WD					
Wagon	HT00W	5401	**19675**	**22950**	**24500**
Add Power Sunroof			**425**	**475**	**475**
LEXUS					
1997 LX450-6 Cyl.-4WD					
Wagon	J88	4971	**13200**	**15775**	**17100**
Add Power Sunroof			**350**	**400**	**400**
LEXUS					
1996 LX450-6 Cyl.-4WD					
Wagon	J88	4971	**11975**	**14425**	**15675**
Add Power Sunroof			**275**	**325**	**325**

LINCOLN

BODY TYPE	Model No.	Weight	Trade-In	Retail	High Retail
LINCOLN					
2004 AVIATOR-V8-AWD					
Utility Luxury (2WD)	U68	4818	**26950**	**30600**	**32425**
Utility Ultimate (2WD)	U68		**27850**	**31625**	**33500**
Utility Luxury	U88		**28025**	**31825**	**33700**
Utility Ultimate	U88		**28925**	**32775**	**34675**
Add Audiophile Stereo System (Std. Ultimate)			**425**	**475**	**475**
Add Navigation System			**750**	**850**	**850**
Add Power Sunroof			**725**	**825**	**825**
Add Rear Entertainment System			**600**	**675**	**675**
Add Theft Recovery System			**100**	**125**	**125**
2004 NAVIGATOR-V8-4WD					
Utility (2WD)	U27	5708	**29525**	**33400**	**35325**
Utility Ultimate (2WD)	U27		**31625**	**35625**	**37600**
Utility	U28	5969	**31250**	**35250**	**37225**
Utility Ultimate	U28		**33350**	**37625**	**39675**
Add Navigation System			**750**	**850**	**850**
Add Power Running Boards (Ultimate)			**350**	**400**	**400**
Add Power Sunroof (Std. Ultimate)			**725**	**825**	**825**
Add Rear Entertainment System			**600**	**675**	**675**
Add Theft Recovery System			**100**	**125**	**125**
LINCOLN					
2003 AVIATOR-V8-AWD					
Utility Luxury (2WD)	U68	4834	**23225**	**26600**	**28300**
Utility Premium (2WD)	U68		**24125**	**27550**	**29275**
Utility Luxury	U88	5002	**24250**	**27700**	**29425**
Utility Premium	U78		**25150**	**28650**	**30425**
Add Audiophile Stereo System (Std. Premium)			**375**	**425**	**425**
Add Navigation System			**650**	**725**	**725**
Add Power Sunroof			**675**	**775**	**775**
Add Rear Entertainment System			**500**	**575**	**575**
Add Theft Recovery System			**75**	**100**	**100**
2003 NAVIGATOR-V8-4WD					
Utility (2WD)	U27	5760	**26525**	**30100**	**31925**

TRUCKS

SEE TRUCK OPTION PAGE FOR ADDITIONAL OPTIONS

BODY TYPE	Model No.	Weight	Trade-In	Retail	High Retail
Utility Ultimate (2WD)	U27		**28225**	**32025**	**33900**
Utility	U28	5994	**28000**	**31800**	**33675**
Utility Ultimate	U28		**29700**	**33600**	**35525**
Add Navigation System			**650**	**725**	**725**
Add Power 3rd Row Seat (Std. Ultimate)			**175**	**200**	**200**
Add Power Running Boards (Ultimate)			**300**	**350**	**350**
Add Power Sunroof			**675**	**775**	**775**
Add Rear Entertainment System			**500**	**575**	**575**
Add Theft Recovery System			**75**	**100**	**100**
LINCOLN					
2002 BLACKWOOD-V8					
Utility 4D	W05	5700	**23975**	**27400**	**29125**
Add Navigation System			**550**	**625**	**625**
Add Theft Recovery System			**75**	**100**	**100**
2002 NAVIGATOR-V8-4WD					
Utility (2WD)	U27	5424	**19200**	**22300**	**23850**
Utility	U28	5774	**20575**	**23775**	**25375**
Add Compact Disc Player			**125**	**150**	**150**
Add Navigation System			**550**	**625**	**625**
Add Power Sunroof			**625**	**700**	**700**
Add Rear Entertainment System			**400**	**450**	**450**
Add Theft Recovery System			**75**	**100**	**100**
LINCOLN					
2001 NAVIGATOR-V8-4WD					
Utility (2WD)	U27	5396	**16075**	**18825**	**20250**
Utility	U28	5746	**17275**	**20250**	**21725**
Add Compact Disc Player			**125**	**150**	**150**
Add Navigation System			**500**	**575**	**575**
Add Power Sunroof			**575**	**650**	**650**
Add Rear Entertainment System			**350**	**400**	**400**
Add Theft Recovery System			**50**	**75**	**75**
LINCOLN					
2000 NAVIGATOR-V8-4WD					
Utility (2WD)	U27	5393	**14075**	**16700**	**18075**
Utility	U28	5723	**15075**	**17775**	**19150**
Add Compact Disc Player			**100**	**125**	**125**
Add Navigation System			**450**	**500**	**500**
Add Power Sunroof			**525**	**600**	**600**
LINCOLN					
1999 NAVIGATOR-V8-4WD					
Utility (2WD)	U27		**12050**	**14550**	**15825**
Utility	U28		**12875**	**15425**	**16725**
Add Power Sunroof			**475**	**550**	**550**
LINCOLN					
1998 NAVIGATOR-V8-4WD					
Utility (2WD)	U27	5150	**11175**	**13575**	**14800**
Utility	U28	5557	**11875**	**14325**	**15575**
Add Power Sunroof			**425**	**475**	**475**

BODY TYPE	Model No.	Weight	Trade-In	Retail	High Retail

MAZDA

BODY TYPE	Model No.	Weight	Trade-In	Retail	High Retail
MAZDA					
2004 TRIBUTE-V6					
Utility 4D DX (4 Cyl, 5 Spd)	Z02	3050	**12075**	**14550**	**15525**
Utility 4D LX	Z04	3321	**15300**	**18000**	**19050**
Utility 4D ES	Z06	3321	**15950**	**18700**	**19775**
Utility 4D DX (4WD, 4 Cyl, 5 Spd)	Z92	3207	**13150**	**15725**	**16750**
Utility 4D LX (4WD)	Z94	3491	**16375**	**19150**	**20225**
Utility 4D ES (4WD)	Z96	3491	**17025**	**19900**	**21000**
Add Power Seat (Std. ES)			**200**	**225**	**225**
Add Power Sunroof			**575**	**650**	**650**
Add Rear Entertainment System			**600**	**675**	**675**
Add Running Boards			**150**	**175**	**175**
Add Theft Recovery System			**100**	**125**	**125**
2004 MPV-V6					
Wagon LX	LW28	3029	**14675**	**17350**	**18375**
Wagon ES	LW28		**17075**	**19950**	**21050**
Add All-Sport Package			**400**	**450**	**450**
Add Dual Power Sliding Doors (Std. ES)			**600**	**675**	**675**
Add Power Sunroof			**575**	**650**	**650**
Add Rear Entertainment System			**600**	**675**	**675**
Add Theft Recovery System			**100**	**125**	**125**
2004 B2300 PICKUP-4 Cyl.-5 Spd.					
Base	R12D	3009	**7375**	**9375**	**10075**
SE-5	R12D		**8650**	**10775**	**11525**
SE Cab Plus 2D	R16D	3180	**10650**	**12925**	**13650**
2004 B3000 PICKUP-V6-5 Spd.					
DS	R12U	3239	**9500**	**11700**	**12450**
DS Cab Plus 2D	R16U	3408	**11500**	**13925**	**14675**
SE Cab Plus 4D	R46U	3325	**11800**	**14225**	**15000**
2004 B4000 PICKUP-V6-5 Spd.-4WD					
DS Cab Plus 4D (2WD)	R46E	3408	**12100**	**14600**	**15375**
Base Cab Plus 2D	R17E	3687	**13250**	**15825**	**16625**
SE Cab Plus 2D	R17E		**14000**	**16625**	**17450**
SE Cab Plus 4D	R47E	3687	**14500**	**17150**	**17950**
B SERIES PICKUP OPTIONS					
Add Off-Road Pkg.			**300**	**350**	**350**
Add Aluminum/Alloy Wheels (B2300 Base)			**325**	**375**	**375**
Add Automatic Trans.			**575**	**650**	**650**
Add Compact Disc Player (Base)			**100**	**125**	**125**
Add Cruise Control (Std. SE-5)			**200**	**225**	**225**
Add Power Door Locks			**175**	**200**	**200**
Add Power Windows			**200**	**225**	**225**
Add Running Boards			**150**	**175**	**175**
Add Theft Recovery System			**100**	**125**	**125**
Add Tilt Steering Wheel (Std. SE-5)			**150**	**175**	**175**
Deduct W/out Air Conditioning			**700**	**700**	**700**
MAZDA					
2003 TRIBUTE-V6					
Utility 4D DX (4 Cyl, 5 Spd)	Z02	3045	**10750**	**13075**	**14000**

TRUCKS

SEE TRUCK OPTION PAGE FOR ADDITIONAL OPTIONS

BODY TYPE	Model No.	Weight	Trade-In	Retail	High Retail
Utility 4D LX	Z04	3309	**13950**	**16575**	**17625**
Utility 4D ES	Z06	3309	**14525**	**17200**	**18225**
Utility 4D DX (4WD, 4 Cyl, 5 Spd)	Z92	3201	**11775**	**14225**	**15175**
Utility 4D LX (4WD)	Z94	3474	**14975**	**17675**	**18725**
Utility 4D ES (4WD)	Z96	3474	**15550**	**18275**	**19325**
Add Power Seat (Std. ES)			**175**	**200**	**200**
Add Power Sunroof			**525**	**600**	**600**
Add Rear Entertainment System			**500**	**575**	**575**
Add Running Boards			**125**	**150**	**150**
Add Theft Recovery System			**75**	**100**	**100**
2003 MPV-V6					
Wagon LX SV	LW28		**12825**	**15375**	**16375**
Wagon LX	LW28	3794	**13475**	**16050**	**17075**
Wagon ES	LW28		**14875**	**17550**	**18600**
Add All-Sport Package			**350**	**400**	**400**
Add Dual Power Sliding Doors			**500**	**575**	**575**
Add Power Sunroof			**525**	**600**	**600**
Add Rear Air Conditioning (Std. ES)			**150**	**175**	**175**
Add Rear Entertainment System			**500**	**575**	**575**
Add Theft Recovery System			**75**	**100**	**100**
2003 B2300 PICKUP-4 Cyl.-5 Spd.					
Base	R12D	3008	**6300**	**8175**	**8925**
SE-5	R12D		**7100**	**9075**	**9775**
SE Cab Plus 2D	R16D	3214	**9100**	**11250**	**11975**
2003 B3000 PICKUP-V6-5 Spd.					
DS	R12U	3271	**7900**	**9950**	**10675**
DS Cab Plus 2D	R16U	3486	**9900**	**12125**	**12850**
SE Cab Plus 4D	R46U		**10200**	**12450**	**13175**
2003 B4000 PICKUP-V6-5 Spd.-4WD					
DS Cab Plus 4D (2WD)	R46E		**10600**	**12875**	**13600**
Base Cab Plus 2D	R17E		**11850**	**14275**	**15050**
SE Cab Plus 2D	R17E	3762	**12450**	**14975**	**15750**
SE Cab Plus 4D	R47E	3762	**12950**	**15500**	**16300**
B SERIES PICKUP OPTIONS					
Add Off-Road Pkg.			**275**	**325**	**325**
Add Aluminum/Alloy Wheels (B2300 Base)			**275**	**325**	**325**
Add Automatic Trans.			**525**	**600**	**600**
Add Compact Disc Player (Base)			**75**	**100**	**100**
Add Cruise Control			**175**	**200**	**200**
Add Power Door Locks			**150**	**175**	**175**
Add Power Windows			**175**	**200**	**200**
Add Running Boards			**125**	**150**	**150**
Add Theft Recovery System			**75**	**100**	**100**
Add Tilt Steering Wheel			**125**	**150**	**150**
Deduct W/out Air Conditioning			**650**	**650**	**650**
MAZDA					
2002 TRIBUTE-V6					
Utility 4D DX (4 Cyl, 5 Spd)	U07B	3091	**9525**	**11750**	**12650**
Utility 4D DX	U071	3292	**10725**	**13025**	**13950**
Utility 4D LX	U091		**12575**	**15125**	**16125**
Utility 4D ES	U091		**13075**	**15650**	**16650**
Util 4D DX (4WD, 4 Cyl, 5 Spd)	U06B	3245	**10525**	**12825**	**13725**
Utility 4D DX (4WD)	U061	3455	**11725**	**14175**	**15125**

BODY TYPE	Model No.	Weight	Trade-In	Retail	High Retail
Utility 4D LX (4WD)	U081		13575	16175	17200
Utility 4D ES (4WD)	U081		14075	16725	17775
Add Power Seat (Std. ES)			150	175	175
Add Power Sunroof			475	550	550
Add Running Boards			100	125	125
Add Theft Recovery System			75	100	100
2002 MPV-V6					
Wagon LX	LW28	3794	11750	14200	15150
Wagon ES	LW28	3812	13550	16150	17175
Add Power Seat (Std. ES)			150	175	175
Add Power Sunroof			475	550	550
Add Rear Air Conditioning (Std. ES)			150	175	175
Add Theft Recovery System			75	100	100
2002 B2300 PICKUP-4 Cyl.-5 Spd.					
Base	R12D	2994	5125	6900	7750
SE-5	R12D		5925	7775	8600
2002 B3000 PICKUP-V6-5 Spd.					
DS	R12U	3276	6675	8625	9400
DS Cab Plus 2D	R16U	3356	8625	10750	11500
Cab Plus 2D (4WD)	R17U	3488	10875	13175	13925
2002 B4000 PICKUP-V6-5 Spd.-4WD					
DS Cab Plus 4D (2WD)	R46E		9225	11400	12125
Cab Plus 4D	R47E	3638	11475	13900	14650
B SERIES PICKUP OPTIONS					
Add Off-Road Pkg.			250	300	300
Add Aluminum/Alloy Wheels (Base 2WD)			225	250	250
Add Automatic Trans.			475	550	550
Add Compact Disc Player (Base)			75	100	100
Add Cruise Control			150	175	175
Add Power Door Locks			125	150	150
Add Power Windows			150	175	175
Add Running Boards			100	125	125
Add Theft Recovery System			75	100	100
Add Tilt Steering Wheel			100	125	125
Deduct W/out Air Conditioning			600	600	600
MAZDA					
2001 TRIBUTE-V6					
Utility 4D DX (4 Cyl, 5 Spd)	U07B	3091	8325	10425	11350
Utility 4D DX	U071	3291	9425	11600	12500
Utility 4D LX	U091		11075	13425	14350
Utility 4D ES	U091		11450	13875	14825
Util 4D DX (4WD, 4 Cyl, 5 Spd)	U06B	3245	9225	11400	12300
Utility 4D DX (4WD)	U061	3455	10325	12575	13475
Utility 4D LX (4WD)	U081		11975	14425	15400
Utility 4D ES (4WD)	U081		12400	14925	15900
Add Aluminum/Alloy Wheels (DX)			175	200	200
Add Power Sunroof			425	475	475
Add Theft Recovery System			50	75	75
2001 MPV-V6					
Wagon DX	LW28	3657	8475	10575	11525
Wagon LX	LW28		9375	11550	12450
Wagon ES	LW28		10625	12900	13825

TRUCKS

SEE TRUCK OPTION PAGE FOR ADDITIONAL OPTIONS

BODY TYPE	Model No.	Weight	Trade-In	Retail	High Retail
Add Aluminum/Alloy Wheels (Std. ES)			175	200	200
Add Power Sunroof			425	475	475
Add Rear Air Conditioning (Std. ES)			125	150	150
Add Rear Entertainment System			350	400	400
Add Theft Recovery System			50	75	75
Deduct W/out Cruise Control			125	125	125
Deduct W/out Power Door Locks			100	100	100
Deduct W/out Power Windows			125	125	125
2001 B2300/2500 PICKUP-4 Cyl.-5 Spd.					
SX	R12C/D	2960	4450	6150	6925
SE	R12C/D		5225	7000	7850
2001 B3000 PICKUP-V6-5 Spd.-4WD					
DS (2WD)	R12U		5925	7775	8600
SE (2WD)	R12U		5725	7550	8350
SE	R13U	3380	8075	10150	10875
DS Cab Plus 2D (2WD)	R16U		7825	9875	10600
SE Cab Plus 2D (2WD)	R16U	3164	7625	9650	10375
SE Cab Plus 4D (2WD)	R16U		8125	10225	10950
SE Cab Plus 2D	R17U	3571	10125	12375	13100
2001 B4000 PICKUP-V6-5 Spd.-4WD					
DS Cab Plus 4D (2WD)	R16E		8875	11025	11750
SE Cab Plus 4D	R17E		11025	13375	14125
B SERIES PICKUP OPTIONS					
Add Aluminum/Alloy Wheels (SX)			175	200	200
Add Automatic Trans.			425	475	475
Add Compact Disc Player (SX)			50	75	75
Add Cruise Control (Std. B4000)			125	150	150
Add Power Door Locks (Std. B4000)			100	125	125
Add Power Windows (Std. B4000)			125	150	150
Add Running Boards			75	100	100
Add Theft Recovery System			50	75	75
Add Tilt Steering Wheel (Std. B4000)			100	125	125
Deduct W/out Air Conditioning			550	550	550
MAZDA					
2000 MPV-V6					
Wagon DX	LW28	3657	6250	8125	8975
Wagon LX	LW28	3657	7050	9025	9875
Wagon ES	LW28	3677	8350	10450	11375
Add Aluminum/Alloy Wheels (Std. ES)			125	150	150
Add Power Sunroof			375	425	425
Add Rear Air Conditioning (Std. ES)			100	125	125
Add Rear Entertainment System			250	300	300
Deduct W/out Cruise Control			100	100	100
Deduct W/out Power Door Locks			75	75	75
Deduct W/out Power Windows			100	100	100
2000 B2500 PICKUP-4 Cyl.-5 Spd.					
SX	R12C	3025	3525	5100	5825
SE	R12C	3025	4225	5900	6700
SE Cab Plus 2D	R16C	3210	6025	7900	8725
2000 B3000 PICKUP-V6-5 Spd.-4WD					
SX (2WD)	R12V	3025	3975	5625	6400
SE (2WD)	R12V	3025	4675	6400	7200
SE	R13V	3441	6675	8600	9375

BODY TYPE	Model No.	Weight	Trade-In	Retail	High Retail
SE Cab Plus 2D (2WD)	R16V	3210	**6475**	**8400**	**9150**
SE Cab Plus 4D (2WD)	R16V		**6825**	**8775**	**9550**
SE Cab Plus 4D	R17V	3585	**8825**	**10975**	**11725**
2000 B4000 PICKUP-V6-5 Spd.-4WD					
SE Cab Plus 4D (2WD, AT)	R16X	3210	**7650**	**9700**	**10425**
SE Cab Plus 4D	R17X		**9275**	**11475**	**12200**
B SERIES PICKUP OPTIONS					
Add Aluminum/Alloy Wheels (SX)			**125**	**150**	**150**
Add AT (Std. B4000 Cab Plus 2WD)			**375**	**425**	**425**
Add Compact Disc Player (Std. SE)			**50**	**75**	**75**
Add Cruise Control (Std. B4000)			**100**	**125**	**125**
Add Power Door Locks (Std. B4000)			**75**	**100**	**100**
Add Power Windows (Std. B4000)			**100**	**125**	**125**
Add Running Boards			**50**	**75**	**75**
Add Tilt Steering Wheel (Std. B4000)			**75**	**100**	**100**
Deduct W/out Air Conditioning			**500**	**500**	**500**
MAZDA					
1999 B2500 PICKUP-4 Cyl.-5 Spd.					
SX	R12C	2998	**3150**	**4675**	**5450**
SE	R12C	2998	**3800**	**5400**	**6150**
SE Cab Plus 2D	R16C	3210	**5200**	**6975**	**7825**
SE Cab Plus 4D	R16C	3210	**5400**	**7175**	**7950**
1999 B3000 PICKUP-V6-5 Spd.-4WD					
SE	R13V	3423	**6000**	**7850**	**8675**
SE Cab Plus 2D (2WD)	R16V	3210	**5600**	**7400**	**8200**
SE Cab Plus 4D (2WD)	R16V	3210	**5800**	**7625**	**8425**
SE Cab Plus 2D	R17V	3616	**7400**	**9400**	**10125**
SE Cab Plus 4D	R17V	3616	**7600**	**9625**	**10350**
1999 B4000 PICKUP-V6-5 Spd.-4WD					
SE (2WD)	R12X	2998	**4425**	**6100**	**6875**
SE Cab Plus 2D (2WD, AT)	R16X	3210	**6150**	**8025**	**8775**
SE Cab Plus 4D (2WD, AT)	R16X	3210	**6350**	**8250**	**9000**
SE Cab Plus 2D	R17X	3616	**7750**	**9800**	**10525**
SE Cab Plus 4D	R17X	3616	**7950**	**10000**	**10725**
B SERIES PICKUP OPTIONS					
Add Aluminum/Alloy Wheels (SX)			**75**	**100**	**100**
Add AT (Std. B4000 Cab Plus 2WD)			**325**	**375**	**375**
Add Cruise Control (Std. B4000)			**75**	**100**	**100**
Add Power Door Locks (Std. B4000 4WD)			**50**	**75**	**75**
Add Power Windows (Std. B4000 4WD)			**75**	**100**	**100**
Add Tilt Steering Wheel (Std. B4000)			**50**	**75**	**75**
Deduct W/out Air Conditioning			**450**	**450**	**450**
MAZDA					
1998 MPV-V6					
Wagon LX	LV52	3730	**4050**	**5700**	**6550**
Wagon ES	LV52	3730	**4700**	**6425**	**7325**
Wagon LX (4WD)	LV52	4120	**4600**	**6300**	**7175**
Wagon ES (4WD)	LV52	4120	**5200**	**6975**	**7925**
Add Aluminum/Alloy Wheels (LX 2WD)			**50**	**75**	**75**
Add Power Sunroof			**275**	**325**	**325**
Add Rear Air Conditioning			**50**	**75**	**75**
Add Rear Bucket Seats (LX)			**50**	**75**	**75**
Deduct W/out Air Conditioning			**400**	**400**	**400**

TRUCKS

SEE TRUCK OPTION PAGE FOR ADDITIONAL OPTIONS

BODY TYPE	Model No.	Weight	Trade-In	Retail	High Retail
1998 B2500 PICKUP-4 Cyl.-5 Spd.					
SX	R12C	3220	**2875**	**4350**	**5100**
SE	R12C	3220	**3425**	**5000**	**5800**
SE Cab Plus	R16C	3420	**4775**	**6500**	**7300**
1998 B3000 PICKUP-V6-5 Spd.-4WD					
SX	R13U	3620	**4775**	**6500**	**7300**
SE	R13U	3620	**5325**	**7100**	**7875**
SE Cab Plus (2WD)	R16U	3500	**5075**	**6825**	**7650**
SE Cab Plus	R17U	3780	**6675**	**8600**	**9375**
1998 B4000 PICKUP-V6-5 Spd.-4WD					
SE Cab Plus (2WD)	R16X	3580	**5175**	**6950**	**7800**
SE Cab Plus	R17X	3820	**6775**	**8725**	**9500**
B SERIES PICKUP OPTIONS					
Add Aluminum/Alloy Wheels (SX)			**50**	**75**	**75**
Add Automatic Trans.			**275**	**325**	**325**
Add Cruise Control			**50**	**75**	**75**
Add Power Windows			**50**	**75**	**75**
Deduct W/out Air Conditioning			**400**	**400**	**400**
MAZDA					
1997 MPV-V6					
Wagon LX	LV52	3790	**3300**	**4850**	**5750**
Wagon ES	LV52	3790	**4000**	**5625**	**6475**
Wagon LX (4WD)	LV52	4105	**3700**	**5300**	**6125**
Wagon ES (4WD)	LV52	4105	**4400**	**6100**	**6950**
Add Power Sunroof			**200**	**225**	**225**
Deduct W/out Air Conditioning			**250**	**250**	**250**
1997 B2300 PICKUP-4 Cyl.-5 Spd.					
Base	R12A	2989	**2550**	**3975**	**4700**
SE	R12A	3059	**2975**	**4475**	**5225**
SE Cab Plus	R16A	3355	**3975**	**5600**	**6375**
1997 B4000 PICKUP-V6-5 Spd.-4WD					
Base	R13X	3242	**4050**	**5700**	**6475**
Base Cab Plus	R17X	3497	**5050**	**6800**	**7625**
SE Cab Plus (2WD)	R16X	3637	**4175**	**5850**	**6650**
SE Cab Plus	R17X	3637	**5475**	**7275**	**8050**
B SERIES PICKUP OPTIONS					
Add SE-5 Trim			**125**	**150**	**150**
Add Automatic Trans.			**175**	**200**	**200**
Add Cruise Control			**50**	**75**	**75**
Add Power Windows			**50**	**75**	**75**
Deduct W/out Air Conditioning			**250**	**250**	**250**
MAZDA					
1996 MPV-V6					
Wagon DX	LV52	3730	**2425**	**3825**	**4600**
Wagon LX	LV52	3730	**2700**	**4150**	**4950**
Wagon ES	LV52	3730	**3300**	**4850**	**5750**
Wagon LX (4WD)	LV52	4045	**3100**	**4625**	**5500**
Wagon ES (4WD)	LV52	4045	**3700**	**5300**	**6125**
Add Power Sunroof			**150**	**175**	**175**
Deduct W/out Air Conditioning			**150**	**150**	**150**
1996 B2300 PICKUP-4 Cyl.-5 Spd.					
Base	R12A	2927	**2000**	**3350**	**4000**

TRUCKS

BODY TYPE	Model No.	Weight	Trade-In	Retail	High Retail
SE	R12A	3003	**2200**	**3575**	**4250**
Base Cab Plus	R16A	3197	**2900**	**4375**	**5125**
SE Cab Plus	R16A	3197	**3100**	**4625**	**5400**
Base (4WD)	R13A	3242	**3200**	**4725**	**5500**
1996 B3000 PICKUP-V6-5 Spd.					
SE Cab Plus	R16U	3283	**3225**	**4775**	**5575**
Base Cab Plus (4WD)	R17U	3548	**4225**	**5900**	**6700**
1996 B4000 PICKUP-V6-5 Spd.-4WD					
SE	R13X	3545	**3625**	**5225**	**5950**
SE Cab Plus	R17X	3829	**4525**	**6225**	**7000**
LE Cab Plus (2WD)	R16X	3552	**3575**	**5150**	**5875**
LE Cab Plus	R17X	3884	**4775**	**6500**	**7300**
B SERIES PICKUP OPTIONS					
Add Automatic Trans.			**125**	**150**	**150**
Deduct W/out Air Conditioning			**150**	**150**	**150**
MAZDA					
1995 MPV-V6					
Wagon L	LV52	3745	**1775**	**3075**	**3750**
Wagon LX	LV52	3745	**2000**	**3350**	**4075**
Wagon LXE	LV52	3745	**2500**	**3925**	**4725**
Wagon LX (4WD)	LV52	4040	**2350**	**3750**	**4525**
Wagon LXE (4WD)	LV52	4040	**2850**	**4325**	**5150**
1995 B2300 PICKUP-4 Cyl.					
Base	R12A	2927	**1850**	**3175**	**3800**
SE	R12A	3003	**2000**	**3350**	**4000**
Base Cab Plus	R16A	3197	**2650**	**4100**	**4825**
SE Cab Plus	R16A	3283	**2800**	**4275**	**5000**
Base (4WD)	R13A	3242	**2950**	**4450**	**5200**
1995 B3000 PICKUP-V6					
SE	R12U	3112	**2075**	**3425**	**4075**
SE Cab Plus	R16U		**2875**	**4350**	**5100**
Base Cab Plus (4WD)	R17U	3548	**3825**	**5450**	**6200**
1995 B4000 PICKUP-V6					
SE Cab Plus	R16X	3497	**2975**	**4475**	**5225**
LE Cab Plus	R16X	3552	**3175**	**4700**	**5475**
SE (4WD)	R13X	3545	**3275**	**4825**	**5625**
SE Cab Plus (4WD)	R17X	3829	**4075**	**5725**	**6500**
LE Cab Plus (4WD)	R17X	3884	**4275**	**5950**	**6750**

TRUCKS

MERCEDES-BENZ

BODY TYPE	Model No.	Weight	Trade-In	Retail	High Retail
MERCEDES-BENZ					
2004 M CLASS-V6/V8-4WD					
Utility 4D ML350	AB57	4819	**27275**	**30975**	**32825**
Utility 4D ML500	AB75	4874	**31475**	**35475**	**37450**
Add Sport Appearance Pkg.			**1075**	**1200**	**1200**
Add Bose Stereo System			**425**	**475**	**475**
Add Compact Disc Player (ML350)			**175**	**200**	**200**
Add Navigation System (ML350)			**750**	**850**	**850**
Add Running Boards			**150**	**175**	**175**
Add Theft Recovery System			**100**	**125**	**125**
Deduct W/out Leather Seats			**575**	**575**	**575**
Deduct W/out Power Seat			**275**	**275**	**275**

SEE TRUCK OPTION PAGE FOR ADDITIONAL OPTIONS

BODY TYPE	Model No.	Weight	Trade-In	Retail	High Retail
Deduct W/out Power Sunroof			725	725	725
MERCEDES-BENZ					
2003 M CLASS-V6/V8-4WD					
Utility 4D ML320	AB54	4786	23675	27075	28775
Utility 4D ML350	AB57	4819	24375	27800	29525
Utility 4D ML500	AB75	4874	27375	31125	32975
2003 M CLASS-V8-4WD					
Utility 4D ML55 AMG	AB74	5073	34075	38650	40725
MERCEDES-BENZ OPTIONS					
Add Sport Pkg. (ML320/350/500)			975	1100	1100
Add Bose Stereo System (Std. ML55)			375	425	425
Add Compact Disc Player (ML320/350)			150	175	175
Add Navigation System (ML350)			650	725	725
Add Running Boards			125	150	150
Add Theft Recovery System			75	100	100
Deduct W/out Leather Seats			525	525	525
Deduct W/out Power Seat			250	250	250
Deduct W/out Power Sunroof			675	675	675
MERCEDES-BENZ					
2002 M CLASS-V6/V8-4WD					
Utility 4D ML320	AB54	4730	20875	24100	25700
Utility 4D ML500	AB75	4795	23025	26400	28100
2002 M CLASS-V8-4WD					
Utility 4D ML55 AMG	AB74	4980	29775	34000	35925
MERCEDES-BENZ OPTIONS					
Add Sport Pkg. (ML320/500)			900	1000	1000
Add Bose Stereo System (Std. ML55)			325	375	375
Add Compact Disc Player (ML320)			125	150	150
Add Power Sunroof (Std. ML55)			625	700	700
Add Rear Entertainment System			400	450	450
Add Running Boards			100	125	125
Add Theft Recovery System			75	100	100
Deduct W/out Leather Seats			475	475	475
Deduct W/out Power Seat			225	225	225
MERCEDES-BENZ					
2001 M CLASS-V6/V8-4WD					
Utility 4D ML320	AB54	4320	17175	20100	21575
Utility 4D ML430	AB72	4420	18675	21725	23250
2001 M CLASS-V8-4WD					
Utility 4D ML55 AMG	AB74	4550	24975	28750	30525
MERCEDES-BENZ OPTIONS					
Add Sport Pkg. (ML320/430)			850	950	950
Add Bose Stereo System (Std. ML55)			275	325	325
Add Compact Disc Player (ML320)			125	150	150
Add Power Skyview Top			1125	1275	1275
Add Power Sunroof (Std. ML55)			575	650	650
Add Running Boards			75	100	100
Add Theft Recovery System			50	75	75
Deduct W/out Leather Seats			425	425	425
Deduct W/out Power Seat			200	200	200
MERCEDES-BENZ					
2000 M CLASS-V6/V8-4WD					
Utility 4D ML320	AB54	4586	15075	17775	19150

TRUCKS

BODY TYPE	Model No.	Weight	Trade-In	Retail	High Retail
Utility 4D ML430	AB72	4696	**16175**	**18950**	**20375**
2000 M CLASS-V8-4WD					
Utility 4D ML55 AMG	AB74	4861	**21975**	**25475**	**27125**
MERCEDES-BENZ OPTIONS					
Add Bose Stereo System (Std. ML55)			**225**	**250**	**250**
Add Compact Disc Player (ML320)			**100**	**125**	**125**
Add Power Skyview Top			**1025**	**1150**	**1150**
Add Power Sunroof (Std. ML55)			**525**	**600**	**600**
Add Running Boards			**50**	**75**	**75**
Deduct W/out Leather Seats			**375**	**375**	**375**
Deduct W/out Power Seat			**175**	**175**	**175**
MERCEDES-BENZ					
1999 M CLASS-V6/V8-4WD					
Utility 4D ML320	AB54	4387	**12175**	**14675**	**15950**
Utility 4D ML430	AB72	4552	**13175**	**15750**	**17075**
Add Bose Stereo System			**175**	**200**	**200**
Add Power Skyview Top			**925**	**1050**	**1050**
Add Power Sunroof			**475**	**550**	**550**
Deduct W/out Leather Seats			**325**	**325**	**325**
Deduct W/out Power Seat			**150**	**150**	**150**
MERCEDES-BENZ					
1998 M CLASS-V6-4WD					
Utility 4D ML320	AB54	4322	**11075**	**13425**	**14650**
Add Power Sunroof			**425**	**475**	**475**
Deduct W/out Leather Seats			**275**	**275**	**275**
Deduct W/out Power Seat			**125**	**125**	**125**

MERCURY

BODY TYPE	Model No.	Weight	Trade-In	Retail	High Retail
MERCURY					
2004 MOUNTAINEER-V6					
Wagon	U66	4374	**16475**	**19275**	**20375**
Wagon Luxury	U66		**17175**	**20100**	**21225**
Wagon Premier	U66		**19575**	**22700**	**23875**
Wagon (AWD)	U86	4523	**17550**	**20550**	**21675**
Wagon Luxury (AWD)	U86		**18250**	**21300**	**22450**
Wagon Premier (AWD)	U86		**20650**	**23850**	**25075**
Add 4.6L V8 Engine			**400**	**450**	**450**
Add Audiophile Stereo System (Std. Premier)			**300**	**350**	**350**
Add Leather Seats (Std. Luxury, Premier)			**450**	**500**	**500**
Add Power Sunroof (Std. Premier)			**575**	**650**	**650**
Add Rear Air Conditioning			**200**	**225**	**225**
Add Rear Bucket Seats			**200**	**225**	**225**
Add Rear Entertainment System			**600**	**675**	**675**
Add Running Boards (Std. Luxury, Premier)			**150**	**175**	**175**
Add Theft Recovery System			**100**	**125**	**125**
Deduct W/out 3rd Row Seat			**200**	**200**	**200**
2004 MONTEREY-V6					
Wagon 4D	A20	4434	**15175**	**17875**	**18925**
Wagon 4D Luxury	A20		**18025**	**21025**	**22175**
Wagon 4D Premier	A20		**18475**	**21525**	**22675**

SEE TRUCK OPTION PAGE FOR ADDITIONAL OPTIONS

BODY TYPE	Model No.	Weight	Trade-In	Retail	High Retail
Add Rear Entertainment System			600	675	675
Add Theft Recovery System			100	125	125
MERCURY					
2003 MOUNTAINEER-V6					
Wagon	U66	4328	14675	17325	18350
Wagon Luxury	U66		15550	18275	19325
Wagon Premier	U66		17225	20150	21275
Wagon (AWD)	U86	4490	15700	18425	19500
Wagon Luxury (AWD)	U86		16575	19375	20475
Wagon Premier (AWD)	U86		18250	21275	22425
Add 4.6L V8 Engine			350	400	400
Add Leather Seats (Std. Luxury, Premier)			400	450	450
Add Power Sunroof (Std. Premier)			525	600	600
Add Rear Air Conditioning			150	175	175
Add Rear Entertainment System			500	575	575
Add Running Boards (Std. Luxury, Premier)			125	150	150
Add Theft Recovery System			75	100	100
Deduct W/out 3rd Row Seat			175	175	175
MERCURY					
2002 MOUNTAINEER-V6					
Wagon	U66	4170	12675	15225	16225
Wagon Luxury	U66		13175	15750	16775
Wagon (AWD)	U86	4410	13675	16300	17325
Wagon Luxury (AWD)	U86		14175	16825	17875
Add 4.6L V8 Engine			300	350	350
Add Audiophile Stereo System			200	225	225
Add Leather Seats (Std. Luxury)			350	400	400
Add Power Sunroof			475	550	550
Add Rear Air Conditioning			150	175	175
Add Running Boards			100	125	125
Add Theft Recovery System			75	100	100
2002 VILLAGER-V6					
Wagon	V11	3997	8575	10700	11650
Wagon Sport	V12	4050	10700	13000	13925
Wagon Estate	V14	4050	11975	14450	15425
Add Aluminum/Alloy Wheels (Base)			225	250	250
Add AutoVision Entertainment System			400	450	450
Add Compact Disc Player			75	100	100
Add Leather Seats (Std. Estate)			350	400	400
Add Power Seat (Base Wagon)			150	175	175
Add Power Sunroof			475	550	550
Add Rear Air Conditioning (Base Wagon)			150	175	175
Add Theft Recovery System			75	100	100
MERCURY					
2001 MOUNTAINEER-V6					
Wagon	U66	4200	8675	10825	11775
Wagon (4WD/AWD)	U76/86	4450	9575	11800	12700
Add 5.0L V8 Engine			250	300	300
Add Compact Disc Player			50	75	75
Add Leather Seats			300	350	350
Add MACH Stereo System			150	175	175
Add Power Seat			125	150	150

TRUCKS

BODY TYPE	Model No.	Weight	Trade-In	Retail	High Retail
Add Power Sunroof			**425**	**475**	**475**
Add Theft Recovery System			**50**	**75**	**75**
2001 VILLAGER-V6					
Wagon	V11	3997	**7150**	**9125**	**10000**
Wagon Sport	V12	4050	**8950**	**11100**	**11975**
Wagon Estate	V14	4050	**10000**	**12250**	**13150**
Add Aluminum/Alloy Wheels (Base)			**175**	**200**	**200**
Add AutoVision Entertainment System			**350**	**400**	**400**
Add Compact Disc Player			**50**	**75**	**75**
Add Leather Seats (Std. Estate)			**300**	**350**	**350**
Add Power Seat (Base Wagon)			**125**	**150**	**150**
Add Power Sunroof			**425**	**475**	**475**
Add Rear Air Conditioning (Base Wagon)			**125**	**150**	**150**
Add Theft Recovery System			**50**	**75**	**75**
MERCURY					
2000 MOUNTAINEER-V6					
Wagon	U66	4050	**6550**	**8450**	**9325**
Wagon (4WD/AWD)	U76/86	4250	**7350**	**9375**	**10250**
Add 5.0L V8 Engine			**225**	**250**	**250**
Add Compact Disc Player			**50**	**75**	**75**
Add Leather Seats			**250**	**300**	**300**
Add MACH Stereo System			**100**	**125**	**125**
Add Power Seat			**100**	**125**	**125**
Add Power Sunroof			**375**	**425**	**425**
2000 VILLAGER-V6					
Wagon	V11	3847	**6025**	**7875**	**8800**
Wagon Sport	V12	3962	**7225**	**9225**	**10100**
Wagon Estate	V14	3962	**8025**	**10100**	**11025**
Add Aluminum/Alloy Wheels (Base)			**125**	**150**	**150**
Add Compact Disc Player			**50**	**75**	**75**
Add Leather Seats (Std. Estate)			**250**	**300**	**300**
Add Power Seat (Base Wagon)			**100**	**125**	**125**
Add Power Sunroof			**375**	**425**	**425**
Add Rear Air Conditioning (Base Wagon)			**100**	**125**	**125**
Add Rear Entertainment System			**250**	**300**	**300**
MERCURY					
1999 MOUNTAINEER-V6					
Wagon	U52	3876	**5550**	**7350**	**8250**
Wagon (4WD/AWD)	U54/U55	4113	**6325**	**8225**	**9075**
Add 5.0L V8 Engine			**225**	**250**	**250**
Add Leather Seats			**225**	**250**	**250**
Add MACH Stereo System			**75**	**100**	**100**
Add Power Seat			**75**	**100**	**100**
Add Power Sunroof			**325**	**375**	**375**
1999 VILLAGER-V6					
Wagon	V11	4003	**5525**	**7325**	**8200**
Wagon Sport	V11	4003	**6525**	**8450**	**9325**
Wagon Estate	V11	4003	**6925**	**8875**	**9775**
Add Aluminum/Alloy Wheels (Base)			**75**	**100**	**100**
Add Leather Seats			**225**	**250**	**250**
Add Power Seat			**75**	**100**	**100**
Add Power Sunroof			**325**	**375**	**375**

SEE TRUCK OPTION PAGE FOR ADDITIONAL OPTIONS

BODY TYPE	Model No.	Weight	Trade-In	Retail	High Retail
Add Rear Air Conditioning			75	100	100
MERCURY					
1998 MOUNTAINEER-V6					
Wagon	U52	4139	4725	6450	7350
Wagon (4WD/AWD)	U54/U55	4374	5400	7200	8075
Add 5.0L V8 Engine			200	225	225
Add Leather Seats			175	200	200
Add MACH Stereo System			50	75	75
Add Power Seat			50	75	75
Add Power Sunroof			275	325	325
1998 VILLAGER-V6					
Van GS	V14		3675	5275	6100
Wagon GS	V11	4003	4275	5950	6825
Wagon LS	V11	4003	5075	6825	7750
Wagon Nautica	V11	4003	5350	7125	8000
Add 3rd Row Seat (GS)			100	125	125
Add Aluminum/Alloy Wheels (Std. Nautica)			50	75	75
Add Leather Seats (Std. Nautica)			175	200	200
Add Power Seat			50	75	75
Add Power Sunroof			275	325	325
Add Rear Air Conditioning			50	75	75
Add Rear Bucket Seats (Std. Nautica)			50	75	75
Deduct W/out Air Conditioning			400	400	400
Deduct W/out Cruise Control			50	50	50
Deduct W/out Power Windows			50	50	50
MERCURY					
1997 MOUNTAINEER-V8					
Wagon	U52	4143	3950	5575	6425
Wagon (AWD)	U55	4378	4550	6250	7125
Add Leather Seats			150	175	175
Add Power Seat			50	75	75
Add Power Sunroof			200	225	225
1997 VILLAGER-V6					
Van GS	V14		3175	4700	5575
Wagon GS	V11	3871	3525	5100	5900
Wagon LS	V11	3964	4125	5775	6650
Wagon Nautica	V11		4425	6125	7000
Add Leather Seats (Std. Nautica)			150	175	175
Add Power Seat			50	75	75
Add Power Sunroof			200	225	225
Deduct W/out Air Conditioning			250	250	250
Deduct W/out Cruise Control			50	50	50
Deduct W/out Power Windows			50	50	50
MERCURY					
1996 VILLAGER-V6					
Van GS	V14	3677	2650	4100	4900
Wagon GS	V11	3805	3000	4500	5350
Wagon LS	V11	3937	3550	5125	5925
Wagon Nautica	V11	3937	3800	5400	6225
Add Power Sunroof			150	175	175
Deduct W/out Air Conditioning			150	150	150

BODY TYPE	Model No.	Weight	Trade-In	Retail	High Retail
MERCURY					
1995 VILLAGER-V6					
Van GS	V14		**2025**	**3375**	**4100**
Wagon GS	V11	3870	**2225**	**3600**	**4350**
Wagon LS	V11	3870	**2725**	**4175**	**4975**
Wagon Nautica	V11	4015	**2925**	**4400**	**5225**

MITSUBISHI

BODY TYPE	Model No.	Weight	Trade-In	Retail	High Retail
MITSUBISHI					
2004 OUTLANDER-I4-AWD					
Utility 4D LS (2WD)	X31	3240	**12325**	**14825**	**15600**
Utility 4D LS	Z31	3461	**13450**	**16025**	**16850**
Utility 4D XLS (2WD)	X41	3240	**12825**	**15375**	**16175**
Utility 4D XLS	Z41	3461	**14700**	**17375**	**18175**
Add Aluminum/Alloy Wheels (Std. XLS)			**300**	**350**	**350**
Add Infinity Stereo (Std. XLS AWD)			**250**	**300**	**300**
Add Leather Seats			**350**	**400**	**400**
Add Power Sunroof (Std. XLS AWD)			**525**	**600**	**600**
Add Theft Recovery System			**100**	**125**	**125**
2004 ENDEAVOR-V6-AWD					
Utility 4D LS (2WD)	M21	3847	**15425**	**18125**	**19175**
Utility 4D LS	N21	4079	**16350**	**19125**	**20200**
Utility 4D XLS (2WD)	M31	3902	**16475**	**19250**	**20350**
Utility 4D XLS	N31	4134	**17400**	**20375**	**21500**
Utility 4D Limited (2WD)	M41	3935	**21225**	**24450**	**25675**
Utility 4D Limited	N41	4156	**22150**	**25450**	**26700**
Add Leather Seats (Std. Limited)			**450**	**500**	**500**
Add Power Sunroof (Ex. Limited)			**575**	**650**	**650**
Add Rear Entertainment System			**600**	**675**	**675**
Add Running Boards			**150**	**175**	**175**
Add Theft Recovery System			**100**	**125**	**125**
Deduct W/out Power Sunroof (Limited)			**575**	**575**	**575**
2004 MONTERO SPORT-V6-4WD					
Utility Sport LS (2WD)	S21	3970	**13725**	**16325**	**17350**
Utility Sport LS	T21	4240	**15050**	**17750**	**18800**
Utility Sport XLS (2WD)	S31		**14725**	**17400**	**18425**
Utility Sport XLS	T31		**16050**	**18800**	**19875**
2004 MONTERO-V6-4WD					
Utility 4D Limited	W51	4718	**22750**	**26075**	**27350**
MONTERO SPORT/MONTERO OPTIONS					
Add Infinity Stereo (XLS)			**300**	**350**	**350**
Add Leather Seats (Std. Limited)			**450**	**500**	**500**
Add Power Sunroof (XLS)			**575**	**650**	**650**
Add Rear Entertainment System			**600**	**675**	**675**
Add Running Boards (LS)			**150**	**175**	**175**
Add Theft Recovery System			**100**	**125**	**125**
Deduct W/out Cruise Control			**200**	**200**	**200**
Deduct W/out Power Sunroof (Limited)			**575**	**575**	**575**
MITSUBISHI					
2003 OUTLANDER-I4-AWD					
Utility 4D LS (2WD)	X31	3240	**10825**	**13150**	**13900**

TRUCKS

SEE TRUCK OPTION PAGE FOR ADDITIONAL OPTIONS

BODY TYPE	Model No.	Weight	Trade-In	Retail	High Retail
Utility 4D LS	Z31	3461	**12200**	**14700**	**15475**
Utility 4D XLS (2WD)	X41		**11300**	**13700**	**14450**
Utility 4D XLS	Z41		**12425**	**14950**	**15725**
Add Aluminum/Alloy Wheels (LS 2WD)			**250**	**300**	**300**
Add Infinity Stereo System			**200**	**225**	**225**
Add Leather Seats			**300**	**350**	**350**
Add Power Sunroof			**475**	**550**	**550**
Add Theft Recovery System			**75**	**100**	**100**
2003 MONTERO SPORT-V6-4WD					
Utility Sport ES (2WD)	S21	3835	**10500**	**12775**	**13675**
Utility Sport ES	T21	4105	**11725**	**14150**	**15100**
Utility Sport LS (2WD)	S21	3945	**12000**	**14475**	**15450**
Utility Sport LS	T21	4215	**13225**	**15800**	**16825**
Utility Sport XLS (2WD)	S31	3970	**13300**	**15875**	**16900**
Utility Sport XLS	T31	4240	**14525**	**17175**	**18200**
Utility Sport Limited (2WD)	S41	4065	**15500**	**18225**	**19275**
Utility Sport Limited	T41	4340	**16725**	**19525**	**20625**
2003 MONTERO-V6-4WD					
Utility 4D XLS	W31	4718	**16375**	**19150**	**20225**
Utility 4D Limited	W51	4784	**19675**	**22800**	**24000**
Utility 4D 20th Anniversary	W61	4784	**20375**	**23550**	**24750**
MONTERO SPORT/MONTERO OPTIONS					
Add Aluminum/Alloy Wheels (ES)			**275**	**325**	**325**
Add Infinity Stereo (XLS)			**250**	**300**	**300**
Add Leather Seats (Std. Limited, Annv)			**400**	**450**	**450**
Add Power Sunroof (Std. Limited, Annv)			**525**	**600**	**600**
Add Rear Air Conditioning (Std. Anniversary)			**175**	**200**	**200**
Add Running Boards (ES)			**125**	**150**	**150**
Add Theft Recovery System			**75**	**100**	**100**
MITSUBISHI					
2002 MONTERO SPORT-V6-4WD					
Utility Sport ES (2WD)	S21	3835	**8650**	**10775**	**11725**
Utility Sport ES	T21	4105	**9950**	**12200**	**13100**
Utility Sport LS (2WD)	S21	3945	**10150**	**12400**	**13300**
Utility Sport LS	T21	4215	**11450**	**13875**	**14825**
Utility Sport XLS (2WD)	S31	3970	**11300**	**13700**	**14650**
Utility Sport XLS	T31	4240	**12600**	**15150**	**16150**
Utility Sport Limited (2WD)	S41	4065	**13050**	**15600**	**16600**
Utility Sport Limited	T41	4340	**14350**	**17000**	**18050**
2002 MONTERO-V6-4WD					
Utility 4D XLS	W31	4600	**13975**	**16575**	**17625**
Utility 4D Limited	W51	4735	**17025**	**19900**	**21000**
MITSUBISHI OPTIONS					
Add Aluminum/Alloy Wheels (ES)			**225**	**250**	**250**
Add Infinity Stereo (XLS)			**200**	**225**	**225**
Add Leather Seats (Std. Limited)			**350**	**400**	**400**
Add Power Sunroof (Std. Limited)			**475**	**550**	**550**
Add Rear Air Conditioning (Montero)			**150**	**175**	**175**
Add Running Boards (ES)			**100**	**125**	**125**
Add Theft Recovery System			**75**	**100**	**100**
MITSUBISHI					
2001 MONTERO SPORT-V6-4WD					
Utility Sport ES (2WD)	S21	3835	**7250**	**9225**	**10100**
Utility Sport ES	T21	4095	**8500**	**10625**	**11575**

BODY TYPE	Model No.	Weight	Trade-In	Retail	High Retail
Utility Sport LS (2WD)	S21	3945	**8750**	**10875**	**11825**
Utility Sport LS	T21	4205	**10000**	**12250**	**13150**
Utility Sport XLS (2WD)	S31	3960	**9350**	**11525**	**12425**
Utility Sport XLS	T31	4220	**10600**	**12875**	**13800**
Utility Sport 3.5 XS (2WD)	S31	4010	**9400**	**11575**	**12475**
Utility Sport 3.5 XS	T31	4275	**10650**	**12925**	**13850**
Utility Sport Limited (2WD)	S41	4065	**11200**	**13575**	**14525**
Utility Sport Limited	T41	4330	**12450**	**14975**	**15950**
2001 MONTERO-V6-4WD					
Utility 4D XLS	W31	4540	**12300**	**14800**	**15775**
Utility 4D Limited	W51	4675	**15200**	**17900**	**18950**
MITSUBISHI OPTIONS					
Add Infinity Stereo (Sport XLS)			**150**	**175**	**175**
Add Leather Seats (Std. Limited)			**300**	**350**	**350**
Add Power Sunroof (Std. Limited)			**425**	**475**	**475**
Add Rear Air Conditioning (Montero)			**125**	**150**	**150**
Add Running Boards (ES)			**75**	**100**	**100**
Add Theft Recovery System			**50**	**75**	**75**
MITSUBISHI					
2000 MONTERO SPORT-V6-4WD					
Utility Sport ES (2WD)	S21	3810	**6475**	**8400**	**9275**
Utility Sport LS (2WD)	S31	3835	**7775**	**9825**	**10725**
Utility Sport LS	T31	4075	**9050**	**11200**	**12075**
Utility Sport XLS (2WD)	S31	3835	**8350**	**10450**	**11375**
Utility Sport XLS	T31	4075	**9625**	**11825**	**12725**
Utility Sport Limited (2WD)	S41	4020	**9575**	**11800**	**12700**
Utility Sport Limited	T41	4260	**10850**	**13175**	**14100**
2000 MONTERO-V6-4WD					
Utility 4D	R51	4520	**9650**	**11875**	**12775**
Utility 4D Endeavor	R51	4645	**10900**	**13250**	**14175**
MITSUBISHI OPTIONS					
Add Infinity Stereo (Sport XLS)			**100**	**125**	**125**
Add Leather Seats (Std. Endeavor)			**250**	**300**	**300**
Add Power Sunroof (Std. Endeavor, Limited)			**375**	**425**	**425**
Add Running Boards (LS)			**50**	**75**	**75**
MITSUBISHI					
1999 MONTERO SPORT-V6-4WD					
Sport ES (2WD, 4 Cyl., 5 Spd.)	S21	3510	**4525**	**6225**	**7100**
Utility Sport LS (2WD)	S31	3755	**6725**	**8650**	**9525**
Utility Sport LS	T31	4005	**7650**	**9700**	**10600**
Utility Sport XLS (2WD)	S31	3755	**7275**	**9275**	**10150**
Utility Sport XLS	T31	4005	**8200**	**10300**	**11225**
Utility Sport Limited (2WD)	S41	3955	**8375**	**10475**	**11400**
Utility Sport Limited	T41	4145	**9300**	**11500**	**12400**
1999 MONTERO-V6-4WD					
Utility 4D	R51	4431	**8350**	**10450**	**11375**
MITSUBISHI OPTIONS					
Add Infinity Stereo (Std. Spt Ltd.)			**75**	**100**	**100**
Add Leather Seats (Std. Sport Ltd.)			**225**	**250**	**250**
Add Power Seat			**75**	**100**	**100**
Add Power Sunroof (Std. Sport Ltd.)			**325**	**375**	**375**
Deduct W/o Automatic Trans. (Ex. Sport ES)			**325**	**325**	**325**
Deduct W/out Air Conditioning			**450**	**450**	**450**

SEE TRUCK OPTION PAGE FOR ADDITIONAL OPTIONS

BODY TYPE	Model No.	Weight	Trade-In	Retail	High Retail
MITSUBISHI					
1998 MONTERO SPORT-V6-4WD					
Sport ES (2WD, 4 Cyl., 5 Spd.)	S21	3500	**3600**	**5175**	**5975**
Utility Sport LS (2WD)	S31	3755	**5775**	**7600**	**8500**
Utility Sport LS	T31	3980	**6750**	**8675**	**9550**
Utility Sport XLS (2WD)	S41	3865	**6375**	**8275**	**9125**
Utility Sport XLS	T41	4110	**7350**	**9350**	**10225**
1998 MONTERO-V6-4WD					
Utility 4D	R51	4431	**7700**	**9725**	**10625**
MITSUBISHI OPTIONS					
Add Infinity Stereo (Std. XLS)			**50**	**75**	**75**
Add Leather Seats (Std. XLS)			**175**	**200**	**200**
Add Power Seat			**50**	**75**	**75**
Add Power Sunroof (Std. XLS)			**275**	**325**	**325**
Deduct W/o Automatic Trans. (Ex. Sport ES)			**275**	**275**	**275**
Deduct W/o Cruise (Ex. Sport ES)			**50**	**50**	**50**
Deduct W/o Power Windows (Ex. Sport ES)			**50**	**50**	**50**
Deduct W/out Air Conditioning			**400**	**400**	**400**
MITSUBISHI					
1997 MONTERO SPORT-V6-4WD					
Sport ES (2WD, 4 Cyl., 5 Spd.)	S21	3435	**2700**	**4150**	**4950**
Utility Sport LS (2WD)	S31	3735	**4875**	**6625**	**7525**
Utility Sport LS	T31	3955	**5650**	**7475**	**8375**
Utility Sport XLS	T41	4020	**6100**	**7975**	**8900**
1997 MONTERO-V6-4WD					
Utility 4D LS	R41	4385	**5650**	**7475**	**8375**
Utility 4D SR	R51	4440	**6500**	**8425**	**9300**
MITSUBISHI OPTIONS					
Add Leather Seats (Std. XLS)			**150**	**175**	**175**
Add Power Seat (Std. SR)			**50**	**75**	**75**
Add Power Sunroof (Std. SR, XLS)			**200**	**225**	**225**
Deduct W/o Automatic Trans. (Ex. Sport ES)			**175**	**175**	**175**
Deduct W/o Cruise (Ex. Sport ES)			**50**	**50**	**50**
Deduct W/o Power Windows (Ex. Sport ES)			**50**	**50**	**50**
Deduct W/out Air Conditioning			**250**	**250**	**250**
MITSUBISHI					
1996 MONTERO-V6-4WD					
Utility 4D LS	R41	4290	**4450**	**6150**	**7025**
Utility 4D SR	R51	4465	**5150**	**6925**	**7850**
Add Power Sunroof (Std. SR)			**150**	**175**	**175**
Deduct W/out Air Conditioning			**150**	**150**	**150**
Deduct W/out Automatic Trans.			**125**	**125**	**125**
1996 PICKUP-4 Cyl.-5 Spd.					
Mighty Max	S21	2600	**1750**	**3050**	**3650**
Add Automatic Trans.			**100**	**125**	**125**
Deduct W/out Air Conditioning			**100**	**100**	**100**
MITSUBISHI					
1995 MONTERO-V6-4WD					
Utility 4D LS	R41	4275	**3400**	**4950**	**5850**
Utility 4D SR	R51	4440	**3925**	**5550**	**6400**
1995 PICKUP-4 Cyl.					
Mighty Max	S21	2600	**1550**	**2800**	**3425**

BODY TYPE	Model No.	Weight	Trade-In	Retail	High Retail
NISSAN					
NISSAN					
2004 PATHFINDER-V6-4WD					
Utility 4D SE (2WD)	R09X	3871	19300	22400	23575
Utility 4D LE (2WD)	R09X	3985	21450	24700	25950
Utility 4D SE	R09Y	4131	20375	23550	24750
Utility 4D LE	R09Y	4304	22525	25850	27125
Add Bose Stereo System (Std. LE)			300	350	350
Add Leather Seats (Std. LE)			450	500	500
Add Power Seat (Std. LE)			200	225	225
Add Power Sunroof (Std. LE)			575	650	650
Add Rear Entertainment System			600	675	675
Add Theft Recovery System			100	125	125
2004 MURANO-V6-AWD					
Utility SL (2WD)	AZ08T	3828	23275	26400	27700
Utility SE (2WD)	AZ08T	3832	24075	27250	28550
Utility SL	AZ08W	3960	24450	27650	28950
Utility SE	AZ08W	3964	25250	28500	29825
Add Touring Pkg			500	575	575
Add Bose Stereo System			300	350	350
Add Leather Seats			450	500	500
Add Navigation System			600	675	675
Add Power Sunroof			575	650	650
Add Rear Entertainment System			600	675	675
Add Theft Recovery System			100	125	125
2004 ARMADA-V8-4WD					
Utility 4D SE (2WD)	AA08A	5013	25025	28500	30000
Utility 4D SE Off-Road (2WD)	AA08A		26825	30425	31975
Utility 4D LE (2WD)	AA08A	5051	27225	30925	32500
Utility 4D SE	AA08B	5290	26750	30325	31875
Utility 4D SE Off-Road	AA08B		28550	32375	34000
Utility 4D LE	AA08B	5328	28950	32800	34425
Add Bose Stereo System (SE Base)			350	400	400
Add Leather Seats (SE Base)			525	600	600
Add Navigation System			650	725	725
Add Power Sunroof			625	700	700
Add Rear Bucket Seats			200	225	225
Add Rear Entertainment System			600	675	675
Add Theft Recovery System			100	125	125
2004 QUEST-V6					
Van 3.5 S	BV28	4012	17575	20550	21675
Van 3.5 SL	BV28	4061	18575	21625	22775
Van 3.5 SE	BV28	4175	21875	25150	26400
Add Aluminum/Alloy Wheels (S)			325	375	375
Add Leather Seats (Std. SE)			450	500	500
Add Navigation System			600	675	675
Add Rear Entertainment System			600	675	675
Add Running Boards			150	175	175
Add Skyview Roof Pkg. (Std. SE)			825	925	925
Add Theft Recovery System			100	125	125

SEE TRUCK OPTION PAGE FOR ADDITIONAL OPTIONS

BODY TYPE	Model No.	Weight	Trade-In	Retail	High Retail
Deduct W/out 3rd Row Seat			200	200	200
Deduct W/out Rear Bucket Seats			200	200	200
2004 FRONTIER PICKUP-V6-5 Spd.					
King Cab Standard (4 Cyl.)	DD26T		11300	13725	14475
King Cab XE (4 Cyl.)	DD26T	3240	12025	14500	15275
King Cab XE	ED26T	3647	13325	15900	16700
King Cab XE (4WD)	ED26Y	3932	15675	18425	19250
King Cab SVE (4WD)	MD26Y	3990	17325	20300	21175
King Cab SC (4WD, AT)	MD26Y	4025	18200	21225	22100
2004 FRONTIER CREW CAB-V6					
Crew Cab XE (5 Spd.)	ED2(7/9)(T/X)	3821	14675	17350	18150
Crew Cab LE	ED2(7/9)(T/X)		16675	19475	20325
Crew Cab SC	MD2(7/9)(T/X)	3934	16950	19825	20675
Crew XE (4WD, 5 Spd.)	ED2(7/9)Y	4093	17025	19900	20750
Crew Cab SVE (4WD)	MD2(7/9)Y	4229	18750	21825	22725
Crew Cab SC (4WD)	MD29Y	4352	19300	22400	23300
FRONTIER OPTIONS					
Add Aluminum/Alloy Wheels (Standard, King Cab XE)			300	350	350
Add Automatic Trans. (Std. LE, SC, Crew SVE)			475	550	550
Add CD Player (Standard, King Cab XE)			100	125	125
Add Cruise Control (XE)			175	200	200
Add Leather Seats (Std. LE)			350	400	400
Add Power Door Locks (XE)			150	175	175
Add Power Windows (XE)			175	200	200
Add Rockford Fosgate Stereo			250	300	300
Add Running Boards (Std. LE, SC Crew)			150	175	175
Add Theft Recovery System			100	125	125
Add Tilt Steering Wheel (XE)			125	150	150
Deduct W/out Air Conditioning			575	575	575
2004 TITAN PICKUP KING CAB-V8					
King Cab XE	AA06A	4966	17875	20900	22250
King Cab SE	AA06A		18950	22050	23375
King Cab LE	AA06A		21450	24700	26100
King Cab XE (4WD)	AA06B	5287	20875	24100	25475
King Cab SE (4WD)	AA06B		21950	25250	26675
King Cab LE (4WD)	AA06B		24450	27900	29375
2004 TITAN PICKUP CREW CAB-V8					
Crew Cab XE	AA07A	5019	20075	23225	24575
Crew Cab SE	AA07A		20700	23900	25275
Crew Cab LE	AA07A		23200	26575	28025
Crew Cab XE (4WD)	AA07B	5341	23075	26450	27900
Crew Cab SE (4WD)	AA07B		23700	27100	28550
Crew Cab LE (4WD)	AA07B		26200	29750	31275
TITAN OPTIONS					
Add Off-Road Pkg.			350	400	400
Add Aluminum/Alloy Wheels (XE)			375	425	425
Add Navigation System			650	725	725
Add Power Seat (Std. LE)			225	250	250
Add Power Sunroof			625	700	700
Add Rear Entertainment System			600	675	675
Add Rockford Fosgate Stereo (Std. LE)			350	400	400
Add Running Boards (Std. LE)			150	175	175
Add Theft Recovery System			100	125	125

BODY TYPE	Model No.	Weight	Trade-In	Retail	High Retail
2004 XTERRA-V6					
Utility 4D XE (4 Cyl., 5 Spd.)	DD28T	3589	**13300**	**15875**	**16900**
Utility 4D XE	ED28T	3760	**15000**	**17675**	**18725**
Utility 4D SE	ED28T	3857	**15825**	**18575**	**19650**
Utility 4D SE SC	MD28T	3911	**17150**	**20075**	**21200**
Utility 4D XE (4WD)	ED28Y	4046	**16075**	**18825**	**19900**
Utility 4D SE (4WD)	ED28Y	4156	**16900**	**19725**	**20825**
Utility 4D SE SC (4WD)	MD28Y	4200	**18225**	**21250**	**22400**
Add Leather Seats			**450**	**500**	**500**
Add Rockford Fosgate Stereo (Std. SE)			**300**	**350**	**350**
Add Running Boards (4 Cyl.)			**150**	**175**	**175**
Add Sunroof			**325**	**375**	**375**
Add Theft Recovery System			**100**	**125**	**125**
Deduct W/out Auto Trans. (Ex. 4 Cyl.)			**575**	**575**	**575**
Deduct W/out Cruise Control			**200**	**200**	**200**
Deduct W/out Power Locks			**175**	**175**	**175**
Deduct W/out Power Windows			**200**	**200**	**200**
Deduct W/out Tilt Steering Wheel			**150**	**150**	**150**
NISSAN					
2003 PATHFINDER-V6-4WD					
Utility 4D SE (2WD)	R09X	3871	**16350**	**19125**	**20200**
Utility 4D LE (2WD)	R09X	3985	**18150**	**21175**	**22325**
Utility 4D SE	R09Y	4131	**17375**	**20350**	**21475**
Utility 4D LE	R09Y	4304	**19175**	**22275**	**23450**
Add Bose Stereo System (Std. LE)			**250**	**300**	**300**
Add Leather Seats (Std. LE)			**400**	**450**	**450**
Add Power Seat (Std. LE)			**175**	**200**	**200**
Add Power Sunroof (Std. LE)			**525**	**600**	**600**
Add Rear Entertainment System			**500**	**575**	**575**
Add Theft Recovery System			**75**	**100**	**100**
2003 MURANO-V6-AWD					
Utility SL (2WD)	AZ08T	3801	**21975**	**25000**	**26250**
Utility SE (2WD)	AZ08T	3806	**22775**	**25900**	**27175**
Utility SL	AZ08W	3955	**23075**	**26200**	**27475**
Utility SE	AZ08W	3960	**23875**	**27050**	**28350**
Add Bose Stereo System			**250**	**300**	**300**
Add Leather Seats			**400**	**450**	**450**
Add Navigation System			**500**	**575**	**575**
Add Power Sunroof			**525**	**600**	**600**
Add Rear Entertainment System			**500**	**575**	**575**
Add Theft Recovery System			**75**	**100**	**100**
2003 FRONTIER PICKUP-V6-5 Spd.					
King Cab Standard (4 Cyl.)	DD26T		**10150**	**12400**	**13125**
King Cab XE (4 Cyl.)	DD26T	3240	**10875**	**13200**	**13950**
King Cab XE	ED26T	3647	**11875**	**14325**	**15100**
King Cab SE (AT)	ED26T	3692	**13675**	**16300**	**17125**
King Cab SC	MD26T	3692	**13750**	**16375**	**17200**
King Cab XE (4WD)	ED26Y	3932	**14225**	**16875**	**17700**
King Cab SVE (4WD)	MD26Y	3990	**15700**	**18450**	**19275**
King Cab SE (4WD, AT)	ED26Y	4025	**16025**	**18800**	**19650**
King Cab SC (4WD)	MD26Y	3990	**16100**	**18875**	**19725**
2003 FRONTIER CREW CAB-V6					
Crew Cab XE (5 Spd.)	ED2(7/9)(T/X)	3821	**13100**	**15675**	**16475**
Crew Cab SE	ED2(7/9)(T/X)	3883	**14575**	**17250**	**18050**

SEE TRUCK OPTION PAGE FOR ADDITIONAL OPTIONS

BODY TYPE	Model No.	Weight	Trade-In	Retail	High Retail
Crew Cab SC	MD2(7/9)(T/X)	3934	**15200**	**17900**	**18725**
Crew XE (4WD, 5 Spd.)	ED2(7/9)Y	4093	**15450**	**18175**	**19000**
Crew Cab SVE (4WD)	MD2(7/9)Y	4229	**17025**	**19900**	**20750**
Crew Cab SE (4WD)	ED2(7/9)Y	4211	**17625**	**20625**	**21500**
Crew Cab SC (4WD)	MD2(7/9)Y	4229	**17550**	**20550**	**21425**
FRONTIER OPTIONS					
Add Aluminum/Alloy Wheels (Standard, King Cab XE)			**250**	**300**	**300**
Add Automatic Trans. (Std. SE, Crew SVE/SC)			**425**	**475**	**475**
Add CD Player (Standard, King Cab XE)			**75**	**100**	**100**
Add Cruise Control (XE)			**150**	**175**	**175**
Add Leather Seats (Std. Crew SE 4WD)			**300**	**350**	**350**
Add Power Door Locks (XE)			**125**	**150**	**150**
Add Power Windows (XE)			**150**	**175**	**175**
Add Rockford Fosgate Stereo (Std. Crew SE 4WD)			**200**	**225**	**225**
Add Running Boards (Std. SE, Crew SC)			**125**	**150**	**150**
Add Sunroof (Std. Crew SE 4WD)			**225**	**275**	**275**
Add Theft Recovery System			**75**	**100**	**100**
Add Tilt Steering Wheel (XE)			**100**	**125**	**125**
Deduct W/out Air Conditioning			**525**	**525**	**525**
2003 XTERRA-V6					
Utility 4D XE (4 Cyl., 5 Spd.)	DD28T	3589	**12425**	**14950**	**15925**
Utility 4D XE	ED28T	3760	**14025**	**16650**	**17700**
Utility 4D SE	ED28T	3857	**14775**	**17450**	**18475**
Utility 4D SE SC	MD28T	3911	**16100**	**18875**	**19950**
Utility 4D XE (4WD)	ED28Y	4046	**15050**	**17750**	**18800**
Utility 4D SE (4WD)	ED28Y	4156	**15800**	**18550**	**19625**
Utility 4D SE SC (4WD)	MD28Y	4200	**17125**	**20075**	**21200**
Add Leather Seats			**400**	**450**	**450**
Add Rockford Fosgate Stereo (Std. SE)			**250**	**300**	**300**
Add Running Boards (4 Cyl.)			**125**	**150**	**150**
Add Sunroof			**275**	**325**	**325**
Add Theft Recovery System			**75**	**100**	**100**
Deduct W/out Auto Trans. (Ex. 4 Cyl.)			**525**	**525**	**525**
Deduct W/out Cruise Control			**175**	**175**	**175**
Deduct W/out Power Locks			**150**	**150**	**150**
Deduct W/out Power Windows			**175**	**175**	**175**
Deduct W/out Tilt Steering Wheel			**125**	**125**	**125**
NISSAN					
2002 PATHFINDER-V6-4WD					
Utility 4D SE (2WD)	R09X	3871	**14175**	**16825**	**17875**
Utility 4D LE (2WD)	R09X	3985	**15375**	**18100**	**19150**
Utility 4D SE	R09Y	4131	**15175**	**17875**	**18925**
Utility 4D LE	R09Y	4304	**16375**	**19175**	**20275**
Add Bose Stereo System (Std. LE)			**200**	**225**	**225**
Add Leather Seats			**350**	**400**	**400**
Add Navigation System			**400**	**450**	**450**
Add Power Seat			**150**	**175**	**175**
Add Power Sunroof (Std. LE)			**475**	**550**	**550**
Add Rear Entertainment System			**400**	**450**	**450**
Add Theft Recovery System			**75**	**100**	**100**
Deduct W/out Automatic Trans.			**475**	**475**	**475**
2002 FRONTIER PICKUP-V6-5 Spd.					
King Cab Standard (4 Cyl.)	DD26S		**8950**	**11100**	**11825**
King Cab XE (4 Cyl.)	DD26S	3196	**9650**	**11850**	**12600**

BODY TYPE	Model No.	Weight	Trade-In	Retail	High Retail
King Cab XE	ED26T	3608	**10550**	**12825**	**13550**
King Cab SE (AT)	ED26T	3687	**11775**	**14200**	**14975**
King Cab SC	MD26T	3718	**12350**	**14850**	**15625**
King Cab XE (4WD)	ED26Y	3885	**12900**	**15450**	**16250**
King Cab SE (4WD, AT)	ED26Y	3989	**14125**	**16750**	**17575**
King Cab SC (4WD)	MD26Y	4026	**14700**	**17350**	**18150**
2002 FRONTIER CREW CAB-V6					
Crew Cab XE (5 Spd.)	ED2(7/9)(T/X)	3780	**11775**	**14200**	**14975**
Crew Cab SE	ED2(7/9)(T/X)	3870	**13075**	**15625**	**16425**
Crew Cab SC	MD2(7/9)(T/X)	3907	**13675**	**16275**	**17100**
Crew XE (4WD, 5 Spd.)	ED2(7/9)Y	4048	**14125**	**16750**	**17575**
Crew Cab SE (4WD)	ED2(7/9)Y	4163	**15425**	**18125**	**18950**
Crew Cab SC (4WD)	MD2(7/9)Y	4221	**16025**	**18775**	**19625**
FRONTIER OPTIONS					
Add Aluminum/Alloy Wheels (Standard, King Cab XE)			**200**	**225**	**225**
Add Automatic Trans. (Std. SE, Crew SC)			**375**	**425**	**425**
Add CD Player (Standard, King Cab XE)			**75**	**100**	**100**
Add Cruise Control (Std. SC, Crew SE)			**125**	**150**	**150**
Add Leather Seats			**250**	**300**	**300**
Add Power Door Locks (Std. SC, Crew SE)			**100**	**125**	**125**
Add Power Windows (Std. SC, Crew SE)			**125**	**150**	**150**
Add Rockford Fosgate Stereo			**150**	**175**	**175**
Add Running Boards (XE)			**100**	**125**	**125**
Add Sunroof			**200**	**225**	**225**
Add Theft Recovery System			**75**	**100**	**100**
Add Tilt Steering Wheel (XE)			**75**	**100**	**100**
Deduct W/out Air Conditioning			**475**	**475**	**475**
2002 QUEST-V6					
Van GXE	N15	3984	**11700**	**14125**	**15075**
Van SE	N16	4056	**12800**	**15350**	**16350**
Van GLE	N17	4064	**13500**	**16100**	**17125**
Add Compact Disc Player (Std. SE, GLE)			**75**	**100**	**100**
Add Leather Seats (Std. GLE)			**350**	**400**	**400**
Add Power Seat (Std. GLE)			**150**	**175**	**175**
Add Power Sunroof			**475**	**550**	**550**
Add Rear Air Conditioning (Std. SE, GLE)			**150**	**175**	**175**
Add Rear Bucket Seats (GXE)			**150**	**175**	**175**
Add Running Boards			**100**	**125**	**125**
Add Theft Recovery System			**75**	**100**	**100**
2002 XTERRA-V6					
Utility 4D XE (4 Cyl., 5 Spd.)	DD28T	3570	**11225**	**13600**	**14550**
Utility 4D XE	ED28T	3731	**12750**	**15275**	**16275**
Utility 4D XE SC	MD28T	3888	**13850**	**16450**	**17500**
Utility 4D SE	ED28T	3831	**13425**	**16000**	**17025**
Utility 4D SE SC	MD28T	3906	**14350**	**16975**	**18025**
Utility 4D XE (4WD)	ED28Y	4034	**13750**	**16350**	**17375**
Utility 4D XE SC (4WD)	MD28Y	4156	**14850**	**17525**	**18575**
Utility 4D SE (4WD)	ED28Y	4115	**14425**	**17075**	**18100**
Utility 4D SE SC (4WD)	MD28Y	4183	**15350**	**18050**	**19100**
Add Rockford Fosgate Stereo (Std. SE)			**200**	**225**	**225**
Add Running Boards (Std. SE, SC)			**100**	**125**	**125**
Add Sunroof			**250**	**300**	**300**
Add Theft Recovery System			**75**	**100**	**100**
Deduct W/out Auto Trans. (Ex. 4 Cyl.)			**475**	**475**	**475**

SEE TRUCK OPTION PAGE FOR ADDITIONAL OPTIONS

BODY TYPE	Model No.	Weight	Trade-In	Retail	High Retail
Deduct W/out Cruise Control			150	150	150
Deduct W/out Power Locks			125	125	125
Deduct W/out Power Windows			150	150	150
Deduct W/out Tilt Steering Wheel			100	100	100
NISSAN					
2001 PATHFINDER-V6-4WD					
Utility 4D XE (2WD)	R07/9X	3871	11925	14400	15375
Utility 4D SE (2WD)	R07/9X	3940	12525	15075	16075
Utility 4D LE (2WD)	R07/9X	3985	13525	16125	17150
Utility 4D XE	R07/9Y	4131	12825	15375	16375
Utility 4D SE	R07/9Y	4250	13425	16025	17050
Utility 4D LE	R07/9Y	4299	14425	17100	18125
Add Leather Seats			300	350	350
Add Navigation System			350	400	400
Add Power Seat			125	150	150
Add Power Sunroof (Std. LE)			425	475	475
Add Rear Entertainment System			350	400	400
Add Theft Recovery System			50	75	75
Deduct W/out Automatic Trans.			425	425	425
2001 FRONTIER PICKUP-V6-5 Spd.					
XE (4 Cyl.)	DD21S		6125	8000	8825
King Cab XE (4 Cyl.)	DD26S		7825	9875	10600
King Cab XE	ED26T		8625	10750	11500
King Cab SE	ED26T		9325	11525	12250
King Cab SC	MD26T		10175	12425	13150
King Cab XE (4WD)	ED26Y		10625	12925	13650
King Cab SE (4WD)	ED26Y		11325	13750	14500
King Cab SC (4WD)	MD26Y		12175	14675	15450
2001 FRONTIER CREW CAB-V6-5 Spd.					
Crew Cab XE	ED27T		10250	12525	13250
Crew Cab SE	ED27T		10900	13225	13975
Crew Cab SC	MD27T		11500	13925	14675
Crew Cab XE (4WD)	ED27Y		12250	14775	15550
Crew Cab SE (4WD)	ED27Y		12900	15450	16250
Crew Cab SC (4WD)	MD27Y		13750	16375	17200
FRONTIER OPTIONS					
Add Aluminum/Alloy Wheels (XE Reg/King Cab)			150	175	175
Add Automatic Trans.			325	375	375
Add CD Player (XE Reg/King Cab)			50	75	75
Add Cruise Control			100	125	125
Add Leather Seats			200	225	225
Add Power Door Locks (Std. SC, Crew SE)			75	100	100
Add Power Windows (Std. SC, Crew SE)			100	125	125
Add Running Boards (XE)			75	100	100
Add Sunroof			175	200	200
Add Theft Recovery System			50	75	75
Add Tilt Steering Wheel (Std. King Cab SC)			75	100	100
Deduct W/out Air Conditioning			425	425	425
2001 QUEST-V6					
Van GXE	N15	3915	9750	11975	12900
Van SE	N16	4003	10700	13000	13925
Van GLE	N17	4057	11550	13975	14925
Add Compact Disc Player (Std. SE, GLE)			50	75	75
Add Leather Seats (Std. GLE)			300	350	350

BODY TYPE	Model No.	Weight	Trade-In	Retail	High Retail
Add Power Seat (Std. GLE)			**125**	**150**	**150**
Add Power Sunroof			**425**	**475**	**475**
Add Rear Air Conditioning (Std. SE, GLE)			**125**	**150**	**150**
Add Rear Bucket Seats (GXE)			**125**	**150**	**150**
Add Running Boards			**75**	**100**	**100**
Add Theft Recovery System			**50**	**75**	**75**
2001 XTERRA-V6					
Utility 4D XE (4 Cyl., 5 Spd.)	DD28T	3504	**9650**	**11875**	**12775**
Utility 4D XE	ED28T	3668	**11425**	**13850**	**14800**
Utility 4D SE	ED28T	3821	**11975**	**14450**	**15425**
Utility 4D XE (4WD)	ED28Y	3933	**12325**	**14850**	**15825**
Utility 4D SE (4WD)	ED28Y	4092	**12875**	**15425**	**16425**
Add Running Boards (Std. SE)			**75**	**100**	**100**
Add Theft Recovery System			**50**	**75**	**75**
Deduct W/out Auto Trans. (Ex. 4 Cyl.)			**425**	**425**	**425**
Deduct W/out Cruise Control (Ex. 4 Cyl.)			**125**	**125**	**125**
Deduct W/out Power Locks (Ex. 4 Cyl.)			**100**	**100**	**100**
Deduct W/out Power Windows (Ex. 4 Cyl.)			**125**	**125**	**125**
Deduct W/out Tilt Steering Wheel			**100**	**100**	**100**
NISSAN					
2000 PATHFINDER-V6-4WD					
Utility 4D XE (2WD)	R07S	3886	**9550**	**11750**	**12650**
Utility 4D SE (2WD)	R07S	3907	**10150**	**12400**	**13300**
Utility 4D LE (2WD)	R07S	3947	**11000**	**13350**	**14275**
Utility 4D XE	R07Y	4111	**10375**	**12625**	**13525**
Utility 4D SE	R07Y	4158	**10975**	**13300**	**14225**
Utility 4D LE	R07Y	4157	**11825**	**14275**	**15225**
Add Leather Seats			**250**	**300**	**300**
Add Power Seat			**100**	**125**	**125**
Add Power Sunroof (Std. LE)			**375**	**425**	**425**
Deduct W/out Automatic Trans.			**375**	**375**	**375**
Deduct W/out Cruise Control			**100**	**100**	**100**
Deduct W/out Power Door Locks			**75**	**75**	**75**
Deduct W/out Power Windows			**100**	**100**	**100**
2000 FRONTIER PICKUP-V6-5 Spd.					
XE (4 Cyl.)	DD21S	3032	**4875**	**6625**	**7450**
King Cab XE (4 Cyl.)	DD26S	3173	**6425**	**8350**	**9100**
King Cab XE	ED26T	3382	**7125**	**9125**	**9825**
King Cab SE	ED26T	3452	**7750**	**9800**	**10525**
King Cab XE (4WD, 4 Cyl.)	DD26Y	3633	**8300**	**10400**	**11125**
King Cab XE (4WD)	ED26Y	3911	**9000**	**11175**	**11900**
King Cab SE (4WD)	ED26Y	3967	**9625**	**11850**	**12600**
2000 FRONTIER CREW CAB-V6-5 Spd.					
Crew Cab XE	ED27T	3742	**8675**	**10825**	**11575**
Crew Cab SE	ED27T	3813	**9400**	**11600**	**12325**
Crew Cab XE (4WD)	ED27Y	4034	**10550**	**12850**	**13575**
Crew Cab SE (4WD)	ED27Y	4108	**11275**	**13700**	**14450**
FRONTIER OPTIONS					
Add Aluminum/Alloy Wheels (XE Reg/King Cab)			**100**	**125**	**125**
Add Automatic Trans.			**300**	**350**	**350**
Add Compact Disc Player (Std. SE)			**50**	**75**	**75**
Add Cruise Control (Std. Crew SE)			**75**	**100**	**100**
Add Power Locks (Std. Crew SE)			**50**	**75**	**75**

TRUCKS

SEE TRUCK OPTION PAGE FOR ADDITIONAL OPTIONS

BODY TYPE	Model No.	Weight	Trade-In	Retail	High Retail
Add Power Windows (Std. Crew SE)			75	100	100
Add Running Boards (Std. SE)			50	75	75
Add Sunroof			150	175	175
Add Tilt Steering Wheel (Std. SE)			50	75	75
Deduct W/out Air Conditioning			375	375	375
2000 QUEST-V6					
Van GXE	N11	3830	8075	10150	11075
Van SE	N11	3950	8675	10800	11750
Van GLE	N11	3986	9575	11775	12675
Add Aluminum/Alloy Wheels (GXE)			125	150	150
Add Compact Disc Player (Std. GLE)			50	75	75
Add Leather Seats (Std. GLE)			250	300	300
Add Power Seat (Std. GLE)			100	125	125
Add Power Sunroof			375	425	425
Add Rear Air Conditioning (Std. SE, GLE)			100	125	125
Add Running Boards			50	75	75
2000 XTERRA-V6					
Utility 4D XE (4 Cyl., 5 Spd.)	DD28T	3504	7600	9625	10525
Utility 4D XE	ED28T	3668	9275	11450	12350
Utility 4D SE	ED28T	3821	9800	12025	12900
Utility 4D XE (4WD)	ED28Y	3933	10075	12325	13225
Utility 4D SE (4WD)	ED28Y	4092	10600	12900	13825
Add Compact Disc Player (Std. V6)			50	75	75
Add Running Boards (Std. SE)			50	75	75
Deduct W/out Auto Trans. (Ex. 4 Cyl.)			375	375	375
Deduct W/out Cruise Control (Ex. 4 Cyl.)			100	100	100
Deduct W/out Power Locks (Ex. 4 Cyl.)			75	75	75
Deduct W/out Power Windows (Ex. 4 Cyl.)			100	100	100
Deduct W/out Tilt Steering Wheel			75	75	75
NISSAN					
1999 PATHFINDER-V6-4WD					
Utility 4D XE (2WD)	R05S	3720	7200	9175	10050
Utility 4D LE (2WD)	R05S	3830	8300	10400	11325
Utility 4D XE	R05Y	3980	7950	10025	10950
Utility 4D SE	R05Y	4065	8525	10650	11600
Utility 4D LE	R05Y	4075	9050	11225	12100
1999.5 PATHFINDER-V6-4WD					
Utility 4D XE (2WD)	R07S		8000	10050	10975
Utility 4D SE (2WD)	R07S		8575	10675	11625
Utility 4D LE (2WD)	R07S		9200	11375	12275
Utility 4D XE	R07Y		8750	10900	11850
Utility 4D SE	R07Y		9325	11525	12425
Utility 4D LE	R07Y		9950	12200	13100
1999/1999.5 PATHFINDER OPTIONS					
Add Bose Premium Stereo (Std. LE)			75	100	100
Add Leather Seats (Std. 1999 LE)			225	250	250
Add Power Seat			75	100	100
Add Power Sunroof			325	375	375
Deduct W/out Automatic Trans.			325	325	325
Deduct W/out Cruise Control			75	75	75
Deduct W/out Power Door Locks			50	50	50
Deduct W/out Power Windows			75	75	75

BODY TYPE	Model No.	Weight	Trade-In	Retail	High Retail
1999 FRONTIER PICKUP-4 Cyl.-5 Spd.					
XE	DD21S	2999	**4475**	**6175**	**6950**
King Cab XE	DD26S	3149	**5875**	**7725**	**8550**
King Cab SE	DD26S	3215	**6275**	**8175**	**8925**
XE (4WD)	DD21Y	3499	**6125**	**8000**	**8825**
King Cab XE (4WD)	DD26Y	3633	**7525**	**9550**	**10275**
King Cab XE (4WD, V6)	ED26Y	3911	**8125**	**10225**	**10950**
King Cab SE (4WD, V6)	ED26Y	3967	**8525**	**10650**	**11375**
Add Aluminum/Alloy Wheels (XE)			**50**	**75**	**75**
Add Automatic Trans.			**250**	**300**	**300**
Add Cruise Control			**50**	**75**	**75**
Add Power Windows			**50**	**75**	**75**
Add Sunroof			**125**	**150**	**150**
Deduct W/out Air Conditioning			**325**	**325**	**325**
1999 QUEST-V6					
Van GXE	N11	3830	**6500**	**8400**	**9275**
Van SE	N11	3950	**7000**	**8950**	**9850**
Van GLE	N11	3991	**7600**	**9625**	**10525**
Add Aluminum/Alloy Wheels (GXE)			**75**	**100**	**100**
Add Leather Seats (Std. GLE)			**225**	**250**	**250**
Add Power Seat (Std. GLE)			**75**	**100**	**100**
Add Power Sunroof			**325**	**375**	**375**
Add Rear Air Conditioning (Std. SE, GLE)			**75**	**100**	**100**
NISSAN					
1998 PATHFINDER-V6-4WD					
Utility 4D XE (2WD)	R05S	3734	**5950**	**7800**	**8725**
Utility 4D LE (2WD)	R05S	3789	**7000**	**8975**	**9875**
Utility 4D XE	R05Y	3994	**6650**	**8575**	**9450**
Utility 4D SE	R05Y	4079	**7200**	**9200**	**10075**
Utility 4D LE	R05Y	4034	**7700**	**9725**	**10625**
Add Bose Premium Stereo (Std. LE)			**50**	**75**	**75**
Add Leather Seats (Std. LE)			**175**	**200**	**200**
Add Power Seat			**50**	**75**	**75**
Add Power Sunroof			**275**	**325**	**325**
Deduct W/out Automatic Trans.			**275**	**275**	**275**
Deduct W/out Cruise Control			**50**	**50**	**50**
Deduct W/out Power Windows			**50**	**50**	**50**
1998 FRONTIER PICKUP-4 Cyl.-5 Spd.					
Base	D21S	2925	**3300**	**4850**	**5650**
XE	D21S	3046	**3975**	**5600**	**6375**
King Cab XE	D26S	3187	**5275**	**7050**	**7825**
King Cab SE	D26S	3231	**5700**	**7525**	**8325**
XE (4WD)	D21Y	3568	**5475**	**7275**	**8050**
King Cab XE (4WD)	D26Y	3683	**6775**	**8725**	**9500**
King Cab SE (4WD)	D26Y	3740	**7200**	**9200**	**9900**
Add Automatic Trans.			**200**	**225**	**225**
Add Cruise Control (Std. SE)			**50**	**75**	**75**
Add Power Windows (Std. SE)			**50**	**75**	**75**
Deduct W/out Air Conditioning			**275**	**275**	**275**
1998 QUEST-V6					
Van XE	N11	3865	**4100**	**5750**	**6600**
Van GXE	N11	4008	**5150**	**6900**	**7825**
Van GLE	N11	4008	**5950**	**7800**	**8725**

SEE TRUCK OPTION PAGE FOR ADDITIONAL OPTIONS

BODY TYPE	Model No.	Weight	Trade-In	Retail	High Retail
Add Aluminum/Alloy Wheels (XE)			**50**	**75**	**75**
Add Leather Seats (Std. GLE)			**175**	**200**	**200**
Add Power Sunroof (Std. GLE)			**275**	**325**	**325**
Add Rear Air Conditioning (XE)			**50**	**75**	**75**
Add Rear Bucket Seats (XE)			**50**	**75**	**75**
NISSAN					
1997 PATHFINDER-V6-4WD					
Utility 4D XE (2WD)	R05S	3720	**5000**	**6750**	**7675**
Utility 4D LE (2WD)	R05S	3775	**5900**	**7750**	**8675**
Utility 4D XE	R05Y	3980	**5600**	**7400**	**8300**
Utility 4D SE	R05Y	4065	**6050**	**7925**	**8850**
Utility 4D LE	R05Y	4020	**6500**	**8425**	**9300**
Add Leather Seats (Std. LE)			**150**	**175**	**175**
Add Power Seat			**50**	**75**	**75**
Add Power Sunroof			**200**	**225**	**225**
Deduct W/out Air Conditioning			**250**	**250**	**250**
Deduct W/out Automatic Trans.			**175**	**175**	**175**
Deduct W/out Cruise Control			**50**	**50**	**50**
Deduct W/out Power Windows			**50**	**50**	**50**
1997 QUEST-V6					
Van XE	N11	3871	**3650**	**5250**	**6050**
Van GXE	N11	3964	**4150**	**5800**	**6675**
Add Leather Seats			**150**	**175**	**175**
Add Power Sunroof			**200**	**225**	**225**
Deduct W/out Cruise Control			**50**	**50**	**50**
Deduct W/out Power Windows			**50**	**50**	**50**
1997 PICKUPS-4 Cyl.-5 Spd.					
Base	D11S	2815	**2750**	**4200**	**4925**
XE	D11S	2820	**3275**	**4825**	**5625**
King Cab XE	D16S	2945	**4275**	**5950**	**6750**
King Cab SE	D16S	3095	**4475**	**6175**	**6950**
XE (4WD)	D11Y	3395	**4575**	**6275**	**7075**
King Cab XE (4WD)	D16Y	3550	**5575**	**7375**	**8175**
King Cab SE (4WD)	D16Y	3645	**5775**	**7600**	**8400**
Add Automatic Trans.			**125**	**150**	**150**
Deduct W/out Air Conditioning			**150**	**150**	**150**
NISSAN					
1996 PATHFINDER-V6-4WD					
Utility 4D XE (2WD)	R05S	3850	**4100**	**5750**	**6600**
Utility 4D LE (2WD)	R05S		**4900**	**6650**	**7550**
Utility 4D XE	R05Y	4135	**4700**	**6425**	**7325**
Utility 4D SE	R05Y	4295	**5100**	**6850**	**7775**
Utility 4D LE	R05Y	4215	**5500**	**7300**	**8175**
Add Power Sunroof			**150**	**175**	**175**
Deduct W/out Air Conditioning			**150**	**150**	**150**
Deduct W/out Automatic Trans.			**125**	**125**	**125**
1996 QUEST-V6					
Van XE	N11	3871	**3400**	**4950**	**5850**
Van GXE	N11	3964	**3900**	**5525**	**6375**
Add Power Sunroof			**150**	**175**	**175**

TRUCKS

BODY TYPE	Model No.	Weight	Trade-In	Retail	High Retail
1996 PICKUPS-4 Cyl.-5 Spd.					
Base	D11S		**2375**	**3775**	**4475**
XE	D11S		**2625**	**4075**	**4775**
King Cab XE	D16S		**3525**	**5100**	**5825**
King Cab SE	D16S		**3725**	**5325**	**6075**
XE (4WD)	D11Y		**3825**	**5450**	**6200**
King Cab XE (4WD)	D16Y		**4725**	**6450**	**7250**
King Cab SE (4WD)	D16Y		**4925**	**6675**	**7500**
Add Automatic Trans.			**100**	**125**	**125**
Deduct W/out Air Conditioning			**100**	**100**	**100**
NISSAN					
1995 PATHFINDER-V6-4WD					
Utility 4D XE (2WD)	D17	3850	**2550**	**3975**	**4775**
Utility 4D LE (2WD)	D17	4085	**3200**	**4725**	**5600**
Utility 4D XE	D17	4135	**3150**	**4675**	**5550**
Utility 4D SE	D17	4295	**3500**	**5075**	**5875**
Utility 4D LE	D17	4215	**3800**	**5400**	**6225**
1995 QUEST-V6					
Van XE	N11	3876	**2700**	**4150**	**4950**
Van GXE	N11	3993	**3075**	**4600**	**5450**
1995 PICKUPS-4 Cyl.					
Base	D11	2805	**2200**	**3575**	**4250**
XE	D11	2860	**2400**	**3800**	**4500**
Base (V6)	D12	3130	**2325**	**3725**	**4400**
King Cab XE	D16	2960	**3200**	**4725**	**5500**
King Cab XE (V6)	D16	3170	**3325**	**4875**	**5675**
XE (4WD)	D11	3390	**3500**	**5075**	**5800**
King Cab XE (4WD)	D16	3525	**4300**	**5975**	**6775**
King Cab XE (4WD, V6)	D16	3805	**4425**	**6125**	**6900**
King Cab SE (4WD, V6)	D16	3895	**4575**	**6275**	**7075**

OLDSMOBILE

BODY TYPE	Model No.	Weight	Trade-In	Retail	High Retail
OLDSMOBILE					
2004 BRAVADA-1/2 Ton-I6-AWD					
Utility 4D (2WD)	S13	4417	**18750**	**21800**	**22975**
Utility 4D	T13	4600	**19825**	**22950**	**24150**
Add Bose Stereo System			**300**	**350**	**350**
Add Power Sunroof			**575**	**650**	**650**
Add Rear Entertainment System			**600**	**675**	**675**
Add Theft Recovery System			**100**	**125**	**125**
2004 SILHOUETTE-V6					
Extended Wagon GL 4D	X03	3948	**13450**	**16025**	**17050**
Extended Wagon GLS 4D	X03*		**15600**	**18325**	**19375**
Ext. Wagon Premiere 4D	X13*		**17550**	**20525**	**21650**
Add All Wheel Drive			**1100**	**1225**	**1225**
Add Left Power Sliding Door (GLS)			**300**	**350**	**350**
Add Right Power Sliding Door (GL)			**300**	**350**	**350**
Add Theft Recovery System			**100**	**125**	**125**

* V as the 1st position of the model # denotes AWD

SEE TRUCK OPTION PAGE FOR ADDITIONAL OPTIONS

BODY TYPE	Model No.	Weight	Trade-In	Retail	High Retail
OLDSMOBILE					
2003 BRAVADA-1/2 Ton-I6-AWD					
Utility 4D (2WD)	S13	4442	**16075**	**18850**	**19925**
Utility 4D	T13	4628	**17100**	**20025**	**21150**
Add Bose Stereo System			**250**	**300**	**300**
Add Power Sunroof			**525**	**600**	**600**
Add Rear Entertainment System			**500**	**575**	**575**
Add Theft Recovery System			**75**	**100**	**100**
2003 SILHOUETTE-V6					
Extended Wagon GL 4D	X0/23	3948	**11900**	**14350**	**15325**
Extended Wagon GLS 4D	X03*		**13850**	**16450**	**17500**
Ext. Wagon Premiere 4D	X13*		**15500**	**18225**	**19275**
Add All Wheel Drive			**1000**	**1125**	**1125**
Add Left Power Sliding Door (GLS)			**250**	**300**	**300**
Add Right Power Sliding Door (GL)			**250**	**300**	**300**
Add Theft Recovery System			**75**	**100**	**100**
* V as the 1st position of the model # denotes AWD					
OLDSMOBILE					
2002 BRAVADA-1/2 Ton-I6-AWD					
Utility 4D (2WD)	S13	4442	**13750**	**16350**	**17375**
Utility 4D	T13	4628	**14750**	**17425**	**18450**
Add Bose Stereo System			**200**	**225**	**225**
Add Power Sunroof			**475**	**550**	**550**
Add Rear Entertainment System			**400**	**450**	**450**
Add Theft Recovery System			**75**	**100**	**100**
2002 SILHOUETTE-V6					
Extended Wagon GL 4D	X0/23	3948	**10225**	**12475**	**13375**
Extended Wagon GLS 4D	X03*		**12125**	**14625**	**15600**
Ext. Wagon Premiere 4D	X13*		**13425**	**16000**	**17025**
Add All Wheel Drive			**900**	**1000**	**1000**
Add Aluminum/Alloy Wheels (GL)			**225**	**250**	**250**
Add Left Power Sliding Door (GLS)			**250**	**300**	**300**
Add Rear Air Conditioning (GL)			**150**	**175**	**175**
Add Right Power Sliding Door (GL)			**250**	**300**	**300**
Add Theft Recovery System			**75**	**100**	**100**
* V as the 1st position of the model # denotes AWD					
OLDSMOBILE					
2001 BRAVADA-1/2 Ton-V6-4WD					
Utility 4D	T13	4068	**9575**	**11800**	**12700**
Add Bose Stereo System			**150**	**175**	**175**
Add Power Sunroof			**425**	**475**	**475**
Add Theft Recovery System			**50**	**75**	**75**
2001 SILHOUETTE-V6					
Extended Wagon GL 4D	X0/23	3948	**7925**	**9975**	**10875**
Extended Wagon GLS 4D	X03		**9625**	**11850**	**12750**
Ext. Wagon Premiere 4D	X13		**10525**	**12800**	**13700**
Add Aluminum/Alloy Wheels (GL)			**175**	**200**	**200**
Add Power Sliding Door (GL)			**225**	**250**	**250**
Add Rear Air Conditioning (GL)			**125**	**150**	**150**
Add Theft Recovery System			**50**	**75**	**75**

BODY TYPE	Model No.	Weight	Trade-In	Retail	High Retail
OLDSMOBILE					
2000 BRAVADA-1/2 Ton-V6-4WD					
Utility 4D	T13	4049	**7350**	**9375**	**10250**
Add Bose Stereo System			**100**	**125**	**125**
Add Power Sunroof			**375**	**425**	**425**
2000 SILHOUETTE-V6					
Extended Wagon GL 4D	X03	3948	**6300**	**8200**	**9050**
Extended Wagon GLS 4D	X03	3948	**7800**	**9850**	**10750**
Ext. Wagon Premiere 4D	X13	3948	**8150**	**10250**	**11175**
Add Aluminum/Alloy Wheels (GL)			**125**	**150**	**150**
Add Compact Disc Player (Std. Premiere)			**50**	**75**	**75**
Add Power Seat (GL)			**100**	**125**	**125**
Add Power Sliding Door (GL)			**200**	**225**	**225**
Add Rear Air Conditioning (GL)			**100**	**125**	**125**
Add Rear Bucket Seats (GL)			**100**	**125**	**125**
OLDSMOBILE					
1999 BRAVADA-1/2 Ton-V6-4WD					
Utility 4D	T13	4068	**6450**	**8375**	**9250**
Add Bose Stereo System			**75**	**100**	**100**
Add Power Sunroof			**325**	**375**	**375**
1999 SILHOUETTE-V6					
Wagon GS 4D	U03	3746	**4850**	**6575**	**7475**
Extended Wagon GL 4D	X03	3942	**5375**	**7150**	**8025**
Extended Wagon GLS 4D	X03	3942	**6575**	**8500**	**9375**
Ext. Wagon Premiere 4D	X03	3942	**7075**	**9050**	**9900**
Add Aluminum/Alloy Wheels (GS, GL)			**75**	**100**	**100**
Add Leather Seats (Std. GLS, Premiere)			**225**	**250**	**250**
Add Power Seat (GL)			**75**	**100**	**100**
Add Power Sliding Door (GL)			**175**	**200**	**200**
Add Rear Air Conditioning (Std. Premiere)			**75**	**100**	**100**
Add Rear Bucket Seats (GS, GL)			**75**	**100**	**100**
OLDSMOBILE					
1998 BRAVADA-1/2 Ton-V6-4WD					
Utility 4D	T13	4049	**5250**	**7025**	**7900**
Add Power Sunroof			**275**	**325**	**325**
1998 SILHOUETTE-V6					
Wagon GS 4D	U03	3746	**4100**	**5750**	**6600**
Extended Wagon GL 4D	X03	3948	**4600**	**6300**	**7175**
Extended Wagon GLS 4D	X03	3948	**5600**	**7400**	**8300**
Add Aluminum/Alloy Wheels (GS, GL)			**50**	**75**	**75**
Add Leather Seats (Std. GLS)			**175**	**200**	**200**
Add Power Seat (GL)			**50**	**75**	**75**
Add Power Sliding Door (GL)			**150**	**175**	**175**
Add Rear Air Conditioning			**50**	**75**	**75**
Add Rear Bucket Seats (GS, GL)			**50**	**75**	**75**
OLDSMOBILE					
1997 BRAVADA-1/2 Ton-V6-4WD					
Utility 4D	T13	4023	**4600**	**6300**	**7175**
Add Power Sunroof			**200**	**225**	**225**

SEE TRUCK OPTION PAGE FOR ADDITIONAL OPTIONS

BODY TYPE	Model No.	Weight	Trade-In	Retail	High Retail
1997 SILHOUETTE-V6					
Wagon	U06	3721	3025	4550	5400
Extended Wagon 3D	X06	3843	3425	5000	5900
Extended Wagon GL 3D	X06	3843	3825	5450	6275
Extended Wagon GL 4D	X03	3948	3975	5600	6450
Extended Wagon GLS 3D	X06	3843	4675	6400	7300
Extended Wagon GLS 4D	X03	3948	4825	6550	7450
Add Leather Seats			150	175	175
Add Power Sunroof			200	225	225
OLDSMOBILE					
1996 BRAVADA-1/2 Ton-V6-4WD					
Utility 4D	T13	4184	3875	5500	6325
1996 SILHOUETTE-V6					
Wagon	U06	3739	2200	3575	4325
OLDSMOBILE					
1995 SILHOUETTE-V6					
Wagon	U06	3689	1900	3225	3925

PLYMOUTH

BODY TYPE	Model No.	Weight	Trade-In	Retail	High Retail
PLYMOUTH					
2000 VOYAGER-V6					
Voyager	W/P25	3536	3900	5525	6375
Voyager SE	W/P45		5050	6800	7725
Grand Voyager	W/P24	3836	5125	6875	7800
Grand Voyager SE	W/P44		6025	7875	8800
Add 3rd Row Seat (Base Voyager)			100	125	125
Add Aluminum/Alloy Wheels (SE)			125	150	150
Add Compact Disc Player			50	75	75
Add Left Sliding Door (Base Voyager)			250	300	300
Add Power Seat			100	125	125
Add Rear Air Conditioning			100	125	125
Add Rear Bucket Seats			100	125	125
Deduct 4 Cyl. Engine			400	400	400
Deduct W/out Air Conditioning			500	500	500
Deduct W/out Cruise Control			100	100	100
Deduct W/out Power Door Locks			75	75	75
Deduct W/out Power Windows			100	100	100
Deduct W/out Tilt Steering Wheel			75	75	75
PLYMOUTH					
1999 VOYAGER-V6					
Voyager	P25	3516	2950	4450	5300
Voyager SE	P45	3711	4150	5825	6700
Voyager Expresso	P45		4600	6325	7200
Grand Voyager	P24	3683	4050	5700	6550
Grand Voyager SE	P44	3812	5050	6800	7725
Grand Voyager Expresso	P44		5500	7300	8175
Add 3rd Row Seat (Base Voyager)			100	125	125
Add Aluminum/Alloy Wheels (SE, Expresso)			75	100	100
Add Left Sliding Door (Base Voyager)			225	250	250
Add Power Seat			75	100	100

BODY TYPE	Model No.	Weight	Trade-In	Retail	High Retail
Add Rear Air Conditioning			75	100	100
Add Rear Bucket Seats			75	100	100
Deduct 4 Cyl. Engine			300	300	300
Deduct W/out Air Conditioning			450	450	450
Deduct W/out Cruise Control			75	75	75
Deduct W/out Power Door Locks			50	50	50
Deduct W/out Power Windows			75	75	75
Deduct W/out Tilt Steering Wheel			50	50	50
PLYMOUTH 1998 VOYAGER-V6					
Voyager	P25	3533	2200	3575	4325
Voyager SE	P45	3533	3500	5075	5875
Voyager Expresso	P45		3900	5525	6375
Grand Voyager	P24	3706	3300	4850	5750
Grand Voyager SE	P44	3706	4400	6075	6925
Grand Voyager Expresso	P44		4800	6525	7425
Add 3rd Row Seat (Base Voyager)			100	125	125
Add Aluminum/Alloy Wheels (SE, Expresso)			50	75	75
Add Left Sliding Door (Base Voyager)			200	225	225
Add Power Seat			50	75	75
Add Rear Air Conditioning			50	75	75
Add Rear Bucket Seats			50	75	75
Deduct 4 Cyl. Engine			200	200	200
Deduct W/out Air Conditioning			400	400	400
Deduct W/out Cruise Control			50	50	50
Deduct W/out Power Windows			50	50	50
PLYMOUTH 1997 VOYAGER-V6					
Voyager	P25	3879	1950	3275	3975
Voyager SE	P45	3879	2900	4375	5200
Grand Voyager	P24	4262	2650	4100	4900
Grand Voyager SE	P44	4262	3600	5175	5975
Add Rallye Trim			175	200	200
Add Left Sliding Door			150	175	175
Add Power Seat			50	75	75
Deduct 4 Cyl. Engine			150	150	150
Deduct W/out Air Conditioning			250	250	250
Deduct W/out Cruise Control			50	50	50
Deduct W/out Power Windows			50	50	50
PLYMOUTH 1996 VOYAGER-V6					
Voyager	P25	3528	1700	2975	3650
Voyager SE	P45	3696	2350	3750	4525
Grand Voyager	P24	3680	2200	3575	4325
Grand Voyager SE	P44	3766	2850	4325	5150
Add Rallye Trim			150	175	175
Deduct 4 Cyl. Engine			150	150	150
Deduct W/out Air Conditioning			150	150	150
PLYMOUTH 1995 VOYAGER-V6					
Voyager	H25	3287	1125	2300	2875
Voyager SE	H45	3439	1500	2750	3400
Voyager LE	H55	3620	1750	3050	3725

TRUCKS

SEE TRUCK OPTION PAGE FOR ADDITIONAL OPTIONS

BODY TYPE	Model No.	Weight	Trade-In	Retail	High Retail
Grand Voyager	H24	3530	**1375**	**2600**	**3225**
Grand Voyager SE	H44	3638	**1750**	**3050**	**3725**
Grand Voyager LE	H54	3776	**2000**	**3350**	**4075**
Add Rallye Trim			**125**	**150**	**150**
Add Sportwagon Trim			**125**	**150**	**150**
Add All Wheel Drive			**350**	**400**	**400**
Deduct 4 Cyl. Engine			**125**	**125**	**125**

PONTIAC

PONTIAC
2004 AZTEK-V6

BODY TYPE	Model No.	Weight	Trade-In	Retail	High Retail
Utility 4D	A03	3779	**11750**	**14175**	**15125**
Utility 4D (AWD)	B03	4043	**12650**	**15175**	**16175**
Add Aluminum/Alloy Wheels			**325**	**375**	**375**
Add Leather Seats			**450**	**500**	**500**
Add Power Seat			**200**	**225**	**225**
Add Power Sunroof			**575**	**650**	**650**
Add Rear Entertainment System			**600**	**675**	**675**
Add Theft Recovery System			**100**	**125**	**125**
Deduct W/out Cruise Control			**200**	**200**	**200**

2004 MONTANA-V6

BODY TYPE	Model No.	Weight	Trade-In	Retail	High Retail
Wagon 4D	U0/23	3803	**11900**	**14350**	**15325**
Wagon Extended 4D	X03*	3942	**13250**	**15825**	**16850**
Wagon Ext. 4D Luxury	X13*	3942	**15950**	**18700**	**19775**
Add All Wheel Drive			**1100**	**1225**	**1225**
Add Aluminum/Alloy Wheels (Std. Ext.)			**325**	**375**	**375**
Add Leather Seats			**450**	**500**	**500**
Add Left Power Sliding Door			**300**	**350**	**350**
Add Power Seat (Std. Luxury)			**200**	**225**	**225**
Add Rear Air Conditioning (Std. Luxury)			**200**	**225**	**225**
Add Rear Bucket Seats (Std. Luxury)			**200**	**225**	**225**
Add Right Power Sliding Door			**300**	**350**	**350**
Add Theft Recovery System			**100**	**125**	**125**

* V as the 1st position of the model # denotes AWD

PONTIAC
2003 AZTEK-V6

BODY TYPE	Model No.	Weight	Trade-In	Retail	High Retail
Utility 4D	A03	3779	**10250**	**12500**	**13400**
Utility 4D (AWD)	B03	4043	**11050**	**13400**	**14325**
Add Aluminum/Alloy Wheels			**275**	**325**	**325**
Add Leather Seats			**400**	**450**	**450**
Add Power Seat			**175**	**200**	**200**
Add Power Sunroof			**525**	**600**	**600**
Add Rear Entertainment System			**500**	**575**	**575**
Add Theft Recovery System			**75**	**100**	**100**
Deduct W/out Cruise Control			**175**	**175**	**175**

2003 MONTANA-V6

BODY TYPE	Model No.	Weight	Trade-In	Retail	High Retail
Wagon 4D	U0/23	3803	**10425**	**12700**	**13600**
Wagon Extended 4D	X03*	3942	**11625**	**14050**	**15000**
Wagon Ext. 4D Luxury	X13*		**14125**	**16750**	**17800**
Add Thunder Pkg.			**700**	**800**	**800**
Add All Wheel Drive			**1000**	**1125**	**1125**

BODY TYPE	Model No.	Weight	Trade-In	Retail	High Retail
Add Aluminum/Alloy Wheels (Std. Luxury)			275	325	325
Add Leather Seats (Std. Thunder)			400	450	450
Add Left Power Sliding Door			250	300	300
Add Power Seat (Std. Luxury)			175	200	200
Add Rear Air Conditioning (Std. Luxury)			150	175	175
Add Rear Bucket Seats (Std. Luxury)			175	200	200
Add Right Power Sliding Door			250	300	300
Add Theft Recovery System			75	100	100

* V as the 1st position of the model # denotes AWD

PONTIAC

2002 AZTEK-V6

BODY TYPE	Model No.	Weight	Trade-In	Retail	High Retail
Utility 4D	A03	3779	8850	11000	11950
Utility 4D (AWD)	B03	4043	9550	11750	12650
Add Aluminum/Alloy Wheels			225	250	250
Add Leather Seats			350	400	400
Add Power Seat			150	175	175
Add Power Sunroof			475	550	550
Add Theft Recovery System			75	100	100
Deduct W/out Cruise Control			150	150	150

2002 MONTANA-V6

BODY TYPE	Model No.	Weight	Trade-In	Retail	High Retail
Wagon 4D	U0/23	3803	9425	11625	12525
Wagon Extended 4D	X03*	3942	10525	12800	13700
Wagon Ext. 4D Luxury	X13*		12625	15150	16150
Add Thunder Pkg.			625	700	700
Add All Wheel Drive			900	1000	1000
Add Aluminum/Alloy Wheels (Std. Luxury)			225	250	250
Add Leather Seats (Std. Thunder)			350	400	400
Add Left Power Sliding Door			250	300	300
Add Power Seat (Std. Luxury)			150	175	175
Add Rear Air Conditioning (Std. Luxury)			150	175	175
Add Rear Bucket Seats (Std. Luxury)			150	175	175
Add Right Pwr Sliding Door (Std. Luxury)			250	300	300
Add Theft Recovery System			75	100	100

* V as the 1st position of the model # denotes AWD

PONTIAC

2001 AZTEK-V6

BODY TYPE	Model No.	Weight	Trade-In	Retail	High Retail
Utility 4D	A03	3779	7000	8950	9850
Utility 4D GT	A03		7650	9675	10575
Utility 4D (AWD)	B03		7700	9725	10625
Utility 4D GT (AWD)	B03		8350	10450	11375
Add Compact Disc Player (Std. GT)			50	75	75
Add Leather Seats			300	350	350
Add Power Seat			125	150	150
Add Power Sunroof			425	475	475
Add Rear Bucket Seats (GT)			125	150	150
Add Theft Recovery System			50	75	75
Deduct W/out Cruise Control			125	125	125

2001 MONTANA-V6

BODY TYPE	Model No.	Weight	Trade-In	Retail	High Retail
Wagon 4D	U0/23	3730	7025	9000	9900
Wagon Extended 4D	X03	3942	7975	10050	10975
Wagon Ext. 4D Luxury	X13		9825	12050	12925
Add Aluminum/Alloy Wheels (Std. Luxury)			175	200	200
Add Leather Seats			300	350	350

TRUCKS

SEE TRUCK OPTION PAGE FOR ADDITIONAL OPTIONS

BODY TYPE	Model No.	Weight	Trade-In	Retail	High Retail
Add Power Seat (Std. Luxury)			125	150	150
Add Power Sliding Door (Std. Luxury)			225	250	250
Add Rear Air Conditioning (Std. Luxury)			125	150	150
Add Rear Bucket Seats (Std. Luxury)			125	150	150
Add Theft Recovery System			50	75	75
PONTIAC					
2000 MONTANA-V6					
Wagon 4D	U0/23	3803	5500	7300	8175
Wagon Extended 4D	X03	3942	6300	8200	9050
Wagon Ext. 4D Luxury	X13		7250	9250	10125
Add Aluminum/Alloy Wheels (Std. Luxury)			125	150	150
Add Compact Disc Player (Std. Luxury)			50	75	75
Add Leather Seats			250	300	300
Add Power Seat			100	125	125
Add Power Sliding Door			200	225	225
Add Rear Air Conditioning			100	125	125
Add Rear Bucket Seats			100	125	125
Deduct W/out Power Windows			100	100	100
PONTIAC					
1999 MONTANA-V6					
Wagon 3D	U06	3730	4350	6025	6875
Wagon 4D	U03	3780	4575	6275	7150
Wagon Extended 4D	X03	3942	5375	7150	8025
Add Aluminum/Alloy Wheels			75	100	100
Add Leather Seats			225	250	250
Add Montana Vision System			200	225	225
Add Power Seat			75	100	100
Add Power Sliding Door			175	200	200
Add Rear Air Conditioning			75	100	100
Add Rear Bucket Seats			75	100	100
Deduct W/out Cruise Control			75	75	75
Deduct W/out Power Windows			75	75	75
PONTIAC					
1998 TRANS SPORT-V6					
Wagon SE 3D	U06	3730	3800	5400	6225
Wagon SE 4D	U03	3780	4000	5625	6475
Wagon SE Extended 4D	X03	3942	4600	6300	7175
Add Montana Trim			350	400	400
Add Aluminum/Alloy Wheels			50	75	75
Add Leather Seats			175	200	200
Add Power Seat			50	75	75
Add Power Sliding Door			150	175	175
Add Rear Air Conditioning			50	75	75
Add Rear Bucket Seats			50	75	75
Deduct W/out Cruise Control			50	50	50
Deduct W/out Power Windows			50	50	50
PONTIAC					
1997 TRANS SPORT-V6					
Wagon SE	U06	3702	3200	4725	5600
Wagon SE Extended 3D	X06	3825	3600	5175	5975
Wagon SE Extended 4D	X03	3920	3750	5350	6175
Add Montana Trim			250	300	300
Add Leather Seats			150	175	175

TRUCKS

BODY TYPE	Model No.	Weight	Trade-In	Retail	High Retail
Add Power Seat			50	75	75
Add Power Sliding Door			125	150	150
Add Power Sunroof			200	225	225
Deduct W/out Cruise Control			50	50	50
Deduct W/out Power Windows			50	50	50

PONTIAC
1996 TRANS SPORT-V6

BODY TYPE	Model No.	Weight	Trade-In	Retail	High Retail
Wagon SE	U06	3593	2200	3575	4325

PONTIAC
1995 TRANS SPORT-V6

BODY TYPE	Model No.	Weight	Trade-In	Retail	High Retail
Wagon SE	U06	3523	1900	3225	3925

PORSCHE

PORSCHE
2004 CAYENNE-V8-4WD

BODY TYPE	Model No.	Weight	Trade-In	Retail	High Retail
Utility 4D (V6)	AA29P	4785	37600	42100	44275
Utility 4D S	AB29P	4950	46100	51075	53525
Utility 4D Turbo	AC29P	5200	68800	75275	78450
Add Advanced Off-Road Pkg.			1500	1675	1675
Add 4-Zone Air Conditioning			400	450	450
Add Bose Stereo System (V6)			425	475	475
Add Navigation System (Std. Turbo)			750	850	850
Add Self-Leveling Suspension (Std. Turbo)			1350	1500	1500
Add Theft Recovery System			100	125	125
Deduct W/out Power Sunroof			725	725	725

PORSCHE
2003 CAYENNE-V8-4WD

BODY TYPE	Model No.	Weight	Trade-In	Retail	High Retail
Utility 4D S	AB29P	4949	41375	46100	48400
Utility 4D Turbo	AC29P	5192	62275	68400	71375
Add 4-Zone Air Conditioning			350	400	400
Add Navigation System (Std. Turbo)			650	725	725
Add Self-Leveling Suspension (Std. Turbo)			1250	1400	1400
Add Theft Recovery System			75	100	100
Deduct W/out Power Sunroof			675	675	675

SATURN

SATURN
2004 VUE-V6

BODY TYPE	Model No.	Weight	Trade-In	Retail	High Retail
Utility 4D (4 Cyl.)	Z(2/3)3	3207	13400	16000	17025
Utility 4D	Z53	3478	15700	18450	19525
Utility 4D Red Line	Z53		16400	19175	20275
Utility 4D (AWD, 4 Cyl.)	Z43	3381	14675	17350	18375
Utility 4D (AWD)	Z63	3630	16875	19675	20775
Utility 4D Red Line (AWD)	Z63		17575	20550	21675
Add Aluminum/Alloy Wheels (4 Cyl.)			325	375	375
Add Compact Disc Player (4 Cyl. 2WD)			100	125	125
Add Leather Seats			450	500	500
Add Power Seat			200	225	225

TRUCKS

SEE TRUCK OPTION PAGE FOR ADDITIONAL OPTIONS

BODY TYPE	Model No.	Weight	Trade-In	Retail	High Retail
Add Power Sunroof			575	650	650
Add Rear Entertainment System			600	675	675
Add Running Boards			150	175	175
Add Theft Recovery System			100	125	125
Deduct W/out Automatic Trans.			575	575	575
Deduct W/out Cruise Control			200	200	200
Deduct W/out Power Door Locks			175	175	175
Deduct W/out Power Windows			200	200	200
SATURN					
2003 VUE-V6					
Utility 4D (4 Cyl.)	Z(2/3)3	3179	11925	14375	15350
Utility 4D	Z53	3396	13650	16250	17275
Utility 4D (AWD, 4 Cyl.)	Z43	3361	12950	15500	16500
Utility 4D (AWD)	Z63	3491	14950	17625	18675
Add Aluminum/Alloy Wheels (Std. AWD V6)			275	325	325
Add Compact Disc Player (4 Cyl.)			75	100	100
Add Leather Seats			400	450	450
Add Power Sunroof			525	600	600
Add Running Boards (AWD)			125	150	150
Add Theft Recovery System			75	100	100
Deduct W/out Automatic Trans.			525	525	525
Deduct W/out Cruise Control			175	175	175
Deduct W/out Power Door Locks			150	150	150
Deduct W/out Power Windows			175	175	175
SATURN					
2002 VUE-V6					
Utility 4D (4 Cyl.)	Z(2/3)3	3172	10475	12750	13650
Utility 4D (AWD, 4 Cyl.)	Z43	3340	11350	13750	14700
Utility 4D (AWD)	Z63	3470	13050	15600	16600
Add Aluminum/Alloy Wheels (Std. AWD V6)			225	250	250
Add Compact Disc Player (4 Cyl.)			75	100	100
Add Power Sunroof			475	550	550
Add Theft Recovery System			75	100	100
Deduct W/out Automatic Trans.			475	475	475
Deduct W/out Cruise Control			150	150	150
Deduct W/out Power Door Locks			125	125	125
Deduct W/out Power Windows			150	150	150

SUZUKI

BODY TYPE	Model No.	Weight	Trade-In	Retail	High Retail
SUZUKI					
2004 VITARA HARD TOP-V6-4WD					
Utility 4D LX (2WD)	TE(5/6)2V	2899	10425	12700	13425
Utility 4D LX	TD(5/6)2V	3020	11375	13800	14550
Add Aluminum/Alloy Wheels			300	350	350
Add Theft Recovery System			100	125	125
Deduct W/out Automatic Trans.			475	475	475
2004 GRAND VITARA HARD TOP-V6-4WD					
Utility 4D LX (2WD)	TE62V	3108	12975	15525	16325
Utility 4D EX (2WD)	TE62V	3108	14225	16850	17675
Utility 4D LX	TD62V	3230	14125	16775	17600
Utility 4D EX	TD62V	3230	15375	18100	18925

BODY TYPE	Model No.	Weight	Trade-In	Retail	High Retail
Add Aluminum/Alloy Wheels (Std. EX)			300	350	350
Add Theft Recovery System			100	125	125
Deduct W/out Automatic Trans.			475	475	475
Deduct W/out Cruise Control			175	175	175
2004 XL-7 HARD TOP-V6-4WD					
Utility 4D LX (2WD)	TY92V	3582	14250	16875	17700
Utility 4D EX (2WD)	TY92V	3682	15500	18225	19050
Utility 4D LX	TX92V	3704	15400	18125	18950
Utility 4D EX	TX92V	3803	16650	19450	20300
Add Running Boards (EX)			150	175	175
Add Theft Recovery System			100	125	125
Deduct W/out 3rd Row Seat			200	200	200
Deduct W/out Automatic Trans.			475	475	475
SUZUKI					
2003 VITARA-4 Cyl.-4WD					
Utility 2D Soft Top (2WD)	TC52C	2679	7225	9225	9925
Utility 2D Soft Top	TA52C	2800	8375	10475	11200
Utility 4D Hard Top (2WD)	TE52V	2855	8400	10525	11250
Utility 4D Hard Top	TD52V	2976	9550	11750	12500
Add Aluminum/Alloy Wheels			250	300	300
Add Theft Recovery System			75	100	100
Deduct W/out Automatic Trans.			425	425	425
2003 GRAND VITARA HARD TOP-V6-4WD					
Utility 4D (2WD)	TE62V	3075	10525	12800	13525
Utility 4D	TD62V	3163	11625	14050	14825
Add Theft Recovery System			75	100	100
Deduct W/out Automatic Trans.			425	425	425
2003 XL-7 HARD TOP-V6-4WD					
Touring 4D (2WD)	TY92V	3516	11925	14375	15150
Limited 4D (2WD)	TY92V	3751	12975	15525	16325
Touring 4D	TX92V	3638	13025	15575	16375
Limited 4D	TX92V	3693	14100	16725	17550
Add Running Boards (Limited)			125	150	150
Add Theft Recovery System			75	100	100
Deduct W/out 3rd Row Seat			175	175	175
Deduct W/out Automatic Trans.			425	425	425
SUZUKI					
2002 VITARA-4 Cyl.-4WD					
JLS 2D Soft Top (2WD)	TC52C	2679	5750	7550	8350
JLX 2D Soft Top	TA52C	2800	6750	8675	9450
JLS 4D Hard Top (2WD)	TE52V	2932	6850	8775	9550
JLX 4D Hard Top	TD52V	3053	7850	9900	10625
Add Aluminum/Alloy Wheels			200	225	225
Add Theft Recovery System			75	100	100
Deduct W/out Automatic Trans.			375	375	375
2002 GRAND VITARA HARD TOP-V6-4WD					
JLS 4D (2WD)	TE62V	3152	8325	10425	11150
JLX 4D	TD62V	3285	9425	11625	12350
Limited 4D (2WD)	TE62V	3119	9800	12025	12750
Limited 4D	TD62V	3252	10900	13200	13950
Add Aluminum/Alloy Wheels (Std. Ltd.)			200	225	225

TRUCKS

SEE TRUCK OPTION PAGE FOR ADDITIONAL OPTIONS

BODY TYPE	Model No.	Weight	Trade-In	Retail	High Retail
Add Theft Recovery System			**75**	**100**	**100**
Deduct W/out Automatic Trans.			**375**	**375**	**375**
2002 XL-7 HARD TOP-V6-4WD					
Standard 4D (2WD)	TY92V	3560	**8525**	**10625**	**11350**
Plus 4D (2WD)	TY92V		**9425**	**11625**	**12350**
Touring 4D (2WD)	TY92V		**10225**	**12475**	**13200**
Limited 4D (2WD)	TY92V	3626	**10675**	**12950**	**13675**
Standard 4D	TX92V	3682	**9625**	**11825**	**12575**
Plus 4D	TX92V		**10525**	**12800**	**13525**
Touring 4D	TX92V	3704	**11325**	**13725**	**14475**
Limited 4D	TX92V	3748	**11775**	**14200**	**14975**
Add Aluminum/Alloy Wheels (Standard)			**200**	**225**	**225**
Add Theft Recovery System			**75**	**100**	**100**
Deduct W/out Automatic Trans.			**375**	**375**	**375**
SUZUKI					
2001 VITARA-4 Cyl.-4WD					
JS 2D Soft Top (2WD)	TC03C	2624	**4475**	**6150**	**6925**
JLS 2D Soft Top (2WD)	TC52C	2690	**4975**	**6700**	**7525**
JX 2D Soft Top	TA03C	2745	**5425**	**7225**	**8000**
JLX 2D Soft Top	TA52C	2811	**5925**	**7775**	**8600**
JS 4D Hard Top (2WD)	TE52V	2866	**5575**	**7375**	**8175**
JLS 4D Hard Top (2WD)	TE52V		**5900**	**7725**	**8550**
JX 4D Hard Top	TD52V	2987	**6525**	**8450**	**9200**
JLX 4D Hard Top	TD52V		**6850**	**8800**	**9575**
Add Aluminum/Alloy Wheels			**150**	**175**	**175**
Add Theft Recovery System			**50**	**75**	**75**
Deduct W/out Air Conditioning			**425**	**425**	**425**
Deduct W/out Automatic Trans.			**325**	**325**	**325**
2001 GRAND VITARA HARD TOP-V6-4WD					
JLS 4D (2WD)	TE62V	3064	**6625**	**8550**	**9325**
JLS Plus 4D (2WD)	TE62V		**7175**	**9150**	**9850**
JLX 4D	TD62V	3197	**7700**	**9725**	**10450**
JLX Plus 4D	TD62V		**8250**	**10325**	**11050**
Limited 4D (2WD)	TE62V		**8025**	**10100**	**10825**
Limited 4D	TD62V		**9100**	**11250**	**11975**
Add Aluminum/Alloy Wheels (Std. Plus, Ltd.)			**150**	**175**	**175**
Add Theft Recovery System			**50**	**75**	**75**
Deduct W/out Automatic Trans.			**325**	**325**	**325**
2001 XL-7 HARD TOP-V6-4WD					
Standard 4D (2WD, 5 Spd.)	TY92V	3582	**7450**	**9475**	**10200**
Plus 4D (2WD)	TY92V		**8425**	**10525**	**11250**
Touring 4D (2WD)	TY92V	3626	**9125**	**11300**	**12025**
Limited 4D (2WD)	TY92V		**9525**	**11725**	**12475**
Standard 4D (5 Spd.)	TX92V	3703	**8525**	**10625**	**11350**
Plus 4D	TX92V		**9500**	**11700**	**12450**
Touring 4D	TX92V	3748	**10200**	**12450**	**13175**
Limited 4D	TX92V		**10600**	**12875**	**13600**
Add Aluminum/Alloy Wheels (Standard)			**150**	**175**	**175**
Add Compact Disc Player (Standard)			**50**	**75**	**75**
Add Theft Recovery System			**50**	**75**	**75**
Deduct W/out AT (Ex. Standard)			**325**	**325**	**325**

BODY TYPE	Model No.	Weight	Trade-In	Retail	High Retail
SUZUKI					
2000 VITARA-4 Cyl.-4WD					
JS 2D Soft Top (2WD)	TC03C	2602	**3575**	**5150**	**5875**
JLS 2D Soft Top (2WD)	TC52C	2690	**3975**	**5600**	**6375**
JX 2D Soft Top	TA03C	2723	**4575**	**6300**	**7100**
JLX 2D Soft Top	TA52C	2811	**4975**	**6725**	**7550**
JS 4D Hard Top (2WD)	TE52V	2866	**4575**	**6275**	**7075**
JLS 4D Hard Top (2WD)	TE52V	2866	**4825**	**6550**	**7350**
JX 4D Hard Top	TD52V	2987	**5575**	**7400**	**8200**
JLX 4D Hard Top	TD52V	2987	**5825**	**7675**	**8475**
Add Aluminum/Alloy Wheels			**100**	**125**	**125**
Add Compact Disc Player			**50**	**75**	**75**
Deduct W/out Air Conditioning			**375**	**375**	**375**
Deduct W/out Automatic Trans.			**300**	**300**	**300**
2000 GRAND VITARA HARD TOP-V6-4WD					
JLS 4D (2WD)	TE62V	3064	**5850**	**7700**	**8525**
JLS Plus 4D (2WD)	TE62V	3064	**6350**	**8250**	**9000**
JLX 4D	TD62V	3197	**6875**	**8825**	**9600**
JLX Plus 4D	TD62V	3197	**7375**	**9375**	**10075**
Limited 4D (2WD)	TE62V	3064	**6800**	**8750**	**9525**
Limited 4D	TD62V	3197	**7825**	**9875**	**10600**
Add Aluminum/Alloy Wheels (Std. Plus, Ltd.)			**100**	**125**	**125**
Add Compact Disc Player (Std. Plus, Limited)			**50**	**75**	**75**
Deduct W/out Automatic Trans.			**300**	**300**	**300**
SUZUKI					
1999 VITARA-4 Cyl.-4WD					
JS 1.6 2D Soft Top (2WD)	TC03C	2602	**2675**	**4125**	**4850**
JS 2.0 2D Soft Top (2WD)	TC52C	2690	**3000**	**4500**	**5250**
JX 1.6 2D Soft Top	TA03C	2723	**3750**	**5375**	**6125**
JX 2.0 2D Soft Top	TA52C	2811	**4075**	**5725**	**6500**
JS 4D Hard Top (2WD)	TE52V	2866	**3625**	**5200**	**5925**
JS Plus 4D Hard Top (2WD)	TE52V	2866	**3775**	**5375**	**6125**
JX 4D Hard Top	TD52V	2987	**4700**	**6425**	**7225**
JX Plus 4D Hard Top	TD52V	2987	**4850**	**6600**	**7425**
Add Aluminum/Alloy Wheels			**50**	**75**	**75**
Deduct W/out Air Conditioning			**325**	**325**	**325**
Deduct W/out Automatic Trans.			**250**	**250**	**250**
1999 GRAND VITARA HARD TOP-V6-4WD					
JS 4D (2WD)	TE62V	3064	**5000**	**6750**	**7575**
JS Plus 4D (2WD)	TE62V	3064	**5450**	**7250**	**8025**
JLX 4D	TD62V	3197	**5925**	**7775**	**8600**
JLX Plus 4D	TD62V	3197	**6375**	**8275**	**9025**
Add Aluminum/Alloy Wheels (Std. Plus)			**50**	**75**	**75**
Deduct W/out Automatic Trans.			**250**	**250**	**250**
SUZUKI					
1998 X-90-4 Cyl.-5 Spd.-4WD					
Utility 2D (2WD)	LA	2326	**2275**	**3675**	**4350**
Utility 2D	LB	2469	**3275**	**4800**	**5600**
Add Automatic Trans.			**200**	**225**	**225**
Deduct W/out Air Conditioning			**275**	**275**	**275**
1998 SIDEKICK-4 Cyl.-5 Spd.-4WD					
JS 2D Convertible (2WD)	TC	2337	**2150**	**3525**	**4175**

SEE TRUCK OPTION PAGE FOR ADDITIONAL OPTIONS

BODY TYPE	Model No.	Weight	Trade-In	Retail	High Retail
JX 2D Convertible	TA	2480	**3150**	**4675**	**5450**
JS 4D Hard Top (2WD)	TE	2624	**2650**	**4100**	**4825**
JX 4D Hard Top	TD	2756	**3650**	**5250**	**5975**
JS Sport 4D Hard Top (2WD)	TE	2822	**3150**	**4700**	**5475**
JX Sport 4D Hard Top	TD	2954	**4150**	**5800**	**6575**
JLX Sport 4D Hard Top	TD	2954	**4500**	**6200**	**6975**
Add Automatic Trans.			**200**	**225**	**225**
Deduct W/out Air Conditioning			**275**	**275**	**275**
SUZUKI					
1997 X-90-4 Cyl.-5 Spd.-4WD					
Utility 2D (2WD)	LA	2346	**1600**	**2875**	**3500**
Utility 2D	LB	2500	**2500**	**3925**	**4625**
Add Automatic Trans.			**125**	**150**	**150**
Deduct W/out Air Conditioning			**150**	**150**	**150**
1997 SIDEKICK-4 Cyl.-5 Spd.-4WD					
JS 2D Convertible (2WD)	TC	2339	**1650**	**2925**	**3550**
JX 2D Convertible	TA	2546	**2550**	**3975**	**4700**
JS 4D Hard Top (2WD)	TE	2593	**2050**	**3400**	**4050**
JX 4D Hard Top	TD	2756	**2950**	**4450**	**5200**
JS Sport 4D Hard Top (2WD)	TE		**2550**	**3975**	**4700**
JX Sport 4D Hard Top	TD	2954	**3050**	**4575**	**5350**
JLX Sport 4D Hard Top	TD	2954	**3450**	**5025**	**5750**
Add Automatic Trans.			**125**	**150**	**150**
Deduct W/out Air Conditioning			**150**	**150**	**150**
SUZUKI					
1996 X-90-4 Cyl.-5 Spd.-4WD					
Utility 2D (2WD)	LA	2321	**1400**	**2625**	**3225**
Utility 2D	LB	2493	**2200**	**3575**	**4250**
Add Automatic Trans.			**100**	**125**	**125**
Deduct W/out Air Conditioning			**100**	**100**	**100**
1996 SIDEKICK-4 Cyl.-5 Spd.-4WD					
JS 2D Convertible (2WD)	TC	2339	**1325**	**2550**	**3125**
JX 2D Convertible	TA	2546	**2125**	**3500**	**4150**
JS 4D Hard Top (2WD)	TE	2632	**1675**	**2950**	**3600**
JX 4D Hard Top	TD	2747	**2475**	**3900**	**4600**
JX Sport 4D Hard Top	TD	2917	**2625**	**4075**	**4775**
JLX Sport 4D Hard Top	TD		**2825**	**4300**	**5025**
Add Automatic Trans.			**100**	**125**	**125**
Deduct W/out Air Conditioning			**100**	**100**	**100**
SUZUKI					
1995 SAMURAI-4 Cyl.-4WD					
JL Convertible	JC	2059	**1425**	**2650**	**3250**
1995 SIDEKICK-4 Cyl.-4WD					
JS 2D Convertible (2WD)	TC	2253	**1175**	**2350**	**2900**
JX 2D Convertible	TA	2436	**1925**	**3250**	**3875**
JS 4D Hard Top (2WD)	TE	2571	**1475**	**2725**	**3325**
JX 4D Hard Top	TD	2762	**2225**	**3600**	**4275**
JLX 4D Hard Top	TD	2917	**2325**	**3725**	**4400**

BODY TYPE	Model No.	Weight	Trade-In	Retail	High Retail
TOYOTA					
TOYOTA					
2004 4RUNNER-V6-4WD					
Wagon 4D SR5 (2WD)	ZU14R	4035	**21325**	**24550**	**25800**
Wagon 4D Sport (2WD)	ZU14R	4065	**22000**	**25275**	**26525**
Wagon 4D Limited (2WD)	ZU17R	4055	**25775**	**29300**	**30650**
Wagon 4D SR5	BU14R	4290	**22700**	**26050**	**27325**
Wagon 4D Sport	BU14R	4330	**23375**	**26750**	**28050**
Wagon 4D Limited	BU17R	4310	**27150**	**30900**	**32275**
2004 4RUNNER-V8-4WD					
Wagon 4D SR5 (2WD)	ZT14R	4220	**22325**	**25625**	**26900**
Wagon 4D Sport (2WD)	ZT14R	4260	**23000**	**26350**	**27625**
Wagon 4D Limited (2WD)	ZT17R	4245	**26775**	**30375**	**31750**
Wagon 4D SR5	BT14R	4475	**23700**	**27100**	**28400**
Wagon 4D Sport	BT14R	4515	**24375**	**27825**	**29125**
Wagon 4D Limited	BT17R	4495	**28150**	**31950**	**33350**
4RUNNER OPTIONS					
Add 3rd Row Seat			**200**	**225**	**225**
Add JBL Stereo System			**300**	**350**	**350**
Add Navigation System			**600**	**675**	**675**
Add Power Sunroof			**575**	**650**	**650**
Add Rear Entertainment System			**600**	**675**	**675**
Add Theft Recovery System			**100**	**125**	**125**
2004 LAND CRUISER-V8-4WD					
Wagon	HT05J	5390	**43350**	**48175**	**50200**
Add Navigation System			**750**	**850**	**850**
Add Rear Entertainment System			**600**	**675**	**675**
Add Theft Recovery System			**100**	**125**	**125**
Deduct W/out Running Boards			**150**	**150**	**150**
2004 SEQUOIA-V8-4WD					
Utility SR5 (2WD)	ZT34A	5070	**27075**	**30750**	**32300**
Utility Limited (2WD)	ZT38A	5100	**30425**	**34350**	**36025**
Utility SR5	BT44A	5270	**29250**	**33100**	**34750**
Utility Limited	BT48A	5295	**32600**	**36825**	**38550**
Add Leather Seats (Std. Limited)			**525**	**600**	**600**
Add Power Sunroof (Std. Limited)			**625**	**700**	**700**
Add Rear Entertainment System			**600**	**675**	**675**
Add Theft Recovery System			**100**	**125**	**125**
Deduct W/out Running Boards			**150**	**150**	**150**
2004 SIENNA-V6					
Wagon 5D CE	ZA23C	4120	**19775**	**22650**	**23825**
Wagon 5D LE	ZA23C*	4120	**20725**	**23650**	**24875**
Wagon 5D XLE	ZA22C*	4165	**23525**	**26675**	**27975**
Wagon 5D Limited	ZA22C*	4310	**27675**	**31200**	**32600**
Add All Wheel Drive			**1100**	**1225**	**1225**
Add Aluminum/Alloy Wheels (Std. XLE, Limited)			**325**	**375**	**375**
Add JBL Stereo System (Std. XLE, Limited)			**300**	**350**	**350**
Add Leather Seats (Std. Limited)			**450**	**500**	**500**
Add Navigation System			**600**	**675**	**675**
Add Power Sliding Door (LE)			**300**	**350**	**350**

TRUCKS

SEE TRUCK OPTION PAGE FOR ADDITIONAL OPTIONS

BODY TYPE	Model No.	Weight	Trade-In	Retail	High Retail
Add Power Sunroof (Std. Limited)			575	650	650
Add Rear Entertainment System			600	675	675
Add Running Boards			150	175	175
Add Theft Recovery System			100	125	125
Deduct W/out Cruise Control			200	200	200

* B as the 1st position of the model # denotes AWD

2004 TACOMA PICKUP-4 Cyl.-5 Spd.

BODY TYPE	Model No.	Weight	Trade-In	Retail	High Retail
Base	NL42N	2750	10975	13175	
PreRunner (AT)	NM92N	3095	13375	15800	
Base X-Cab	VL52N	2950	13325	15725	
PreRunner X-Cab (AT)	SM92N	3270	15725	18275	
PreRunner X-Cab (V6, AT)	SN92N	3355	17225	19950	
Base (4WD)	PM62N	3290	14075	16525	
Base X-Cab (4WD)	WM72N	3470	16425	19000	
Base X-Cab (4WD, V6)	WN72N	3515	18025	20800	
Limited X-Cab (4WD, V6)	WN72N		20925	23850	

2004 TACOMA PICKUP DOUBLE CAB-V6-AT

BODY TYPE	Model No.	Weight	Trade-In	Retail	High Retail
PreRunner (4 Cyl.)	GM92N	3430	16850	19450	
PreRunner	GN92N	3475	18350	21150	
PreRunner Ltd.	GN92N		21200	24150	
Base (4WD)	HN72N	3705	19875	22750	
Limited (4WD)	HN72N		22425	25525	

TACOMA OPTIONS

BODY TYPE	Model No.	Weight	Trade-In	Retail	High Retail
Add SR5 Trim			675	750	
Add TRD Off-Road (Std. Limited)			675	750	
Add Aluminum/Alloy Wheels (Std. PreRunner, Ltd., D-Cab)			300	350	
Add AT (Std. PreRunner, Double Cab)			475	550	
Add CD Player (Std. Limited)			100	125	
Add Cruise Control (Std. Limited)			175	200	
Add Power Door Locks (Std. Limited)			150	175	
Add Power Windows (Std. Limited)			175	200	
Add Running Boards			150	175	
Add Theft Recovery System			100	125	
Add Tilt Wheel (Std. Limited, D-Cab)			125	150	
Deduct W/out Air Conditioning			575	575	

2004 TUNDRA PICKUP-V8

BODY TYPE	Model No.	Weight	Trade-In	Retail	High Retail
Base (V6)	JN321	3925	13125	15700	16900
SR5 Access Cab (V6)	RN341	4160	18925	22000	23375
SR5 Access Cab	RT341	4450	20275	23450	24825
Limited Access Cab	RT381	4400	21675	24950	26350
SR5 (4WD)	KT441	4490	19075	22175	23500
SR5 Access Cab (4WD, V6)	BN441	4435	21725	25000	26400
SR5 Access Cab (4WD)	BT441	4725	23075	26450	27900
Limited Access Cab (4WD)	BT481	4675	24475	27925	29400

2004 TUNDRA PICKUP DOUBLE CAB-V8

BODY TYPE	Model No.	Weight	Trade-In	Retail	High Retail
SR5 Double Cab	ET341	4725	21875	25150	26575
Limited Double Cab	ET381	4780	23275	26650	28100
SR5 Double Cab (4WD)	DT441	4965	24675	28125	29600
Limited Double Cab (4WD)	DT481	5020	26075	29625	31150

TUNDRA OPTIONS

BODY TYPE	Model No.	Weight	Trade-In	Retail	High Retail
Add TRD Off-Road (SR5)			600	675	675
Add Aluminum/Alloy Wheels (Base)			375	425	425
Add Leather Seats			525	600	600

TRUCKS

BODY TYPE	Model No.	Weight	Trade-In	Retail	High Retail
Add Power Seat			225	250	250
Add Power Sunroof			625	700	700
Add Rear Entertainment System			600	675	675
Add Running Boards			150	175	175
Add StepSide Bed			625	700	700
Add Theft Recovery System			100	125	125
Deduct W/out Air Conditioning			750	750	750
Deduct W/out Automatic Trans.			625	625	625
Deduct W/out Cruise Control (Ex. Base)			225	225	225
Deduct W/out Power Door Locks (Ex. Base)			200	200	200
Deduct W/out Power Windows (Ex. Base)			225	225	225
Deduct W/out Tilt Steering Wheel			175	175	175
2004 RAV4-4 Cyl.-4WD					
Utility 4D (2WD)	GD20V	2897	16150	18700	19525
Utility 4D	HD20V	3119	17200	19925	20775
Add L Pkg.			400	450	450
Add Sport Pkg.			350	400	400
Add Aluminum/Alloy Wheels			300	350	350
Add Leather Seats			350	400	400
Add Power Sunroof			525	600	600
Add Running Boards			150	175	175
Add Theft Recovery System			100	125	125
Deduct W/out Automatic Trans.			475	475	475
2004 HIGHLANDER-V6-4WD					
Utility 4D (2WD, 4 Cyl.)	(G/D)D21A	3520	19325	22175	23350
Utility 4D (2WD)	(G/D)P21A	3650	20675	23600	24800
Utility 4D Limited (2WD)	(G/D)P21A		22625	25725	27000
Utility 4D (4 Cyl.)	HD21A	3750	20400	23300	24500
Utility 4D	EP21A	3935	21950	24975	26225
Utility 4D Limited	EP21A		23700	26875	28175
Add 3rd Row Seat (Std. V6 4WD, Ltd.)			200	225	225
Add Aluminum/Alloy Wheels (Std. Ltd.)			325	375	375
Add Leather Seats			450	500	500
Add Navigation System			600	675	675
Add Power Seat (Std. Limited)			200	225	225
Add Power Sunroof			575	650	650
Add Rear Entertainment System			600	675	675
Add Running Boards			150	175	175
Add Theft Recovery System			100	125	125
TOYOTA					
2003 4RUNNER-V6-4WD					
Wagon 4D SR5 (2WD)	ZU14R	4025	20200	23375	24575
Wagon 4D Sport (2WD)	ZU14R	4065	20800	24000	25225
Wagon 4D Limited (2WD)	ZU17R	4035	24650	28100	29425
Wagon 4D SR5	BU14R	4280	21575	24825	26075
Wagon 4D Sport	BU14R	4320	22175	25475	26750
Wagon 4D Limited	BU17R	4290	26025	29575	30925
2003 4RUNNER-V8-4WD					
Wagon 4D SR5 (2WD)	ZT14R	4155	21000	24225	25450
Wagon 4D Sport (2WD)	ZT14R	4195	21600	24850	26100
Wagon 4D Limited (2WD)	ZT17R	4165	25450	28950	30275
Wagon 4D SR5	BT14R	4410	22375	25700	26975
Wagon 4D Sport	BT14R	4450	22975	26325	27600
Wagon 4D Limited	BT17R	4420	26825	30425	31800

TRUCKS

SEE TRUCK OPTION PAGE FOR ADDITIONAL OPTIONS

BODY TYPE	Model No.	Weight	Trade-In	Retail	High Retail
4RUNNER OPTIONS					
Add JBL Stereo System			250	300	300
Add Navigation System			500	575	575
Add Power Sunroof			525	600	600
Add Running Boards (Std. Limited)			125	150	150
Add Theft Recovery System			75	100	100
2003 LAND CRUISER-V8-4WD					
Wagon	HT05J	5390	37475	41975	43825
Add Navigation System			650	725	725
Add Rear Entertainment System			500	575	575
Add Theft Recovery System			75	100	100
Deduct W/out Running Boards			125	125	125
2003 SEQUOIA-V8-4WD					
Utility SR5 (2WD)	ZT34A	5070	24575	28025	29500
Utility Limited (2WD)	ZT38A	5100	27275	30975	32550
Utility SR5	BT44A	5270	26650	30225	31775
Utility Limited	BT48A	5295	29350	33225	34875
Add Leather Seats (Std. Limited)			475	550	550
Add Power Sunroof			575	650	650
Add Rear Air Conditioning (Std. Limited)			150	175	175
Add Rear Entertainment System			500	575	575
Add Theft Recovery System			75	100	100
Deduct W/out Power Seat			200	200	200
Deduct W/out Running Boards			125	125	125
2003 SIENNA-V6					
Wagon 5D CE	ZF19C	3919	15075	17775	18825
Wagon 5D LE	ZF13C	3932	16575	19375	20475
Wagon 5D Symphony	ZF13C	3932	17250	20225	21350
Wagon 5D XLE	ZF13C	3932	17925	20925	22075
Add Aluminum/Alloy Wheels (Std. Symphony, XLE)			275	325	325
Add Dual Power Sliding Doors (XLE)			500	575	575
Add Leather Seats			400	450	450
Add Power Sliding Door			250	300	300
Add Power Sunroof			525	600	600
Add Rear Bucket Seats (CE, LE)			175	200	200
Add Rear Entertainment System			500	575	575
Add Running Boards			125	150	150
Add Theft Recovery System			75	100	100
Deduct W/out Cruise Control			175	175	175
Deduct W/out Power Door Locks			150	150	150
Deduct W/out Power Windows			175	175	175
2003 TACOMA PICKUP-4 Cyl.-5 Spd.					
Base	NL42N	2750	9725	11775	12525
PreRunner (AT)	NM92N	3095	12125	14475	15250
Base X-Cab	VL52N	2950	12075	14400	15175
PreRunner X-Cab (AT)	SM92N	3270	14475	16950	17775
PreRunner X-Cab (V6, AT)	SN92N	3355	15925	18475	19300
Base (4WD)	PM62N	3290	12825	15200	16000
Base X-Cab (4WD)	WM72N	3470	15175	17700	18525
Base X-Cab (4WD, V6)	WN72N	3515	16775	19375	20225
Limited X-Cab (4WD, V6)	WN72N		19475	22325	23225
2003 TACOMA PICKUP DOUBLE CAB-V6-AT					
PreRunner (4 Cyl.)	GM92N	3430	15700	18250	19075

TRUCKS

BODY TYPE	Model No.	Weight	Trade-In	Retail	High Retail
PreRunner	GN92N	3475	**17150**	**19875**	**20725**
PreRunner Ltd.	GN92N		**19750**	**22625**	**23525**
Base (4WD)	HN72N	3705	**18575**	**21375**	**22275**
Limited (4WD)	HN72N		**20925**	**23850**	**24775**
TACOMA OPTIONS					
Add SR5 Trim			**625**	**700**	**700**
Add TRD Off-Road (Std. Limited)			**625**	**700**	**700**
Add Aluminum/Alloy Wheels (Std. PreRunner, Ltd., D-Cab)			**250**	**300**	**300**
Add AT (Std. PreRunner, Double Cab)			**425**	**475**	**475**
Add CD Player (Std. Limited)			**75**	**100**	**100**
Add Cruise Control (Std. Limited)			**150**	**175**	**175**
Add Power Door Locks (Std. Limited)			**125**	**150**	**150**
Add Power Windows (Std. Limited)			**150**	**175**	**175**
Add Running Boards			**125**	**150**	**150**
Add StepSide Bed			**300**	**350**	**350**
Add Sunroof			**225**	**275**	**275**
Add Theft Recovery System			**75**	**100**	**100**
Add Tilt Wheel (Std. Limited, D-Cab)			**100**	**125**	**125**
Deduct W/out Air Conditioning			**525**	**525**	**525**
2003 TUNDRA PICKUP-V8					
Base (V6)	JN321	3925	**11275**	**13675**	**14775**
SR5 Access Cab (V6)	RN341	4160	**17000**	**19875**	**21175**
SR5 Access Cab	RT341	4450	**18250**	**21275**	**22625**
Limited Access Cab	RT381	4400	**19550**	**22675**	**24025**
SR5 (4WD)	KT441	4490	**16950**	**19825**	**21125**
SR5 Access Cab (4WD, V6)	BN441	4435	**19700**	**22825**	**24175**
SR5 Access Cab (4WD)	BT441	4725	**20950**	**24150**	**25525**
Limited Access Cab (4WD)	BT481	4675	**22250**	**25550**	**26975**
Add TRD Off-Road (SR5)			**550**	**625**	**625**
Add Aluminum/Alloy Wheels (Base)			**325**	**375**	**375**
Add Leather Seats			**475**	**550**	**550**
Add Power Seat			**200**	**225**	**225**
Add Running Boards			**125**	**150**	**150**
Add StepSide Bed			**550**	**625**	**625**
Add Theft Recovery System			**75**	**100**	**100**
Deduct W/out Air Conditioning			**700**	**700**	**700**
Deduct W/out Automatic Trans.			**575**	**575**	**575**
Deduct W/out Cruise Control (Ex. Base)			**200**	**200**	**200**
Deduct W/out Power Door Locks (Ex. Base)			**175**	**175**	**175**
Deduct W/out Power Windows (Ex. Base)			**200**	**200**	**200**
Deduct W/out Tilt Steering Wheel			**150**	**150**	**150**
2003 RAV4-4 Cyl.-4WD					
Utility 4D (2WD)	GH20V	2711	**14475**	**16950**	**17775**
Utility 4D	HH20V	2877	**15725**	**18275**	**19100**
Add L Pkg.			**350**	**400**	**400**
Add Sport Pkg.			**300**	**350**	**350**
Add Aluminum/Alloy Wheels			**250**	**300**	**300**
Add Cruise Control			**150**	**175**	**175**
Add Leather Seats			**300**	**350**	**350**
Add Power Door Locks			**125**	**150**	**150**
Add Power Sunroof			**475**	**550**	**550**
Add Power Windows			**150**	**175**	**175**
Add Running Boards			**125**	**150**	**150**

TRUCKS

SEE TRUCK OPTION PAGE FOR ADDITIONAL OPTIONS

BODY TYPE	Model No.	Weight	Trade-In	Retail	High Retail
Add Theft Recovery System			**75**	**100**	**100**
Deduct W/out Air Conditioning			**525**	**525**	**525**
Deduct W/out Automatic Trans.			**425**	**425**	**425**
2003 HIGHLANDER-V6-4WD					
Utility 4D (2WD, 4 Cyl.)	GD21A	3485	**18075**	**20850**	**22000**
Utility 4D (2WD)	GF21A	3660	**19425**	**22275**	**23450**
Utility 4D Limited (2WD)	GF21A		**21075**	**24025**	**25250**
Utility 4D (4 Cyl.)	HD21A	3715	**19125**	**21950**	**23125**
Utility 4D	HF21A	3880	**20475**	**23375**	**24575**
Utility 4D Limited	HF21A		**22125**	**25175**	**26425**
Add Aluminum/Alloy Wheels (Std. Ltd.)			**275**	**325**	**325**
Add Leather Seats			**400**	**450**	**450**
Add Power Seat (Std. Limited)			**175**	**200**	**200**
Add Power Sunroof			**525**	**600**	**600**
Add Running Boards			**125**	**150**	**150**
Add Theft Recovery System			**75**	**100**	**100**
TOYOTA					
2002 4RUNNER-V6-4WD					
Wagon 4D SR5 (2WD)	GN86R	3740	**17950**	**20975**	**22125**
Wagon 4D Limited (2WD)	GN87R	3795	**20650**	**23850**	**25075**
Wagon 4D SR5	HN86R	4070	**19550**	**22675**	**23850**
Wagon 4D Limited	HN87R	4115	**22250**	**25575**	**26850**
Add Sport Pkg. (SR5)			**400**	**450**	**450**
Add Leather Seats (Std. Limited)			**350**	**400**	**400**
Add Power Sunroof			**475**	**550**	**550**
Add Running Boards (Std. Limited)			**100**	**125**	**125**
Add Theft Recovery System			**75**	**100**	**100**
2002 LAND CRUISER-V8-4WD					
Wagon	HT05J	5115	**30900**	**34875**	**36550**
Add Navigation System			**550**	**625**	**625**
Add Theft Recovery System			**75**	**100**	**100**
Deduct W/out Running Boards			**100**	**100**	**100**
2002 SEQUOIA-V8-4WD					
Utility SR5 (2WD)	ZT34A	5070	**20925**	**24150**	**25525**
Utility Limited (2WD)	ZT38A	5100	**22925**	**26275**	**27725**
Utility SR5	BT44A	5270	**22825**	**26150**	**27600**
Utility Limited	BT48A	5295	**24825**	**28275**	**29775**
Add Leather Seats (Std. Limited)			**425**	**475**	**475**
Add Power Sunroof			**525**	**600**	**600**
Add Rear Air Conditioning (Std. Limited)			**150**	**175**	**175**
Add Theft Recovery System			**75**	**100**	**100**
Deduct W/out Power Seat			**175**	**175**	**175**
Deduct W/out Running Boards			**100**	**100**	**100**
2002 SIENNA-V6					
Wagon 5D CE	ZF19C	3919	**13225**	**15800**	**16825**
Wagon 5D LE	ZF13C	3932	**14725**	**17400**	**18425**
Wagon 5D Symphony	ZF13C		**15275**	**17975**	**19025**
Wagon 5D XLE	ZF13C	3932	**15975**	**18725**	**19800**
Add Aluminum/Alloy Wheels (Std. Symphony, XLE)			**225**	**250**	**250**
Add Dual Power Sliding Doors (XLE)			**500**	**575**	**575**
Add Leather Seats			**350**	**400**	**400**
Add Power Sliding Door			**250**	**300**	**300**

TRUCKS

BODY TYPE	Model No.	Weight	Trade-In	Retail	High Retail
Add Power Sunroof			475	550	550
Add Rear Bucket Seats (CE, LE)			150	175	175
Add Rear Entertainment System			400	450	450
Add Running Boards			100	125	125
Add Theft Recovery System			75	100	100
Deduct W/out Cruise Control			150	150	150
Deduct W/out Power Door Locks			125	125	125
Deduct W/out Power Windows			150	150	150
2002 TACOMA PICKUP-4 Cyl.-5 Spd.					
Base	NL42N	2750	8650	10725	11475
PreRunner (AT)	NM92N	3095	10650	12875	13600
Base X-Cab	VL52N	2990	10850	13100	13850
PreRunner X-Cab (AT)	SM92N	3270	12850	15275	16075
S-Runner X-Cab (V6)	VN52N	3125	12450	14850	15625
PreRunner X-Cab (V6, AT)	SN92N	3355	14250	16750	17575
Base (4WD)	PM62N	3290	11600	13900	14650
Base X-Cab (4WD)	WM72N	3470	13800	16275	17100
Base X-Cab (4WD, V6)	WN72N	3515	15200	17775	18600
Limited X-Cab (4WD, V6)	WN72N		17550	20425	21300
2002 TACOMA PICKUP DOUBLE CAB-V6-AT					
PreRunner (4 Cyl.)	GM92N	3430	14325	16825	17650
PreRunner	GN92N	3475	15725	18325	19150
PreRunner Ltd.	GN92N		17775	20650	21525
Base (4WD)	HN72N	3705	16900	19575	20425
Limited (4WD)	HN72N		19050	22000	22900
TACOMA OPTIONS					
Add SR5 Trim			575	650	650
Add TRD Off-Road (Std. Limited)			575	650	650
Add Aluminum/Alloy Wheels (Std. Pre/S-Runner, Ltd., D-Cab)			200	225	225
Add AT (Std. PreRunner, Double Cab)			375	425	425
Add CD Player (Std. Limited X-Cab)			75	100	100
Add Cruise Control (Std. Limited)			125	150	150
Add Power Door Locks (Std. Limited)			100	125	125
Add Power Windows (Std. Limited)			125	150	150
Add Running Boards			100	125	125
Add StepSide Bed			275	325	325
Add Sunroof			200	225	225
Add Theft Recovery System			75	100	100
Add Tilt Wheel (Std. Limited, Double Cab)			75	100	100
Deduct W/out Air Conditioning			475	475	475
2002 TUNDRA PICKUP-V8					
Base (V6)	JN321	3795	9125	11300	12325
SR5 Access Cab (V6)	RN341	4088	14425	17075	18275
SR5 Access Cab	RT341	4276	15525	18250	19500
Limited Access Cab	RT381	4402	16725	19525	20825
SR5 (4WD)	KT441	4262	14225	16850	18075
SR5 Access Cab (4WD, V6)	BN441	4320	16925	19775	21075
SR5 Access Cab (4WD)	BT441	4518	18025	21050	22400
Limited Access Cab (4WD)	BT481	4644	19225	22325	23650
Add TRD Off-Road (SR5)			500	575	575
Add Aluminum/Alloy Wheels (Base)			275	325	325
Add Compact Disc Player (Std. Limited)			100	125	125
Add Leather Seats			425	475	475

SEE TRUCK OPTION PAGE FOR ADDITIONAL OPTIONS

TRUCKS

BODY TYPE	Model No.	Weight	Trade-In	Retail	High Retail
Add Power Seat			175	200	200
Add Running Boards			100	125	125
Add Theft Recovery System			75	100	100
Deduct W/out Air Conditioning			650	650	650
Deduct W/out Automatic Trans.			525	525	525
Deduct W/out Cruise Control (Ex. Base)			175	175	175
Deduct W/out Power Door Locks (Ex. Base)			150	150	150
Deduct W/out Power Windows (Ex. Base)			175	175	175
Deduct W/out Tilt Steering Wheel			125	125	125
2002 RAV4-4 Cyl.-4WD					
Utility 4D (2WD)	GH20V	2711	13300	15700	16500
Utility 4D	HH20V	2877	14450	16925	17750
Add L Pkg.			350	400	400
Add Aluminum/Alloy Wheels			200	225	225
Add Compact Disc Player			75	100	100
Add Cruise Control			125	150	150
Add Leather Seats			250	300	300
Add Power Door Locks			100	125	125
Add Power Sunroof			425	475	475
Add Power Windows			125	150	150
Add Running Boards			100	125	125
Add Theft Recovery System			75	100	100
Deduct W/out Air Conditioning			475	475	475
Deduct W/out Automatic Trans.			375	375	375
2002 HIGHLANDER-V6-4WD					
Utility 4D (2WD, 4 Cyl.)	GD21A	3485	16550	19125	20200
Utility 4D (2WD)	GF21A	3660	18000	20750	21875
Utility 4D Limited (2WD)	GF21A		19500	22350	23525
Utility 4D (4 Cyl.)	HD21A	3715	17525	20275	21400
Utility 4D	HF21A	3880	18975	21800	22975
Utility 4D Limited	HF21A		20475	23375	24575
Add Aluminum/Alloy Wheels (Std. Ltd.)			225	250	250
Add Leather Seats			350	400	400
Add Power Seat (Std. Limited)			150	175	175
Add Power Sunroof			475	550	550
Add Running Boards			100	125	125
Add Theft Recovery System			75	100	100
TOYOTA					
2001 4RUNNER-V6-4WD					
Wagon 4D SR5 (2WD)	GN86R	3740	15125	17825	18875
Wagon 4D Limited (2WD)	GN87R	3795	16925	19775	20875
Wagon 4D SR5	HN86R	4070	16625	19425	20525
Wagon 4D Limited	HN87R	4115	18425	21475	22625
Add Leather Seats (Std. Limited)			300	350	350
Add Power Sunroof			425	475	475
Add Running Boards (Std. Limited)			75	100	100
Add Theft Recovery System			50	75	75
Deduct W/out Air Conditioning			550	550	550
Deduct W/out Power Windows			125	125	125
2001 LAND CRUISER-V8-4WD					
Wagon	HT05J	5115	25950	29475	31000
Add 3rd Row Seat			125	150	150
Add Navigation System			500	575	575

TRUCKS

BODY TYPE	Model No.	Weight	Trade-In	Retail	High Retail
Add Rear Air Conditioning			125	150	150
Add Theft Recovery System			50	75	75
Deduct W/out Running Boards			75	75	75
2001 SEQUOIA-V8-4WD					
Utility SR5 (2WD)	ZT34A	5070	18150	21175	22525
Utility Limited (2WD)	ZT38A	5100	19650	22775	24125
Utility SR5	BT44A	5270	19675	22800	24150
Utility Limited	BT48A	5295	21175	24400	25800
Add Compact Disc Player (Std. Limited)			100	125	125
Add Leather Seats (Std. Limited)			375	425	425
Add Power Sunroof			475	550	550
Add Rear Air Conditioning (Std. Limited)			125	150	150
Add Theft Recovery System			50	75	75
Deduct W/out Power Seat			150	150	150
Deduct W/out Running Boards			75	75	75
2001 SIENNA-V6					
Wagon 5D CE	ZF19C	3919	10950	13300	14225
Wagon 5D LE	ZF13C	3932	12350	14875	15850
Wagon 5D XLE	ZF13C	3932	13500	16100	17125
Add Aluminum/Alloy Wheels (Std. XLE)			175	200	200
Add Dual Power Sliding Doors (XLE)			450	500	500
Add Leather Seats			300	350	350
Add Power Sliding Door			225	250	250
Add Power Sunroof			425	475	475
Add Rear Bucket Seats (LE)			125	150	150
Add Rear Entertainment System			350	400	400
Add Running Boards			75	100	100
Add Theft Recovery System			50	75	75
Deduct W/out Cruise Control			125	125	125
Deduct W/out Power Door Locks			100	100	100
Deduct W/out Power Windows			125	125	125
2001 TACOMA PICKUP-4 Cyl.-5 Spd.					
Base	NL42N	2750	7500	9500	10225
PreRunner (AT)	NM92N	3095	9200	11375	12100
Base X-Cab	VL52N	2990	9375	11550	12275
PreRunner X-Cab (AT)	SM92N	3279	11075	13450	14200
S-Runner X-Cab (V6)	VN52N	3125	10925	13225	13975
PreRunner X-Cab (V6, AT)	SN92N	3355	12375	14875	15650
Base (4WD)	PM62N	3290	10300	12550	13275
Base X-Cab (4WD)	WM72N	3470	12175	14675	15450
Base X-Cab (4WD, V6)	WN72N	3515	13475	16050	16875
Limited X-Cab (4WD, V6)	WN72N		15600	18325	19150
2001 TACOMA PICKUP DOUBLE CAB-V6-AT					
PreRunner (4 Cyl.)	GM92N	3430	12625	15150	15950
PreRunner	GN92N	3475	13925	16525	17350
PreRunner Ltd.	GN92N		15825	18550	19375
Base (4WD)	HN72N	3705	15400	18100	18925
Limited (4WD)	HN72N		17300	20275	21150
TACOMA OPTIONS					
Add SR5 Trim			525	600	600
Add TRD Off-Road (Std. Limited)			525	600	600
Add Aluminum/Alloy Wheels (Std. Pre/S-Runner, Ltd., D-Cab)			150	175	175

TRUCKS

SEE TRUCK OPTION PAGE FOR ADDITIONAL OPTIONS

BODY TYPE	Model No.	Weight	Trade-In	Retail	High Retail
Add AT (Std. PreRunner, Double Cab)			325	375	375
Add CD Player (Std. Limited X Cab)			50	75	75
Add Cruise Control (Std. Limited)			100	125	125
Add Power Door Locks (Std. Limited)			75	100	100
Add Power Windows (Std. Limited)			100	125	125
Add Running Boards			75	100	100
Add StepSide Bed			250	300	300
Add Sunroof			175	200	200
Add Theft Recovery System			50	75	75
Add Tilt Wheel (Std. Limited, Double Cab)			75	100	100
Deduct W/out Air Conditioning			425	425	425
2001 TUNDRA PICKUP-V8					
Base (V6)	JN321	3795	7850	9925	10975
SR5 Access Cab (V6)	RN341	4088	12900	15450	16625
SR5 Access Cab	RT341	4276	13800	16425	17650
Limited Access Cab	RT381	4402	14900	17600	18825
SR5 (4WD)	KT441	4321	12550	15100	16275
SR5 Access Cab (4WD, V6)	BN441	4320	15250	17975	19225
SR5 Access Cab (4WD)	BT441	4518	16150	18925	20200
Limited Access Cab (4WD)	BT481	4644	17250	20225	21550
Add TRD Off-Road (SR5)			450	500	500
Add Aluminum/Alloy Wheels (Base)			225	250	250
Add Compact Disc Player (Std. Limited)			100	125	125
Add Leather Seats			375	425	425
Add Power Seat			150	175	175
Add Running Boards			75	100	100
Add Theft Recovery System			50	75	75
Deduct W/out Air Conditioning			600	600	600
Deduct W/out Automatic Trans.			475	475	475
Deduct W/out Cruise Control (Ex. Base)			150	150	150
Deduct W/out Power Door Locks (Ex. Base)			125	125	125
Deduct W/out Power Windows (Ex. Base)			150	150	150
Deduct W/out Tilt Steering Wheel			100	100	100
2001 RAV4-4 Cyl.-4WD					
Utility 4D (2WD)	GH20V	2711	12200	14700	15475
Utility 4D	HH20V	2877	13175	15750	16550
Add L Pkg.			300	350	350
Add Aluminum/Alloy Wheels			150	175	175
Add Compact Disc Player			50	75	75
Add Cruise Control			100	125	125
Add Leather Seats			200	225	225
Add Power Door Locks			75	100	100
Add Power Sunroof			375	425	425
Add Power Windows			100	125	125
Add Running Boards			75	100	100
Add Theft Recovery System			50	75	75
Deduct W/out Air Conditioning			425	425	425
Deduct W/out Automatic Trans.			325	325	325
2001 HIGHLANDER-V6-4WD					
Utility 4D (2WD, 4 Cyl.)	GD21A	3485	14400	17050	18075
Utility 4D (2WD)	GF21A	3660	15800	18550	19625
Utility 4D Limited (2WD)	GF21A		17200	20150	21275
Utility 4D (4 Cyl.)	HD21A	3715	15350	18075	19125
Utility 4D	HF21A	3880	16750	19550	20650

TRUCKS

BODY TYPE	Model No.	Weight	Trade-In	Retail	High Retail
Utility 4D Limited	HF21A		**18150**	**21175**	**22325**
Add Aluminum/Alloy Wheels (Std. Ltd.)			**175**	**200**	**200**
Add Leather Seats			**300**	**350**	**350**
Add Power Seat (Std. Limited)			**125**	**150**	**150**
Add Power Sunroof			**425**	**475**	**475**
Add Running Boards			**75**	**100**	**100**
Add Theft Recovery System			**50**	**75**	**75**
TOYOTA					
2000 4RUNNER-V6-4WD					
Wagon 4D (2WD, 4 Cyl.)	GM84R	3440	**10200**	**12450**	**13350**
Wagon 4D SR5 (2WD)	GN86R	3600	**13425**	**16025**	**17050**
Wagon 4D Limited (2WD)	GN87R	3710	**14825**	**17500**	**18525**
Wagon 4D (4 Cyl, 5 Spd)	HM84R	3725	**11000**	**13325**	**14250**
Wagon 4D SR5	HN86R	3885	**14600**	**17250**	**18275**
Wagon 4D Limited	HN87R	3975	**16000**	**18750**	**19825**
Add Compact Disc Player (Std. Limited)			**50**	**75**	**75**
Add Leather Seats (Std. Limited)			**250**	**300**	**300**
Add Power Sunroof			**375**	**425**	**425**
Add Running Boards (Std. Limited)			**50**	**75**	**75**
Deduct W/out Air Conditioning			**500**	**500**	**500**
Deduct W/out AT (Ex. HM84R)			**375**	**375**	**375**
Deduct W/out Cruise Control			**100**	**100**	**100**
Deduct W/out Power Door Locks			**75**	**75**	**75**
Deduct W/out Power Windows			**100**	**100**	**100**
Deduct W/out Tilt Steering Wheel			**75**	**75**	**75**
2000 LAND CRUISER-V8-4WD					
Wagon	HT05J	5115	**21600**	**24850**	**26250**
Add 3rd Row Seat			**100**	**125**	**125**
Add Rear Air Conditioning			**100**	**125**	**125**
Deduct W/out Running Boards			**50**	**50**	**50**
2000 SIENNA-V6					
Wagon 4D CE	GF19C	3759	**8475**	**10575**	**11525**
Wagon 5D CE	ZF19C	3880	**8825**	**10950**	**11900**
Wagon 5D LE	ZF13C	3890	**9975**	**12200**	**13100**
Wagon 5D XLE	ZF13C	3945	**10975**	**13300**	**14225**
Add Aluminum/Alloy Wheels (Std. XLE)			**125**	**150**	**150**
Add Leather Seats			**250**	**300**	**300**
Add Power Sliding Door			**200**	**225**	**225**
Add Power Sunroof			**375**	**425**	**425**
Add Rear Air Conditioning (4D CE)			**100**	**125**	**125**
Add Rear Bucket Seats (LE)			**100**	**125**	**125**
Add Running Boards			**50**	**75**	**75**
Deduct W/out Cruise Control			**100**	**100**	**100**
Deduct W/out Power Door Locks			**75**	**75**	**75**
Deduct W/out Power Windows			**100**	**100**	**100**
2000 TACOMA PICKUP-4 Cyl.-5 Spd.					
Base	NL42N	2580	**6425**	**8350**	**9100**
PreRunner (AT)	NM92N	3035	**7925**	**10000**	**10725**
Base X-Cab	VL52N	2760	**8075**	**10150**	**10875**
PreRunner X-Cab (AT)	SM92N	3175	**9575**	**11800**	**12550**
Base X-Cab (V6)	VN52N	2910	**9275**	**11475**	**12200**
PreRunner X-Cab (V6, AT)	SN92N	3280	**10775**	**13075**	**13825**
Base (4WD)	PM62N	3215	**8825**	**10975**	**11725**

SEE TRUCK OPTION PAGE FOR ADDITIONAL OPTIONS

BODY TYPE	Model No.	Weight	Trade-In	Retail	High Retail
Base X-Cab (4WD)	WM72N	3360	**10475**	**12750**	**13475**
Base X-Cab (4WD, V6)	WN72N	3425	**11675**	**14100**	**14875**
Limited X-Cab (4WD, V6)	WN74N	3430	**13125**	**15700**	**16500**
Add SR5 Trim			**475**	**550**	**550**
Add TRD Off-Road			**475**	**550**	**550**
Add Aluminum/Alloy Wheels (Std. PreRunner, Ltd.)			**100**	**125**	**125**
Add Auto Trans. (Std. PreRunner)			**300**	**350**	**350**
Add Compact Disc Player (Std. Limited)			**50**	**75**	**75**
Add Cruise Control (Std. Limited)			**75**	**100**	**100**
Add Power Door Locks (Std. Limited)			**50**	**75**	**75**
Add Power Windows (Std. Limited)			**75**	**100**	**100**
Add Running Boards			**50**	**75**	**75**
Add StepSide Bed			**225**	**250**	**250**
Add Sunroof			**150**	**175**	**175**
Add Tilt Steering Wheel (Std. Limited)			**50**	**75**	**75**
Deduct W/out Air Conditioning			**375**	**375**	**375**
Deduct W/out Power Steering			**50**	**50**	**50**
2000 TUNDRA PICKUP-V8					
Base (V6)	JN321	3795	**6900**	**8875**	**9925**
SR5 Access Cab (V6)	RN341	4088	**11725**	**14175**	**15300**
SR5 Access Cab	RT341	4276	**12425**	**14950**	**16100**
Limited Access Cab	RT381	4402	**13375**	**15975**	**17175**
SR5 (4WD, V6)	KN441	4123	**10325**	**12600**	**13675**
SR5 (4WD)	KT441	4321	**11025**	**13400**	**14500**
SR5 Access Cab (4WD, V6)	BN441	4320	**13725**	**16350**	**17575**
SR5 Access Cab (4WD)	BT441	4518	**14425**	**17100**	**18300**
Limited Access Cab (4WD)	BT481	4664	**15375**	**18100**	**19350**
Add TRD Off-Road (SR5 4WD)			**400**	**450**	**450**
Add Aluminum/Alloy Wheels (Base)			**175**	**200**	**200**
Add Compact Disc Player (Std. Limited)			**75**	**100**	**100**
Add Leather Seats			**325**	**375**	**375**
Add Power Seat			**125**	**150**	**150**
Add Running Boards			**50**	**75**	**75**
Deduct W/out Air Conditioning			**550**	**550**	**550**
Deduct W/out Automatic Trans.			**425**	**425**	**425**
Deduct W/out Cruise Control (Ex. Base)			**125**	**125**	**125**
Deduct W/out Power Door Locks (Ex. Base)			**100**	**100**	**100**
Deduct W/out Power Windows (Ex. Base)			**125**	**125**	**125**
Deduct W/out Tilt Steering Wheel			**75**	**75**	**75**
2000 RAV4-4 Cyl.-4WD					
Utility 4D (2WD)	GP10V	2668	**8325**	**10425**	**11150**
Utility 4D	HP10V	2723	**9150**	**11325**	**12050**
Add L Pkg.			**300**	**350**	**350**
Add Aluminum/Alloy Wheels			**100**	**125**	**125**
Add Compact Disc Player			**50**	**75**	**75**
Add Cruise Control			**75**	**100**	**100**
Add Leather Seats			**150**	**175**	**175**
Add Power Door Locks			**50**	**75**	**75**
Add Power Sunroof			**325**	**375**	**375**
Add Power Windows			**75**	**100**	**100**
Add Running Boards			**50**	**75**	**75**
Deduct W/out Air Conditioning			**375**	**375**	**375**
Deduct W/out Automatic Trans.			**300**	**300**	**300**

BODY TYPE	Model No.	Weight	Trade-In	Retail	High Retail
TOYOTA					
1999 4RUNNER-V6-4WD					
Wagon 4D (2WD, 4 Cyl.)	GM84R	3485	**8600**	**10750**	**11700**
Wagon 4D SR5 (2WD)	GN86R	3600	**11250**	**13675**	**14625**
Wagon 4D Limited (2WD)	GN87R	3710	**12450**	**15000**	**15975**
Wagon 4D (4 Cyl.)	HM84R	3770	**9625**	**11850**	**12750**
Wagon 4D SR5	HN86R	3930	**12275**	**14800**	**15775**
Wagon 4D Limited	HN87R	3975	**13475**	**16075**	**17100**
Add Leather Seats (Std. Limited)			**225**	**250**	**250**
Add Power Sunroof			**325**	**375**	**375**
Deduct W/out Air Conditioning			**450**	**450**	**450**
Deduct W/out Automatic Trans.			**325**	**325**	**325**
Deduct W/out Cruise Control			**75**	**75**	**75**
Deduct W/out Power Door Locks			**50**	**50**	**50**
Deduct W/out Power Windows			**75**	**75**	**75**
Deduct W/out Tilt Steering Wheel			**50**	**50**	**50**
1999 LAND CRUISER-V8-4WD					
Wagon	HT05J	5115	**18075**	**21100**	**22450**
Add 3rd Row Seat			**100**	**125**	**125**
Add Power Sunroof			**475**	**550**	**550**
Add Rear Air Conditioning			**75**	**100**	**100**
Deduct W/out Leather Seats			**325**	**325**	**325**
1999 SIENNA-V6					
Wagon 4D CE	GF19C	3759	**6850**	**8800**	**9700**
Wagon 5D CE	ZF19C	3880	**7150**	**9125**	**10000**
Wagon 5D LE	ZF13C	3890	**8150**	**10225**	**11150**
Wagon 5D XLE	ZF13C	3890	**9050**	**11200**	**12075**
Add Aluminum/Alloy Wheels (Std. XLE)			**75**	**100**	**100**
Add Leather Seats			**225**	**250**	**250**
Add Power Sliding Door			**175**	**200**	**200**
Add Power Sunroof			**325**	**375**	**375**
Add Rear Air Conditioning (4D CE)			**75**	**100**	**100**
Add Rear Bucket Seats (LE)			**75**	**100**	**100**
Deduct W/out Cruise Control			**75**	**75**	**75**
Deduct W/out Power Door Locks			**50**	**50**	**50**
Deduct W/out Power Windows			**75**	**75**	**75**
1999 TACOMA PICKUP-4 Cyl.-5 Spd.					
Base	NL42N	2567	**5475**	**7275**	**8050**
PreRunner (AT)	NM92N	3035	**6825**	**8775**	**9550**
Base X-Cab	VL52N	2747	**7075**	**9075**	**9775**
PreRunner X-Cab (AT)	SM92N	3175	**8425**	**10550**	**11275**
Base X-Cab (V6)	VN52N	2897	**8075**	**10175**	**10900**
PreRunner X-Cab (V6, AT)	SN92N	3280	**9425**	**11625**	**12350**
Base (4WD)	PM62N	3202	**7575**	**9625**	**10350**
Base X-Cab (4WD)	WM72N	3347	**9175**	**11350**	**12075**
Base X-Cab (4WD, V6)	WN72N	3412	**10175**	**12425**	**13150**
Limited X-Cab (4WD, V6)	WN74N	3417	**11375**	**13800**	**14550**
Add SR5 Trim			**450**	**500**	**500**
Add TRD Off-Road			**450**	**500**	**500**
Add Aluminum/Alloy Wheels (Std. PreRunner, Ltd.)			**50**	**75**	**75**
Add Auto Trans. (Std. PreRunner)			**250**	**300**	**300**
Add Cruise Control (Std. Limited)			**50**	**75**	**75**
Add Power Windows (Std. Limited)			**50**	**75**	**75**

SEE TRUCK OPTION PAGE FOR ADDITIONAL OPTIONS

TRUCKS

BODY TYPE	Model No.	Weight	Trade-In	Retail	High Retail
Add Sunroof			125	150	150
Deduct W/out Air Conditioning			325	325	325
1999 RAV4-4 Cyl.-4WD					
Utility 2D Soft Top (2WD)	XP10V	2547	5700	7500	8300
Utility 2D Soft Top	YP10V	2723	6525	8450	9200
Utility 4D (2WD)	GP10V	2668	7075	9050	9750
Utility 4D	HP10V	2844	7925	10000	10725
Add L Pkg.			250	300	300
Add Aluminum/Alloy Wheels			50	75	75
Add Cruise Control			50	75	75
Add Power Sunroof			275	325	325
Add Power Windows			50	75	75
Deduct W/out Air Conditioning			325	325	325
Deduct W/out Automatic Trans.			250	250	250
TOYOTA					
1998 4RUNNER-V6-4WD					
Wagon 4D (2WD, 4 Cyl.)	GM84R	3485	6150	8025	8875
Wagon 4D SR5 (2WD)	GN86R	3565	8750	10900	11850
Wagon 4D Limited (2WD)	GN87R	3610	9850	12075	12950
Wagon 4D (4 Cyl.)	HM84R	3735	7200	9200	10075
Wagon 4D SR5	HN86R	3895	9800	12025	12900
Wagon 4D Limited	HN87R	3940	10900	13200	14125
Add Leather Seats (Std. Limited)			175	200	200
Add Power Sunroof			275	325	325
Deduct W/out Air Conditioning			400	400	400
Deduct W/out Automatic Trans.			275	275	275
Deduct W/out Cruise Control			50	50	50
Deduct W/out Power Windows			50	50	50
1998 LAND CRUISER-V8-4WD					
Wagon	HT05J	4971	16775	19575	20875
Add 3rd Row Seat			100	125	125
Add Power Sunroof			425	475	475
Deduct W/out Leather Seats			275	275	275
1998 SIENNA-V6					
Wagon 4D CE	GF19C	3759	5925	7775	8700
Wagon 4D LE	GF13C	3825	6825	8775	9675
Wagon 5D LE	ZF13C	3891	7025	9000	9900
Wagon 5D XLE	ZF13C	4055	7825	9875	10775
Add Aluminum/Alloy Wheels (Std. XLE)			50	75	75
Add Leather Seats			175	200	200
Add Power Sliding Door			150	175	175
Add Power Sunroof			275	325	325
Add Rear Air Conditioning			50	75	75
Add Rear Bucket Seats (LE)			50	75	75
Deduct W/out Cruise Control			50	50	50
Deduct W/out Power Windows			50	50	50
1998 TACOMA PICKUP-4 Cyl.-5 Spd.					
Base	NL42N	2566	4700	6425	7225
Base X-Cab	VL52N	2746	6300	8200	8950
PreRunner X-Cab (AT)	SM92N	3175	7500	9525	10250
Base X-Cab (V6)	VN52N	2896	7100	9100	9800
PreRunner X-Cab (V6, AT)	SN92N	3280	8300	10400	11125

TRUCKS

BODY TYPE	Model No.	Weight	Trade-In	Retail	High Retail
Base (4WD)	PM62N	3201	**6600**	**8525**	**9300**
Base X-Cab (4WD)	WM72N	3346	**8200**	**10300**	**11025**
Base X-Cab (4WD, V6)	WN72N	3411	**9000**	**11175**	**11900**
Limited X-Cab (4WD, V6)	WN74N	3416	**10150**	**12400**	**13125**
Add SR5 Trim			**400**	**450**	**450**
Add TRD Off-Road			**400**	**450**	**450**
Add Auto Trans. (Std. PreRunner)			**200**	**225**	**225**
Add Cruise Control (Std. Limited)			**50**	**75**	**75**
Add Power Windows (Std. Limited)			**50**	**75**	**75**
Add Sunroof			**100**	**125**	**125**
Deduct W/out Air Conditioning			**275**	**275**	**275**
1998 T100 PICKUP-V6					
Base (4 Cyl.)	JM11D	3320	**5125**	**6900**	**7750**
Base X-Cab	TN12D	3550	**7925**	**10000**	**10725**
SR5 X-Cab	TN14D	3600	**8825**	**10975**	**11725**
Base X-Cab (4WD)	UN22D	4005	**9525**	**11750**	**12500**
SR5 X-Cab (4WD)	UN24D	4040	**10425**	**12700**	**13425**
Add Aluminum/Alloy Wheels			**50**	**75**	**75**
Deduct W/out Air Conditioning			**400**	**400**	**400**
Deduct W/out Automatic Trans.			**275**	**275**	**275**
Deduct W/out Cruise Control (Ex. JM11D)			**50**	**50**	**50**
Deduct W/out Power Windows (Ex. JM11D)			**50**	**50**	**50**
1998 RAV4-4 Cyl.-4WD					
Utility 2D (2WD)	XP10V	2568	**4600**	**6300**	**7100**
Utility 2D Soft Top (2WD)	XP10V	2592	**4600**	**6300**	**7100**
Utility 2D	YP10V	2701	**5475**	**7275**	**8050**
Utility 2D Soft Top	YP10V	2786	**5475**	**7275**	**8050**
Utility 4D (2WD)	GP10V	2712	**5900**	**7725**	**8550**
Utility 4D	HP10V	2789	**6775**	**8725**	**9500**
Add L Pkg.			**250**	**300**	**300**
Add Cruise Control			**50**	**75**	**75**
Add Power Sunroof			**225**	**275**	**275**
Add Power Windows			**50**	**75**	**75**
Deduct W/out Air Conditioning			**275**	**275**	**275**
Deduct W/out Automatic Trans.			**200**	**200**	**200**
TOYOTA					
1997 4RUNNER-V6-4WD					
Wagon 4D (2WD, 4 Cyl.)	GM84R	3485	**5500**	**7300**	**8175**
Wagon 4D SR5 (2WD)	GN86R	3565	**7900**	**9950**	**10850**
Wagon 4D Limited (2WD)	GN87R	3610	**9100**	**11275**	**12175**
Wagon 4D (4 Cyl.)	HM84R	3735	**6100**	**7975**	**8900**
Wagon 4D SR5	HN86R	3895	**8500**	**10625**	**11575**
Wagon 4D Limited	HN87R	3940	**9700**	**11925**	**12850**
Add Leather Seats (Std. Limited)			**150**	**175**	**175**
Add Power Sunroof			**200**	**225**	**225**
Deduct W/out Air Conditioning			**250**	**250**	**250**
Deduct W/out Automatic Trans.			**175**	**175**	**175**
Deduct W/out Cruise Control			**50**	**50**	**50**
Deduct W/out Power Windows			**50**	**50**	**50**
1997 LAND CRUISER-6 Cyl.-4WD					
Wagon	HJ85J	4834	**13100**	**15675**	**16875**
Add Power Sunroof			**350**	**400**	**400**

TRUCKS

SEE TRUCK OPTION PAGE FOR ADDITIONAL OPTIONS

BODY TYPE	Model No.	Weight	Trade-In	Retail	High Retail
Deduct W/out Leather Seats			**250**	**250**	**250**
Deduct W/out Power Seat			**100**	**100**	**100**
1997 PREVIA-4 Cyl.					
Wagon DX S/C	GK12M	3755	**5900**	**7750**	**8675**
Wagon DX S/C All-Trac	HK22M	3975	**6300**	**8200**	**9050**
Wagon LE S/C	GK13M	3875	**6550**	**8475**	**9350**
Wagon LE S/C All-Trac	HK23M	4095	**6950**	**8900**	**9800**
Add Dual Sunroof			**300**	**350**	**350**
Add Leather Seats			**150**	**175**	**175**
Deduct W/out Air Conditioning			**250**	**250**	**250**
Deduct W/out Cruise Control			**50**	**50**	**50**
Deduct W/out Power Windows			**50**	**50**	**50**
1997 TACOMA PICKUP-4 Cyl.-5 Spd.					
Base	NL42N	2560	**4125**	**5775**	**6550**
Base X-Cab	VL52N	2745	**5575**	**7375**	**8175**
Base (4WD)	PM62N	3190	**5725**	**7550**	**8350**
Base X-Cab (4WD)	WM72N	3345	**7175**	**9175**	**9875**
SR5 X-Cab (4WD, V6)	WN74N	3405	**8425**	**10525**	**11250**
Add LX Trim			**250**	**300**	**300**
Add Automatic Trans.			**125**	**150**	**150**
Add Sunroof			**50**	**75**	**75**
Add V6 Engine (Std. SR5 X-Cab)			**450**	**500**	**500**
Deduct W/out Air Conditioning			**150**	**150**	**150**
1997 T100 PICKUP-V6					
Base (4 Cyl.)	JM11D	3320	**4625**	**6350**	**7150**
Base X-Cab	TN12D	3550	**6525**	**8450**	**9200**
SR5 X-Cab	TN14D	3600	**7325**	**9325**	**10025**
Base X-Cab (4WD)	UN22D	4005	**8125**	**10200**	**10925**
SR5 X-Cab (4WD)	UN24D	4040	**8925**	**11075**	**11800**
Deduct W/out Air Conditioning			**250**	**250**	**250**
Deduct W/out Automatic Trans.			**175**	**175**	**175**
Deduct W/out Cruise Control (Ex. JM11D)			**50**	**50**	**50**
Deduct W/out Power Windows (Ex. JM11D)			**50**	**50**	**50**
1997 RAV4-4 Cyl.-4WD					
Utility 2D (2WD)	XP10V	2469	**3800**	**5400**	**6150**
Utility 2D	YP10V	2646	**4625**	**6350**	**7150**
Utility 4D (2WD)	GP10V	2612	**4900**	**6650**	**7475**
Utility 4D	HP10V	2789	**5725**	**7550**	**8350**
Add Dual Sunroof			**100**	**125**	**125**
Add Power Sunroof			**150**	**175**	**175**
Deduct W/out Air Conditioning			**150**	**150**	**150**
Deduct W/out Automatic Trans.			**125**	**125**	**125**
TOYOTA					
1996 4RUNNER-V6-4WD					
Wagon 4D (2WD, 4 Cyl.)	GM84R		**4650**	**6375**	**7250**
Wagon 4D SR5 (2WD)	GN86R		**6500**	**8425**	**9300**
Wagon 4D (4 Cyl.)	HM84R		**5250**	**7025**	**7900**
Wagon 4D SR5	HN86R		**7100**	**9075**	**9925**
Wagon 4D Limited	HN87R		**8200**	**10300**	**11225**
Add Power Sunroof			**150**	**175**	**175**
Deduct W/out Air Conditioning			**150**	**150**	**150**
Deduct W/out Automatic Trans.			**125**	**125**	**125**

ADJUST FOR MILEAGE - DEDUCT FOR RECONDITIONING

BODY TYPE	Model No.	Weight	Trade-In	Retail	High Retail
1996 LAND CRUISER-6 Cyl.-4WD					
Wagon	HJ85J	4751	**11600**	**14025**	**15150**
Add Power Sunroof			**275**	**325**	**325**
1996 PREVIA-4 Cyl.					
Wagon DX S/C	GK12M	3755	**5000**	**6750**	**7675**
Wagon DX S/C All-Trac	HK22M	3975	**5400**	**7200**	**8075**
Wagon LE S/C	GK13M	3875	**5600**	**7400**	**8300**
Wagon LE S/C All-Trac	HK23M	4095	**6000**	**7850**	**8775**
Add Dual Sunroof			**225**	**250**	**250**
Deduct W/out Air Conditioning			**150**	**150**	**150**
1996 TACOMA PICKUP-4 Cyl.-5 Spd.					
Base	NL42N	2560	**3325**	**4875**	**5675**
Base X-Cab	VL52N	2740	**4625**	**6350**	**7150**
Base (4WD)	PM62N	3185	**4825**	**6550**	**7350**
Base X-Cab (4WD)	WM72N	3340	**6125**	**8000**	**8825**
SR5 X-Cab (4WD, V6)	WN74N	3400	**7025**	**9000**	**9775**
Add LX Trim			**100**	**125**	**125**
Add Automatic Trans.			**100**	**125**	**125**
Add V6 Engine (Std. SR5 X-Cab)			**300**	**350**	**350**
Deduct W/out Air Conditioning			**100**	**100**	**100**
1996 T100 PICKUP-V6					
Base (4 Cyl.)	JM11D	3320	**3700**	**5300**	**6050**
Base X-Cab	TN12D	3550	**5450**	**7250**	**8025**
SR5 X-Cab	TN14D	3600	**6150**	**8025**	**8775**
Base X-Cab (4WD)	UN22D	4005	**6750**	**8700**	**9475**
SR5 X-Cab (4WD)	UN24D	4040	**7450**	**9475**	**10200**
Deduct W/out Air Conditioning			**150**	**150**	**150**
Deduct W/out Automatic Trans.			**125**	**125**	**125**
1996 RAV4-4 Cyl.-4WD					
Utility 2D (2WD)	XP10V	2469	**2900**	**4375**	**5125**
Utility 2D	YP10V	2646	**3700**	**5300**	**6050**
Utility 4D (2WD)	GP10V	2612	**4000**	**5625**	**6400**
Utility 4D	HP10V	2789	**4800**	**6525**	**7325**
Deduct W/out Air Conditioning			**100**	**100**	**100**
Deduct W/out Automatic Trans.			**100**	**100**	**100**
TOYOTA					
1995 4RUNNER-V6-4WD					
Wagon 4D SR5 (2WD)	N29V	3760	**4425**	**6125**	**7000**
Wagon 4D SR5 (4 Cyl.)	N37W	3825	**4625**	**6350**	**7225**
Wagon 4D SR5	N39W	4165	**5025**	**6775**	**7700**
1995 LAND CRUISER-6 Cyl.-4WD					
Wagon	J81W	4751	**10000**	**12250**	**13300**
1995 PREVIA-4 Cyl.					
Wagon DX	C11R	3615	**3550**	**5125**	**5925**
Wagon DX S/C	C13R	3755	**3900**	**5525**	**6375**
Wagon LE	C12R	3735	**4100**	**5750**	**6600**
Wagon LE S/C	C14R	3875	**4450**	**6150**	**7025**
Wagon DX All-Trac	C21S	3835	**3950**	**5575**	**6425**
Wagon DX S/C All-Trac	C23S	3975	**4300**	**5975**	**6850**
Wagon LE All-Trac	C22S	3955	**4500**	**6200**	**7075**
Wagon LE S/C All-Trac	C24S	4095	**4850**	**6600**	**7500**

TRUCKS

SEE TRUCK OPTION PAGE FOR ADDITIONAL OPTIONS

BODY TYPE	Model No.	Weight	Trade-In	Retail	High Retail
1995 PICKUPS-4 Cyl.					
Base	N81A	2690	**2600**	**4025**	**4725**
DX	N81P	2750	**2800**	**4275**	**5000**
DX X-Cab	N93P	2990	**3800**	**5400**	**6150**
SR5 X-Cab (V6)	N93G	3135	**4350**	**6025**	**6800**
DX (4WD)	N01P	3400	**3700**	**5300**	**6050**
DX X-Cab (4WD)	N13P	3585	**4700**	**6425**	**7225**
SR5 X-Cab (4WD, V6)	N13G	3880	**5250**	**7025**	**7800**
Add V6 Engine (Std. SR5 X-Cab)			**250**	**300**	**300**
1995 TACOMA PICKUP-4 Cyl.					
Base	N41B	2580	**2975**	**4475**	**5225**
Base X-Cab	N53B	2760	**4075**	**5725**	**6500**
Base (4WD)	N61C	3215	**4275**	**5950**	**6750**
Base X-Cab (4WD)	N73C	3370	**5375**	**7150**	**7925**
SR5 X-Cab (4WD, V6)	N73K	3430	**6175**	**8050**	**8800**
Add V6 Engine (Std. SR5 X-Cab)			**250**	**300**	**300**
1995 T100 PICKUP-V6					
Base (4 Cyl.)	D10D	3350	**3200**	**4725**	**5500**
Base	D11E	3420	**3450**	**5025**	**5750**
DX	D11E	3460	**3625**	**5225**	**5950**
DX X-Cab	D12E	3580	**4725**	**6450**	**7250**
SR5 X-Cab	D12F	3630	**5275**	**7050**	**7825**
DX 1-Ton	D11G	3550	**3925**	**5550**	**6300**
DX (4WD)	D21E	3945	**4725**	**6450**	**7250**
DX X-Cab (4WD)	D22E	4075	**5825**	**7650**	**8450**
SR5 X-Cab (4WD)	D22F	4110	**6375**	**8275**	**9025**

VOLKSWAGEN

BODY TYPE	Model No.	Weight	Trade-In	Retail	High Retail
VOLKSWAGEN					
2004 TOUAREG-V6-AWD					
Utility 4D	B/Z	5086	**27350**	**31100**	**32950**
Utility 4D (V8)	C/E/F	5300	**31150**	**35150**	**37125**
Utility 4D TDI (V10)	H	5825	**51250**	**56525**	**59125**
Add 4-Zone Air Conditioning			**400**	**450**	**450**
Add Adjustable Air Suspension (Std. TDI)			**1350**	**1500**	**1500**
Add Navigation System			**750**	**850**	**850**
Add Theft Recovery System			**100**	**125**	**125**
Add VW Premium Stereo System			**425**	**475**	**475**
Deduct W/out Leather Seats			**575**	**575**	**575**
Deduct W/out Power Seat			**275**	**275**	**275**
VOLKSWAGEN					
2003 EUROVAN-V6					
Van GLS	K	4288	**18100**	**21125**	**22275**
Van MV	M	4478	**19150**	**22250**	**23425**
Van MV Weekender	N	5236	**27500**	**31275**	**32675**
Add Compact Disc Player			**75**	**100**	**100**
Add Power Sunroof (Ex. Weekender)			**525**	**600**	**600**
Add Theft Recovery System			**75**	**100**	**100**

TRUCKS

BODY TYPE	Model No.	Weight	Trade-In	Retail	High Retail
VOLKSWAGEN					
2002 EUROVAN-V6					
Van GLS	K	4288	**15925**	**18675**	**19750**
Van MV	M	4478	**16875**	**19725**	**20825**
Van MV Weekender	N	5236	**20925**	**24150**	**25375**
Add Compact Disc Player			**75**	**100**	**100**
Add Power Sunroof (Ex. Weekender)			**475**	**550**	**550**
Add Theft Recovery System			**75**	**100**	**100**
VOLKSWAGEN					
2001 EUROVAN-V6					
Van GLS	K	4285	**13950**	**16575**	**17625**
Van MV	M	4474	**14800**	**17475**	**18500**
Van MV Weekender	N		**18100**	**21125**	**22275**
Add Compact Disc Player			**50**	**75**	**75**
Add Power Sunroof (Ex. Weekender)			**425**	**475**	**475**
Add Theft Recovery System			**50**	**75**	**75**
VOLKSWAGEN					
2000 EUROVAN-V6					
Van GLS	K	4220	**12425**	**14925**	**15900**
Van MV	M	4438	**13175**	**15725**	**16750**
Van MV Weekender	N		**15700**	**18425**	**19500**
Add Compact Disc Player			**50**	**75**	**75**
Add Power Sunroof (Ex. Weekender)			**375**	**425**	**425**
Add Rear Bucket Seats (GLS)			**100**	**125**	**125**
VOLKSWAGEN					
1999 EUROVAN-V6					
Van GLS	K	4220	**10800**	**13125**	**14050**
Van MV	M	4348	**11450**	**13875**	**14825**
Van MV Weekender	N	4438	**13600**	**16200**	**17225**
Add Power Sunroof (Ex. Weekender)			**325**	**375**	**375**

VOLVO

BODY TYPE	Model No.	Weight	Trade-In	Retail	High Retail
VOLVO					
2004 XC90-5 Cyl./I6 Turbo-AWD					
Utility 2.5T (FWD)	C(N/Y)59	4361	**29800**	**33700**	**35625**
Utility 2.5T	C(M/Z)59		**31325**	**35325**	**37300**
Utility T6	C(M/Z)91	4638	**32825**	**37075**	**39100**
Add Navigation System			**750**	**850**	**850**
Add Rear Entertainment System			**600**	**675**	**675**
Add Theft Recovery System			**100**	**125**	**125**
Add Volvo Premium Stereo System			**425**	**475**	**475**
Deduct W/out 3rd Row Seat			**200**	**200**	**200**
Deduct W/out Leather Seats			**575**	**575**	**575**
Deduct W/out Power Sunroof			**725**	**725**	**725**
Deduct W/out Rear Air Conditioning			**200**	**200**	**200**
VOLVO					
2003 XC90-5 Cyl./I6 Turbo-AWD					
Utility 2.5T (FWD)	C(N/Y)59	4450	**27200**	**30875**	**32725**
Utility 2.5T	C(M/Z)59	4450	**28625**	**32450**	**34325**

TRUCKS

SEE TRUCK OPTION PAGE FOR ADDITIONAL OPTIONS

BODY TYPE	Model No.	Weight	Trade-In	Retail	High Retail
Utility T6	C(M/Z)91		**29875**	**33775**	**35700**
Add Navigation System			**650**	**725**	**725**
Add Theft Recovery System			**75**	**100**	**100**
Add Volvo Premium Stereo System			**375**	**425**	**425**
Deduct W/out 3rd Row Seat			**175**	**175**	**175**
Deduct W/out Leather Seats			**525**	**525**	**525**
Deduct W/out Power Sunroof			**675**	**675**	**675**
Deduct W/out Rear Air Conditioning			**150**	**150**	**150**

TRUCKS

Vehicle Identification Numbers are printed on a small metal plate usually located on the left side of the dashboard visible through the windshield. Some models and makes place the VIN plate on the inside of the left windshield pillar.

The Vehicle Identification Number's tenth digit represents the vehicle model year. This will be true on all vehicles since 1981. Please refer to the following chart for model year indicator codes.

Code	Model Year	Code	Model Year
A	1980	S	1995
B	1981	T	1996
C	1982	V	1997
D	1983	W	1998
E	1984	X	1999
F	1985	Y	2000
G	1986	1	2001
H	1987	2	2002
J	1988	3	2003
K	1989	4	2004
L	1990	5	2005
M	1991	6	2006
N	1992	7	2007
P	1993	8	2008
R	1994	9	2009

ACURA	www.acura.com	800-862-2872
AUDI	www.audiusa.com	800-822-2834
BMW	www.bmwusa.com	800-831-1117
BUICK	www.buick.com	800-521-7300
CADILLAC	www.cadillac.com	800-458-8006
CHEVROLET	www.chevrolet.com	800-222-1020
CHRYSLER	www.chrysler.com	800-992-1997
DODGE	www.dodge.com	800-992-1997
FORD	www.fordvehicles.com	800-392-3673
GMC	www.gmc.com	800-462-8782
HONDA	www.hondacars.com	800-999-1009
HUMMER	www.hummer.com	800-732-5493
HYUNDAI	www.hyundaiusa.com	800-633-5151
INFINITI	www.infiniti.com	800-662-6200
ISUZU	www.isuzu.com	800-255-6727
JAGUAR	www.jaguarusa.com	800-452-4827
JEEP	www.jeep.com	800-992-1997
KIA	www.kia.com	800-333-4542
LAND ROVER	www.landroverusa.com	800-637-6837
LEXUS	www.lexus.com	800-255-3987
LINCOLN	www.lincolnvehicles.com	800-392-3673
MAZDA	www.mazdausa.com	800-222-5500
MERCEDES-BENZ	www.mbusa.com	800-222-0100
MERCURY	www.mercuryvehicles.com	800-392-3673
MINI	www.miniusa.com	866-467-6464
MITSUBISHI	www.mitsucars.com	800-222-0037
NISSAN	www.nissanusa.com	800-647-7261
OLDSMOBILE	www.oldsmobile.com	800-442-6537
PONTIAC	www.pontiac.com	800-762-2737
PORSCHE	www.porsche.com	800-545-8039
SAAB	www.saabusa.com	800-955-9007
SATURN	www.saturn.com	800-553-6000
SCION	www.scion.com	866-707-2466
SUBARU	www.subaru.com	800-782-2783
SUZUKI	www.suzuki.com	800-934-0934
TOYOTA	www.toyota.com	800-331-4331
VOLKSWAGEN	www.vw.com	800-822-8987
VOLVO	www.volvocars.us	800-458-1552